# THE ALBERTA ADVANTAGE

## AN ANTHOLOGY OF PLAYS

# The Alberta Advantage:

## An Anthology of Plays

**The Third Ascent** by Frank Moher

**Gravel Run** by Conni Massing

**The Red King's Dream** by David Belke

**Blowfish** by Vern Thiessen

**Selling Mr. Rushdie** by Clem Martini

**Excavations** by Eugene Stickland

**The Exquisite Hour** by Stewart Lemoine

**Coal Valley: The Making of a Miner** by Katherine Koller

**Kabloona Talk** by Sharon Pollock

**While My Mother Lay Dreaming** by Doug Curtis

Edited by Anne Nothof

Playwrights Canada Press
Toronto · Canada

**Playwrights Canada Press**
*The Canadian Drama Publisher*
215 Spadina Avenue, Suite 230, Toronto, Ontario CANADA M5T 2C7
416-703-0013 fax 416-408-3402
orders@playwrightscanada.com • www.playwrightscanada.com



This book would be twice its cover price were it not for the support of Canadian taxpayers through the Government of Canada Book Publishing Industry Development Programme, the Canada Council for the Arts, the Ontario Arts Council, and the Ontario Media Development Corporation.

Canada
The Canada Council for the Arts
Le Conseil des Arts du Canada
ONTARIO ARTS COUNCIL
CONSEIL DES ARTS DE L'ONTARIO
Ontario
Ontario Media Development Corporation
Société de développement de l'industrie des médias de l'Ontario

Front cover image "Mud Spirits" by Jim Davies. Oil on panel, 14" x 16".
Courtesy of Jim Davies and Scott Gallery, Edmonton.
Production Editor and Cover Design: Micheline Courtemanche

**Library and Archives Canada Cataloguing in Publication**

The Alberta advantage : an anthology of plays / edited by Anne Nothof.

ISBN 978-0-88754-783-6

1. Canadian drama (English)--Alberta. 2. Canadian drama (English)--21st century. I. Nothof, Anne

PS8315.5.A43A43 2008 C812'.608097123 C2008-902596-2

First edition: May 2008
Printed and bound by Canadian Printco at Scarborough, Canada.

# Acknowledgements

My thanks to the playwrights for enriching the lives of Albertans, and to Playwrights Canada Press for bringing their plays to a wider audience.

Anne Nothof

# Contents

# Introduction

"The Alberta Advantage" has long been a political marketing slogan for the economic and business resources of the province. The title of this anthology, however, underscores the wealth of the theatre activity in Alberta: the wide range of subjects and the diversity of styles in Alberta theatre for the past twenty-five years. *The Alberta Advantage* includes plays which reflect the extensive and varied dramatic landscape—the people, politics, history and culture of Alberta. It features playwrights with a substantive body of produced work, but whose works have limited exposure through publication. It also features playwrights who may not have achieved wide recognition through production and publication, but whose work merits national and international exposure. The selection attempts to be inclusive – in terms of gender and location of playwrights, and dates of the plays. Several of these plays have been published in single volumes which have gone out of print; several are published for the first time; but all have been professionally produced on Alberta stages, with one notable exception.

Of the conspicuous omissions, several previously published Alberta plays should be highlighted here: *Mieko Ouchi: Two Plays: The Blue Light and The Red Priest* (2007); Vern Thiessen's *Apple* (2002), *Einstein's Gift* (2003), *Shakespeare's Will* (2005), *The Courier and Other Plays* (2006) and *Vimy* (2008). Both Ouchi and Thiessen move beyond a specific Alberta region, and interrogate complex ethical and political issues in terms of history and art. The plays of Brad Fraser, published by Playwrights Canada Press and NeWest Press, are typically set in the violent interstices of an urban environment which may reference any large Western city, and are not specific to Edmonton or Calgary. The satirical sociological plays of Edmontonian Chris Craddock address problems endemic to teenagers, such as drug abuse and family dysfunction – in *Naked at School: Three Plays for Teens* (NeWest 2001), for example. Lyle Victor Albert enacts the challenges of living with cerebral palsy in his monologues, *Scraping the Surface* and *Objects in the Mirror* (NeWest 2000) and Marty Chan considers the dilemmas occasioned by mixed race relationships in *Mom, Dad, I'm Living with a White Girl* (Playwrights 2002). Ronnie Burkett's miniature gothic stories have travelled across Europe, although his marionettes had their origins in Calgary. Stephen Massicotte has also expanded his theatrical horizons since graduating from the University of Calgary – from the prairie landscape in *Mary's Wedding* (Playwrights 2002) to Oxford University in *The Oxford Roof Climber's Rebellion* (Playwrights 2007). Sharon Pollock's extensive contribution to Albertan, Canadian and international theatre is evident in the three-volume *Collected Works* (Playwrights 2005–08). The play included in this anthology, *Kabloona Talk*, has been chosen for its specifically Alberta setting and because it is little known, having been performed only once as a staged reading at a workshop organized by Alberta Playwrights Network in Calgary in 2005.

For the purposes of inclusion in this collection, playwrights are identified as "Albertan" if they have written plays while resident in the province – particularly plays that thematically reflect the region and the people. Some were born and began their careers in theatre elsewhere—such as Vern Thiessen—who may also be identified as a Manitoban Mennonite; others were born and raised in Alberta, and established themselves as produced playwrights in the province, but have since lived and worked for many years elsewhere – Frank Moher, for example. However, Moher returns to his roots regularly, and his plays are imbued with an Alberta sensibility – reacting to the righteous political and religious inclinations of the province.

## A Brief History of Alberta Theatre

The history of Alberta theatre is long and rich, reflecting the necessity of making and performing plays in communities across the province since the first settlers transplanted their cultural heritages to new lives on foreign soil. Informal theatrical occasions, including dramatic readings and recitations, date before the 1880s in church and town halls, hotels and barns. With the arrival of the railroad in Calgary and Edmonton, the population grew rapidly, as did the level of theatre activity, including touring professional troupes from the United States in the early 1890s. In 1892, to accommodate these players, Edmonton's sheriff and chief auctioneer, W.S. Robinson, constructed the town's first theatre, on the second floor of a frame building on Jasper Avenue with stores on the ground floor – a popular and pragmatic design for frontier theatre spaces. Robertson's Hall functioned as the city's main theatre for fifteen years until it burned down in 1906 – a common tragic conclusion for many early stages. From 1904, plays were also staged in the larger Thistle Rink in the spring and summer until it, too, was destroyed by fire.

The "golden years" of early professional theatre in Edmonton witnessed the construction of several large and opulent theatres, including three "Empires," which mounted vaudeville and plays by American, British and Canadian touring companies. The first Empire was built in 1906, a vaudeville house with four shows a day. It was renamed the Bijou in 1907 and functioned as a movie house, then converted to the Queen City Meat Market in 1911, which burned down in 1953. The Edmonton Opera House, also constructed in 1906, was remodelled in 1909 as the Second Empire and participated in the American Pantages circuit via Calgary. In January 1913, Sarah Bernhardt, at the age of sixty-eight, performed the death of young Parisian courtesan Marguerite Gauthier in the fifth act of *La Dame aux Camélias* by Alexandre Dumas fils at the second Empire Theatre for one matinee and one evening show. She was on tour with Martin Beck's New York company, providing a tragic finale to the vaudeville acts which comprised the first half of the show. This event is celebrated in Stewart Lemoine's 2006 comedy, *At the Zenith of the Empire*, written for his company, Teatro la Quindicina. In his play, he paraphrases her euphoric response to Edmonton: "I see around me a ravishingly beautiful city… in the very new future. And I don't mean beautiful buildings and trees and hills. I mean beautiful thoughts. …And life in your city is not going to be lived as it is lived elsewhere, and that will be the charm of it. You're being challenged to live free of old notions… (117, 118).

The third Empire Theatre was built in 1920 with seating for 1,477 in the auditorium and box seats. Following the Second World War it was converted to a movie theatre and then a popular dance hall named the Trocadero until 1981 when it was pulled down to make way for an office tower. Residential stock companies performed at the Lyceum (formerly the Opera House), and enjoyed strong local support, since the touring companies typically stayed for only one or two performances.

Amateur theatre found a focus in the establishment of the Edmonton Amateur Dramatic Company in 1886, which toured in Alberta and British Columbia, and the Garrick Club in 1900. The Edmonton Operatic and Dramatic Society staged Gilbert and Sullivan operettas annually between 1904 and 1920. Theatre also flourished on the campus of the University of Alberta during the 1920s with an Inter-year Play Competition including students from most faculties, and attracting audiences from the community as well as the campus. This vibrant amateur theatre tradition was given particular impetus by Elsie Park Gowan with her Edmonton Community Players (1945), and by Jack McCreath with Theatre Associates (1959), which performed in an old schoolhouse in the Walterdale flats. Since 1974, amateur theatre has been enthusiastically enacted by the company in the Walterdale Playhouse, a renovated fire hall in the Strathcona district. Walterdale Theatre Associates has produced many new plays by Alberta playwrights such as Brad Fraser, Warren Graves, Wilfred Watson, Gordon Pengilly, Sharon Pollock, Eugene Stickland and Scott Sharplin.

In Calgary, the Calgary Amateur Music and Dramatic Club, formed in 1884, performed in the unusually commodious Hull's Opera House after its construction in 1893. The much more opulent Grand Theatre opened in 1912. Constructed by Senator James Lougheed, the grandfather of former Conservative Premier Peter Lougheed, the Grand seated 1,350 in seats upholstered in green leather, 810 on the main floor and 540 in the gallery, with twelve loges and twelve boxes for the more conspicuously affluent and a sunken orchestra pit with its own orchestra. Its ambitious roster included touring vaudeville groups and luminaries such as Sarah Bernhardt (1913 and 1918) and Sir Johnston Forbes-Robinson, who inaugurated the theatre with a performance in *The Passing of the Third Floor Back*. In 1918, it accommodated five operas by the San Carlo Opera Company. During and after World War I, the Grand was also used by amateur groups, including a production of a new Alberta operetta, *The Highwood Trail*, by the Calgary Operatic Society in 1921. By 1921, as in Edmonton, a plethora of theatres housed touring productions, including the Capitol, the Royal, the Princess, the Monarch, the Empire and the Lyric, most of which have long since disappeared from the scene. The happy exception to this lost theatre tradition is the Grand, which in 2006 was restored from its 1937 conversion to a movie theatre and now functions as a multi-use performance venue and a home base for Theatre Junction.

Between the wars, Alberta theatre was performed by enthusiastic amateurs throughout the province in Red Deer, Camrose, Medicine Hat, Lethbridge, Banff and Coaldale, to name a few. Because of the drought and the Depression, and the demise of travelling companies, communities initiated their own entertainments. In 1929, the Drama League, which became a model for the Dominion Drama Festival, was formed in Alberta by Sterndale Bennett, Elizabeth Sterling Haynes and others. Working for the University of Alberta's Department of Extension, Haynes travelled throughout the province conducting workshops, lecturing and directing; she also assisted in the founding of the Banff Centre for the Arts with E.A. Corbett in 1933, setting the stage for the beginnings of a distinctive Alberta dramaturgy.

Two women playwrights gave Alberta communities and their history a voice – in live performances and on the radio. Gwen Pharis Ringwood's folk plays and community pageants enacted the rituals and customs of peoples from diverse cultures which made up the uniqueness of small Alberta towns. Elsie Park Gowan's stage plays examined the restricted lives of rural women in Alberta, and her epic radio plays and pageants comprised a social history of Edmonton. Ringwood grew up in the small southern Alberta towns where her father taught, and developed an appreciation for the distinctive nature of each community:

> Our population is a heterogeneous one and our manners and customs vary greatly from region to region. We have villages when speech and action and thought is in the light, quick rhythm of the French. Again a Ukrainian town seems to have a slower, outwardly stolid rhythm but underneath run the deep, passionate undercurrents of feeling and a lusty broad humour. We have towns with the flavour of a quiet English village or a slightly aggressive American town; we have industrious German settlements, mining towns with a preponderance of Latin names, the cow towns when the flavour and play-acting of the ranching industry have their way, the northern town with its feeling of the fur trade and the dog team. (quoted in Anthony 27–28)

Ringwood graduated from the University of Alberta and worked part time as a secretary for the Department of Extension's director of drama, Elizabeth Sterling Haynes, and then at the Banff Centre for the Arts as registrar. In 1938, while studying playwriting in North Carolina, she created the one-act prairie tragedy, *Still Stands the House*, one of the most frequently performed plays in the history of Canadian theatre. In Edmonton, during the war, she wrote her Alberta folk plays: *Jack the Joker* (Banff 1944), about the life of the notorious Calgary newspaper editor, Bob Edwards; *The Rainmaker* (Banff 1945), set in Medicine Hat during the drought of 1921; and *Stampede* (University of Alberta 1946), about the Black cowboy and rancher, "Nigger John." Ringwood also wrote historical pageants to celebrate community anniversaries: an Edmonton pageant on Methodist missionary John McDougall and Chief Maskapetoon to commemorate the seventieth anniversary of the Methodist Church in 1940; and *Look Behind You Neighbour* for the fiftieth anniversary of Edson, Alberta in 1961.

Elsie Park Gowan studied history at the University of Alberta, where she was president of the Dramatic Society. She also acted in several plays directed by Elizabeth Sterling Haynes, including James Barrie's *Shall We Join the Ladies?*, which represented Edmonton in the first Alberta Drama League Festival in 1930. Between 1930 and 1958 she was active in the Edmonton Little Theatre, and acted in roles for the University of

Alberta's Department of Drama from its inception in 1946. Her first play, *Homestead* (1932), was written when she was a lonely teacher in a small town, and first produced at the Drumheller Music Festival. The University of Alberta Dramatic Club entered *God Made the Country* in the Alberta Regional Dominion Drama Festival, and it was subsequently produced at the Grand Theatre in Calgary in 1935. This play reflects Gowan's preoccupation with the plight of isolated rural women who struggled to survive in constrictive marriages and harsh environments. *Back to the Kitchen, Woman!* anticipates women's liberation; *One Who Looks at the Stars* (1946) portrays an interracial marriage; *Breeches from Bond Street* (1949) enacts the fate of a mail-order bride in southern Alberta. Her three-act comedy, *The Last Caveman*, premiered at the Edmonton Little Theatre in 1938 and in 1946–47 was toured by the western professional company, Everyman Theatre, under the direction of Sydney Risk. It depicts the hardships encountered in Alberta by a family lured to Canada by CPR propaganda in the early 1920s.

With limited opportunities for stage production, Gowan began to write extensively for radio, including two historical series co-written with her friend, Gwen Pharis Ringwood: *New Lamps for Old* (1936–37) and *The Building of Canada*, commissioned by the University of Alberta radio station, CKUA. Both series were later broadcast nationally by the CBC. Between 1939 and 1958, Gowan wrote about 250 radio scripts. She also wrote historical pageants for celebrations in Edmonton and Jasper: *Who Builds a City* (1954), *The Jasper Story* (1956), *Portrait of Alberta* (1956) and *A Treaty for the Plains* (1977). Their common uplifting theme is the realization of personal and community dreams through a united spirit in a frontier environment.

## Edmonton

The first professional theatre between Winnipeg and Vancouver in thirty years was established by Edmonton lawyer, Joe Shoctor, in 1965 in a former Salvation Army building, and appropriately named the Citadel. During its early years, the Citadel produced only one Canadian play, Gratien Gelinas's *Yesterday the Children were Dancing*, but it did help to develop a theatre culture in the city. The Citadel flourished during the oil boom of the late 1970s under Artistic Director John Neville (1973 to 1978), who orchestrated the construction of a multi-staged theatre complex. Neville also actively encouraged the production of Canadian plays by Tremblay, Lazarus, Freeman and Pollock (*A Compulsory Option* in 1973 and *The Komagata Maru Incident* in 1977). Under the artistic direction of yet another British import, Peter Coe, the Citadel poured its resources into wanna-be Broadway musicals, but also staged important Canadian plays such as George Ryga's *The Ecstasy of Rita Joe* (1978/79 season), Sharon Pollock's *One Tiger to a Hill* (1979/80) and John Gray's *Billy Bishop Goes to War* (1979/80). The Citadel also programmed W.O. Mitchell's *The Kite* (1981/82), *The Black Bonspiel of Wullie MacCrimmon* (1982/83) and *Back to Beulah* (1987/88), and during the tenure of Artistic Director Robin Phillips the plays of John Murrell also made an appearance: *Democracy* (1991/92) in the small Rice venue and *Waiting for the Parade* (1991/93) on the large proscenium Shoctor stage. Artistic Director Duncan McIntosh committed the resources of the Citadel to the premiere of *South of China* (1997), an ambitious epic by Raymond Storey, who had worked with Theatre Network before his departure to Toronto. When Shoctor hired Edmonton native and former artistic director of Edmonton's Phoenix Theatre, Bob Baker, in 1999, hopes were high for more Canadian, if not Albertan content for the Citadel. Baker obliged with a premiere of a Depression-era political murder-mystery, *The Aberhart Summer* (2000) by Conni Massing, *Doing Leonard Cohen* (2002) by One Yellow Rabbit's Blake Brooker and three new plays by Vern Thiessen: *Einstein's Gift* (MacLab stage, 2003), *Shakespeare's Will* (Rice stage, 2005) and *Vimy* (MacLab 2007).

Theatre 3 was founded as an "alternative" to the Citadel in 1970 by Mark Schoenberg, a professor at the University of Alberta, focusing more on non-commercial works. Theatre 3 offered a season of all-Canadian plays in 1972/73 and premiered Pollock's *Blood Relations* in 1980, as well as Frank Moher's adaptation of a short story by Henry Kreisel, *The Broken Globe* (1976). Following its closure in 1981, it was reborn as the Phoenix Theatre, which featured a controversial American and British modern repertoire and developed a young and hip Edmonton audience under the leadership of Bob Baker, followed by Jim Guedo, until it, too, encountered financial difficulties and closed in 1997.

The two "alternative" theatres in Edmonton, with a specific mandate to develop and produce Canadian plays, have been Theatre Network and Workshop West, and during the 1980s Edmontonians enjoyed a wealth of new Alberta plays. Between 1985 and 1995, seventy per cent of Theatre Network productions were scripted by Edmonton writers. It was founded as a non-equity collective in 1975 by a group of University of Alberta BFA students, including Tanya Ryga and Mark Manson. Its original objective was to produce plays about Alberta for Albertans, and its first productions were collective social satires, docu-dramas and community plays, including *Hard Hats and Stolen Hearts: A Tar Sands Myth* (with Gordon Pengilly, 1977) which toured throughout Alberta, the Northwest Territories and to Newfoundland and Toronto. Other significant early productions were George Ryga's *Seven Hours to Sundown* (1976) and Sharon Pollock's *Tracings*. Under Artistic Director Stephen Heatley, the theatre supported playwrights-in-residence and developed mentorship relationships with its playwrights. In 1981, it became part of the Theatresports network and established partnerships with other theatres in Alberta and across Canada.

Theatre Network's premieres of Alberta plays have included the musical *Country Chorale* (1982) by Raymond Storey and John Roby, with k.d. lang in the chorus; *Wolfboy* (1982), Brad Fraser's first play; *The Deer and the Antelope Play* (1983) with Edmonton actor Paul Gross, a graduate from the University of Alberta's BFA programme; *Odd Jobs* (1985) by Frank Moher, nominated for the Governor General's Literary Award for drama; *The Mail-Order Bride* (1988) by Robert Clinton, winner of the Alberta Culture Playwriting competition; *The Last Bus* by Raymond Storey; *The Third Ascent* (1988) by Frank Moher, winner of a Sterling for Outstanding New Play; *Elephant Shoes* (1990) and *Uncle Joe Again* (1991) by Ian Fergusson; *Castrato* (1992) by Greg Nelson, also winner of a Sterling; a revised form of *Martin Yesterday* (1998) by Brad Fraser; *Scraping the Surface* (1996) by Lyle Victor Albert (Sterling winner). Theatre Network has also hosted productions by Calgary puppeteer Ronnie Burkett, including *Tinka's New Dress*, *Street of Blood*, *Happy* and *10 Days on Earth*.

New play development, music, dance and poetry are now showcased in the annual NeXtFest Arts Festival, initiated in 1996 under the directorship of Bradley Moss. Stage productions have included *SuperEd* by Chris Craddock, *Tuesdays and Sundays* by Daniel Arnold and Medina Hall (anthologized in *NeXtFest*, NeWest Press, 2000); and the premiere of *Metis Mutt* by Sheldon Elter (2003), an autobiographical monologue which exposes racism without losing its sense of humour. Elter subsequently performed *Metis Mutt* at the Magnetic North Theatre Festival in Ottawa in 2003 and toured it throughout Canada and in New Zealand.

Workshop West was established in Edmonton in 1978 by Gerry Potter, a graduate from the University of Alberta. Its original mandate was three-fold: to give Edmonton a chance to share in the explosion of new Canadian theatre by producing shows that had proved popular elsewhere; to give Alberta playwrights more access to the stage; and to develop playwriting talent in Alberta. In 1985, Workshop West initiated a "Playwriting Ensemble" of eight theatre artists. Over the next two years, the ensemble worked collectively to produce new works, including *It's your Turn to get Up*, and to adapt stories from other media, such as *Sweatlodge Tails* and *The Rich Man*, based on the novels by Henry Kreissel. It also worked with Alberta playwrights Brad Fraser, Frank Moher, Marty Chan, Conni Massing, Stewart Lemoine, Ronnie Burkett and Vern Thiessen. In 2000, Ron Jenkins became artistic director and in the 2001/02 season he won the Sterling Award for best director for the Workshop West production of *Mesa* by Doug Curtis. He initiated the KaBoom! Theatre Performance series, featuring new and unusual Canadian plays, and Playwrights Garage, which featured fifteen-minute readings of new works. For the past seventeen years, Workshop West has also hosted the Loud 'N' Queer Cabaret, a festival of gay performing arts.

University of Alberta professor, David Barnet, founded Catalyst Theatre in 1977 as a social-action theatre. The mandate of Catalyst was "to promote and practise the use of theatre for public education and as a catalyst for social change." It commissioned works about alcoholism, drug and sexual abuse, Native rights, immigration and suicide, as well as initiating its own plays. These were performed in found spaces and sometimes toured in the province. In 1979, Barnet hired Jan Selman (now head of the Drama Department at the University of Alberta) as artistic director. In 1985, Ruth Smillie became artistic director for a ten-year period. Initially, many of the works were created collectively. A notable exception to the collective approach was Frank Moher's *Odd Jobs*, written for a co-production with Theatre Network in 1985. It addresses issues of unemployment and old age in a sensitive, imaginative way and has been produced around the world – from Los Angeles to Tokyo.

In 1996, co-directors Jonathan Christenson and Joey Tremblay committed "to creating original Canadian work that explores new possibilities for the theatrical art form and the process through which it is created, to exposing the work locally, nationally and internationally and to challenging the artists and audiences who participate in the a mixed season of American, Irish, British and Canadian works; and many of Belke's plays have travelled across Canada and the United States.

The Varscona is also home to Teatro la Quindicina, a collective of actors and playwright and founder, Stewart Lemoine, whose work also originated at the Fringe. He co-wrote his first play, *All These Heels*, for the Fringe in 1982, and provided a new play nearly every summer until he ended his association with the Festival in 2003, preferring to focus his attention on developing a season of plays for his company.

## Calgary

Theatre Calgary, founded in 1968, was the first professional theatre company in Stampede City. Its origins are in the merger of Workshop 14, an amateur theatre company formed in the 1940s by the students of Betty Mitchell, drama teacher at Calgary's Western Canada High School; and The Musicians' and Actors' Club (MAC), which staged short plays and excerpts from musicals in the old Isis movie house in the 1960s. Under the direction of Kenneth Dyba, playwright and novelist, MAC 14 staged its productions in a converted tractor house. It also toured the province, and in 1967 among its company, the "Prairie Players," was Sharon Pollock, performing in *Mary, Mary*, a play which convinced her that she could write better ones.

The first artistic director of the newly named Theatre Calgary was Christopher Newton (1968–1971), who produced two of his own plays, *You Stay Here, The Rest Come Along With Me* and *Trip*, and invited Toronto actors to his seasons. Artistic director Harold G. Baldridge (1973–1978) directed the premiere production of Sharon Pollock's *Walsh* (1973) and W.O. Mitchell's *Back to Beulah* (1976). Rick McNair (1978–1984) encouraged the production of Canadian plays and formed a travelling theatre troupe which brought plays to schools in Western Canada. McNair commissioned and produced an adaptation of Robert Kroetsch's novel, *The Words of My Roaring* and of W.O. Mitchell's stories, *The Black Bonspiel of Wullie MacCrimmon* (1979) and *The Kite* (1981). He also directed John Murrell's *Farther West* (1982) and premieres of Pollock's *Whiskey Six Cadenza* (1983) and *Doc* (1984). Sharon Pollock then assumed the position of artistic director for three months, resigning after a difference of opinion with the board over the prerogatives of artistic direction. In 1985, the company moved to the 750-seat proscenium Max Bell Theatre in the Epcor Centre for the Performing Arts. During his tenure as artistic director from 1985 to 1991, Martin Kinch introduced George Walker's plays to Calgary and hired Alberta writer, Gordon Pengilly, as playwright-in-residence. Dennis Garnhum, appointed artistic director in September 2005, has followed the formula for professional theatre seasons in Canada: including one musical and one Canadian play, without prioritizing Alberta works. The 2007 production of *The Wars*, adapted by Garnhum from Timothy Findley's novel, was the first premiere of a Canadian play at Theatre Calgary in nineteen years.

Since its inception in 1972, Alberta Theatre Projects has fostered a close connection with Alberta plays and writers. It was the first Alberta theatre to dedicate itself to the production of Canadian works, commissioning local plays based on historical themes, and performing in the old Canmore Opera House in Heritage Park. Now located in the Martha Cohen Theatre, also part of the Epcor Centre for the Performing Arts, ATP has produced the early works of W.O. Mitchell, such as *The Devil's Instrument* (1977), the premiere of John Murrell's *A Great Noise, A Great Light* (1976), set in Calgary during Aberhart's rise to power and *Waiting for the Parade* (1977). Sharon Pollock's *The Wreck of the National Line Car* (1978) and *Generations* (1981) also premiered at ATP, while she was playwright-in-residence, following Murrell's tenure. ATP has also produced the works of Edmonton playwrights Frank Moher (*Prairie Report* in 1989 and *Odd Jobs* in 1994), Robert Clinton (*The Mail Order Bride* in 1990), and Raymond Storey (*The Glorious Twelfth* in 1994).

ATP has featured an annual new play festival since 1987, which includes four fully developed mainstage productions of Canadian plays, platform performances and readings. PlayRites has premiered many Alberta plays: *Gravel Run* (1988), *Sky Geezers* (1992), *The Aberhart Summer* (1999) and *The Myth of Summer* (2005) by Conni Massing; *Kidnapping the Bride* (1991), *Tolstoy's Wife* (1997) and *Weather* (1999) by Frank Moher; *The Colour of Coal* (1988), *A Change of Mind* (1991) and *Illegal Entry* (1995) by Clem Martini; *Some Assembly Required* (1994), *Sitting on Paradise* (1996), *A Guide to Mourning* (1998), *Appetite* (2000), *Midlife* (2002) and *All Clear* (2004) by Eugene Stickland; *Unidentified Human Remains and the True Nature of Love* (1989) and *The Ugly Man* (1992) by Brad Fraser; *Waves* (1989) by Lyle Victor Albert; *Respectable* (2001) and *The Knowing Bird* (2007) by Ron Chambers; *The Red Priest* (2003) and *The Blue Light* (2006) by Mieko Ouchi; and *Mary's Wedding* (2002) by Stephen Massicotte. Many of these plays have since been produced in Edmonton theatres and across the country. The current artistic director of ATP is Bob White, who has established a close relationship with the Banff Centre in the development of new Alberta plays.

Lunchbox Theatre is the longest running lunchtime theatre in the world: it has offered one-act plays in Calgary's city centre since 1975 and has commissioned and premiered more than sixty Canadian works, many of them by Alberta playwrights such as Clem Martini, Eugene Stickland and Gordon Pengilly. The Loose Moose Theatre Company, founded in 1977 by Keith Johnstone and Mel Tonkin, still performs theatresports, hosting local groups and international competitions.

Theatre Junction, an ensemble theatre company founded in Calgary in 1991 by Mark Lawes, has as its mandate the creation and performance of challenging works by local, national and international playwrights. It places itself at the "junction" of different manifestations of performance art. Premieres of Alberta plays have included three by Sharon Pollock: *Moving Pictures* (1999), *End Dream* (2000) and *Angel's Trumpet* (2001). In 2006, Theatre Junction relocated from a small theatre space in the basement of the Southern Jubilee Auditorium to the newly restored Grand Theatre, and reconfigured the resident company of artists as a multidisciplinary group from theatre, dance, music, literary and visual arts.

Theatre in Calgary has taken on a more radical, experimental dimension since the founding of One Yellow Rabbit in 1982 by Michael Green and Blake Brooker, later joined by dancer and performance artist Denis Clarke. The company's approach is transgressive and multi-disciplinary, and to this end they have performed works like John Murrell's *Death in New Orleans*, Brad Fraser's *The Ugly Man* and their own work, such as *Doing Leonard Cohen* (1997), which enacts Cohen's poems and novel, *Beautiful Losers*, through text, dance and puppetry. Michael Green is also founder and curator of the High Performance Rodeo (1987), Calgary's annual international festival of the alternative arts, which hosts a wide range of works—dance, comedy, interdisciplinary and performance art. Every January it extends audience experience and provokes controversy, hosting a range of theatre practitioners including Teatro la Quindicina's production of *Caribbean Muskrat* (2003) by Stewart Lemoine and Josh Dean; Daniel MacIvor's *Cul-de-Sac* (2004); and Chris Craddock and Steve Pirot's *Faithless* (2005).

The Ghost River Theatre Company also extends theatre practice in Calgary. Founded in Calgary in 1991 as a text-based theatre with a focus on storytelling, it then moved the text into performance, incorporating movement and music, and now specializes in a hybrid form of theatre called "rock 'n roll storytelling." Since 1992, the Company has travelled across the country, appearing at various Fringe Festivals, with Doug Curtis as storyteller, Lester Quitzau on guitar and Peter Moller as comedic/percussion sidekick. Ghost River became the subject of national controversy in 2001 when it mounted *An Eye for an Eye: An Oil and Gas, Piss and Vinegar Cabaret*. The production performed the ongoing saga of environmental protestor/terrorist/preacher Wiebo Ludwig and the death of a local girl on Ludwig's farm. It played in the National Arts Centre as Alberta's centennial contribution.

Calgary's theatre scene has been doing a brisk business in the twenty-first century, with new companies, such as Ground Zero, Sage, Mob Hit and Downstage, inhabiting found spaces and opulent new theatre venues, like the Vertigo Theatre, with two stages at the base of the Calgary Tower, the larger stage producing only murder mysteries, one of which has included Sharon Pollock in the cast. There is little fear of competition in the theatre communities of Calgary and Edmonton. "I say bring it on, the more the better," says Theatre Network executive director Bradley Moss. "Something new elevates all of us. If something new comes in and becomes successful, that's what makes a scene." (Quoted in *Edmonton Journal* 9 Oct 2007.)

## Lethbridge

As George Mann ironically points out in his detailed study of theatre in Lethbridge, "it was the two major institutions of social control, the Church and the NWMP, which provided the community with its first local musical and dramatic entertainment" (5) at the end of the nineteenth century, before the arrival of the railway. Most of these amateur events were fundraisers for charitable activities, performed in church and recreation halls. During the mid-1890s, Captain R. Burton Deane, an inspector in the NWMP, used his theatre experience in England to good effect in the production of melodrama and comedy. His initiatives were continued by another British immigrant, and member of the NWMP, Tim Dunne, who organized a Literary Society comprising the employees of the Alberta Railway and Coal Company. Touring professional stock companies also provided a range of entertainments from their repertoires, and by the early twentieth century, more modest versions of the opulent theatres in Calgary and Edmonton were housing their performances, as well as films. Despite their optimistic names—the Monarch, the Empress and the Majestic—all had brief lifespans.

During the 1920s and 30s, with the falling-off of touring companies, it was the local amateur "Little Theatre" groups which took the initiative in play production in Lethbridge. In 1923, E.G. Sterndale Bennett and his wife, Belle, established The Playgoers Club of Lethbridge, as an artistic enterprise rather than a charitable one, and building on a British dramatic tradition initiated by their predecessors. They also brought to the city their considerable acting skills and their desire to train new theatre practitioners, until their departure for Toronto in 1932. With his second wife, Hilda Church, Bennett created the Canadian Theatre School in Toronto, the first full-time organization dedicated to the development of professional theatre practitioners in Canada. The development of amateur theatre was given a further incentive through participation in the Alberta Drama League, until its disbandment in 1968, and the participation of local educators such as George Mann in the Playgoers Club. In 1971, the University of Lethbridge established a Drama Department, opening up opportunities for the production of contemporary Canadian plays by students and providing institutional support for Alberta playwrights, such as Ron Chambers, who studied drama at the university, and has been a faculty member since 1988. His plays have been produced at the Edmonton Fringe (*Leather Leather*, 1998); at Theatre Network (*Dirt*, 1996, *Marg Szkaluba [Pissy's Wife]*, 1994); at Workshop West (*17 Dogs*, 2003), ATP (*Respectable*, 2001, *The Knowing Bird*, 2007); and at Theatre Passe Muraille (*Pretty Blue*, 1994). In 1993, he wrote the text for a dance theatre work with Lisa Doolittle, entitled *Into Africa*, performed at the university and subsequently by One Yellow Rabbit in Calgary.

## A Short Survey of Playwrights

As is abundantly evident from the preceding abbreviated history of Alberta theatre, the relationship of playwrights and theatre companies in the province is symbiotic: playmaking is a communal, collective process, and in Alberta, it originates and flourishes through a network of associations, mentoring and friendships. Plays developed in one space may migrate to full productions in another. Plays which premiere at ATP's playRites Festival, and are workshopped at the Banff Centre, often travel north to Edmonton theatres the following year; Mieko Ouchi's *The Red Priest*, for example. And the traffic also flows in the other direction. Highway 2 is a busy cultural corridor. The Alberta Playwrights Network, incorporated in 1985, also plays an important role in supporting its members through mentorship, dramaturgy and public readings. In 1998 Sharon Pollock was elected president and has actively encouraged the new works of Alberta playwrights. In 2007, the president was Eugene Stickland, and the Edmonton liaison was David Belke.

## FRANK MOHER

Like many Alberta playwrights, directors and actors, Frank Moher studied at the University of Alberta. For the past thirty years, first in Edmonton, and now from his home base on Gabriola Island, he has written more than twenty-five plays and has taught playwriting at the University of Alberta, the University of British Columbia and Malaspina University-College. He has also written extensively for magazines and newspapers, including *The Globe and Mail, Saturday Night, Alberta Report* and *backofthebook.ca.*

His most popular work, *Odd Jobs*, premiered at Theatre Network , Edmonton, 1985. It was nominated for a Governor General's Literary Award, a Chalmers Award and won the Los Angeles Drama League Award in 1993. It has been produced across Canada, in the United States, New Zealand, Japan and Ireland. Among his other plays, *The Broken Globe* premiered at Theatre Three in 1976; *Down For The Weekend* at Northern Light Theatre in 1980; *The Third Ascent* at Theatre Network in 1988; *Kidnapping the Bride* at Alberta Theatre Projects in 1991; *Supreme Dream* at Theatre Network, 1995; *Tolstoy's Wife* at Alberta Theatre Projects, 1997; and *Big Baby* at playRites 2006.

Moher's works are typically aimed at political, social and/or moral conundrums, whether in a comic or a tragic mode. He has challenged the fundamentalist politics of Alberta, instigated and perpetuated by long successions of strong majority governments dominated by paternalistic leaders since the ascendancy of William Aberhart in 1935 – the religious rhetoric translated into a business agenda, in which the unexamined economic imperatives of capitalism have assumed the values of a fundamentalist religion. However, Moher does not oversimplify the conflict of values in his plays: he believes that "drama should act as a catalyst to thought," that "thinking is social action" (Interview).

In *Prairie Report* (Workshop West 1988), the conflict of conservative versus liberal values is appropriately set in a newsroom presided over by a benign patriarch, a thinly-disguised portrait of Ted Byfield, the former publisher of *Alberta Report*, and the voice of fundamentalist politics in Alberta, who treated most of his employees with a sort of "bemused benevolence" (Preface 9), and who took a paternal interest in Moher's work as a review editor for *Alberta Report*. In this play, Moher shows that in any extreme, unexamined view, there is a potential for the abuse of power, whether it be on the right or the left of the political spectrum.

Moher demonstrates the much more horrific consequences of the ascendancy of the politics of the righteous in *The Third Ascent*. The protagonist is Henry Stimson, the United States Secretary for War during World War II, whose political philosophy had devastating consequences beyond his country. In *The Third Ascent*, Stimson aspires to become an "invincible warrior" by climbing Chief Mountain, located just south of the Canadian border in Montana, and which he describes as jutting out onto the prairies "as if leading the peaks of Montana into battle" (9). Guided by Thomas, a Blood Indian from the Cardston area, he makes three attempts to climb the mountain; on the first two he is successful, but his third attempt is imagined; he has been defeated by his own moral culpability in the decision to drop an A-bomb on Hiroshima. Moher intersects three different time frames: 1891 when Stimson was a young idealistic lawyer, making his first ascent; 1921 when he worked as an ambitious "servant" of the government; and sometime after the bombing of Hiroshima, when he was in his eighties. In this way, Moher shows the extent to which "the past inhabit[s] the present, accusing it and exacting a terrible revenge for it" (Nicholls, review B6). Thomas, his Native guide, also comes to a realization of the destructive consequences of compromising the beliefs of his people, an awakening that coincides with his discovery of Stimson's terrible decision.

## CONNI MASSING

Conni Massing is a graduate of the MFA playwriting program at the University of Alberta, and writes for theatre, film and television. She has been writer-in-residence at Theatre Network (1988–92), Playwrights' Workshop Montreal (1994) and the National Theatre School (1995). She also teaches stage and screenwriting. She has written sixteen plays, including *Gravel Run, Sky Geezers, Dustsluts, The Aberhart Summer, Homesick* and *The Myth of Summer*, which have been produced in both Edmonton and Calgary. *The Aberhart Summer* premiered at Great West Theatre Company, Fort MacLeod in 1994, directed by David Mann; and was subsequently presented at Alberta Theatre Projects as part of playRites 1999 and at the Citadel Theatre in January, 2000. Both of these productions were directed by Stephen Heatley, who was instrumental in the development of the play. *The Aberhart Summer* is an adaptation of a political murder mystery by Bruce Allen Powe, set during the early years of Social Credit in Alberta. It touches on the ongoing problem of how Canada deals with outsiders (whether they are immigrants, religious minorities or the sexually suspect) and how Canada's political machines are greased by cronyism.

Massing's plays are typically characterized by a quirky sense of humour, an ironic consideration of contemporary dysfunctional family life and a keen ear for colloquial dialogue. *Homesick* (Workshop West Theatre 2000, directed by David Mann) is a portrait of a prairie family with secrets that finally force their way out of the past in bizarre, grotesque ways, when a long absent daughter returns home for a funeral.

The gothic comedy *Gravel Run* was first produced by Alberta Theatre Projects in Calgary for novaplayRites '88, as part of the Olympic Arts Festival. It was subsequently performed in Edmonton at Theatre Network, again directed by Stephen Heatley and then transferred to the 25th Street Theatre in Saskatoon as part of the Carlton Trail exchange of plays. Massing grew up in a small town in Alberta and wanted to dramatize its eccentricities and its strong individuality in a non-naturalistic style. *Gravel Run* is the portrait of a family whose tribal customs are peculiar to rural Alberta – the gravel run and the bush party being but two. The others are more sinister, and yet perpetuated all in the best interests of family cohesion.

In *Gravel Run*, a claustrophobic domestic interior is established through clutter: every dust collector and trashy trinket is lovingly preserved and displayed as accumulated family history. The Sorenson family appears, at first, to be a typical

Canadian nuclear family: Papa loved to hunt, Mama loves to cook and to assemble photos of her ideal family; son Billy works as a car wrecker; daughter Leona has just returned from five years at university, bringing with her a fiancé, an anthropologist who is intrigued by the social rituals of his prospective in-laws.

Gothic comedy seems a peculiar phenomenon of the prairies. Saskatchewan contributions to the genre include *Cold Comfort* by Jim Garrard, *Canadian Gothic* by Joanna McClelland Glass and *Sky* by Connie Gault. They are characterized by sexual deviancy and latent or overt domestic violence; in each play the family relationships become twisted and distorted. The female protagonists attempt to escape the family trap by defying conventional social patterns of behaviour.

## DAVID BELKE

David Belke's dramatic forte is the closely observed comic rituals of social loners and eccentrics. His plays sympathetically scrutinize the foibles of human nature and often have a strong moral underpinning which informs the confusions of his characters. He graduated from the University of Alberta with a B.Ed, and has worked in many aspects of theatre production, including stage design and acting in the weekly Rapid Fire Theatre improvs at the Varscona Theatre.

His familiarity with and love for Shakespeare are evident in his satiric spoofs on the complexities and absurdities of Shakespeare's plots and characters: in *The Maltese Bodkin* the characters from *Richard III* are transplanted to a "B-movie" private-eye scenario. In *The Red King's Dream*, Steven Tudor plays the role of a Shakespearean fool and quotes his favourite playwright liberally.

Belke has written two apocalypse plays: *Blackpool and Parrish*, in which personifications of good and evil play a game of chess to determine the fate of humanity; and *Riders of the Apocalypse (The Reunion Tour)*, a sequel in which Death has some reservations about her profession. In *Another Two Hander or Two* Belke turns a rehearsal of Bernard Shaw's *Village Wooing* into a comedy which replicates the confusions of Shaw's characters. In *That Darn Plot*, a playwright is haunted by the characters he has created from his personal life as he struggles to write one more play. *Ten Times Two* is a moral sex fable which tracks a relationship through five hundred years of encounters. *Becoming Sharp* investigates the ways in which the author of popular murder mysteries is upstaged by the young woman she hires as a ghostwriter. Several of his comedies allude to the whimsical, fantastical rabbit-hole world of *Alice in Wonderland*: *The Red King's Dream* (1996), *Between Yourself and Me* (2001) and *The Raven and the Writing Desk* (2006), the title of which references a riddle asked of Alice by the Mad Hatter at their tea party, and to which there is no answer.

Belke's riddles are typically about human relationships – love and friendship, misunderstandings and confusions. In *The Red King's Dream*, the innocent protagonist, Steven Tudor, is enticed away from his orderly but limited reality into a chaotic fantasy world of possibilities when he falls in love with his neighbour. His job as a maker of indices is to find the logic in the nonsense, and his life is rigorously controlled by his editor, whose role mirrors that of the Red Queen. His friend, Amy, introduces an element of spontaneity and personal mayhem into his life, but neither woman upsets his balance until he meets Zoe, who assumes the role of Alice in his imagination. Their witty repartee is both amusing and informative, with occasional Wildian aphorisms on love and marriage. The play also explores the positive and negative attributes of solitary life versus living with another, and undertakes a sociological study of "love." Like the protagonist in Lemoine's play, *The Exquisite Hour*, Steven explores the world through encyclopedias, and discovers all kinds of esoteric details which broaden his understanding of life. And like Lemoine's plays, most of his works, including *The Red King's Dream*, were written for production at the annual Edmonton Fringe Festival, and performed in the Varscona Theatre. Both playwrights investigate the imaginative possibilities of language and music in their comedies, creating fantastical worlds as preferred alternatives to limiting mundane reality.

## VERN THIESSEN

Thiessen's works are historically and philosophically ambitious: they are often engaged in ethical debates on a personal and political level, ranging across cultures and histories to consider the possibility of exercising humanist values despite betrayals and compromises and the possibility of faith and belief in a world bent on self-destruction. His plays range in style from introspective monologue to Theatre of the Absurd to historical epic. Several explore the cultural contradictions and "outsider" status of his "German-speaking-Russian-Mennonite-turned-Canadian" heritage (quoted in Dyck Fehderau, "Introduction," *The Courier and Other Plays* iii). Thiessen's self-reflexive monologue, *The Courier* (Agassiz Theatre, Winnipeg 1987) explores this Mennonite cultural complexity. Thiessen himself undertook the role of David Dyck, a young Mennonite from the Russian Ukraine, working as a courier for the Nazis in 1945 in occupied Czechoslovakia, and eventually coming to terms with his identity and his loyalties. In his "sequel" monologue, *Back to Berlin* (Solo Collective, Vancouver 2005), Thiessen again interrogates the identity of his conflicted protagonist by imagining a visit to the "ol' country" by an eighty-year-old Mennonite and his reluctant middle-aged son, although as the son points out, his father was not even a real German. He was born in Russia: "A German speaking Mennonite living on a colony in the Russian Ukraine. All very confusing" (*The Courier and Other Plays* 37). In *Einstein's Gift*, Thiessen again returns to his roots and compares the philosophies and beliefs of physicist Albert Einstein and chemist Fritz Haber in respect to their scientific research and the ironic and tragic consequences of their work. Thiessen's epic portrait of World War I, *Vimy* (Citadel 2007), enacts the emergence of a national consciousness through the memories of four young Canadians on the battlefield and during their painful recovery process in a hospital, attended by a hovering Angel of Life and Death personified by a nurse.

In his monologue, *Shakespeare's Will* (Citadel Theatre 2005), Thiessen focuses on the life and times of Anne Hathaway, following the death of her long absent husband. Shakespeare's wife finally has her say about the casual personal betrayals so often attendant on genius, and the price paid by those who live in its shadow, in order that it may shine more brilliantly. *Shakespeare's Will* is an introspective memory play, an extended extemporization on life, death, love and marriage which speaks back to the male-centred soliloquies in Shakespeare's tragedies.

Thiessen's earlier play, *Blowfish*, is, like *Shakespeare's Will*, a memory play in the form of a monologue. Commissioned by Workshop West Theatre in 1995, it was extensively workshopped by several theatres across the country, and opened on November 6, 1996 at the Commerce Place in downtown Edmonton, with a symposium banquet for the audience. *Blowfish* explores the possibility of living humanist values through an extended philosophical monologue, spoken by a caterer named Lumiere. His life unfolds as a series of disasters that test his beliefs, but which finally inform his beliefs. He formulates a philosophy of dying, which is integral to his philosophy of living, and he takes his cue from Socrates – whose dying provided the opportunity for one last symposium with his followers. A humanist philosophy that values rationality and self-determination is defined through interrogation and debate, not through fixed systems or ideologies. Thiessen's play employs a Socratic mode of inquiry that activates and energizes doubt and irony, pitting the chaotic, irrational forces of a tornado against the positive cohesive elements of family as a microcosm of human society.

Vern Thiessen has played many roles in the Edmonton theatre community since his graduation from the MFA playwriting program at the University of Alberta – actor, playwright, dramaturge, teacher. He has been playwright-in-residence at Workshop West, where he co-founded the Playwrights Garage Development Program with Ron Jenkins, and at the Blue Heron Arts Centre in New York. He has also been an Honorary Research Fellow in Playwriting at the University of Alberta. He was the literary liaison for the Alberta Foundation for the Arts, president of the Playwrights Guild of Canada from 2002–04, president of the Writers Guild of Alberta and an Artistic Associate of Dramaturgy and Play Development at the Citadel Theatre.

## CLEM MARTINI

Clem Martini has a BFA from the University of Calgary, where he is now a professor in the Drama Department. He writes plays, film scripts and fiction, particularly for young people. With Kathleen Foreman he has written a book on theatresports – *Something Like a Drug* (Red Deer Press, 1995); and on playwriting – *The Blunt Playwright* (Playwrights, 2006). Martini is a three-time winner of the Alberta Writers Guild Drama prize and a Governor General's Literary Award nominee for his anthology of one-act plays, *Three Martini Lunch* (Red Deer Press, 2000), which includes *Conversations with My Neighbour's Pit Bull*, *House of Glass* and *Up On The Roof*. These microcosmic portraits of urban angst comment on larger issues of violence, racism and individual responsibility and choice.

Martini's plays have been produced in Alberta and across Canada, thirteen of them at Calgary's Lunchbox Theatre, including *Afterlife* (2005), *The Replacement* (2004), *Turnaround* (1999), *Bite Me* (1997), *Borrow Me* (1997) and *Up On The Roof* (1995). His full-length play, *Illegal Entry*, was produced at Alberta Theatre Projects in 1995 and *Selling Mr. Rushdie* at Workshop West Theatre in 1997.

Clem Martini's works exhibit a strong social conscience and a quirky sense of humour, often focusing on the lives of troubled teens. *Selling Mr. Rushdie* explores Western culture's obsession with fame and wealth and challenges the notion of freedom of speech – whether it can go too far, or whether it is ineffective compared to violent action. Three teens from a residential school for young offenders, working in a seedy bar, kidnap a man who claims to be Salman Rushdie. They then attempt to figure out how they will claim the million dollar *fatwa* reward, even though the man now denies that he is Rushdie; however, he proves to be a formidable opponent, demonstrating the power of words to both persuade and confuse.

## EUGENE STICKLAND

Born in Regina in 1956, Eugene Stickland graduated with a Masters in Fine Arts from York University and began his career developing plays with Act IV Theatre Company. In 1989, he returned to Regina and co-founded Laughing Dog Theatre. Since 1989, he has lived in Calgary where he was playwright-in-residence at Alberta Theatre Projects until 2004. He also supervised the educational programming at ATP, including the Student Writers Group and the Theatreblitz! Festival, and was the Canadian delegate to the World Interplay Festival for young playwrights in Australia. Many of his plays have premiered at the ATP playRites Festival, including *Some Assembly Required* (1994), which has been produced more than thirty times across Canada, and in French translation as *Noël de force* at Compagnie Jean-Duceppe. Other playRites premieres include: *Sitting on Paradise* (1996), *A Guide to Mourning* (1998)—the winner of four Betty Mitchell Awards—*Appetite* (2000), *Midlife* (2002) and *All Clear* (2004). A full-length version of his one-act play, *Closer and Closer Apart*, a study of Alzheimer's disease, which premiered in 1999 at Lunchbox Theatre in Calgary, opened at Theatre Network in Edmonton in its 2007 season. *Excavations* premiered at Theatre Network in 2002 and won the 1995 Alberta Playwriting Award.

His plays are characterized by black humour and an absurdist philosophy. They often consider the farcical conundrums of dysfunctional families, failed relationships and endgame scenarios, and satirize the materialist, corporate culture of Alberta. *Excavations* is one of his darker plays, anticipating the apocalypse in *All Clear*. Set in the borderland of Saskatchewan and Alberta, where the landscape has resisted intrusion for millennia, it foreshadows the extinction of the human race in the demise of the dinosaurs. Science and religion are but weak defences, and communication, meaningful relationships and collective action are virtually impossible.

## STEWART LEMOINE

Lemoine's plays are highly imaginative, witty comedies of manners, combining exotic locales with quirky characters. The dialogue is original, the plots fantastical, the themes philosophical. They are contemporary fairy tales for adults, which juxtapose the strange and the familiar, and drawing on the talent for comedy of his company of actors, Teatro la Quindicina. *Shockers Delight!* (1993) is an inquiry into the nature of friendship and love, set in university in the 1950s and in a reconstructed and fantastical Biedermeier era to make possible a reconciliation and acceptance of tragic loss. *Pith!* (1997) dramatizes the imaginary journey from a Rhode Island manor to a hotel in New Orleans and the jungles of Panama and Ecuador by a grieving widow and her companion, escorted by a mysterious sailor who conjures up scenarios and stories that enable a final acceptance of death and a celebration of life. *The Margin of the Sky* (2003) locates a Canadian playwright in Los Angeles, inventing romantic scenarios that express the creative possibilities of the imagination: the sky is not the limit. In all of Lemoine's plays, the creative imagination is a means by which fantasies become psychological realities, often transforming lives and offering the possibility of hope and redemption. They explore ways of achieving balance in a precarious world – through humour, imagination, loyalty and friendship.

Many of his early plays premiered at the Edmonton Fringe Festival, beginning with his first work, *All These Heels*, in 1982. For two decades he provided a new play (sometimes two) for nearly every annual Fringe, always using it as an opportunity to experiment with extravagantly imaginative premises, eccentric characters and exotic locales; e.g. *Cocktails at Pam's*, (1986), *The Swift Hotel* (1990) and *Two Tall, Too Thin* (1992). Lemoine ended his association with the Fringe in 2002 with the production of *The Exquisite Hour* in the Strathcona Legion.

The name, Teatro La Quindicina is serendipitous: an actor happened to be reading Graham Greene's *Travels with My Aunt* during the production of Lemoine's first Fringe play. The company comprises a core group of Edmonton actors who have a long-term relationship with Lemoine and his plays, and for whom Lemoine often constructs his roles: Jeff Haslam and Kate Ryan, for example, the duo in his play, *The Exquisite Hour*, which was reprised at the Varscona by 2007 with the same actors. This is a funny, poignant vignette, a closely observed portrait of the interplay of two personalities – the one introverted and literal, the other imaginative and inquisitive. Zack's realization of the limitations of life, one of Lemoine's finest pieces of writing, was appropriately read by Haslam at the memorial service for Edmonton theatre historian, John Orrell, but its resonance is timeless. Lemoine was presented with a copy of Orrell's history of early Edmonton theatres, *Fallen Empires*, and from that encounter he was inspired to write his work about the visit of Sarah Bernhardt to Edmonton in 1913 *At the Zenith of the Empire*. The theatre community connections in Alberta run deep.

## KATHERINE KOLLER

Edmonton playwright and businesswoman Katherine Koller writes for radio, stage and screen. Her first plays were produced at the Edmonton Fringe Festival. *Cowboy Boots and a Corsage* (1991) tells the story of a resilient woman attempting to save what's left of her family and her legacy by working at a bar. It was revised and produced at FemFest!: A Festival of One-Act Plays by Women, in Winnipeg, June 7–15, 2003 and a radio version was broadcast by the CBC. Other radio plays for the CBC include *Magpie* and *Going to the Dump*. Jagged Edge Lunchbox Theatre in Edmonton has produced three of her one-act comedies: *The Early Worm Club* (2000), *Starter Home* (2001) and *Magpie* (2001). Two new one-acts were produced in 2007: *Perdu* at Walterdale Playhouse in Edmonton and *Intimacy, Inc.* at Alumnae Theatre in Toronto.

Her full-length play, *Coal Valley: The Making of a Miner*, was commissioned by the Town of Drumheller and the Historic Atlas Coal Mine to celebrate the Year of the Coal Miner. It was produced in February 2005 by the Sloughfoot Stubble Jumpers at the Royal Tyrrell Museum Theatre, Drumheller. As the granddaughter of an underground coal miner, Koller took a particular interest in the subject. This epic work outlines the history of coal mining in the Drumheller valley, and the creation and dissolution of a community through fifty years of a miner's life, from a young boy working with the ponies in 1914 until he closes the last mine as a pit boss. In the protagonist's friendship with a Polish immigrant miner, Koller evokes the strong male bonding forged through work underground and through her portrait of their wives, the resilience, courage and strength of the women. The play also indirectly comments on the social conditions of the current oil boom in Alberta – a shortage of housing, a large influx of diverse peoples from abroad, the precarious working conditions of a resource-based economy. Primarily, however, like the plays of Ringwood, it is about the creation of an Alberta community by individuals working together, despite differences, to create a future for their families.

In 2006, Koller received an Alberta Short Term Residency and a Production Residency at the Banff Centre and a grant from the Alberta Foundation for the Arts to write another play about a threatened way of life on the prairies. *The Seed Savers* was inspired by the story of Saskatoon-area farmer Percy Schmeiser, who decided against growing genetically modified canola, and fought back against Monsanto when the company claimed that it had found its patented canola in his fields. Again, Koller focuses on events in terms of a family: farmers for fifty years are faced with losing their farm and their home. Pride, prairie will and a Black granddaughter named Sky give them the strength to stand up against the Monolith Company for the farmers' right to save their own seed. Like Sharon Pollock's prairie play, *Generations*, *The Seed Savers* also portrays intergenerational friction and casts the land as a character. It was first performed as a staged reading at the conference, "West-words: Assessing Western Canadian Playwriting at the Millennium" held at the University of Saskatoon, May 2007, with the Schmeiser family in the audience.

## SHARON POLLOCK

Although she was born in New Brunswick, Sharon Pollock has long identified Alberta as her home. As she has succinctly explained: "You don't always come from the place you're born in. The trick is to recognize it" (quoted in O'Grady 21). Her second full-length play, *Walsh* (1973), was produced by Theatre Calgary, where she also had a brief tenure as artistic director; *One Tiger to a Hill* opened at the Citadel Theatre in Edmonton; and *Blood Relations* (1980), her best-known work, was first produced by Edmonton's Theatre Three. Alberta Theatre Projects premiered *Generations* in 1980 and Theatre Calgary premiered *Whiskey Six Cadenza* in 1983 and *Doc* in 1984. She produced

*Saucy Jack* (1993) and *Death in the Family* (1993) in her own Garry Theatre, which she founded in the run-down Inglewood district in Calgary in an attempt to create a theatre that was close to the pulse of the community, not as a commodity or cultural industry (Much 20). Three of her recent plays, *Moving Pictures* (1999), *End Dream* (2000) and *Angel's Trumpet* (2001) premiered at Theatre Junction in Calgary; and *Man Out of Joint* (2006) premiered at the Vertigo Theatre, also in Calgary. *Kabloona Talk* was presented as a staged reading by Alberta Playwrights Network, where she was playwright-in-residence. She has been a visiting lecturer at the University of Alberta and head of the Playwrights Colony at the Banff Centre for the Arts.

Like *Walsh*, which considers Canadian culpability for the near-genocide of the Sioux Nation, *Kabloona Talk* revisits the historical travesties occasioned by the collision of white authority and Native tradition – this time in Canada's north. It is based on the 1913 killings of two Roman Catholic priests by two Inuit in the Northwest Territories and their subsequent trials in Alberta in 1917. When the first Inuit was acquitted in Edmonton, a new trial was ordered in Calgary, where both were found guilty. As with all of her "history" plays, Pollock researched the story thoroughly, and then extemporized on the factual details to provide the basis for a complex moral, political and social debate, and to interrogate received notions of justice, responsibility and freedom. The play also indirectly examines the current consequences of the colonization of the North and its vast resources, and issues of Canadian sovereignty in the Arctic. The debate takes place in a private room off the courtroom following the Edmonton jury's surprising verdict, and is conducted by four white men (or *kabloona* in Inuit): the judge, the prosecutor, a young and idealistic defence lawyer and a mysterious visitor who is there to make sure that a "correct" solution be found in order to establish the incontrovertibility of white Canadian law in every jurisdiction. The Inuit are absent from the scene, as they have been in the construction of Canada's history. Pollock also felt strongly that their voices not be "appropriated" by a white playwright.

Pollock believes in the social and cultural importance of the playwright in Canadian society, yet she resists national or regional labels. She believes in "the power of metaphor and a shared cultural literacy [that] make almost anything possible. It is important to reach beyond specific interests that address specific audiences... to things which govern many people's lives" (Nothof, Interview 179).

## DOUG CURTIS

Like many Alberta theatre practitioners, Doug Curtis is a man for all seasons: playwright, director, actor and storyteller. He was born in Edmonton in 1964 and studied at the Banff Centre for the Arts and at the University of Calgary.

He has performed in his own stories and in the works of others at theatres and festivals in Edmonton and Calgary, across the country, and on CBC Radio and in film. In 1991, he created Ghost River Theatre, a company dedicated to combining live music and storytelling. He has also collaborated with other playwrights and theatres in the development of new plays. His political satire, *The Climate: A Province in Decline* (1997, co-written with Ken Cameron and Laura Parkin, features the mayor of a western city who finds his next job as premier of Alberta. Curtis developed *Mesa* (2001), about an odd couple's archetypal Alberta winter trip south to Arizona, with Workshop West Theatre. The divergent philosophies of Paul, a thirty-five-year-old wanna-be artist, and his grandfather-in-law, Bud, a ninety-three-year-old, long retired bank manager, are played off against each other, showing their inadequacies and their strengths. Curtis's stories and plays are often autobiographical. *The Ian Parkinson Project* (2005), a surreal musical inspired by his own diaries, is a record of the effects of having Parkinson's disease.

*While My Mother Lay Dreaming* (2006) has its origins in a family incident: returning home one night as a teenager, Curtis found his mother lying on the verandah, contemplating the stars, after slipping on a patch of ice. Curtis looks back to his teenage years in the Calgary suburbs during the oil boom in the early 1980s, a period which prefigures the Alberta scene twenty-five years later: skyrocketing oil prices, thousands of people moving to Calgary, no affordable housing, global tension. Ralph Klein is beginning his long reign in Alberta politics as the mayor of Calgary. The presidency of Ronald Regan anticipates that of George Bush. The unseasonably warm weather hints at climate change. Curtis was writing the play "as kind of an environmental warning, the idea that our economic structure is flawed." He challenges the assumption that "the only way to maintain this lifestyle is to continually mass produce" (quoted in www.beatroute.ca). The disintegrating nuclear family in the play suggests a general social breakdown, as making money becomes the prime motivator. Individuals are losing or have lost a sense of community. Friendship and love are elusive and precarious. The mother's dream is a nightmare. Yet *While My Mother Lay Dreaming* is a comic coming-of-age story which portrays the synchronicities in life – "the coincidence of events that seem related but are not obviously caused one by the other," as the young Ontario immigrant, Jennifer, points out. The surreal juxtaposition of events suggests a dreamscape; as in David Belke's *The Red King's Dream*, the characters imagine more positive possibilities for themselves in a consumerist and materialistic world.

## Bibliography

Anthony, Geraldine. *Gwen Pharis Ringwood.* New York: Twayne, 1981.

Bennett, Susan and Penny Farfan. "'At War with Commercial Entertainment and Mediocrity': Interview with High Performance Rodeo Founder and Curator Michael Green." *Canadian Theatre Review* 124 (Fall 2003): 6–21.

Benson, Eugene, and L. W. Conolly, eds. *The Oxford Companion to Canadian Theatre.* Toronto: Oxford University Press, 1989.

Day, Moira. *The Hungry Spirit: Selected Plays and Prose by Elsie Park Gowan.* Edmonton: NeWest Press, 1992.

Goffin, Jeffrey. "'Canada's Finest Theatre': The Sherman Grand." *Theatre Research in Canada* 8.2 (Fall 1987): 193–203.

Lemoine, Stewart. *At the Zenith of the Empire.* Edmonton: NeWest Press, 2006.

Mann, George. *Theatre Lethbridge: A History of Theatrical Production in Lethbridge, Alberta (1885–1988).* Calgary: Detselig, 1993.

———. *Sterndale Bennett: A Man for All Theatre.* Lethbridge: Lethbridge Historical Society, 2004.

Moher, Frank. *Prairie Report.* Winnipeg: Blizzard Publishing, 1990.

———. Interview with Anne Nothof. November, 1988.

Morrow, Martin. *Wild Theatre: The History of One Yellow Rabbit.* Banff: Banff Centre Press, 2003.

Much, Rita. "Theatre by Default: Sharon Pollock's Garry Theatre." *Canadian Theatre Review* 82 (Spring 1995): 19–22.

Nicholls, Liz. "Literate Play whacks right, left with gusto," *Edmonton Journal*, 22 October 1988: F1.

Nothof, Anne. "Reacting to the Right[eous]: the Political Plays of Frank Moher, Lyle Victor Albert, Raymond Storey, and Greg Nelson," *Prairie Forum* 21.1 (Spring 1996): 75–98.

———. "Introduction: Stewart Lemoine's Canadian Comedia," *A Teatro Trilogy: Selected Plays by Stewart Lemoine.* Edmonton: NeWest Press, 2004. 1–9.

———. "Introduction: Sarah Bernhardt's Edmonton Apotheosis at the Empire," *At the Zenith of the Empire* by Stewart Lemoine. Edmonton: NeWest Press, 2007. 1–9.

———. "Making Community History: The Radio Plays of Ringwood and Gowan," *Edmonton: The Life of a City.* Ed. Bob Hesketh and Frances Swyripa. Edmonton: NeWest Press, 1995. 170–177.

———. Interview with Sharon Pollock. *Sharon Pollock: Essays on her Works.* Toronto: Guernica Editions, 2000. 167–179.

———, Ed. *Canadian Theatre Encyclopedia* (www.canadiantheatre.com).

O'Grady (Nothof), Anne. "Sharon Pollock: Theatre Relations." *Athabasca University Magazine* 8.3 (1983/84): 21–23.

Orrell, John. *Fallen Empires.* Edmonton: NeWest Press, 2006.

Smith, Donald B. *Calgary's Grand Story: the making of a prairie metropolis from the viewpoint of two heritage buildings.* Calgary: University of Calgary Press, 2005.

Stewart, E. Ross. *The History of Prairie Theatre.* Toronto: Simon & Pierre, 1984.

———. "Alberta, Theatre in." *Oxford Companion to Canadian Drama.* Ed. Eugene Benson and L.W. Conolly. Toronto: Oxford, 1989. 9–12.

Thiessen, Vern. *The Courier and Other Plays.* Toronto: Playwrights Canada Press, 2006.

Wagner, Anton. "Elsie Park Gowan: Distinctively Canadian," *Theatre History in Canada* 8.1 (Spring 1987): 68–82.

Wattling, Shari, ed. *Theatre 100: Celebrating 100 Theatre Practitioners Over 100 Years.* Calgary: Alberta Playwrights' Network, 2006.

# The Third Ascent

By Frank Moher

# About
# Frank Moher

Frank Moher's plays have been seen internationally, at theatres including South Coast Rep (Costa Mesa, California), the Canadian Stage Company (Toronto), Workshop West Theatre (Edmonton), the Asolo Theater (Sarasota, Florida), Alberta Theatre Projects (Calgary), The Mingei Theatre (Tokyo) and Dodona Theatre (Prishtina, Kosova). They include *Pause, The Broken Globe, Down for the Weekend, Odd Jobs, Sliding for Home* (with Gerald Reid), *The Third Ascent, Prairie Report, Kidnapping the Bride, Farewell, McLuhan: The Musical* (with Gerald Reid), *Supreme Dream* (with Rhonda Trodd), *All I Ever Wanted, Tolstoy's Wife, Weather, Big Baby* and *Moonbound!* (with Dave Clarke). His plays are published by the Playwrights Guild of Canada and online by ProPlay.

Recipient of the Alberta Culture Playwriting Award, the City of Edmonton Cultural Achievement Award and the Alberta Achievement Award, Frank has also won a Los Angeles Drama-Logue Award for Writing (for *Odd Jobs*), the Edmonton Sterling Award for Outstanding New Play (for both *The Third Ascent* and *Prairie Report*), and is included in the Alberta Playwrights' Network publication *Theatre 100: Celebrating 100 Theatre Practitioners over 100 Years.* He has taught at the University of British Columbia and the University of Alberta, and is currently an instructor in dramatic writing at Vancouver Island University. He has also worked extensively as a literary manager and dramaturge, including creating the online script workshop E-script, and writes regularly for various newspapers and magazines, among them backofthebook.ca. His website is at frankmoher.com.

*The Third Ascent* was first produced by Theatre Network, Edmonton on January 28, 1988 with the following company:

| | |
|---|---|
| TOM | Raul Tome |
| TOMMY | Bill Davidson |
| THOMAS | David Mann |
| HANK | Michael Spencer-Davis |
| HENRY | Kent Gallie |
| STIMSON | Len Crowther |

Directed by Stephen Heatley
Set and Costumes Designed by Daniel van Heyst
Lighting Designed by Robin Ayles
Percussionist: Doug Blackley
Stage Manager: Terri Gillis

---

*The Third Ascent* was written with the assistance of a grant from the Alberta Playwrights Network, and developed through the workshop program at Theatre Network, with the assistance of the Canada Council for the Arts.

## Characters

HANK is Stimson in his twenties.
HENRY is Stimson in his fifties.
STIMSON is Stimson in his eighties.
TOM is Thomas at age twelve.
TOMMY is Thomas at forty-two.
THOMAS is Thomas in his seventies.

## Note

This play is written for six actors.

The actor playing STIMSON plays only that one role. The actors playing HANK, HENRY, TOM, TOMMY and THOMAS also play all the other roles in the play.

The first ascent takes place in 1891, the second in 1921, and the third some time after the bombing of Hiroshima.

Ideally, the play will be done with a cast of Aboriginal, Asian and white actors, with colour-blind casting (i.e., Aboriginal actors play white and Asian characters, etc.) A Japanese child should play the role of the Japanese boy.

# The Third Ascent

## Act One

*A three-level set. These levels can be used horizontally to represent Stimson's three ascents of Chief Mountain at three different periods in his life, or they can be used vertically to indicate movement up the mountain.*

*In the dark, percussion.*

*Then, movement on all three levels – TOM and HANK at the top, TOMMY and HENRY at middle, THOMAS and STIMSON at stage level. Ropes and climbing gear are hauled on, backpacks removed, binoculars called into play.*

**TOM** Mr. Stimson!

**TOMMY** Hey, Stimson!

**HANK** Over here, Tom!

**THOMAS** Put your pack by that boulder there. We won't go any farther tonight.

**TOMMY** Is there any way 'round there?

**HANK** Try pulling it up!

**STIMSON** Why is the last part the hardest?

**HENRY** I shouldn't have come here. I don't know why I did.

**TOM** Mr. *Stimson.*

**TOMMY** Hey, Stimson!

**THOMAS** Because we're a couple of old farts, Henry. That's why.

**HANK** All together now – pull!

**STIMSON** Is this your idea of a stroll?

**TOMMY** Pretty big mountain, eh, Stimson?

**THOMAS** Pretty big mountain. Gets bigger every year—

*The upper levels clear. STIMSON and THOMAS remain, STIMSON straggling behind.*

**STIMSON** *(winded)* Lord! I am too old for this!

**THOMAS** Buck up, Stimson. You're just used to people carrying your bags for you.

**STIMSON** *(sitting)* No one carries my bags for me, Tommy.

**THOMAS** Bullshit. I just carried this. *(He puts STIMSON's pack down.)* We'll go 'round the east side tomorrow. That way no one can see us.

**STIMSON** Is it really so awful, Tommy?

**THOMAS** What?

**STIMSON** Climbing the mountain.

**THOMAS** I don't say it's awful. *(He scans the mountain.)* I just say we're not supposed to do it.

*Light change. STIMSON steps forward.*

**STIMSON** The decision to bomb Hiroshima was almost totally mine. Or rather the decision *not* to bomb Kyoto was mine. I was offered a list of four potential targets by General Groves: Kokura, Hiroshima, Niigata and Kyoto. Kyoto was the choice of the military because they supposed its population of intellectuals would then put pressure on the Japanese government to end the war. But I said no. It seemed to me that Kyoto, with its great history and its religious significance for the Japanese, was an inappropriate target for the atom bomb. I had visited the city as Governor General of the Philippines, and I had liked it very much. It also occurred to me that while the people of Hiroshima might not be supremely well educated, still, they could not misunderstand the importance of our discovery. Nobody could. I did not mention this fact to General Groves. I did not suppose he would appreciate it.

*Laughter. The Yale University Law School dorms, 1884. HANK is with three of his law schoolmates: GULLIVER, SUTTON and WESKER and a professor, DR. POINDEXTER. They drink brandy.*

**GULLIVER** And then what will you do, Stimson?

**SUTTON** Jump off the top!

**WESKER** What *will* you do when you get to the top of this mountain, Stimson? Commune with the gods?

**HANK** The view will be rather impressive, I suppose. *(His CLASSMATES find this very funny.)*

**SUTTON** *(laughing wildly)* The view – The view— ! The view will be rather – impressive! *(He laughs.)*

**GULLIVER** If he's still alive to see it.

**DR. POINDEXTER** *(raising his brandy)* Hear hear, Stimson!

**WESKER** To Henry Stimson. Our little mountain climber.

**GULLIVER** To Hank. The things you don't find out about people! *(They toast him. HANK rises angrily.)*

creation of that work." Their productions include *Elephant Wake* (Edmonton Fringe 1995), a lament for a dying French culture on the prairies, subsumed by an Anglophone hegemony. In the 1996/97 season, the *Abundance Trilogy* explored the dark side of life in Alberta through the lives of the misfits and marginalized, and invited the audience to participate as voyeurs of the gothic tales which unfolded. Christenson, Tremblay and designer Bretta Gerecke developed *The House of Pootsie Plunket* in 1999, a satiric recasting of "Bonanza" style television melodrama in an Alberta environment, with Greek myth underpinnings. In 2000, the collaborative team at Catalyst initiated *The Blue Orphan*, a collage of poetic text and imagery, and for the 2006/07 season Christenson (writer/director/composer) and Gerecke (designer) created an imaginative extemporization on Mary Shelley's gothic novel, *Frankenstein*, which explores the tragic possibilities of both the "Creature" and his Creator.

Like Catalyst, Northern Light has morphed through different mandates and production strategies since its founding in 1975 by Scott Swan (artistic director), Allan Lysell (administrative director) and Angela and Merrilyn Gann (actors) as a lunchtime theatre. It expanded to evening performance of full-length plays in 1976, and in 1979 established a "playwrights unit" for reading and workshopping new plays, including works by Gordon Pengilly, Tony Bell, Frank Moher and Ben Tarver, with Moher as dramaturge. Subsequent directors have featured diverse seasons, becoming more adventurous and provocative, most recently under the direction of playwright and actor Trevor Schmidt, who includes his own works such as *Water's Daughter* and *Blood Oranges* in his seasons.

Edmonton boasts the highest number of professional theatres per capita of any Canadian city. Most are engaged in developing new plays and many have been initiated by talented graduates from the University of Alberta and Grant MacEwan College theatre programs, intent on creating their own style of theatre. "Indie" companies such as Kill Your Television and Trunk, for example, may produce one or more plays a year and have linked up to package their independent productions in an "Indie5" series. Others, such as Azimuth, have originated as social action theatre and tour the province, playing primarily to schools. Many Edmonton theatre groups, playwrights and plays have their origins in the Edmonton International Fringe Theatre Festival – the largest annual expression of the creativity and ingenuity of theatre makers in North America. Since 1981, when it was founded by Edmonton Pied Piper, Brian Paisley, it has expanded to include twelve stages scattered throughout the Old Strathcona region, and eleven "Bring Your Own Venues," constructed by the playmakers in churches, bars, libraries and alleys. Productions are not vetted, chosen by lottery from amongst applicants at home and abroad. Although many are angst-ridden monologues or stand-up comedies, new Alberta plays often emerge from the chaos, which may have a life beyond the Fringe. For fifteen years, David Belke has written an annual full-length comedy for the Fringe, including *The Red King's Dream*. Belke's original production group, Acme Theatre Company, joined forces with Shadow Theatre, which also originated in the Fringe with the production of Sam Shepherd's *Fool for Love* in 1989 by artistic director, John Hudson, and friends from the University of Alberta. Shadow Theatre now remounts Belke's Fringe plays and his other new works in the Varscona Theatre venue as part of

**HANK** You really are a stupid lot of buggers, did you know that?

**GULLIVER** Ohh.

**SUTTON** Ohhhhhhh.

**WESKER** Did you hear that, Dr. Poindexter? He called us a stupid lot of buggers.

**HANK** Chief Mountain happens to be a very sacred place to the Indians of the area. And climbing it happens to be a test of strength.

**GULLIVER** *(Indian caricature)* Ugh.

**SUTTON** Me heap big impressed.

**HANK** And if I ever get to the top—*if* I get to the top—I will have accomplished a lot more than any of you ponces, lounging about Yale law school and drinking your glasses of port!

**WESKER** Brandy.

**HANK** Brandy!

**SUTTON** We really must make a drinker out of Stimson.

**GULLIVER** Oh, come now Stimson, we're only having fun. We're really very impressed with your exploits, and we wish you nothing but a successful climb. Isn't that right, gentlemen?

**SUTTON, WESKER & DR. POINDEXTER** Hear hear. Hear hear.

*SUTTON and WESKER break up laughing.*

**GULLIVER** Dr. Poindexter. Would you care to propose a toast?

**DR. POINDEXTER** *(rising)* To Stimson. Our most courageous student. May he be safe on his travels through the Indian territories. And may he return, his strength well proved, to guide our young land farther down the road to justice and prosperity. And so may you all.

**GULLIVER, SUTTON, WESKER & HANK** Hear hear! Hear hear!

**DR. POINDEXTER** To the men of the Yale Law School. You are America's future.

*Percussion: three beats.*

**TOM** *(moving to the top level)* They say that only one man has ever climbed to the top! They say that when he got there he met the thunderbird – and was never seen again.

**HANK** *(moving to join him)* Uh, that's not true, actually.

**TOM** No?

**HANK** No. Actually, the *first* brave to climb the mountain was a Flathead warrior, and he came away invincible. He couldn't be killed in battle.

**TOM** Oh.

**HANK** At least that's what they say. The first person to climb the mountain from *your* tribe climbed it because the buffalo had disappeared, and he needed to know where they'd gone. And then, of course, some believe that the first person up the mountain was a *woman* whose husband had been killed in battle, and so she wanted to throw herself and her baby off. So. What do you think about that?

**TOM** *(unpacking)* You sure know a lot about Chief Mountain.

**HANK** Yes. Well, I suppose I do. *(He strides around.)* I've brought something special with me. It's called a camera. It's going to be difficult to lug up the mountain. But I do want to document our trip. How old are you, Tom?

**TOM** Twelve.

**HANK** Twelve. Yes, well, you'll want to have some mementos, too. *(pause)* I've also had a change of heart. I think we should go up the east face. Right here.

**TOM** Right here?

**HANK** Mm.

**TOM** But – we can't.

**HANK** Why not?

**TOM** Because – well, look at it!

**HANK** Yes, straight up, fifteen hundred feet. We meet our king, eyeball to eyeball. Hm?

**TOM** Then I'm going back. *(He starts to pack his gear.)*

**HANK** Tom.

**TOM** I'm not going up that way. *(He starts to go.)*

**HANK** Tom! *(TOM stops.)* I'll give you an extra dollar if you climb the east face with me. And who knows? Maybe someday they'll tell legends about you. *(Pause. TOM holds his hand out for the dollar.)* Oh, no. When we get back to Cardston. As agreed. *(TOM goes back to putting up the tent.)* Atta boy.

**TOM** All that stuff about the thunderbird?

**HANK** Yes?

**TOM** I don't believe all that.

**HANK** You don't, eh? Well. We soon shall see.

**THOMAS** *(on another level, to STIMSON)* I don't know, Stimson. I don't know why you come up here.

**TOMMY** *(on another level, to HENRY)* See, the first thing you gotta do is get people interested. If you can get people interested, you can sell 'em just about anything.

**STIMSON** *(Light change. STIMSON addresses the audience.)* I first came into the service of the President in 1906. I had been a partner in the law firm of Root and Clarke and I was a member of the New York County Republican Committee, when President Roosevelt—that is Theodore Roosevelt—appointed me U.S. attorney for the Southern District of New York. I liked Teddy Roosevelt – he wore his prejudices on his sleeve.

In 1910, I ran for governor in New York and was firmly trounced. Not only did my opponents humiliate me, but I finished behind most of my own ticket, as well. The cads. Thereafter, I toyed with elected office but when President Taft appointed me Secretary of War, I felt somehow I had found my place. Serving. A servant. I don't mind calling myself a servant. Servants sometimes run the household.

**TAFT** *(Elsewhere on stage, with his back to the audience. STIMSON watches.)* Stimson!

**STIMSON** Yes, Mr. President?

**TAFT** What the hell's wrong with the army?!

**HENRY** Well, there's nothing really *wrong* with it, sir. It just needs some reorganization.

**TAFT** Well, then reorganize it, would you? Goddammit. We're preparing to fight the Hun!

Randall Read
Theatre Network 1990 production
*photo by Ian Scott*

**HENRY** Yes, sir. Anything… in particular you want done, Mr. President?

**TAFT** No, goddammit. You're the goddamn Secretary of War!

**HENRY** Yes, Mr. President.

**STIMSON** *(to the audience)* You see what I mean.

The conduct of World War II, however, was a different matter entirely. Franklin Roosevelt was a different president; so was Harry Truman. The issues were a great deal more complicated, or so they seemed to me. The world was less innocent. And S-1 changed everything.

**BARD** *(approaching)* Mr. Secretary?

**STIMSON** Yes?

**BARD** May I see you?

**STIMSON** Of course, Mr. Bard. The Navy is always welcome in my office. *(BARD enters.)* I'm just putting some papers in order. Mrs. Stimson doesn't like me working so late, but it seems this is the only time left for this sort of thing. And you?

**BARD** Well, I had a late dinner with the Secretary of the Navy.

**STIMSON** Ah, yes.

**BARD** He does go on.

**STIMSON** Yes.

**BARD** And then I came back here to draft a memo. It's concerning the Franck report. I thought perhaps you should be the first to read it. *(He holds it out to STIMSON. STIMSON does not take it.)*

**STIMSON** Well, I think I would rather hear it from you.

**BARD** Of course.

**STIMSON** I think that would be better.

*Pause.*

**BARD** Dr. Franck proposes a demonstration of the bomb before we use it. He proposes that we explode it on a deserted Pacific atoll so that—

**STIMSON** *Yes,* Mr. Bard, I have read his report.

**BARD** I'm afraid that I agree with him, Mr. Secretary.

**STIMSON** Ah, yes?

**BARD** Well, not in every respect. But enough that I am going to have to change my own opinion. I am going to have to dissent from the findings of the Interim Committee. I hope you will understand.

*Pause.*

**STIMSON** Mr. Bard—

**BARD** Which is why I wanted to see you as quickly as possible.

**STIMSON** Mr. Bard… we have been over this ground before.

**BARD** I know we have, but—

**STIMSON** Certainly, I can understand that we are all still grappling with this, how shall I say, momentous decision we have made. But the decision has been made. You were there.

**BARD** But the decision can be reversed.

**STIMSON** Can it?

**BARD** I think it can, in light of our scientists' disagreements.

**STIMSON** But our scientists are not disagreed. They have told us, a demonstration of the bomb before dropping it is not possible, or at least not advisable. They are not disagreed. Dr. Franck is disagreed!

*Pause.*

**BARD** But surely his views should be taken into consideration.

**STIMSON** They have been.

**BARD** Have they, Mr. Secretary? I am not sure. *(pause)* In any event. I don't propose a demonstration. I propose that we provide the Japanese with information about atomic power and a warning. Then if they do not respond, we may act.

**STIMSON** I see.

**BARD** In our own best interests, of course.

**STIMSON** Yes. *(beat)* Well, I hope you will put your recommendation into letter form to the President. I will see that he reads it.

**BARD** Mr. Secretary.

**STIMSON** *(shaking his hand)* Mr. Bard.

*BARD goes. A SCIENTIST appears on one of the levels.*

**SCIENTIST** Estimated altitude of detonation: One thousand eight hundred and fifty feet. Estimated number of deaths: ten thousand.

*HENRY, GULLIVER and ROOT, pheasant hunting. HENRY and GULLIVER are about fifty. ROOT is in his sixties.*

**GULLIVER** The problem with you, Stimson, is you think we're still at Yale. You think we go in for all that Skull-and-Bones, secret handshakes, let's all be frat brothers shit. But we don't. In the world of jurisprudence, it is every man for himself.

**HENRY** You mean every cad for himself.

**ROOT** Pheasant at two o'clock!

**HENRY, GULLIVER & ROOT** *(They raise their rifles and shoot.)* Blam, blam! Blam, blam! Blam, blam! *(pause)* Missed.

**HENRY** I wonder how three such brilliant lawyers can be such damnable pheasant hunters.

**ROOT** Perhaps it's because you two keep talking.

**GULLIVER** Perhaps.

**HENRY** Have you ever actually shot any pheasant in this field, Mr. Root?

**ROOT** Oh, for chrissakes, Stimson, you're fifty years old. Call me Elihu.

**HENRY** *(uncomfortably)* Elihu.

**ROOT** Besides, we're out of the office. No, I haven't shot any pheasant in this field. But I intend to. Now let's go.

**GULLIVER** Uh, without me, I'm afraid.

**HENRY** Giving up so soon, Gulliver?

**GULLIVER** I'm going to sit here and commune with nature. You'll understand that I'm sure, Stimson.

**HENRY** I understand your feet are sore.

**GULLIVER** By the way, did you know, Mr. Root, that Stimson is going out to sit on top of a mountain again this summer?

**ROOT** That true, Stimson?

**HENRY** Well, it's not exactly a *mountain*—

**GULLIVER** You'd better watch him, Mr. Root. Next thing, he'll want to go off and become a monk!

*HENRY grimaces at GULLIVER, then moves to catch up with ROOT, who has moved to another part of the field. Lights fade on GULLIVER, rubbing his feet.*

**ROOT** *(looking for birds)* I don't know where they've gone, Stimson. I think we are shooting at phantoms. *(Pause. They stand there.)* So how are you anyway? Everything all right?

**HENRY** Oh. Yes, thank you, sir.

**ROOT** Don't think so.

**HENRY** Sir?

**ROOT** Don't think so. Something… down at the mouth about you lately. Didn't get to be senior partner without learning to be a judge of men.

**HENRY** Yes, Mr.… Elihu. *(pause)* Well, I have been a little tired lately.

**ROOT** Tired.

**HENRY** Yes.

**ROOT** You're not very happy out of the White House, are you? Not very happy out of public life?

**HENRY** No, sir. I don't believe I am.

**ROOT** No. Well, there'll be a place for you again soon, soon as we get this piker Harding out of office. Y'know, sometimes that man makes me ashamed to be a Republican. Hard-on, my wife calls him. Hard-on! Ha, ha, ha, ha, ha! *(ROOT enjoys this joke immensely. HENRY is embarrassed.)* And this mountain business. What's the deal there?

**HENRY** The deal, sir?

**ROOT** Went to the mountains myself once. Didn't like 'em. Came home.

**HENRY** Well, as I say, it's not really a *mountain.* It's more of a hill, a *large* hill, about three thousand feet. And *sheer*, especially the crown. It's a particularly beautiful place. Beautiful and awesome, and with a mysterious sort of… presence.

**ROOT** Presence! Presents are something you give! *(He grins. HENRY smiles back.)* Well, don't spend too much time mooning about your mountains, Henry. Remember—Republicans are men of action. Action! Speaking of which—you heard about all that trouble in Nicaragua?

**HENRY** Yes.

**ROOT** *Somebody* oughta take care of it. Pheasant at eight o'clock.

**ROOT & HENRY** *(They raise their rifles and shoot again.)* Blam, blam! Blam! Blam! Blam, blam, blam! *(pause)* Missed again.

**STIMSON** *(from another level, to HENRY)* He never did shoot any pheasant, you know.

**HENRY** What's that?

**STIMSON** Root. He was the worst hunter I'd ever seen.

**TOMMY** *(on another level)* Hey, Stimson. Come on up here. I got something to show you.

**HENRY** *(moving to him)* Can I help you with the fire, Tom?

**TOMMY** Nope. But you could hand me that backpack there. *(HENRY does. TOMMY indicates the mountain.)* Y'see that, Stimson? That's the east face. That's the side we climbed up last time we was up here.

**HENRY** Yes. I remember.

**TOMMY** Pretty hard to believe, eh? Pretty hard to believe we even tried. Then again, you weren't too bright in those days, even if you had been to law school.

**HENRY** Well, thank you very much.

**TOMMY** Now you're much smarter, I can tell. Hey and I'm much smarter, too. Take you up the easy side this time; charge you ten times as much!

*He laughs. HENRY smiles.*

**HENRY** I don't mind paying you well, Tom.

**TOMMY** No, huh?

**HENRY** No. After all… I'd never have found it without you.

*Pause. They work.*

**TOMMY** So, hey, Stimson. You think we taught them Germans a lesson over there?

**HENRY** Where?

**TOMMY** In Europe. The war.

**HENRY** I think we were lucky to get out alive. If the Germans learned any lesson, that is strictly a bonus.

**TOMMY** Oh, yeah?

**HENRY** I cannot tell you how unprepared the American army was. First, to have to stand by while Mr. Woodrow Wilson dithered and philosophized and tried to call a spade a shovel. And then to get over there and find our forces in utter chaos – well. It was more than I could stomach.

**TOMMY** You went over there?

**HENRY** I fought.

**TOMMY** Yeah? No kidding. Hey how about that, Stimson – you got more guts than I thought. *(He slaps HENRY heartily on the back and starts to collect wood for the fire.)* Yeah, well, I been doin' things, too, you wouldn't figure. Didn't save the world, maybe. But it sure as hell saved my ass.

**HENRY** What's that?

**TOMMY** Well, I had me a job puttin' a road inna Glacier for awhile there. And then I had a job buildin' houses. And then I had me a job where I was supposed to watch for bootleggers runnin' whiskey through the pass. Only nobody gives a shit about Prohibition anymore, least of all the Mounties. An' then when I realized that even if I saw somebody, I probably wouldn't stop 'em – well. That job lasted about two weeks.

**HENRY** Alcohol is the curse of your people, Tom.

**TOMMY** *(TOMMY regards STIMSON coolly for a moment.)* Hey, Stimson. You can call me Tommy now. That's what people call me. *(pause)* Anyway. Now that I got a few bucks together, I don't know what I'm gonna do next. But it's gonna be something good. That much I know.

*Quietly, TOMMY prepares his bed for the night. HENRY leans back, staring up at the mountain. Percussion – a faint rattle. After a moment:*

**HENRY** Do you think it's still up there, Tommy?

**TOMMY** What's that?

**HENRY** The skull. The old buffalo skull. The old Flathead's pillow. Do you remember? We found it last time we were up there. And we built a cairn for it, to protect it from the rain. And we held it… and all that good medicine flowed into us. Do you think it's still there? I hope it is. I like to think it is.

**TOMMY** Is that why you come up here? To find that old *skull*?

**HENRY** Something like that.

**TOMMY** *(smiles)* Why Henry. You ol' witch doctor. You shoulda told me. I coulda bought you one in town.

*Movement and voices on all three levels. Percussion.*

**TOM** Storm.

**STIMSON** Lightning.

**TOMMY** You think the thunderbird's waiting for us, Stimson? I think it's probably watchin' us right now.

**HANK** Any sign of our base camp, Tom?

**TOM** No.

**HENRY** We could be in for some weather.

**HANK** We could go up this chimney here.

**THOMAS** The weather'll be clear tomorrow. We can start as soon as it's light.

*Pause.*

*Lights up on STIMSON, PETER JAY DAVIS, who is STIMSON's assistant, and Jimmy BYRNES, who is—at this point—the Director of War Mobilization. DAVIS takes notes. BYRNES eats licorice "Nibs." In STIMSON's office.)*

**STIMSON** Do you think we should just open up our files to the Japanese?

**DAVIS** No, sir.

**STIMSON** Do you think we should stop work?

**DAVIS** No.

**STIMSON** Well, do you think we should use S-1 at all, Peter Jay?

*Pause.*

**DAVIS** It doesn't matter what I think, Mr. Secretary. What matters is that the military and we are in agreement.

**BYRNES** *(South Carolina accent)* Well, I don't mind telling you what I think, gentlemen.

**STIMSON** I'm sure you don't, Jimmy.

**BYRNES** I think the military would much rather invade than drop this bomb. But if we let 'em go in there with their hip pistols out, the Japanese might get a little upset. Licorice, Peter Jay?

**DAVIS** No, thank you, Mr. Byrnes.

**BYRNES** And then just watch the casualty figures rise.

**STIMSON** Is that the official position of the war mobilization office, Jimmy?

**BYRNES** I try not to adopt "positions," Henry. I leave that sort of thing to you boys here.

**DAVIS** Well, according to General Marshall—

**BYRNES** General Marshall is dreaming—

**DAVIS** The number of casualties in the first thirty days of an invasion would number no more than thirty thousand. And if we accept the estimate prepared for the Joint Chiefs—

**STIMSON** I'm afraid I don't accept their estimate, Peter Jay.

**DAVIS** No?

**STIMSON** No. It strikes me also as a little undercooked. *(BYRNES laughs.)* Don't forget that I have spent much time in Japan. And it is the hilliest and most treacherous terrain you could imagine. What's more, the Japanese will fight to the death for their Emperor. That is their glory and their downfall. So I would place the casualty figure quite a bit higher than thirty thousand. Perhaps nearer… a million. And that would be in 1946 alone.

*Pause.*

**BYRNES** One million American lives.

**STIMSON** Possibly.

**BYRNES** Versus how many Japanese if we use S-1?

**DAVIS** Well, actually that figure has been revised upwards as well.

**BYRNES** To?

**DAVIS** Twenty thousand.

*Pause.*

**BYRNES** Well then, frankly, gentlemen, I do not know why we are arguing. *(beat)* Licorice, Henry?

**STIMSON** No, thank you, Jimmy.

**BYRNES** I'll leave you two alone.

*BYRNES goes. DAVIS starts to go also.*

**DAVIS** I'll prepare a summary for—

**STIMSON** Peter Jay. *(DAVIS stops, turns)* You don't think we should use S-1, do you?

**DAVIS** Mr. Secretary—

**STIMSON** No, I want to know!

*Pause.*

**DAVIS** I agree with Mr. Bard. I think we should issue a warning to the Japanese and see if that isn't enough. But no, I don't think we should use this bomb.

**STIMSON** I see.

**DAVIS** I don't think it should ever be used.

*Pause.*

**STIMSON** You know… I knew a man once—Elihu Root—I knew him first when I was about the age that you are now. And he used to tell me: assume the worst and believe the best.

**DAVIS** Meaning?

**STIMSON** Meaning… there will be other ways to end this war.

*Pause.*

**DAVIS** I hope so, Mr. Secretary. I'll go prepare my notes.

*DAVIS goes. STIMSON stands for a moment, then turns to the audience.*

**STIMSON** I first heard of Chief Mountain in the summer of 1884, my first summer in the Rockies. I first saw it two years later, for by then I had made it an annual matter to take some time off in the summer months to go hiking and hunting in the West. I would take with me two rifles, a volume of Shakespeare's sonnets and my well-worn copy of Canon Farrar's *The Early Days of Christianity.*

Chief Mountain sits on the very northwestern fringe of Montana, just below the Canadian border. It is called the Chief because it juts out onto the prairies as if leading the peaks of Montana into battle. Also, because when viewed from a certain angle, it looks very like the profile of an Indian chief.

*STIMSON and THOMAS, at stage level. STIMSON reading from Shakespeare's sonnets.*

"Whilst I alone did call upon thy aid,
My verse alone had all thy gentle grace.
But now my gracious numbers are decay'd
And my sick Muse doth give another place.
I grant, sweet love, thy lovely argument
Deserves—"

**THOMAS** What's that? A poem?

**STIMSON** Yes. A poem.

**THOMAS** What's it mean?

**STIMSON** Well, that's a good question. What's it mean? *(He reopens the book.)* "Whilst I alone did call upon thy aid, My verse alone had all thy gentle grace." Well, this means that Shakespeare was once the only one writing poems to his beloved. And so his poems contained all the… grace that her beauty inspired. *(reading)* "But now my gracious numbers are decay'd, And my sick Muse doth give another place." In other words, now she has taken up another suitor, and so Shakespeare's poems are no longer as grand as they used to be. "I grant, sweet love, thy lovely argument—"

**THOMAS** Sounds like a lot of bullshit.

*Beat.*

**STIMSON** Well, yes. Well, I suppose it is. *Lovely*… bullshit. But bullshit all the same. *(STIMSON closes the book.)* Perhaps I'll read this later. *(pause)* Lovely night. *(pause)* I think I can see the river down there. *(pause)* Do you know… that both times I have climbed this mountain I have returned to the East and met up with the most extraordinary good luck? It's true. The last time, I returned and was named Governor General of the Philippines. Well, that was some time later, but you get the idea. And the first time, I returned and stumbled upon "Highhold," my country home.

**THOMAS** It's called *what*?

**STIMSON** "Highhold." It's located on Long Island.

**THOMAS** Your house has a name?

**STIMSON** Well, yes. Well, I gave it a name. *(lightly)* Why don't you give your house a name?

**THOMAS** I don't think so, Henry.

**STIMSON** You don't think it needs one?

**THOMAS** I don't have a house.

*Pause.*

**STIMSON** Oh. Oh, yes. Well, it's just as well, they're hell to keep up. *(pause)* You, uh… did have plans to build something the last time I was up here, didn't you?

**THOMAS** Oh. I expect so.

**STIMSON** What was that?

**THOMAS** *(rising)* I'm sure you remember much better than me. Did you want to spend the day up there tomorrow, or is it just up and down?

**STIMSON** Well. I expect I will want to spend *some* time up there.

**THOMAS** Fine. Just so I know.

*Pause.*

**STIMSON** A *restaurant!* That was it! You were going to open up a little Chinese restaurant in Cardston!

**THOMAS** Oh, yeah. I guess that was it.

**STIMSON** You were going to sell Chinese food to the Mormons! That's what you told me! The very first Indian to sell Chinese food to the Mormons!

**THOMAS** Yeah. Well, I guess I was.

**STIMSON** Did you do it?

**THOMAS** For a while, yeah.

**STIMSON** And?

**THOMAS** And what?

**STIMSON** How did it go?

**THOMAS** I'm standin' here before you, aren't I?

**STIMSON** Yes, but—

**THOMAS** I'm not selling Chinese food, am I?

**STIMSON** I understand, but—

**THOMAS** You see any Mormons around here?

**STIMSON** Tommy—

**THOMAS** *Well then, how the fuck do you think it went? It didn't! I closed the fucking shithouse down!*

*Pause.*

**STIMSON** I'm sorry. I shouldn't have asked.

**THOMAS** Yeah. Well, it don't matter anyway. Stupid goddamn thing. Shouldn't of tried it anyway. A Indian sellin' Chinese food – who's gonna come? Not the Mormons, that's for sure. They wouldn't of come in if they were starving. And not the Indians, either. They just thought I was crazy. *(pause)* Only ones who used to come in were the Chinese. They used to love my cooking. I never did figure that one out. *(pause)* Anyway. Lasted about six months, then I shut 'er down. Sold 'er to a white guy from Lethbridge, and you know what? Within two weeks that place was packed. Every night. Packed.

**STIMSON** Well. I hope you made some money from the sale.

**THOMAS** Ha. That's when I started bringin' people up here. To pay off the bills.

**STIMSON** You what?

**THOMAS** Oh, I coulda walked away from it, eh, but I don't do that kinda thing. I don't accept no handouts and I don't run away from my bills.

*Pause.*

**STIMSON** You bring other people up this mountain?

**THOMAS** Well, I don't do it much anymore. But I used to bring up four, five parties a year.

**STIMSON** Why?

**THOMAS** Whaddaya mean, why.

**STIMSON** Why? Why would you do something like that? You know how important this mountain is. You know that better than I.

**THOMAS** Nobody knows how to be a Indian as good as you, Stimson.

**STIMSON** I don't mean—

**THOMAS** Nobody knows how to be an Indian as good as you, Stimson. You're the best goddamn Indian I ever seen! *(beat)* Whaddaya mean, why'd I bring 'em up here. To make money! Whaddaya think?

**STIMSON** Well, there must have been other ways you could make money.

**THOMAS** Oh yeah? And what are those, *huh*? What are those?

**STIMSON** Well, you could… herd horses.

**THOMAS** Horses! Ha!

**STIMSON** You *could* have lived on the reservation!

**THOMAS** Don't tell me what I could or couldn't do, okay? I'm tired of guys like you tellin' me what I could or couldn't do. Ya come up here, ya turn the land into some kinda *dude ranch*, and then you tell me this mountain is *sacred* or some kinda bullshit like that. Well, this mountain ain't sacred, Stimson. It used ta be sacred, but it ain't sacred anymore.

**STIMSON** I didn't—

**THOMAS** An' if you wanna know who's responsible for that, just take a look in a mirror! I wouldn't even of brought people up here if it hadn't been for you! I wouldn't even of thought of the idea if you hadn't given it to me first! *(pause)* So don't gimme none of that bullshit.

**STIMSON** I'm sorry.

**THOMAS** And quit apologizin'. That don't make it better.

*Pause.*

**STIMSON** I didn't mean to... upset you, it just... caught me by surprise, that's all. *(THOMAS just "humphs." Pause.)* Anyway. I don't apologize. But I guess I... understand. *(pause)* Um... here. Here. I have something to show you. I was going to show you tomorrow. But I think I'll show you now. *(He moves to his pack.)* Actually, I *do* want to spend some time up there. I'll show you why. *(He draws out an old bison skull. He holds it out to THOMAS.)* Do you see? Do you see, Thomas? I brought it along to replace the one that was up there. Do you remember? And who knows. Maybe *we'll* become invincible.

*STIMSON smiles. THOMAS stares at him for a moment, then quickly turns and walks away. STIMSON stands there, the skull slowly dropping in his arms.*

**TOMMY** *(on another level)* Halfway there, Stimson. Halfway there!

**GULLIVER** *(on another level with his brandy)* Some people just can't be dissuaded. Our Henry is one of those.

*Percussion: three beats.*

**SCIENTIST** When will you be seeing the President, Dr. Franck?

**FRANCK** I won't be seeing the President. I hope to see the Secretary of War.

*Light change. DAVIS moves to meet FRANCK and ARTHUR COMPTON, both scientists on the Manhattan Project.*

**DAVIS** Dr. Compton!

**COMPTON** Hello, Peter Jay.

**DAVIS** This is a surprise.

**COMPTON** Is it? I thought I'd wired the Secretary that we were coming. My goodness me. Well! I'd like to introduce Dr. James Franck of our Chicago lab. It was Dr. Franck who developed the metals for S-1.

**DAVIS** How do you do.

**FRANCK** *(German accent)* How do you do.

**DAVIS** You've been doing some amazing work in the Chicago laboratory.

**FRANCK** Thank you. I wish I could say I was proud of it.

**COMPTON** Dr. Franck has a report that he would like to give to the Secretary. It represents the views of a number of the scientists working on the project. Not *my* views, but—

**FRANCK** When will the Secretary be available?

**DAVIS** Well, he's in a meeting right now.

**FRANCK** Fine then. We will wait until he is done.

*They sit. Light change.*

**STIMSON** *(to the audience)* What most attracted me to the mountain was the wealth of myth and lore that clung to it. For one, the Blood Indians in Alberta had made a standing offer to their southern neighbours, the Piegans, of fifty horses to anyone who could run around its base in a day. For another, the summit of the mountain was said to be the home of the thunderbird, that terrible creature from who the thunder and the lightning sprang.

**DAVIS** *(approaching COMPTON and FRANCK)* Gentlemen! My apologies for the delay. Secretary Stimson asks me to extend his greatest good wishes, and to accept your report so that he may peruse it while he is away.

**FRANCK** Then he is refusing to see us?

**DAVIS** I'm sorry. His day is very full.

**COMPTON** My goodness me.

**FRANCK** Well, perhaps then we can see him tomorrow.

**DAVIS** I'm afraid he will be away.

**FRANCK** From his office?

**DAVIS** From the city.

*Pause.*

**FRANCK** Then I shall have to see him now.

*FRANCK makes for the "door." STIMSON, on the other side, does not react.*

**DAVIS** Dr. Franck.

**COMPTON** James. *James.*

**DAVIS** There is no point in going in there, the Secretary is already gone!

**FRANCK** Then you listen to me. The only reason I came onto this project was because I was assured—assured by you, Arthur—that I would be allowed to make my views known at the appropriate time.

**DAVIS** And so you—

**FRANCK** I am *not* being heard! *We* are not being heard – this report is the work of some of the Project's most eminent scientists, most of it is not even written by me! If you ignore me now, you are condemning to death tens of thousands of people. Unnecessarily! Horribly! Without any warning! And all because scientists like you, Arthur, are afraid to tell the politicians what you think! *(beat)* Well, I will not be treated this way, I will not allow you to ignore me, not when I know that the Secretary is standing behind that door! *(STIMSON does not move.)* Please, tell him… that I will return in the morning. Or he may reach me at my hotel. Arthur has the number.

*FRANCK goes. Pause. DAVIS sits.*

**COMPTON** If you… could ask him just once more, Peter Jay.

**DAVIS** *(pause; weary)* Leave me the number, Arthur. I'll do what I can.

*Percussion: a rattle. Lights fade on DAVIS and COMPTON. Lights narrow on STIMSON.*

**STIMSON** *(to the audience)* For centuries, that lonesome summit had lain unconquered. *(percussion, music)* Then, it is said, a young Indian brave of the Flathead tribe had set out to make its spirit his own. For eight days and nights he travelled eastward into the mountains, carrying with him a sacred bison skull for his pillow. He climbed the east face of the mountain, grabbing at its black walls with his bare hands, choking down each gasp of panic when they seemed to want to thrust him off and down. Until finally he reached the summit. And there, for four days and nights, he fasted, sleeping in the great cleft that one sees from far out on the prairie. On the first night, the thunderbird came to him and threatened to hurl him off if he did not go down the next day. But he refused to go, and spent the next day pacing the summit, chanting his warrior song and waving his peace pipe in the air as an offering. Again the spirit appeared to him, and again— !… Until finally, on the fourth night, the spirit yielded, smoked the pipe with the brave, and gave him good medicine to serve him the rest of his life. *(percussion out)* In 1891, I had been the first white man to climb that mountain. And, there at the top, we found the old bison skull the Flathead brave had left behind. What joy I felt to hold it in my hands! What exhilaration to discover that the legend was true! How amazing to think that the Indian brave might have been made invincible! What mystery was here! What… awe!

*STIMSON stands lost in the moment. TOMMY and HENRY, drunk, singing.*

**HENRY & TOMMY** "Counter March! Right about!
Hear those wagon soldiers shout,
While those caissons go rolling along."

**HENRY** "For it's Hi! Hi! Hee! In the Field Artillery,
Call off your numbers loud and strong!"

**HENRY & TOMMY** "And where'er we go,
You will always know
That those caissons are rolling along!"

*They laugh, then sit.*

**TOMMY** Well, if that don't scare off the thunderbird, nothin' will.

**HENRY** Ahhhh, you shoulda been there, Tommy. With the cannons booming and the marchers drumming and the shells whizzing by. Whizzzzzzzz-bang. Whizzzzzz-bang. I was a lieutenant colonel, Tommy—a very important position.

**TOMMY** What was the most dangerous thing you ever seen?

**HENRY** *(confidentially, melodramatically)* Once, when when we were in France—*very* close to the fighting—I saved the whole regiment from burning down. Yep. Battery gun blew up and the whole camp would have died if it hadn't been for me.

**TOMMY** Really?

**HENRY** Yep.

**TOMMY** Who blew it up—the Germans?

**HENRY** No.

**TOMMY** Who then?

**HENRY** *(mumbling)* We did.

**TOMMY** Who?

**HENRY** We did. We were practising our gunnery training and the gun blew up!

**TOMMY** *(laughing)* You blew up your own gun?

**HENRY** No, goddammit, *I* didn't do it, the *gunners* did it and *I* put it out. Organized the whole camp, an' you know what we did? We threw sand on it.

**TOMMY** *(finds this very funny)* You put it out with sand?

**HENRY** All right, that's it, I'm not tellin' you any more war stories.

**TOMMY** No, no, that's very interesting, Stimson. Gives me a good idea of what it musta been like there.

**HENRY** Ohh, it was a great time, Tommy. A great… adventure! And I would of fought, too. If they'd let me. *(He swigs from a bottle.)* Hey. Hey. Y'know what? This is the first time I've been drunk in… ever. *(TOMMY laughs.)* No no, I think that's true. Never got drunk in law school, was too busy gettin' grades. Never got drunk in the White House, though the president sure as hell did. Can't get drunk at the office, goddamn Elihu might walk in. I have never been drunk in my life.

**TOMMY** That's okay, Henry. I like you anyhow.

**HENRY** It's you. You're the reason I can get drunk up here, Tommy.

**TOMMY** Is that good?

**HENRY** It's wonderful.

**TOMMY** Well, okay then. Why doncha get me a job in the White House? Oh. That's right. You're not in the White House anymore, are you?

**HENRY** Goddamn Harding. Goddamn Harding! Hard-on! Ha, ha, ha, ha, ha, ha! That's what… somebody calls him.

**TOMMY** Who's Hard-on?

**HENRY** *(amazed)* The President of the United States of America! Don't you know *anything*?

**TOMMY** I may not know much, Stimson. But I do know the President of the United States isn't named Hard-on. *(HENRY considers this. TOMMY rolls over.)* Anyway. I don't want a job in the White House. Gonna carve me out my own little niche. Hey, hey: did I tell you what one of my plans is?

**HENRY** For what?

**TOMMY** For my money! All the money I got saved! Plus what you're gonna give me tomorrow.

**HENRY** All right.

**TOMMY** Hey, by the way, I wancha ta know I wouldn't do this for just anybody.

**HENRY** Do what?

**TOMMY** Take ya up the mountain. I wouldn't do this for most people. But you – I know you respect what's up here. So. *(pause, then confidentially)* I'm gonna open me up… a little café. Sell Chinese food to the Mormons. Hey, whaddaya think? Think you'd buy Chinese food from me?

**HENRY** I'm not Mormon.

**TOMMY** Well, I ain't Chinese! But that's the idea, see? That's what'd get people interested.

**HENRY** *Why*?

**TOMMY** Well, because! I'd be the first Indian sellin' Chinese food to the Mormons. Prob'ly get my picture in the newspaper or somethin'.

**HENRY** What for?

**TOMMY** *Because!* It's *unusual!* Newspapers love that kind of stuff!

**HENRY** I see…. Well, of *course* I'd buy Chinese food from you. If it was any *good*.

**TOMMY** Ohh, this is gonna be the best, Stimson, you wait and see. You oughta meet my partner. Hair like an angel and cooks like one, too. *(They snigger.)*

**HENRY** Well, here. Here. I wish to make a small contribution.

**TOMMY** No, no, no.

**HENRY** Or an *investment*, think of this as an *investment*—

**TOMMY** I don't want your money, Stimson.

**HENRY** Oh. You don't want my money?

**TOMMY** Not until tomorrow.

**HENRY** Oh. *(pause)* Well, if you ever need a loan, you'll know where to come. *(He puts his money away. Pause.)* Yep. Yep. Chinese food to the Mormons. *(pause)* Hey, whaddaya think, Tommy? Think you could give me a job?

**TOMMY** I dunno. How do ya look in an apron? *(They laugh.)* Yeah, sure. I'll give you a job. What the hell. Might open up two. *(pause, dreaming)* Then once I got that goin'… I might try opening a store. Or maybe I'll buy me some race horses. Who knows what I might do?

**STIMSON** *(on another level)* Tell him it's not going to work.

**HENRY** What?

**STIMSON** Tell him! My God, we were so stupid!

*Percussion: three beats.*

*REPORTERS pursuing STIMSON.*

**REPORTER ONE** Mr. Secretary! Will you be accompanying the President to Potsdam?

**REPORTER TWO** Mr. Secretary! Will the Russians be entering the war in the Pacific?

**REPORTER ONE** Mr. Secretary! Do you have any comment on the appointment of James Byrnes as Secretary of State?

**STIMSON** Yes, I will comment upon that. *(The REPORTERS gather around him, scribbling.)* Mr. Byrnes will make a fine Secretary of State. He brings to the position a deep love of America and a long friendship with President Truman. I look forward to working with him. Now if you will excuse me, I have work to do.

**REPORTERS** *(as they disperse)* Thank you, Mr. Secretary. Thank you.

*STIMSON moves to BYRNES and TRUMAN, who—like TAFT earlier—we do not fully see.*

**STIMSON** Mr. President!

**BYRNES** Hello, Henry.

**STIMSON** *(surprised to see him)* Jimmy. I thought you were in Europe.

**BYRNES** Yes. Well, I had to cancel my plans. The President asked me to stay close by.

**STIMSON** Mr. President. I have just received a request that the test date be set back two days.

**TRUMAN** *(still unseen)* Two days!

**STIMSON** Yes, to July sixteenth.

**TRUMAN** Goddammit! What's the matter with those people?!

**BYRNE** Tell General Groves no.

**STIMSON** The request comes from Dr. Oppenheimer.

**BYRNES** Then tell Dr. Oppenheimer no. The President and Mr. Churchill must have the results before them at Potsdam. I thought that was understood.

**STIMSON** Yes, but even if the test is pushed back two days, Mr. President, you will still be able to use the information.

**BYRNES** If the thing works.

**STIMSON** I suspect it is more likely to work if we listen to Dr. Oppenheimer.

**TRUMAN** Oh, all right! But two days only. Tell 'em any longer than that and they goddamn might as well not bother.

**STIMSON** *(with a glance to BYRNES)* Yes, sir. *(moving to TRUMAN)* May I also suggest that we decide now how best to break the news of S-1 to the Russians. Mr. Churchill can be trusted, of course, but Stalin—

**BYRNES** Yes. Well, the President and I have been discussing that, Henry, and we feel that the best strategy would be to tell the Russians nothing at all.

*Beat.*

**STIMSON** But surely—

**BYRNES** They have no need to know.

**STIMSON** Yes, but surely if we hope to establish some sort of arrangement with them later—

**BYRNES** What sort of arrangement?

**STIMSON** For the disposition of Manchuria. For the control of atomic power.

**BYRNES** If you ask me, we have enough "arrangements" with the Russians already. We have all the "arrangements" we need.

*Pause.*

**TRUMAN** Jimmy's right, Henry.

**STIMSON** But Mr. President—

**TRUMAN** Mr. Stalin does not need our help. *(rising)* Come into the next room with me, Jimmy.

**BYRNES** Yes, Mr. President.

**TRUMAN** We can talk about this some more.

*BYRNES and TRUMAN exit. Percussion – chimes tolling twelve. STIMSON turns out towards the audience.*

**STIMSON** When first I saw the pictures from the test site, I thought: it must have been something like that, that night, on that mountain. To confront a force so primeval and pure. To know that it could save or destroy you. To stand with it rising thousands of feet in the air… and know that it was the most horrible sight you had ever seen… and that you had just climbed three thousand feet… to see it.

*Chimes finish. The other actors stand looking up. Percussion: a low rumbling, building. Suddenly, a bright white light pours down upon the actors, save STIMSON, from high above. They stand looking up at it, awestruck. STIMSON stares out. Percussion peaks, fades. Lights fade.*

*Morning light. THOMAS and STIMSON. STIMSON throws items to THOMAS, who packs them for the climb. They work quietly, rhythmically for a moment.*

You want to eat before we start, Thomas?

**THOMAS** Nope.

**STIMSON** No. Well, we'll be up there by noon.

*They work. THOMAS stops, turns to STIMSON. STIMSON is about to throw something when he sees THOMAS and stops.*

**THOMAS** Hey, Stimson. I'm sorry I yelled at you last night. I don't know what I was doin'.

**STIMSON** That's quite all right, Thomas.

**THOMAS** It's just that you're *not* an Indian. And you're not supposed to be up here. And I'm not supposed to be taking you up, but I don't have any choice, I need the money. And I don't see—

**STIMSON** *Thomas.* I said it's all right.

*Pause.*

**THOMAS** Yeah, well, anyway. I was just feelin' mad. *(Pause. They work.)* It's a good thing I didn't *biff* you.

**STIMSON** What's that?

**THOMAS** Hit you. You'd probably sue me or somethin'. Being a lawyer and all.

**STIMSON** No, I'd just, uh… biff you back.

**THOMAS** Ha. That'd be something, eh? Two old assholes, goin' at it eight hundred feet in the air. You'd be better off suing me.

**STIMSON** Actually, I don't do much of that anymore.

**THOMAS** What. Fighting?

**STIMSON** Law. I haven't practised law in years. Decades.

**THOMAS** I thought that was what you did.

**STIMSON** Well, it was until I got back into public life. Actually, I did arrange to have Goerring and that lot tried.

**THOMAS** Who?

**STIMSON** Goerring. The Nazis.

**THOMAS** *You* did that?

**STIMSON** Yes. As Secretary of War.

**THOMAS** Well, hey! You're a bigger deal than I thought. *(pause)* Well, that was a good job, givin' it to those Nazis. Stickin' people in ovens. An Indian would never do that.

**STIMSON** No?

**THOMAS** Well, no, eh, 'cause an Indian knows the difference between real war and a coward's war. Like when the Nazis dropped that bomb on the Japanese and killed I don't know how many thousand—

**STIMSON** That wasn't the Nazis.

**THOMAS** What?

**STIMSON** That wasn't the Nazis, that was… us.

**THOMAS** Who?

**STIMSON** *Us.* The United States.

**THOMAS** You did that?

**STIMSON** Yes.

**THOMAS** Well, not you personally.

**STIMSON** Yes. I had something to do with it. *(pause)* I hardly see that it's the same as putting people in ovens. Frankly, I am astonished. The connection would never occur to me.

*Pause.*

**THOMAS** Well, frankly I am "astonished." I just assumed that was the Nazis.

*Pause.*

**STIMSON** Well, I hardly think it's worth sorting out now. We have a climb ahead of us.

*STIMSON works. THOMAS watches him. Pause.*

**THOMAS** *(quietly)* How much did you have to do with that?

**STIMSON** I'm sorry?

**THOMAS** How much?

**STIMSON** I made the decision.

**THOMAS** You did.

**STIMSON** I made the recommendation to the President.

**THOMAS** Uh-huh.

**STIMSON** I helped choose the cities. I chose the date. I was the Secretary of War.

**THOMAS** Yeah, I got that.

**STIMSON** I do not think it is worth debating now! To be honest, I am quite proud of what we did. We saved at least a million lives.

*THOMAS moves to pick up his gear.*

What are you doing?

**THOMAS** Going back down.

**STIMSON** *Now*?

**THOMAS** Yeah, now. Go find your own way up the mountain. I'm not taking you up.

*Beat. He throws down his own gear, grabs up STIMSON's and starts throwing it off the mountain.*

Get off the mountain. *Get off the mountain.* Fucking Nazi! Get off the mountain *now!*

**STIMSON** No.

**THOMAS** I'm not taking you up. I need the money, but I don't need it that bad. *This mountain is holy!* If I took you up there, it'd be to *throw you off! (pause)* You got nothing to climb with. It's all down there. Go on down now. Go down.

*They stand watching each other.*

**HANK** *(on another level, to Tom)* The cumuli. And the snow on the mountains. It's so beautiful up here. *(pause)* Let's go.

*End of Act One.*

## Act Two

**STIMSON** There was no third ascent. I climbed Chief Mountain precisely twice: once when I was twenty-four, again when I was fifty-three. I died in my home at Highhold, in October of 1950. I was eighty-three years old.

*THOMAS and STIMSON on the middle level, as at the end of Act One.*

You can't leave.

**THOMAS** Oh no? *(starting to go)* See you, Stimson. Write when you get there.

**STIMSON** But what will I do?

**THOMAS** Climb it yerself!

**STIMSON** I can't climb it myself, you just—

**THOMAS** Look, Henry, what you do or don't do ain't my concern anymore. If I'd known what kind of man you was, I wouldn't of brought you up here at all. So if you're stuck on this ledge for a coupla years or so, that's fine by me.

*He continues to go.*

**STIMSON** And all the others you brought up here. Did you know what kind of men they were, too?

**THOMAS** *(THOMAS stops, turns)* They didn't drop bombs on people.

**STIMSON** No. But it seems to me you've become awfully discriminating all of a sudden. You've been taking just anybody up this mountain for quite a while, why stop now? Besides. Are you prepared to refund my money?

**THOMAS** No.

**STIMSON** No. Well then. I thought you said you don't run away from your debts.

*Pause.*

**THOMAS** I go first, you stay at least five feet behind.

**STIMSON** Fine.

**THOMAS** No talkin'.

**STIMSON** All right.

**THOMAS** And this is the last time.

**STIMSON** Fine.

*Pause. THOMAS looks around for remaining gear. There isn't any, save the pack containing the buffalo skull. He picks it up.*

**THOMAS** Let's go.

**ROOT** *(on another level)* Upward! Ever upward, Henry!

**TOM** *(on another level)* My father says he seen the thunderbird once – but I don't believe him. I don't believe in all that.

*Percussion: three beats.*

**STIMSON** I see no reason to drive the Emperor from power. He is willing to cooperate with us. And frankly, we need his help.

**MARSHALL** He is willing to *cooperate* with us?

**STIMSON** I think so, General Marshall.

**MARSHALL** Then who have I been fighting for the last three years?

**DAVIS** Our problem is not Hirohito. Our problem is their Secretary of War.

**STIMSON** Stubborn buggers, Secretaries of War.

**BYRNES** I'll say.

**STIMSON** Almost as stubborn as Secretaries of State.

**MARSHALL** Well, I don't suppose it matters what we put in the declaration. We are threatening to destroy them, after all.

**BYRNES** Yes, but we're not telling them how, are we? Are we?

**MARSHALL** No.

**STIMSON** No.

**BYRNES** Well then, do not expect them to give up.

**DAVIS** They're a lot more likely to give up if we allow them to save face.

**BYRNES** And you do not think they will see this as a sign of weakness?

**DAVIS** No!

**BYRNES** Well then, I reluctantly say, Mr. Davis, that you do not know the Japanese mind.

*Pause.*

**STIMSON** Well, I do.

**MARSHALL** What's that, Henry?

**STIMSON** I *do*. I have spent much time on the home island. And I think that qualifies me to speak as much as any man in this room. And I say that so long as the Japanese lay down their arms immediately, we should allow their Emperor to remain. That is what I have put in the Declaration and that will be my recommendation to the President. Any remarks? Jimmy?

*After a moment, BYRNES sullenly shakes his head "No."*

Good then. You may all go have your dinners.

*Percussion: three beats.*

**HANK** *(looking out)* I cannot believe I am up here! I cannot believe I made it this far! *(turning to TOM and a large box camera)* Now, here. Here. I have set the camera up. All you have to do is take the photograph.

**TOM** The what?

**HANK** The *photo-graph.* You don't know what that is, do you? Well, I will stand there, and you will stand here. And when I tell you, you are to pull the slide out of this box. And then you pull this lever.

**TOM** What for?

**HANK** Well, that will place my… image, my… face—me—upon the plate. And then I will be able to take it into a darkroom and have a picture made up, so that everyone will know that I was up here. *(TOM starts to back away in terror.)* Oh no, now look, there's nothing to be afraid of. *(TOM continues backing away.)* I know! We'll take a picture of you, too! *(TOM turns and runs.)* Tom. Tom! *(HANK grabs him and hauls him back.)* Look, how about this: if you take a picture of me, I'll give you another dollar when we get back to Cardston.

*TOM regards him and then moves to stand warily by the camera. HANK moves to his posing place.*

All right. Now stay right there. And don't do anything until I tell you. *(posing)* Ha. Wait'll I get these pictures back to Hawthorne Hall. They'll have to double their intake of brandy when they see this! *(He shouts.) I hereby claim this mountain on behalf of Yale men everywhere.* Quick, take the picture.

**TOM** Wait!

**HANK** What?

**TOM** Under your foot. What are you standing on?

*HANK looks down. He has placed one foot on an old bison skull, lying atop the mountain. He regards it, disbelieving. Percussion. TOM moves to pick it up. HANK turns into the next scene, with GULLIVER, SUTTON and WESKER.*

**HANK** It was the old Flathead's pillow! It was the bison skull he took with him when he first climbed the mountain!

**GULLIVER** Oh, come now, Stimson. You don't really expect us to believe that, do you?

**WESKER** You don't really expect us to believe in invincible old warriors?

**HANK** *You* can believe what you want.

**SUTTON** Pretty convincing imitation of a mountain climber, mind you.

**GULLIVER** Yes, we'll have to get these touched up and published in the paper.

**HANK** *(grabbing for the photos)* Give me those!

**WESKER** Stimson has a great future ahead of him as a model, wouldn't you say, Sutton?

**SUTTON** A great future. A great, great future.

**HANK** You are a stupid lot of nincompoops. And those are my pictures, so give them back! *(He gets them.)*

**GULLIVER** What I can't believe, Hank, is that you actually dragged a camera all the way up a mountain just so you could come home with these.

**HANK** Well, I knew you wouldn't believe me if I didn't. I knew you wouldn't believe me anyway, but at least this way you have to think about it. And I wanted to show you! I wanted you to see what it's like up there!

**SUTTON** Stunning.

**WESKER** Absolutely breathtaking. Where's my glass?

**HANK** Not that I'd ever been up there before. But I knew what it would be like. And you know what? It was just like I thought it would be. *(pause)* And when I held that bison skull in my hands… I could feel the good medicine coming into me. Oh, you can scoff and laugh all you like, but it's an experience you'll never have. I could feel myself becoming stronger, nobler and wiser. And ready! Ready to serve my country and serve my god and go out into the world and make it better. This nation will do more to improve the world than any that has gone before it, I really believe that now. And we'll be the ones to do it. Us, the men in this room. You know that, don't you? We have a great responsibility before us.

*Pause.*

**SUTTON** Yes, but we'll all have to climb that mountain first, won't we?

**GULLIVER** You save the world for us, Stimson. We'd rather drink.

*Lights cross fade to STIMSON, also regarding the photo. A moment passes.*

**STIMSON** I don't know what happened.

**HANK** You betrayed me.

**STIMSON** What's that?

**HANK** You betrayed me. That's all.

*Pause. Then STIMSON turns.*

**STIMSON** Byrnes. Byrnes!

**BYRNES** Hello, Henry. Licorice?

**STIMSON** Would you please put that ridiculous candy away!

*BYRNES registers STIMSON's anger, does so.*

Have you seen this?

**BYRNES** What is it?

**STIMSON** It's the Declaration I prepared for the President. The part about the Emperor is missing.

**BYRNES** Ah, yes. Well, the President wanted it that way, Henry. He is the President, you know.

**STIMSON** Did you do this?

**BYRNES** I don't know what you mean.

**STIMSON** Did you talk to him?

**BYRNES** Of course I talked to him, I am his Secretary of State! *(pause)* The President believes, as I do, that the surrender must be unconditional to be any good at all. Get into bargaining with them about whether or not they keep their Emperor, and we have lost the upper hand. There is also the small matter of the next election. We have been telling the people for eighteen months that Hirohito breathes fire and eats babies. What are they to think if we suddenly tell them that he's not so bad after all?

**STIMSON** But the Japanese will not be able to accept these terms!

**BYRNES** Well then, we are prepared for that. Aren't we? *(pause)* Is that all?

**STIMSON** No.

**BYRNES** Well, I am afraid that will have to be all, Henry. I am out of time.

*BYRNES starts to go.*

**STIMSON** Mr. Davis tells me that the Japanese have asked the Russians to negotiate a truce. Is that true? *(beat)* I am the Secretary of War! I deserve to know these things!

**BYRNES** Well, obviously you do know these things.

**STIMSON** From you! Not from my assistant!

**BYRNES** Yes, it is true the Japanese approached the Russians. We told the Russians to ignore them. They did as they were told.

**STIMSON** Why?

**BYRNES** Because they are afraid of us, Henry. They know we have something and they are afraid of us.

**STIMSON** I mean why did we not pursue these overtures from the Japanese?

**BYRNES** Because who knows what in the hell is meant by them? Who knows what the Japanese want? Because we have already spent two billion dollars on your bomb, Henry, and we're not gonna leave it sitting in the warehouse! *(pause)* You really are the most incredibly naive man, Henry. Forgive me for saying so. But I do not know how you came to be Secretary of War. I truly do not.

*BYRNES goes. STIMSON stands for a moment, then turns to the audience. He is vaguely dazed, disoriented.*

**STIMSON** What I find… most striking now… is the absolute hypocrisy of those who would judge us. To them, of course, I am nothing but a criminal and a war-mongerer. And our decision is the inevitable result of a military machine gone mad. Do they really think a decision of this magnitude could be made so callously? Do they really believe we had nothing on our minds but winning the war?

The Japanese replied to the Potsdam Declaration by taking a position of *mokusatsu*. This was translated by the Domei News Agency as meaning they would "ignore" it. We learned later that in fact they had intended the word's other meaning, which is to "withhold comment." But what were we to do if their own news agency did not understand their intentions? *What were we to do?*

*Sound of wind and rain. TOMMY and HENRY huddle under a tarp. They call out over the storm.*

**TOMMY** Helluva day you picked for a climb, Henry!

**HENRY** But it was so clear the last time we were up here!

**TOMMY** What?

**HENRY** Clear! There was hardly any wind! *(pause)* I'm going out there again!

**TOMMY** Aw, leave it alone, Henry!

**HENRY** No! I have to find it now! *(He pulls TOMMY closer.)* If this keeps up we'll have to go down! If we have to go down before we find the skull I don't know if I can get up here again! I don't know if I'll ever be back here! It was just over there, I'm sure it was! I remember – the cairn was near the edge of the cliff!

**TOMMY** All right. Then I'll come with you!

**HENRY** No! No!

**TOMMY** You look over on that side! I'll look over here!

**HENRY** But—

**TOMMY** Just shuddup and start looking, Henry! I wanna get going!

*HENRY starts to go. ROOT sweeps in and leads him another way.*

**ROOT** Henry, my boy! Henry! Drop what you're doing and come with me.

*Sound of wind, rain out. ROOT leads HENRY over to the figure of COOLIDGE, whom—like the other Presidents—we do not see.*

President Coolidge, I would like you to meet Mr. Henry L. Stimson! A colleague of mine and a very good lawyer.

**HENRY** Yes, we've... met, Mr. President.

**COOLIDGE** We have?!

**HENRY** Yes, you uh... shook my hand at the nominating convention.

**COOLIDGE** Oh, that's right! Goddammit! I oughta write these things down. Well, listen, Stimson, on Elihu's recommendation here, I wanna send you to the Philippines.

**HENRY** The—?

**COOLIDGE** Philippines. As Governor General.

**ROOT** Because you did such a good job in Nicaragua.

**COOLIDGE** That you did, that you did! Gettin' those rebels to sit down and talk. Now there's a problem we won't have to deal with again! *(ROOT beams. Pause.)* Well?

**HENRY** Well what, sir?

**COOLIDGE** The Philippines, goddammit, whaddaya say?

**ROOT** What the President has in mind, Henry, is a little negotiation, a little gentle persuasion, you know, the kind of thing you're good at. Get the nationalists to tone down things a bit – and get our own people to stop being such a bunch of cusses! Isn't that about it, Mr. President?

**COOLIDGE** Absolutely, Elihu. Exactly what I would've said!

**ROOT** I don't even know why we're asking. You're obviously not going to say no!

**HENRY** Well... no—

**ROOT** Good! Good! I'll fill him in on the details, Mr. President. You have better things to do. *(He leads HENRY away.)* Oh, I know it's halfway around the world, Henry, but think of this: that means it's halfway home, too. And you'll be able to get over to Japan every once in awhile – that oughta break things up. *(They stop.)* The reason we like to turn to you, Henry... is because you're the kind of man who can get things started.Who can get things rolling. Oh, anybody can run a government, but without the ones who were there at the beginning... you're an initiator, Henry. That's what I'd call you. An initiator.

*Percussion: three beats.*

*The sound of wind and rain, even louder.*

**TOMMY** *(yelling over the storm)* Any sign of it over there, Henry?

**HENRY** No! Not yet! I can't see a thing! *(HENRY moves farther down. He sees something in the distance.)* There it is.

**TOMMY** What?

**HENRY** I see it! It's over here!

*HENRY runs to the cairn. TOMMY follows a distance behind. HENRY stops, looking down into the cairn. Sound of wind and rain peaks, stops. Pause.*

It's gone, Tommy. The skull is gone.

*Music: a Japanese lute. HANK crosses to directly opposite HENRY and begins to build a rock cairn on the spot that HENRY stares at. TOM hands him the stones. As this continues, STIMSON speaks.*

**STIMSON** Hiroshima was bombed on the morning of... well, that is all history. You know all that. The death toll was rather higher than we expected. We had thought twenty thousand people would die. Seventy thousand died in Hiroshima. Seventy-four in Nagasaki.

That is not news to you. It was news to us then.

By dropping the atomic bomb, I believe we saved at least a million American lives. By dropping the bomb, we may also have saved a million Japanese lives. We also put an end to the fire raids which had already killed one hundred thousand people in Tokyo, and destroyed or irreparably damaged such centres of culture and history as Coventry, Berlin, London, Cologne. We put an end to the military blockade which was causing such hardship in Japan. *We knew what we were doing.* But there were circumstances. Circumstances which I very much fear history has obscured rather than made clearer.

There is an assumption that distance makes clearer the nature of an event or deed. But it is not so. Study a painting from the middle of the gallery floor and you will see its total effect, yes. But stand with your eyes inches from the canvas and you will begin to see the brushstrokes, the draughtsmanship, the choices of brush and colour that passed through the artist's mind as he stood in that exact same spot. It is only close up that an event can be understood; distance in time or geography only *seems* to make the event simpler. That is why there was debate in Chicago, and doubt in Los Alamos, as to what we were doing. That is why you sit there now and wonder at our hard-heartedness. But it was not that simple. It was not that simple. That is what I want you to know.

*HENRY turns away from the cairn, which is now almost fully constructed in front of him. He goes; TOMMY follows. HANK places the last rock on the cairn, then moves to pick up the bison skull. He starts to put it in place in the cairn, then hesitates and gives it to TOM to do so. TOM places the bison skull in the cairn, as lights cross-fade to DAVIS being pursued by REPORTERS.*

**REPORTER ONE** Mr. Davis, why was there a second bombing at Nagasaki?

**REPORTER TWO** Mr. Davis, where is the Secretary of War?

**REPORTER ONE** Mr. Davis, is it true that the Japanese had tried to open peace negotiations through the Russians?

**DAVIS** Your questions will have to wait for the Secretary, gentlemen. I am not empowered to answer them.

**REPORTER TWO** Mr. Davis, is it true that the Russians were planning to occupy Manchuria?

**REPORTER ONE** Mr. Davis, where *is* the Secretary of War?

**DAVIS** The Secretary is resting at his country home, gentlemen. I suggest that we leave him to do so.

*The REPORTERS and DAVIS leave. Lights up on STIMSON. He is seated. He wears a fine dressing gown. He looks ashen. He reads from a book of Shakespeare's sonnets.*

**STIMSON** "How can I then return in happy plight,
That am debarred the benefit of rest?
When day's oppression is not eased by night,
But day by night, and night by day, oppressed?
And each, though enemies to either's reign,
Do in consent shake hands to torture me."

*He stops. Puts the book down. Looks out.*

*Light shift. STIMSON still seated. He stares at nothing. OLD GULLIVER is there. He drinks brandy.*

**OLD GULLIVER** Well, the gods have finally conspired to destroy me, Henry. I have been kicked upstairs. I am to become an eminence grise at the law firm, a sort of Hirohito of Fifth Avenue.

**STIMSON** Congratulations, Gulliver.

**OLD GULLIVER** Thank you. I do not think Root would be pleased. *(pause)* I want you to join me.

**STIMSON** To what?

**OLD GULLIVER** Come back to the law firm, Henry. Join me in stately desuetude.

**STIMSON** Good God, Gulliver. I am almost eighty years old.

**OLD GULLIVER** So what? So am I. Almost. We can go for long lunches. We can walk in Battery Park. It will be like old times.

*Pause.*

**STIMSON** No, thank you, Gulliver. I think not.

**OLD GULLIVER** When you are ready.

**STIMSON** Thank you. No.

*Pause.*

**OLD GULLIVER** You aren't going to stay on in Washington, are you?

**STIMSON** No.

**OLD GULLIVER** No. I didn't think so. Working with Truman. It must be like working with a haberdasher.

**STIMSON** He *was* a haberdasher.

**OLD GULLIVER** Yes, Henry. *I know. (pause)* Well? What will you do then? If you won't come work with me.

**STIMSON** I shall stay here.

**OLD GULLIVER** And?

**STIMSON** *(rising; tense; anger building)* Why must I have everything planned? Why? Because you ask me? I shall grow flowers. I will putter. I will host picnics for the local children. I shall do what I want, Gulliver, and it might not involve you! *(pause)* I'm sorry. *(pause)* I'm sorry. Perhaps I should go to bed. *(He starts to go.)*

**OLD GULLIVER** Poor Henry. *(Pause. STIMSON stops.)* Poor Henry. No, I shouldn't have asked you. You're much too good for us. *(pause)* Poor Henry. A good man cast among swine. The world doesn't want to be saved. What is he to do? Wars are declared. Bombs are dropped. Women and children are killed, my, my, my. What an insult to his senses! Sixty years I have known you, Henry. And you are still living in agony.

*Pause.*

**STIMSON** Get out, Gulliver.

**OLD GULLIVER** What?

**STIMSON** *(firm with controlled fury)* Get *out.* Go *home.*

*After a moment, OLD GULLIVER goes. Light shift. STIMSON still in his chair.*

*(a deadness in his voice)* I wait for the dinner bell. I look out over the ocean. Some evenings there is a sunset. Some evenings there is nothing. I read Shakespeare's sonnets. I play parcheesi to pass the time.

Why do I think back to that mountain? Where I have not visited for thirty years. Why do I think of Tommy now – why do I wonder if he is still alive? In my mind I climb the mountain. I am nearly at the top. I can feel the breeze blowing down off the summit. I can hear the beat of the thunderbird's wings. *(long pause)*

I go for walks above the ocean. I watch the gardener do his work. Sometimes a neighbour comes over – I listen without hearing. I build castles with toothpicks. I host picnics for the local children. I am… in Highhold.

*Pause. A dinner bell tinkles. STIMSON rises laboriously from his chair, starts to move off. Percussion, low, building. STIMSON stands stock still for a moment. Suddenly, he collapses. Darkness. Percussion. Voices.*

**ROOT** Come pheasant hunting with me, Henry!

**TOM** Don't go too close to the edge!

**TOMMY** Halfway there, Stimson! Halfway there!

**GULLIVER** Our Henry was one of—

**HANK** You betrayed me.

**THOMAS** Tell him.

**HENRY** Tell him!

**BYRNES** Licorice, Henry?

**TOMMY** Pretty big mountain, eh, Stimson?

**THOMAS** Pretty big mountain. Gets bigger every—

*Sound stops. Light up on DAVIS.*

**DAVIS** Mr. Secretary.

**STIMSON** *(STIMSON turns.)* Peter Jay.

**DAVIS** I can only see you for a few minutes, I'm afraid. My day is very busy.

**STIMSON** *(STIMSON moves to him.)* How are you, Peter Jay?

**DAVIS** Very well, thank you.

**STIMSON** You're moving to the State Department, I hear.

**DAVIS** Yes, that's right.

**STIMSON** Well, good. Good. Good for you. *(pause)* Uh, I've come back to Washington because I'm hoping to submit a proposal to the President. I hope to impress upon him the need to control atomic power now that we—

**DAVIS** To *control* it, sir?

**STIMSON** Yes, that's right, now that we—

**DAVIS** To *control* it, sir? Isn't it a little late for that?

*Pause.*

**STIMSON** Well, yes. We can't take back what has happened, if that's what you mean. But I do believe we can—

**DAVIS** I'm sorry, Mr. Secretary, I really must be going.

**STIMSON** If you could help me draw up—

**DAVIS** Perhaps we can get together next—

**STIMSON** Peter Jay, *listen to me!*

*Pause. DAVIS stops and turns.*

**DAVIS** No, Mr. Secretary. I have listened enough. *(pause)* You told me once that there would be no need to use the bomb. That there would be other ways to end the war. And I believed you, sir, and I take full responsibility for believing you. But I ask you: did you really believe it yourself? *(pause)* Did you really believe that? *(pause)* It seems to me now that what has happened was as inevitable on that day as if the bomb bay doors had already opened. Because you were outmanoeuvered, Mr. Secretary. You have always believed that the force of a good idea will prevail over the power of men and machines. But it is not so. I see that now. *(pause)* So yes, I will help you with your proposal, or whatever it is you want to do. You are a good man and I respect you for that. But I will not be so naive this time as to believe that hoping, or wishing, or believing that something will happen is enough to make it so. Naïveté can kill people, Mr. Secretary. I see that now, too. *(pause)* Please see my secretary. She can set up some time next week.

*DAVIS goes. STIMSON stands there. Percussion, loud, building. Peaks. An odd, coloured light rises onstage. FRANCK appears.*

**FRANCK** Mr. Secretary.

**STIMSON** *(turning, befuddled)* Yes?

**FRANCK** I am James Franck. I worked on S-1.

**STIMSON** Oh, yes, Dr. Franck. Please, I was just…

*His voice trails off.*

**FRANCK** You have been very busy lately.

**STIMSON** Yes.

**FRANCK** But you are not so busy now.

**STIMSON** No. No. Is there something I can—

**FRANCK** I have come to tell you that I will speak out against what we have done, Mr. Secretary. I will speak out against you. I will take your name in vain.

*Pause.*

**STIMSON** Yes. Well, I stand advised of your enmity, Dr. Franck. Thank you for informing me.

*STIMSON turns away.*

**FRANCK** I have worked twice now for governments that made murder their official policy. It is time for me to atone, would you not say?

**STIMSON** You may do as you please.

**FRANCK** And perhaps you as well.

**STIMSON** Dr. Franck. We were all chastened by the outcome of this horrible war. It is something we cannot repeat. Let us concentrate on that. *(pause, then quickly)* You may be interested to know that I was not the sole author of the Potsdam Declaration. I wished to include a clause that would have allowed the Japanese to retain their monarchy but I was overruled by… others. As it is, we have ended up letting them keep their Emperor anyway, so yes, I agree with you, the bombing need not have happened. But I am only one man. I am not the government incarnate!

**FRANCK** And that is your defense, Mr. Secretary?

**STIMSON** I am not offering you a defense, Dr. Franck, I am offering you an explanation! *(pause)*

**FRANCK** Where were you when I tried to see you?

**STIMSON** When?

**FRANCK** In June. I tried to see you. You would not see me.

**STIMSON** Ah, yes. Well, I was rather busy then. Just as I am rather busy now.

**FRANCK** You were standing in your office, weren't you?

**STIMSON** I was out of the city!

**FRANCK** The first time. I was standing on one side of the door. And you were standing on the other. *(pause)* And when you left the city, where did you go?

**STIMSON** I don't think—

**FRANCK** To Europe? To Russia? Some very important state dinner?

**STIMSON** I don't remember and I do not think it is your concern!

**FRANCK** Or were you, in fact, still in Washington, Mr. Secretary. That is what my friends tell me. They tell me that you did not leave the city at all! *(pause)* If you had seen me, you might have changed your mind.

**STIMSON** I very much doubt that.

**FRANCK** If you had seen me—

**STIMSON** Your letter was widely circulated, Dr. Franck. I am sure it was taken into consideration.

**FRANCK** But if you had seen me—

**STIMSON** *Yes, perhaps, if I had seen you, perhaps I would have changed my mind!*

*Pause.*

**FRANCK** But you didn't. You didn't see me. You stayed in your office. *(pause)* You are no better than the men who destroyed my homeland, Mr. Secretary. You are no better than the Nazis. You do not like that comparison, it outrages you. You say, oh, I wanted to stop the bombing, but others would not let me. But *when you might have done something, you did nothing at all.* I denounce you, Mr. Secretary. I denounce you as a war criminal.

*FRANCK spits in STIMSON's face.*

You have made criminals of us all.

*FRANCK goes. Percussion, building. STIMSON stands there. Percussion peaks. Pause. Japanese lute music. White light floods the stage. HENRY and a JAPANESE OFFICIAL appear. A young Japanese BOY gambols about nearby. STIMSON watches.*

**JAPANESE OFFICIAL** These woods are over four centuries old. The people come here from Tokyo to worship at the shrines. Or they simply come for the quiet. It is very quiet, once you are among the trees.

**HENRY** They remind me of certain woods at home.

**JAPANESE OFFICIAL** In the Philippines?

**HENRY** No, not in the Philippines – the islands are not my home. No, I mean in the West of America. *(They start to go. The BOY runs by them.)* That boy. Who is he?

**JAPANESE OFFICIAL** I don't know. I shall ask.

*The JAPANESE OFFICIAL calls out to the BOY in Japanese. The BOY replies.*

He says he is the groundskeeper's son. He is one of the groundskeepers' sons. We have fourteen.

*The JAPANESE OFFICIAL calls to the BOY in Japanese. Then, to HENRY.*

I have told him to come meet a great American.

**HENRY** Oh, no, really, it's not necessary. It's not true.

**JAPANESE OFFICIAL** Please. He will be able to tell all his friends he has met the Governor General of the Philippines!

*The boy runs up to them, bows. HENRY bows gracefully back. The boy speaks in Japanese.*

He asks is it true that you come from America? *(The JAPANESE OFFICIAL speaks.)* I have told him that it is true, but that now you are visiting from Manila. *(The BOY speaks to STIMSON.)* He says he has many uncles in America and that they say everyone there is rich. He wants to know if this is true.

**HENRY** *(Smiling)* Tell him it is not true, but that everyone there is given the chance to be.

*The JAPANESE OFFICIAL does. The BOY replies.*

**JAPANESE OFFICIAL** He asks if you can take him there.

**HENRY** Tell him I'm sure when he is older, if his father lets him, he may come to America. *(The JAPANESE OFFICIAL does.)* All right then?

**JAPANESE OFFICIAL** Yes. I think he is disappointed.

*HENRY and the JAPANESE OFFICIAL start off. Suddenly, the BOY runs after them and starts tugging at HENRY'S jacket, jabbering in Japanese.*

**HENRY** What – what does he want?

*The JAPANESE OFFICIAL speaks harshly to the BOY. The BOY continues jabbering and tugging at HENRY.*

What does he say?

**JAPANESE OFFICIAL** Nothing. It is foolishness, Colonel Stimson.

**HENRY** No, I want to know!

*The JAPANESE OFFICIAL pulls the BOY off HENRY and throws him to the ground. The BOY kneels there, bowing to HENRY.*

**JAPANESE OFFICIAL** He says that if you will take him to America, he will leave his father and do your bidding. He will be your servant.

**HENRY** Servant?

*The BOY speaks again.*

**JAPANESE OFFICIAL** Son.

*Pause.*

**HENRY** Tell him to stand up. *(The JAPANESE OFFICIAL does.)* Tell him that in America we do not bow before others.

*The JAPANESE OFFICIAL does. Slowly, the BOY stands. HENRY crouches before him. He takes a small card from his wallet and gives it to him.*

This is my card. This is where I live. This is my name. Henry Stimson. When you are eighteen, you write to me here, and have your father write to me, too. And if he agrees… I will see that you are allowed to come to America. Do you understand?

*The BOY looks at the card, looks at HENRY, nods.*

Good. Write in your own language. I will understand.

*They regard each other for a moment, then the BOY starts to run off. At a distance, stops to look back at HENRY again.*

**STIMSON** This is my card. This is where I live. This is my name. Henry. Stimson.

*Blackout. In the dark, sound of percussion, very loud.*

*(more quickly)* This is my card. This is where I live. This is my name. Henry—

*A deafening crash of thunder drowns out his name. A brilliant white light from high above pours down upon STIMSON. He peers up at it in terror, slowly drops to his knees. Meanwhile, on another level, the figure of FRANCK appears.*

**FRANCK** *(reading from his report)* The military advantages and the saving of American lives achieved by the sudden use of atomic bombs against Japan may be outweighted by a wave of horror and revulsion sweeping over the rest of the world.

*Here the figure of BARD joins in the reading. He begins at the beginning, so that they do not speak in unison, but softly, so that FRANCK is still heard.*

From this point of view, a demonstration of the new weapon might be made, before the eyes of all the United Nations on the desert or a barren island.

*They are joined by HANK and DAVIS. Again, they begin at the beginning.)*

If the United States were to be the first to release this new means of indiscriminate destruction on mankind— *(THOMAS joins in, as above.)* —she would sacrifice public support throughout the world, precipitate the race for armaments, and prejudice the possibility of reaching an international agreement on the future control of such weapons.

**STIMSON** I—*am not*—*a criminal!* I knew what we had done! I wrote, I wrote to the President – you will find the papers in my files! That our ability to destroy ourselves was now complete. That upon us fell responsibility for the future of civilization. That man's very relationship to his universe had been wholly and forever altered. *This* is history! *This* is what is written down! *This is what I stand by*, not what you would prefer to think of me, *not* what time in its infinite hypocrisy preaches! *This!*

Yes, we might have exploded it on some deserted Pacific island – but what if it had not gone off? What if it had not worked? Yes, we might have given the Japanese some warning, but would they have believed us? We might as well have told them we walked among the gods as that we had mastered the power of the sun!

There is… in every system… an *inertia*… whereby the possible becomes the inevitable, and what might have been is forgotten in the rush towards *what is.* Like the gravity that sucks a bomb towards its target… like the force that draws the sap through the tree… a power of the universe we have not mastered. That masters us. A mystery still unhewn.

*(On another level, THOMAS faces out.)* Oh, Thomas. *Thomas!* I stand upon the top of Chief Mountain. I stand here alone. I wait for the judgement of the thunderbird. Why does he not come to me? Why does he not appear? I have climbed the east face of the mountain. Come to me! *Come to me!*

*Pause. STIMSON stands searching the sky. The Japanese BOY breaks position, runs a few steps, stops, looks at STIMSON. STIMSON looks to him, reaches out. The BOY runs away.*

**HANK** *(looking out)* Light.

**TOMMY** It's clearing.

**TOM** I think we had better head down now.

**HENRY** Maybe some tourists got it.

**HANK** What if it is his pillow?

**TOMMY** Maybe the thunderbird got it.

**HENRY** I don't want to know.

**TOM** *(THOMAS rises and starts to move up.)* Come on, Mr. Stimson!

**STIMSON** Go, you silly fool. Go.

**TOMMY** We could be back before dinnertime, Henry!

**THOMAS** Hey, Stimson. We better head down now. It's gettin' late.

*STIMSON does not move,THOMAS moves to sit beside him. Looks around.*

I come up here sometimes. Just for myself. Clean up a little bit. Clean up the tourists' junk. Still. All the times I been up here. Winter. Nighttime. Sleep under the stars. If there's any thunderbird up here… I ain't seen him. *(pause)* I don't say it's right what I done, Henry. But I done it. So, what can I do? Come up here. Clean up a bit. Don't lie to myself. Most of all, don't lie to myself, Henry. That helps. *(pause)* Oh. Hey. Here. I brung ya something. Ya left it over there.

*He reaches into the pack, pulls out the bison skull.*

Thought you might want it. It was about the only thing I didn't throw off.

*Pause.*

**STIMSON** Put it on the cairn, Thomas.

**THOMAS** No. You put it on the cairn.

*He holds it out to STIMSON. STIMSON takes it. Moves to the cairn, places it on top. They are still, looking at it.*

**HENRY** *(on another level, singing)*
"For it's Hi! Hi! Hee! In the Field artillery,

Call off your number loud and strong!
And where'er we go,
You will always know
That those caissons are rolling along."

*The light narrows to a pinspot on the bison skull. Fade.*

*The End.*

# Gravel Run

By Conni Massing

## About
# Conni Massing

Conni is an award-winning writer working in theatre, film, radio and television. Recent stage credits include the hit comedy *The Myth of Summer*, premiered by Alberta Theatre Projects in 2005 and an adaptation of Bruce Allen Powe's *The Aberhart Summer* (Alberta Theatre Projects/Citadel Theatre). Conni has worked as a television series story editor on "The Beat," "North of 60," "The Adventures of Shirley Holmes" and was most recently the story consultant on the Anaid Productions/Life Network documentary series "Taking it Off" and "Family Restaurant" (The Food Network). Film projects include two feature-length screenplays, "Procreation" and "Death Rocks," both funded through Telefilm. She is currently writing a book about road trips.

*Gravel Run* received its premiere at novaplayRites '88, Alberta Theatre Projects' annual festival of new plays, on January 6th, 1988 with the following company:

| | |
|---|---|
| PAPA | Ray Hunt |
| MAMA | Pat Armstrong |
| BILLY | Weston McMillan |
| LEN | Brian Linds |
| LEONA | Christine MacInnis |

Directed by Stephen Heatley
Set and Light Design by Warren Carrie
Costumes by Joan Murphy
Original Music by Allan Rae
Stage Manager: Charlotte Green

## Characters

PAPA is about sixty.
MAMA is in her mid-fifties.
BILLY is in his early twenties.
LEONA is in her early twenties.
LEN is in his late twenties.

## Setting

The action is set in a small Canadian prairie town and takes place in the living room and dining room of the Sorenson home. The living room is dominated by Papa Sorenson's collection of jars: multicoloured, labelled and shelved. The jars, which are filled with rendered animal fat, are carefully positioned in front of a window so that they are illuminated by natural light. The remaining living room furniture is extremely well-worn but meticulously cared for. The furniture is layered with doilies and pillows; the walls are covered with plaques and plates. The dining room area is graced with a worn chrome and arborite dinette set and decorated with spoon racks and knick-knacks of every description.

## Note

At times characters speak simultaneously; a slash (/) indicates when an overlap of voices begins.

# Gravel Run

## Act One

### Scene One

*As the lights fade up, PAPA is by the window examining his fat jars, holding them up to the light. He whistles "When You Wish upon a Star" (Ned Washington and Leigh Harline) and goes through an elaborate ritual of "reading" the jars. After holding a jar up to the light and rolling it carefully from side to side, he stomps on the floor to see if that affects the patterns in the fat. Then he warms the jar in his armpit. He spreads a newspaper out beside him and compares his predictions with the forecasts in the paper.*

**PAPA** *(to his jar)* I'll tell you one thing, they're wrong about the rain. It's gonna be hot isn't it? *(reads)* Highs of fifteen. Precipitation. *(derisive snort)* Now you know and I know it's not going to rain. Heat's hanging' in the air like a ton of rocks and that's the way it's gonna stay. *(new jar)* Now what's all this? You're a regular tornado in a jar, ain't ya? *(pause)* And it's not the weather… no, sir… what's up? *(pause)* Something's gonna happen, isn't it?

*MAMA enters, carrying a plate of food. PAPA does not acknowledge her.*

**MAMA** I brought you a bite. *(pause)* I brought you some food, Papa. And a letter.

**PAPA** *(continues to stare at this jars)* Looks good, Mama. Thank you.

**MAMA** Cold roast beef and beet pickles and *(pause)* spiders' eggs. And some mice stuffed with cabbage.

*PAPA reacts but makes no move to acknowledge MAMA.*

**PAPA** This new fat's a marvel, all right. It's caribou, you know.

**MAMA** Mona phoned a minute ago. Their house burned down last night.

**PAPA** What I really need is some human fat. I had a talk with Ed Hemeyer. He's having an operation.

**MAMA** Mona says someone shot the prime minister.

**PAPA** Reckon I'll just kill Ed. That might be easier.

**MAMA** The kitchen's on fire.

**PAPA** Of course, the tidal wave might kill him first.

**MAMA** Mona says she saw flames licking around the eavestroughs. But I told her you probably wouldn't care if the whole house burned down, long as you saved your jars.

*PAPA sighs softly, takes the plate from MAMA and looks directly at her for the first time.*

**PAPA** *(without enthusiasm)* This looks good, Mama. You must be the best cook in the whole county. And you certainly have a knack for spiders' eggs.

**MAMA** This letter. It's from Leona.

**PAPA** Is that right?

**MAMA** She's coming home.

**PAPA** Now Mama…

**MAMA** Read it. *(hands him the letter)*

**PAPA** Says she'll be here Monday. That's… tonight.

**MAMA** I knew she'd come back.

**PAPA** She says "we," Mama. She's got someone with her.

**MAMA** She says "big news." She has big news—

**PAPA** Wonder what that could be—

**MAMA** Won't it be nice to have everyone home, Papa? Billy and Leona and…

**PAPA** Mama, Sarah's not coming.

**MAMA** I bet I know what that big news is – I'm gonna start cooking right now. A roast of beef, a turkey… I'll get Billy to bring up ham from the freezer. I better get started—

**PAPA** Now Mama… why don't you just rest a minute? Just stay and talk a minute?

**MAMA** And scalloped potatoes. You know how Leona loves them.

**PAPA** Well now, you better cook some fish.

**MAMA** What?

**PAPA** Just in case, Mama. In case Leona's engaged.

**MAMA** *(after a pause)* I don't think Leona likes fish. Do you remember?

**PAPA** Sure I remember, Mama. I brought a nine-pound pike to your folks' house. I gave it to you to clean. A nine-pound pike and a diamond ring in the pocket.

**MAMA** Some people don't like picking the bones out. Besides, it's only really good when it's fresh—

**PAPA** It was fresh all right. But we had a set-to about something. You made me so damn mad I threw the ring at you. So, you cooked that pike with a diamond in its guts.

**MAMA** No, I just can't remember whether Leona even likes fish.

**PAPA** Your mother almost choked on that diamond. "Do fish have teeth" she says, polite as can be. And you grabbed it from her and said – "Oh, for Lord's sake, Mama. We're getting married." Do you remember that, Mama? I haven't thought about that in years. Do you remember?

**MAMA** *(after a pause)* I remember the engagement party. Everyone in pale dresses eating sandwiches...

**PAPA** It was a barbecue, steaks and homemade beer.

**MAMA** Everyone in the district came—

**PAPA** Just your folks and my brother—

**MAMA** And the dancing. Waltzing on the lawn—

**PAPA** We barbecued steaks and had a good laugh about the diamond in the fish guts—

**MAMA** All those people—

**PAPA** Mama... try to remember. Don't you remember?

**MAMA** Of course I do. I've got pictures of the whole thing. People in white dresses, dancing on the lawn. I have the photos – I'll show them to you.

**PAPA** No, Mama. That's all right. You better... get cooking.

**MAMA** I'll make some pie. Raspberry pie. It's her favourite. And Sarah likes it, too.

**PAPA** Mama, there's just no way in the world Sarah could get here in time. She's just too busy.

**MAMA** I guess... I guess you're right.

**PAPA** That's right, Mama. No way in the world.

**MAMA** You done with your plate?

**PAPA** *(He hasn't touched a bite.)* Yes, Mama. Thank you.

**MAMA** Would you care—

**PAPA** No pie, Mama. I'm saving' room for supper. I'll track down Billy and make sure he's home in time.

**MAMA** Oh, don't tell him. Let's have a surprise. Billy will sure be surprised, won't he?

**PAPA** Yep. He sure will.

*MAMA starts to exit.*

Mama, your hair… there's something different about your hair. It's a different colour.

**MAMA** I dyed it. I want everything to be the same, Papa. The same as when she left.

**PAPA** Mama, you—*(pause)* It's nice, Mama. It's real nice.

*As lights fade a thumping noise is heard.*

## Scene Two

*BILLY and PAPA are in the living room waiting for supper. PAPA sits on the couch, resigned to his fate. BILLY wanders around the room, idly banging a baseball bat on the floor.*

**BILLY** Gonna rain?

**PAPA** *(after a pause)* Nope.

**BILLY** *(leans close to PAPA's face)* That's good. Real good.

**PAPA** Yep.

**BILLY** *(after a pause)* You sure?

**PAPA** *(leans close to BILLY's face)* I'd bet my life on it.

**BILLY** *(nodding toward the kitchen)* What's going on?

**PAPA** Mama's makin' supper.

**BILLY** It's nine o'clock.

**PAPA** That's right. I haven't eaten since breakfast.

**BILLY** It smells like dead meat.

**PAPA** It smells good.

**BILLY** I gotta go to work. I got a late shift.

**PAPA** You just stay put.

**BILLY** What's goin' on?

**PAPA** Mama wants you here for supper.

**BILLY** Why don't you just tell me? Whisper it in my ear. Write me a note.

**PAPA** It's a surprise. You know how Mama likes a surprise.

*BILLY swings his bat up from underneath the table and throws it at PAPA. PAPA catches it. They crouch over the bat, do a hand-over-hand game. PAPA caps the top of the bat and wins.*

It'll be hot as blazes tomorrow. You hear me?

*BILLY nods slowly. MAMA enters in high spirits. She is carrying an armload of games, cards and photo albums.*

**MAMA** Billy! There's my Billy… how's my boy?

*MAMA ruffles BILLY'S hair and pinches his cheeks.*

**BILLY** Great, Mama. Couldn't be better—

**MAMA** That's good to hear. That's always good to hear. Papa, what'll it be? Norwegian Whist or Scrabble?

**PAPA** No more Scrabble 'til you buy a dictionary.

**MAMA** Billy, what do you want to play?

**BILLY** Whatever you like, Mama.

**PAPA** I could eat a horse, Mama. How about some pickles or something?

**MAMA** Do you want to play cards, Billy?

**PAPA** Just to take the edge off.

**BILLY** Are we having a party, Mama?

**MAMA** You just wait and see!

**BILLY** It must be my birthday.

**MAMA** It's a special occasion.

**PAPA** Maybe we could have some crackers and cheese while we're waiting.

**MAMA** Could you deal the cards, Papa? I feel like Norwegian Whist.

**BILLY** I had a birthday just last month, Mama. And the month before.

**PAPA** That's more than most people get in a lifetime, Billy.

**MAMA** I thought I could work on my photo albums while we're waiting. While we're playing whist.

**PAPA** We usually have popcorn while we play whist.

**BILLY** What are we waiting for?

**MAMA** Supper, Bill. I've been cooking all day.

*PAPA has dealt the cards.*

**BILLY** I know, Mama. I can smell it.

**PAPA** You gonna call Mona for the other partner?

**BILLY** But I'm not very hungry—

**MAMA** Mona always cheats at whist – why don't we play Scrabble instead?

**PAPA** We need a dictionary—

**MAMA** I'll get out some crackers.

*PAPA sets out the board.*

**BILLY** Now let me see. Papa's birthday is in September. You were born in December. And I was born in March. So, what's the occasion?

**MAMA** I know when your birthday is, Billy. Pick your letters.

**BILLY** You know I love Scrabble, Mama, but not tonight—

**MAMA** It improves your vocabulary.

**BILLY** I gotta go to work, Mama.

**MAMA** I've been cooking all day—

**PAPA** It sure smells good—

**BILLY** I'm not really that hungry, Mama.

**MAMA** You just tell them that you can't come to work—

**BILLY** I'd need a reason—

**MAMA** This is a pretty good reason.

**BILLY** Someone would have to die for me to get off work, Mama. Now if there's no birthday and no deaths in the family, I'll just have to go. That's all there is to it.

*BILLY pulls on his jacket and starts to leave. He gets halfway across the room and then stops. Pause.*

**MAMA** Who loves you, Billy? Does your boss love you?

**BILLY** Mama, just tell me what's the surprise—

**MAMA** Who's the only person in the world who really loves you, Billy? I think you know. And the person is just asking you to be here for the surprise. Please.

**BILLY** *(pause)* All right, Mama. *(pause)* For a bit. I'll stay for a bit.

**PAPA** Pick your letters, son.

*MAMA opens the photo album and starts to sort photos. PAPA pokes BILLY under the table with the baseball bat, makes an elaborate gesture – "just go along with it." BILLY picks some letters.*

**BILLY** Toilet. T-o-i-l-e-t. Fourteen points.

**PAPA** Crackers. C-r-a-c-k-e-r-s. Eighty-two points.

*MAMA makes her word.*

Mama… that's not a word. Cr-orp.

**BILLY** What does it mean?

**MAMA** It's… a machine.

**PAPA** It's not a word, Mama.

**MAMA** Yes, it is.

**BILLY** Does Mona have a dictionary?

**MAMA** No—

**PAPA** If we could have a little something to eat, maybe we could allow just this one word.

**BILLY** I wanna know what a crorp is—

**PAPA** Or some pickles.

**MAMA** Do you want a little snack, Billy? To tide you over?

**BILLY** No thanks, Mama.

**PAPA** I wouldn't mind a snack.

**MAMA** I don't want to spoil your appetite.

**PAPA** Well then, it's not a word. I've never heard of it.

**MAMA** I better check on the roast – and the pie. I made lemon meringue, Billy…

**BILLY** I am not hungry. I'll play Scrabble but I'm not touching a bite until someone tells me what's going on—

**PAPA** *(warning)* Billy…

**MAMA** I wanted it to be a surprise.

**BILLY** I'm just about dead from the suspense.

**PAPA** Mama, he can wait.

**MAMA** Why don't I just show him a picture. / He can guess. Let's see if he can guess.

**BILLY** *(looking at picture)* Who's that?

**MAMA** It's Leona, silly. When she came home for my birthday last year.

**BILLY** Mama, Leona never—

**PAPA** Billy—

**BILLY** All right, Mama. What about Leona?

**MAMA** Leona's coming home, Billy. Tonight.

*BILLY looks at PAPA to confirm this. He jumps up from the table and whoops with joy.*

**BILLY** Well, I'll be dammed! She's really coming?

**PAPA** Anytime now—

*The phone rings.*

**MAMA** *(as she exits)* That might be her now.

**BILLY** Well now, that's a surprise all right.

**PAPA** That ain't the half of it, son.

**BILLY** Won't she be happy to see you…

**PAPA** You're not too old to take over my—

**BILLY** Am I old enough to go hunting?

*PAPA picks up BILLY'S bat. They stare at one another.*

**PAPA** Almost, Billy. Almost.

**MAMA** *(as she enters)* That was Mona. She says a car just pulled up. A foreign car. Red. They have… luggage and—

*The doorbell rings. Everyone freezes.*

**BILLY** They? They? She brought someone with her?

*The lights fade.*

## Scene Three

*LEONA and LEN enter, well-dressed, loaded up with parcels. A long silence. The family members stare at one another. LEN smiles expectantly, oblivious to the tension.*

**LEONA** I didn't know if we had the right house.

*Another pause.*

**LEN** But here we are. *(pause)* I'm Len.

**LEONA** Mama… what's all that stuff in the front yard—/ all those ceramic animals and—

**MAMA** Len? I'm Leona's—

**LEN** You must be Leona's mother—

**BILLY** It's been a long time, Leona / a very long time.

**LEONA** I rang the doorbell because / I didn't know if it was the—

**PAPA** It's good to see you, Leona—

**LEN** And you're Billy? I'm Len—

**MAMA** I did a little cooking. Didn't know when you'd get here—

**LEONA** Mama… /neither did I.

**BILLY** William James. Billy.

**PAPA** Len? Your name is Len?

**LEN** Yes, sir—

**BILLY** My friends / call me Blitz—

**PAPA** Good to meet you.

**LEN** Blitz? A nickname – that's / something I've never had.

**LEONA** Mama, how are you? / You look… fine.

**MAMA** Papa wanted to eat before you got here / but I knew the minute—

**LEN** Something certainly smells wonderful—

**LEONA** Why didn't anyone come to the door though? Mama, why didn't / you come to—

**BILLY** *(to PAPA)* You never said anything about Leona bringing home a friend.

*There is an uncomfortable silence.*

**LEONA** Len's an anthropologist.

**BILLY** *(after a pause)* Oh… well, that's different then.

**LEN** What do you do, Billy?

**BILLY** I work at Cliff's Wreck and Tow. That usually requires a university degree but they let me stay on because I'm a good worker. I go to accidents and pull cars apart. Then I take 'em back to the yard and smash them down to playing card size.

**LEN** That sounds… interesting.

**LEONA** Something smells awfully good, Mama—

**MAMA** I did a little cooking. Billy, could you get some plates?

**BILLY** I'm glad you're finally home, Leona.

**PAPA** Billy, get the plates.

*PAPA is discreetly following BILLY around the room with the baseball bat. LEN helps MAMA clear the table.*

**BILLY** I was beginning to wonder, you know. So was—

**PAPA** Billy, help your mama bring the food out.

**BILLY** Why don't you help her?

**PAPA** Go on, now.

**BILLY** I won't eat.

**MAMA** He's a picky eater.

**PAPA** Now that you're home you've brought his appetite back, though.

**BILLY** You got my appetite in one of those bags, Leona?

**LEN** I thought it might be a nice idea to come bearing gifts. *(laughs a little at his own joke)* Leona picked them out, of course, but… I'd like you to think they're from both of us.

**LEONA** They're… presents.

**MAMA** Isn't that nice? Now who wants coffee?

**BILLY** I want to know what's in the packages.

**LEONA** *(after a pause)* All right Billy, you first.

*LEONA hands a parcel to BILLY. He opens it slowly, eyes on LEONA. It's a custom steering wheel, made of shiny chrome.*

**BILLY** Well now, that's real thoughtful of you, Leona.

**LEONA** You like it?

**MAMA** What is it?

**LEN** That's what I said, too.

**PAPA** Looks like a steering wheel. Couldn't afford the rest of the car, eh?

**LEONA** And Mama…

**MAMA** *(opening the gift)* Now what's all this?

**LEONA** It's a photo album. With pictures… from the last five years. My room in residence. Convocation—

**MAMA** *(closing it abruptly)* I imagine we could look at it later—

**LEN** I took some of the shots actually—

**PAPA** Can I see it?

**MAMA** No! I've… I've already got one.

**LEONA** You've already got what?

**MAMA** Pictures from when you were gone—

**LEONA** But Mama…

**PAPA** Do I get a present?

**LEONA** *(after a pause)* Of course… of course you do.

**PAPA** *(opens his gift)* It's…

**BILLY** It's a red hat! A hunting cap!

*BILLY laughs. LEONA and PAPA stare at one another. LEN beams, unaware of the tension.*

**MAMA** Is there a present for Sarah?

**LEN** Sarah?

**MAMA** Sarah's our oldest daughter. She looks more like me than… Leona.

**LEN** Leona? Was there a gift for… your sister?

**LEONA** Oh, Mama… I'm sorry. We didn't buy anything for… Mama, it's so nice to see you. Are you happy to see me? You haven't even touched me – no one's even touched me yet.

*LEONA hugs MAMA. MAMA nervously pats her on the back, embarrassed by this show of feeling.*

**MAMA** Well now, what's all the fuss. You're here, aren't you? It hardly seems like you've been away. What's all the fuss?

**BILLY** Just seems like yesterday, Leona.

*The lights fade.*

## Scene Four

*After dinner, PAPA is slumped over the table, his head between his hands. BILLY is lying on the floor, picking out a slow repetitive rhythm on his guitar. He is wearing the red cap. LEONA paces nervously. LEN is telling a story to MAMA.*

**LEN** They take the young girl to a tent up in the mountains, you see, to initiate her into the secrets of marriage. Meanwhile, the men of the village are taking the groom through his paces. Tests of strength, bravery – many things that would be considered extremely barbaric by our standards – self-inflicted pain – which the young bridegroom bears without making a sound. What my professor didn't know was that the tribesmen thought he had his eye on the young bride. And that's where the trouble started.

**MAMA** What kind of trouble?

**LEN** Well, I didn't really mean to dominate the conversation like this.

**MAMA** It's very interesting—

**BILLY** I have a story—

**LEONA** Len has lots of stories—

**LEN** But they're probably only truly interesting to me—

**MAMA** Oh no, I don't think so. I'd like to hear all your stories. Can I get you some coffee?

**LEN** Thank you, yes. That was a lovely meal.

**MAMA** Thank you. I hope you saved room for pie.

*PAPA groans loudly.*

I have five different kinds.

**LEONA** Maybe we could take a little break between courses, Mama.

**MAMA** We could just get settled with dessert and then we'll hear about that trouble your professor had.

**LEN** Mmmm… dessert. I expect I could be persuaded.

**MAMA** Papa, what kind of pie do you want?

**PAPA** No more, please, Mama.

**MAMA** Lemon Meringue?

**PAPA** I don't want anything.

**MAMA** Maybe a little wedge of each kind if you can't make up your mind.

**PAPA** I can't do it. I cleaned out the garage yesterday, Mama, and I took that load out to the dump. You said I wouldn't have to eat any pie.

**MAMA** Papa, we have company.

**PAPA** *(after a pause)* All right, Mama. Just a little.

**MAMA** Leona, I made raspberry. Do you want saskatoon and raspberry or just the one?

**LEN** Did I hear saskatoon?

**LEONA** I'm so full—

**LEN** *(to PAPA)* You're a lucky man – do you get pie every day?

**PAPA** Sometimes twice.

**LEONA** No thanks, Mama. Really. Maybe Len—

**MAMA** Don't you like raspberry anymore?

**LEN** Come on, Leona…

**MAMA** You've always loved raspberry pie—

**LEONA** I guess I forgot about that—

*PAPA shoots LEONA a glance.*

**MAMA** Just a little piece, I baked it specially for you.

**LEONA** All right, Mama. Just a little. Billy, you haven't eaten anything. Why aren't you eating?

**MAMA** *(to LEN)* Did I hear someone mention saskatoon pie?

**BILLY** *(to LEONA)* It's not my birthday.

**MAMA** Now, who wants more roast beef before I bring the pie?

*Pause.*

**LEN** I'll have a little. And I'd love some saskatoon pie. I'm quite full but I just can't seem to stop eating.

*PAPA and BILLY stare at LEN resentfully. Pause.*

**MAMA** Where did you find this flatterer, Leona?

**LEONA** They grow them on trees in the city.

**MAMA** Well, I'll get the pie and then we can hear about your professor at that wedding.

**LEN** Well, I suppose the story's quite appropriate in a way—

*LEN laughs and takes LEONA's hand. BILLY stops playing.*

**BILLY** How's that?

**MAMA** Well now… is this the big news?

**BILLY** Big news?

**LEN** What do you say, Leona? Should we – spill the beans, as it were?

**LEONA** Well, yes…

**BILLY** You're moving home?

**MAMA** Papa and I figured it out on our own—

**LEONA** Mama, Len and I are engaged.

**LEN** We're getting married.

**MAMA** Well, isn't that wonderful! Of course we thought—

**BILLY** Surprise, surprise—

**PAPA** Billy why don't you go down to the cellar and get some—

**MAMA** I should phone Mona—

**PAPA** She's probably lip-reading through the picture window.

**BILLY** That's big news all right—

**PAPA** Billy, wine!

**BILLY** Well, I'd just like to be the first to kiss the bride—

*BILLY kisses LEONA on the mouth. They both look a little uncomfortable when the kiss ends.*

**MAMA** Isn't that nice?

**BILLY** Congratulations, Leona.

**PAPA** Congratulations, Leona... Len—

*LEN shakes hands with PAPA. LEONA watches MAMA.*

**LEN** Certainly nice to finally meet you, sir.

**LEONA** Mama... are you happy— / happy I'm getting married?

**MAMA** Well, it's short notice to plan a wedding— / but we can manage.

**PAPA** *(to BILLY)* I told you to get the wine, Billy—

**LEONA** Mama, listen—

**BILLY** That wine's skunky anyhow—

**MAMA** I'm sure we can get the Legion Hall—

**LEONA** Mama—

**PAPA** *(to BILLY)* I like skunky wine—

**MAMA** The reception is no trouble – The Ladies' Auxiliary is still doing roast beef at five dollars a head. That includes the midnight lunch and all the salads. Now, the church might not be so easy unless you wanted the Catholic Church. Are you... Catholic, Len?

**LEONA** Mama, we haven't set a date.

**MAMA** Well, you can set a date now, can't you?

**LEN** We hadn't really discussed—

**LEONA** We don't know when we're getting married—

**MAMA** We can do it all here—

**LEONA** We're just here for a couple of days—

**MAMA** It's sure cheaper than the city. Not as fancy—

**BILLY** Just dropped in for a little visit, eh?

**MAMA** We could all pitch in—

**LEN** Now, Leona, maybe we should talk about this—

**LEONA** Mama, no! I don't want anyone pitching in. We just aren't ready yet – not ready to set a date.

*There is an uncomfortable silence.*

Well... are we still having pie? I'd like some of your pie, Mama.

**MAMA** Yes... yes... I'll get it.

**LEN** Can I help you with anything?

**MAMA** Yes... that would be nice. Very nice.

*LEN and MAMA exit.*

**PAPA** Why'd you bother, Leona? Why'd you bother coming home?

**LEONA** Because I'd had just about long enough to forget why I left—

**PAPA** It would mean a lot to Mama if you'd just go along—

**LEONA** I'm supposed to "go along" with my own—

**BILLY** What's the matter, Leona? Cold Feet?

*The sound of a plate smashing is heard offstage.*

**LEN** *(offstage)* Mrs. Sorenson? Are you all right?

*LEN and MAMA enter.*

*(whispering)* Is she all right? She just stopped talking...

**PAPA** *(goes to MAMA)* It's all right, Mama. All right...

**BILLY** *(to LEONA)* Oh, you've really done it now—

**LEN** She hasn't said a word – she dropped a plate—

**PAPA** Mama, you try and talk now. Just try—

**MAMA** It's all my fault...

**PAPA** Now Mama—

**LEONA** What's she talking about?

**BILLY** She was like this for days after you left—

**LEN** Should we call a doctor?

**PAPA** Leona, please... just a little family party...

**LEONA** Mama—

*MAMA focuses on LEONA.*

Mama, I'm here. I'm home, Mama. Leona's home.

**MAMA** *(after a long pause)* You're home.

**LEONA** Yes, Mama.

**MAMA** I just thought it wouldn't be any trouble.

**LEN** Whatever you want is all right with me, Leona—

**LEONA** *(after a pause)* We'll talk about it, Mama. We'll talk—

**MAMA** Oh, Leona, it would be lovely. Please…

**BILLY** We'll all pitch in.

**LEONA** We're only here for a few days, Mama.

*Pause. MAMA regains her spirits.*

**MAMA** Of course you are. Well now – I was getting some pie, wasn't I?

**LEN** And I was helping you…

*MAMA smiles sweetly at the group and exits on LEN's arm.*

**PAPA** Thank you Leona…

**LEONA** I'm not doing it for you.

*BILLY laughs, picks up his guitar. As lights fade on scene BILLY plays a slightly "off" version of "Here Comes the Bride" (Richard Wagner). It ends suddenly and BILLY laughs in darkness.*

## Scene Five

*As lights go up we see MAMA sitting by the window with her eyes closed, rocking back and forth. LEN enters wearing a housecoat.*

**LEN** I couldn't sleep… first night in a strange house.

**MAMA** Shh…

**LEN** I'm sorry.

**MAMA** I'm just… catching the tail end of a dream. I'm… standing smack in the middle of a road. A gravel road in the middle of the prairie. There's a half-ton truck raising up the dust. Coming toward me. The headlights blend right in with the stars. It's coming right for me… but I stay put. And then…

**LEN** *(whispering)* Then what?

**MAMA** I see who's driving… it's always the same. I see who's driving and I can't get out of the way. He's coming right for me. And I…

**LEN** Yes?

**MAMA** Then I always wake up.

*Pause. MAMA opens her eyes, smiles at LEN.*

I used to sit here and wait for them at night, Len. That's why I'd come to this window to try to finish off that dream. I can see the driveway from here. I worried. So I used to wait for them, for Leona and Billy and… Nelson Eddy.

**LEN** Nelson Eddy. That's a peculiar name.

**MAMA** Yes, I suppose. His mother was a fan of Jeanette MacDonald and – but I expect Leona's told you all about Nelson Eddy.

**LEN** I… expect she has.

**MAMA** I can't help feeling it was partly my fault, you know. But we thought – they might get married, you see. And so, I felt like he was part of the family. I felt I could tell him things, Len. You understand, don't you?

**LEN** Of course… you felt you could… confide—

**MAMA** And so I did. I told him things. I talked to him. Only he wasn't part of the family. He wasn't. It turned out badly then.

**LEN** Turned out badly?

**MAMA** Papa never liked him in the first place. Nelson Eddy just wasn't part of the family. *(pause)* Not like you. I wanted you to know that. That I feel you're part of the family now.

**LEN** That's one of the nicest things anyone's ever said to me, Mrs. Sorenson. I've never really felt like I was part of a family.

**MAMA** Now that you're here, maybe I'll stop having that dream about Nelson Eddy. Driving his truck down the middle of the road. All the dust, it's enough to blind you. *(pause)* We're very happy, Papa and I. We worried about Leona being alone. But now that you're here… well, I knew the minute we met you that you were different. *(pause)* Different from Nelson Eddy.

*LEONA enters in a nightgown.*

Leona, are you still up?

**LEONA** You're not feeding Len again, are you?

**MAMA** I never even thought to ask – did you want anything, Len? There's cold roast beef and—

**LEN** I'm perfectly all right. That was a lovely dinner, Mrs. Sorensen.

**MAMA** Why don't you call me Mama?

**LEN** All right, Mama.

**MAMA** Well, I think I can sleep now. It was nice talking to you, Len.

**LEN** Good night. Good luck with the… truck.

**MAMA** Thank you. Good night.

**LEONA** Good night, Mama.

*MAMA exits.*

Truck?

**LEN** Your mother was having a dream… about a truck. And a… Nelson Eddy.

**LEONA** What did she say about Nelson Eddy?

**LEN** An old beau of yours apparently.

**LEONA** Apparently…

**LEN** But then we never discuss old romances. Leona's "let bygones be" clause…

**LEONA** Believe me, you're better off. *(pause)* I just had a dream about him, too. Only he wasn't with me, he was… with Sarah.

**LEN** Sarah… your sister… is she included under bygones?

**LEONA** Yes. I mean, I'm not even sure she exists.

**LEN** I see – part of the family mythology.

**LEONA** No… no, she's very real to me. She's the good girl, the only girl for Mama. She's like the only girl in the family.

**LEN** Fascinating…

**LEONA** This is not an anthropological case study, Len. We don't talk about it. We just go along.

**LEN** Go along?

**LEONA** Len, I'm sorry I didn't tell you… things. I thought you'd be amused, superior and bored stiff.

**LEN** I'm not bored. I'm—

**LEONA** You're fascinated.

**LEN** Isn't it only natural that I'm interested? It's your family – it's part of you.

**LEONA** Sometimes I'm not so sure about that. I don't feel anything like them. I don't even look like them.

**LEN** But they're a real family, Leona. You don't understand what it's like being an only child, Leona. My parents… well, they're not like yours. When I graduated from university they sent me a telex. A telex, Leona.

**LEONA** Len, I'm sorry. But my family isn't—

**LEN** Your mother is delightful and your father and Billy seem… sincere. I've only been here a few hours. All I know is it's important that they like me.

**LEONA** Well, Len – knowing about Nelson Eddy and Sarah is not going to make anyone like you.

**LEN** Are you all right?

**LEONA** I just need some sleep, that's all. Some sleep without dreams.

*LEN holds out his arms for an embrace.*

Oh… yes. *(hugs LEN unenthusiastically)* Sorry… it feels funny in this house.

*The lights fade.*

## Scene Six

*PAPA is in the living room examining jars with newspaper at hand. Morning light streams in the window. PAPA is wearing his red cap.*

**LEONA** *(offstage)* Len! Len! *(pause)* Mama!

*Pause as LEONA searches the other rooms in the house.*

Where is everyone?

**PAPA** I'm in here, Leona.

*LEONA comes to the doorway of the living room, wearing a housecoat. She watches PAPA for a moment. LEONA begins singing "Bee-Bop-A-Lula" (Gene Vincent and B. Davis).*

**LEONA** *(singing, taunting)* Bee-bop-a-loola…

*PAPA reacts but does not turn around to look at LEONA. After a pause she continues.*

Bee-bop-a-loola… she's my baby.

**PAPA** Damn it, Leona!

**LEONA** *(louder)* Bee-bop—

**PAPA** Leona, stop it!

**LEONA** What do you want to hear?

**PAPA** Anything but that!—

**LEONA** Does it remind you of someone?

**PAPA** I know you want to fight—

**LEONA** Yes, I wanna fight!

**PAPA** I'm not gonna fight with you, Leona.

*PAPA turns to his jars, determined to ignore LEONA. PAPA begins to hum "When you Wish upon a Star." LEONA stares at him for a moment.*

**LEONA** What's with the jars? I thought you had a hobby.

**PAPA** Leona...

**LEONA** I thought you had a pastime—

**PAPA** I quit that years ago. I stopped—

**LEONA** You always loved hunting...

*LEONA picks up one of the jars. PAPA rushes toward her.*

**PAPA** Don't touch that – you'll wreck the patterns!

**LEONA** I want to know why you quit hunting!

*PAPA grabs LEONA's arm to get the jar. They struggle. This turns into a rather awkward wrestling match, LEONA holding the jar and striking at PAPA while he restrains her.*

*(as they wrestle)* You tell me, Papa!

**PAPA** I quit – after the accident.

**LEONA** The "accident"—

**PAPA** Stop it – you'll break the jar!

**LEONA** Why'd you do it, Papa?

**PAPA** You don't understand—

**LEONA** You tell me—

*PAPA wrestles the jar away from LEONA.*

**PAPA** It was an accident. But it was... for the best. The best for Mama.

**LEONA** *(The anger seems to have left her.)* For Mama...

**PAPA** I'm sorry, Leona. I am.

*Long pause. PAPA reaches out and tweaks LEONA's nose. She stares at him, astonished. PAPA pinches his thumb between the next two fingers.*

I got your nose...

**LEONA** You got my nose?

**PAPA** Don't you remember? See, I got your nose.

*LEONA stands up, stares at PAPA for a moment.*

**LEONA** No, I don't. I don't remember.

*PAPA returns to his jars.*

**PAPA** I never did thank you for the cap, Leona. It fits just perfect.

**LEONA** Good, Papa. I thought of you when I saw it.

*LEN enters, a camera around his neck, wearing a sweater.*

**LEN** There you are! I had a great time. You should have come—

**LEONA** No one woke me up—

**LEN** Your mother and I had breakfast in the Chinese café. Then we went to the farmer's market, the Legion Hall and the United Church thrift sale. Your mother bought me this sweater—

**LEONA** The Legion Hall?

**LEN** It's second-hand. Two bits. Can you believe it? We're going back tomorrow.

**PAPA** Small-town life ain't so bad then?

**LEN** So far it's been very interesting. I shot nearly a whole roll of film—

**LEONA** Of what?

**LEN** People – everyone's very friendly.

**LEONA** They're curious.

**PAPA** Yep.

**LEN** Say, what's in the jars?

**PAPA** Rendered animal fat.

**LEN** You don't say. Now what's that for?

**PAPA** Predicting the weather. There's patterns in the fat – swirls and spots. I study them and I can see rain, hail, snow… I predicted every storm last year. I see other things too. Events, changes. I can't change the past. But if I study my jars, I can get an idea of what to expect.

*PAPA and LEONA stare at one another. LEN examines the jars.*

**LEONA** You got any human fat in those jars, Papa?

**PAPA** I aim to.

**LEN** You know, I think I might have read something about this. The Indians have great faith in the healing powers of bear fat. I wonder if there's any relationship—

**PAPA** I could tell you how it works if you're interested.

**LEN** I'd love to hear more about it.

**MAMA** *(offstage)* Leona, could you give me a hand?

**LEONA** Coming!

**PAPA** Now come on over here where the light's proper so you can see.

**LEN** Okey-doke.

**LEONA** Okey-doke?

## Scene Seven

*In the darkness we hear guitar strumming, a standard country and western chord progression. Lights fade up on BILLY playing guitar. BILLY hears LEONA in another room of the house. He considers for a moment and then picks up the pace and volume of his strumming. LEONA enters the room, lured by the music.*

**LEONA** Hi, Billy… what are you playing?

**BILLY** C… G… G7… *(continues to strum)*

**LEONA** It's… nice. I was just going to—

**BILLY** *(changes chords, new tune)* Singalong with old Bill…?

**LEONA** What?

**BILLY** You don't remember how, do you?

**LEONA** *(Pause. She's got it now.)* Maybe.

**BILLY** Pick a topic. Any topic. *(strums louder)*

**LEONA** Trucks.

*The game is one BILLY and LEONA invented and played often before LEONA left.*

**BILLY** A tender ballad about… trucks. *(pause, sings)* You are the attendant in the parking lot of my heart…

**LEONA** *(thinks fast, sings)* I've given you the keys but your love for me won't start…

**BILLY** *(singing)* You've given me a ticket… that says that we must part…

**LEONA** *(singing)* And if I don't pay you'll tow me… *(She can't finish it.)*

**BILLY** *(to the rescue)* To the cheating hearts wreckin' yard!

*BILLY won, new round.*

**LEONA** You are the bluebell in the garden of my soul…

**BILLY** *(picking up the pace)* I'd love to plant you but I'd have to dig a hole…

**LEONA** We'd need lots of sunshine to let our sweet love grow…

**BILLY** 'Cause my bluebell left our town and dealt me a blow…

*BILLY plays a finishing chord. The game is over. Pause.*

**LEONA** Why didn't you ever visit me, Billy? Just for the weekend. We could have gone for a drink, gone to the movies – hell, we could have driven around in your truck for all I care.

**BILLY** What do I need to go to the city for, Leona? All those movies show up here eventually. Why, right this very minute the town cinema's showing "Gone with the Wind"—

**LEONA** I thought maybe you were scared to come to the city. I know I was—

**BILLY** You know how Mama gets. She has to have one of us here.

**LEONA** I know, but just for the weekend or something—

**BILLY** Why didn't you come home? I missed you.

**LEONA** I got busy. I just – I couldn't.

**BILLY** But now you're here. I installed my new steering wheel this morning. It's real pretty. Looks like old times in that truck. Let's go for a run out to the lake and crack a mickey—

**LEONA** No, I better not. Mama's run off with Len again. They went out this morning and… rented a hall. I better track them down…

**BILLY** Rented a hall – for a family party—

**LEONA** Mama wants to invite a few aunts and uncles. Len doesn't seem to mind and I just…

**BILLY** Wanna keep Mama happy… *(back to the song game)* All I ever wanted was a wedding for my Ma… we're just plain and simple folks… my bouquet was made of straw… *(stops)* Why don't you just come for a little lemon gin? For old times' sake.

**LEONA** *(after a pause)* No, Billy. Once was enough of that.

**BILLY** Suit yourself. Have to admit I had my hopes up when I heard you were coming home. I still do.

**LEONA** I wouldn't if I were you—

**BILLY** Even when you turn up with this spit and polish boy—

**LEONA** I'm sorry you don't like him, Billy.

**BILLY** Where'd you find him, Leona? Through some kind of protection agency?

**LEONA** I'm going to marry him, Billy.

**BILLY** You knew you couldn't come back alone 'cause you'd get sucked back into the centre of the house. It's got a gravitational force, this place, like magic—

**LEONA** For you, maybe.

**BILLY** He sure is different from Nelson Eddy. I'll say that. Does he know about Nelson Eddy?

**LEONA** Do you know about Nelson Eddy?

**BILLY** Nope, not really. Mama gave him an earful, that's all I know. I think he actually wanted to meet Sarah after all the buildup.

**LEONA** Does she even know why I left?

**BILLY** I don't know – we don't talk about Nelson Eddy around here.

**LEONA** Do we talk about Sarah? I mean, does Mama—

**BILLY** Yep. Sarah gets more wonderful every day.

**LEONA** Does she ever talk about me?

**BILLY** She does now, Leona. That's all we think about now – the upcoming nuptials. *(pause)* Come for a drink, Leona. Please...

**LEONA** No. Sorry.

*BILLY starts strumming on his guitar again.*

You got a girlfriend now, Billy?

**BILLY** I had one but she left town.

**LEONA** That's too bad.

**BILLY** Yep. She's getting married to someone else.

**LEONA** Oh, Billy... I'm sorry.

**BILLY** So am I. We got along real good. She was like a sister to me.

**LEONA** Is that right?

**BILLY** *(singing)* Oh, she was like a sister to me... we even had bunk beds... she was as sweet as could be...

*Lights snap to black.*

## Scene Eight

*Dining room. MAMA is sitting at the table with a stack of photo albums and glue and paper in front of her. She is taking out old pictures, pasting in new ones and labelling them. She is humming "Good night, Irene" (traditional) to herself.*

**MAMA** *(singing)* Good night, Irene... good night, Irene... I'll— *(stops, unable to remember the words)* Good night, Irene...

*LEONA enters and watches her for a moment.*

Good night... Irene... Jolene...

**LEONA** *(gently)* It's Irene, Mama.

**MAMA** I know, I know. I can't remember—

**LEONA** I'll see you in my dreams.

**MAMA** That's right. I know that.

**LEONA** Of course you do. Mama, have you seen Len?

**MAMA** Len? I sent him to get the decorations. He'll be back in time for supper.

**LEONA** Decorations? *(pause)* I've hardly seen him today. And I haven't had a chance to talk to you, either.

**MAMA** Would Saturday be all right with you? I think we can get everything done by Saturday.

**LEONA** Well, I'll have to talk to Len—

**MAMA** It's all right with Len...

**LEONA** Well, I guess it's set then. *(pause)* Do you like the album I gave you? I left room at the back so that you could add pictures—

**MAMA** That's just what I'm doing. I thought it might be nice to have a photo album by the guest book. Beth Hemeyer did that when her boy got married. She even had his birth certificate and a lock of hair.

**LEONA** I suppose I need a birth certificate to get my marriage licence. Do you have it? Do you have a lock of my baby hair?

**MAMA** Well, no. I don't think so, honey. You know how it is. You save every little button for the first few years and then you just sort of run out of steam.

**LEONA** Yes... I know. Do you have a lock of Sarah's baby hair?

**MAMA** Yes. It was brown and curly, even when she was a baby. She really did look a lot like me.

**LEONA** Can I see ?

*MAMA hands LEONA an album. LEONA starts to look through it.*

She's very pretty. She looks... different in every picture, doesn't she?

**MAMA** What do you mean?

**LEONA** Nothing. It's just... I've never seen some of these pictures before. Here she is... playing a violin. Is that Sarah, Mama?

**MAMA** Of course it is. She took lessons... at the school. They wanted her to go on but she... just didn't care to.

**LEONA** Do you remember when I took piano lessons, Mama?

**MAMA** *(uncertainly)* Yes…

**LEONA** The teacher—Mrs. Harris—is she still alive? She used to rap my knuckles with a ruler when I was playing.

**MAMA** Sarah's teacher was a tyrant, too. But she kept a stiff upper lip.

**LEONA** Do you have any pictures of me playing the piano? You could put those in the photo album.

**MAMA** I expect I do…

**LEONA** They should be here somewhere. You have all these shots of Sarah and I know there were pictures of me. At least I think there were.

**MAMA** Of course there's pictures, honey. Somewhere here…

*MAMA continues to cut and paste. Long pause.*

**LEONA** There's a picture in the album I gave you of my twenty-first birthday. *(pause)* I don't know if you can tell from the picture but the cake is shaped like a merry-go-round. There was even money in it. Len took a lot of the more recent pictures in there… I put in a few from my convocation – when I graduated from university… because I thought you'd be proud… *(pause)* I wish you could have been there, Mama. The one on the first page is taken in the office where I work. *(frustration creeping in)* Do you want to hear about my job, Mama? How much money I make? What I take for lunch? Mama… *(leaning over her to point out a picture)* You see this is where I work— *(pause)* Where's the picture, Mama? Did you take it out? *(pause)* Where did you get all these pictures? This isn't me—

**MAMA** It's a picture of you at the Dominion Day picnic, Leona. Last summer.

**LEN** *(offstage)* Mission accomplished!

**LEONA** Mama, I wasn't here—

**LEN** *(as he enters with arm-loads of packages)* I got everything on the list and more. Your dad and Billy just drove up after me, so we've got a full crew.

*LEN goes to a corner of the room and starts to unpack the boxes.*

**LEONA** Mama, I'm sorry I went away but you can't change it—

**MAMA** Why don't I put all this away for now so we can make those decorations?

**LEN** *(opening out a paper bell)* Leona, look at this. Pop culture at its finest, wouldn't you say? Leona.

*Lights fade.*

## Scene Nine

*BILLY and PAPA in the living room, with a box of pop-up paper bells between them. PAPA pulls a bell out of the box and demonstrates to BILLY.*

**PAPA** There's clips on the sides, see?

**BILLY** Fascinating.

**PAPA** Look – the sooner we get this over with—

**BILLY** I'm listening.

**PAPA** You grab them in the middle and fan 'em out. Then you clip them back together. *(bell snaps back to flat shape)* Dammit!

**BILLY** Mind if I try?

*BILLY successfully assembles a bell.*

**PAPA** Smartass.

**BILLY** How many of these anyway?

**PAPA** *(wearily)* Mama says we need about two hundred.

**BILLY** Gosh, I hope there's a couple left over for the window of my truck.

**PAPA** Billy, you be careful. You be damn careful. You know what Mama's been like. So just—

**BILLY** I know my place, Papa. Don't you worry about a thing.

*LEN and LEONA enter.*

**LEN** I certainly didn't know—

**LEONA** You might have consulted me. It's a wedding not a damn handicraft sale!

**LEN** I didn't think it mattered—

**LEONA** They're remodelled bleach bottles with artificial flowers in them.

**BILLY** Looks real pretty—

**LEONA** You stay out of this!

**LEN** *(to PAPA)* They're centrepieces for the tables. I thought Leona knew—

**BILLY** Oh, it's just nuptial nerves—

**LEONA** Listen you—

**PAPA** Billy!

**MAMA** *(as she enters)* Isn't this going to be fun?

**LEONA** Mama, why are we doing this now? Isn't this supposed to be done at the hall?

**MAMA** Beth Hemeyer did her son's decorations ahead. It'll save a fuss. Now – you and Len can twist the streamers and tape the middle. Papa and Billy can do the bells.

**BILLY** Look, Mama. I already did one!

*PAPA shoots BILLY a warning glance.*

**MAMA** I've got the guest list here, and you kids have to decide what you want to eat.

*LEN and LEONA stretch out lengths of crêpe paper and twist them from both ends. BILLY and PAPA assemble bells. MAMA sits at the table with her lists.*

I talked to Myra Stuart and she seemed to think roast beef would be best.

**BILLY** *(to PAPA)* You're falling behind, old man.

**MAMA** Leona?

**LEONA** What about Cornish game hens, Mama?

**MAMA** Oh, not for this many people, Leona.

**LEONA** For this many people?

**MAMA** Besides, I don't think I've ever seen a game hen in a store here.

**BILLY** *(to PAPA)* How about some wild meat?

**PAPA** Shut up, Billy.

**MAMA** How about turkey and roast beef, Leona? It's far enough away from Christmas that people wouldn't mind turkey—

**LEONA** Oh, I'm sure they wouldn't mind.

**MAMA** *(goes to PAPA)* No, Papa… you have to clip it so—

**LEN** *(to LEONA)* You're just bubbling over aren't you?

**MAMA** *(to PAPA)* So, it will stay opened up. There, you see?

**LEONA** *(to LEN)* What's the point?

**MAMA** What did those people in that village eat, Len?

**LEN** I beg your pardon?

**MAMA** In the village your professor was in – what did they eat for the wedding?

**LEN** Oh… I think it was…

**LEONA** They butter up the bride and then roast her over a pit—

*BILLY laughs. PAPA silences him with a sharp elbow to the ribs.*

**MAMA** If you don't want to do decorations, Leona... just say so.

**LEONA** I'm sorry, Mama. It was a joke. Len, what did they eat?

**LEN** Hmmm... yams, I think.

**MAMA** Isn't that funny? Well, we could have yams.

**LEONA** Why not?

**MAMA** Mona has a jelly mould in the shape of a wedding bell. She says we could borrow it.

**LEONA** I don't know if we really want – jellied salad, Mama.

*BILLY tapes a bell to the middle of a length of crêpe paper.*

**BILLY** *(to LEONA)* That mould would go real nice with the centrepieces.

**PAPA** *(undoing two of BILLY's bells)* I don't think you got these quite right after all, Billy.

**BILLY** What the hell—

**MAMA** Oh, did you like those centrepieces, Leona? Myra made them.

*LEN tugs on the streamer and shoots LEONA a glance. She tugs back and rips the streamer.*

**LEONA** *(to LEN)* Don't you start, too!

**MAMA** Start what?

**BILLY** My bells are squashed. Now how could that have happened?

**LEONA** Mama – listen. They're – someone's obviously gone to a lot of work on them. But I think maybe I'd rather have – wildflowers or something. On the tables—

**MAMA** I understand, honey, but Myra's coming to the wedding, you know, and when she sees that you—

**LEONA** Myra's coming to the wedding?

**MAMA** If you don't want her to come I can tell her—

**LEONA** Who is coming anyway?

**MAMA** I've got the list right here—

**LEONA** *(looking at list)* Who's Ossie Toffling?

**LEN** *(to LEONA)* Twist.

**PAPA** He always comes right away when we call about the furnace.

**LEONA** But who is he?

**LEN** Leona, your end…

**BILLY** *(taping a bell to crêpe paper, takes LEN's end of the paper)* Here, you pop bells. I'll twist.

*LEN sits with PAPA.*

**LEONA** Mama, I don't know most of these people. How many people have you got on this list anyway?

**MAMA** About three hundred.

**LEONA** No, Mama. We just can't. You can't. What about Len's relatives?

**MAMA** Well, I already asked Len about that if you really want to know.

**LEN** It's all right, Leona. My family is too busy to come. As usual they're just… too busy.

**MAMA** That's a real shame.

**LEN** Yes, it is a shame. At any rate, they live so far away—

**LEONA** That's still no reason to turn this into a county fair—

**PAPA** We'll pay for the reception, Leona—

**LEN** I wouldn't dream of letting you—

**LEONA** I don't care if the government pays for it! I don't know any of these people—

**MAMA** Well, I know them, Leona. Your Papa and I—

**BILLY** Twist your end, Leona.

**MAMA** It's our party, too—

**LEONA** Of course, Mama, but—

**BILLY** *(looking over MAMA's shoulder)* What do you know? Al Johnson.

**MAMA** I asked Al if he'd MC—

**LEONA** I never liked him, Mama.

**MAMA** He said he'd be delighted—

**BILLY** Did he get his charges cleared?

**PAPA** *(warning)* Billy… *(to LEN)* Al's a town councilman.

**LEN** He's up on charges?

**BILLY** He got caught—

**MAMA** Billy, please. You know how people talk. You know how people are, Billy.

**BILLY** *(after a pause)* I know, Mama. I know.

**MAMA** We can ask someone else as a backup in case Al's not available.

**LEONA** I will not have Al at my wedding—

**MAMA** Maybe Billy could fill in—

**BILLY** Hell, no – I'd rather be best man. I've never had a tuxedo before.

**MAMA** It'd sure be nice to see this boy dressed up for once—

**PAPA** *(to MAMA)* Maybe we better let the kids have who they want for—

**LEONA** Mama, you said it was going to be a small family wedding. Then it was aunts and uncles – but now you've got half the town on that list. Please, Mama—

*MAMA leaps to her feet, very angry.*

**MAMA** We've never had a chance to have a party, Leona. All these people have invited us to their weddings and they always ask about you. I'd just like a chance to show people a good time.

**LEONA** I know, Mama, but—

**MAMA** Please, Leona. We haven't seen you in so long. We'd like to have a party.

*LEONA looks around the room for help. Long pause.*

**LEONA** I'd like to have a party, too, Mama. *(pause)* Maybe you and I could go over the guest list. It's just that I've never laid eyes on most of these people—

**MAMA** Of course you have. You grew up here, after all.

**LEONA** Yes, I know but—

**BILLY** Do I get to be best man?

**LEONA** Oh, for God's sake, Billy. Sure you can be best man. At this rate we might as well have Sarah for the maid of honour, too!

**PAPA** Leona!

**MAMA** Oh, would you like that, honey?

**PAPA** Leona didn't mean it, Mama—

**LEONA** How do you know?

**PAPA** Mama, no. She couldn't get here on short notice.

**MAMA** Leona would like to see Sarah—

**PAPA** *(to MAMA)* She'd need longer notice, Mama.

**LEONA** How much notice would she need?

**PAPA** Mama, come on in the kitchen for a minute. We should talk—

**MAMA** *(pulls away from PAPA)* Papa could go and get her. Couldn't you Papa? I know she wouldn't miss it for the world.

**PAPA** Now, Mama…

**MAMA** She'll be here.

*Lights fade.*

## Scene Ten

*LEN is in the living room examining the animal fat jars. BILLY enters the room quietly, sneaks up behind LEN. He has a wedding bell, which he smashes shut just behind LEN'S head.*

**BILLY** Ha!

**LEN** What the hell! Oh, Billy – you startled me.

**BILLY** Sorry, Len. Wedding bells make you nervous, eh?

*BILLY laughs. LEN reluctantly joins in.*

**LEN** So, you just came from work. How was… work?

**BILLY** Just a routine night. I'd like to hear about your work, Len. I was going to go to a party, you know, and then I thought – maybe old Len would like to go along for a drink.

**LEN** I don't know. Maybe I… better not.

**BILLY** Too bad. Well then, you leave me no choice, Len.

*BILLY backs LEN down with his hand in his back pocket as if he's going to draw a gun. Just when LEN's starting to look very nervous, BILLY pulls a mickey out of his back pocket.*

Care for a sip?

**LEN** Well, I… all right. *(sips gingerly)* Thank you.

**BILLY** So, your work. What exactly is it you're doing?

**LEN** I'm trying to link some of our contemporary North American traditions to their roots in primitive cultures. Rites of passage, for instance – the first hunt, the ritual aspects of—

**BILLY** The first hunt, eh? The first hunt and the last hunt. We have those traditions here. We've got all kinds of… traditions. Like gravel runs. You ever been on a gravel run, Len? That's kind of a tradition around here.

**LEN** Gravel… what was it?

**BILLY** You load up the truck with beer and drive. Back roads, ditches – under the stars, Len. Then you go to a bush party.

**LEN** A bush party.

**BILLY** Lord God, Leonard. Where did you grow up? Leona's never told you about gravel runs and bush parties? What about racing on the quarter mile?

**LEN** I really don't think so.

**BILLY** Well then, she hasn't told you much, has she? *(pause)* About our… traditions.

**LEN** They sound… fascinating.

**BILLY** Yep. You sure I can't twist your arm, Len? Let's go out and have a few… native customs.

**LEN** Well, I just don't know what Leona's plans are—

**BILLY** Her and Mama are off wrapping cake. You and I'd be all thumbs. *(pause)* I'd like to get to know you better, Len. After all, I'm gonna be your best man. Come on… what do you say?

**LEN** I suppose it might be interesting.

**BILLY** I can almost guarantee that, Len. You'll have a time, all right. Besides. I think someone oughta let you in on a few family secrets.

**LEN** Family secrets?

**BILLY** Trust me, Len. We'll have a hell of a time.

*End of Act One.*

# Act Two

## Scene One

*In the darkness we hear doors creaking open, suppressed giggling, whispering. Lights fade up as LEN and BILLY sneak into the house looking like they've been on a three-day drunk. They are carrying what appears to be part of a tree. LEN is much more drunk than BILLY and he's wearing the red cap. BILLY comes in quietly singing "A Good Hearted Woman" (Waylon Jennings).*

**BILLY** *(singing quietly)* A good-hearted woman in love with a good-timin' man…

**LEN** *(off-key and loud)* She loves him in spite of his wicked ways that she don't understand…

**BILLY** Shh… shush now. You'll wake the whole damn house up.

**LEN** I'll tell the world—

**BILLY** You got the rye?

**LEN** *(pulls an empty bottle out of his pocket)* It's all gone.

**BILLY** Shh… other one, in your hip pocket. The flask, the mickey, the nectar of life—

**LEN** Yeah, sure… I got it.

*LEN pulls a half-empty mickey of Five Star out of his pocket. Both men slump into chairs. BILLY has leaned the wood up against a chair.*

**BILLY** Here's to you and here's to me—and if any thing should happen—to hell with you and here's to me.

**LEN** That's the best time… I've ever had. Ever.

**BILLY** Scout's honour?

**LEN** Yep.

**BILLY** Screw the scouts. You ever in the scouts?

**LEN** You bet. I got my badges.

**BILLY** I bet you do. Hunting? You got a hunting badge?

**LEN** No such thing. Scouts don't hunt. They track, they birdwatch, they cook beetles over an open fire. But they don't hunt.

**BILLY** You ever been hunting?

**LEN** No my father was a conser – conservationist. Goddammit, that's hard to say.

**BILLY** The old man used to hunt big game. That's where he got the animal fat. Leona never told you that, eh?

**LEN** No… she never said nothin'.

**BILLY** *(a little frustrated)* Len, your language has deteriorated over the past twenty-four hours. You notice that?

**LEN** I don't – mind – that bush party was fun.

**BILLY** Yeah, that's fun all right.

**LEN** That girl – that Edith girl. She was throwing up.

**BILLY** Oh, she'll be all right.

**LEN** Is she your girlfriend?

**BILLY** She likes fast cars.

**LEN** Me, too.

**BILLY** Yeah, you turned into a regular Sterling Moss there, didn't you? A regular Northern Dancer in a half-ton truck.

**LEN** You're no slouch, either. When you were driving in and out of the ditches I – thought you were trying to scare me—

**BILLY** Nah…

**LEN** Edith was scared. I never seen anyone throw up that much—

**BILLY** Lenny, Lenny… I have never seen – I have – get a grip on yourself.

**LEN** You called me Lenny. No one's called me Lenny for years. I had a friend once… called me Lenny. My best friend.

**BILLY** So, what are you fixing to do with that wood Leonard?

**LEN** I dunno. It's kinda cute. "Nelson Eddy and Leona – live and love forever."

**BILLY** You could varnish it up – make it into a clock. Hang it above your bed or something.

**LEN** Hell of an idea.

**BILLY** Or you could glue dry macaroni to it and spray-paint it silver. Put it at the head table.

**LEN** Why not?

**BILLY** What the hell's the matter with you, man? Your grammar's gone to shit and now you've lost your taste.

**LEN** Nah… I'll just wake Leona up and show it to her. She'll laugh.

**BILLY** Well, I don't know that she'll laugh, exactly.

**LEN** Sure… high school sweetheart. This Nelson Eddy – he still in town?

**BILLY** Nope.

**LEN** What happened to him? Left town or something? Is he heartbroken?

**BILLY** He's dead.

**LEN** What… what the hell?

**BILLY** Hunting accident. Got shot in the head. One of the things I've been trying to tell you.

**LEN** What happened?

**BILLY** He forgot to wear his red cap. That's what Papa said. "He weren't wearin' a red cap. It's his own damn fault."

**LEN** Leona must have been – that would be very upsetting.

**BILLY** He was my best friend. Leona never told you *that*?

**LEN** No… she didn't. We never talk about old romances.

**BILLY** That's awful funny she never told you. Nelson Eddy was—

**LEN** Nope, no – I don't wanna know. I don't wanna compro— *(can't get the word out)* —screw anything up. She never told me so I don't wanna know—

**BILLY** Well then, I guess you don't wanna know about me, either.

**LEN** Are you a family secret?

**BILLY** Well, let me put it to you this way, Len. What would you say if I told you I know where Leona's birthmark is?

**LEN** What are you talking about?

**BILLY** The three of us used to go out together, Len. Nelson Eddy and Leona – and me. Just like you and I did tonight with Edith. We used to get a case of beer… each… and go for long drives. Then we'd stop by the side of the road. Leona would lean right to Nelson Eddy and make him the happiest man alive. Then she'd lean right over to the other side of the truck and make me even happier.

**LEN** I don't believe you—

**BILLY** It's heart-shaped, Len. And it's right… *(leans over and touches LEN)* on the inside of her thigh—

**LEN** Well, you – what are you tryin' to say here? A birthmark doesn't prove a damn thing. Not a damn thing.

**BILLY** *(laughs)* Oh, Len… Len you're decent, aren't you? You think about it, Len. You sure you wanna marry the white-haired girl? You sure?

**LEN** *(after a pause)* Well, I'll tell you something, Billy. Even if I believed you and well, I just don't believe it – but even if I did… it wouldn't make a damn bit of difference. Not a damn bit.

**BILLY** Is that right?

**LEN** That's right.

*Long pause. Both men are dejected: BILLY has run out of ideas and LEN's mood is deflated. LEN takes a long pull on the bottle.*

I don't know why you went and said that, Billy. I was having... such a good time. I was thinking I'd like to stay on after the wedding. I mean, I could work on my thesis. I could—

**BILLY** *(a glimmer of an idea)* Is that so? *(pause)* You like it here, don't you?

**LEN** Well, I... it's a good life, Billy. It's... you work all day and then you go... driving trucks and—

**BILLY** We know how to have a good time all right—

**LEN** Drinking whisky out under the stars, sitting on a bale of hay. Watchin' the wood smoke curl up to the clouds. You know, my clothes smell like wood smoke. My clothes haven't smelled this way since I was a little boy. I went to camp... once.

**BILLY** *(after a pause)* Listen, Lenny. I might as well admit to something. All that stuff I said about Leona, well, I was lying, of course.

**LEN** I don't know why you went and said that—

**BILLY** I just... it was sort of a test. I guess it was sort of like your village in Africa, where they take the groom off and put him through his paces. I just got a little carried away, that's all.

**LEN** Well, I guess you did.

**BILLY** My own sister, Len. Isn't it only natural that I'd wanna make sure you really loved her?

**LEN** Well, I didn't believe you anyway. After all, your name isn't carved in the tree trunk here.

**BILLY** *(after a pause)* No, it isn't is it? *(pause)* So I wanna apologize.

**LEN** It's all right, Billy.

**BILLY** 'Cause I wouldn't wanna wreck the party

**LEN** *(wistfully)* It was... fun.

**BILLY** I'm glad, Len. There's more where that came from. Lots more. You can do your thesis during the day, tuck Leona in and you and me can hit the road. Hell, we could even... go hunting sometime. Just you and me.

**LEN** Why not? I got a red cap—

**BILLY** You hang on to that cap. You'll need that if we go out in the bush. Hell, how about tomorrow?

**LEN** Ahh, shit, Billy. Can't. I told Mama I'd go – look for suits—

**BILLY** Oh, that's all right. Lots of time to go hunting now that you're staying on for a bit.

**LEN** I'd like to… I really would. Singin' and drinkin' and driving under the stars. And this birch carving. I couldn't be happier if I'd found an Indian burial ground.

**BILLY** You gonna show that to Leona?

**LEN** Maybe she'd like to have it. A keepsake. *(pours the last of the rye over the wood)* I christen you… I christen you Nelson Eddy.

**BILLY** Well, that's the last of the rye. It's time for bed, old boy. I'm gonna put a little of that wedding cake under my pillow.

**LEN** You're s'posed to dream about the girl you're gonna marry. Maybe you'll dream about that Edith girl.

**BILLY** Christ, I hope not.

**LEN** I think I'll sit up for a while yet.

**BILLY** Len – you're sure about this, eh? You're gonna stay on after the wedding?

**LEN** Damn right.

*BILLY smiles sweetly at LEN and starts to leave.*

Billy… what was that song you were singin' – when we were pushing the truck out of the ditch?

**BILLY** "Bee-bop-a-loola…"

**LEN** Thanks. Good night.

*BILLY exits. LEN begins to hum the song, enjoying memories of the night. Suddenly he bursts into an extremely loud, off-key version of "Bee-Bop-A-Lula."*

Bee-bop… ba… loola… she's my baby.

*LEONA enters wearing a nightgown. She sees the wood, reacts. She covers LEN's mouth to silence him. Snap to black.*

## Scene Two

*PAPA at his jars, carefully rearranging them in order to make room for a new jar. BILLY enters.*

**BILLY** Howdy, Pop.

**PAPA** Morning, Billy.

**BILLY** Whatcha doing? Wanna take me to a baseball game? How about some ice cream?

**PAPA** You drinkin' again, Billy? It's not even noon yet.

**BILLY** Heck no, Pop.

**PAPA** *(pointing to a new jar)* That lined up right? I left my damn bifocals at the Legion.

**BILLY** *(moves the jar a little)* There. Straight as an arrow. What is it this time? Rabbit? Frogs? Newts?

**PAPA** It's Ed Hemeyer.

**BILLY** What?

**PAPA** Ed Hemeyer. He had one of those operations where they vacuum the fat out. He saved some for me.

**BILLY** He always was mighty thoughtful. He used to stop me in the street and give me Juicy Fruit gum.

**PAPA** Well now, I guess he just had a few too many sticks.

**BILLY** Yeah…

*BILLY moves around the room, restless.*

**PAPA** What's on your mind, boy?

**BILLY** It's Len. Len… likes it here.

**PAPA** He eats enough.

**BILLY** He's almost like one of the family, isn't he?

**PAPA** Almost.

**BILLY** Well, he's sure looking forward to meeting Sarah.

**PAPA** He better look forward to something else.

**BILLY** I just wondered what you were going to tell him. When you explain things. Like Nelson Eddy and Sarah. I expect he'll want to know all the details. Len's just like that.

**PAPA** Len's just here for three more days, Billy.

**BILLY** I don't know about that. I think he's gonna stay on for a bit.

**PAPA** I doubt that. Wild horses couldn't keep Leona here.

**BILLY** Oh, I don't know – guess it depends—

**PAPA** Get it out of your head, Billy.

**BILLY** I guess it depends on me. If I go away like I'm plannin' to, Leona will have to stay for Mama.

**PAPA** You're not going anywhere, son.

**BILLY** I'm gonna tell Cliff to ram his car-crusher up his ass. I'm thinking of going to California, Papa. I've never seen the ocean.

**PAPA** You can't go, Billy.

**BILLY** *(after a pause)* I can't stay, either.

**PAPA** You know damn well you're scared to set foot out of this town.

**BILLY** I'm not scared. You're the one that's scared. Mama's expecting you to bring Sarah home for the wedding. Len's got his heart set on it, too.

**PAPA** He'll get over it.

**BILLY** You gonna help him get over it, Papa? *(a long pause)* I told him, you know. I told Len – about Nelson Eddy not wearing a red hat.

**PAPA** Did you tell him what happened?

**BILLY** Now, how could I do that? You never told me—

**PAPA** You were there, Billy.

**BILLY** He was my best friend, dammit!

**PAPA** *(after a pause)* I'm sorry, Billy. It all happened in a split second. I don't know…

*Long pause.*

**BILLY** *(softly)* Maybe if he'd kept his mouth shut about Sarah? Len's expecting Sarah for the wedding. So is Mama. What are you going to tell them? Papa?

**PAPA** Billy… she doesn't remember. Mama just doesn't—

**BILLY** Doesn't remember what?

*PAPA turns to his jars.*

Suit yourself, old man. The wedding's in three days. I'm gonna walk down the aisle in my shiny new suit, push some roast beef around on my plate and then… we'll see, won't we?

**PAPA** I wouldn't make any travel plans if I was you, son. Len and Leona are getting married. Then they're gonna go. That leaves you, Billy.

**LEN** *(as he enters)* Morning, Mr. Sorenson. Morning, Blitz.

**PAPA** Morning, Len.

**LEN** I feel fantastic.

**BILLY** Is that a fact?

**LEN** Anyone seen Leona?

**PAPA** Her and Mama went to look at dresses or something.

**LEN** Ahh…

**PAPA** Billy! Mama wanted you to run some errands, didn't she?

**BILLY** I imagine she did. *(pause)* You keep staring at your grease, Papa. You tell me what the weather's like in California… you let me know.

**PAPA** I'll do that, son.

**BILLY** *(as he exits)* See you later.

**PAPA** Well, Len…

**LEN** You can predict weather that far away?

**PAPA** Sometimes. Mostly depends on how big the disturbance is.

**LEN** That's quite… incredible.

**PAPA** I can show you – I've got it written down.

**LEN** Oh, I believe you. There's a lot of places in the world where they predict the weather with… naturalistic processes. It's quite common really.

**PAPA** That a fact?

**LEN** There's a tribe in India that uses spiders. The spiders are trapped in small ceramic bowls, placed on the ground. Then the… weatherman checks the patterns at dawn. It's like reading a teacup.

**PAPA** Spiders? Sounds crazy to me.

**LEN** Well… yes. Rendered fat is actually quite a lot more scientific.

**PAPA** Let me tell you something, Len. *(slight pause)* Farmers round here are always asking me about the weather but I know people think I'm crazy. And if they knew what I was doing now…

**LEN** What's that?

**PAPA** Well, Len… I think there's other things…

**LEN** Other things?

**PAPA** I think I can get a notion about… some human events from these jars. Guess that's what I've wanted all along. I just want to have an idea what to expect. So I can do something before it's too late.

**LEN** Well, it does seem reasonable… I mean, certainly anything's possible and… with the success you've had with the weather it seems…

**PAPA** *(picks up Ed Hemeyer jar)* That's just exactly what I thought, Len. That's what I thought. Now look at this new jar. Look how it's…

**LEN** Crystallized… yes…

**PAPA** It's got me worried. It's something pretty big. It's some kind of… major disruption. Some kind of major change.

**LEN** It would seem to…

**PAPA** I just wish I knew for sure. I have a notion it might be family, Len. Our family.

**LEN** Is it something to do with Sarah?

**PAPA** What do you know about Sarah?

*A door slams shut offstage.*

**LEN** Nothing, sir. I just—

**PAPA** That'll be Mama and Leona. We can talk about this later.

**LEN** All right.

*LEN smiles uncertainly and exits. PAPA returns to his jar of human fat.*

*(offstage)* Mornin', Mama.

**MAMA** *(offstage)* Mornin', Len.

*MAMA enters carrying a plate of food.*

Brought you a bite, Papa. Some meat loaf. I knew you wouldn't eat while we were out.

**PAPA** Mama, there's quite a ruckus in my new jar.

**MAMA** We ordered the flowers. I guess I'm going to have a bouquet too.

**PAPA** This ruckus—

**MAMA** Of course, there's still the midnight lunch to sort out. Betty Brookson is set on hazelnut squares. I told her Len was allergic to hazelnuts.

**PAPA** The patterns are different—

**MAMA** 'Course it went in one ear and out the other. I said, what about your peanut butter round-up cake, Betty. And she—

**PAPA** *(grabs MAMA by the shoulders)* Mama! I think it's Sarah—

**MAMA** Papa, I'm so excited about seeing Sarah. It's been… so long. Leona's never asked to see her before. I want Leona to see her. *(pause)* Now, why don't you have a bite, Papa? It's almost time to start supper.

*MAMA exits. PAPA looks over at his jars.*

## Scene Three

*LEN and LEONA at the dining room table writing their vows. LEN is dressed in blue jeans, plaid shirt and maybe even some brand new cowboy boots.*

**LEN** To have and to hold?

**LEONA** Sounds like real estate.

**LEN** But I've always liked that. How about cherish?

**LEONA** Cherish 'til we perish—

**LEN** Leona…

**LEONA** To have and to hold is fine.

**LEN** Well, if you're not happy with it—

**LEONA** It's fine. All right. Are we still having this Kahlil Gibran reading?

**LEN** No, not necessarily. Your mama suggested a poem.

**LEONA** Oh no… it's not "The Cremation of Sam McGee" is it?

**LEN** Of course it's not—

**LEONA** She loves that poem.

**LEN** It's a… traditional piece which… equates marriage with a good cake recipe.

**LEONA** Yeah?

**LEN** I know it sounds hokey but it's really quite clever. The ingredients it takes to make a good marriage and a good… cake. What makes a good cake rise and—

**LEONA** *(quoting)* "The beauty's in the batter when a love cake's in the making. What makes it sweet and so complete—" Oh, for crying out loud, Len. She's got you sold on having Lydia Harmon sing "My Best to You" at the bloody signing of the register and now this—

**LEN** She's a friend of the family—

**LEONA** She can't sing! She was kicked in the throat by a cow—

**LEN** She what?

**LEONA** Oh, never mind. She sings like an angel. But this poem—

**LEN** I think it's kind of important to her. I'm not sure but I think she might have written it. She wants Sarah to recite it at the reception.

**LEONA** God help me I wish I'd never mentioned her. Now that Mama thinks Sarah's coming she's really gone into high gear. It's not my wedding anymore – it's a homecoming party for Sarah.

**LEN** We don't have to decide right now, about the poem.

**LEONA** I hope not. So where were we?

**LEN** Cherish, to have and to hold.

**LEONA** Oh, right.

**LEN** You still haven't forgiven me, have you?

**LEONA** Do you want the bit about "'til death do us part"?

**LEN** Leona, I'm sorry about dragging that tree into the house.

**LEONA** What are you sorry about? Did I say anything? It's just a hunk of birch, Len.

**LEN** It's gone now. I put it in Billy's truck.

**LEONA** Fine.

**LEN** *(after a pause)* What was Nelson Eddy like, Leona?

**LEONA** Why?

**LEN** I know we agreed but I just… I'd like to know.

**LEONA** He wore tight jeans.

**LEN** Yeah?

**LEONA** Yeah.

**LEN** Leona, it's important to me.

**LEONA** He smelled like whisky and Export A cigarettes. It was a nice smell. He had lashes an inch long. Curly lashes. / And he wore tight jeans.

**LEN** Is that why you… fell in love with him?

**LEONA** Len…

**LEN** Please.

**LEONA** All right. I guess I liked… he'd do anything for a nickel. He was always on the edge of doing something unacceptable. He was wild.

**LEN** He sounds rather… imposing.

**LEONA** He had an awful temper. He had a signet ring that was all scratched from banging his fist into walls. He had green eyes, like a cat, only they were huge. And lips. Big, purple lips that tasted like whisky and cigarettes. But mostly whisky.

**LEN** He was a drinker.

**LEONA** No, Len. He wasn't a "drinker." Not any more than Billy's a drinker. *(pause)* He was a lot like Billy actually. Quite a lot.

**LEN** Billy can drink, all right.

**LEONA** But you can't, can you? A little too much hooch makes you dig up graveyards and sing songs that don't belong to you.

**LEN** You see – you're still mad.

**LEONA** You were never meant to know.

**LEN** Know what? That you had a boyfriend in high school. That seems to me a pretty standard confidence between two people who are getting married—

**LEONA** Oh, that ain't the half of it.

**LEN** So, what's the other half of it?

*Pause. LEONA doesn't respond.*

Billy said Nelson Eddy was killed in a hunting accident.

**LEONA** An accident?

**LEN** Well, yes...

**LEONA** Then you know all about it. He was killed in a hunting accident.

**LEN** Because he wasn't wearing a red hat.

**LEONA** *(laughs)* That's right. That's what Papa said. And Papa would know.

**LEN** Wait just a minute here—

**LEONA** I left town shortly afterwards. Three hours later.

**LEN** Now hold on, Leona. You're not accusing your own father of—

**LEONA** I never accused anybody of anything. Rest in peace – good riddance. The only person I talked to before I left was Mama.

**LEN** What?

**LEONA** He had a big mouth. Big lips, remember? One of the things I liked best about him. He used to pull into that driveway singing "Bee-Bop" at the top of his lungs. When he wasn't singing he was talking. It wasn't a good quality in this family. If you know something you keep it to yourself.

**LEN** Your mother was telling me, she used to wait up for you. She worried a lot—

**LEONA** Look, Len – the less you know the better off you'll be. Rest in peace. Nelson Eddy just wasn't well liked around here.

**LEN** He was well liked by you and Billy.

**LEONA** We... had a hell of a good time.

**LEN** *(after a pause)* Why did you fall in love with me?

**LEONA** You were... different from anyone I'd ever met before. You'd never farmed a quarter section, gone to a drive-in or de-horned cattle...

**LEN** Leona, I like it here.

**LEONA** I'm glad, Len. A nice place to visit.

**LEN** It's peaceful.

**LEONA** Are you crazy? I've hardly slept since we've been here—

**LEN** It's simple. Things are simpler—

**LEONA** I keep having nightmares—not the scary monster kind—the slow, creepy ones where everything quietly goes wrong.

**LEN** I really like your family. And they like me—

**LEONA** I had one last night that Mama stood up in church and disowned me. "She's not my daughter – we're not paying for this." People started jumping through stained glass windows—

**LEN** Leona, you're not listening to me. I said I like it here. I wouldn't mind staying for awhile. I wouldn't mind—

**LEONA** Len, are you serious?

**LEN** I mean it—

**LEONA** You're getting sucked into the centre of the house—

**LEN** I know what's happening to me – I like it. You didn't think I'd fit in, did you?

**LEONA** Oh, you're fitting in all right. You're – where did you get those clothes anyway?

**LEN** Mama bought the shirt for me and I bought the jeans—

**LEONA** What the hell's happening to you?

**LEN** Why did you bring me here if you didn't think they'd like me?

**LEONA** I wanted Mama to – I wanted her to stop worrying – I wanted to make her happy.

**LEN** Well, she's happy, isn't she?

**LEONA** Oh sure – she's delirious.

**LEN** Well, if you're having second thoughts, I guess now's the time to say.

**LEONA** I'm having second thoughts about the damn three-ring circus. It's not our wedding—

**LEN** Then whose wedding—

**LEONA** I just want – damn it, Len. I know all the conventional wisdom about weddings being for the parents. But this is different. This is all for Mama and I don't think she even knows it. This wedding—

**LEN** This wedding or this marriage?

**LEONA** The wedding, Len. For God's sake, you know what I mean. That poem and the Legion Hall and – oh, never mind. I'll be fine as soon as we get out of this goddamn house, as soon as Mama… *(pause)* You've changed, that's all.

**LEN** So have you. You're unhappy. But I'm having fun. And I think your mother would appreciate it if we didn't rush off after the wedding.

**LEONA** Yes, I know. I know she'd appreciate it.

**LEN** *(after a pause)* Where were we then? The vows.

**LEONA** What? Oh… I don't know.

**LEN** 'Til death do us part. How do you feel about that?

*Lights snap to black.*

## Scene Four

*MAMA enters with a plate of cookies. She sets them on the sideboard and begins to clear the snack remains from the table onto a tray. She hums happily while she does this.*

**LEN** *(offstage)* Can I get you anything?

**MAMA** No, thank you.

**LEN** *(after he enters)* There is nothing quite like a glass of cold milk after a meal of chocolate cake—

**MAMA** Good?

**LEN** Magnificent, Mama. Magnificent.

**MAMA** Do you really think so?

*MAMA presents LEN with the plate of cookies.*

**LEN** But I can't eat another bite. I'm not used to eating so much this time of night.

**MAMA** I told you to save room for a cocoa puff.

**LEN** Well, they sure smell good…

**MAMA** They're fresh, right out of the oven. And they're spiked.

**LEN** Spiked?

**MAMA** It's my special recipe. Cocoa and vodka.

**LEN** Well, let me see – I guess I can choke one down. *(He eats.)* Mmmm…

**MAMA** Good?

**LEN** Mmmm… real good.

**MAMA** It's nice to hear the sound of smacking lips at the table. Makes it feel like a home. You're a very good eater.

**LEN** It's one thing I excel at.

**MAMA** Does Leona cook for you?

**LEN** Well, we're both… pretty busy. I guess we eat out a lot.

**MAMA** Have another. Have another puff.

**LEN** Well, I guess… they are good.

**MAMA** I made them just for you.

**LEN** How much vodka is in these anyway?

**MAMA** 'Bout a mickey – but it's a big batch—

**LEN** This is your own recipe?

**MAMA** Yep. Sometimes, when I'm feeling a little blue… I mix up a batch. It's sort of a home remedy.

**LEN** Good for the spirits.

**MAMA** I just bake a dozen and eat them on a dreary afternoon. It makes me feel so much better.

**LEN** I bet. These things pack quite a wallop.

**MAMA** Have another?

**LEN** Oh, I better not. I should be heading off to bed here…

**MAMA** Just one more…

**LEN** I don't…

**MAMA** Open wide…

*MAMA presses a cocoa puff between LEN's lips. He chews it slowly, staring at MAMA.*

**LEN** Mmmm…

**MAMA** Now, tell me a story.

**LEN** What?

**MAMA** Tell me a story about yourself. Whatever you like. You're getting married to Leona and we hardly know you.

**LEN** I could tell you another story about… New Guinea, if you like.

**MAMA** All right… or something about your childhood. When you were growing up. I'm so sorry your parents can't come to the wedding, you know. We could have found out all about you.

**LEN** Yes, well… I'm sorry, too. They're very busy people, my parents. And it was short notice. Mom has a conference and Dad never seems to have time to…

**MAMA** Did your mother work?

**LEN** Oh yes… she had to when I was a kid. So I didn't get to see her that much. And she didn't have time to bake. So… this is… great. Like a second childhood.

**MAMA** That's a nice thing to say, Len.

**LEN** I mean, I can only imagine what it must have been like to grow up in this house. Coming home from school, slamming the screen door and boom – the smell of fresh bread slaps you in the face. So you yell – "Whatcha makin' Mom?" and you would say—

**MAMA** Oatmeal bread. Careful… it's hot!

**LEN** And then you get ice-cold butter out of the fridge, rip open a bun and the butter melts just like that. You stuff yourself and then you stick your hand into the bread-keeper and presto – there's cookies and…

**MAMA** You get out of there – those are for dessert.

**LEN** But I have some anyway – and then I – watch TV until supper time. Then we have roast beef and potatoes and I even eat my carrots because I know…

**MAMA** You know there's cookies – and pie.

**LEN** And cold milk to wash it down! Then just before I go to bed I say – "Ahh, come on…"

**MAMA** Maybe just one last sliver.

**LEN** Yeah! Yeah… and then I… *(He has run out of steam.)* go to sleep.

**MAMA** That was a lovely story.

**LEN** Yes… yes, it was.

**MAMA** *(pause)* I'd like to tell you a story too, Len.

**LEN** All right.

**MAMA** Sometime I'd like to tell you all about Sarah.

**LEN** I'd like that very much.

**MAMA** Shh… it's a secret. One last cocoa puff?

**LEN** *(taking a cookie and a bite)* Well… I guess…

**MAMA** You missed a crumb.

*LEN reaches up to his face. MAMA beats him to it, gently brushing the crumb away.*

There...

## Scene Five

*LEONA is standing on a chair by the dining room table in a wedding dress. The dress is all fluffs and ruffles, quite hideous. LEONA has the look of someone resigned to her fate.*

**LEONA** Mama! Mama... I'm waiting.

*BILLY sneaks into the room, puts his hands over LEONA's eyes. He hums "Here Comes the Bride."*

Len, is that you? Len!

**BILLY** *(singing)* Here comes the bride—

**LEONA** Billy—

*LEONA starts to get off the chair. BILLY appears in front of her and lifts her down off the chair.*

**BILLY** Well, well, well...

**LEONA** Where's Mama? She's supposed to pin up this damn dress.

**BILLY** I was supposed to tell you, Len took her to buy some "tape"?

**LEONA** Bias tape. Why did Len have to take her? Why couldn't you take her?

**BILLY** Because I wanted to talk to you—

**LEONA** She could have driven herself—

**BILLY** No, Papa's got the Chevy. He went to get Sarah.

**LEONA** Oh yeah? What's he doing – driving around the block?

**BILLY** I think I know where he went.

**LEONA** It doesn't matter what we think, Billy. Mama thinks Sarah's coming home.

**BILLY** Well, the old man better have a good story when he gets back.

**LEONA** She even bought a damn dress for Sarah. Pink polyester, size seven.

**BILLY** You look like you could use a drink.

*BILLY hands a mickey to LEONA.*

**LEONA** *(takes a swig)* Oh, why not? *(pause)* So you wanted to talk to me?

**BILLY** *(after a pause)* Is that what you're wearing to the wedding?

**LEONA** No kidding.

**BILLY** Think you'll be able to wear it afterwards? If I was you I'd make it into doilies.

**LEONA** Shut up. I'm gonna get through this, Billy. Somehow…

**BILLY** What – the wedding or the marriage?

**LEONA** Aren't you supposed to be at work?

**BILLY** I'm gonna quit work.

**LEONA** Why?

**BILLY** I'm thinking of going to California. I'm taking my guitar and a case of beer. Longest gravel run I've ever been on. *(pause)* Wanna come?

**LEONA** Don't tempt me—

**BILLY** I mean it—

**LEONA** No you don't… and neither do I. Besides, you can't leave Mama.

**BILLY** Looks like you can't, either.

**LEONA** We're only staying a few days after the wedding—

**BILLY** Sure.

**LEONA** Len likes it here! *(takes a good big swig, chokes)* Damn it, Billy. Why don't you ever spend the extra dollar and get something that doesn't taste like—

**BILLY** Lemon gin?

**LEONA** I thought I recognized this—

**BILLY** I wanted to talk about old times. The night of the lemon gin. You remember that? My God, you were sick—

**LEONA** I bet Mona remembers—

**BILLY** What?

**LEONA** Me driving the truck up and down the street – you and Nelson Eddy standing in the back with your lily-white asses pointed in her general direction. I always wondered if she saw us—

**BILLY** She turned her lights off but she never said anything—

**LEONA** What was she supposed to say? "Alice, I was just waiting up for your kids as usual when suddenly the moon came out—"

**BILLY** Two of them!

**LEONA** Give me another drink of that—

**BILLY** Careful, she is probably watching us right now—

**LEONA** *(toast to the window)* Here's to you, Mona.

*BILLY unzips his pants.*

**BILLY** Get a load of this, Mona—

*LEONA lifts her dress slightly.*

**LEONA** All together now—

*They can't quite bring themselves to go through with it.*

**BILLY** What have you got on underneath that thing anyway?

**LEONA** What? Oh... the standard issue. Virginal white panty hose. With runs in them.

**BILLY** Let's see.

*LEONA lifts up her dress and exposes a run in her panty hose. BILLY pulls at the run, causing a much larger run to develop*

**LEONA** Oooh... that looks lovely. Let me try—

**BILLY** It just goes like sixty—

**LEONA** Renegade wedding socks—

**BILLY** *(pulling another run)* A run in the marital fabric—

**LEONA** The bride wore... ribbons of white nylon—

**BILLY** Are those the socks you're wearing to the wedding?

**LEONA** Oh, hell... why not?

**BILLY** You not gonna get cold feet, are you?

**LEONA** I will if I wear these—

**BILLY** Not in California. Hell, we could take Mama with us.

**LEONA** Sure, Billy. If you got Mama outside of town limits, she'd turn into a pillar of salt. And so would you.

**BILLY** I've never been anywhere, Leona. I wouldn't even mind that so much if you stayed here.

**LEONA** Why don't you go for a few days right after the wedding? I'll be here for Mama and you could...

**BILLY** I don't wanna go by myself. I – can I ask you something?

**LEONA** Shoot.

*She takes another big drink.*

**BILLY** If you weren't getting married and if Mama didn't... turn into a pillar of salt, wouldn't it be fun to load up the truck and go? Buy some beer, or some of that Mai Tai shit and drive and drive and— *(runs out of steam)*

**LEONA** It would be… a hell of a good time, Billy.

**BILLY** *(pause)* Remember after we mooned Mona we went out to the lake? 'Cause there was supposed to be a party?

**LEONA** *(uneasy)* Sure… yeah, I remember—

**BILLY** Only there wasn't anyone there. So we sat in the truck listening to that damn party tape. Then you and Nelson Eddy got romantic—

**LEONA** I wish to hell Mama would get back so I could take off this dress.

**BILLY** You and Nelson Eddy – I took off for a while. Then I climbed back into the truck so quiet you didn't even hear me. The tape deck was blasting and you were kissing Nelson Eddy. Then you turned around and kissed me. Like you didn't know the difference between us or something—

**LEONA** Billy, shut up…

**BILLY** Nelson Eddy thought it was a great joke. He laughed, we all laughed. But I'll tell you something – when you two took off to carve your initials in that tree, I wanted to come with you. I wanted to carve my initials, too.

**LEONA** Why are you telling me this, Billy?

**BILLY** You're getting married tomorrow. So it's my last chance.

**LEONA** Last chance?

**BILLY** *(after a pause)* I love you Leona. I've probably loved you for ten years. Maybe more. And that night… that night was the only time I thought… you might love me, too. Just for a second… I thought you might. Leona…

**LEONA** I'm in my wedding dress, Billy.

**BILLY** Did you love me? Just for that second – that one second? Just say it, for shit's sake.

**LEONA** Billy…

**BILLY** Say it. You loved me. You did—

**LEONA** I did!

**BILLY** *(a whoop of joy)* I knew it! Damnit, I knew it! Nothing matters a damn now that I've heard you say that.

**LEONA** Billy, that was years ago. I'm getting married tomorrow.

**BILLY** You don't want to, Leona. I can tell—

**LEONA** Yes, I do, Billy. I have to do it. I have to—

**BILLY** Why? Can you give me one good reason why?

*MAMA's laughter is heard offstage.*

**LEONA** *(nodding toward the sound of MAMA's voice)* You know why…

**LEN** *(offstage)* Well, you only do it once, after all!

*LEN and MAMA enter loaded up with parcels.*

**MAMA** Leona! The groom's not supposed to see you in your dress!

**LEN** Oops! Guess I better leave—

**BILLY** It's bad luck—

**MAMA** Billy, get that cover off the couch and put it around Leona—

**LEONA** Really – I could just take if off—

**LEN** I'll close my eyes—

**MAMA** It's not hemmed yet. Just leave it on for now—

**LEONA** Did you get the bias tape?

**MAMA** Yes, and I picked up more place-cards just in case—

**LEONA** Did you find my birth certificate, Mama? We have to get the licence today.

**MAMA** Billy, did you wash your truck?

**LEONA** It's not in the photo album. You said you knew where it was.

**MAMA** Now where'd I put that tape?

**BILLY** When the hell's Papa getting back? He seems to be avoiding most of the work—

**MAMA** Is Papa back?

**LEONA** Mama, are you listening to me? I need my birth certificate so we can get our marriage licence.

**MAMA** I don't have it, Leona! We lost it.

**LEONA** Don't get upset. We'll just go to a notary public and—

**BILLY** *(looking out the window)* There's the old man now and he's— *(stops himself)*

**MAMA** It's Papa? He's back?

*PAPA enters. MAMA turns to face him. They stare at one another.*

**MAMA** Papa…

**PAPA** Mama, did anyone phone while I was gone?

**MAMA** Where's Sarah?

**PAPA** Mama… she's dead. Sarah's dead.

*Everyone freezes. Lights fade.*

## Scene Six

*It's the day of the wedding. There are several wedding presents piled on the dining room table. LEONA is sitting at the table in her wedding dress. She stares at the presents, decides to open one. It's a framed landscape, possibly a velvet painting: ugly. LEONA reacts, searching for the card.*

**LEONA** *(reading)* Special wishes for a special couple on this special day. Truly yours, Mona.

*MAMA appears at the entrance to the room, dressed for the wedding. LEONA goes to her, seats her in a chair. She kneels in front of MAMA.*

Mama, could you do up this hook and eye? At the top? Please?

*MAMA slowly lifts her arms to fasten LEONA's dress, then lowers them, when LEONA speaks. LEONA doesn't notice.*

I feel like it's my fault, Mama. I was the one that wanted Sarah to come home. And now… it's almost like I killed her. I'm sorry I'm not Sarah, Mama. I can never live up to your… I'm sorry I left home. I'm sorry I came back.

**MAMA** *(very quietly)* No… Leona…

**LEONA** Mama! Mama…

*PAPA enters, wearing his suit and the red cap.*

**PAPA** What do I say again? I can't keep it in my head.

**LEONA** He'll say something about you giving up a daughter. You say – "her mother and I do." Then you smile—

**PAPA** He's gonna ask me a question?

**LEONA** Don't worry, Papa. It'll come to you.

**PAPA** Do you think she's happy? I did everything on her list. The flowers and the place cards and – I wish she'd say—

**LEONA** You did just fine, Papa. I'm sure she knows that.

**PAPA** *(after a pause)* I should have told her a long time ago. I know that. She thought it was all her fault and it made her feel better to pretend…. And I let her do it all these years. All these years I just tried to make Mama happy. Everything I've done, Leona – it's all been for Mama.

**LEONA** I know, Papa. I know what you mean.

**PAPA** I can hardly think straight with this suit on – it's grabbin' me in all the wrong places— Do I look all right?

**LEONA** You look just fine… except for the hat. I don't think it really suits you after all.

*LEONA takes the hat off PAPA's head and smooths his hair down.*

**PAPA** I can't remember what I'm supposed to say, Leona.

**LEONA** You just say whatever comes into your head, Papa. It'll be all right.

*BILLY enters dressed in a tuxedo.*

**BILLY** *(whistling)* Wow… you look good enough to ride in my truck.

**PAPA** You done those decorations?

**BILLY** Damn thing looks like a parade float.

**PAPA** Oh no – the bouquets! They have to go to the church.

*PAPA exits.*

**BILLY** Can I kiss the bride?

**LEONA** No, Billy.

**BILLY** Last chance… going, going, going—

*LEONA kisses him quickly.*

**LEONA** Gone. *(pause)* Now get out of here. Mama's…

**BILLY** *(kneels beside MAMA, holds her hand)* Mama… you sure look nice.

**LEONA** I want you to know that I think you should go to California, Billy. I'm going to stay on for a while. I'll stay for Mama and you should—

**BILLY** I told you I don't want to go by myself. And you know damn well I won't leave when Mama's like this. *(pause)* Leona, I wish you—

**LEONA** Mama's gonna be fine.

**BILLY** So where's my replacement bridesmaid?

**LEONA** She's getting dressed.

**BILLY** Never thought I'd be walking down the aisle with Mona.

*LEN enters.*

Leonard, for God's sake observe the traditions. You can't see the bride in her dress—

**LEONA** Billy!

**BILLY** Maybe I'll just put some finishing touches on the nuptial truck.

*BILLY exits.*

**LEN** Well… the big day…

**LEONA** You got something on your mind, Len?

**LEN** I wish there was time to talk. But I guess the best thing right now is just to… get through this. For Mama's sake, I mean.

**LEONA** Just get through the wedding… or the marriage?

**LEN** You know what I mean.

**LEONA** I do.

**LEN** I'll just… see if I've forgotten anything…

**LEONA** Len, maybe…

**LEN** *(a nervous laugh)* I guess I'll see you later.

**LEONA** Yes.

*LEN attempts to embrace LEONA but his heart isn't in it. They stare at each other for a long moment, then LEN exits. LEONA kneels in front of MAMA and takes her hands.*

**MAMA** Leona…

**LEONA** Mama, listen to me. I don't love him. This is all like a dream. Len's some strange ghost that fades in and out and when he fades out, I don't even think about him. But Mama, you know what's funny? If I have your blessing, I'll marry him. I'm getting married in an hour and all I care about is you. I have to know if this what you want—I need your blessing—because this is all for you. The white dress, the roast beef and that long walk down the aisle. *(pause)* I'm gonna turn around and look at you, Mama. Just before I get to the altar I'm gonna turn and look at you. And if you don't give me some kind of sign, I swear to God I'll hitch up my dress and run in the other direction. I just need you to tell me…

*It's just barely audible but MAMA is humming the first few notes of "Good night, Irene."*

Mama…

**MAMA** I'll see you in my dreams. The words came back. I used to sing you to sleep with that. Do you remember?

*LEONA nods quickly.*

I was just remembering the first time I saw you. Hair so blonde it was almost white. And red cheeks. Red apple cheeks. You were so healthy you looked like you had a fever. Do you remember the first time you put a tooth out for the tooth fairy?

**LEONA** Yes, Mama.

**MAMA** I lifted up your head when you were sleeping and put a dollar bill under the pillowcase. But I forgot to take the tooth. You knew something was up but you never blinked.

**LEONA** I forgot about that.

**MAMA** I… forgot too. Do you still play the piano, Leona? All those lessons… you still play, don't you?

**LEONA** Sometimes.

**MAMA** Remember the time you played a piano duet at the music festival with the Jarvis girl? You did your very best but you didn't win. The Jarvis girl cried all the way home. We even stopped at the Payless for orange floats to take her mind off it. You never cried. And the time you stood up for Billy in that tangle with the Olsen kid. Billy told him… that his sister, Sarah, was away at a school for extra-smart kids. Little Jim Olsen laughed and Billy tore into him and your knees were knocking together but you pulled that Olsen kid's socks down and stopped the fight. Were you in grade four? Grade four? You weren't very old and your hair was still white, you asked me what a towhead was because someone called you – your lips quivered and your eyes got shiny but you never cried… even at that dance when…

*Pause. MAMA is uncertain about continuing.*

Val Pearson and Jacqueline Dandeneau
*photographer unknown*

**LEONA** The crushed velvet skirt, Mama. That dance? Beth Hemeyer made that thing, down to my ankles.

**MAMA** It's not her fault, Leona. She didn't have her bifocals and she—

**LEONA** I had to wear it – she was a chaperone.

*They both laugh. MAMA takes LEONA's hands and whirls her around.*

**MAMA** I feel like a kite, Leona. Feel like I might fly away any minute.

**LEONA** Mama… I'm supposed to get married. In an hour. All those people. All that food.

**MAMA** Turn around.

*LEONA turns around. MAMA hesitates for a moment and then rips the dress down her back. She throws her bouquet in the air.*

*(singing loudly)* Good night, Irene, Good night, Irene…

*LEONA joins in.*

**LEONA & MAMA** I'll see you in my dreams…

*Lights fade.*

## Scene Seven

*PAPA sits in front of his jars whistling "When You Wish Upon a Star." He goes through his ritual of warming the jar. MAMA enters with two plates of food. They sit down together and eat.*

**MAMA** Cold turkey. And some beet pickles.

**PAPA** *(takes a bite)* Thank you, Mama. I expect we'll be eating cold turkey for a few days yet, eh?

**MAMA** I expect so. Well?

**PAPA** See that squiggle… that swirl?

**MAMA** It's all kind of rosy… pinkish.

**PAPA** According to my calculations that's a heat spell… real nice and hot.

**MAMA** There'd be some breeze though, wouldn't there?

**PAPA** Oh, you bet. It's right by the ocean, after all. Mmmm… did you make these pickles?

**MAMA** What do you think? You don't see any earthquakes, do you?

**PAPA** Oh no – nothing like that. Just a nice solid heat snaking down the California coast.

**MAMA** Well, that's nice. They'll like that.

**PAPA** They sure will.

*LEN enters, dressed in BILLY's clothes and carrying a plate.*

**LEN** Looks good, Mama. Mind if I join you?

*LEN joins MAMA and PAPA on the couch. They beam at one another as the lights fade.*

*The End.*

# The Red King's Dream

By David Belke

# About
# David Belke

David Belke was born in Winnipeg but was raised and continues to flourish in Edmonton, Alberta. He graduated from the University of Alberta with a B.Ed and where he also studied stage design. He fills many different roles in the theatre: performer, producer, designer, teacher, award-winning playwright. His first full-length play was produced for the 1990 Edmonton Fringe Theatre Festival, the largest theatre festival in North America. Since then he has written a new play for each subsequent year becoming one the Fringe's mainstays and one of the city's favourite playwrights. His plays have been performed across Canada, as well as in the United States, England and Northern Ireland. David currently works as resident playwright with Edmonton's Shadow Theatre where he is also an Artistic Associate. Shadow Theatre usually produces one of David's plays a year, either a premiere or a remount. A multiple Sterling Award winner, David also received Samuel French Inc.'s prestigious Canadian Playwrights' Award for 2000; Samuel French Inc. has since published four of his plays. In addition, he is a cast member of Edmonton's long-running comedy institution, Die-Nasty, the live improvised soap opera. He also serves as a member of the Varscona Theatre Alliance Board and as the Alberta representative on the National Council of the Playwrights Guild of Canada.

*The Red King's Dream* was originally presented by Shadow Theatre at the 1996 Edmonton Fringe Theatre Festival with the following company:

| | |
|---|---|
| STEVEN Tudor | Christopher Craddock |
| AMY Mathias | Kristine Baker |
| Katherine RAPELL | Coralie Cairns |
| ZOE Pryce | April Banigan |

Directed by John Sproule
Set and Costume Design by David Belke
Wonderland Costumes Designed by Iain Little
Stage Manager: Paul Bezaire
Graphic Design by Chris Belke

---

The Christmas edition of *The Red King's Dream* was presented by Shadow Theatre at the New Varscona Theatre in December 1999 with the following company:

| | |
|---|---|
| STEVEN Tudor | Matt Baram |
| AMY Mathias | Rhonda NuGent |
| Katherine RAPELL | Blair Wensley |
| ZOE Pryce | April Banigan |

Directed by John Hudson
Designer: David Belke
Wonderland Costumes Designed by Iain Little
Stage Manager: Wayne Paquette
Graphic Design by Chris Belke

---

Note: *The Red King's Dream* was followed by two sequels: *Between Yourself and Me* (2001) and T*he Raven and the Writing Desk* (2006).

## Characters

STEVEN Tudor is a thirty-three-year-old index writer working out of his home.

AMY Mathias is Steven's best friend, an elementary school music teacher and jazz singer in her early thirties.

Katherine RAPELL* is Steven's boss, an editor with Dinah House Publishing and is in her late thirties or forties.

ZOE Pryce is the woman Steven quite probably, and very likely, loves. A graduate student in anthropology with a specialization in Polynesian culture, she is in her late twenties to early thirties.

## Setting

The present, around November and December, in and about the apartment of Steven Tudor.

*Rapell: accent on the second syllable (ra-PELL)

# The Red King's Dream

## Act One

### Scene One

*The apartment of STEVEN Tudor. It is a simple bachelor's residence, perhaps a little cramped by the encroaching walls of books. The living room is lined to overflowing with bookshelves. The furniture is simple. A dilapidated couch sits in the centre of the room, beside which sits an end table with a phone, to the left is a work station with a computer and printer, as well as galleys for upcoming books. On the opposite side of the room is a dinette set. A doorway to the right leads into the kitchen and another hallway to the left leads to the apartment's other rooms (bathroom, bedroom, etc.). The entry door leading to the apartment hallway and other apartments is upstage and just off centre. The whole apartment gives an impression of a drab, quiet and very ordered existence.*

*We are in a dream-like cue. STEVEN is sleeping on his computer keyboard. A voice offstage speaks.*

**VOICE** "The Red King's Dream. From *Through the Looking Glass and What Alice Found There.* Plural pages sixty-three through sixty-five inclusive."

*With jazzy underscoring, AMY and RAPELL enter as Tweedle-dee and Tweedle-dum. They discover the sleeping STEVEN.*

**AMY & RAPELL** "Come and look at him."

**RAPELL** The brothers cried.

*ZOE, dressed as Alice curiously pops into the room. The Tweedles each take one of Alice's hands and pull her into the room as they speak. They end up by the sleeping STEVEN.*

**AMY** And they each took one of Alice's hands and led her to where the King was sleeping.

**RAPELL** "Isn't he a lovely sight?"

**AMY** Said Tweedle-dum.

**ZOE** Alice couldn't say honestly that he was.

**AMY** "He's dreaming now."

**RAPELL** Said Tweedle-dee.

**AMY** "And what do you think he's dreaming about"?

**ZOE** "Nobody can guess that."

**RAPELL** Said Alice.

**AMY** "Why about you!"

**RAPELL** Tweedle-dee exclaimed.

**AMY** "And if he left off dreaming about you, where do you suppose you'd be?"

**ZOE** "Where I am now, of course."

**RAPELL** Said Alice.

**AMY** "Not you! You'd be nowhere. Why you're only a kind of thing in his dream."

**RAPELL** Tweedle-dee retorted contemptuously. "If that there King were to wake—"

**AMY** Added Tweedle-dum.

**RAPELL** "You'd go out—bang—just like a candle!"

**ZOE** "I shouldn't!"

**AMY** Alice exclaimed indignantly.

**ZOE** "Besides, if I'm only a sort of thing in his dream, what are you, I should like to know?"

**RAPELL** "Ditto."

**AMY** Said Tweedle-dum. "Ditto, ditto."

**RAPELL** Cried Tweedle-dee.

**AMY** "Hush. You'll be waking him, I'm afraid."

*The lights shift into reality as STEVEN rouses himself from sleep. The fantasy characters dash off. Once STEVEN is awake, he notices the presence of the audience. With a warm manner, he addresses them.*

**STEVEN** Hello. My name is Steven Tudor. And this is my life.

*STEVEN bustles to work as he talks.*

I write indices. That's the plural of index. My title is assistant editor with Dinah House Publications. Dinah House specializes in the publication of biographies and historical references, some how-to books, some school texts. But all I do is write indices. I even get to work out of my home. Which means there is no excuse for me not to be doing what I'm doing.

As a child, I would read all the time. Read. And notate. Take down the reference, mark the page number, create an index. It's just a matter of finding the logic in the nonsense. Going through the maze of text and finding the framework that binds the meaning.

No one reads indices. They just look things up. Search for a word, find a page number, abandon the index. It's a shame. I think I make very good indices. It's my life.

This is also my life.

*AMY enters the apartment at a run. STEVEN stays glued to his work table.*

**AMY** Hiya Heckle.

**STEVEN** *(to audience)* Heckle. She can get away with calling me that.

**AMY** I need some help.

**STEVEN** I'm busy, Jeckle.

**AMY** Just looking for the rhyming dictionary.

**STEVEN** *(to audience)* Amy teaches music at an elementary school.

**AMY** Working on a new song for the group.

**STEVEN** But she spends most nights singing with this jazz quartet.

**AMY** I need a rhyme for vermicelli.

**STEVEN** Vermicelli?

**AMY** I'm working on an Italian restaurant theme. What rhymes with vermicelli?

**STEVEN** Mary Shelley?

**AMY** Who's that?

**STEVEN** Creator of *Frankenstein*. Born 1797, died 1851. Married to Percy Bysshe Shelley, the romantic poet.

**AMY** Doesn't sound like jazz.

**STEVEN** She died miserable and impoverished.

**AMY** That's jazz. Any other choices?

**STEVEN** Cancelli. Donatelli. Franco Zefferelli.

**AMY** Ooh. I like that one. I like that. Can I write that down?

**STEVEN** I don't mind.

**AMY** You're an inspiration, Heckle.

**STEVEN** I am not.

**AMY** *(making a note on one of STEVEN's index cards)* Well, you're something. Yeah. That's it. That's good.

**STEVEN** Don't lose that. That's important. That's the Mary Pickford years.

**AMY** Mine now.

**STEVEN** Amy…

**AMY** Shhh. I'm on a roll. Italian. Battalion. Rapscallion.

*Katherine RAPELL imperiously steps through the door. She is regally flamboyant and is almost never at rest.*

**RAPELL** Steven! Darling!

**STEVEN & AMY** Hello, Ms. Rapell.

**RAPELL** It's Katherine. How many times must I tell you? It's Katherine. Just got back from St. Augustine. You must go some time.

**STEVEN** I couldn't.

**RAPELL** Of course not, dear. You're always here, aren't you? So dependable.

**STEVEN** All I need is my work.

**RAPELL** Our work.

**STEVEN** I'm happy where I am.

**RAPELL** And I'm happy you're happy. We're all so very happy.

**AMY** Vino. Keno…

**RAPELL** How's the Fairbanks biography?

**AMY** Dino. Reno…

**RAPELL** I told Bradshaw we'd have it ready for bed tomorrow.

**AMY** San Bernardino…

**STEVEN** *(handing RAPELL the index)* It's ready now.

**AMY** Maybe some scat.

**RAPELL** Looks good.

**AMY** Do you like scat?

**RAPELL** No.

**STEVEN** Yes.

*AMY does some scat under the next few lines.*

**RAPELL** What took you so long?

**STEVEN** I'm precise.

**RAPELL** I don't want precision in an index, *tovarisch.*

**STEVEN** What?

**RAPELL** Nobody reads the damn things anyway.

**STEVEN** I do.

**RAPELL** I need volume. The bigger the index, the more respected the book.

**AMY** What rhymes with bolognaise?

**RAPELL** Helen Hayes.

**AMY** That could work.

**RAPELL** Here's your next assignment. *(passing the manuscript)*

**STEVEN** Great!

*The phone rings. AMY picks it up.*

**RAPELL** It's another biography.

**STEVEN** Lewis Carroll.

**RAPELL** Charles Darwin.

**AMY** Hello?

**STEVEN** Charles Dodgson.

**RAPELL** Whatever.

**AMY** Steven. It's your mother.

**RAPELL** He'll call back.

**STEVEN** I'll call back.

**AMY** You'll call back?

**STEVEN** I'll call back.

**AMY** *(to phone)* He'll call back.

**RAPELL** I'll need this in a month.

**STEVEN** But I still have the *Medieval Agricultural History.*

**RAPELL** Do them both.

**STEVEN** It's ten volumes.

**RAPELL** Then do it first.

**AMY** *(holding out the phone)* She wants to talk.

**RAPELL** I need you working, darling.

**STEVEN** *(to AMY)* Not now.

**AMY** Steven…

**STEVEN** Katherine?

**RAPELL** I'm counting on you, sweetheart.

**AMY** *(to phone)* Do you have a rhyme for calamari?

**RAPELL** You mustn't get backed up.

**AMY** It's fried squid.

**STEVEN** I'm just taking my time.

**AMY** No, I can't explain it.

**RAPELL** I'm counting on you.

**AMY** Steven. Your mom…

**STEVEN** It's my mom…

**RAPELL** *(taking the phone from AMY)* Mrs. Tudor. Your son is dead. Call back later. *(hangs up)* Now he can work.

**AMY** That was his mother.

**RAPELL** She shouldn't call at inappropriate times.

**AMY** That was incredibly rude.

**RAPELL** My dear, please. We're on company time. Work, work, work.

**AMY** Steven's his own man.

**RAPELL** Oh?

**AMY** He can talk to whoever he wants to.

**RAPELL** And what business is it of yours?

*The phone rings and continues to do so.*

**AMY** Steven's my friend.

**RAPELL** Ours, dear. Steven is ours.

**AMY** He can do what he likes.

**RAPELL** Not on my time.

**AMY** And what about his time?

**RAPELL** I've paid for that, too.

*Avoiding confrontation, STEVEN addresses the audience again. The women and the phone fade away.*

**STEVEN** I take great pride in the fact that my life has maintained a certain static quality. All I need is in this room. When I look around, all I see is the reflection of the certainty of my life. As safe as a specimen preserved under glass. Nothing gets through a looking glass.

Nothing real anyway. Nothing logical. Nothing to worry about.

Nothing ever changes.

And that's good.

Really.

*Blackout.*

## Scene Two

*Another day. STEVEN is toiling at his desk when AMY bursts into the room. She is returning from work, a whirlwind of frazzled energy. She throws herself on STEVEN's couch.*

**AMY** Good God. Those kids are driving me nuts. You can't hold a civilized conversation with an eight-year-old. Trust me, they aren't human. I need a drink, Heckle.

**STEVEN** I don't drink, Jeckle.

**AMY** Why do I keep doing this to myself? Thank God I have the quartet, or else I'd really go insane. It's like babysitting twenty-five tone-deaf brats, and what's worse, instead of putting them all down for nappies, you have some lamebrain curriculum to follow. Today it was classical music.

**STEVEN** That's nice.

**AMY** Like anyone under four feet tall knows the first thing about classical music. But there it is. Introduce them to Bach. Bach, for God's sake. As far as those kids are concerned, the three B's are Batman—

**STEVEN** Barney—

**AMY** —and barfing. I swear, one of these days I'm just going to go nuts. I'm off to grab a nap. Rehearsal tonight. Thank God for jazz. Jazz is my anchor. By the way, someone is moving in down the hall. Bye. *(exits)*

**STEVEN** *(to audience)* And that's how I received the first inkling that there was change coming to my immediate environment. Further information was to follow.

*Another day. AMY bursts in as before. Only this time she has just returned from rehearsal.*

**AMY** You know what the worst thing about music is? That's right. Musicians. Like you can ever get a straight answer out of a bass player. I'd be better off in a barbershop quartet. I'll tell you, if it wasn't for Richard, I'd go nuts. God, I need a drink.

**STEVEN** I don't drink, Jeckle.

**AMY** And just when I think we're getting somewhere, that maybe we're on the verge of becoming this tight professional group, then ole Freddie chirps up and says that it ain't jazz if it's written down. He says that ole Louis Armstrong couldn't read music. And I say, Freddie, the day you play like Louis Armstrong plays, is the day you can say what Louis Armstrong says.

**STEVEN** Clever.

**AMY** That should have been the end of it, but then suddenly we're all in this ridiculous argument about what Louis Armstrong would have to say about our sound, and then I point out we don't have a sound, and that's the end of rehearsal. Do you know what's wrong with these guys?

**STEVEN** "Full of sound and fury signifying nothing."

**AMY** That's Shakespeare, isn't it?

**STEVEN** *Macbeth.* Act Five.

**AMY** Why?

**STEVEN** Why what?

**AMY** Why the quote?

**STEVEN** I was being clever?

**AMY** Don't. What are you going to do when you finally meet someone who knows what you're talking about?

**STEVEN** Marry them.

**AMY** And if it's a guy?

**STEVEN** I'll get them to marry you.

**AMY** Too late. I'm going out with Richard tonight. Richard is my anchor. I'm off to catch forty winks. By the way, have you met that new woman who moved in today? I haven't. God, I need a life. *(exits)*

**STEVEN** *(to audience)* So. The new neighbour was a woman. It's amazing the kind of intelligence one can gather just by being observant of the activities in one's vicinity.

*Night. Fresh from her date with Richard, AMY slowly enters in a cloud of depression. She collapses on STEVEN's couch.*

**AMY** You never really know a person do you?

**STEVEN** Who don't we know?

**AMY** Richard.

**STEVEN** Ah.

**AMY** Here I thought that he really cared about me. I thought that we were two people who shared a respect and affection for one another, but I guess I was just fooling myself. I spend three hours waiting for him at the restaurant. Three hours. Do you know how long that is?

**STEVEN** One hundred and eighty minutes?

**AMY** At least. And when I finally phone him, he's with Caroline.

**STEVEN** Who?

**AMY** His ex.

**STEVEN** Girlfriend?

**AMY** Wife. There he is, renewing acquaintances with the woman he only last week called the she-demon of Sherbrooke, Quebec, and did he even have the courtesy to call me? No. Left me stranded.

**STEVEN** Like the Franklin Expedition.

**AMY** What?

**STEVEN** Never mind.

**AMY** I'm not feeling too clever tonight.

**STEVEN** Don't let it get you down. The guy was an idiot.

**AMY** How do you know?

**STEVEN** He let you get away.

*Pause. A grateful AMY kisses his forehead.*

**AMY** Thanks, Heckle.

**STEVEN** Any time, Jeckle.

**AMY** I better head back to the apartment. It's one o'clock in the morning and I have lesson plans to write. Thank God for teaching. If it wasn't for those kids, I'd go nuts. Work is my anchor.

**STEVEN** I know. Good night.

**AMY** Good night.

*AMY departs. STEVEN watches the door close and, after a moment, returns to his work. He is well into it when the door buzzer rings. STEVEN is puzzled by this unfamiliar sound.*

*There is another buzz and STEVEN crosses to the intercom. He studies the buzzer to see if he can figure out what is responsible for this unexpected phenomenon.*

*There is another buzz. Since there is no escape, STEVEN presses the intercom button.*

**STEVEN** *(uncertain)* Hello?

**ZOE** *(speaking through intercom)* Excuse me. Sorry.

**STEVEN** Pardon?

**ZOE** I'm sorry. I know it's late.

**STEVEN** It's one fifteen.

**ZOE** Sorry. I saw your light on.

**STEVEN** I'm working.

**ZOE** Oh, good. I was afraid I'd wake someone up.

**STEVEN** Who is this?

**ZOE** My name is Zoe Pryce. And you must be Steven Tudor.

**STEVEN** How do you know?

**ZOE** Your name is on the mailbox. I need your help, Steven.

**STEVEN** My help?

**ZOE** I'm locked out. I just moved in down the hall.

**STEVEN** Oh. Hi.

**ZOE** Hi.

**STEVEN** So we're neighbours.

**ZOE** Just across the courtyard.

**STEVEN** Then welcome.

**ZOE** Thanks.

**STEVEN** So. How are you finding everything?

**ZOE** I'm locked out. Listen, I don't know anybody in the building. I accidentally left my keys in the apartment and I need to be buzzed in.

**STEVEN** Why me?

**ZOE** Your lights were on. I know you don't know me, but I'd really like to get into my apartment right now.

**STEVEN** I don't know.

**ZOE** I really live here.

**STEVEN** How would I know?

**ZOE** Ask me what colour the hall carpet is.

*STEVEN opens the front door and looks out into the hall while keeping his finger on the intercom button.*

**STEVEN** What colour is the hall carpet?

**ZOE** Lavender.

**STEVEN** I'd say it was more of a mauve.

**ZOE** Lavender, mauve, whatever. It proves I live here. Now will you buzz me in?

**STEVEN** I don't know. That was your question.

**ZOE** How would I know if I didn't live in the building?

**STEVEN** What's your apartment number?

**ZOE** Six ten. Listen, I know you don't want to take any chances here, but—

**STEVEN** What's the super's name?

**ZOE** Derek Flores.

**STEVEN** Derek? Mr. Flores is a Derek?

**ZOE** Yes.

**STEVEN** Really?

**ZOE** He asked me to call him Derek.

**STEVEN** He asked me never to call him.

**ZOE** Is this going to take much longer? I'm feeling a little abandoned here.

**STEVEN** Like the Franklin Expedition.

**ZOE** *(beat)* At least Franklin had the rest of the *Erebus* crew to keep him company. Although I think a more apt comparison to my situation might be that of Napoleon during his St. Helena exile. Desperate, lonely and trapped by his own misfortune.

**STEVEN** History major?

**ZOE** Anthropology. I'm taking a graduate degree.

**STEVEN** Really? In what?

**ZOE** Cultural anthropology with a specialization in Southern Polynesia.

**STEVEN** Anthropology has never been a major interest of mine. I'm more of a history buff myself. But I do find Margaret Mead's studies quite gripping.

**ZOE** She was a role model for me.

**STEVEN** I find it disturbing how her work has been so denigrated in recent years. Certainly, *Coming of Age in Samoa* may have some factual errors—

**ZOE** Misinterpretation of facts, I would say.

**STEVEN** —but that does nothing to undermine the value of her observations.

**ZOE** Especially when you consider… *(catching herself)* Listen. Steven. Maybe I am starting to feel a bit like the Franklin Expedition. Can you buzz me in?

**STEVEN** Oh. Yes. Certainly. Sorry. *(He presses the appropriate button. Pause. He suddenly presses the intercom button again.)* It's been nice talking to you. Nice. *(He releases the button. Pause.)* Well. That was interesting.

*Blackout.*

## Scene Three

*The next day. STEVEN is working at his computer. RAPELL enters with a carry-all and a plate of brownies. She is talking to someone unseen in the hall.*

**RAPELL** By all means. I'm sure you're quite right. It's been a pleasant encounter. We must do this again some time. Definitely. Goodbye. *(With some difficulty handling her burdens, RAPELL closes the door.)* Yeesh. *(then seeing STEVEN)* Stephanopolis. How is my bright-eyed hermit today?

**STEVEN** Don't you ever knock?

**RAPELL** *(placing the brownies on the coffee table)* Why should I knock when I have a key?

**STEVEN** I don't recall giving you a key.

**RAPELL** I had Derek make up a copy for me. A very helpful man, your super. He's a super super. *(pause)* You're not expected to laugh at my jokes, dear, but it is polite to at least acknowledge that some attempt at humour has been made.

*STEVEN makes a feeble, forced laugh, which heartens RAPELL. She sits on the couch and pulls out a book from her carry-all. She holds it out for STEVEN.*

**STEVEN** What have you got for me?

**RAPELL** The latest Dinah House release. *Dusty Hefty: The Voice of the Underground.*

**STEVEN** Dostoevsky.

**RAPELL** Whatever. Not exactly what you'd call the most cheery of Christmas releases, but *c'est la vie.* I thought I'd bring you a copy hot off the press, since you weren't at the release party last night.

**STEVEN** I wasn't invited to the release party.

**RAPELL** Would you have gone?

**STEVEN** It would have been nice to be invited.

**RAPELL** Steven. You work best by yourself. We both know that, my reclusive little worker bee. I don't want you disturbed by the other drones.

**STEVEN** I was thinking...

**RAPELL** Oh dear.

**STEVEN** Maybe I would like to meet them sometime. They could come here and—

**RAPELL** But I don't want you to meet them. I want to protect you. I want you to be my very own special little helper.

**STEVEN** But—

**RAPELL** You just concentrate on work. That's what I love about you, dear. You never play the martyr.

**STEVEN** I would have liked to have been invited.

**RAPELL** I just paid you a compliment. Don't make me a liar. You're my good right hand and I need you working. I don't think you realize how precarious things are for us back at the office.

**STEVEN** Precarious?

**RAPELL** *(helping herself to a brownie)* Well, you know Bradshaw has never really liked me. Personality conflict or something. But you know how a petty little man like him can blow things out of proportion.

**STEVEN** Actually, I always liked Mister—

**RAPELL** Did you know he actually suggested I find work at another company? After all the years I've spent at Dinah House? The nerve of the man. Well, we've certainly showed him, haven't we, my special little helper?

**STEVEN** Have we?

**RAPELL** We're one of the most productive editing teams the firm has. And as long as I have my writers and my spell check and my ten hours sleep, everything'll be fine. Oh. And you, of course. Couldn't do it without you. You're a treasure. An absolute treasure.

**STEVEN** Thank you.

**RAPELL** So if there's anything I could do to make your life easier, don't be afraid to ask.

**STEVEN** Well, actually, remember when I said I'd like a little more time for Christmas? Maybe another few days. Things have been so hectic...

**RAPELL** More vacation time?

**STEVEN** That would be nice.

**RAPELL** And where would you spend your vacation?

**STEVEN** Um. Here.

**RAPELL** And where do you work?

**STEVEN** Here.

**RAPELL** Then if you're not going anywhere, why don't you just work through your vacation, hmmm?

**STEVEN** Um. *(beat)* Okay. I guess.

**RAPELL** I envy you. I really do. Working in the comfort of your own home. Worker's paradise as far as I can see. Karl Marx would be proud.

**STEVEN** I wouldn't know.

**RAPELL** Not that I could ever handle it, but it's ideal for you. I want to see the index compiled for that medieval thingy by the end of the week. And remember the Lewis Carroll. I'm leaving in a week and I want you caught up with my work before I'm gone.

**STEVEN** Gone? Gone where?

**RAPELL** *(pronouncing it the way it's spelt)* Majorca. That's in Greece, darling.

**STEVEN** I know.

**RAPELL** Nicky and I are feeling an absolute crying need to romp again on the ancient soil of his ancestors.

**STEVEN** Nicky is Portuguese.

**RAPELL** His uncle owns a hotel on the island. The secret of a good marriage is not to think about things too deeply. In any case, I'll see you tomorrow some time. Cheerio, my deario. *(heading for the exit)* By the way, there are brownies there.

**STEVEN** Leftovers from the party?

**RAPELL** No. Of course not. What are you thinking? I ran into some young woman in the hallway. I said I was on my way to see you and she asked me to deliver those to you. She said they were thanks for last night.

*STEVEN dashes for the door and looks both ways down the hall, there is no sign of ZOE.*

So what did you do? Water her geraniums? Give her directions to the library?

**STEVEN** I buzzed her.

**RAPELL** *(laughing)* I know you, Steven, so I know not to assign a risqué interpretation to such a statement, but I shall make the observation that that is a very vague and intriguing statement. I just thought I should mention that. Ta ta for now.

*RAPELL moves to exit, but STEVEN intercepts her.*

**STEVEN** Wait! What is she like?

**RAPELL** Who?

**STEVEN** Who? Her. The person who gave you the brownies.

**RAPELL** You're the one who buzzed her.

**STEVEN** Is she nice?

**RAPELL** I suppose.

**STEVEN** She's smart.

**RAPELL** I didn't notice.

**STEVEN** She's a graduate student.

**RAPELL** I wouldn't know.

**STEVEN** What does she look like?

**RAPELL** Don't you know?

**STEVEN** I talked to her over the intercom.

**RAPELL** Figures.

**STEVEN** So…?

**RAPELL** *(sighing)* You're taxing my memory, Steven. She's young. Twenties I would say. A little shorter than me.

**STEVEN** That fits.

**RAPELL** Brunette. Green eyes.

**STEVEN** Attractive?

**RAPELL** I don't make value judgments.

**STEVEN** Inoffensive?

**RAPELL** I suppose. Perhaps even pretty.

**STEVEN** Possibly pretty.

**RAPELL** Probably pretty.

**STEVEN** So to summarize; Zoe is in her twenties—

**RAPELL** Late twenties, to be perfectly frank.

**STEVEN** Fine. Late twenties, to be perfectly frank.

**RAPELL** Always strive for perfection, I say.

**STEVEN** A little shorter than you, brunette, green eyes and possibly pretty.

**RAPELL** Probably pretty. I stand by my statement. *(getting up to leave)* Now, if we're done here, I'm late.

**STEVEN** You're late?

**RAPELL** For a very important date.

**STEVEN** Thank you, Ms. Rapell. I appreciate your efforts.

**RAPELL** Good boy. *(She crosses to the brownies and picks them up, plate and all.)* I'm taking these. I've earned them I think. Keep up the good work. *(exits, but leaves the door open)*

**STEVEN** *(to audience)* I just wanted to learn a little more about that person I talked to the night before. I was simply curious, that's all.

*ZOE is briefly seen through the open door crossing the hall.*

**ZOE** Hi, Steven.

*STEVEN springs to the door and frantically looks left and right down the hall. Seeing nothing, he returns to his apartment more than a little perplexed.*

**STEVEN** Curiouser and curiouser. Perhaps I am becoming territorial in my old age. Certainly the knowledge of a new intruder on my hunting grounds was making me as attentive as a watchdog.

When I go to pick up my mail I find myself bracing for an encounter with someone possibly, probably pretty.

But after five days without hearing another word from the elusive Miss—was it Miss?—Pryce I began to feel that I won back some more of my self control. Then, with one simple elevator ride, one simple trip to pick up my mail, things turned topsy turvy.

*Blackout.*

## Scene Four

*The elevator. STEVEN reads a letter as he presses his floor button. The doors are about to close when there is a shout.*

**ZOE** Hold the elevator!

*STEVEN holds the door. ZOE dashes in. STEVEN remains focused on his letter.*

Thanks.

*ZOE reaches to press her button and then pauses.*

We're on the same floor.

*STEVEN looks up from his letter and sees ZOE. She is beautiful. The doors close. ZOE spies the address on STEVEN's envelope.*

Tudor? Steven Tudor? Hi. I'm glad we've finally met. Thanks for letting me in that other night. Did you get the brownies I sent over? I'm Zoe Pryce.

**STEVEN** Um.

**ZOE** By the way, I'll be wanting that plate back.

**STEVEN** Um. Hi.

**ZOE** Hi. I guess we'll be running into each other all the time. Since we're in the same building and all.

**STEVEN** Um.

*The floor bell rings.*

**ZOE** Oops. Here's the floor. See you around. You know, you don't look a thing like I expected you to look. See you. *(exits)*

**STEVEN** Uh. What do you mean I don't look… *(The doors close.)* Wait. That was my floor.

*Blackout.*

## Scene Five

**STEVEN** *(addressing the audience)* Now what the hell was that? Was that a dream? And if so, who dreamt it? I was obviously distracted. The problem was that I had no basis for making a judgment on what I was feeling. I've never had these sort of feelings before. How can a reasonable course of action be developed if I can't understand the events that shaped the dilemma? I can't—

*The phone rings, STEVEN picks it up.*

Hello, Mother. No. I just knew it was you. Yes, Mum. I'm working, Mum. Yes, in my home. I like it better than an office. I'm more comfortable. I'm my own boss. No, I don't write my own paycheques. No, I don't have a secretary. No, I can't give myself a raise. You're right. I'm a bad boss.

*There is a knock on the door.*

Just hold on. I've got someone at the door, Mum. I have to answer the door, Mum. No, I am not making this up. I'm not trying to get rid of you. There is someone at my door. Just hold on, will you, Mum. Please, just…. Yes. Yes. Just hold on.

*All this time STEVEN has been moving towards the door with the receiver cradled between his ear and shoulder. He opens the door. ZOE is revealed. STEVEN is immediately flustered.*

**ZOE** Hi. I wasn't sure you'd be home on a Saturday night.

**STEVEN** Always. Come in. Hi.

**ZOE** Hi.

**STEVEN** *(suddenly remembering the phone)* Mum. I'll call you back, okay? There's someone here, Mum. No. Really.

**ZOE** If this is a bad time for you, I could come back.

**STEVEN** No. That's fine. I'm only talking to my mother. Have a seat. *(He directs ZOE to a chair while he continues on the phone.)* Mum. I've got to go. Mum. Mum. Mother. When I said I was only talking to my mother, I was.... Of course I think you're important. No. I want you to call me. It's just... I have a guest. I'm sorry. *(pause)* It's a she. I just met her a few days ago. Sort of. *(beat)* I buzzed her. No, Mum. Nothing like that, Mum. I'll call back, Mum. As soon as.... Yes, Mum.

**ZOE** I can come back.

**STEVEN** No. Stay.

**ZOE** I just came for my plate.

**STEVEN** I'll get it right away. Just let me... *(back to phone)* Goodbye, Mum. Goodbye.... Yes. A she. I've had visitors before. No. Really. I'll tell you later. Goodbye, Mum. Bye, Mum. Love you, too. Bye, Mum. Bye, Mum. Bye, Mum. Bye, Mum. *(Hangs up the phone and turns to ZOE. Pause.)* That was my mother.

**ZOE** I know.

**STEVEN** Right.

*Silence.*

So. How are you?

**ZOE** I'm fine. I came for my plate.

**STEVEN** I know. I don't have it.

**ZOE** You don't?

**STEVEN** My boss took the plate.

**ZOE** But you said you'd get it.

**STEVEN** Yes.

**ZOE** Right away.

**STEVEN** Yes.

**ZOE** But your boss took the plate.

**STEVEN** My boss took the plate. I… *(STEVEN darts into the kitchen and returns with a plate.)* I thought I'd give you one of mine.

**ZOE** It's not the same.

**STEVEN** But if you need a plate…

**ZOE** I've got other plates.

**STEVEN** Good.

**ZOE** *(beat)* So how were the brownies?

**STEVEN** They looked good.

**ZOE** Didn't you have any?

**STEVEN** My boss took the brownies.

**ZOE** They were for you.

**STEVEN** Thanks.

**ZOE** You're welcome. *(pause)* Maybe I should go.

**STEVEN** No! I mean, okay. If you want. It's just, if we're going to be neighbours, maybe we should get to know one another.

**ZOE** I really should go. I'm working on a paper.

**STEVEN** Anthropology?

**ZOE** My thesis. Tribal funeral customs in Tahiti.

**STEVEN** I love that.

**ZOE** You're familiar with Tahitian funeral rites?

**STEVEN** Sort of. *(indicating his bookshelves)* I always like to learn.

**ZOE** *(taking in the enormity of STEVEN's book collection)* Wow.

**STEVEN** Have you been at the university long?

**ZOE** This is my final year. *(picking up a plastic card from the shelf)* What's that?

**STEVEN** My library gold card. It allows me to get books delivered.

**ZOE** From the library around the corner?

**STEVEN** Others, too.

**ZOE** And this?

**STEVEN** Those are the galleys for a book I'm working on.

**ZOE** Galleys?

**STEVEN** Preliminary pages sent by the printers. *(ZOE starts skimming through the pages.)* Lewis Carroll.

**ZOE** Charles Dodgson.

**STEVEN** Same man.

**ZOE** Different names.

**STEVEN & ZOE** Whatever.

**ZOE** You're working on this?

**STEVEN** Yes. I'm an assis… editor with Dinah House Publishing.

**ZOE** I love Lewis Carroll. I used to read him all the time when I was a little girl.

**STEVEN** Me, too. I mean, when I was a boy. I never got it, though.

**ZOE** *(chuckling)* They're nonsense books. What's there to get?

**STEVEN** It just seems to me that if something runs over a hundred pages, it ought to make some sort of sense.

**ZOE** So. Is it any good? The biography?

**STEVEN** I've just started. It's very informative. Did you know that Lewis Carroll was a university professor?

**ZOE** Mathematics professor at Oxford?

**STEVEN** Yes.

**ZOE** It's been a while since I read any of his books. I'd sort of like to try them again. I could use a little humour in my life right now.

**STEVEN** *(making a beeline to a bookshelf)* Just hold on.

**ZOE** What?

**STEVEN** I think I have…. Yes. Here. *(delivers a yellow paperback book to ZOE)*

**ZOE** *(reading the title) The Annotated Alice*?

**STEVEN** It's *Wonderland* and *Through the Looking Glass* in a single volume. It has footnotes and annotations throughout. It's quite an interesting read. It explains things. It reveals some of the underlying structure beneath the absurdity. If I had this when I was first reading Carroll, maybe I would have enjoyed it more.

**ZOE** I bet.

**STEVEN** Did you know that many of Carroll's so-called nonsense passages are actually based on solid scientific and philosophical foundations? Tweedle-dee and Tweedle-dum are based on enantiomorphic geometric theory. Humpty Dumpty's syntactical meaning is based on medieval nominal meaning. There is a fundamental logic to the nonsense.

**ZOE** Not everything is logical.

**STEVEN** Everything has its own logic. You just have to look for it.

**ZOE** *(amused)* Then what is it?

**STEVEN** I don't know.

**ZOE** I better go. I've got ten pages to write tonight. Thanks for the book. Are you sure you don't mind me taking it?

**STEVEN** I'm getting enough Lewis Carroll these days.

**ZOE** Right. Thanks. And when you get that plate back...

**STEVEN** I'll bring it right over to your apartment.

**ZOE** Thanks. Good night, Steven Tudor.

**STEVEN** Good night, Zoe Pryce.

*ZOE exits. STEVEN stares after her for a moment and then makes a frantic leap for the phone. He desperately taps out a phone number.*

Hello? Ms. Rapell? I need that plate. Now!

*Blackout.*

## Scene Six

*We are in the dream cue again. STEVEN dozes on the couch.*

**VOICE** "*Through the Looking Glass.* Chapter Two. Plural pages thirty-three through thirty-five. Abridged."

*RAPELL enters as the Red Queen.*

**RAPELL** Alice set out at once. She had not been walking a minute before she found herself face to face with the Red Queen.

**ZOE** *(entering as Alice)* She had grown a great deal since Alice first found her in the ashes. She had been only three inches high, and here she was, half a head taller than Alice herself.

**RAPELL** "Where do you come from?"

**ZOE** Said the Red Queen.

**RAPELL** "Look up, speak nicely and don't twiddle your fingers all the time."

**ZOE** Alice attended to all these directions and explained, "I've lost my way."

**RAPELL** "I don't know what you mean by your way."

**ZOE** Said the Red Queen.

**RAPELL** "All the ways around here belong to me – but why did you come out here at all?"

**ZOE** Alice wondered a little at this.

**RAPELL** "It is time for you to answer now. Open your mouth a little wider when you speak and always say 'Your Majesty.'"

**ZOE** I just moved in down the hall. *(indicating STEVEN)* He helped me.

**RAPELL** "That there king is mine."

**ZOE** Said the Red Queen.

**RAPELL** "And you are to stay away from him. You understand?"

**ZOE** But…

**RAPELL** "You understand"?

**ZOE** "Yes, your Majesty."

**RAPELL** "Very well, then."

**ZOE** "But…"

**RAPELL** "But what?"

**ZOE** "I think he likes me."

**AMY** *(offstage)* Thanks, Heckle.

The Looking Glass *characters scurry off. It is now evening as STEVEN suddenly awakes.*

**STEVEN** What? What was that?

*AMY, dressed to the nines, enters from the kitchen with a loaf of bread.*

**AMY** Thanks for the loaf. You're a life saver. *(heads for the hall)*

**STEVEN** What do you need the bread for?

**AMY** My famous bread pudding. I'm cooking dinner for Tremaine.

**STEVEN** Who's Tremaine?

**AMY** Tremaine. The guy I'm going out with. You know. Tremaine.

**STEVEN** First time I've heard you mention him.

**AMY** Oh, come on. You know. Tremaine. The guy.

**STEVEN** What guy?

**AMY** The guy I'm going out with. Him.

**STEVEN** Tremaine?

**AMY** We've gone out before. That Tremaine.

**STEVEN** Him?

**AMY** That's right.

**STEVEN** I have no idea who you're talking about.

**AMY** I'm still going out with him.

**STEVEN** Who is he?

**AMY** He's a jazz dancer. You know what that means.

**STEVEN** It means he's a thin, pale smoker who dresses in black leotards.

**AMY** He's also very flexible. I'll come back later and tell you which way he bends.

**STEVEN** Okay.

**AMY** What was that?

**STEVEN** What?

**AMY** What you just said.

**STEVEN** I said okay.

**AMY** But it was the way you said it.

**STEVEN** How did I say it?

**AMY** You said it like you think I shouldn't be seeing him again.

**STEVEN** Well…

**AMY** Don't you like Tremaine?

**STEVEN** I barely know Tremaine.

**AMY** Oh. *(brightening)* That's right. So how can you judge?

**STEVEN** Okay.

*AMY slams the door and turns to face STEVEN. She waits for an answer.*

It's just…

**AMY** What?

**STEVEN** He's a dancer?

**AMY** Yes.

**STEVEN** A jazz dancer?

**AMY** What is it?

**STEVEN** You have a bad history with dancers.

**AMY** Do I?

**STEVEN** Especially jazz dancers.

**AMY** I do not.

**STEVEN** They always abandon you.

**AMY** They do not.

**STEVEN** I could show you the statistics.

**AMY** You have statistics?

**STEVEN** It's mostly anecdotal evidence. But I'm sure I could draw up a chart…

**AMY** I do not get abandoned. I get along really well with jazz dancers. Most of them. And besides, this is Tremaine we're talking about. He's not going to drop me.

**STEVEN** The last one you dated did.

**AMY** That was different. That was Graham.

**STEVEN** I thought that was Marcus.

**AMY** No, that was Graham. Marcus was the choreographer who dropped me in a week.

**STEVEN** And then there was Nelson and Edgar and Ron.

**AMY** And Felix and Pat.

**STEVEN** And Jeremy. Who could forget Jeremy?

**AMY** I had. Thanks for reminding me.

**STEVEN** Sorry.

**AMY** It's all right.

**STEVEN** *(sensing something is wrong)* What is it?

**AMY** It's just…. It's just after all that and all of them…. You begin to wonder if you're ever going to find the right one.

**STEVEN** Maybe some people just aren't made for falling in love, Jeckle.

**AMY** You don't really believe that do you?

**STEVEN** I do.

**AMY** Great. That's just what I need to hear before a date. *(She heads for the exit, then pauses.)* You know, you're lucky. You've got peace and quiet and the books you love. Your life is perfect. For you. But for me, it's once more into the game.

*AMY exits. STEVEN ponders for a moment.*

**STEVEN** Perfect.

*After a brief hesitation, STEVEN crosses to the phone and checks a number written there. After a moment's consideration, he dials.*

Hello. Steven Tudor here. Yes. I was just wondering.... Well, actually to get to the point, I need to get that *Annotated Alice* back for a moment. I was just working on the index and I came across a reference I need to check, and what with the library closed.... No. Just for a moment. Then you can have it right back. Right. See you shortly. Bye. Thank you.

*He hangs up, carefully folds the paper and puts it in his pocket, sits on the couch and momentarily basks in a feeling of accomplishment, then suddenly snaps bolt upright.*

Now what have I done?

*Blackout.*

## Scene Seven

*Later that night. ZOE is at work on STEVEN's computer. STEVEN watches her nervously from the couch. He has some work spread out on the coffee table, but his heart isn't really in it.*

**ZOE** Wow! Look at this. It's Bleriot's text on English-Tahitian custom fusion on Pitcairn Island. Can I download it?

**STEVEN** Sure. Depending on copyright, of course.

**ZOE** Of course. I can't believe the site access you have on this computer.

**STEVEN** It's for my work.

**ZOE** You didn't tell me you could access the Library of Congress.

**STEVEN** What have you got there?

**ZOE** This is one of the rarest textbooks on the subject. Bleriot spent two years on the island just after the turn of the nineteenth century, documenting the mixing of cultures between the Bounty crew and their Tahitian counterparts.

**STEVEN** Fascinating.

**ZOE** They lived in isolation for decades. A unique opportunity to see the result of two separate and distinct cultures forced to interact for survival. Like, which customs prevailed? The European or the Polynesian? *(reading the screen)* Available for copy. Great, great. Oh, this is great. I could kiss you. *(beat)* Steven...

**STEVEN** Yes?

**ZOE** Do you have a blank disc?

**STEVEN** I always keep one in the B drive. Just punch it in.

**ZOE** *(reading the screen)* It's really big. I might need more than one disc.

**STEVEN** I'll get another.

**ZOE** Thank you, Steven. This is just great.

**STEVEN** It's nice to have someone over who appreciates my database. If you need any more atypical information, don't be afraid to come over.

**ZOE** I don't want to be a nuisance.

**STEVEN** It wouldn't be.

**ZOE** I've tied up your computer for five hours.

**STEVEN** I don't mind. Really.

**ZOE** You're a doll.

**STEVEN** Come over any time.

**ZOE** Any time?

**STEVEN** Sure.

**ZOE** Steven?

**STEVEN** Yes?

**ZOE** I need the second disc.

**STEVEN** Oh. *(STEVEN hands ZOE the disc. She plugs in the new one and starts the download again.)* So. You've been working on your Master's.

**ZOE** Yes.

**STEVEN** Four years? At the same university?

**ZOE** Yes. So?

**STEVEN** So. So nothing. It's just.... Well, if you've been studying at the same place for some time, you must have been staying somewhere in town. And since this building isn't very near the university...

**ZOE** Yes. I had a place.

**STEVEN** So? Why did you move here?

**ZOE** Things happen.

**STEVEN** I'm sorry. I'm prying.

**ZOE** *(pause)* I was sharing this place. With this guy. Darren. We'd been going together for the past few years. But then.... Well, you know how it goes. *(STEVEN doesn't.)* It was rather painful at the end. And when it was all over, well, I couldn't stay there. Too many painful memories, you know.

*Silence.*

**STEVEN** So. He died.

*There is a silence that is explosively broken by ZOE's laughter.*

What? What?

**ZOE** Darren didn't die. I wish. He left me. The bastard ran off with a freshman sociology student.

**STEVEN** You can't trust sociologists.

**ZOE** That was two months ago. You know how it is.

**STEVEN** *(truthfully)* No.

**ZOE** *(chuckles)* You make me laugh, Steven Tudor. Thanks. You know, I haven't even seen a movie or gone on a date since he left. I don't think I could handle any more stress right now. Especially in the romance department. I just need to focus on my thesis. That's all I can handle right now. *(ZOE returns to the computer as STEVEN digests this very important piece of information.)* So, here I am.

**STEVEN** *(beat)* Zoe?

**ZOE** Yes, Steven?

**STEVEN** *(beat)* You're going to need a third disc.

*STEVEN gives ZOE the disc. She puts it in the drive.*

**ZOE** Just a little bit left. Thanks again, Steven.

**STEVEN** You're welcome.

**ZOE** Did you find the reference you were looking for?

**STEVEN** What?

**ZOE** The one in the Alice book.

**STEVEN** Oh…

**ZOE** It's right there on the table.

**STEVEN** Oh. Good. I'll just…

*STEVEN picks up the book. He quickly pages through it making a hastily improvised effort to look something up. He barely looks at the book.*

Oh, yes. There it is. Tiger Lily. Whew. That's a load off my mind. Good thing you brought that over. Saved me some time, you did. *(ZOE is gathering the discs together and preparing to go.)* Oh. Are you leaving already?

**ZOE** It's six-thirty in the morning.

**STEVEN** Oh.

**ZOE** Thanks for everything.

**STEVEN** If you ever want to use my computer again…

**ZOE** Great. I appreciate it. *(pause)* I better go.

**STEVEN** *(bringing her the book)* Don't forget this.

**ZOE** You might need it again.

**STEVEN** If I need to look something up again, I'll just give you another call.

*STEVEN and ZOE are by the hall door.*

**ZOE** Sorry. I talked all night.

**STEVEN** You make the study of cargo cults truly fascinating.

**ZOE** There's an exhibit at the museum. Do you want to go?

**STEVEN** I don't go to museums.

**ZOE** You don't?

**STEVEN** I… I'm a homebody. I've got everything I need here. But why don't you go? And then you could tell me all about it?

**ZOE** You're sure?

**STEVEN** Pretty sure.

**ZOE** Oh. Well. I should get—

**STEVEN** One more thing. I was just wondering—

*Suddenly, AMY steps through the door and rushes into the kitchen without actually acknowledging anyone in the room. She is still dressed in her clothes from the date.*

**AMY** *(rushing through)* I never want to see another man for as long as I live. God, I need a drink. I'll take anything as long as it's served on the rocks and has a straw. God, Heckle, what a disaster. *(She re-enters the living room and freezes when she spots ZOE.)* Who are you?

**STEVEN** Amy Mathias. This is Zoe Pryce. Our new neighbour.

**AMY** Hi.

**ZOE** Hi.

**AMY** You're the one he buzzed?

**ZOE** Yes.

**AMY** What happened? Get locked out again?

**ZOE** No. I don't know what happened that night. I guess I was distracted, and the next thing I knew, I was stranded.

**STEVEN** Like the Franklin Expedition.

**ZOE** Yes.

*STEVEN and ZOE laugh and share a moment that is noted by AMY.*

**AMY** So… how are you finding it?

**ZOE** I'm still getting to know people in the building. I haven't been getting out a lot.

**AMY** Getting over a bad relationship?

**ZOE** How do you…?

**AMY** That's what I do whenever it goes sour for me. Stay at home, open a bag of chips and watch TV. I've been watching a lot of TV lately.

**ZOE** I've been thinking of getting cable.

**AMY** Sometimes I just leave it on all day.

**ZOE** Some days I feel like a Neilsen family.

**AMY** Doesn't even matter what's on.

**ZOE** You just let your mind go blank.

**AMY** Just sit and watch.

**ZOE** Sit and watch.

*AMY and ZOE sadly sigh. Beat.*

**STEVEN** *(trying to join in)* Actually, I like to read.

**AMY** *(to ZOE)* So, if you didn't get locked out, what brings you over to this neck of the woods?

**ZOE** Steven's been letting me use his computer.

**AMY** Has he? Well, Heckle's a good neighbour.

**STEVEN** I try.

**ZOE** Heckle?

**STEVEN** What? Oh. I'm Heckle. She's Jeckle.

**ZOE** Why?

**STEVEN** Mr. Flores calls us that.

**AMY** He saw us in the hall together so often he began calling us Heckle and Jeckle.

**ZOE** So, you're a couple?

**STEVEN** No. Never a couple.

**AMY** But always a pair.

**STEVEN** A subtle but important distinction.

**ZOE** I better get going. Thanks again, Steven. *(to AMY)* Nice meeting you.

**AMY** Me, too.

**ZOE** *(back to STEVEN)* I'll see you. Bye. *(exits)*

**AMY** Kind of late to be using the computer.

**STEVEN** Kind of early to be dropping by.

**AMY** Never bothered you before.

**STEVEN** Still doesn't. Do you want a 7-Up?

**AMY** If that's what you've got.

**STEVEN** That's what I've got.

**AMY** Then that's what I'll have. *(STEVEN exits to the kitchen.)* She seems nice enough.

**STEVEN** *(from the kitchen)* She is.

**AMY** *(to herself)* They all seem nice at the beginning. *(pause)* Steven?

**STEVEN** Yes?

**AMY** Have you ever been in love?

**STEVEN** What?

**AMY** I was just asking if you've ever been in love.

*STEVEN bursts from the kitchen with a glass of 7-Up in his hand.*

**STEVEN** Who, me? Why?

**AMY** I was just thinking. Maybe I'm fooling myself. Now that Tremaine has shown his true colours…

**STEVEN** What happened?

**AMY** I thought he was sweet and witty and wonderful and beautiful.

**STEVEN** So?

**AMY** He thought I was selling him short.

**STEVEN** Oh.

**AMY** I'm taking myself out of the game for a while. Maybe you're right about me falling in love with the wrong people.

**STEVEN** So you're taking a sabbatical?

**AMY** *(chuckling)* Yes. I believe so.

**STEVEN** *(pause)* You know what I believe?

**AMY** What?

**STEVEN** I truly believe that, for some people, love is a needless complication that is better left unexplored.

**AMY** People like who, for instance?

**STEVEN** Sir Isaac Newton. One of the foremost scientific geniuses of all time, and he died a virgin.

**AMY** He was also a miserable old bastard despised by everyone who met him.

**STEVEN** Nonetheless, I maintain that there are people who are just not designed to experience love.

**AMY** People like me.

**STEVEN** Hardly. I was thinking of… other people. I believe that there are people who are simply destined to die alone and unloved.

**AMY** Steven…

**STEVEN** Now hear me out. Such people, I imagine, must have been solitary children. Much happier sitting at home reading a book than going outside and playing with other youngsters. By the time these people reach the age where dating or other emotional contacts meant something, they lack the skills to do anything about it.

**AMY** You don't need any special skills to love someone. After all these years around me, I would have thought you'd have figured that out.

**STEVEN** Perhaps. But you need special skills to act on those feelings. And so lacking experience in the customs, rituals or expectations of social interaction, these people live secure in the knowledge that they shall never be swept away by the ecstatic tides of lusty love. Such people must lead lives of great calm and equilibrium, devoted to much more rational pursuits. Such people are, I think, to be admired.

**AMY** It sounds like you've given this a great deal of thought.

**STEVEN** I have.

**AMY** It's amazing how so much thought can produce such a sack of rubbish.

**STEVEN** It is not.

**AMY** It is, too.

**STEVEN** It is not.

**AMY** It is, too.

**STEVEN** It is not.

**AMY** God, I feel like I'm back at the school.

*RAPELL bursts through the door. She looks like she has just left an all night party and is still a little tipsy. She carries a shopping bag.*

**RAPELL** Steven! Compadre! Ah. My little church mouse with company. I hope I'm interrupting something.

**AMY** We were just discussing how stupid Steven is.

**RAPELL** *(finding a chair)* Fascinating.

**STEVEN** Ms. Rapell…

**RAPELL** Katherine.

**STEVEN** It's six-thirty in the morning. What are you doing here?

**RAPELL** I brought back your plate. You made it sound mind-bogglingly important, and so I brought it back as soon as I could.

**STEVEN** I called you six days ago.

**RAPELL** Well, I had to have it washed, didn't I? *(to AMY)* So. How stupid is Steven?

**AMY** Steven believes there are people incapable of feeling love.

**STEVEN** I didn't say that.

**RAPELL** What did you say?

**STEVEN** I said that lacking certain social skills, it is only right and natural that certain people lead a solitary life.

**RAPELL** I wish you had said the other thing. It was much more intelligent.

**STEVEN** Listen, it's early and I'm tired…

**AMY** Do you have my drink?

**STEVEN** What? Oh. Yes. *(delivers her drink)*

**AMY** You know what I think?

**STEVEN** I think you think you want to go home.

**AMY** I think he's afraid of allowing himself to be vulnerable. That he's come up with all these reasons why he can't fall in love.

**STEVEN** I wasn't talking about myself.

**AMY** You were, too.

**STEVEN** I was not.

**AMY** You were, too.

**STEVEN** I was not.

**AMY** You were—

**STEVEN** Amy! Just drop it. Okay?

**AMY** Okay.

**STEVEN** So that's the end of this?

**AMY** The end. Suits me.

**STEVEN** Fine.

**AMY** Fine.

**STEVEN** Fine.

*STEVEN and AMY head for the exit.*

**RAPELL** So if what you suggest is true, then Steven could actually fall in love with someone and never even admit it to himself?

**AMY** *(re-entering the room)* Yes.

**STEVEN** I was talking about other people.

**RAPELL** Why, that's absolutely tragic.

**AMY** It is.

**RAPELL** Who knows how many times he might have fallen in love in the past and never admitted it to himself?

**STEVEN** I have never fallen in love.

**RAPELL** How would you know?

**STEVEN** I think I'd know if I fell in love.

**RAPELL** I doubt it.

**AMY** Have you ever found yourself asking questions about someone you barely know just because you want to learn more about them?

**STEVEN** Never.

**RAPELL** Have you ever found yourself in the bushes outside someone's house staring through their bedroom window with a camera and a pair of binoculars?

*STEVEN and AMY pause to stare at RAPELL before AMY dives in again.*

**AMY** Have you ever spoken someone's name for no other reason than it gave you pleasure to say it?

**RAPELL** Have you ever found yourself in such synchronization with someone that you say the same thing at the same time?

**AMY** Have you ever found yourself unable to take your eyes off someone?

**RAPELL** Have you ever found yourself struck speechless by the mere sight of someone?

**STEVEN** No. Now I am going straight to bed. I take it the two of you know the way out? Good night. Good night. *(starts for the bedroom)*

**RAPELL** Steven, dear.

**STEVEN** *(freezing in his exit)* What?

**RAPELL** *(removing ZOE's plate from her shopping bag)* You want your plate?

*STEVEN huffily takes the plate and then tenderly holds it. He exits to the bedroom. There is a moment's silence.*

**AMY** He just hasn't been himself lately.

**RAPELL** How so?

**AMY** When I arrived this morning…

**RAPELL** What?

**AMY** Nothing. Steven is entitled to his privacy.

**RAPELL** Except from us.

**AMY** Except from us.

*They share a laugh.*

**RAPELL** Well, I'm feeling a mite peckish. Shall we see what Steverino has hidden away in his larder?

**AMY** Some people would call that burglary.

**RAPELL** I call it take-out breakfast.

**AMY** Why don't you join me? How does bread pudding for breakfast sound?

**RAPELL** Quite esoteric, actually.

**AMY** Great. *(They start to leave.)* I could use the company right now.

**RAPELL** Bad morning?

**AMY** The worst.

**RAPELL** Bad night?

**AMY** Also the worst.

**RAPELL** Bad date?

**AMY** The worst in the world.

**RAPELL** Couldn't be.

**AMY** Why not?

**RAPELL** Because I was the one who had to suffer through the worst date in the world.

**AMY** Oh, come on.

**RAPELL** No, really.

**AMY** What was so bad?

**RAPELL** *(as they exit)* Well, I'm sure you've heard of the La Brea Tar Pits…

*Fade-out.*

## Scene Eight

*STEVEN strides to the elevator.*

**STEVEN** *(muttering to himself)* In love. Would I know if I was in love? What is love anyway? Just a word. And I know when I'm in a word. Semantical meaning is defined by people. Not the other way around. I know what I'm doing. I know what I'm feeling. It's not like there's a systematic test to verify your feelings is there? Why isn't this elevator moving? *(Pause, then STEVEN remembers and presses the button for his floor.)* Okay. That was a mistake. Simple mistake. Anyone could… could…

*The bell rings announcing arrival at a floor. The doors open and ZOE enters the elevator.*

**ZOE** Hi, Steven.

*STEVEN opens his mouth, but nothing comes out.*

**RAPELL** *(voice-over)* Have you ever found yourself struck speechless by the mere sight of someone?

**ZOE** Boy, these elevators take forever to get started, don't they?

*ZOE reaches over and presses the floor button again a number of times. STEVEN can't take his eyes off her.*

**AMY** *(voice-over)* Have you ever found yourself unable to take your eyes off someone?

**ZOE** Here we go.

**ZOE & STEVEN** Well…. I don't… *(They laugh.)* What were… *(They laugh again.)*

**RAPELL** *(voice-over)* Have you ever found yourself in such synchronization with someone that you say the same thing at the same time?

*The floor bell rings.*

**STEVEN** Here we are.

**ZOE** Yes. See you later, Steven.

**STEVEN** See you.

*ZOE exits.*

**AMY** *(voice-over)* Have you ever spoken someone's name for no other reason than it gave you pleasure to say it?

**STEVEN** *(smiling)* Zoe…

*The idyll is broken by shocked revelation. Panicking, he addresses the audience.*

Can it be? This is beyond me. This was totally unlike anything I had ever felt before. But what to do about it? What was my next step?

There is only one thing a man can do when he finds himself caught in the throes of passion. I went to the library.

*Consults his computer.*

The catalogue at the central library lists over five hundred different references for the word love, ranging from romantic love, to love of country, to self love and a large number of variations in between. I obviously had no reason to worry. Surely at least one volume would have something to say about the state I found myself in. After all, it was just a simple biological imperative.

Wasn't it?

The first step was to determine whether or not I was truly in love or if it was merely infatuation. When in search of such distinctions I always like to turn to the *Oxford Universal Dictionary*. It's clear, concise and the section on abbreviations is one of the most amusing passages I have found in any reference book. It is a subtle wit, I admit.

Infatuate. Verb transitive. Affect – person – with extreme folly; inspire with extravagant passion.

Well, I suppose I could attest to the passion, although I'm not sure I could call it extravagant. I'm not sure I'm capable of extravagance. And there is nothing so disturbing as to discover that one is possibly affected by the extremity of folly.

The definition for the word love fills an entire page. So much for Oxonian clarity and conciseness. But to summarize: Love. Noun. Also verb transitive or intransitive. Warm affection. Attachment. Likeness or fondness. Paternal benevolence?

So maybe it wasn't love. Certainly what I was feeling didn't seem to fit the definition.

There doesn't seem to be a word about the quick skip of the pulse experienced whenever you see her in the hall. There doesn't seem to be a reference for the way her name slowly slips into your thoughts.

Zoe.

The way the sudden sight of her inspires a complete dissatisfaction with your clothing choice for the day as well as a certainty in the absolute benevolence of the universe. Her turn of phrase, her sharpness of intellect, the way she can talk about cultural anthropology and somehow make it even more fascinating than English syntax drift during the Cromwellian period.

Her face, her hair, her voice. The way her perfume lingers in one's memory. I think it's perfume. I'm not sure what perfume smells like. Maybe that's just her. Maybe she just naturally exudes aromatic essences into the atmosphere like a hyacinth. What a happy accident of genetics that would be.

She's there and I want to be there. She speaks and I want to listen. She looks at me and I want to hide. I want to fill my life with her.

Infatuation may be defined as folly, but love is thoroughly, absolutely, fundamentally, exquisitely indefinable. And the conclusion is: I am in love with Zoe Pryce. Every piece of data, every scrap of information, every second of every minute of every day of the last few weeks all point to one inescapable conclusion that defies all hypotheses. Without a doubt and beyond all expectation, I am in love!

The world is turned upside down. I have stepped through the looking glass and all previous frames of reference are meaningless. I am Fate's pawn. Fair is foul and foul is fair! Bring on the folly! Steven Tudor is in love!

*Beat.*

I wonder if I should tell her?

*Blackout.*

*End of Act One.*

# Act Two

## Scene One

*The apartment is bathed in a dreamlike lighting cue. AMY is perched on a stool and dressed in a beatnik fashion. She exudes a bohemian attitude as jazzy music plays under. Seated on the floor is STEVEN, immersed in the books and papers spread around him on the floor. It is a royal mess of research.*

**AMY** *(performing like a beat poet)* 'Twas brillig and the slithy toves
Did gyre and gimble in the wabe
All mimsy were the borogroves
And the mome raths outgrabe.

*(fortissimo)* Beware the Jabberwock, my son!

*ZOE runs in dressed like Alice.*

**ZOE** *(indicating STEVEN)* "Hush. You'll be waking him, I'm afraid."

**AMY** Beware the Jubjub bird!

**RAPELL** *(entering as the Red Queen)* Well, it's no use your talking about "waking him."

**AMY** *(fortissimo)* And shun *(sotto)* the frumious bandersnatch.

**RAPELL** You know very well you're not real.

**AMY** He took his vorpal sword in hand.

**ZOE** I am real.

**AMY** Long time the manxome foe he sought.

**RAPELL** You won't make yourself a bit realer by crying.

**AMY** Then rested he by the tumtum tree.

**ZOE** I am real!

**AMY** And stood a while in thought.

**ZOE** Steven?

**AMY** And as in uffish thought he stood.

**ZOE** *(shaking STEVEN)* Steven?

**AMY** The Jabberwock with eyes of flame—

**ZOE** Steven, am I real or aren't I?

**AMY** —came whiffling through the tulgey wood—

**RAPELL** *(to ZOE)* You can't do that.

**AMY** —and burbled as it came.

**RAPELL** You're breaking convention.

**AMY** One, two, one, two—

**ZOE** Well, I'm not going to stand here—

**AMY** —and through and through.

**ZOE** —and be dismissed as a figment of someone's imagination.

**AMY** He left it dead—

**RAPELL** Well, look how you're dressed.

**AMY** —and with its head—

**ZOE** *(looking at her costume for the first time)* Good grief. Steven…

**AMY** *(fortissimo)* He went galumphing back!

**RAPELL** Oh, lay off the *Jabberwocky* already!

**AMY** Sorry.

**ZOE** Steven? What's real here? Is this really me?

**STEVEN** *(still engrossed in research)* That's what I'm trying to figure out.

*The women look at each other.*

**RAPELL** He thinks too much, our boy.

**ZOE** *(indicating her costume)* I just want to know what this is.

**AMY** I don't think that's you.

**RAPELL** Symbolism again?

**AMY** I think so.

**ZOE** Okay. Then I'm going to change. Coming?

**RAPELL** Sure. Why not? The metaphor's lost its potency anyway.

*RAPELL and ZOE head for the exit.*

**AMY** Wait. What about him?

**RAPELL** Are you kidding? He's deeper into fantasy than any of us.

*The women leave. STEVEN remains deep in concentration. The lights shift to the normal apartment cue. It is two days after Act One. STEVEN notices the audience.*

**STEVEN** The more I think about it, the more I'm convinced that Zoe and I were meant to be.

Consider our similar intellects, our interest in esoteric topics, the fact that, out of all the people in the building, she called me. It wasn't coincidence. It wasn't Fate. It was just one of those things that was meant to be. Like grunion migration or continental drift. She's intelligent, cogent, well tempered, well read, sympathetic, empathetic, studious and ambitious within an appropriately scholastic scale. She understands me when I drop obscure historical references and has proven herself more than able to expand on my inferences. She is thoughtful, generous, amiable and is further blessed with the ability to bake brownies. The fact that she is probably pretty is a dividend.

There is no denying it. Zoe Pryce is the perfect woman. For me. The only question is what to do about it.

*STEVEN returns to the tangle of books just as RAPELL sweeps in. She is just back from vacation and carries a brightly wrapped package.*

**RAPELL** Steven, *ma petite amis.* I just got… *(taking in the mess)* Oh my God!

**STEVEN** Hello.

**RAPELL** Steven, child. What have you done to the place?

**STEVEN** I'm working.

**RAPELL** The Lewis Carroll opus?

**STEVEN** Private research. *(RAPELL reaches to examine one of the papers, but STEVEN intercepts her.)* How was Greece? Did Nicky have a good time?

**RAPELL** Nicky? I suppose he had a good time. Give Nicky a ball of string and a colouring book and he'll have a good time. So where is the index?

*STEVEN makes some vague motion to the workspace. RAPELL crosses and examines the detritus by the computer.*

**STEVEN** So…. How did you and Nicky meet?

**RAPELL** *(concentrating on her search)* As I recall, it had something to do with moonlight, beaches and an outrageous amount of Kahlua. Where's the rest of the index?

**STEVEN** That's it.

**RAPELL** This isn't finished. It's nowhere near finished.

**STEVEN** I've been busy.

**RAPELL** The Carroll biography was supposed to be done today.

**STEVEN** It'll get done.

**RAPELL** Today?

**STEVEN** It'll get done.

**RAPELL** Steven. Are you in need of a severe reprimand?

**STEVEN** No.

**RAPELL** This isn't like you. You've always been so reliable in the past.

**STEVEN** I'm sorry.

**RAPELL** Sorry doesn't put bread on the Rapell family table. Just get down to work. I need an index, a fat one and Lord knows I can't do it myself. We're behind schedule and we can't afford to wallow in the jejune.

**STEVEN** If you need help, I'm sure I could help you edit—

**RAPELL** Help? Me?

**STEVEN** I've been thinking I need a change. And as far as the job goes, it seems like I've been running as fast as I can and getting nowhere.

**RAPELL** In our business it takes all the running you can do to keep in the same place. If you want to get somewhere else, you must run at least twice as fast as that, and you're simply not suited to such exertions.

**STEVEN** But editing…

**RAPELL** My dear boy, since when have you got into to your head that you could edit? That requires meeting people, dear. And if there's two things you are totally unsuited for, it's meetings and people.

**STEVEN** *(beat)* It'll get done. I promise.

**RAPELL** Good. You frightened me for a moment, *ma petite.* Let's not talk about change, shall we? Not when we have everything just the way we like it.

*AMY enters with a full head of steam.*

**AMY** Tell me. Why did God create field trips? Who ever thought that children could learn anything outside a school? Oh. Hi, Katherine.

**RAPELL** It's Ms. Rapell. I'm on business.

**AMY** Sorry.

**RAPELL** And I'll thank you not to disturb Steven during work hours. *(sweetly back to STEVEN)* I'll pop by tomorrow and see how you're getting along. *(remembering her package)* Oh. And this is for you.

**STEVEN** What is it?

**RAPELL** A Christmas present. A souvenir from Greece.

**STEVEN** *(unconvincingly)* Thank you.

**RAPELL** I look forward to your gift to me. And remember, Steven, I want you working. Toodles.

**AMY** Toodles.

*RAPELL exits. STEVEN opens his gift.*

Steven. Never turn your back on that woman.

**STEVEN** I should have warned you. She'll only let you call her Katherine when she wants something from you.

**AMY** And you put up with that?

**STEVEN** What else can I do?

**AMY** You can always give her a stiff uppercut. What is it?

**STEVEN** Two bottles of duty free Ouzo.

*AMY reaches for the bottles. STEVEN pulls them from her reach and takes the bottles to the kitchen.*

**AMY** You don't drink.

**STEVEN** That's right.

**AMY** Okayyy. What happened to your apartment?

**STEVEN** *(returning)* I'm working. I need music.

**AMY** Working on what?

**STEVEN** A project. I'm doing research on romantic love.

**AMY** What happened? Get swept away by those lusty tides?

**STEVEN** It's a private project.

**AMY** You have enough material here to write a book.

**STEVEN** *(leaping on the idea)* That's what I'm doing. I'm writing a book.

**AMY** You are?

**STEVEN** Yes. I need some music.

**AMY** What kind of book?

**STEVEN** It's hard to put into words.

**AMY** That's a problem for a book.

**STEVEN** I'm researching the evolution of romantic love through the ages. From chivalry to the modern day.

**AMY** Why this sudden interest?

**STEVEN** It's not so sudden.

**AMY** You're right. It's completely unbelievable.

**STEVEN** Remember that conversation we had about falling in love? Well, you convinced me that I am sorely ignorant. I decided that I should look into the subject. And as long as I am researching the topic and gathering all this information, I might as well put my efforts to good use and write a book.

**AMY** So I inspired you to write a book?

**STEVEN** Okay.

**AMY** Me?

**STEVEN** Sure.

**AMY** *(pause, then smiling)* Cool. Do you need any help?

**STEVEN** I need some music. To get a feel for the emotional content of the subject.

**AMY** What kind of music?

**STEVEN** Ballads. Romantic songs. Evocative instrumentals. Love music. Do you have anything like that?

**AMY** Sure. I'll just go pick out a few of my favourites.

**STEVEN** That would be helpful.

**AMY** I'll be right back. *(heads for the door and then pauses)* So I inspired you to write a book?

**STEVEN** That's right.

**AMY** Cool. *(exits)*

*As STEVEN speaks, he cleans his apartment.*

**STEVEN** *(to audience)* What could I say? I was still figuring all this out myself.

I have decided to expand my relationship with Zoe. I have to find out if my love for her is reciprocated or is capable of being reciprocated. Now, this is a rather delicate situation. Some middle ground must be traversed. Push too hard and I might be rejected. Be too timid and the opportunity might be lost forever.

It is from such questions that military campaigns are lost and won.

The first step is obvious. I must allow Zoe to get to know me. It seems like the easiest way to accomplish this initial goal is through a "date."

According to almost every volume I've read, the first date is the moment that either builds or destroys a relationship. It is sobering to consider that balanced upon this delicate fulcrum lies the entire genetic destiny of the human race.

For ease of social interaction, I decided that the most effective locale for such an endeavour would be some place comfortable for both of us.

*There is a knock on the door. STEVEN opens it. There is ZOE with textbooks.*

**ZOE** Hi.

**STEVEN** Hi.

**ZOE** Thanks for letting me use your computer. *(She heads for the work station.)*

**STEVEN** No problem. *(to the audience)* And so the date begins.

*Blackout.*

## Scene Two

*Later that night. ZOE is working on the computer. STEVEN is sitting on the couch with the Carroll galleys and a notepad. STEVEN watches ZOE. ZOE is intent on the screen.*

**STEVEN** How's your work going?

**ZOE** Fine.

**STEVEN** Good.

**ZOE** A lot of material.

**STEVEN** There is. *(pause)* It's amazing what you can access through the internet, isn't it? It's better than being there.

**ZOE** What's that?

**STEVEN** As long as you have a computer and modem, you can reach anywhere from the comfort of your own home.

**ZOE** I know.

**STEVEN** Even Tahitian funeral rites.

**ZOE** Hmm-mmm.

**STEVEN** Let Tahiti come to you.

**ZOE** Right.

**STEVEN** Right.

**ZOE** *(pause, then with excitement)* Oh. I had an offer to go to the South Pacific.

**STEVEN** What?

**ZOE** Professor Hudson asked me to join him on a trip to Western Samoa.

**STEVEN** Samoa?

**ZOE** They're doing a field study starting in the new year. It's quite the honour to be asked.

**STEVEN** But you're studying Tahiti.

**ZOE** That's right.

**STEVEN** That's not Tahiti.

**ZOE** It's Polynesia.

**STEVEN** It's not the same.

**ZOE** No, it's not.

**STEVEN** So you might as well stay.

**ZOE** I wasn't really planning on going.

**STEVEN** Good.

**ZOE** Not right away. I'm too deep into my thesis right now.

**STEVEN** I think that's for the best.

**ZOE** Yes.

**STEVEN** Would you like some Ouzo?

**ZOE** What?

**STEVEN** I've got some Ouzo in the fridge. Would you like some?

**ZOE** Not really. I need to concentrate. But go ahead and have some if you like.

**STEVEN** I don't drink. *(pause)* Would you like some food?

**ZOE** No, thanks.

**STEVEN** I've got lots.

**ZOE** Maybe later.

**STEVEN** Okay.

*STEVEN pauses. Then with deliberate casualness he strolls over to his sound system. He turns on music. Romantic strings.*

**ZOE** *(without thinking)* Could you turn that off?

*STEVEN hastily switches off the music.*

I'm so sorry. It's your apartment. If you want to listen to music…

**STEVEN** No. That's all right.

**ZOE** I don't mind.

**STEVEN** If you want quiet…

**ZOE** I'm just trying to concentrate.

**STEVEN** I know.

**ZOE** But if you want music…

**STEVEN** I don't.

**ZOE** Are you sure?

**STEVEN** I don't care. *(pause)* I just thought that you might like to hear some music.

**ZOE** I don't.

**STEVEN** To relax things a bit.

**ZOE** It's a little distracting right now.

**STEVEN** I know.

**ZOE** I'm trying to concentrate on my work.

**STEVEN** *(to audience)* Me, too. At least we're talking. It took an hour and a half, but we're talking. Not about us. Yet. But at least the foot is in the door. Now we can move on to more personal topics. Likes, dislikes. Family history. It's all going… somewhat according to plan.

*STEVEN casually strolls over to ZOE and the computer. He peers over her shoulder.*

What are you working on?

**ZOE** Hmm? Oh. Just looking at some descriptions on burial totems.

**STEVEN** Do you like burial totems?

**ZOE** Pardon?

**STEVEN** Are they better than other totems?

**ZOE** They're not better. Just different.

**STEVEN** Right. Different.

**ZOE** It's not a matter of liking one or the other.

**STEVEN** You know what I like? Encyclopedias.

**ZOE** Do you?

**STEVEN** I do. They're so substantial. Just full of facts and figures. I could spend days just reading from volume A to volume Z. Aardvark to zymase. Do you know what zymase is?

**ZOE** No.

**STEVEN** Well, let's get the encyclopedia and find out!

**ZOE** No, thanks.

**STEVEN** It'll be fun.

**ZOE** No, that's fine.

**STEVEN** Okay.

**ZOE** I'm working right now.

**STEVEN** Okay.

*STEVEN hovers. ZOE is starting to feel annoyed when the intercom buzzes. Pause. The buzzer sounds again.*

Excuse me. I'll just go get that.

**ZOE** Of course.

*STEVEN crosses to the intercom. ZOE tries to concentrate on her work.*

**STEVEN** *(to intercom)* Hello?

**RAPELL** *(from intercom)* Steven child, *c'est moi.* I seem to have misplaced your key. Be a dear and ring me in will you?

**STEVEN** *(glancing over at ZOE)* You can't come in right now. *(pause, waits for a response, then)* Ms. Rapell?

**RAPELL** I'm sorry, darling. I didn't quite get that last part.

**STEVEN** I'm in the middle of something right now.

**RAPELL** I refuse to believe that.

**STEVEN** Can you come back tomorrow?

**RAPELL** I need the index, Steven. Bradshaw is pressuring me, dear.

**STEVEN** You'll get it tomorrow.

**RAPELL** But I'm here now.

**STEVEN** But I'm not. See you tomorrow. *(STEVEN leaves the intercom. He strolls over to ZOE.)* You know what else I like? *(There is an explosive buzz from the intercom.)* Excuse me.

*Back at the intercom again, STEVEN presses the button. But before he can even open his mouth:*

**RAPELL** *(from intercom)* Did you hang up on me? Did you actually hang up on me? I'm down in the lobby, darling. Don't think I can't get in there if I really want to.

**STEVEN** *(blurting)* I'm working on the Carroll index right now, Ms. Rapell. You'll have it in the morning. If that's not good enough for you, then you can find someone else to do your work for you. But in the meantime, allow me to work at my own pace in my own way. All right?

**RAPELL** No. It is not—

**STEVEN** Good night. *(He ends the communication, takes a moment to settle himself and strolls back to ZOE.)* Do you know what else I like?

**ZOE** No.

**STEVEN** I like clocks. I like the way they just keep on working through the night, through the day. Just marking the hours, never stopping. There's a certain intensity of purpose about clocks that I like a lot.

**ZOE** Steven. Maybe I will have some food now.

**STEVEN** Hungry?

**ZOE** Apparently.

**STEVEN** I'll get something from the kitchen.

**ZOE** That would be nice.

**STEVEN** I'll be right back.

**ZOE** Thanks.

*STEVEN retreats into the kitchen and ZOE breathes a sigh of relief. She returns to her work. She is well into typing when STEVEN returns and places two china plates on the table. He returns to the kitchen. After a moment or two, he returns with silverware which he precisely sets in the appropriate relation to the plates. ZOE watches all this from a corner of her eye, although she makes a game attempt to concentrate on her task. But a horrible fascination is starting to overtake her. STEVEN returns from another trip to the kitchen with linen napkins which he professionally folds and places on the plates. Another trip to the kitchen yields candles, which he lights. Finally, he returns from the kitchen with a salad bowl. Placing careful servings of salad on each plate, he tries to make light conversation.*

**STEVEN** So. Do you have any hobbies?

**ZOE** *(urgently getting up)* Maybe I'd better go.

**STEVEN** Are you sure?

**ZOE** I think I should.

**STEVEN** We were doing so well.

**ZOE** Yes. It's just…

**STEVEN** What?

**ZOE** Steven. You made a salad.

**STEVEN** So?

**ZOE** This doesn't happen when people are working. This never happens in study hall.

**STEVEN** *(improvising)* Oh, come on. You don't think I made that salad for you, do you?

**ZOE** Well…

**STEVEN** It's just leftovers I had lying around, that's all.

**ZOE** Oh.

**STEVEN** I thought you might appreciate a nutritious snack, that's all. It's not like I prepared a meal for you.

**ZOE** Of course not.

**STEVEN** I'll just eat by myself. You can work if you like. And I'll sit here and eat. And watch.

**ZOE** And watch?

**STEVEN** Watch you work?

**ZOE** I better go.

**STEVEN** Do you have to?

**ZOE** There's something going on here, Steven.

**STEVEN** No there isn't. *(pause)* Why don't you join me and we can discuss it?

**ZOE** I think we better say good night. Before we get into some uncomfortable territory.

**STEVEN** Are you sure?

**ZOE** I'm sure.

**STEVEN** Do you want to take home some salad?

**ZOE** No. Thank you. Good night, Steven.

**STEVEN** Good night.

*ZOE exits. STEVEN is despondent.*

*(to audience as he cleans up)* So. It's over before it began. But this isn't a failure. We're still friends and that's okay, too. Right? Right. Eventually she'll sense what I'm feeling for her. She'll figure it out. If we're meant to be together, she'll eventually put it all together. I can wait if I have to. I can do that. I'm sure. I'm a rational human being. Now there's only one question left to answer. What am I going to do with all that pasta in the kitchen?

*RAPELL bursts through the door.*

**RAPELL** All right. What's all this then?!

*Blackout.*

## Scene Three

*STEVEN is standing in the elevator. The bell rings. A cautious ZOE enters.*

**STEVEN** Going down? *(ZOE nods. STEVEN presses the button. Pause.)* About last night…

**ZOE** Thanks for letting me use your computer.

**STEVEN** My pleasure. *(pause)* You can use it any time.

**ZOE** That's all right.

**STEVEN** *(long pause)* There's a documentary on the South Pacific on TV tonight—

**ZOE** I'm working on my thesis.

**STEVEN** Of course you are.

*Floor bell rings, ZOE starts to exit.*

Maybe some other time.

**ZOE** Maybe. *(exits)*

**STEVEN** I'll see you around… I pressed too hard. What an idiot I am. *(starting to pound his own head in frustration)* Idiot. Idiot. Idiot. Idiot. Idiot…

*This is the sight that greets AMY as she enters the elevator. She says nothing, but watches STEVEN. Eventually, he becomes aware of her presence and springs into some semblance of normalcy.*

Hi, Jeckle.

**AMY** Going up?

**STEVEN** Sure.

**AMY** *(pressing the button, beat)* Working on the book last night?

**STEVEN** That's right.

**AMY** I saw Zoe go into your apartment.

**STEVEN** She was helping me.

**AMY** I heard you put on my music.

**STEVEN** I did.

**AMY** Was that part of your research?

**STEVEN** Yes.

**AMY** Get much work done?

**STEVEN** Nothing. It was a disaster.

*The floor bell rings.*

**AMY** Steven. What's going on?

**STEVEN** I was just.... The book. I think I'm going to have to give it up.

**AMY** That's too bad. *(reaching for his hand)*

**STEVEN** *(pulling away)* Yes.

**AMY** Maybe I'll call you tonight.

**STEVEN** Sure. Do that.

**AMY** Right.

**STEVEN** Right.

*STEVEN exits.*

**AMY** *(to audience)* I know he's not telling me things. After seven years of teaching elementary students, I can tell when someone's lying. Steven's just going through a phase, that's all. I can tell. I go through phases all the time. I just never thought...

We all need anchors in our lives. Something to give us something we can count on. Something we can trust. Something we can hold and call our own. I always thought he was the most anchored person I knew. But while I was out looking for one to call my own, Steven found a new anchor. He's changing. Right before my eyes. And I can only watch. I hope it's for the best.

I just never thought you would be one of the ones to drop me.

*Fade-out.*

## Scene Four

*It is night in STEVEN's apartment. He is talking on the phone to his mother.*

**STEVEN** Yes, Mum. Things are going fine. The new neighbour? Well, I haven't seen her in a while. Not since.... No. I can't call her. It would look, well, it would look like she was right about what she thought I thought I was doing when I didn't or at least I wasn't. *(beat)* It does too make sense. She was over and I think that maybe I was... too forward with her, maybe. Mother. Mother. Mother. This is not a breakthrough.

*There is a knock on the door.*

Someone's at the door, Mum. I've got to go. Bye. Love you, too. Yes. Bye. I promise I'll get out more. *(another knock)* Bye. Bye. Bye.

*STEVEN hangs up and crosses to the door. He opens it to reveal ZOE. She is dressed as if just preparing to go to bed, pajamas and a robe. She has been crying, but she is working hard to keep her emotions under control.*

**ZOE** Hi.

**STEVEN** *(surprised)* Hi.

**ZOE** I need to use your computer.

**STEVEN** You do?

**ZOE** Right now. Is that okay?

**STEVEN** Sure.

*ZOE quickly crosses to the computer and starts typing furiously.*

Is something wrong?

**ZOE** No, no. I'm fine. I just need to work, that's all. I just need to keep my mind off things.

**STEVEN** Keep your…

**ZOE** I mean focused. I need to keep my mind focused.

**STEVEN** What's wrong?

**ZOE** *(typing)* Wrong? Nothing's wrong. Why would you think that something's wrong?

*STEVEN silently crosses over to the computer. He turns it on.*

**STEVEN** Give it a second to boot up. *(pause)* Do you want to talk about it?

**ZOE** No.

**STEVEN** Okay.

**ZOE** I should go.

**STEVEN** Okay.

*ZOE remains seated in the chair. Pause.*

**ZOE** I'd better go.

**STEVEN** If you want. *(Pause. Everything remains frozen.)* Do you want something to drink?

**ZOE** What do you have?

**STEVEN** Water, 7-Up, Diet Coke, some lemonade and a bottle of Ouzo.

**ZOE** *(crying anew)* Bring the bottle.

*STEVEN quickly runs to the kitchen and re-enters with the Ouzo. ZOE takes a long swig directly from the bottle.*

**STEVEN** What happened?

**ZOE** I got a phone call. God. You'd think I was beyond this by now.

**STEVEN** You got a phone call…

**ZOE** Yes. It was Darren.

**STEVEN** You mean…

**ZOE** Yes. That Darren. Darren the bastard.

**STEVEN** What did he say?

**ZOE** He said…. This is so stupid. I'm over him, for God's sake. He said…. I mean this is the first time I've heard from him since… since the event.

**STEVEN** Since he ran off with the sociology student. Sorry. What did he say?

**ZOE** He said he and Sandy…

**STEVEN** The sociologist.

**ZOE** He said that he and Sandy have gotten engaged.

**STEVEN** Engaged? To be married?

**ZOE** In all the time we were together, do you know how often Darren and I discussed getting married?

**STEVEN** Three times?

**ZOE** Well, maybe we didn't discuss it, but I suggested it. And every time, I mean every time, Darren rejected the idea. And then he meets this, this, this airhead…

**STEVEN** The sociologist.

**ZOE** Sandy.

**STEVEN** Her.

**ZOE** And he asks her to marry him. How could he?

**STEVEN** I don't know.

**ZOE** I can't take this anymore.

**STEVEN** Can't take what?

**ZOE** Him. Her. Them. Me.

**STEVEN** Didn't you tell me you wanted nothing more to do with Darren?

**ZOE** That's right. He's a horrible person.

**STEVEN** Didn't you say you wanted him out of your life?

**ZOE** The bastard.

**STEVEN** Right. Bastard.

**ZOE** Bastard!

**STEVEN** Didn't you tell me you were glad to be rid of him?

**ZOE** I am. I'm glad he's gone.

**STEVEN** Bastard!

**ZOE** Bastard!

**STEVEN** Then you should be happy. He's not marrying you. He's marrying Sandy the sociologist. *(ZOE breaks into fresh tears.)* Am I missing something here?

**ZOE** Oh, Steven. Poor Steven. You really don't get it, do you?

**STEVEN** Not yet.

**ZOE** Look. How can I make you understand?

**STEVEN** Explain it to me.

**ZOE** Darren and I lived together for three years before…

**STEVEN** The event.

**ZOE** Yes. And they were good years. I can still tell you what his favourite TV shows are and what he likes on his pizza and what his allergies are.

**STEVEN** Allergies?

**ZOE** Cats and nutmeg. I thought as long as I loved him, he would love me.

**STEVEN** It doesn't always work that way.

**ZOE** But it should, shouldn't it?

**STEVEN** But you can't let him influence your life this way.

**ZOE** I know. You're right. And you know what the worst part is?

**STEVEN** What?

**ZOE** I'm invited to the wedding.

**STEVEN** Are you going?

**ZOE** No. Of course not. I can't sit there and watch…

**STEVEN** The bastard.

**ZOE** Get married to that…

**STEVEN** Sociologist. Why not?

**ZOE** Because…. Because…. We had something special.

**STEVEN** I understand. *(beat)* It makes you wonder, though…

**ZOE** What?

**STEVEN** Nothing.

**ZOE** You were going to say something.

**STEVEN** Just a thought.

**ZOE** What is it?

**STEVEN** Well, if they're getting married so soon after…

**ZOE** The event.

**STEVEN** It makes you wonder…

**ZOE** What?

**STEVEN** How long were they seeing each other while the two of you were still together?

**ZOE** How long?

**STEVEN** I doubt Darren ran off with her on first viewing, and it's very unlikely they would have decided to get married without having some sort of long-term relationship. It would probably indicate that Darren was seeing Sandy for quite some period of time while the two of you were still living together.

**ZOE** Darren was seeing Sandy?

**STEVEN** Maybe.

**ZOE** While we were still together?

**STEVEN** It seems entirely possible.

**ZOE** While the two of us were living together?

**STEVEN** I'm probably wrong.

**ZOE** You're right.

**STEVEN** I am?

**ZOE** It's only logical.

**STEVEN** Darren and Sandy have probably been seeing each other for quite some time now.

**ZOE** How long?

**STEVEN** There's no basis for—

**ZOE** *How long!?*

**STEVEN** Perhaps a year?

**ZOE** A year?!

**STEVEN** Maybe two.

**ZOE** Why that…

**STEVEN** Bastard?

**ZOE** All that time we were together and he was seeing that… that…

**STEVEN** Possibly others, too.

**ZOE** I'll kill him. I swear, I'll kill him. I'll murder him. Or even worse…

**STEVEN** What?

**ZOE** I'll go to the wedding. That'll teach him.

**STEVEN** Zoe…

**ZOE** That bastard. All the time we were living together…

**STEVEN** Zoe, please…

**ZOE** And all those phone conversations he had. And I paid for the bills. My scholarship paid for those bills.

**STEVEN** Zoe…

**ZOE** I could just—

**STEVEN** Zoe! Let it go. *(beat)* We've all been hurt by people we've loved.

**ZOE** *(pause)* I'll… let it go.

**STEVEN** Good.

**ZOE** *(beat)* So you don't think I should go to the wedding?

**STEVEN** Of course not. But I think you should send Darren a gift.

**ZOE** You do?

**STEVEN** Yes. Look on the shelf. I wrote the index for a book on bomb making.

**ZOE** *(smiles)* You make me laugh, Steven Tudor.

**STEVEN** I try.

**ZOE** You're a good friend.

*ZOE gives STEVEN a friendly kiss. She then looks at the bottle in her hand.*

I should go. Thanks for caring.

**STEVEN** I do. Care.

*ZOE starts to exit.*

Zoe, do you want to come over Saturday night?

**ZOE** What?

**STEVEN** I'm having a party.

**ZOE** A party?

**STEVEN** A… a Christmas party. My annual Christmas party. I have one every year. In my apartment.

**ZOE** Really?

**STEVEN** You know, 'tis the season and all.

**ZOE** Sounds nice.

**STEVEN** I'd like it if you could come.

**ZOE** What time?

**STEVEN** Around eight?

**ZOE** Should I bring anything?

**STEVEN** You don't—

**ZOE** How about some homemade eggnog?

**STEVEN** Sure. Eggnog. That's nice. Never can have enough eggnog.

**ZOE** Great. So. Eight. Saturday. I'll bring the eggnog. See you then. *(exits)*

*STEVEN stares after her and then turns to the audience.*

**STEVEN** I know what you're thinking. And you're right. I wasn't planning to have a party. But one thing is for certain. I'm going to have one now.

*Blackout.*

## Scene Five

*The night of the party in STEVEN's apartment. Some Christmas decorations have been ineptly added to the room. AMY enters in party regalia.*

**AMY** Hiya, Heckle. *(surveys the empty room)* Nice party.

**STEVEN** *(from the kitchen)* I'm expecting more people any time now.

**AMY** Mr. Flores sends his regrets.

**STEVEN** Well, maybe less people.

*STEVEN enters from the kitchen with more decorations. He is wearing a Santa hat.*

**AMY** There are other people coming?

**STEVEN** Of course. All my friends.

**AMY** I'm here.

**STEVEN** *(putting up decorations)* Cute.

**AMY** Nice hat.

**STEVEN** I've got hats for everyone. I don't want anyone to feel left out.

**AMY** Heaven forbid. Here. Do you want a hand with that?

**STEVEN** Thanks. I'm sort of new at this. *(AMY helps with decorations.)* So. How was rehearsal last night?

**AMY** Really good. I think we're really starting to pull together. And get this. We got a gig.

**STEVEN** Someone hired you?

**AMY** Yes.

**STEVEN** To perform?

**AMY** Yes.

**STEVEN** Congratulations.

**AMY** It's just an office party and we're supposed to do nothing but Christmas carols. But you never know. There might be room for a little scat between "The Little Drummer Boy" *(Katherine K . Davis)* and "Joy to the World" *(Isaac Watts and Lowell Mason).*

**STEVEN** It's a start.

**AMY** You should come.

**STEVEN** You don't need me.

**AMY** You'd be surprised. *(STEVEN uncomfortably exits to the kitchen.)* So. A party. What brought this on?

**STEVEN** *(from the kitchen)* Do I need a reason to have a party?

**AMY** Yes.

**STEVEN** *(re-entering with Santa hats)* Well, it's Christmas. And I just thought it would be nice to celebrate this year. 'Tis the season, you know.

**AMY** So I heard.

**STEVEN** I just want to spend some time with all my friends.

**AMY** Me?

**STEVEN** Of course.

**AMY** Zoe?

**STEVEN** She's coming.

**AMY** And suddenly everything makes sense.

**STEVEN** *(pause)* I think I love her.

**AMY** What was that?

**STEVEN** I said... I love her.

**AMY** You do?

**STEVEN** I do.

**AMY** Are you sure?

**STEVEN** Of course.

**AMY** Really?

**STEVEN** I've been doing the research.

**AMY** Ah. *(pause)* Have you told her?

**STEVEN** No. But she likes me. I let her use my computer. We talk. She shares her problems with me. I help her.

**AMY** Let me give you one small warning. Friends never fall in love with friends.

**STEVEN** Never?

**AMY** Never.

**STEVEN** Not even if one of them really, truly loves the other?

**AMY** Not in my experience.

**STEVEN** *(pause)* You're wrong.

**AMY** Steven...

**STEVEN** What makes you such an expert? You've never had a relationship that has lasted more than two weeks! *(brain catching up to mouth)* Oh, God. Amy. I'm sorry. I...

**AMY** No. That's fine. You're right. I...

**STEVEN** I was upset. I mean... I'm sorry.

**AMY** No. That's all right. You're just a little confused right now. You're saying things... I mean, you're in love. That's great. I mean... I wish.... Excuse me, I think I have to go to the bathroom.

**STEVEN** Amy...

**AMY** Great party, Steven.

*AMY runs to the bathroom. STEVEN begins to follow when RAPELL bursts in.*

**RAPELL** Tidings of goodwill, fellow celebrants! I found my key. *(taking in the room)* Dear heavens. Am I the first to arrive? I'm never the first to arrive. I better go. I can't be first.

*She exits. STEVEN runs after her into the hall.*

**STEVEN** *(offstage)* No, don't. You're not first. Amy's here, Ms. Rapell. Please, come in. Please. Please. Please.

*RAPELL sullenly re-enters. She is now wearing a Santa hat. She drops on to the couch. An anxious STEVEN follows close behind.*

Where's Nicky?

**RAPELL** Nicky had a small accident. He pulled a muscle AbFlexing.

**STEVEN** Is he okay?

**RAPELL** Darling, he is simply marvellous. I haven't received the revised Carroll index yet.

**STEVEN** I know.

**RAPELL** There are twenty-three errors in that index.

**STEVEN** I'm sorry.

**RAPELL** You never make errors. At least, you never have before. Something on your mind, sweetheart? Something I should know about?

**STEVEN** *(presenting a plate of cheese and crackers)* Hors d'oeuvres?

**RAPELL** *(examining the plate with distaste)* You were right to phrase that as a question. *(A sulking AMY re-enters.)* And here's Ms. Mathias.

**AMY** Ouzo?

**STEVEN** In the fridge. *(holding up the Santa hat)* Hat?

*AMY grabs the hat and exits in the manner of someone looking for something break.*

**RAPELL** And in a party mood I see. *(pause)* So, are we going to be decorating the tree?

**STEVEN** I couldn't get one delivered.

**RAPELL** Then what are we going to do at this party?

**STEVEN** We could talk. Get to know one another better.

**RAPELL** Swell. *(silence)* How was the Ouzo?

**STEVEN** Fine. It's good.

**RAPELL** You don't have to give me my gift tonight. I can be patient.

**STEVEN** Oh. Good.

*There is a long silence as STEVEN and RAPELL sit on the couch. Finally, RAPELL crosses to the kitchen and calls to AMY.*

**RAPELL** Why don't you join us, my dear? The party is just getting rolling.

*AMY joins STEVEN and RAPELL. Time passes in silence. AMY sits. STEVEN sits. RAPELL sits. Everybody sits. Wearing Santa hats.*

**STEVEN** I can get out the *Trivial Pursuit.*

**RAPELL** *(getting up)* Well, this has been a simply marvellous party, Stephini. We must do this again next time.

**STEVEN** No. Don't go. The party's just starting. Not everybody's here yet.

**AMY** Of course not.

**RAPELL** You mean someone else actually agreed to come to this mausoleum?

**STEVEN** *(to AMY)* Why don't you put on some music?

**AMY** Okay. *(remains seated)*

**STEVEN** Amy?

**AMY** I'm trying to decide what best suits the occasion.

**RAPELL** How about "Show Me the Way to Go Home"?

*There is a knock at the door.*

**STEVEN** That's her. You can't go. Just wait. The party's just getting started. *(crosses to the door)*

**RAPELL** Her? Her who?

**AMY** Steven's new friend.

**RAPELL** Friend?

**AMY** Friend.

**RAPELL** Oh. You mean "friend."

**STEVEN** *(opening the door)* Zoe! Hello.

**ZOE** *(with pitcher of eggnog)* Hi.

**RAPELL** *(sizing her up)* Interesting.

**ZOE** Sorry I'm late.

**STEVEN** You arrived at just the right time.

**ZOE** I brought the eggnog. I hope it's enough. *(taking in the largely empty room)* It looks like I'm not the only one who's late.

**STEVEN** No. This is everyone.

**ZOE** Oh. *(looking at the jug)* I guess I brought enough.

**STEVEN** Some people couldn't make it and then there was… I mean…. You know Amy, of course.

**ZOE** Hi. Merry Christmas.

**AMY** *(beat)* I need a drink. *(exits to the kitchen)*

**STEVEN** And you've met my boss.

**ZOE** Yes. Hello.

**RAPELL** Pleasure to make your acquaintance.

**ZOE** Actually, we've met. In the hallway?

**RAPELL** What a pleasant little distraction you would make.

**ZOE** Excuse me?

**STEVEN** Do you want something to drink?

**ZOE** *(handing over the pitcher)* Eggnog.

**STEVEN** Yes. I'll get you a glass.

**ZOE** Do you have a punch bowl?

**STEVEN** I'm sure I do. Somewhere. Just wait here. I'll find something.

*STEVEN exits to the kitchen. RAPELL sizes up ZOE.*

**RAPELL** Zoe, is it?

**ZOE** Yes. And you're Ms. Rapell?

**RAPELL** But you can call me Katherine. Known our dear Steven long?

**ZOE** I just moved into the building.

**RAPELL** Do tell! And when might that have been?

**ZOE** Just about a month ago.

**RAPELL** About the time of the Carroll biography.

**ZOE** What was that?

**RAPELL** So, tell us, what have you and dear old Steverooney been up to?

*STEVEN pulls AMY from the kitchen. STEVEN has a large saucepot. AMY has started with the Ouzo.*

**STEVEN** And how have you two been getting along?

**RAPELL** Swimmingly.

**STEVEN** Zoe's a graduate student.

**AMY** Oh, don't gush, Steven.

**STEVEN** Why don't you put something on the CD player?

**RAPELL** Why don't I help you?

**AMY** Help me?

**RAPELL** It'll give us a chance to chat.

*RAPELL and AMY cross to the other side of the room where the sound system is. STEVEN turns his attention to ZOE.*

**STEVEN** I couldn't find a punch bowl, but I think this will be big enough.

**ZOE** It'll do in a pinch. *(She pours the eggnog into the pot.)*

**STEVEN** *(not even realizing he is saying it)* Zoe…

**ZOE** What?

**STEVEN** What?

**ZOE** You said my name.

**STEVEN** Did I? Sorry. I just like saying your name. I'm glad you could make it.

**ZOE** Me, too. Steven…. Can I just say something?

**STEVEN** Okay.

**ZOE** I may be overstepping the bounds, but… I really think you should get out more.

**STEVEN** Me? Out? Why?

**ZOE** Because there is more to life than this room. You have so much more to give the world than indexes.

**STEVEN** Indices.

**ZOE** Same thing.

**STEVEN & ZOE** Whatever.

**STEVEN** I don't know. I have trouble with people.

**ZOE** You're a lovely man, Steven. You're gentle… intelligent…

**STEVEN** *(embarrassed)* I'll get some cups.

**ZOE** *(taking his hand so he won't leave)* It just seems such a waste to me. You lock yourself up in this apartment when you've got so much to give.

**STEVEN** Everything I need is here.

**ZOE** No. You deserve the extras.

**STEVEN** You think so?

**ZOE** You've helped me through a very difficult time. And I just think you should go out there and show the rest of the world what kind of terrific person you are. *(STEVEN tries to speak, but he is tongue-tied.)* I'm sorry. Maybe I'm sticking my nose in where it doesn't belong.

**STEVEN** No. I appreciate the candour. It's nice to know you're thinking about me.

**ZOE** Give it some thought, okay?

**STEVEN** Sure.

**ZOE** *(pouring eggnog into cups)* Right. Do you want to try some of my eggnog? *(STEVEN is staring at her.)* Steven? Steven?

**STEVEN** *(recovering)* Sure. *(sips)*

**ZOE** What do you think?

**STEVEN** It seems to be missing something.

**ZOE** Like what?

**STEVEN** I don't know. My mother's eggnog had that sprinkly stuff on top.

**ZOE** Nutmeg. Darren was allergic to nutmeg.

**STEVEN** Oh. Sorry. I didn't mean to—

**ZOE** *(brightening)* So let's get all the nutmeg we can, shall we?

**STEVEN** We shall?

**ZOE** I want so much nutmeg, Darren will break into hives on the other side of the city.

**STEVEN** Revenge can be sweet.

**ZOE** Or spicy. Show me your kitchen.

*STEVEN and ZOE run into the kitchen like school kids. RAPELL watches them closely as AMY goes through STEVEN's CDs.*

**AMY** The closest thing he has to a Christmas album is "The Sound of Music" *(Richard Rogers and Oscar Hammerstein II).*

**RAPELL** Let's pass, shall we? One can hear "The Lonely Goatherd" only so many times in one's life. *(pause)* Has she been spending a lot of time over here?

**AMY** She uses the computer.

**RAPELL** Whatever for?

**AMY** They had music on one night.

**RAPELL** He should be working.

**AMY** And now he's throwing this party.

**RAPELL** The poor boy's not concentrating.

**AMY** Next thing you know, he'll be giving barbecues.

**RAPELL** He's being distracted from my work.

**AMY** I guess it had to happen sooner or later.

**RAPELL** What?

**AMY** He told me.... He said that he...

**RAPELL** Don't tell me he thinks he's in love? With her?

**AMY** *(best face)* I'm happy for him. I really am.

**RAPELL** She's just taking of advantage of him.

**AMY** I thought I was his best friend.

**RAPELL** You just pick out some music and I'll take care of everything.

**AMY** Okay.

*RAPELL crosses over to where STEVEN and ZOE have returned from the kitchen. They're having a taste of the heavily spiced eggnog.*

**ZOE** Oh. That's awful.

**STEVEN** Too much nutmeg?

**ZOE** That's not nutmeg. I think it's paprika.

**RAPELL** Steven, darling! Aren't you forgetting your hosting duties?

**STEVEN** Sorry?

**RAPELL** The *Trivial Pursuit*, boy. I thought we were promised a ripping game of psycho-intellectual gamesmanship.

**STEVEN** You want to play? Now?

**RAPELL** Oh, I think we simply must, don't you? Zoe?

**ZOE** If everybody's up for it.

**RAPELL** Then fetch it. Bring on *la belle jeu.*

**STEVEN** Just give me a minute to find it. And remember everyone, I'm green.

*An eager STEVEN exits.*

**RAPELL** Nice boy, isn't he?

**ZOE** Yes. Want some Hungarian eggnog?

**RAPELL** Thank you. No. But he's a little odd, too, wouldn't you say?

**ZOE** Odd? Steven? A little shy maybe.

**RAPELL** It's always the shy ones, isn't it?

**ZOE** Excuse me?

*A music selection starts playing: "You Always Hurt the One You Love" (Allan Roberts and Doris Fisher).*

**AMY** There. How's that?

**ZOE** It's not very Christmassy.

**RAPELL** Why don't you find another one, dear? Something pleasant?

*AMY turns off the music and searches the CDs again.*

**RAPELL** You don't know Steven very well, do you?

**ZOE** I like to think we're friends.

**RAPELL** That's how it always starts.

**ZOE** What do you mean?

**RAPELL** You know how obsessive the quiet ones are. They fixate on a person.

**ZOE** Fixate? Steven?

**RAPELL** They have so little in their lives. And then someone new comes along. They start getting a little compulsive—

**ZOE** Now wait a minute. Are we talking about Steven?

**RAPELL** Who else?

**AMY** Are *The Rolling Stones* Christmassy?

**RAPELL** I'd say they're the anti-Christmassy.

**AMY** No?

**RAPELL** No. *(AMY returns to her search.)* Did you see the index he wrote for the Carroll book?

**ZOE** No.

**RAPELL** Your name appears over and over in it.

**ZOE** My name?

**RAPELL** I'm sure he doesn't even realize he's doing it. But it's par for the course.

*STEVEN re-enters with the game.*

**STEVEN** I've got the game.

**RAPELL** Wonderful, darling. Now why don't you go get me a drink before we start?

**STEVEN** Pepsi?

**RAPELL** Whatever. *(STEVEN goes to the kitchen.)* He puts up such a good front, doesn't he? But it'll only be a matter of time before he's camped outside your front door and following you from street corner to street corner...

**ZOE** Oh, come on...

**RAPELL** You must have noticed how attentive he's been to you.

**ZOE** He's just being friendly.

**RAPELL** Of course he is. They always are.

*STEVEN re-enters with a Pepsi.*

**STEVEN** Here's your Pepsi.

**RAPELL** Oh, that wasn't for me. That was for dear Amy. Why don't you give that to her and find out what colour she wants to be?

**STEVEN** Okay.

*STEVEN smiles at ZOE as he crosses to AMY.*

**RAPELL** He's taken a liking to you, I can tell.

**ZOE** And I like him.

**RAPELL** Of course you do. That's what makes it all so sad. It starts so innocently.

**ZOE** Why are you telling me all this?

**RAPELL** I like Steven. I really do. Why else would I keep bailing him out?

**ZOE** Bailing him out? Steven is not a criminal.

**RAPELL** Of course not. But before you know it.... You just have to watch for the signs.

**ZOE** What kind of signs?

**RAPELL** Has he ever been struck speechless by the mere sight of you?

**ZOE** I wouldn't say speechless...

**RAPELL** Have you ever found him unable to take his eyes off you?

**ZOE** I don't—

**RAPELL** Has he ever said your name for no other reason than it has given him pleasure?

**ZOE** Yes. Yes, he has.

**RAPELL** There you are, then. It's already started. But I'm sure you have nothing to worry about. After all, up until recently, stalking was a perfectly acceptable form of courtship.

**ZOE** I can't deal with this. I'm still—

**RAPELL** It's rather flattering really. Until the end.

**ZOE** The end?

**RAPELL** Maybe I'm wrong. Maybe he just wants to be your pal and nothing more. There's only one sure way of finding out. Just ask him if he's in love with you. If he says you're just friends, then everything's fine. If not.... All you have to do is ask.

*STEVEN and AMY join RAPELL and ZOE.*

**STEVEN** Prepare to be pursued! Amy's going to be blue.

**AMY** *(a little tipsy)* Because I'm feeling kind of blue.

**RAPELL** Ask him.

**ZOE** I'm not going to ask him.

**RAPELL** All right. But don't blame me.

**STEVEN** Hey Zoe. What colour do you want to be?

**ZOE** Colour?

**STEVEN** For *Trivial Pursuit.* Ms. Rapell?

**RAPELL** I think I'll just watch. I don't want to miss a moment.

**ZOE** Maybe I should go home.

**STEVEN & RAPELL** You can't leave.

**RAPELL** We've just started the game. I just love *Trivial Pursuit*, don't you? It's all so simple. You ask a question. You get an answer. And if the right question is asked, you get the answer to everything. Isn't that right, Steven?

**STEVEN** Exactly. The foundation of the scientific method.

**RAPELL** I must imagine you are quite the expert at this game.

**STEVEN** I don't want to brag...

**RAPELL** Zoe has a question for you, Steven.

**STEVEN** Really?

**AMY** What's going on here?

**STEVEN** I'm willing to answer any question.

April Banigan, Matt Baram, Blair Wensley and Rhonda NuGent
Shadow Theatre 1999 production
*photo by Ian Jackson (photo courtesy of* The Edmonton Journal*)*

**RAPELL** Good for you. You see, Zoe? Steven wants to give you the answer. And darling, you know you have to ask.

**STEVEN** Go ahead, Zoe.

**ZOE** Steven… I don't want to do this.

**STEVEN** Don't worry. Ask me anything. I'm ready.

**ZOE** Steven…

**STEVEN** Anything for you.

*RAPELL looks significantly at ZOE. ZOE braces herself.*

**ZOE** Steven…?

**RAPELL** If you don't ask, then I will.

**ZOE** Steven…

**STEVEN** Yes?

**ZOE** Do you like me?

**STEVEN** Of course I do. Is that the question?

**RAPELL** No. The next one is for all the marbles.

**AMY** Is this "Truth or Consequences"? Did I miss something?

**STEVEN** Zoe?

**ZOE** Steven. Are you in love with me?

*STEVEN is surprised. He looks about the room. AMY turns away. RAPELL shows him encouragement.*

**STEVEN** Yes. I love you, Zoe.

**ZOE** You do?

**STEVEN** *(moving in)* Yes. I do. With all my heart.

*STEVEN moves toward ZOE, but she backs away.*

**ZOE** No.

**STEVEN** What is it?

**ZOE** I can't… I don't know… I've got to go.

**STEVEN** But Zoe…

*STEVEN reaches out to touch her. ZOE flinches at his touch.*

**ZOE** Don't…

*ZOE runs to the door. STEVEN calls to her.*

**STEVEN** Zoe. I love you. I really do.

*ZOE freezes. RAPELL motions her out. ZOE dashes out the door. A concerned AMY follows. STEVEN starts to follow as well, but he is intercepted by RAPELL.*

**RAPELL** What have you done, Steven? What have you done? You've really gone and done it this time.

**STEVEN** But…

**RAPELL** What were you thinking? You've pushed too far.

**STEVEN** I have?

**RAPELL** You have. And it's really just as well. She never really cared about you, you know.

**STEVEN** Zoe…

**RAPELL** The only people who care about you are right here in this room. Nobody else does and nobody else ever will.

**STEVEN** No, I…

**RAPELL** I'm sorry, pumpkin, but I must be honest. And the fact is you are simply not designed to experience love. There are people in this world, dear child, who are destined to die alone and unloved. And you are one of those people.

**AMY** *(re-entering, sobered up)* What did you say to her?

**RAPELL** I'm only telling you this because I can't let you remain trapped in this silly little daydream of yours. It's time to wake up to reality. You know I'm right.

**STEVEN** But I'm in love.

**RAPELL** You don't know. You can't know. You've never been in love, child. And you never will be.

**STEVEN** I have to go to her.

**RAPELL** You love her? It's all over. Accept it. You have to stay here, darling. Right here in this apartment. This is your world. Right here. Safe, certain, never changing…

**AMY** Steven…

**RAPELL** And that's fine. That's good. For you, Steven. This is your life, Steven Tudor.

**STEVEN** I don't know what—

**RAPELL** You don't need her. Not when you've got all this. Your computer, your books, your work…

**STEVEN** My work.

**RAPELL** *(manoeuvring him to the computer)* That's right. And you've been neglecting it, haven't you? Poor boy. Why don't you just pull yourself together and I'll turn on the computer? It's just what you need right now. Put your brain to work and give that poor silly heart some rest.

*As she has been listening AMY has drifted behind RAPELL.*

**AMY** Ms. Rapell?

**RAPELL** *(turning to AMY)* Call me Katherine.

*AMY decks RAPELL, who collapses in a heavy heap behind the couch.*

**STEVEN** Amy!

**AMY** Go. Talk to her.

**STEVEN** But…

**AMY** Go, Heckle. Now.

*STEVEN dashes out the door. AMY is left with the unconscious RAPELL. With not a little wonder, she looks at her fist and then discovers a smile of triumph.*

Well, if this is Christmas, I can hardly wait to see what he has planned for New Year's Eve.

*Blackout.*

## Scene Six

*It's two days later, in STEVEN's apartment. He is on the phone.*

**STEVEN** The Lewis Carroll is all over and done with. I've just emailed it over, Mr. Bradshaw. I'm sure it'll be fine. Thank you, sir. When can I.... Yes, sir. I'll be waiting here for the messenger. No, sir. I look forward to my next assignment. Thank you, sir. I was in need of a change. Thank you, Mr. Bradshaw. Goodbye, Mr. Bradshaw.

*STEVEN hangs up the phone. There is a knock on the door. STEVEN opens the door. It is ZOE.*

**ZOE** Hello.

**STEVEN** Hi.

**ZOE** May I come in?

**STEVEN** Of course. By all means. *(ZOE enters.)* How are you? I haven't seen you since...

**ZOE** Amy told me what happened. I'm sorry, Steven. I thought...

**STEVEN** I know what you thought. It's all right.

**ZOE** I'm sorry about leaving. I'm sorry about what happened.

**STEVEN** Don't be. Ms. Rapell can be very convincing.

**ZOE** But I shouldn't have believed it.

**STEVEN** How could you believe otherwise? You barely know me. *(pause)* Anyway, I'm not working for Ms. Rapell any more. No one is working for Ms. Rapell any more. If I stay the course, I might even be considered for my own editorship. I might really be my own boss.

*Silence.*

**ZOE** I'm not in love with you, Steven.

**STEVEN** I know.

**ZOE** I thought we were friends.

**STEVEN** We still are. I hope.

**ZOE** Yes. If you want.

**STEVEN** I do.

**ZOE** Me, too.

**STEVEN** Then that's it, then.

**ZOE** Yes. *(beat)* Steven, if I knew how you felt...

**STEVEN** I know. Nothing more needs to be said.

**ZOE** *(pause)* So. Friends.

**STEVEN** Always. And if you ever want to use my computer again...

**ZOE** I won't be needing the computer any time soon. I told Professor Hudson I'd be joining him in Samoa.

**STEVEN** So you'll be putting your thesis on hold?

**ZOE** For at least a year.

**STEVEN** And you'll be moving out?

**ZOE** Yes.

**STEVEN** I see.

**ZOE** But I'll be back.

**STEVEN** Good. *(pause)* When do you leave?

**ZOE** Next week.

**STEVEN** That soon? We'll have to do something together before you go.

**ZOE** Yes. But not another party.

**STEVEN** No. Not another party.

*There is silence. After a moment, ZOE gets up and crosses to STEVEN. She awkwardly, sweetly, sincerely gives him a kiss. STEVEN is speechless. Pause.*

**ZOE** I'd better get going. I have to get my life organized.

**STEVEN** Don't we all?

*ZOE crosses to the exit.*

Oh. Wait a minute. *(STEVEN rushes to the kitchen and quickly returns.)* Here. It's your plate.

**ZOE** I still have your book.

**STEVEN** Keep it. It's a Christmas present. From me to you.

**ZOE** Thank you. I'm sorry. I didn't get you anything.

**STEVEN** You've given me so much already.

**ZOE** *(pause)* Goodbye, Steven Tudor.

**STEVEN** Goodbye, Zoe Pryce.

**STEVEN & ZOE** *(pause)* See you. *(beat)* Bye.

*They share the moment. And then ZOE exits. We slowly shift into the dream cue again. STEVEN addresses the audience.*

**STEVEN** My name is Steven Tudor. And this was my life.

Zoe left on the plane this morning. Amy and I drove her to the airport. Zoe and I spent the whole ride talking about recent developments in Polynesian politics, advances in the aviation industry and Bernoulli's Principle. I think Amy was incredibly bored, but she didn't say a word. Good old Jeckle. It was a very sentimental goodbye at the departure lounge. I was crying. Zoe was crying. And Amy complained we were acting like her students again. And then she started crying. It was very embarrassing. Not at all the way logical adults should act. I enjoyed it a great deal.

*AMY drifts into the apartment, dreamlike.*

Amy didn't say a word all the way back. Not until we got home.

**AMY** Heckle?

**STEVEN** What is it, Jeckle?

**AMY** You're my anchor. You know that?

**STEVEN** I know.

*AMY smiles wistfully and gently kisses STEVEN. She exits with a glance in his direction.*

I'm going to see Amy perform tonight. In all the years I've known her, I've never heard her sing. Not on stage. In front of an audience of strangers. I want to hear that.

*Lights come up, isolating ZOE. She is sitting on the plane, reading* The Annotated Alice.

**ZOE** "You've woken me out of such a lovely dream…"

*STEVEN crosses to the door and, for the first time, puts on a coat.*

**STEVEN** I've lived the last month as if I were in a dream.

**ZOE** Said Alice.

**STEVEN** Unsure if I was the dreamer…

**ZOE** "And you've been along with me…"

**STEVEN** Or just a thing in someone else's dream.

**ZOE** *(closing the book)* "All through the Looking Glass world."

**STEVEN** There is only one logical conclusion.

**ZOE** *(smiling at the memory)* Steven… *(and she fades from view)*

**STEVEN** It really doesn't matter who dreamed the dream. It doesn't matter if I was the dreamer or just a pawn in someone else's fantasy. The important thing is the dream itself. A dream of love. And someday, if I'm lucky, there will be another dream. The looking glass will open wide again, the Red King will doze and I'll be carried away by fantasy, folly and affection.

**VOICE** The Red King's Dream.

**STEVEN** At least one can always hope.

**VOICE** *Through the Looking Glass and What Alice Found There.*

**STEVEN** Can't one?

*And STEVEN steps out his door into the wide, scary, mysterious world. He pauses in the door frame feeling the enormity of the undertaking and then, having made up his mind, closes it behind him.*

*Fade-out.*

*The End.*

# Blowfish

By Vern Thiessen

# About
# Vern Thiessen

Vern Thiessen is one of Canada's most produced playwrights. His work has been seen across Canada, the United States and Europe, including *Shakespeare's Will*, *Apple*, *Einstein's Gift*, *Blowfish*, *Vimy* and *The Resurrection Of John Frum*. Vern is the recipient of numerous awards, including the Elizabeth Sterling Haynes Award for Outstanding New Play, The City of Edmonton Arts Achievement Award, The University of Alberta Alumni Award for Excellence, The Canadian Jewish Playwriting Competition and the Governor General's Literary Award, Canada's highest honour for playwriting. He has also been nominated for several Alberta Literary Awards and the prestigious Siminovitch Prize in Theatre. Vern received his BA from the University of Winnipeg and an MFA from the University of Alberta. He has served as Playwright in Residence at Workshop West Theatre (where he founded the Playwrights' Garage program) and the Citadel Theatre in Edmonton. He is a Past President of both the Playwrights Guild of Canada and the Writer's Guild of Alberta.

*Blowfish* was commissioned by Workshop West Theatre in 1995. It was subsequently given public workshops at: Workshop West's Springboards Festival, in February 1996; Alberta Theatre Projects' playRites Festival, in March 1996; and the Saskatchewan Playwrights Centre's Spring Festival of New Plays, in May 1996.

*Blowfish* was further developed and co-produced by Northern Light Theatre (Edmonton) and the National Arts Centre, Ottawa. It opened November 6, 1996 at Commerce Place (Edmonton), with the following company:

| | |
|---|---|
| LUMIERE | John Kirkpatrick |
| CELLIST | Christine Hanson |
| ASSISTANTS | Adam Blocka, David Chapman |
| | Nicola Devine, Emily Dykes |
| | Kirsten Kilburn, Becca Murtha |
| | Trina Pozzolo, Ian Rowe |

Directed by DD Kugler
Designed by Bretta Gerecke
Stage Manager: Susan Hayes
Catering: Gourmet Goodies

---

*Blowfish* transferred to the Studio Theatre of the National Arts Centre (Ottawa) on November 28, 1996, with the following company:

| | |
|---|---|
| LUMIERE | John Kirkpatrick |
| CELLIST | Christine Hanson |
| ASSISTANTS | Heather Jopling, Susan Hayes |

Directed by DD Kugler
Designed by Bretta Gerecke
Stage Manager: Susan Hayes
Catering: Chef Kurt Waldele and the NAC catering staff
Studio Chief: Jim Reynolds

## Characters

LUMIERE
ASSISTANTS

In the original production, LUMIERE played all of the following incidental characters. The assistants may appear as these characters, but preferably only as shadows of LUMIERE's memory and not in any naturalistic way.

BRIAN MULRONEY
MILA MULRONEY
MOM
FLETCHER
TROOPER
GUARD
WAITRESS
GREEKS
SECRETARY
VOICE

## Notes

*Blowfish* runs approximately eighty minutes, which does not include the intermission where the meal is served.

*Blowfish* was originally performed using live music and real food. It is highly recommended that producers include some form of food, be it a buffet, a sit-down meal or munchies. Music and/or sound also play a crucial role in this play. As in the original production, live music/sound may be used to set the play's mood; entertain the audience during intermission; establish leitmotifs for various characters, stories and time periods; or inspire images of weather that appear frequently throughout the play.

# Blowfish

## Act One

*A room. A long table with food. Large knives. A musician plays. Perhaps various screens that project images. The mood is charmed elegance, calculated opulence, precise lushness. As LUMIERE greets his guests, he treats them to an assortment of beverages and hors d'oeuvres. LUMIERE, a man in his mid-thirties, is dressed impeccably. Nevertheless, his demeanour is edgy and a bit ragged. He leads the catering, along with numerous ASSISTANTS. When people have had time to settle, LUMIERE begins.*

**LUMIERE** Hello. And thank you for coming.

My name is Lumiere. I am a caterer, and what I have for you tonight is a fête, a special event. I've requested your presence here this evening—and you have been so good as to oblige—for a variety of reasons. Number one: to eat. As much as you like. We have victuals to meet your every dining desire; we have foodstuffs to tantalize your discerning palate; we have edibles that will nourish your mind, as well as your soul; we have it all. Number two: to listen. To me. Tell a few stories, nothing too dull or overly long, I promise. Just a few anecdotes to help you digest and, hopefully, in the process, entertain and... enlighten you. Number three: to observe, to witness, to...

But more on that later. Until then, rest, relax and be assured that throughout this evening's event, I am here to serve you – my esteemed guests.

Let me tell you a story.

*Thunder threatens in the distance.*

---

**LUMIERE** The brand new 1979 Ford barrels down Highway 3 and turns off onto a dirt road. Gravel and dust fly.

The driver is not speeding.

He is sixteen years old and this is his first day driving by himself after acquiring his Alberta driver's licence.

He is not stoned.
He is not drunk.
He is not careless.

His parents are loving and encouraging, but do not spoil him. He makes his own lunches. He does his own homework. Occasionally he masturbates. But he always cleans up afterwards, and is fully cognizant of its moral implications and biological purpose. He mows the lawn Saturdays. He plays ball with his... brother.

He goes for his driver's licence as soon as he turns sixteen. And—like most teenagers—as soon as he receives it, he goes to his father and asks him for the keys, who, after a number of questions and warnings, gives the keys to his son, who happily—but not deliriously—starts the engine.

A taste of freedom. The brink of adulthood. His whole life before him.

The brand new 1979 Ford barrels down Highway 3 and turns off onto a dirt road. Gravel and dust fly.

*Thunder threatens.*

The clouds brew all day long in the western sky. Now, in the early evening, a swirling storm boils onto the dirt-and-gravel road. Hail splatters the windshield of the 1979 Ford, making the teen's visibility less than desirable. A cold coil of wind sends the brand new Ford twisting and turning on the wet road.

The teen does not panic. He brakes normally.
Cold rain. Loose gravel. A deep ditch. Metal and fibreglass fly.
A piece of the Ford's frame,
Through the windshield,
Through the nose,
To the brain.

*Pause.*

The teen never speaks intelligibly again. He cannot communicate, he cannot walk unaided and his nose runs endlessly. The family wonders who is responsible for this – God? or Fate? or Ford?

Later, the teen's brother and the teen's parents send him to an institution, where everyone who visits the teen (now a man) takes him to be defective from birth, or crazy, or both.

He will… die.

Eventually.

Would anyone like some more?

---

*The ASSISTANTS attend to people as needed.*

**LUMIERE** As I said, my name is Lumiere, and I am a caterer.

I might remind you at this time that caterers are not chefs, although like chefs we prepare a great deal of the meal. Unlike chefs, caterers do not indulge themselves in the food. We are rarely overweight. We don't wear tall hats. We do not taste the soup and say "a little more salt." We rarely have fits of anger and never throw dishes at our serving staff, as do chefs. We forgo ego.

Unlike chefs, my most important role is not to create the food, but to serve the food. To you. To make the most mundane hors d'oeuvre exciting, and the most exotic seem irresistible. To ensure the napkin is properly folded, the soup spoon precisely placed, the room lovingly lit to match the desired atmosphere and mood. The smallest detail must be perfect. Timing is everything.

For the caterer, food is only the medium. My calling is to create ceremony, to realize ritual.

A birthday party, for example, demands not only a cake, but the perfect cake that—along with specifically chosen candles and carefully selected liqueurs—creates an atmosphere of friendly fun, savoury celebration, a yearning for youth and acceptable indulgence. Wedding receptions require an illusion of intimacy: bouquets of benevolence, lighting, sublime spirits, a miraculous meal, an atmosphere heavy with hope.

Funerals? Well!

*A number of ASSISTANTS equipped with nail files, clippers and pumice stones begin to give LUMIERE a manicure.*

Food is comforting, and after a long day of weeping and keening, eating a sandwich brings much-needed relief and nourishment to the grieving body. Whether the funeral is a sombre service for a solitary stranger, or a spectacular soirée for a celebrated socialite, a few rudimentary rules are essential:

Nothing gooey, nothing gaudy. Nothing bitter, nothing bony. Nothing too hard to chew, too hard to digest, too much like the human body, like human flesh, like—

Well, you get my drift.

*He inspects his nails.*

*(to ASSISTANTS)* Thank you. *(They leave.)*

I confess it: I am fascinated by food and distracted by death.

---

**LUMIERE** There are, after all, only four things in this world that link us as human beings:

Number one: Food. We all have to eat.
Number two: Death. We all have to die.
Number three: The Weather…

*A fulmination.*

And number four: Politics.

Without weather, we have no food. Without food, we have death. And the common thing about food, death and the weather, is that we have no control over any of them. Let's face it, if you had to go out and sow an acre of oats, you wouldn't know where to begin. You wouldn't know how to forecast a storm if a wavering barometer stared you in the face. And you certainly wouldn't know how to bury a dead person, now would you?

Would you?

Politics is people. People like you and me. People converging in groups: families, churches, governments, unions and political parties. The farmer, the weatherman, the undertaker. We give those people the unthankful job of trying to control things that are, for the most part, uncontrollable. Politicians, on the other hand, have been given the task of serving the public's hope that some things in life actually may be controllable: terrorism, unemployment, specialty channels, assisted suicide…

---

**LUMIERE** My parents were the kind of people who religiously voted—against the trend. If the Grits got in, they voted Conservative. If the Tories were strong, they voted NDP. And part of this Canadian electoral rite was to attend a campaign rally, in which my mother would inevitably embarrass everyone involved by holding up *me and my brother* as an example of everything that had gone wrong in the country. We were "the children whose parents couldn't afford to buy them a ball glove," or "the boys whose parents had to pay too much tax."

Mom knew how to work these things. She would descend on the candidate and ask pointed questions; camera bulbs would flash, the candidate's lackey would scribble down my parent's name, and eventually ball gloves would arrive in the mail or banks would call with new scholarship schemes.

And so it happened that in 1984 I graduated from university and—surprise, surprise—I didn't have a job. My dad was at a funeral and my brother was not around, when my mother took me to a Progressive Conservative rally. Not to support them, but to confront them. After all, Brian Mulroney himself would be there.

My mother put on the practical, no-nonsense pantsuit she always wore to these events. We went to the barbecue and waited for the appropriate cue, which came after the speeches, just when the press started to scrum.

Mulroney got up, and for the first time in my life, I couldn't take my eyes off the podium. Standing beside him was the most stunning creature I had ever laid eyes upon. I'll never forget the warm, fall day I first saw her.

Mila…

She was finishing a homemade hors d'oeuvre: a simple cracker, cheddar cheese and half-cherry tomato, with a toothpick. But she lifted it to her lips like it was the finest Russian caviar, like an oyster freshly culled from the warmest, deepest waters. Young, vivacious, friendly, sleek as an otter, legs for days, speaks five languages, beautiful sweater with ruby necklace and matching earrings, cool Jackie O. sunglasses...

I could have devoured her.

**BRIAN** Uh, Mila and I have been campaigning together for sixteen hours every day, and we're going to keep it up seven days a week if you'll promise to send—

**LUMIERE** Whoever to Ottawa. As the applause began, Brian and Mila stepped off the podium into the scrum of reporters. My mother elbowed me out of my reverie, and headed through the crowd like a salmon heads upstream to deliver the precious egg.

**MOM** *(bellows)* Excuse me, excuse me, Mr. Mulroney!

**BRIAN** Uh, Yes?

**MOM** I want to know why my son here can't find a job after three years of university training.

**LUMIERE** My mother failed to understand that a BA doesn't get anyone a job, and certainly not when your degree is in philosophy.

**BRIAN** *(hesitating)* Well...

**MILA** What's your name?

**LUMIERE** That voice. Like a fine claret: smooth, sweet, with a firm finish.

**MILA** What's your name?

**LUMIERE** She looked at me, and she knew. She knew I was mortified. She took me out of the scrum and pulled me to the side, as my mother battled it out with Brian and his assistants.

**MILA** It must be very difficult for someone your age, especially when John Turner drops Celine Hervieux-Payette from the Liberal cabinet. I mean, she's the Youth Minister.

**LUMIERE** I didn't hear much else. I only smelled her soul, revelled in her rays, felt her healing touch. She took down my name and promised to send me the Conservative Party plan on grants and tax credits for youth employment. Which I later received, along with a photo of her and Brian. On the back of the photo she wrote:

**MILA** "Serve others, and others will serve you."

**LUMIERE** I had the photo enlarged, then I cut out Brian, and hung Mila up on my wall. The smaller photo with the note I kept in my pocket for a long time, right up until...

*Pause.*

That chance encounter changed my life.

I was lazy, living at home, and had a philosophy degree. I didn't know what I wanted, I didn't know what I believed in, I had no… vision.

But after meeting Mila, I became a Young Conservative: independent, ambitious, responsible, debt-free, entrepreneurial, driven. I left home, moved to the city and got a job as a security guard in a mall. Being in a mall landed me a job in a pet shop, selling weasels, where I met a man who spent his summers killing rats on the Alberta/Saskatchewan border (Alberta prides itself on being a "rat free" province). I spent the summer poisoning rats, which landed me in Medicine Hat, where I ended up writing instruction manuals for new pesticide-application devices, which led to various freelance writing jobs in Calgary, where I became, for a time, the person who wrote press releases for an organization called Canadians For a Better Canada, whose more radical members were accused of beating a man into unconsciousness. The man recovered, the radicals were convicted and I was out of a job.

But. My work with Canadians For a Better Canada had put me in contact with a number of groups in Ohio, Oklahoma and Texas. And so it happened that I ended up in that part of the world known broadly as "America's Breadbasket."

*A lamenting wind.*

---

**LUMIERE** The first time I met Robert Fletcher was in a corn field in Ohio. He was from the Three Hills area of Alberta, but spent a lot of his time in the States. People who knew Fletcher called him The Prophet.

**FLETCHER** See that?

**LUMIERE** Says Fletcher.

**FLETCHER** Have yourself a good look.

**LUMIERE** He points to a section of rotten, flattened corn crops.

**FLETCHER** That's what I mean. That's what we're trying to stop.

**LUMIERE** I stare at the wilting maize.

The Hopi Indians believed that corn was divinely granted to humanity as the Staff of Life. They dug deep pits in Mother Earth to store the consecrated cornmeal alongside their dead.

We retire to Fletcher's cabin deep in the countryside for beers and burgers. Fletcher was good with a spatula, and he flipped the hamburgers on the barbecue with a certain care, concern and affection that could only come with military training. It has been my experience that military personnel are almost always excellent barbecue chefs.

We eat the burgers in silence, whereafter Fletcher places a dossier labelled "secret" on the clean kitchen table.

**FLETCHER** That corn? That corn could have fed hundreds of people and it was destroyed.

**LUMIERE** Destroyed?

**FLETCHER** Destroyed. There were exactly sixteen twisters in that section of corn within a month. The meteorological chances of that happening are so astronomically small as to be nearly impossible.

**LUMIERE** Wow...

**FLETCHER** Wow is right. They're trying to kill us.

**LUMIERE** Who?

**FLETCHER** The government, that's who!

**LUMIERE** Fletcher carefully opens the dossier and shows me a number of documents. He believed these documents were evidence. Evidence that the CIA and the Pentagon had been secretly manipulating weather systems. With the silent support of the government.

**FLETCHER** They're starving their own people.

**LUMIERE** Why?

**FLETCHER** To test this weapon they know they can't test anywhere else. No different than nuclear testing or chemical warfare. Weather Warfare. It's the next thing.

**LUMIERE** I don't know, Fletcher, don't you think the weather's pretty much a random thing?

**FLETCHER** That's what I used to think... that's just the way I used to think...

---

**LUMIERE** Once upon a time, there was a teenager. This teenager belonged to a family who lived in a small-to-medium-sized home, in a small-to-medium-sized city, in a western province, in a place known as Canada.

The city the teen grew up in was a normal kind of city, and the home the teen grew up in was a normal kind of home, with all the normal, small-to-medium-sized home-like features.

With two exceptions:

Number one: The teen had a brother. A twin. And until he was sixteen, the teen shared a room with this twin brother.

Exception number two: The home of the teen was also the business office of the teen's parents, who were morticians. Or funeral directors, as they liked to call themselves. It was their job to look after people in times of bereavement and grief, and so the teen's home was an important and unusual home.

There was a kind of tunnel.

It connected the house to the funeral home. So that in order to get to the office of the funeral home, one would have to go through the tunnel. And in this tunnel was the "prep" room, or embalming room.

The teen brothers loved and feared the prep room.

Once, the boys were sent to get the Thanksgiving turkey from the deep freeze, which because of the necessity for constant cool conditions, was naturally located in the prep room. Quickly and quietly, the brothers carried the frozen bird across the clean porcelain tiles gleaming under bright fluorescent lights.

Oft times, the faint and muffled cries of grieving customers travelled from the funeral office down the tunnel toward them. Now and then, the brothers peaked through the door to catch a glimpse of their parents "dressing" the body, preparing it for burial. Like juice through a straw, the brothers watched blood drain from the cadavers, and replaced with fluids to better preserve and present them.

Contrary to popular belief, the household of the mortician parents and their twin sons was one full of mirth and levity. The parents loved their sons, the sons loved each other and often the family would play jokes on each other.

Like the time dinner guests were over, and all had retired to the living room for coffee, when suddenly, an eyeball rolled out into the middle of the floor. The guests were transfixed with horror, the parents with embarrassment. One teen bent down and touched it gingerly. Then, he popped it in his mouth.

A gasp from all.

"It's glass!" the teen said, then popped it from his mouth and threw it to his twin brother, whereafter they proceeded to play catch with the glass eyeball. When it was realized that this was nothing more than a teenage prank, and that no morbidity was meant, the family and guests all had a good laugh at death.

When the teen was sixteen, he took an abrupt interest in his parents' work and learned the family trade – its fascinating history and business practices. He learned to polish coffins, drive the hearse, coordinate grave-site activities and assist in prep work.

*Pause.*

Years later… when the parents died unexpectedly, the teen, now a man, insisted on performing the prep himself. The parents had died a violent death and the bodies were not cooperative, making the reconstruction, dressing and embalming procedure a distressing affair.

Slowly, and with great care, the son washes and cleans his mother, manicures her nails, applies her makeup, perfumes her skin and dresses her in the pantsuit she loved to wear.

John Kirkpatrick and Christine Hanson
*photo by Ellis Brothers Photography*

He creates a smooth lather, and dipping the razor in the water, brings the blade to his father's chin. Tears race down the son's skin to his father's, as he scrapes away the final stubble of life.

The son works late into the night.

He speaks to them.

Chastising them.

Reassuring them.

Telling them things he never before dared to voice.

"I love you… I love you so…"

He washes his hands and cleans the instruments. Calls are made: priest, florist, cemetery, stone cutters. Obituaries are written and caskets chosen. Then he lays his parents to rest on a bed of the finest oak.

Finally, dirt is thrown on the caskets, and the oak once more takes root in the earth below.

*LUMIERE leans on a chair. The ASSISTANTS enter with razor, water, mirror, etc.*

You don't mind if I rest for a moment, I hope. You should never see a caterer sitting. Ever. It is very bad manners and can be very disturbing to the customers. But, please, don't be alarmed.

*LUMIERE sits. The ASSISTANTS give him a shave. LUMIERE meditates. Another ASSISTANT enters.*

**ASSISTANT** Sir?

*Pause.*

Sir?

*Pause.*

Sir?

**LUMIERE** *What?!*

*Pause.*

*What?!*

*Pause.*

*I'm busy! Can you not see that I am busy?!*

**ASSISTANT** *(glances at watch)* Sir…

**LUMIERE** How long?

**ASSISTANT** Ten minutes or so, sir.

**LUMIERE** Right.

*Pause. LUMIERE gazes at himself in the mirror. He turns to the ASSISTANTS.*

Thank you.

*The ASSISTANTS leave.*

The main course will be served shortly.

---

**LUMIERE** A long, cold, dark day. A dusty rural road. A big sky. A big hunger. The van barrels across the northern prairie toward Flin Flon. Dust and gravel fly. I pull into the five-star motel – five stars because it's the only one in town.

And I say to myself, I say: "Why? Why in Christ's name did I become a Schwann Meat salesman?"

"Because I love it," I tell myself, and I have yet another drink. The pinball machine whines. The darts are thrown a little too hard. The solids and stripes break against my brain like a hammer against the minerals and rocks that support this scuzzy town. This town…

**WAITRESS** How's everything?

**LUMIERE** The same question, in every town, at every lunch, at every dinner.

Never eat in the Chinese restaurants. Don't assume you'll get brown bread. Make sure it's not really Tang. Salads cost ten dollars—they've got to fly in the lettuce, we're so far north. Always order the clubhouse, it's the hardest thing to get wrong. The waitress comes by.

**WAITRESS** How's everything?

**LUMIERE** "It's fine," I used to say, when I first started this job. "It's fine," I say, as I swallow another clod of rancid veal cutlet, another order of synthetic mashed potatoes, another glass of instant milk.

"It's fine."

Sixteen months after my first meeting with Fletcher; sixteen months after giving the Young Conservative thing another try; after sixteen months trying to sell Schwann Frozen Veal Cordon Bleu, Schwann Frozen Pork Chops and Schwann Frozen Chicken Breasts to rural housewives with *no* dispensable income; after sixteen months, I have moved from one to thirty-five cigarettes a day, from one drink after work to…. After sixteen months, the waitress asks me:

**WAITRESS** How's everything?

**LUMIERE** And for some reason, I say, I say: "Not very good, really. Not very good at all. These potatoes are awful." The shock on her face – unforgettable. I have turned her world upside down.

And I think: Ah hah! If only I could get a good meal; if only I could eat and not consume; if only I could serve and not just sell...

I could change my world.

*Pause.*

That night I am asleep.

"Hello?"

**VOICE** Lumiere?

**LUMIERE** Yes...

**VOICE** I have a message for you.

**LUMIERE** Yes?

**VOICE** It's your parents.

**LUMIERE** Yes?

**VOICE** There's been an accident.

**LUMIERE** Oh?

**VOICE** They're dead. Come back as quick as you can.

**LUMIERE** And I cry such tears of joy, I wail such lamentable happiness, such overwhelmingly awful feelings of felicity fill my soul that I go straight out to the local Chinese restaurant, order the greasiest seafood dinner on the menu, shovel down the fetid shrimp, pay, leaving a good tip, walk out the door and throw-up my entire life. I was saved. Death had saved me.

It was then I decided to go into catering.

*The ASSISTANTS burst in with trays of food and place them near LUMIERE.*

---

*LUMIERE begins to prepare some of the intermission entrees. His creations are simple, yet awe-inspiring. He prepares them with incredible ease in a cool detached state. It is practiced, precise and is not ostentatious in any way.*

**LUMIERE** Food has a way of sounding its purpose, its function, its taste or effect. "Steak" for example. Or: "Fish."

*He continues working, relishing each word.*

Soup.
Oats.
Wiener.
Bread.
Squid.
Chicken.
Paprika.

*Pause.*

Parsley.

*He begins cutting parsley.*

Here's a story:

The year was 399 B.C., and the Greeks had just lost the Peloponnesian War. Needless to say, they were in a mean mood, looking for a scapegoat. Enter Socrates: old, ugly, cynical and—most important of all—a philosopher, the greatest truth-teller of his time.

**GREEKS** That damn Socrates, he's a liar! He doesn't believe in anything! Make him pay a fine!

**LUMIERE** But good old Socrates, he refused to pay the fine. So the government took the next logical step: it decided to execute him. Sometimes telling the truth can get you killed.

The Athenian method of execution was a kind of suicide by lethal injection. A cup of hemlock. Pale and oily, liquid hemlock blocks the sensory and motor neurons, causing convulsions, respiratory failure and, ultimately, Death.

Slowly, Socrates drank the hemlock. Waiting… waiting for it to take effect. Some guests showed up to witness the public passing of their companion and mentor. Socrates, ever practical, asked them to kindly document his demise for posterity. He started to walk in circles, hoping to quicken the poison's path through his system. After a time, Socrates weakened and lay down on a cot kindly provided by the Athenian penal system. The poison spread – to his feet, his hands, his lips. He had a series of long, beautiful convulsions and… died.

Killing rats on the Alberta/Saskatchewan border trained me in a plethora of poisons:

*He relishes them.*

Caustic potash.
Chloroform.
Fungi.
Curare.
Paraquat…

Such beautiful names. But the greatest and oldest and my most favourite of them all, is hemlock. Because…

*Pause.*

Well, because it can be so easily mistaken for parsley.

*He takes a bite of the parsley.*

*An ignition of lightning.*

---

**LUMIERE** The boy dreams. Inside a fish bowl too small. Watching, as silent, formless shadows float by the faded glass.

Entering a tunnel.
Floating through.
Trapped inside.
Screaming.
Screaming for…
Screaming for his brother.
"I love you. I love you so."

---

**LUMIERE** Enjoy your meal. But don't eat too fast. Digest the evening slowly. We wouldn't want you to get sick, now would we?

*LUMIERE exits. The ASSISTANTS cater the meal, during which the intermission takes place.*

## Act Two

*After the intermission, the guests are invited back to their seats by the ASSISTANTS. LUMIERE walks in and mingles with guests. Eventually, he takes a bite of food. He spits it out violently.*

**LUMIERE** *What is this??*

*The ASSISTANTS look to LUMIERE.*

*What is this??*

*He slowly pulls something from his mouth. The ASSISTANTS are horrified.*

Go look!

*The ASSISTANTS look at each other.*

*Go!!*

*The ASSISTANTS leave.*

*Pause.*

My apologies. I am so terribly sorry. What has just occurred is a catering nightmare. Finding hair in one's meal is absolutely revolting. A meal is a ritual. It is sacred and I don't like the idea that anything might disturb its purity.

Then again, the unfortunate truth is that before it hits your plate, food is treated as anything but sacred.

*(to a guest)* That carrot you're eating.

If you consider the time it died being the time it was picked, you are eating something that died three weeks ago. It was cleaned, cut and sent to your grocery store via a plane, or most likely a truck. We paid it homage when we sautéed it in butter, we gave it a good old-fashioned wake when we served it, we placed it on a fine coffin—a plate—and when you shovelled it into your mouth, you buried it six feet under. And like worms nibbling the crust of a corpse, the enzymes in your stomach gnaw at the remains of the carrot, feasting on the chemicals that keep your body alive, while separating the leftovers into a rich, compact fertilizer called… poo.

But we don't like to think of it that way, do we? And so we dice the carrot instead of cutting it, we pour on the vinaigrette to disguise the vegetables; we create sauces to enhance the meat; we wrap it, we can it, we pickle it, freeze it, fry it, broil it, bake it, mash it, poach it, grind it, grill it, blend it, toast it, mince it. Make it beautiful, make it live again, like a mortician, using just the right amount of make-up, resurrects the corpse, makes the dead seem appetizing, seem good to… to…

**LUMIERE** Once upon a time, there was a young boy who lived in a small-to-medium-sized home, in a small-to-medium-sized city, in a western province, in a place known as Canada. Every evening, the boy's mother carefully created dinner to the rhythm of the boy's father turning the pages of his newspaper.

One evening, the family sat down and dug into large helpings of scalloped potatoes, fresh carrots from the garden and roast chicken. As the young boy picked up a drumstick, he could not believe his incredible luck. While the parents used cutlery to wrestle with their thighs and breasts, the young son said: "Look Mom, look Dad, I don't need a knife and fork. I've got meat with a handle."

A pause descended on the table. The young son thought this natural, that meat came with or without handles. The boy's twin laughed, and even the mother could not suppress a smile. The father, however, stood up, and without finishing dinner said: "Come with me."

Father and son travelled in silence. The son feared that he had said something terribly wrong, wondering: "Where is Dad taking me"?

Father and son entered a shop.

"Wait here."

The boy did as he was told, taking in the dimly lit surroundings and plugging his nose against the overwhelming smell of... something. He wasn't quite sure what it was, but the smell was strong, and made his tummy turn.

The father returned with a man.

"Come 'ere," said the man. The boy, holding his father's hand, followed the man down a long tunnel and through a door. The boy could not believe his eyes: in front of him lay a room filled with animals. Sides of beef, legs of lamb and fresh fowl. All of them dead.

"Come 'ere."

The father nudged his son, who stepped forward, the knot in his stomach growing. The man took a chicken, freshly plucked, and put it onto a cutting board.

"This is an animal. This is meat. It was once alive and now it is dead."

With that, the man brought down the blade hard. The boy felt the knot in his stomach grow tighter. The man quickly and efficiently gutted the bird, letting the insides steam out.

The son watched the blood ooze, he saw the chicken's eye look dark and dead, he had visions of his own death, felt the blood drain from his face and as the smell of innards reached the sensitive nerves of the young boy's nose, he leaned over and threw up on the butcher.

And so a mother's meal was wasted.

But a valuable lesson was learned.

---

*An ASSISTANT enters with a piece of paper and a pen.*

**ASSISTANT** Sir?

*Pause. The ASSISTANT lingers.*

**LUMIERE** Yes?

**ASSISTANT** As you requested, sir.

**LUMIERE** Ah.

*LUMIERE reads. The ASSISTANT waits.*

Hmmmm.

*LUMIERE scratches out a word.*

Hmm.

*He writes on the paper. He hands it back to the ASSISTANT.*

Change this.

*The ASSISTANT stares.*

Change this.

*The ASSISTANT stares.*

Change it, or they won't understand.

*The ASSISTANT takes the paper, lingers.*

Thank you.

*The ASSISTANT exits. LUMIERE pours himself a large glass of wine. The ASSISTANTS clear plates.*

It is highly unusual for a caterer to drink with his guests. Usually I save such an indulgence for after the event, when the guests have happily strayed home, full, but wanting more. I pour myself a generous glass of Merlot and sit down to evaluate the evening: What dish could people not get enough of. What dish didn't anyone touch. Did people enjoy themselves, or were they thoroughly bored, etc.

*He takes a sip of wine.*

I take the magnificent mounds of dirty dishes, the half-eaten platters of rotting fish, the glasses caked with calcifying red wine, the smeared cutlery, the creased linen – I take all this glorious waste to the back room. I sit amongst the mess, soaking in the rays of a successful event I have been responsible for, but haven't had time to witness. I sit, close my eyes and nibble on the leftover sounds of the evening: business deals closed and love affairs started, toasts raised and cutlery dropped.

We spend a large part of our existence making things dirty: our clothes, our dishes, our love lives. We spend an even larger percentage of our life cleaning up: clothes, dishes, love lives. Then there is that small percentage, that unique twilight time, that special moment, when we don't clean or filthify, but... watch.

*LUMIERE leads the ASSISTANTS in a chant.*

**LUMIERE & ASSISTANTS**

Dirt
dirt
dirt.

Dirt
dirt
dirt.

Dirt.
dirt.
dirt.
dirt
watch.

*Pause.*

Dirt
dirt
dirt.

Dirt
dirt
dirt.

Dirt.
dirt
dirt.
clean.
dirt.

*Pause.*

Clean
dirt
clean.
Clean.
dirt
clean.

Clean.
dirt
clean
clean
clean.

*Pause.*

Clean
clean
clean.

Clean
clean
clean.

Clean.
clean
clean
clean
watch.

*Pause.*

Clean.
dirt
clean.

Dirt
clean
dirt.

Dirt
dirt
clean
clean
dirt.

*Pause.*

Clean
clean
clean.

Dirt
dirt
dirt
watch.

*Pause.*

Watch.

*Pause.*

Watch.

*Pause.*

**LUMIERE** Anyway.

*Pause.*

We spend so much time making a mess of our lives. Or trying in vain to clean it up. We rarely take the time to just…

*Lightning flares.*

---

**LUMIERE** The boy hears the wind whisper his name. He stands at the window and watches the lightning cast aquarium shadows through rain-smeared curtains onto the floor of his room.

Thunder. His twin brother mumbles, lost in dreams. He turns on his back, his head pointed to one side. The boy waits for lightning to show his twin's face. He sees his brother's eyes move back and forth, sees his lips speak soundless words, dreaming of birth, or death, or both. The boy thinks, this is what I will look like when I die.

Another loud crack and the brother jolts up in his bed:
Screaming.
Shh.
Screaming.
It's okay…
Screaming.
What?
What?

No answer, but heaving with breath the brother collapses in the boy's arms. The boy holds his twin brother tightly, rocking him into a sleep as deep as death.

*A wind moans.*

---

**FLETCHER** You see this…

**LUMIERE** Says Fletcher.

**FLETCHER** This could be the start of a twister.

**LUMIERE** And he's right. We are standing in a field outside Robinson, Texas. Dust blows up from the south. If it's warm enough out on the gulf, the wind spills onto the land, turns into a tornado and makes its way as far north as Oklahoma, killing trees, livestock, people, almost everything in its path. Eventually it loses steam and… kills itself.

*Pause.*

Fletcher points northwest of Robinson.

**FLETCHER** You see that up there, you see that?

**LUMIERE** I look and see spirals of smoke rising from the remnants of the Branch Davidian compound near Waco. The week before, eighty men, women and children died in a fire Fletcher claims the government started. On purpose.

**FLETCHER** To curtail free speech…

**LUMIERE** Says Fletcher.

**FLETCHER** To show their power, to make sure they had control.

**LUMIERE** I watch the rising steam of the compound.

The Romans embalmed their loved ones in balsam, aromatic salt, honey and wax. As friends and family mourned, they lit the body on a gigantic pyre. The soul rose upwards with the smoke and ash, until it reached the gods…

**FLETCHER** You hear about that tornado in Edmonton?

**LUMIERE** Says Fletcher.

**FLETCHER** You hear about that?

**LUMIERE** Sure. My parents, they were killed in that storm.

**FLETCHER** No, not Edmonton, Alberta. I mean that one in Kentucky.

**LUMIERE** There's an Edmonton, Kentucky?

**FLETCHER** That's right. Now. Was there ever a tornado in Edmonton, Alberta before?

**LUMIERE** Not that I know of.

**FLETCHER** Ever been one since?

**LUMIERE** No.

**FLETCHER** You see? You see? That's because it was a test. To see how things worked. There was never a twister in Edmonton, Kentucky before either. You think that's a coincidence?

**LUMIERE** But—

**FLETCHER** Kentucky, Alberta, it's all the same, Lumiere. It's the government, that's who's done it.

**LUMIERE** But, Fletcher—

**FLETCHER** I know these things, Lumiere. I know. They got your brother, they killed your folks, and God knows, they'll get you, too. I can see it.

---

**LUMIERE** Once upon a time there was a man and a woman who fell in love. They married, had twin sons and lived happily in a small-to-medium-sized city, in a western province, in a place known as Canada.

The man and woman worked hard their entire lives, to give their twin sons everything they needed. They taught them about life and how to lead it. They taught them about love and how to give it. They taught them about death. And how to accept it.

The man and woman finished their life's work and decided to enjoy the rest of their adulthood in what we call retirement.

They sold their small-to-medium-sized home and they purchased two new homes. One home was in Arizona, to escape the cold; the other home was a simple, sparse and modest home in a trailer park on the outskirts of a city called Edmonton. The man and woman travelled from home to home, enjoying their retirement, enjoying the fact their children were… taken care of. After all, the man and woman loved each other.

*Pause.*

One hot, muggy Friday afternoon in late July, the man and woman returned from visiting one of their sons. He'd been in an accident, this son, and put in a care home. They had visited him and had returned to their trailer home to make an early dinner.

*A storm gathers.*

There had been strong winds, rain and even hail, on this hot, muggy, Friday afternoon in late July. The man and woman noticed the green hue of storm clouds on the way home and hoped it would not destroy their weekend.

The man and woman entered their trailer home. The man read the newspaper and the woman made dinner, after which the man did the dishes and the woman read the paper. This had been their ritual, their symbol of love and commitment, ever since they could remember.

It was not long after the man had cracked open the paper and the woman had started dinner, that they heard the winds grow stronger, smelled rain in the air, heard hail on their roof and stepped outside to examine their circumstances.

This is what they saw: debris raining down, wind tossing vehicles to and fro, homes on fire…

No sooner had the man and woman raced back into their home, than the lights went out and they heard a sound like a freight train passing outside. The man and woman fell to their knees and crawled under the table. They crawled under the table, held each other tightly, rocked each other back and forth, praying to God and each other, praying:

"I love you. I love you so…"

And then it was over. And a call was made to notify the next of kin, which was me. They told me my parents were dead, there had been a tornado, an accident, they were dead and "please, come home as soon as you can," my parents were dead. They're dead.

---

**LUMIERE** Some time later, I phoned Mila Mulroney.

*He takes out a small picture of MILA.*

She had helped me before. She had told me "Serve others, and others will serve you," which I was trying to do.

I would call, to ask for relief funds, to ask about what insurance policies would or would not cover, about how I could pay for funeral costs and so on. I would call Mila to say: "my mother and father have been killed. And I don't have money to bury them. And my brother is very sick. And I have no money to take care of him. And I don't want a handout, I don't. What I want is… what I want is…"

So I called. And left a message. And I called. And left a message. And I called again and left another message. And I called and left more messages. And I called, and called, and called, and left more and more and more messages. And I kept on calling, over and over and over, until the secretary said:

**SECRETARY** I'm sorry. She's busy.

**LUMIERE** But she said that I—

**SECRETARY** She says she doesn't know you.

**LUMIERE** But she told me to—

**SECRETARY** She says she doesn't know you. And if she doesn't know you, she doesn't know you. Now please, don't keep calling or I'll notify the RCMP.

*LUMIERE rips up the photo. An ASSISTANT enters.*

**ASSISTANT** Sir?

*Pause.*

Sir?

*Pause.*

**LUMIERE** Yes.

**ASSISTANT** Did you want us to…

**LUMIERE** Not yet. Soon.

*The ASSISTANT leaves.*

---

**FLETCHER** I've got it all figured out.

**LUMIERE** Says Fletcher.

**FLETCHER** It's all coming together for me now.

**LUMIERE** Two years after I last saw Fletcher, we are driving down Interstate 33 through northern Oklahoma.

**FLETCHER** The government's after people – you know why?

**LUMIERE** Like you said, Weather Warfare.

**FLETCHER** No. The real reason they're after people, is to get people needing them. That's why. The government's using all these storms to kill the "real" food, so people will rely more on "fake" food: McDonalds, coffee whitener, you know. The less "real" food we have, the worse we eat, the more unhealthy we are, the less successful we are, the more our minds shrivel, the more we need the government, the more government jobs remain secure.

**LUMIERE** Right...

**FLETCHER** And you know why they're after you.

**LUMIERE** I... think so.

**FLETCHER** It's obvious. You're a caterer. You're interested in food, and not only that, you're interested in good food, and making that food look good. You see? It all makes sense.

**LUMIERE** We pass through Beaver County, crossing the North Canadian River. A half hour out of Oklahoma City, a state trooper pulls us over.

**TROOPER** Can I see some ID?

**FLETCHER** What seems to be the trouble, officer?

**TROOPER** There's been a bombing. In Oklahoma City.

**LUMIERE** A... bombing?

And I see a bead of panic masquerading as sweat run down Fletcher's forehead onto his cheek. He hands over his licence, along with both our passports. The trooper heads back to his car to check us out. Fletcher turns to me:

**FLETCHER** Oh, Jesus... Jesus.

**LUMIERE** What, what is it?

**FLETCHER** A couple of guys were talking, we were talking was all, about bombings, about taking action. Shit, and now there's you.

**LUMIERE** Me?

**FLETCHER** If they find out about you, about who you are, they're going to implicate me in this.

**LUMIERE** What?!

**FLETCHER** They killed your folks, they got your brother, they're after you, and now you're in my car!

*Pause.*

**LUMIERE** Fletcher and I are in a county jail for questioning. We hear about what has happened at the Murrah Federal Building.

At lunch, Fletcher is eating fish. He starts to choke on a stray bone.

All I do is watch.

Fletcher is speechless. He cannot call a guard and we are sitting far from other cellmates. He motions for me to help him.

All I do is watch.

I watch as Fletcher gags for air, his face goes blue, his bowels void and his body slumps to the floor. A guard runs over and performs first aid. An ambulance is called.

Twenty-four hours later, I'm allowed to leave. When they hand over my belongings, they ask how I feel.

"Fine. Why?"

**GUARD** Your friend there… Fletcher?

**LUMIERE** He's not my friend, I just hitched a ride.

**GUARD** Whatever, that Fletcher, they took him to the hospital.

**LUMIERE** How… is he?

**GUARD** Dead.

**LUMIERE** Oh.

*Pause.*

I had seen many dead things in my life, but I had never actually witnessed something—someone—die. I knew the beauty of food. I knew the beauty of death. Now I knew the beauty of dying. All you have to do is watch.

*LUMIERE sits.*

---

**LUMIERE** I walk into the care home in the early evening and go to your room.

I stand by your bed and watch the sun's lavender rays pass through avocado curtains and cast aquarium shadows on the floor. A family of fish in a bowl too small, the figures jump out of the bowl and splash to the linoleum, where they squirm and panic until the sun's setting terminates their lengthy, prolonged demise.

You lie on your back, your head pointed to one side. Crisp sheets, cool on your pale skin. A highway of feeding tubes. You haven't tasted a meal in years.

I sit on the chair beside your bed, my hands curled in my lap. Kids at school used to call you a vegetable. I hated that.

*(slowly)* Hi.

It's me.

Sorry I didn't come earlier.

Mom and Dad are dead, you know.

I don't have a lot of money, you see. I don't know how I can take care of you.

I'm not sure who did this to you: God, or the government, or the car.... It doesn't matter. What matters is... what matters is...

*A storm summons.*

There was a storm, you see. It was night and there was a storm. And I got in my car and I drove, just like you. I drove up along Highway 3, just like you. And I turned onto the gravel road, just like you. I went down a ways and I came to the exact spot where you had your accident. And I stopped, and I got out of the car, and I lay on the road, in the pouring rain, just like you did, and I closed my eyes. And I thought about you, about your blood. Draining into the wet wheat, draining into the ditch, into the creek, into the Red Deer River, into the Bow River basin, all of that blood, reaching Drumheller, where you've been in this stupid care-home for sixteen years.

*Silence: no hail, no thunder, no rain. Only a voice.*

**VOICE** Lumiere...

**LUMIERE** Yes?

And it spoke to me, not with words, but with ideas. Thoughts, concerns, beliefs, all spread out in front of me like a luxurious banquet. And I understood. I understood what Fletcher needed, and I understood what Mom and Dad needed, and I understand what you need. Someone to watch, to witness, to honour, to... to remember.

*He produces a vial.*

It won't hurt, I promise you…

*Pause.*

The teen, now a man, sits on the edge of the bed and moves close to his twin brother.

The man slowly takes his brother's head in his hands.

Leaning over, he opens his brother's mouth and pours in the vial of crushed hemlock.

*LUMIERE drinks the vial.*

"I love you. I love you so."

He kisses his brother gently on the mouth.

He waits and waits, until he feels his brother's body convulse. Once. Twice. Three times. At last, he feels his brother's lips begin to cool. Wipes tears from his eyes. Holds him in his arms. Holds him for a long time, rocking him back and forth. Twins again.

*An ASSISTANT enters.*

**ASSISTANT** Sir?

**LUMIERE** What.

**ASSISTANT** Sir, perhaps we should…

**LUMIERE** Now.

**ASSISTANT** Sir?

**LUMIERE** Now!

*The ASSISTANT runs off.*

---

**LUMIERE** I wonder if you would be so kind as to join me in a little toast.

To Mila.
To my dear friend Fletcher.
To my parents.
To my brother.
And of course, to you – my esteemed guests.

*The ASSISTANTS return. They create a death bed with the catering table, linens, left-over food, cutlery and other catering items. Then they complete the "prep": they help LUMIERE remove his jacket and replace it with a new one; apply a death mask of make-up; mist him with perfume.*

As you recall, I asked you here for several reasons. Number one: to eat. And I do hope you've enjoyed your fare. Number two: to listen. To my testament, my…

life. And you have been so very patient in that regard, and I thank you. And number three, to watch, to… witness my passing.

The ritual is almost complete. The body has been prepped, the meal has been served, the obituary written.

*The ASSISTANTS disperse small bags of parsley. Accompanying the parsley is a scroll with LUMIERE's obituary.*

Now that I have served you, I ask that you serve me. And to help you in this task, I want you to take something home.

*During the dispersal of the obituary, LUMIERE slowly circles the death bed. He feels faint. He lays down on the table.*

I love you. I love you so.

*LUMIERE has a series of slow, beautiful convulsions and is dead. The ASSISTANTS stand vigil.*

---

*On the scrolls that accompany the parsley, is written the following:*

This evening, between the hours of eight and ten p.m., Lumiere, renowned caterer, political observer, student of philosophy, surrounded by acquaintances, after much deliberation, by his own hand, peacefully re-joined his loving family.

Guests were treated to an excellent meal catered by the deceased. Musical accompaniment provided a refined atmosphere, not only for the repast, but also for ~~re-living~~ witnessing the life and passing of the caterer. Dress was casual.

In lieu of flowers, please plant, consume, or share the parsley provided.

Lumiere is predeceased by his mother, his father and his brother.

His body, soul and history are survived by no one but you.

*The end.*

# Selling Mr. Rushdie

By Clem Martini

# About
# Clem Martini

A man of many talents, Clem Martini is equally at home writing for adults and young people, whether for live theatre, film or television. He is a three-time winner of the Alberta Writer's Guild Drama Prize, a Governor General's Literary Award Nominee, a National Playwriting Competition winner and is the Past President of the Playwrights Guild of Canada. His text on playwriting, *The Blunt Playwright* has enjoyed tremendous success at universities and colleges across the country. He is currently at work adapting *The Crow Chronicles*, his trilogy of novels for young adults, for the stage. Clem Martini is a Professor of Drama at the University of Calgary where he teaches Playwriting, Screenwriting and Theatre for Young Audiences.

*Selling Mr. Rushdie* was first produced by Workshop West Theatre, Edmonton at the Springboards New Play Festival in 1997 with the following company:

| | |
|---|---|
| CLARENCE | Dave Clarke |
| DAN | Kevin James Kruchkywich |
| GERALD | Murray Utas |
| ELLIE | April Banigan |

Directed by David Mann
Sound Design by Dave Clarke
Fight Director: Raul Tome

## Characters

CLARENCE is a man who looks vaguely like he could be Salman Rushdie.
DAN is young, short and pugnacious.
GERALD is young, skinny and uncertain.
ELLIE is young, attractive and hungry.

# Selling Mr. Rushdie

## Act One

### Scene One – Morning

*A room in the attic of an old home on the outskirts of a city in the American Midwest. CLARENCE lies on a bed, set against the wall of this very spartan seeming room. There's a door which leads to a washroom and a door leading to a hallway. There is a window, a chair and a small table. CLARENCE appears to be asleep. Slowly he wakes.*

**CLARENCE** Whoa. Where is this?

*He sits up and discovers his hands are chained to the bedpost by handcuffs. He jerks against the handcuffs. It's the real thing.*

What have I been up to?

*He glances around the room.*

Hello? Hello?

*ELLIE appears in the doorway which leads to the hall.*

Ah. Hello.

**ELLIE** Hi.

**CLARENCE** I appear to be…

*He lifts his wrist.*

…handcuffed. Would you know anything about this?

**ELLIE** I might.

**CLARENCE** I seem to have my pants on so I assume I haven't done anything dishonourable.

**GERALD** *(from offstage)* Nope.

*GERALD enters.*

And thank your lucky stars you haven't. That's my bed.

*DAN enters.*

**DAN** Will you shut up.

**GERALD** What?

**DAN** Don't tell him where he is.

**GERALD** I didn't.

**DAN** Yeah. You said your bed.

**GERALD** How's that telling him where he is?

**DAN** Your bed.

**GERALD** That doesn't tell him where he is.

**DAN** Ya.

**GERALD** No. He can see it's a bed!

**DAN** It tells him we're somewhere in the area that you live in.

**GERALD** So?

**DAN** We could be anywhere.

**GERALD** What do you mean?

**DAN** In another country or something?

**GERALD** Does this look like another country?

**DAN** It could—

**GERALD** —I don't think so.

**DAN** Just don't give him anything, okay? Don't give him a thing.

**GERALD** All right.

**DAN** Not a thing. It's important.

**GERALD** All right, all right Dan!—

*DAN punches GERALD in the shoulder.*

Ow – or John, or whatever you're calling yourself.

**DAN** Are you gonna remember?

**GERALD** Yes!

**CLARENCE** What's going on? Who are these guys?

**DAN** Your worst nightmare, Solomon.

**CLARENCE** Excuse me?

**GERALD** We've caught you.

**DAN** And now we're gonna turn you in.

**GERALD** For the money.

**CLARENCE** You're kidding? They're kidding? This is a joke, right?

*CLARENCE looks at the three of them.*

**DAN** No joke, Rushdie.

**CLARENCE** Oh, man. I see now. You gave me drinks. We were going to go back to your place. And instead I wake up in *his* bed.

**DAN** See?

*DAN punches GERALD in the shoulder.*

**GERALD** Ow.

**CLARENCE** Handcuffed. And now the three of you? Are going to turn me in? For what? The million-dollar reward? Is that right?

**GERALD** Bingo.

*DAN punches GERALD.*

Ow! Will you cut it out, he knows that already! How does it hurt if he knows it already?

*CLARENCE chuckles.*

**DAN** What? Something's funny?

**CLARENCE** I hate to disappoint you and your friends but you're not going to collect any million dollars.

**ELLIE** I think we are.

**CLARENCE** I'm not Salman Rushdie.

**ELLIE** That's not what you said last night.

**CLARENCE** No, it's not. That's because I lied last night. *I lied.* You understand?

**GERALD** Ya, right. What about all those books you carry. In your briefcase?

**CLARENCE** Anyone can buy books.

**ELLIE** And all those notes and letters?

**CLARENCE** Made up.

**DAN** Ya, right. We got stuff to do. There's water by the bed, with a straw. There's a, you know, pot under the bed. You can figure it out. We'll check back later.

**ELLIE** Be good.

**CLARENCE** Wait a minute—

**DAN** —And don't make a lotta noise, understand?

**GERALD** Not that it'd help anyway.

**CLARENCE** Don't go! Wait! *What's going on*?

**GERALD** Smell ya later.

*The door shuts and they're gone.*

**CLARENCE** Wait! Wait! Listen to me! I lied! *I lied!*

*Blackout.*

## Scene Two – Later

*Lights up. CLARENCE now sits on a heavy office-type chair with metal casters at its base. His legs are shackled together, as are his hands – furthermore, his handcuffs are attached by a short length of chain to another length of chain wrapped around his waist. One last length of chain runs from his waist to the very heavy office chair. GERALD is just in the process of locking this last bit of chain to the base of the chair. Now that we get a chance to take a closer look at CLARENCE we see that he does bear an interesting resemblance to Salman Rushdie.*

**GERALD** There you go.

**CLARENCE** Quite an arrangement.

**GERALD** Good idea, eh? That way, you gotta go, I just wheel you into the washroom, and you take it from there.

**CLARENCE** Very nice. Where's everyone else?

**GERALD** On the moon. I'm not that stupid, eh? They'll be along soon enough.

*GERALD reaches into his backpack.*

Supper. Got some McDonald's for you.

**CLARENCE** Can I not feed myself?

**GERALD** Nope.

**CLARENCE** You could unlock just one hand.

**GERALD** Nope.

**CLARENCE** *One hand.* I'm not going to escape with one hand.

**GERALD** Open.

*CLARENCE opens his mouth. GERALD begins to feed him the burger.*

**CLARENCE** I'm not…

*He swallows.*

…Salman Rushdie. I'm not.

**GERALD** Open.

*CLARENCE receives more burger.*

**CLARENCE** Do I look worried to you?

**GERALD** No.

**CLARENCE** I'm not. And I'd *be* worried if I was Salman, wouldn't I? But the reason I'm not worried is because this isn't *dangerous*, Gerald. *This*, is just stupid. Have you ever seen *The Satanic Verses*?

**GERALD** The what?

**CLARENCE** The book? Salman Rushdie was condemned for writing it? You know? You've got my briefcase, right? It's in there. Just lift it out and look at the jacket cover a minute…

*He swallows.*

…Look at the jacket of the book closely and then look at me. Go on. Look. It's not me, I'm telling you. *Look* at it.

*GERALD looks at it.*

**GERALD** Looks like him to me. Open.

*GERALD feeds him some more burger.*

**CLARENCE** Yes, he's got a beard and I've got a beard and we both wear glasses, but look at my nose, then look at his nose. Look at my lips, then look at his lips. Look at the forehead, for goodness sake.

**GERALD** You explained that all last night to Ellie.

**CLARENCE** I did?

**GERALD** Yeah. The plastic surgery.

**CLARENCE** Oh, right.

**GERALD** It's clever.

**CLARENCE** Yeah, real clever.

**GERALD** Open.

*CLARENCE eats.*

**CLARENCE** And my accent's not the same as Rushdie's.

**GERALD** Explained all that to Ellie, too. Practicing different ways of talking to throw people off. Want a drink?

**CLARENCE** Oh, yeah.

*CLARENCE sucks his drink up through a straw.*

Listen. Listen to me. Even if I was Rushdie—and I'm not—but for the sake of argument, even if I was, how are you going to collect the money?

**GERALD** Send a letter and a photo, I guess. That's what we're working on right now.

**CLARENCE** And you think they're going to just send you your millions? Through the mail? For a picture and a letter? Come on, you've got a brain. You know it's going to be more complicated than that. They're going to want *proof*? And what are you going to do then? Kill me? Fly my dead body to Iran? And what are you going to do at customs, declare me along with the whiskey and chocolates?

**GERALD** Open.

*CLARENCE opens his mouth and accepts more burger.*

Maybe it'd be difficult if that was what we were going to do – but we're not.

**CLARENCE** You're not?

**GERALD** No. We're not going to kill anybody. We're not murderers.

**CLARENCE** —Glad to hear it—

**GERALD** —We're going to let them take care'a that – if that's what they want to do.

**CLARENCE** Them? (*He chews.*) Who?

**GERALD** Them. You know? The Iranians.

**CLARENCE** They—"Them"—are going to laugh at you. They are going to split a gut. Because I'm not Salman Rushdie.

**GERALD** Not what you said last night.

**CLARENCE** I lied. You know what a lie is?

**GERALD** Oh, yeah. I know what a lie is, all right. Open.

**CLARENCE** How much money have you got on you anyway? How 'bout your buddy Dan? It costs a couple'a thousand to fly to Iran. You got that?

**GERALD** We'll tell 'em to come here.

**CLARENCE** Right. Why do I think that's not going to happen? You're going to get in touch with Iran's secret service and just invite them to fly here for a little visit. And how are you going to arrange that without suddenly getting famous? You ever heard of the Secret Service? Their *whole job* is to monitor guys like that and make sure they don't waltz into the country with money and out with bodies.

**GERALD** You finished?

**CLARENCE** I'll have another bite. And who are you going to send this letter and photo to anyway? (*slight pause*) Who?

**GERALD** I don't know.

**CLARENCE** You don't know. You must have an idea.

**GERALD** The Ayatollah I guess.

**CLARENCE** The Ayatollah is dead.

*GERALD is clearly amused by the lack of skill CLARENCE has shown in his ability to lie.*

**GERALD** *Right.*

**CLARENCE** He's dead. Died several years back.

**GERALD** Whatever.

**CLARENCE** Don't believe me. Go to a library. Check it out.

**GERALD** That's fine. I'm sure I believe you.

**CLARENCE** You guys don't even know *who* to get in touch with and you don't know how to get in touch with the guys you'd need to get in touch with if you did know how. Come on. This isn't going to happen. I need a drink.

*CLARENCE sips from a straw.*

Listen. I'll bet this is, what? – your buddy's plan? Right? Am I right? Dan's? And I'll bet he's got you into other fixes before this, hasn't he? Hasn't he?

**GERALD** No.

**CLARENCE** Come on.

**GERALD** I'm not saying nothing.

**CLARENCE** I'll bet you and he have gotten into all kinds'a screwy shit together. Haven't you? I'm just talking to you, we're just talking, there's nothing wrong with that, is there? No big secrets, right? But tell the truth. You've gotten into some trouble before, with him, haven't you?

**GERALD** Maybe.

**CLARENCE** Gimme a couple of fries.

*GERALD feeds CLARENCE some fries.*

And I'll bet… this is pure guess work—

**GERALD** —Save your guesses for when Dan gets here. He should be here any minute—

**CLARENCE** —you tell me if it's the truth, I'll bet if there's been trouble you two got into, it was always *Dan* who got the sweeter deal after, right? Am I right? I need another drink.

*CLARENCE sips from a straw.*

I mean, it's obvious. I mean, you can see he's used to getting his way around people. I'm just saying what anyone can see. Look at me. You know I'm not Salman Rushdie.

**GERALD** I don't know that.

**CLARENCE** Yes, you do. Inside. Even if you can't bring yourself to admit it to me. Even if you can't admit it to yourself right now, you *know* at the back of your mind. And all that's going to happen is—eventually—*someone* is going to get into some really major trouble. Now you think back to what you and Dan have gone through in the past and you tell me who that someone is likely to be. Right now this is kidnapping. You realize that? Kidnapping. That's not shoplifting, that's a big deal. That's a federal offence. I'll tell you the truth. Everyone's got their scam. What I do is I go 'round pretending to be Salman Rushdie. The way I see it, no one gets hurt. I get free meals, free drinks, sympathy and you wouldn't believe the number of girls who get turned on at the idea of being with someone famous on the run. And who am I to say no? But *you're* not going to fall for this BS, are you? You're smarter than that. You don't want to do time for kidnapping a, a *nobody*. 'Cause that would be just plain stupid and I know you're not stupid. You let me go, I'll walk away. I won't go to the police, 'cause – I'll be totally frank with you here, I've got a bit of a record myself. I don't want to mess with the police. *You* tell Dan you were napping in another room. You woke up and I was gone. You don't *know* how I did it. He's going to be pissed at first, but you know he's going to get over it. And then this whole thing is outta your hair. A couple of years from now you're going to joke about this guy you and he picked up that you thought was—

*DAN steps in through the door.*

**DAN** —Isn't *he* something? With words? Got a thousand of them. Just like a real writer would, eh? Sorry for interrupting. Just admiring your little performance.

**GERALD** I wasn't really listening. You know, he was just—

**CLARENCE** —What I just said, does it make sense or not?

**DAN** We catch Mr. Solomon Rushdie, you think he's going to say, "That's me! I am that famous writer dude who fucked with the Ayatollah"? No, you *know* he's going to spin everything he can to convince us he's someone else.

**CLARENCE** There are keys in my briefcase. I'll give you the address. Go to where I'm staying, let yourself in, you'll find ID—

**DAN** —And guess what else we'll find, eh?—

**CLARENCE** —Take my fingerprints. Take them down to the police station. Say someone broke into your place and have them run an ID on them—

**DAN** *(laughs)* Whoooo, is that an idea or what? That's gotta nail it for us, eh? What's going to get us caught quicker than taking Mr. Solomon Rushdie's fingerprints to the police and *asking them* to run an ID for us?? We must look pretty fucking simple, eh?

**GERALD** Ya!

*GERALD chuckles scornfully.*

**CLARENCE** You've got the wrong guy!

**DAN** I got the letter written right here. Couple'a weeks, Gerald, and we're rich.

**CLARENCE** You're an *idiot!* And you are an idiot's idiot!

**DAN** And you're our Clarence, so what's that make you, Mr. Solomon?

**CLARENCE** Salman, it's Salman, not Solomon you fuckwit! For Christ's sake, you don't even know the man's real name! God! I've been kidnapped by Bart and Homer *Simpson*!

**DAN** Right. I guess he's about finished eating, eh?

*DAN grabs a rag and forces it into CLARENCE's mouth. He then winds the cloth around his face. CLARENCE tries to protest throughout – albeit with the rag in his mouth. DAN speaks overtop of the noise.*

There. That's better. I hate arguing after lunch. It's so upsetting for the appetite, eh? Hey, quiet! *Shut up!* Here. Help me wheel him into the closet so we can hear ourselves think.

*Together DAN and GERALD wheel CLARENCE into the closet. DAN shuts the closet door.*

There, that's better. Let 'im chill in there.

**GERALD** Yeah. Though, you think that cloth's a little big for his mouth, maybe?

**DAN** He's got a big mouth.

**GERALD** Huh.

*GERALD looks at the closet.*

**DAN** What?

**GERALD** Which of us do you think he thought was Homer?

**DAN** Who cares! And listen to me, you stop talking to him. He's a writer and you're a moron—

**GERALD** —I'm not a moron—

**DAN** —and you two debatin' each other is the biggest mismatch of the century. You haven't got a chance.

**GERALD** Where's Ellie?

**DAN** Fucked if I know. She should be here. Anyway – here it is.

**GERALD** What?

**DAN** The letter.

**GERALD** Oh, yeah. So what'dja say?

**DAN** I'll read it to ya.

*He opens a folded piece of paper. CLARENCE has continued to bang on the floor and in general make noise in the closet. DAN bangs on the door with his fist.*

Shut up in there! Man.

*He sees something.*

What the fuck is that?

**GERALD** What?

**DAN** That.

**GERALD** Oh, that's a wasp.

**DAN** Eww.

**GERALD** No problem.

*GERALD opens the window and gently shoos the wasp out.*

**DAN** They get in here often?

**GERALD** Every once in a while. There's a nest of 'em 'round back.

**DAN** Ya? Wasps, nests, birds, flowers, it's just like a campin' trip out here, isn't it?

**GERALD** Yeah.

**DAN** I hate camping. We'll have to find a way to get rid of it, eh?

**GERALD** What? The wasp's nest? Naw, you just set out a beer for 'em.

**DAN** What?

**GERALD** Yeah.

**DAN** Get outta here.

**GERALD** I'm tellin' ya.

**DAN** What kinda shit are you talking now?

**GERALD** I'm telling you, you put a jar'a beer—

**DAN** —And then what? Pretzels and pickled eggs and shit like that—

**GERALD** —No. When they buzz round, they take a sip'a the beer—

**DAN** —They got a *brand* they prefer?—

**GERALD** —and *then* after they finish drinking, they can't get outta the jar 'cause they're drunk, and they drown.

**DAN** You're making this up?

**GERALD** No.

**DAN** 'Cause it sounds completely nuts.

**GERALD** I've seen it, man. Them lyin' on their backs in the beer—

**DAN** —I think it's gotta be way easier to just whack 'em hard and kill 'em, but hey. Anyway, as I was saying, here's the letter.

*Enter ELLIE.*

**ELLIE** Hi, what's goin' on?

**DAN** So, you finally got here.

**ELLIE** Don't gimme that "finally" shit. It takes for fucking ever, bussing it, then walkin'. This place might as well be in another freaking country. Where's Rushdie?

*At that moment CLARENCE pounds again and makes a muffled shout.*

What's he doin' in the closet?

**GERALD** Dan read him the riot act 'n told him to shut up.

**ELLIE** It's not workin', hey?

**DAN** Ya.

**ELLIE** No. I can hear him plain as anything.

**DAN** Just let me deal with this, will ya.

**ELLIE** Hey, suddenly you're giving orders. Who's idea was all this in the first place?

**DAN** You came to me. You asked my help. I organized things. But you figure you can do better, do it. Go fer it. You got an idea? No? All right then, just shut up and let me do what I'm doin'. I'm handlin' this. He's quieter now than he was a couple'a minutes ago. Just wait.

**ELLIE** What's that?

**DAN** The letter.

**ELLIE** What letter?

**DAN** Duh! The letter we're writing. The letter that's going to get us our money, that letter. Hel-lo!

**ELLIE** All right, you don't hafta spaz. What's it say?

**DAN** I was going to read it when you interrupted me. "We have caught Mr. Rushdie. If you want him, place a message in *The Globe and Mail* personal ads telling us how you want to arrange things. We will not kill him, that's up to you..." – eh?

**GERALD** Good.

**ELLIE** Yeah.

**DAN** "...*But* we will bring him to you and you can do whatever you want. We still expect to be paid in *full.* Deg."

**ELLIE** What's that?

**DAN** What?

**ELLIE** That Deg thing?

*DAN wheels around and pounds on the closet door.*

**DAN** *Shut up!*

*He returns to ELLIE and GERALD.*

That's our code name.

**ELLIE** Our code name?

**DAN** Yeah, we gotta know the message is for us, right? But we don't want to give up our real names. So, Deg.

**ELLIE** What? You couldn't think up a real name?

**DAN** It's a code name—

**ELLIE** —I *know* it's a code name, but couldn't you think up like a *real* code name?

**DAN** It's made from the initials of our first names, Dan, Ellie, Gerald. Deg.

**ELLIE** They're not going to take anyone named Deg seriously.

**DAN** Ya!

**ELLIE** No, they're going to go, "This is not even a real person—"

**DAN** —The fuck they care about the name—

**ELLIE** —Couldn't you think of something else, Max, or Jesse. Jesse can be a man's or woman's name—

**DAN** —It's just a *name!* A name in a newspaper, they *don't give a fuck, okay*? Okay??

*Pause.*

**ELLIE** Okay. So, now you just, send it?

**DAN** Ya. Then we watch the personals. In the meantime, we shouldn't meet here together. Someone's got to keep an eye on him – you understand that? Keeping an eye on him?

**GERALD** Yeah!

**DAN** But you know, if we're always out here together, someone's going to get suspicious, right?

**ELLIE** And it's a fuck of a long way to walk at the end of the bus line anyway.

**DAN** The bus ride and walk are the least of our worries, okay? – And I can give you a ride back tonight.

**ELLIE** That's a relief. I don't know how long yer busses run out here.

**DAN** Can you put a little in for gas?

**ELLIE** Aw fer fucks sake—

**DAN** Just a bit, I'm not asking you to crack yer retirement savings or anything, I'm just kinda strapped tonight is all.

**ELLIE** *(snorts)* Tonight?

**DAN** Ya, tonight. You gotta problem with that?

**ELLIE** I can put in. Okay? Fuck.

*Pause.*

**DAN** So we'll break it into shifts to take care'a Rushdie. I've written it out.

**GERALD** I can't read your handwriting.

**DAN** That's why I'm going to read it out. I'll watch him to begin with, you watch him over the weekend, and you after that.

**ELLIE** Why me on the weekend.

**DAN** 'Cause you're off work then.

**ELLIE** I could ask for Monday off, or call in sick.

**DAN** Everything's gotta be like regular.

**GERALD** What's the big deal?

**DAN** "What's the big deal?" *Hello?* We've got a person in the closet?

**GERALD** I thought you said no one was watching us when we brought him out here.

**DAN** No one was, like no one usual, like not the regular cops and what have you, but figure it out – there's gotta be special forces, and you know, Interpol and all'a that lookin' for him?

**ELLIE** Who the fuck's Interpol?

**DAN** You know you use "fuck" for everything.

**ELLIE** So?

**DAN** So, that's really fuckin' common.

**ELLIE** So, go fuck yourself and tell me who Interpol is.

**DAN** *Hey! Don't tell me to fuck myself, okay!*

**ELLIE** *And don't you tell me how to fuckin' talk!*

*DAN kicks over a chair.*

**DAN** *I said I don't like that kinda talk and I'm serious. You understand?*

*Pause.*

**ELLIE** Are you goin to tell me or what?

*Slight pause.*

**DAN** Can you just try to talk a little more like a civilized human being? It's like a cop force, all over the world. Like an international CIA.

**GERALD** And you figure they're watching?

**DAN** Well, ya sure.

**GERALD** Here?

**DAN** Not "here," here, Stupid, but they're looking around. And they gotta know that he was last seen in this city, right? So they'll be sending agents to this city to scope it out.

**GERALD** From where?

**DAN** From anywhere. From all over.

**GERALD** Maybe we should just stay out here. The whole time. We could bring some board games out. My dad probably wouldn't care.

**DAN** No, we gotta do things regular-like and you can't ask permission of your dad. Your dad can't know that we're doing something out here—

**GERALD** —I told him already.

**DAN** *You told him?*

**GERALD** Ya.

**DAN** *You told him*?? What, you told him you were kidnapping someone and keeping him here?

**GERALD** No! I told him I was staying out here. So he'd know when he saw the lights on or a car out front or whatever—

**DAN** —You said he doesn't come out here—

**GERALD** —He doesn't. Usually. But every once in a while he'll wander by. So I told him I was hanging out here for a few days—

**DAN** —He didn't ask you what for?

**GERALD** No, what does he care, he doesn't give a shit. He just told me don't wreck the place, no drugs, no booze, no parties. That kinda stuff.

**DAN** Well, if you don't show up at work and you start acting suspicious, *that* is exactly the kind of thing Interpol starts picking up on.

**ELLIE** People who skip work?

**DAN** Ya.

**ELLIE** They gotta have a huge fuckin' file on you.

**DAN** After Rushdie goes missing. They look for anything suspicious after that.

**ELLIE** So you're sending this letter?

**DAN** Yes.

**ELLIE** And we hang out 'til we hear back?

**DAN** Yes.

**ELLIE** And when's that?

**DAN** Pretty quick I'd guess. They probably gotta consult and all that, that could take a day or so. The letter won't get there 'til the weekend. So they won't read it 'til Monday—

**GERALD** Do they have the weekend off?

**DAN** Who?

**GERALD** Muslims.

**DAN** Yes. Everyone's got the weekend off, ya moron.

**GERALD** I'm not a moron, and it's not the same for Muslims.

**DAN** Yeah.

**GERALD** No.

**DAN** Yeah, they have *Saturdays*. That's like their going to church day—

**GERALD** —They don't go to church—

**DAN** —Yeah! Muslim church—

**GERALD** No.

**DAN** Yeah, on Saturdays!

**GERALD** *(to ELLIE)* Do they go to church?

**ELLIE** The fuck I know or care about Muslim church. Will you two shut up, you're givin' me a brain tumour.

**DAN** Look it up. Saturdays.

**GERALD** It's not church.

**DAN** Whatever. We should hear from them next week for sure.

**ELLIE** Okay.

**GERALD** Okay.

**ELLIE** And then we make a deal?

**DAN** Right.

**ELLIE** Great.

**DAN** So in the meantime we'll do shifts. Me first. Then you. Then you.

*Pause. Silence.*

**ELLIE** Say, Rushdie's pretty quiet.

*DAN goes to the door.*

**DAN** 'Kay, you can come out now, Solomon.

*He opens the door.*

Only no more'a yer shit, 'kay? Or back you go.

**ELLIE** Dan? Hey Dan, look.

*She takes CLARENCE by the shoulders.*

Wake up. Ho-ly fuck!

**GERALD** What's wrong?

**ELLIE** His head's flopped over! Omygod, we've killed him.

**DAN** Just chill.

**GERALD** Hey. Wake up.

**ELLIE** He's dead, isn't he?

**DAN** He's not dead.

**GERALD** He's choked.

**ELLIE** He's dead. Oh, man, we killed him and we're all going to be charged with murder.

**GERALD** Do you know CPR?

**DAN** He's not dead. Get some water.

**GERALD** What the fuck do you want with water? He's not thirsty.

**DAN** Just get it.

**GERALD** I *told* you!—

**DAN** —*Get it!*—

**GERALD** —I told you he couldn't stay in there like that—

**DAN** —Here's water – Don't pour it down his throat! Are you nuts! He's passed out! You want him drownin'?—

**ELLIE** —Well, what'm I s'posed to do?

**DAN** Wet a rag.

**ELLIE** You said we wouldn't kill anyone!

**DAN** We haven't killed anyone. What are you doing?

**GERALD** I'm unlocking him.

**DAN** Cut it out.

**GERALD** You think he's going to jump up?

**DAN** And what are you doing?

**ELLIE** You said wet a rag, I'm cooling him off!

**DAN** His head, his head, he doesn't need a sponge bath!

*CLARENCE moans.*

There! See! I told you he wasn't dead.

**GERALD** Ya, well, his hands are *totally* white. There's no circulation.

**DAN** Rub 'em.

**ELLIE** With the cloth?

**DAN** *No! With your hands! Rub his arms and legs with your hands – Jesus what's wrong with you two, grab a fuckin' brain and use it, will ya!*

*Slight pause.*

**GERALD** It's just his arms are going to fall off if we keep him tied up this tight.

**DAN** We're selling him to someone who's going to kill him, the fuck I care if his arms fall off.

*CLARENCE breaks into a fit of coughing.*

**CLARENCE** Give me a drink.

**ELLIE** Here.

**CLARENCE** I couldn't breathe.

**DAN** You can breathe now, right?

**CLARENCE** Yeah.

**DAN** Okay. I want you to listen close then. I'm not going to take any more shit.

**CLARENCE** I'm telling you I lied.

**DAN** *Right.*

**CLARENCE** I lied.

**DAN** Why?

**CLARENCE** 'Cause I thought I was going to make it with her.

**DAN** I really buy that.

**GERALD** Ya.

**DAN** He makes up this *big* story, carries around this briefcase filled with books and everything just so he can sleep with you.

**ELLIE** So what's your point?

**DAN** He didn't even know you when you walked into the lounge. And he had all that stuff with him.

**ELLIE** Yeah, that's right, you didn't even know I existed.

**CLARENCE** Do the homework – would Rushdie, the real Rushdie, a guy who's hunted the world over, walk around a lounge telling every Tom, Dan and Ellie who he was? I don't think so. And what business would Salman Rushdie have being over here in the first place? Has he lived here? Does he have work here? No. The last place he appeared was France, about a week ago. Look it up in the newspapers.

**GERALD** So?

**CLARENCE** So? So, why would he fly all the way from France, Europe, to your lounge a week later? *For happy hour and a piping hot order of Buffalo wings??*

**GERALD** This'd be the last place people'd look for you, right? Right?

**DAN** And that other stuff is just disinformation.

**CLARENCE** 'Scuse me?

**DAN** Y'know, your Secret Service-types leak stuff to the media saying you're in *France*, you're in *New York*—

**CLARENCE** —When in fact I'm in a cheesy lounge trying to hit on the waitress, you guys are *hallucinating*. Rushdie is older than me. Rushdie is balder than me. Rushdie has a bigger vocabulary than me. Rushdie can *write* for God's sake, just have a look at my handwriting, that should tell you something. I don't even write postcards! I'm *not* Rushdie, can't you understand that? You have the *wrong man!!*

**DAN** I forbid you to say that anymore.

*Slight pause.*

**CLARENCE** What?

**DAN** I forbid you to say that anymore. I don't want to hear that anymore—

*Overlapping.*

**CLARENCE** —You can't—

**DAN** —I'm telling you—

**CLARENCE** —"forbid" me to say that I'm—

**DAN** —I don't want to hear that anymore—

**CLARENCE** —not Salman Rushdie—

**DAN** —What did I tell you??—

**CLARENCE** —Because I most certainly *am not* Salman Rushdie—

**DAN** —You stop right there. You stop—

**CLARENCE** —I'm not Salman Rushdie—

**ELLIE** —I'd cool it if I were you—

**DAN** —I'm warning you—

**CLARENCE** —I'm not Salman Rushdie—

**ELLIE** —He's got a fucking temper—

**DAN** —You shut'cher mouth this minute—

**ELLIE** —And he'll lose his freaking mind—

**CLARENCE** —I'm not Salman Rushdie I'm not Salman Rushdie I'm not—

**DAN** —*Shut up!!*—

**CLARENCE** —Salman Rushdie—

*DAN cracks CLARENCE across the face. His head rocks backward with the force of the blow. It takes a moment for him to realize he's been hit. Silence.*

I'm not Salman—

*DAN cracks CLARENCE across the face twice more. Silence.*

**DAN** I'm not going to tell you again. I don't want to hear any more of that "I'm not Salman Rushdie" bullshit. You understand?

*Silence.*

You understand?

**CLARENCE** Yeah.

**DAN** So you won't say it anymore?

**CLARENCE** No.

**DAN** What's that?

**CLARENCE** No!

**DAN** Good.

*Pause.*

**CLARENCE** You can't stop me thinking it.

**DAN** I give a fuck what you think. But you *say* it, and you'll get thumped.

*Pause.*

**CLARENCE** Okay.

**DAN** *(triumphant)* There y' go. In a battle'a words against fists – bet on the fists every time.

**CLARENCE** So… let's say I am Salman Rushdie—

**DAN** *(As in "What did I tell you guys?")* Hey.

**CLARENCE** —I'm not, of course—

**DAN** *(As in "You're this close to getting hit again.")* Hey!

**CLARENCE** —but just for the sake of argument, let's say I am. You, the three of you, are *actually* okay with selling me to someone who's intention it is, eventually, to kill me?

**DAN & GERALD** *("of course")* Ya!

**CLARENCE** —For doing *nothing* but saying something that they didn't like?

**DAN & GERALD** Ya!

*Pause.*

**CLARENCE** Think about this now…. Here's a guy—for now we'll say me—who hasn't done anything to anybody, except to call it the way he saw it, you know, writing a book, expressing his own opinion. *Except*, his opinion so offends the Ayatollah, that he says he mustn't do that anymore. Matter of fact, he declares that this opinion is so offensive that anyone who expresses it must be silenced – killed. And you're going to *help* do that?

*DAN and GERALD look at each other, and then at CLARENCE.*

**DAN & GERALD** Ya!

**CLARENCE** Well. You guys are… *send* your letter, just send your stupid letter and see what happens.

**DAN** Okay.

**CLARENCE** Good.

**DAN** We will. *(to GERALD)* You hear that "...so offends..." business, eh?

**GERALD** Ya.

**DAN** Writer or what, eh?

**CLARENCE** *Fuck.*

**DAN** I'm going to send that letter tonight along with...

*DAN pulls a camera out of his jacket pocket.*

...a picture. So, smile. Smile. You know how to smile. Good.

*He takes the picture.*

Thank you.

*Blackout.*

## Scene Three – Night Three

*DAN sits smoking, drumming his fingers against the wall and looking off. CLARENCE sits, chained up.*

**DAN** Well. *This*, is a drag. This. Is a complete, fucking, draaag. Never thought I'd see the day come when I spent a Friday night in some *guy's* bedroom, with the dude sittin' in a chair, wrapped in chains.

**CLARENCE** I gotta go to the washroom.

**DAN** Agh.

*DAN wheels him into the washroom.*

There.

*CLARENCE stands, hobbles about—still attached by a length of chain to the chair—and closes the washroom door.*

Don't try anything funny.

**CLARENCE** *(from inside)* You mean like stand-up routines?

**DAN** Ha ha, stop it, you're killin' me. *(DAN smokes.)* Ya, it's a drag. You know the one thing that makes it interesting? Hey, I say, you know the one thing that makes it interesting?

**CLARENCE** No.

**DAN** Thinking about what I'm going to do with all that money. Eh? You can do a lot with a million or so bucks. You must make pretty good bread, Solomon. Whady'you do with it?

*The toilet flushes. CLARENCE opens the door, sits on the chair and pushes himself backwards across the floor.*

**CLARENCE** Hang out in bars, buy drinks, tell everyone who I am. The usual.

**DAN** Really, no more. My sides are killing me.

*He smokes.*

Those chains are actually kind of attractive once you get used to them.

*He smokes.*

Y' know, Solomon, you're takin' this pretty good. If I was you, I'd be shittin' bricks.

**CLARENCE** I'm not worried because nothing's going to happen—

**DAN** —Don't start—

**CLARENCE** —I'm not saying why. I'm just saying I know this is going to be a complete waste of time.

**DAN** Ya? Well, you better hope not. Things happened and this turned out to be a complete waste'a time, I'd be plenty pissed.

*DAN ducks suddenly.*

Ah, sonofabitch.

**CLARENCE** What?

**DAN** There's another wasp.

*He rolls up a paper.*

It beats me why people say they go to the country to relax. There's wasps—

*He swats at it and misses.*

—'n bees, 'n ants, 'n every other type of thing designed to bite, stab or otherwise get up your ass.

*Swat.*

There! Once again, man lays the boots to mother nature.

*Pause.*

Hey? Solomon? Hey?

**CLARENCE** What?

**DAN** You play chess?

**CLARENCE** Yeah.

**DAN** You any good?

**CLARENCE** I'm okay.

**DAN** "I'm okay." *Right.* Yer probably one'a those Zen Chess Masters.

**CLARENCE** Yeah, I'm a chess master and a millionaire *and* Salman Rushdie. I'm all of those things. That's why I'm dressed this way, it's my regulation Zen Chess Master's Uniform.

**DAN** Wanta play or not?

**CLARENCE** Is there a board?

**DAN** Ya.

**CLARENCE** Can we make it interesting?

**DAN** Whady'ya mean?

**CLARENCE** Bet something.

**DAN** Like we play and if you win I let you go? Like that?

**CLARENCE** That'd work for me.

**DAN** Why don't we just play for the moon and stars and all'a creation or something else that I'm *really* going to pay you.

**CLARENCE** 'Kay, not my freedom, but say… my freedom of speech? I win, I get to say what I like—

**DAN** —No dice—

**CLARENCE** —For five minutes. That's all. Five minutes of free speech. I get five minutes to try to convince you that I'm not – who you say I am – and you'll sit and listen, that's all. Five minutes. Five minutes isn't going to kill you. And I have to win first. I am, after all, wearing the very attractive chain wear. It's not like I'm going to do anything.

**DAN** So, what if I win?

*Pause.*

**CLARENCE** I autograph that copy of *The Satanic Verses.* Bound to be worth something after you've sold me and I'm dead, right?

*DAN considers it.*

**DAN** 'Kay, rack 'em up.

*DAN lays out a chessboard on a small table in front of CLARENCE. They start setting up the players. DAN holds out his clenched fists.*

Pick.

*CLARENCE chooses, he selects white.*

You go first.

**CLARENCE** How old are you?

**DAN** Two hundred. Your move.

**CLARENCE** How did you and Gerald meet up?

**DAN** I ain't gonna tell you my personal history and I ain't gonna let you find out about the others so you might just as well scratch that little plan'a yours.

**CLARENCE** I never knew I was so transparent.

**DAN** Your move.

*They play quickly and quietly for a few moments.*

**CLARENCE** She your girlfriend?

**DAN** Who? Ellie? *(He snorts.)* Right.

**CLARENCE** You're lucky. She's pretty.

*DAN stops playing.*

**DAN** Whad'ya mean by that?

**CLARENCE** I mean she's pretty.

**DAN** So, I'm lucky to get her?

**CLARENCE** Yeah.

**DAN** I'm lucky? Meaning I'm not good enough for her?—

**CLARENCE** —No—

**DAN** —Well, fuck you—

**CLARENCE** —All I'm saying is—

**DAN** —*She's* lucky to have *me*—

**CLARENCE** —*anyone* would be lucky to have her—

**DAN** —I got her the fucking job she's got. I got her her place. She's got anything, it's because I helped her, she can't put two thoughts together without my help.

**CLARENCE** Okay.

**DAN** I do all her thinkin'. She'd be nowhere without me.

*They play a moment.*

I catch the way you look at us sometimes—

**CLARENCE** —I'm not looking at you *any* way—

**DAN** —Oh, no, I've caught you sometimes, lookin', like what's she doing with *him*, but people have underestimated me all'a my life. 'Cause people don't look hard enough at anything, they think if you haven't been to university you can't use your brain but I can tell you there's plenty'a useless fucks out there don't know *where* their brain is, have got two or three degrees. I got all the smarts I need and I got 'em from the ground up, okay?

**CLARENCE** Okay.

**DAN** Okay. Move.

*They play a moment.*

She can't even read. You know that? I mean that's the reason she thinks you're such a hotshot, it's not 'cause she thinks you're such a great fuckin' writer, cause the book might as well be written in Swahili for all she can tell, she hasn't even cracked the cover – it's just 'cause *you can write*, period.

*They play quietly.*

And you think she's pretty.

*DAN laughs, then stops as he comes to a realization.*

Hey. Now this is pretty fuckin' weird, eh?

**CLARENCE** What?

**DAN** You here. Us catchin' you. I mean, who are we? Nobody from nowhere. And we catch *you*.

**CLARENCE** Yeah. That's pretty fuckin' weird all right.

**DAN** That should tell you something 'bout how the world works.

**CLARENCE** Yeah. It should, I'm just not sure what.

*Pause.*

**DAN** But I'll tell ya, you gotta admire the Ayatollah, eh?

**CLARENCE** Well. No.

**DAN** Well, no, I s'pose not, given your circumstances. He kicked your ass, didn't he? So you're not likely to see it that way, I mean, maybe you see things different—

**CLARENCE** —I think we can pretty well count on that—

**DAN** —but the way I see it is, you write this book. You think to yourself, I can say whatever 'cause I'm Mr. Hotshot Writer and it's all this freedom of speech yakety yak and anyways the Iranians live in shithole Irania, what are they going to do – if they don't like the book, they can fuckin' lump it, right? What can they do? And then this wizened old motherfucker, has gotta be old enough to be my great-grandfather says screw you, I'm not interested in your freedom of expression or your lawyers or your money, I'm gonna have your skinny writer's ass and he says

I say this guy has got to die – and bim bam there's a million bucks tagged on your ass and what're you gonna do about it? Bugger all. You're beat. And here you are. That's very straight up. You gotta admire that. Your move.

**CLARENCE** That's the way you see it?

**DAN** That's the way I see it.

**CLARENCE** That's some pretty heavy analysis. Okay, so tell me. Just how straight up is it to not even *read* a book, then, like you say, tag a million dollars on someone's ass because you *think*, maybe, they said something wrong?

**DAN** I gotta tell you, I can't blame the dude. I couldn't wade through that book'a yours with a shovel and a stick'a dynamite—

**CLARENCE** —Have you tried?—

**DAN** Ya, I've tried. I mean, where is it?

*DAN reaches into CLARENCE's briefcase, fishes out the book and flips through it.*

What is this "Mahound, Gibreel Farishta... Oopervala, the apparition answered, the fellow upstairs..."

*He tosses the book aside.*

I mean gimme a break, the stuff's unreadable, I think you shoulda been sentenced to death just for thinking up summa the fuckin' names'a yer characters. Move.

**CLARENCE** So, you're not a real big believer in freedom of expression?

**DAN** No, Mr. Rushdie, it may surprise you to find out I'm not. Move. Move.

**CLARENCE** So. What do you think about rap?

**DAN** Rap? Fuck rap, that's what I think about rap. As a matter of fact I can't stand that shit, d'zat come as another surprise to you? Or are all us young dudes s'posed to like that boomshakalakalakaboomshakalakalaka-rhyme-n-hop-n-grab-your-nuts type shit? Your move. You think I'm going to get all sentimental 'bout rap and cry big tears over who's having their asses thrown in jail for saying this thing or that? Listen to me, Mr. Potato Head, 'cause I'm about to set you straight 'bout something: There is no freaking freedom of expression, right? Not out there and sure as fuck not in this room.

**CLARENCE** Is that right?

**DAN** Ya, that's right, only in *this* room it's clear, no fairy tale. Out there, you know, it's say one thing, live another. Move, move, move. Lemme tell you, first of all number one, like I said, I tried to read your book and it put me to fucking sleep, and any freedom that allows you to bore me to tears like that is a stupid fucking freedom—your move—and second thing, number two, is like I said, there's no such thing as freedom of speech—

**CLARENCE** —So how exactly is that?—

**DAN** —*unless* you're rich, case in point, 'bout a year ago I go to court for this 'n that, nothing very major, 'n the judge calls me scum. "Scum!" What can I say? Nothing. He's the judge, now can I call his honour scum? Can I say where do you get off calling me scum, you weaselly pucker mouthed peckerhead, no, where's the freedom of speech, there is none – unless you're rich. Move. I lie, it's perjury, you lie it's artistic licence. I lie, it's breach'a contract, yer hotshot politician lies, it's a campaign promise, where's the freedom of speech, there is none. *Now*, my friend, I tell you what you can say, what you can't say, you think it's not fair, I say fuck you, fuck your freedom of speech, there's your freedom of speech, your move.

**CLARENCE** It bother you to know that kind of talk would get you shot in Iran?

**DAN** Not at all, 'cause I'm here.

**CLARENCE** You've got an answer for everything, haven't you?

**DAN** Yup.

**CLARENCE** Got it all worked out?

**DAN** Like to think so, yeah.

**CLARENCE** So, how are you going to get me past the police to whoever it is you're going to contact, *if* you ever contact anybody?

**DAN** I ain't gonna tell you that, 'kay—

**CLARENCE** —And what are you going to do when the police come looking for me at your lounge, as they're going to eventually?—

**DAN** —I don't *have* to tell you that either 'cause—

**CLARENCE** —And what are you going to do when no one answers your letter and Gerald and Ellie start to get bored?

**DAN** —I ain't gonna tell you what my plans are!—

**CLARENCE** —Because you don't have a plan!—

**DAN** —I do have a plan, I just ain't gonna tell you—

**CLARENCE** —"You ain't gonna tell me"—

**DAN** —Matter of fact I'm not gonna tell you fuck all about anything, matter of fact I don't want you to say anything, either, not anything—

*CLARENCE goes to say something but stops as DAN stands and interrupts him.*

—You say anything, anything at all, and I'm gonna break this chair over your fucking head, what about that? Hey, look I'm gonna remove your pawn from the board—*Bingo*—it's gone! You mad about that? Ticked off? Steamed 'bout your loss of democratically elected chess freedoms? Too bad! Hey look! – I'm taking away your bishop, recalled by the Pope to Rome – he's *history*, you want to say something about it? Huh? See freedom's only a freedom when you can deny it to somebody else, and right now I'm chockablock fulla freedom! I am the fucking Grand Wazoo'a Freedom! You want to say something about it? Huh? Do you? Go ahead!

*DAN raises the chair.*

But don't forget I got the chair, right here, and I'd be just as happy to finish this whole shiteroo right here, right now, take your head right off, go ahead say something! Oh, there goes your rook, and there goes your motherfuckin' queen and now it's my move, bim bam, *checkmate Solomon!* Ya! And the big guy wins!

*DAN performs a triumphant dance.*

You lose.

*DAN lowers the chair.*

So. Care to autograph your book, Mr. Rushdie?

*He picks up the book and tosses it to CLARENCE, who catches it. Lights down.*

## Scene Four – Night Four

*Lights up. The length of chain that runs from CLARENCE's waist is just long enough to allow him to lie down on the bed—which is what he does now. Music comes from a tape player sitting in the corner. The room now begins to take on a littered look: comic books, cassettes, overflowing ashtrays. ELLIE emerges from the washroom, continuing her conversation with CLARENCE as she does so. She flips her hair and glances back one more time into the washroom mirror.*

**CLARENCE** Now *she's* crazy.

**ELLIE** And ugly.

**CLARENCE** Mind you, *he's* no treat. Have you ever seen a close up of him?

**ELLIE** Whoa.

**CLARENCE** It's all that touring under those hot lights – he's the dehydrated man. He's *all wrinkles. I mean, drop that man in a jug'a water!*

**ELLIE** But is it any wonder he's still on the road at age fifty or whatever – he's gotta get outta the house! Imagine waking up and looking over at her. In the morning?

*Kill me now!* I mean, we see her at her best. With no make-up and bad hair it's gotta be like waking up to that movie "Aliens" happenin' right there beside you and the alien head popping right up outta the pillow! Ew! And fer sure those are not her real tits.

**CLARENCE** Well. I may be biased but I gotta say, on a balance, he's uglier than she is.

**ELLIE** Ya, sure, but who's got the bread? You can put up with a lotta ugly for the kinda bread Mick Jagger's makin'. But what's Jerry Hall bringin' to the table but mutt ugly and fake tits?

**CLARENCE** Give me a drink will you?

**ELLIE** Ya.

*She takes his empty glass to the washroom. On the way there, she stops to look out the window.*

Spooky out here, eh?

*CLARENCE grunts his ironic agreement.*

The last way you'd want to spend your Saturday night, eh?

**CLARENCE** Couldn't agree more.

*ELLIE pulls the drapes and glances out at the darkness.*

**ELLIE** Gerald says coyotes come out here. And bats. I wouldn't live this far outta downtown for a million bucks – well, maybe a million. And Gerald's dad. Whoa, you wanta talk spooky, now he's fuckin' Mr. Friday the thirteenth. The thought'a him creepin' 'round here to check things out, that's scary. I've seen pictures'a him, he's one ugly old fat dude – one'a those super-religious types that look super, super straight but secretly whack off with a picture of Mary Tyler Moore.

*She looks out a little longer.*

Yeah, do what you want, but don't leave me out here in the boonies.

*She goes into the washroom. Comes out with the glass of water.*

Here.

**CLARENCE** Thanks. Whose hardware is all this anyway?

*He lifts his handcuffs.*

**ELLIE** Dan got a hold of 'em. Scary, huh? There's a kinkier side to Dan than meets the eye.

**CLARENCE** You think you could let me have an arm free?—

**ELLIE** —Fuck off. Don't ask—

**CLARENCE** —Just an arm—

**ELLIE** —Yeah, like those guys who say can I put it in for just a minute—

**CLARENCE** —My arms and legs are killing me—

**ELLIE** —Don't ask. Don't!

**CLARENCE** Okay.

*Pause. ELLIE lights up a smoke.*

That'll give you wrinkles.

**ELLIE** Yeah. Well. I'll smoke 'til I'm slightly textured.

**CLARENCE** "Slightly textured"? That's very clever.

**ELLIE** Well, thank you, Mr. Letterman.

**CLARENCE** No, it is. You ever thought of becoming a VJ?

**ELLIE** What?

**CLARENCE** A VJ. You know? On TV?

**ELLIE** Who? Me?

**CLARENCE** Sure, you could do it. You'd be good at it.

**ELLIE** Ha.

**CLARENCE** I mean it. You got looks, you seem to know about music.

**ELLIE** Yeah, well. I mean, I'm no musical genius, but I know a fuck of a lot more than some'a those dim for brains they got. I mean some'a them don't know their Soundgarden from their Kindergarten, y'know. It's pathetic.

*There's a sound.*

Whoa. What's that?

*There's a sound.*

Oh, fuck.

*She turns down the music and snaps out some of the lights.*

Trust my luck, it'll be Gerald's old man Friday the thirteenth come checking things out.

*She butts out her smoke.*

Sonofabitch.

*She picks up a baseball bat.*

Now don't you say anything. You let out one peep and I'll pop you. I'm not kiddin'.

*They sit in semi darkness. Silence.*

You hear anything?

**CLARENCE** No.

**ELLIE** Well, what the fuck was that?

*She gets up slowly and walks to the doorway. Nothing. She opens the door.*

**CLARENCE** Eeep.

*ELLIE jumps.*

**ELLIE** Hey!

*She delivers a warning look, then glances out the door.*

What's goin' on?

*She creeps out the door. Quiet. Hear her walking. Quiet.*

Gerald? Dan?

*She comes back. Shuts the door.*

Nothin'.

*She goes to the window. Slides the curtains back, peers out. Nothing. Suddenly she shrieks.*

*Whoa! Oh my Gawd!*

*She runs across the room to stand beside CLARENCE.*

Bats! There's a great big motherin' bat hangin' right in the curtain.

*The curtain stirs, we hear a bat.*

Oh, man! I can't stand bats.

**CLARENCE** —Let it out—

**ELLIE** —Yeah, just invite it out—

**CLARENCE** —Open the window—

**ELLIE** —And let a coupla dozen more fly in. No thank you—

**CLARENCE** —It'll fly out—

**ELLIE** —I'm not goin' near that widow. No way. Uh uh.

*It stirs.*

Holy shit!

**CLARENCE** Give me that.

*He points to the baseball bat.*

**ELLIE** As if.

**CLARENCE** Give it to me. I'm not going to do anything to you.

*The bat stirs and ELLIE tosses CLARENCE the baseball bat. Holding it, CLARENCE climbs onto the chair, pushes it across the room. He and the chair land against the wall with a thump. The bat stirs.*

**ELLIE** Ewww!

*ELLIE scuttles to the furthest reaches of the room. CLARENCE stands—and even though his hands are shackled to his waist—he manages, using the baseball bat, to poke at the window and unfasten the latch. The window falls open, the bat launches itself out and flies away.*

**CLARENCE** Now quick, come shut it.

*ELLIE runs over and slams the window shut. They stop and breathe. Everything becomes quiet. CLARENCE tosses her the bat.*

**ELLIE** Wow. That was a trip.

*She pushes CLARENCE back over to the bed. He climbs out of the chair and flops back onto the bed.*

Thanks.

**CLARENCE** No problem.

**ELLIE** I hate bats.

*She sits.*

I mean, I s'pose you guessed that.

*Pause.*

**CLARENCE** So what's the deal? Dan your boyfriend, is that it?

**ELLIE** *(snorts)* Right. In his dreams, maybe. We're buddies. Kinda. Maybe a little more than that once, but—

**CLARENCE** —I thought the way he was talking—

**ELLIE** —Why? What'd he say?

**CLARENCE** Just, y'know—

**ELLIE** —What?—

**CLARENCE** —how much he's helped you out and all.

**ELLIE** How much he's helped me out?

**CLARENCE** Yeah.

**ELLIE** How much he's helped me out? Ha. How?

**CLARENCE** Said he got you your job. Your apartment.

**ELLIE** He said that?

**CLARENCE** Yeah.

**ELLIE** My job? Ya, he got me the job. I'm a waitress. Whoopee do. He's like the bouncer next door in the bar, thinks he's got connections with the president. Apartment? Right. If a garage is an apartment, he got me an apartment. I got no shower and the place reeks'a exhaust and there's oil spots on the carpet. Fuck that guy, he's gotta take credit for every fuckin' thing in my life. It's unreal. An' he keeps settin' me up on dates. Like I'm s'posed to think it's an honour. Here's so and so, they're new in town, take care'a them. "Take care'a them." I'm s'posed to thank him for settin' me up with Mr. Bad Suit, Bad Hair, Bad Breath, Bad Everything. He keeps saying he wants to "manage" me, like who's ever heard of a manager who was a bouncer? And always broke. Man.

*She lights a smoke.*

You think this dress is too tight? I mean, I want it tight, but you don't want anything to make you look like a chubbo.

**CLARENCE** No, it's not too tight.

**ELLIE** No?

**CLARENCE** You look good.

**ELLIE** You think so?

**CLARENCE** Sure. It's what got me here in the first place, right? Say, how old are you?

**ELLIE** How old do you think I am?

**CLARENCE** Twenty-three. I'd say twenty-three. Am I close?

*She shakes her head.*

Older? You don't look older.

*She shakes her head.*

Twenty-one. Less than that? You're less than twenty-one. Twenty? Nineteen? You'll stop me when I get there, right? – Less than nineteen? Eighteen? Seventeen?

**ELLIE** Bingo.

**CLARENCE** Come on, you're seventeen?

*She nods.*

Wow. You look… a lot older.

**ELLIE** Happens all the time. Everyone thinks I'm older than what I am. Always have. It's 'cause I matured early. That's the only way I got the job in the lounge, I'd make better tips other places but they're more suspicious about ID.

**CLARENCE** I bet. Well, you had me fooled. Look… Ellie, I'm being straight with you when I tell you I was just trying to pick you up the other night—

**ELLIE** —Aw. Don't—

**CLARENCE** —I mean, this is just stupid—

**ELLIE** —Don't start that shit, 'kay? Dan *said* specifically no talking about that, and you know I gave my word. I mean, I'm not gonna peg you with the bat or anything, but I'll walk outta here – go outside, get some air 'til you cut it out. And you know I don't want'a do that.

**CLARENCE** I'm not going to say anything. I'm just telling you, in that briefcase there're some keys. You take them and you go to the address written on them, and you open it up. You'll find out everything you need to know about—

**ELLIE** —Don't start—

**CLARENCE** —who I really am. There, that's all. I'm not going to say anything more. You know where the keys are. Think about it.

**ELLIE** Right. I'll think about it.

**CLARENCE** Do that.

**ELLIE** I will.

**CLARENCE** Good.

*Mini pause.*

**ELLIE** But, I *don't* believe it, right? Know why?

**CLARENCE** No. Why?

*Pause.*

**ELLIE** 'Cause. A couple reasons. You smell good for one thing.

**CLARENCE** I smell good?

**ELLIE** Even after a coupl'a days here, you still smell good. I mean, that's something. You're managing to take care'a yourself, even wrapped in chains 'n shit. I mean, you're better groomed than half'a the guys I serve in the bar – most'a them. That's why I was eyeballin' you in the first place.

**CLARENCE** There are a lot of guys beyond that bar, Ellie.

**ELLIE** Ya. I just don't meet 'em.

**CLARENCE** But that doesn't mean—

**ELLIE** —Hey, I'm talkin'. The other thing is, you're different inside. I mean, you *think* different. I mean, I was going over what you said to me in the bar the other night? Remember? 'Bout your life and your writin'? And all the things you've done?

**CLARENCE** —Ellie, it's what I'm telling you—

**ELLIE** Sh! I'm tellin' you, I think that's what's so fuckin' wicked. I mean, you've *done* stuff with your life already. I don't know anyone else who's done anything like what you said. Travel anywhere. Eat anything you want. I've never travelled. Furthest away I've ever even *known* anyone to go was Disneyland. And I mean, Disneyland's cool, but it's still just Disneyland, right? You been to Europe and Asia and all'a that. I never had a hope of going anywhere like that.

*She pushes her chair in closer.*

I like thinking about you. After we picked you up, brought you here, that's all I could do all night. Think about you. Everyone I know lives, just like to get by. Ordinary fucked up lives. Gotta do what someone else says, their mom, their boss, their parole officer. Not you. It's gotta take real balls to say, "I'm gonna write this book. I'm gonna write it and screw everything else, screw it even if I gotta go into hiding, screw it even if someone's gonna *kill* me. This is *my* moment, *my* thoughts. Me. That seems so – right on. That seems so, so – cool. You know? That's somethin'. Somethin' no one can take away. No one can control that. Nobody can touch what you think or feel, right?

*Pause. She butts out her cigarette.*

Listen. I can massage your arms if you're really that uncomfortable. In exchange for the window thing you did.

*She sits on the bed and massages his right arm.*

But no nonsense, right? I'm serious about that baseball bat, I beat the crap outta this one dude who tried to break into my place the other night. I'm no wimp when it comes to crackin' heads.

*She continues massaging.*

That okay?

**CLARENCE** Feels great.

**ELLIE** You like my hands?

**CLARENCE** Yeah. They look nice.

**ELLIE** Small, eh?

**CLARENCE** Very delicate.

**ELLIE** I like 'em.

*She continues massaging.*

One'a my best features, I think.

**CLARENCE** You know how to massage.

**ELLIE** I used to hafta massage my mom's hands. She had arthritis, her hands looked like a lunch sack fulla marbles, they didn't look like hands at all. I used to wonder if my hands'd look like that when I grew up, used to worry that they would, that my hands 'n everything would look like hers 'cause she looked like—oh—she'd scare you the way she looked. She was ugly. Drank heavy. Ate bad. Had teeth like you see on those school health films, like when they're showing you what you don't want'a look like with cavities and swollen gums and.... You know, I been surrounded by *ugly* people most of my life. If I never see another ugly person again, it'll be too soon.

*She kisses him.*

**CLARENCE** Ellie—

**ELLIE** —Sh. Don't say nothing.

*She kisses him again. Lights down.*

## Scene Five - Night Five

*Lights up. Several days have passed. There is a fair accumulation of junk food debris at this point. GERALD sits talking with CLARENCE, who is chained to the chair.*

**GERALD** Do that one again.

**CLARENCE** "I'm smokin'!"

**GERALD** That sounds just like him. Just like him. One more time.

**CLARENCE** "I'm smokin'!"

**GERALD** Too cool. Do some more.

**CLARENCE** Arnie?

**GERALD** Sure.

**CLARENCE** "I'll be back."

**GERALD** That's great.

**CLARENCE** "Abdy-abdy-abdy – that's all folks."

*GERALD laughs immoderately.*

**GERALD** You are so good.

**CLARENCE** "I am not a crook."

*GERALD draws a blank.*

**GERALD** Who's that?

**CLARENCE** Nixon? Former president.

**GERALD** Ri-ight. *(He still doesn't get it.)* Do Jim Carrey again.

**CLARENCE** I need some water.

**GERALD** 'Kay.

*GERALD goes to the washroom with a glass. CLARENCE pulls hard at one of his hands while GERALD is out of the room, trying to slip it through the handcuff loop. He begins imitating an owl as GERALD returns.*

That is a gift, man.

**CLARENCE** What is that, anyway?

**GERALD** What you just did?

**CLARENCE** Yeah. I've heard it at nights here.

**GERALD** And you don't even know what it is?

**CLARENCE** No.

**GERALD** Man! That's amazing, first time you hear it and you can repeat it, just like that. That… that's a miracle, y'know? See, that's how I know you are who you are, in spite of what you say. 'Cause you're talented. Like you see things a different way. You see things *different* – you can't hide that kinda thing. What you just did? That's a barn owl. They're all over the field out there, after yer mice 'n rabbits 'n voles. Hey, did you know that as man spreads all over the world with his cities and everything the one type'a animal that is expanding, too, is the rodent? 'Cause they feed on all'a that junk that man leaves behind, right?

*GERALD finishes a bag of chips and drops the bag without, for even a second, connecting his deeds with his words.*

And I guess maybe the barn owl, too, 'cause they like, feed on rodents.

**CLARENCE** They here all year?

**GERALD** Owls? Naw. Only during the summer and fall. More of 'em now since my dad's gotten older. He used to shoot the crap out of 'em. Come to birds, gophers, squirrels, badgers, snakes or any other creepin', crawlin' kinda thing he was the fuckin' terminator. Was always worried about 'em getting after his chickens, y'know. He had chickens on the freakin' brain, you couldn't do anything might disturb his precious chickens. Couldn't watch TV too loud, couldn't slam the door. You went to the washroom, you felt like you ought to wear a silencer attachment. I told him scientists have proved that when owls are given the choice between a mouse and a chicken, they will take the mouse like ninety-nine percent of the time, but my dad couldn't wrap his pea brain around that kinda mathematical evidence. He'd just blast 'em outta the sky whenever he caught sight'a one. Bang. I remember when I was a kid, I couldn'ta been more 'n five, six, we were walking through the canola, and this great big grey owl—like I'm talkin' *big*, it coulda been as big as me at the time—came floating over top of us like a, a snowflake, like a, like a *dream* it was that quiet, like it wasn't real at all – whoosh! An angel, that's what I thought for a moment. All big 'n feathery like an *angel*. Then my moron dad whipped up this big motherin' over and under he's packin' and Kaboom! – owl feathers everywhere. Double ought shot and everything. Wasn't enough owl left to feather a hummingbird after.

**CLARENCE** How come?

**GERALD** 'Cause he's a pinhead 'n I come from a long line'a pinheads.

**CLARENCE** Is this a very big farm?

**GERALD** 'Bout average, for out here, it's – oh fuck!

**CLARENCE** What?

**GERALD** I'm not s'posed to talk about this place.

**CLARENCE** Relax, relax. I'm not going to say anything. I mean, I'm still locked up, right? We're just talking.

**GERALD** But I *promised*. I'm not going to say anything more about this place.

**CLARENCE** Fine. We're just passing the time. We can talk about something else. So, your dad's a hunter?

**GERALD** He's a fuckin' dork with a fork 'n I don't want to talk about him, neither.

**CLARENCE** Okay.

*Pause.*

So. You guys went to school together?

**GERALD** What the fuck do you care, all right?

**CLARENCE** It's just conversation.

**GERALD** Yeah, well, this conversation is over.

*They sit in silence. Neither of them say anything. GERALD looks off into the distance, shifts in his seat.*

Yeah, we went to school together.

**CLARENCE** From what grade?

**GERALD** Eight. Ellie in grade eight.

**CLARENCE** And Dan?

**GERALD** Don't know. Was a "blended" grade school for young offenders 'n screw-ups, so you kinda had people comin' back for their grade nine who already had full beards and tattoos 'n that kinda thing, y'know.

**CLARENCE** Residential school?

**GERALD** Some of us. Me and Ellie were in residence there. Dan lived with his mom.

**CLARENCE** You weren't living with your dad?

**GERALD** Naw! You kiddin'? Was finished with him long before that. I was thirteen, right? Showering. I'm at an age I want privacy, right? So I lock the door. Well, my old man's got something up his ass about locks, no one can lock nothing but him. He comes in, says he's gotta use the can, tries the door – it's locked. "Unlock the door," he says. I say, "Hold your horses, I'm showering." He freaks. "Open the door, open the door this fucking minute." Rattlin' the door, rattlin' the door. I'm, "Hey, hold on, I'm naked." Boom. He kicks the door down. Picks me up, chucks me out the front door 'n locks it back up. It's winter, right? Snow everywhere, right? I'm naked. That cocksucker won't open the door. Lemme in, I tell him. Apologize, he says. Says I've shown him disrespect. Apologize. I sat out there. I sat out there 'til I thought I was going to freeze to death. I thought no way am I going to apologize and it just gets colder and colder and then I realize he really is. He really is going to let me freeze to death for not openin' the door at the exact precise second he says. So I knock on the door and I apologize. I took off from home that night. Lived with friends for a while. Lived on the streets for a while. Then got picked up for this 'n that, ended up in residency.

**CLARENCE** That's tough.

**GERALD** Fuck of a lot better than living at home. The old man's a major loser, right? I could tell you stories.

**CLARENCE** You got a girlfriend, Gerald?

**GERALD** Me? No.

**CLARENCE** How come?

**GERALD** *(laughs)* Like it's a mystery, right?

**CLARENCE** You like to keep relationships at arm's-length? That it?

**GERALD** Ha.

**CLARENCE** I mean, I thought you and Ellie were…

**GERALD** Me 'n Ellie? I wish. No. She 'n Dan are more…. Not really, but kind of.

**CLARENCE** Yeah?

**GERALD** Off 'n on. More off than on these days.

**CLARENCE** Huh.

*Slight pause.*

**GERALD** Why?

**CLARENCE** It's nothing.

**GERALD** Why?

**CLARENCE** I thought. She seems to like you.

**GERALD** Well, yeah, sure, we're buddies. Like, we actually knew each other longer, too. We went to school longer and all. But. I mean, look at me. I'm not exactly a babe magnet.

**CLARENCE** Huh.

*Slight pause.*

**GERALD** What?

**CLARENCE** I was just thinking about *body language.*

**GERALD** Body language? What's that? You mean like sign language?

**CLARENCE** No, you know, body language.

**GERALD** Haven't got a clue what you're talking about.

**CLARENCE** Look, human beings are just like hairless monkeys, right? When monkeys are together they don't talk with words like we do. They talk with their bodies. You've seen gorillas thump their chests, yeah?

**GERALD** Sure, on the nature programs.

**CLARENCE** Gorilla's way of telling another gorilla to piss off. Humans are the same way.

**GERALD** Right.

**CLARENCE** We don't beat our chest, but you know, the way we stand, how close we get to someone, whether we stare someone in the eye or not, it's all saying something. And around you, Ellie's body language is, well...

**GERALD** What?

**CLARENCE** ...very open.

**GERALD** No way.

**CLARENCE** Yeah.

**GERALD** Right.

**CLARENCE** Sure.

**GERALD** Open?

**CLARENCE** Yeah.

**GERALD** So what's that mean anyway?

**CLARENCE** Like her body gives off signals that are saying she's, open, to you.

**GERALD** Right. Open to me?

**CLARENCE** Yeah.

**GERALD** Fuck off. She's not open to me.

*Mini pause.*

How?

**CLARENCE** Like the way she stares at you. She looks you straight in the eyes. That's a big signal.

**GERALD** Yeah?

**CLARENCE** Oh, yeah.

**GERALD** Of what?

**CLARENCE** That's a very big way of saying you're open. But you… *you* look away. That's saying you're closed. That's like putting up a big sign saying you're not available for business.

**GERALD** Fuck off.

**CLARENCE** I'm telling you.

**GERALD** As if *I'd* say to *her* I was unavailable. *Right.*

**CLARENCE** It's not a conscious thing, it's not something you say to yourself, it's something you're doing *unconsciously.* And I'm telling you, unconsciously she's saying she'd like to get to know you better.

**GERALD** No.

**CLARENCE** Yeah!

**GERALD** And you see this?

**CLARENCE** Yeah, in the couple of times you've both been here, the other day when you came and she was leaving. Like, how close you stand or sit. She'll come up and stand right beside you. You'll move off.

**GERALD** I don't do that. Do I?

**CLARENCE** Sure you do. Think about it. Without even noticing. That's the power of body language. See, you don't even know. You just feel this thing, this force and you react. Maybe you'll feel nervous, or you'll feel like you're in someone's way… and you'll step back. *You don't even think about it*—and bang!—you've said, "I'm not available."

**GERALD** No kiddin'?

**CLARENCE** Yeah.

**GERALD** 'Cause I've felt that. Nervous.

**CLARENCE** Sure. You can tell. Look, here's a series of, whatever you want to call them, experiments, you can try. How close are you to me?

**GERALD** Eight feet.

**CLARENCE** Look me in the eye. From there.

**GERALD** Okay.

**CLARENCE** And don't break it.

*They stare at each other.*

How do you feel?

*Slight pause as they stare at each other.*

**GERALD** Like a really big dork.

**CLARENCE** Stand up straight. I'll look away, and look up to catch your eye – you just keep staring and see how it feels.

*They do it.*

How's that?

**GERALD** I can feel it.

**CLARENCE** Can you feel it?

**GERALD** Yeah, I can.

**CLARENCE** A more powerful feeling?

**GERALD** Yeah. Like I got this, power.

**CLARENCE** That's not something you do very often is it?

**GERALD** I *never* do that.

**CLARENCE** Okay, now, move closer.

**GERALD** It's like you feel a – force.

**CLARENCE** A *force*, that's exactly the right word for it. Now walk around the room with that feeling.

**GERALD** Walk. How?

**CLARENCE** Just walk.

*He walks.*

Ah, ah, ah. You're losing it. Close your eyes.

**GERALD** Why?

**CLARENCE** Just do it. Stand still. Now, see yourself.

**GERALD** You've asked me to close my eyes.

**CLARENCE** In your mind. See yourself in your mind.

**GERALD** Oh. Okay.

**CLARENCE** Now, in your mind, what are you doing?

**GERALD** Just hangin' out.

**CLARENCE** Are you standing straight? Or leaning?

**GERALD** Kinda leaning.

**CLARENCE** Straighten up. Are you smiling or frowning?

**GERALD** I don't know.

**CLARENCE** Imagine you've done something really well and you've been complimented.

**GERALD** For what?

**CLARENCE** Anything.

**GERALD** But, like – for what?

**CLARENCE** What might you be complimented for?

**GERALD** Maybe getting a package to someone on time.

**CLARENCE** Getting a package to someone?

**GERALD** That's what I do, I deliver things, bike courier. If you're late you get reamed out like anything, but sometimes if you're right on time you'll get a tip, or something like that.

*He opens his eyes.*

Oh. I shouldn'ta told you that.

**CLARENCE** It's okay. Close your eyes.

*GERALD closes his eyes.*

Fair enough, you've just been complimented for getting something to someone on time. You're happy.

**GERALD** Did I get a tip?

**CLARENCE** Sure, you got a tip. You're smiling. You're standing tall. You've got your money in your pocket. You feel great. Now, can you see that?

**GERALD** Yes.

**CLARENCE** Can you?

**GERALD** Yeah!

**CLARENCE** Walk around the room – *with that feeling.*

**GERALD** With my eyes closed?

**CLARENCE** Yes.

*GERALD walks.*

Oh, yeah. You look completely different. Your body is talking, and it is talking a completely different language.

**GERALD** It feels different.

**CLARENCE** It is different. Okay, set your chair down here.

**GERALD** Can I open my eyes?

**CLARENCE** Yes.

*He opens his eyes.*

Set it here. I want to see you sit.

**GERALD** Like this?

**CLARENCE** Do it one more time.

**GERALD** Like this?

*He sits and suddenly CLARENCE swings his left arm around GERALD's neck.*

Hey, what the fuck? How'd you get that loose?

**CLARENCE** Don't move or I'll break your neck. Give me the key.

**GERALD** I don't have it.

**CLARENCE** Don't give me that bullshit. Give me the key!

**GERALD** This was all some sort of trick, that it?

*CLARENCE reefs on GERALD's neck.*

I don't have it! I don't.

**DAN** He doesn't.

*DAN stands at the door.*

I have it.

**CLARENCE** Oh fuck. Give it to me, or I'll kill him. I'm not kidding. Tell him.

**GERALD** Ow! He's not kiddin'.

**CLARENCE** Give it to me!

**GERALD** He's not kiddin'! Give it to him! Ow!

**DAN** I guess you'll have to kill him.

**GERALD** What?!

**CLARENCE** I'm not joking!

**GERALD** Ow! He's not kiddin'! He's chokin' me! Dan! *He's chokin' me!*

**DAN** Kill him. Go ahead.

*DAN lights a cigarette and stands watching.*

Kill him!

*CLARENCE stares a moment at DAN, then simply releases GERALD.*

**GERALD** Ow.

*GERALD scrambles back to his feet.*

**DAN** *I told you.* Don't talk to him. Are you going to be careful now?

**GERALD** Yes.

**DAN** Are you?

**GERALD** Yes! Some friend you are. "Kill him." I'll remember that.

**DAN** Fine. And you. Put your hands back up there. Put 'em back up. Gerald, lock him up again.

*GERALD locks CLARENCE's left hand up again. ELLIE enters, limping and in a foul mood. The heel on one of her shoes has broken. She holds it.*

**ELLIE** Look at this! One'a my best pair'a shoes. Now what am I goint'a do with 'em? The freakin' road up here might as well be a freakin' obstacle course. What's goin' on here?

**DAN** Seems Solomon's got a bit'a Houdini in him. Got one of his hands free and was stranglin' the life outta poor old Ger here.

**ELLIE** Man.

*She limps to the window and throws it open.*

The place is like a pig sty. Gerald, whady'ya been doin' out here?

**GERALD** Nothing. Hangin' out. Watching *him.*

**DAN** And doin' a great job'a that.

**GERALD** Fuck yourself. Fuck both'a you. I get my head ripped off, while you watch—

**DAN** —Teach you a lesson—

**GERALD** —and all you two can do is criticize.

**ELLIE** The place reeks!

**GERALD** Fuck you!

**ELLIE** Fuck you!

**DAN** Fucking quit, both'a you!

**GERALD** Fuck you, too!

**ELLIE** Fuck this! I didn't come out here in the middle of the freakin' nowhere to listen to you whine.

**GERALD** You try havin' your head nearly ripped off—

**ELLIE** —Maybe if you were doin' something other than sittin' around eating nachos and Twizzlers.

**GERALD** How do *you* know what I was doin'?

**ELLIE** This is a waste'a time. When are we going to hear something? You said a *week*, this is gettin' stupid—

**GERALD** —Yeah, when are we goin' to hear something?—

**ELLIE** —I'm breakin' the heels off my shoes—

**DAN** —Maybe I've got something to tell you—

**GERALD** —Well, you better have, because I'm sick'a this—

**ELLIE** —Me, too!—

**GERALD** —Sick'a sittin' around, babysitting this psycho—

**CLARENCE** —*Psycho*? Hey, I didn't ask to get babysat—

**DAN** —Hey—

**ELLIE** —Sick'a coming out here, might as well be in another country—

**DAN** —Hey—

**GERALD** —No showers, no TV—

**ELLIE** —I hate this house, this room, this window—

*DAN holds up a newspaper.*

**GERALD** What?

*Pause.*

**ELLIE** What's that?

**GERALD** You heard something? Is that something there?

**DAN** You ready to listen now? Lemme read you what it says.

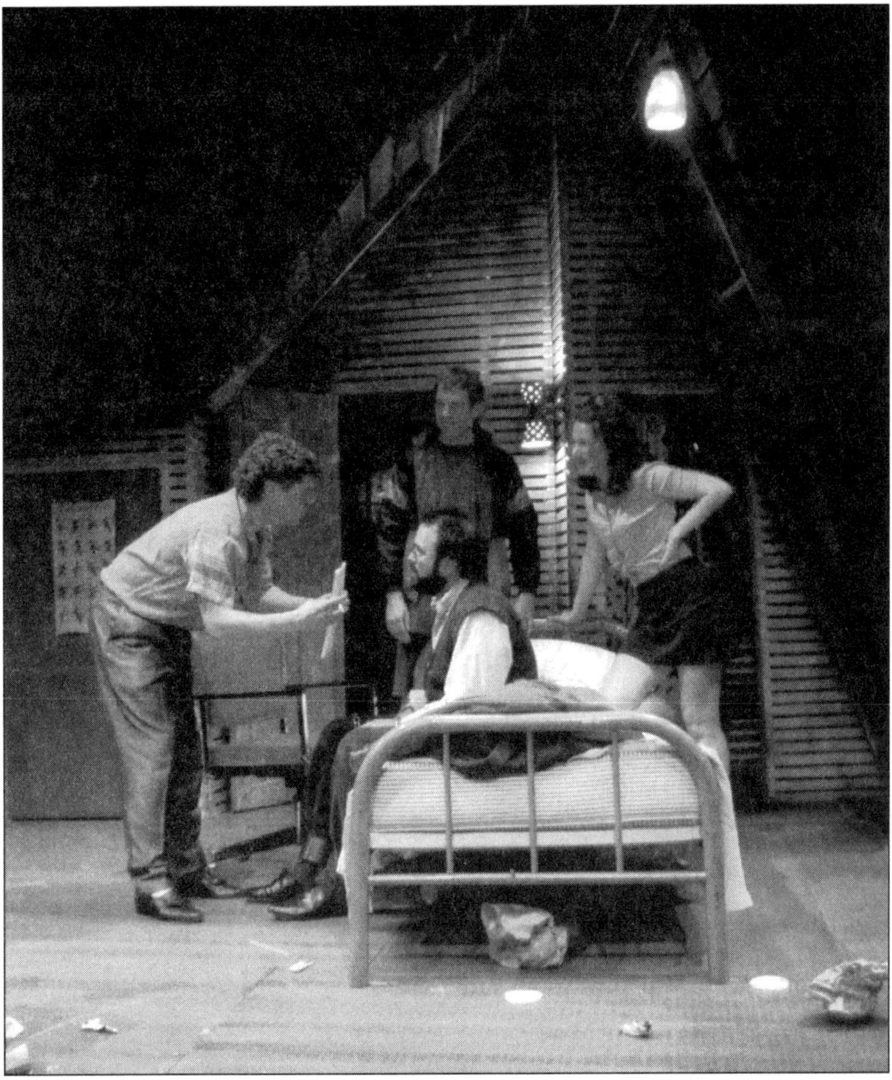

Kevin James Kruchkywich, Murray Utas, Dave Clarke (on bed) and April Banigan
*photo by Ed Ellis*

*He unfolds the newspaper.*

Personal ads. *(reading)* Ahem. "Dear Deg:—

**GERALD** —Deg! Hey that's us! Gimme that!

*GERALD snatches for the paper but DAN pulls it away and continues reading.*

**ELLIE** Let 'im read!

**DAN** "Dear Deg: Very interested. Will require further ID. Send fingerprints."

**ELLIE** You're kiddin'?

**DAN** There it is in black and white.

*ELLIE looks at it and gives DAN a hug and kiss.*

That's more like it.

*DAN gives her a longer, fuller kiss and gropes her a bit. ELLIE backs away slightly.*

**ELLIE** Okay, you don't hafta make a meal of it.

*She looks at the paper again.*

There it is in black and white. So, what address?

**DAN** It's just an address.

**GERALD** Is it like the Iranian embassy or something?

**DAN** The Iranian embassy! Use your head! They're not goin' to have us send something like that to the embassy.

**GERALD** Why not?

**DAN** It's a secret! This's a box number.

*GERALD snatches it and reads it.*

**GERALD** All right!

**ELLIE** Lemme see!

**CLARENCE** This is bullshit. It's somebody pulling your leg—

**ELLIE** —Where's it say it?

**DAN** Right there. "Very interested…"

**CLARENCE** —It's a joke.

**ELLIE** Wow!

**GERALD** We did it!

**ELLIE** Yeah!

*She kisses DAN again.*

**DAN** Gimme your hand.

*DAN grabs CLARENCE's hand and pushes it onto a stamp pad he has produced from his pocket. He then pushes the hand against a piece of paper. He holds the handprint up triumphantly.*

There's your joke, Solomon. There's your joke. Your hand print in the next mail out. Next best thing to a million in our pockets!

**GERALD** Right on!

*GERALD and DAN give each other a high five. Lights snap out.*

*End of Act One.*

# Act Two

## Scene One

*Everyone is in exactly the same positions they were at the end of Act One.*

**DAN** There's your joke, Solomon. There's your joke. Your handprint in the next mail out! Next best thing to a million in our pockets!

**GERALD** Right on!

*They give each other high fives.*

**DAN** Hey – and that's not the only thing we got to celebrate.

**ELLIE** What else?

**DAN** It's downstairs in the car. Hold on.

*DAN exits. GERALD decides to use this moment to practice some of the stuff he's learned from CLARENCE. He begins staring at ELLIE. At first she doesn't think anything of it and looks away as she lights a smoke, but when she glances back up, she finds that he's still staring at her. After putting her cigarettes away, she glances up once more at GERALD and this time confronts him.*

**ELLIE** Gerald! What're you doing?

*Rattled, GERALD folds immediately and breaks eye contact.*

**GERALD** Nothing.

*DAN re-enters at that moment with a spray can in his hand.*

**DAN** Here it is.

**GERALD** What?

**DAN** This!

*He holds up the spray can.*

**ELLIE** So what's that?

**DAN** This is like the wasp version of the atomic bomb – designed to kill them on contact—

**ELLIE** Whady'ya mean, on contact?

**DAN** It means on contact?

**ELLIE** So?

**DAN** So, what?

**ELLIE** So, what's that mean?

**DAN** It means on contact, "on contact," it means when it touches them.

**ELLIE** Like, doesn't everything work that way? I mean, it'd be pretty weird if it worked, you know, while it was still in the can. Like, the wasps just *read* the label or whatever and croaked—

**DAN** It's what it says, I'm just reading what it says, does everything have to be a big deal?

**ELLIE** You're the one trying to make it a big deal, like you try to make everything a big deal—

**DAN** —Suddenly it's on me—

**ELLIE** You said "on contact" like it was something, I was just trying to find out—

**DAN** —Well now, you know. Satisfied?

**ELLIE** Thank you very much.

**DAN** And it works up to twenty feet away, so we can massacre those sonsofbitches without getting stung ourselves. And this is the time to do it, 'cause it's dark and they're tucked in their little wasp beds under their little wasp blankees, asleep, so here you go.

*He tosses the can to GERALD.*

**GERALD** Me.

**DAN** Yeah. You're the wasp expert so you're elected. Besides, you know where the nest is.

**GERALD** So. Whady'ya do with this?

**DAN** Ready, aim, fire. From up to twenty feet away. Directions are all there. Just read it.

*GERALD starts to go, then stops.*

**GERALD** Although, you know, wasps never all sleep at once—

**DAN** Fuck. Most'a them.

**GERALD** —Maybe most of them, but there're always some that stay awake—

**DAN** —Yeah, yeah, okay, so long as they're all in one place it really doesn't matter 'cause the ones that have insomnia will be dead along with their better rested buddies seconds later, 'kay. You gotta flashlight there, brainiac?

**GERALD** Yeah.

**DAN** Then off you go. Kick some'a that wasp butt.

*DAN gives GERALD a push. GERALD shrugs off the push and halts.*

**GERALD** Hey.

**DAN** What now?

**GERALD** What's that sound?

*ELLIE shrinks back.*

**ELLIE** Bats? Is it bats?

**GERALD** No, no. Sh. *(listens)* It's a car motor.

*GERALD rushes to the window.*

**DAN** I didn't hear nothing.

**GERALD** Wait a minute – Fuck, it's my old man!

**DAN** You're kiddin'?

*DAN looks out the window.*

What's he doin' here?

**GERALD** Fucked if I know.

**DAN** Oh, *man.*

**GERALD** Now what? He finds out about this, we're screwed.

**ELLIE** Go down and see him. We'll turn out the lights, pretend we're not here.

**DAN** Chill a minute. 'Kay, my wheels are parked out front so he's going to know someone's with you—

**ELLIE** —Go move your car—

**DAN** —He's right there—

**ELLIE** —*Shit!*—

**DAN** —so let's go out and meet him—

**GERALD** —and do *what*?

**DAN** Bring the wasp spray. He like giving advice?

**GERALD** What?

**DAN** Does he like giving advice?

**GERALD** He's the fucking king of advice. He never fucking stops.

**DAN** Good. He can help us trash the wasp nest and we can find out what he wants before he comes in.

*DAN turns to ELLIE.*

You keep an eye on Solomon here. He says anything, anything at all, you club him. You hear?

**ELLIE** Yeah, yeah.

**DAN** I mean it. You club him hard if he makes so much as a peep.

**ELLIE** I heard you.

**DAN** You understand? You make any noise, any shouting or any'a that shit, she'll club you and I'll come up and kill you.

**ELLIE** You better get going.

**DAN** Keep the door shut until you hear us tell you different.

*DAN and GERALD exit.*

**ELLIE** Not a sound.

**CLARENCE** I heard him.

**ELLIE** Don't think 'cause we've messed 'round that I've gone soft either.

**CLARENCE** Never crossed my mind.

**ELLIE** 'Cause I'm not that way about things. I know what's business. His old man's hard'a hearing anyway.

*ELLIE sits.*

**CLARENCE** Okay.

**ELLIE** Sh.

**CLARENCE** *(whispers)* I thought he was hard of hearing.

**ELLIE** Yeah. Well. Just keep it quiet.

*Pause. We hear, in the distance, a car door slam and, very faintly, the voices of DAN, GERALD and GERALD's old man. Gradually these voices fade as the three go off to hunt wasps.*

**CLARENCE** Ellie?

**ELLIE** Hm?

**CLARENCE** Suppose I was him.

**ELLIE** Who? What're you talking about?

**CLARENCE** Rushdie. Suppose I really *was* Salman Rushdie.

**ELLIE** Yeah. Well. I've already supposed that.

**CLARENCE** I guess. So, you got me.

**ELLIE** Right. We got you. So, sh.

**CLARENCE** So, you tell me. *The Satanic Verses.* You have any idea how much I make off that book.

**ELLIE** No.

*Pause.*

How much?

**CLARENCE** A lot.

**ELLIE** So, how much?

**CLARENCE** Do the math.

**ELLIE** If I could do the math, I wouldn't be here, right? So just tell me.

**CLARENCE** It was a bestseller, right?

**ELLIE** Sh. Yeah? So, it was a bestseller?…

**CLARENCE** Not only here but England and the rest of Europe, too. And it isn't the only book I've written. They're all selling well.

**ELLIE** So how much?

**CLARENCE** And it's British pounds I collect in. You know how much a pound is worth?

**ELLIE** What's your point?

**CLARENCE** Something you and your guys haven't thought about. I can beat the offer of one million easy.

*Pause. She listens for a moment for anyone coming up the stairs.*

**ELLIE** Yeah?

**CLARENCE** Absolutely. And look at the advantages. I pay you cash. I can't take you to court – I can't appear to testify. I can't let anyone know where I am, right? And look what you avoid. No deals with foreign embassies. No transporting me across borders. No charges of kidnapping or accessory to murder. No more waiting. I phone up my people, and they make a deal.

**ELLIE** I don't know—

**CLARENCE** You just want to make money, right? You don't want to make a bunch of Iranians happy?

**ELLIE** We want money, yeah.

**CLARENCE** Well, here I am.

**ELLIE** Yeah.

*Slight pause.*

So, why didn't you say something earlier?

**CLARENCE** Who wants to give a million away. And I didn't know how serious you all were.

**ELLIE** What? Kidnapping you wasn't serious enough?

**CLARENCE** —Besides, I've got to know who I'm dealing with.

*A car door slams. ELLIE pauses to listen.*

**ELLIE** Whady'ya mean?

*CLARENCE chooses his words very carefully.*

**CLARENCE** I have to know something first. Do you love Dan?

**ELLIE** Love Dan? As if. Why?

*Pause.*

**CLARENCE** See, my problem is, who do I deliver the money to?

**ELLIE** You deliver it to us, I mean, what? You're not paying my mom.

**CLARENCE** No, but listen, listen carefully—

**ELLIE** Sh.

*They stop and listen.*

It's nothing.

**CLARENCE** *Who* am I dealing with? I've got to believe that whoever I pay, I only pay once—

**ELLIE** —Once is enough—

**CLARENCE** —*and after that*, I'm free.

**ELLIE** Yeah?

**CLARENCE** So how can I guarantee that that's what's going to happen?

**ELLIE** Why shouldn't it happen? What're you saying?

**CLARENCE** You think all three of you would feel the same way about a deal?

**ELLIE** Sure.

**CLARENCE** The trouble in doing deals like this is if someone figures they can sell someone twice. Or they sell someone and they don't keep their end of the bargain. They don't let them go. I want to make a deal, Ellie. With you—

**ELLIE** —Wait a minute—

**CLARENCE** —With you—

**ELLIE** —I ain't double crossing anyone—

**CLARENCE** —I can trust you, Ellie. I can't trust Dan, I mean would you trust him if you were in my situation? *Do* you trust him?

*Pause.*

Look, everyone still gets paid, only you handle it. This way, no police, no trouble, no negotiating. The other way, the police get involved somewhere along the line. They've got to. Even if you get your money, you'll have to go somewhere else to live, take on a new identity. 'Cause the moment I'm caught – you are too. And for the rest of your life you're an accessory to kidnapping, maybe murder. Right? You won't be able to spend any of that money at the malls in *this* part of the world. You'll be just like me. Hunted.

**ELLIE** I hadn't thought'a that.

**CLARENCE** The other thing is…. This way we could still see each other. If you wanted. If no one else is involved it's just something we two have agreed upon, right? Our private deal. I could take you places, Ellie. Money to burn. We could have fun.

*Pause. She's listening.*

Figure out how you want to do it, but we have to organize how I get out first. You don't have the keys?

**ELLIE** I could get the keys.

**CLARENCE** Could you?

**ELLIE** Sure. Course I could.

**CLARENCE** *Think* about it. Don't say anything to Dan or Gerald yet. Just think about it, and if you can get the keys, then we can make a deal.

*We hear DAN and GERALD somewhere close.*

Okay?

**ELLIE** I'll think about it.

**CLARENCE** But you won't say anything, right Ellie?

**ELLIE** Yeah. Sh.

**CLARENCE** Just between you and me. I'm relying on you.

*He kisses ELLIE. She breaks away as she hears someone on the stairs.*

**ELLIE** Hello? Who is it?

*DAN re-enters triumphantly. GERALD seems somewhat more agitated.*

**DAN** It's okay. He's gone.

**ELLIE** What did he want?

**GERALD** Who knows?

**ELLIE** He didn't want to come in?

**DAN** No.

**GERALD** What a power freak.

**DAN** When he leaned in on you like that, was he checkin' your breath?

**GERALD** 'Course he was. Checkin' my eyeballs, too. See if the pupils are enlarged, eh? He's been doing that kind'a shit since I was eight.

**ELLIE** How'd you get rid of him so quick?

**GERALD** Alls he wanted was to gimme his third degree. What are you doing? Who you got with you? You got any dope? No partying. And a shitload'a useless advice about wasps, make sure you wear gloves—right!—he doesn't *offer* any, don't spray into a breeze – *as if there's a breeze!*

*GERALD throws open the window.*

It's dead fucking calm out there and he's talking about a breeze. Can any'a you feel a breeze? No!

*He glances out the window.*

There he goes, in his big motherin' four-by-four. Never drove anything but them beat up pick-up trucks all his life.

**DAN** Ah, he's not so bad.

*Absently, as he stares out the window.*

**GERALD** Yeah, right.

**DAN** Just super old.

**GERALD** You never had to live with him.

**DAN** Times I've met him, he always seemed okay.

**GERALD** He likes you.

**DAN** He can't be all bad then.

*GERALD leaves the window.*

**GERALD** You're both selfish pricks, what's not to like?

**DAN** Hey!

**ELLIE** So? You do the wasps?

**DAN** D-E-A-D! – those wasps are outta here! Once again modern technology kicks butt – the death spray gets ten big points, mother nature – zippety do dah. Hey, what's that I hear?

**GERALD** What now? He comin' back? I can't hear nothing.

*GERALD returns to the window.*

**DAN** Can't you hear it?

**ELLIE** Me neither, I don't hear a thing.

**DAN** Oh, yeah, I hear it. "Be-eeer." It's the mating call of the Big Frosty Brewski. Time to celebrate! Whady'ya say?

**GERALD** Right on.

**DAN** Whady'ya say?

**ELLIE** Do you have any money?

**DAN** Ah, don't be that way.

**ELLIE** "Ah, don't be that way."

**DAN** C'mon – we just received our letter, we've got Solomon here wrapped in iron, we've sent Mr. Fat and Greasy on his lonely way and we're this close to wrapping our sticky mitts around a million dollars.

*He loops an arm around ELLIE's shoulders.*

Be a pal and loosen up a little.

*She doesn't.*

**ELLIE** So you *don't* have any money?

**DAN** Will you take the stick outta your butt? No, not at this precise moment. But I'll pay you back.

**ELLIE** When?

**DAN** Soon as I got it, now c'mon.

**ELLIE** Why is it you never have any money on you?

**DAN** It's not like I never have money—

**ELLIE** —Pretty close to never—

**DAN** —You should be grateful you got money in the first place, you wouldn't *have* a job if it weren't for me—

**ELLIE** —You want me to kiss your ass every second of every day 'cause you got me a job waiting tables? *Excuse me*, I don't think so—

**DAN** —Hey! Who planned this whole Rushdie thing? You or me? Whose car drove him out here? Who sent the letters? Who wrote the letters?—

**ELLIE** —Yeah, you can write. There's plenty'a others out there who can write, okay?—

**DAN** —Oh, yeah? And where are all these others, hey? Where are they?

*He sticks his head out the window.*

Are they out there? This huge fucking line'a others?

*He withdraws his head.*

'Cause I can't see 'em. All these guys who are dropping dead to hang out with you. I'll tell you where the lineup is, it begins and ends *here! With me!* I am the whole fucking lineup and I have stuck by you when no one else would and now you won't spring a couple of stinking bucks for a lousy case'a beer! But if you want'a forget everything I've done for you, here ya go!

*He wrestles with his shirt and finally rips it off.*

Here you go, you want fucking collateral, take the fucking shirt off my back. Take it! Make sure I pay you back, every fucking cent! Go on!

*He throws the shirt at her. Mini pause.*

**ELLIE** Put yer shirt on.

*She picks it up and tosses it to DAN.*

I didn't say I *wouldn't* pay. I'm just saying I don't want to pay *every* time.

**DAN** C'mon, Ellie, c'mon. You know I'm good for it. Let's party a little.

*He puts his arm around her.*

Can't we party anymore? You and me? You too good for that?

*Slight pause.*

**ELLIE** Fine, fine. *My* pick, though. Let's go.

*DAN slings on his shirt.*

**DAN** You stay here with Prince Charming. And clean up a little. We'll try not to drink it all before we get back.

**GERALD** Ha, fucking ha.

**CLARENCE** Hey, Ellie.

*ELLIE and DAN stop on their way out.*

Get me one, too, will you?

**ELLIE** 'Kay.

**DAN** You're goin' to get *him* one?

**ELLIE** Yeah. One. I mean, I might as well treat *everyone*, eh? Come on.

**CLARENCE** You won't forget?

**ELLIE** No. I won't forget.

*DAN and ELLIE exit.*

**CLARENCE** So. The wasps are dead?

**GERALD** Yeah. The wasps are dead.

*GERALD goes to the window to watch DAN and ELLIE get into the car.*

They're all dead. Everyone'a them, dead.

*He turns away from the window as the car starts.*

Stuff's fast, I'll give it that. Touch is all you need.

**CLARENCE** That right?

**GERALD** Oh, yeah. One of the wasps peeked out – like I said, you're never going to catch all yer wasps sleeping, there's always a couple awake, that's one of their defence mechanisms, eh? – and the spray, you know, just touched it. That was all she wrote. Froze in its tracks. Never moved again. Yeah, that stuff's some eerie shit. See, what Dan doesn't get, though, is that whole circle'a life thing—like, you know, in "The Lion King"?—that's not just stuff for yer big furry things, lions and bears and whatnot, but ugly, puny things like yer wasps and earthworms, too. Guys like Dan, it's just, somethin' gets in their way they figure "kill it," but you don't know if even things you don't think count, count. To something else, right. Or even to themselves. That's all I'm saying.

**CLARENCE** Right.

**GERALD** That's all I'm sayin'.

*Slight pause.*

**CLARENCE** So, I'm surprised your dad'd check on you out here if you two don't get along like you say.

**GERALD** You kiddin'? He likes nothing better than havin' me *out here.*

**CLARENCE** Yeah?

**GERALD** Oh, yeah. He *loves* it. So's he can say, "There's my stupid, no account, shit for brains son, staying at the old house again, back home again. Useless fucker begged me for a place to stay and I caved in. Did I tell you he's a *bike messenger* now? Can you fuckin' believe it? You could train monkeys to do that shit only you'd have to pay 'em more." Oh, he'll go on like that for hours.

*CLARENCE stares a long moment at GERALD.*

What? What're you starin' at?

**CLARENCE** I'm not sure.

**GERALD** Yeah. Well. Quit it, okay.

*CLARENCE continues to stare.*

Hey. I said cut it out.

**CLARENCE** What are you doing, Gerald?

**GERALD** What do you mean? I'm standing here.

**CLARENCE** I'm trying to figure you out – but I can't do it. You hate taking orders from your dad, but you'll take any kind of crap from your buddy Dan. You can't stand the thought of putting wasps down—*wasps, mind you*—but you're happy enough to take part in a venture that would, theoretically at least, end up with me getting killed.

**GERALD** I need the money.

**CLARENCE** There's not going to be any money! There's not going to be any money! You've managed to elude your *father*, he's not the police, he's your *father. That's like the equivalent of sneaking a pack of smokes into your bedroom.* And you only barely did that. You're not going to get away with *kidnapping*!

**GERALD** We done okay so far.

**CLARENCE** You haven't had the smallest sniff of money, and what's more you're not going to because *you know I'm not Rushdie!*

**GERALD** Don't start that again.

**CLARENCE** You know it!

**GERALD** I said don't start!

**CLARENCE** Because you are smarter than everyone gives you credit for.

**GERALD** Right.

**CLARENCE** Because you are smarter than your father gives you credit for and smarter than Dan gives you credit for.

**GERALD** Oh, yeah, I'm so smart what'm I doin' runnin' messages around on a bike?

**CLARENCE** Because you believe whatever people tell you about yourself—

**GERALD** —*Right*—

**CLARENCE** —Sure, your dad says you're a fuck-up, so you must be a fuck-up, so you hang out with anyone so long as you're absolutely certain they'll treat you exactly the way you ought to be treated—

**GERALD** —Screw this—

**CLARENCE** —*like a fuck-up*—

**GERALD** —Like I should listen to you—

**CLARENCE** —Yeah, you should—

**GERALD** —Why?—

**CLARENCE** —'Cause I know!—

**GERALD** —You don't know anything about my life, asshole—

**CLARENCE** —I know only too well what it is be a total screw-up—

**GERALD** —Fuck off, you don't know nothing—

**CLARENCE** —Are you kidding? I spent the better part of my life rehearsing for that part. I *mastered* that part. You get as good as me at that part you get sent away to university, to do something with your life – the operative phrase being "sent away." But university's just a small challenge to as talented a failure as myself and I, of course, *fucked it away*, partied it away, skipped courses, cheated on the tests when I didn't know the material which was virtually every time 'til they'd had enough of me and kicked me out – and why not? It's only what I deserved, wasn't it? So I got the odd job selling appliances, selling cars, selling insurance, bouncing around from one job to another selling whatever product I could, occasionally getting some relief from the unrelenting *fucking boredom* of being me by *pretending* to be someone I'd studied in my English courses, someone smarter than me, someone more talented than me, someone who *wasn't* a fuck-up—

**GERALD** —This is total bullshit—

**CLARENCE** —*Salman Rushdie!* 'Cause when I was him, hey! I was someone a helluva lot better than Clarence Mukherjee, a guy who couldn't do anything more impressive with his life than the odd owl impression—

**GERALD** —This is total, total bullshit—

**CLARENCE** —You *know* it's the truth—

**GERALD** —The fuck I do!—

**CLARENCE** —And you could prove it in a moment. 416-542-5121. Call that number and you'll get my father, he'll tell you everything you need to know, what a screwed up, unenterprising wanker his son is! Tell him! Tell him he's pretending to be Salman Rushdie, tell him three reform school drop outs got him dead drunk and chained him up in some attic and you'll make his fucking day! He'll laugh his head off and have a hundred stories just like it to share with you—

**GERALD** —I'm not listening to this—

**CLARENCE** —4165425121. *Call it!*—

**GERALD** —*Bullshit!*—

**CLARENCE** —You know what's bullshit? *You!* Doing all of this – hiding in the house, running back and forth from town, bunking out here, sending ads to newspapers, this big game of make-believe – and the only reason you're doing it is because you're afraid it's the only game anyone will let you play. *It's pathetic!* Open the briefcase, *take* my keys! Stand up and prove this for yourself, once and for all. Not for me. For you! Or call my dad, makes no difference.

*GERALD goes to the door.*

Where are you going? Outside, pretend I didn't say anything, wait for your friends to come back so you can continue playing at being part of something?

*GERALD turns around and looks at CLARENCE.*

**GERALD** I want to think.

*GERALD exits. Blackout.*

## Scene Two

*Lights up. CLARENCE alone in the room. Enter DAN with a couple of cases of beer under his arm.*

**DAN** Ger? Ger? Where's Ger?

**CLARENCE** You took your time.

**DAN** It's my time, right?

*He puts the beer down.*

He didn't leave you here alone did he?

*GERALD answers from down the hall.*

**GERALD** I'm here.

*DAN steps out onto the landing.*

**DAN** Watch'a doin' out here in the hall?

**GERALD** I was just havin' a smoke outside. Thinking.

**DAN** Don't strain yourself.

*They both re-enter the room.*

Hey, you're not afraid to smoke 'round old Solomon, are ya?

**GERALD** No.

**DAN** Not afraid of his awesome writerly powers, eh?

**GERALD** I just needed some air. Where's Ellie?

**DAN** She jammed out.

**GERALD** What?

**DAN** She's doin' double shift tomorrow or some such shit, didn't feel like doing the drive back and then getting up in the morning. So you know what that means?—

*DAN tosses GERALD a beer.*

**DAN & GERALD** —More for us! Yeah!

*They crack the beers and drink.*

**DAN** There you go. You were looking a little blue. Cabin fever, eh? Eh?

**GERALD** I guess.

**DAN** Don't you worry, we're almost done here. Drink up.

*They drink.*

**GERALD** I've never seen Ellie back off a drink.

**DAN** It's different with chicks. They don't really know how to get shit-face drunk, but it's one of those things that come instinctively to guys.

**CLARENCE** Give me one.

*GERALD pulls a beer from the case. DAN grabs GERALD's arm.*

She said she'd get me one. Don't sweat it. You're all going to be rich soon, right. You can afford to pop for a beer. C'mon, Diamond Jim.

*DAN stares at CLARENCE, then relinquishes the beer.*

**DAN** Yeah, I guess we can afford that. Go ahead. Enjoy.

*DAN tosses CLARENCE a beer.*

Crank'er!

*They drink. They keep drinking. DAN finishes his beer and crushes the beer can between his two hands. CLARENCE finishes his and smashes the can against his forehead. GERALD keeps drinking but eventually, with beer streaming from his nostrils, must stop. He takes a breath and drinks until it's finished.*

**DAN & GERALD** Yeah!

**DAN** Spike another!

*They open another set. DAN tosses CLARENCE a beer.*

**CLARENCE** For me?

**DAN** Is there another fucker wrapped in chains and sittin' there?

*They crack their beers and drink.*

**GERALD** Whoo-oo!

**DAN** Yeah!

**GERALD** That hits the spot.

**DAN** So.

*DAN claps GERALD on the back.*

Way to keep your cool when your old man came out.

**GERALD** Yeah.

**DAN** Thought he was going to stumble onto the whole thing.

**GERALD** He's not smart enough.

**DAN** I don't think he was keen on climbin' the stairs—

*GERALD and DAN laugh.*

**GERALD** I'm not sure the stairs woulda held him.

**DAN** He's a big ol' fart, eh?

**GERALD** A whale, a great big blubbery whale.

**DAN** No kiddin'.

**GERALD** A big blue whale. Fuck, it's amazing, eh? Whales get as big as they do and they only eat this shit that's the size'a the head of a match. You'd have to eat a fuck of a lot, eh?

**DAN** Yeah.

**GERALD** Why is that? Hey? Why has the biggest animal on earth got to eat nothing but like, dust mites?

**DAN** Now, how the fuck should I know?

**GERALD** Don't know. It's just interesting to think—

**DAN** —You know, you watch a bit too much'a that nature shit.

**GERALD** It's the only stuff on TV worth watchin'.

**DAN** It's ruinin' your mind. Your brain's turnin' to nature film mush, I mean, zebras, coyotes, blue whales and I don't know what else – what use is all'a that crap?

**GERALD** It's interesting.

**DAN** It's fucking insane. Go!

*They drain another can of beer. DAN and GERALD belch loudly.*

**DAN & GERALD** Whooooo!

*They crack open two more.*

**DAN** Hey?

**GERALD** What?

**DAN** Your old man's got a shit load'a guns, right? That's what you said, he's a gun collector or something?

**GERALD** Guns? *(snorts)* Yeah.

**DAN** They all shootin' guns?

**GERALD** What other type are there?

**DAN** There are other types.

**GERALD** No.

**DAN** Yeah.

**GERALD** If it don't shoot, it's not a gun.

**DAN** Yeah.

**GERALD** No.

**DAN** There are *show* guns. Blank shootin' guns—

**GERALD** —That's a shootin' gun.

**DAN** No!

**GERALD** You just said. Blank shootin' gun.

**DAN** I mean bullet shootin' real guns. Guns that shoot for real.

**GERALD** Well, all my dad's guns are real bullet shootin' real guns. That's all he's got. Him and his wonderful guns. His collection. His collection of real bullet shootin' real guns.

**DAN** You think you could lift one if you wanted to?

**GERALD** Yeah. Sure. Why?

**DAN** Off this useless fucker.

**GERALD** Right. *(laughs)* Right.

**DAN** What're you laughing about?

**GERALD** We're going to lift one'a my old man's guns and just shoot ol' Rushdie here?

**DAN** Yeah.

**GERALD** You're not serious?

**DAN** Yeah.

**GERALD** I thought we were going to send him—

**DAN** Well, that was BS. You knew that, didn't you? C'mon!

*He slaps the back of GERALD's head.*

**GERALD** What?

**DAN** That was always for someone as dim as Ellie 'cause I knew she was too gutless to follow through. But c'mon – they want him dead, they always said that, they never said pick him up and bring him by for lunch.

**GERALD** What difference does it make to us? Let them do whatever.

**DAN** How're we going to bring him, alive, somewhere without gettin' caught?

**CLARENCE** It's a set up, Gerald.

**DAN** Hey, who gave you permission to beak off?

**CLARENCE** Who's he asked to steal the gun? Who's going to be charged?

**DAN** You think 'cause I've given you a couple'a beers I've invited you to express your opinion?

**CLARENCE** —this is serious shit he's asking you to do, Gerald.

**GERALD** I know! You don't have to tell me.

**DAN** Shut the fuck up!

**CLARENCE** That's right, Gerald, he's ordered me to be quiet, but it's really directed at you. *You* shut up, and do what you're told – 'cause he doesn't want to hear any arguments from me or anybody. Not Ayatollah Dan—

**DAN** —I said *shut up!*

*DAN smashes a glass against CLARENCE's head.*

**CLARENCE** Ah!

**DAN** It's a lotta money, Ger. We don't want'a fuck this up.

**GERALD** No.

**DAN** What do you mean no?

**GERALD** I mean no. I ain't goin' to do it.

**DAN** Yeah. We *are* goin' to do it.

**GERALD** Not me.

**DAN** All right, all right, seems I'm doing all the work here but if you're goin' to be a pussy about it just *get* the gun and I'll pull the trigger. I can handle that.

*Pause.*

**GERALD** This was fucked up from the start. I want out.

**DAN** You want *out*?

**GERALD** Yeah.

**DAN** You want out?

**GERALD** Yeah.

**DAN** And just how do you suggest we do that?

*Slight pause.*

**GERALD** Let 'im go.

**DAN** Let 'im go. You don't know what the fuck you're talking about. *He's seen us!* He's seen your face, my face, Ellie's face, he knows where we work, he's got a good idea where he is right now – we let 'im go and he'll tell the heat and we'll spend the rest of our lives in the joint.

**GERALD** I don't think so.

**DAN** *(laughs)* You don't think. Period. Why *wouldn't* he tell?

**GERALD** I just don't think he would.

**DAN** Well, think again. I have screwed up so badly putting my faith in the stupidest, most fucked up bunch'a head cases that ever walked the earth. You're pissing away the only chance you've ever had to make any serious money, and for what? What is it? I mean, have you fallin' in love with this guy? That it?

**GERALD** No.

**DAN** You got the hots for this guy, that it?

*He slaps GERALD.*

**GERALD** No.

**DAN** No girl'd have you, so you been slippin' it to Solomon here, eh?

*He slaps GERALD.*

**GERALD** No.

**DAN** That's it, isn't it? You're soft on him!

*He tries to slap GERALD. GERALD grabs DAN's wrist and throws it off.*

**GERALD** It ain't me who's been screwing him.

**DAN** What's that s'posed to mean?

**GERALD** You know what I mean. You're just jealous and that's where all'a this is comin' from.

**DAN** Ya dim wit, you don't know what you're talkin' about.

**GERALD** I do. And I ain't goin' to have nothing to do with it. Slappin' me! Big guy. Like it takes a lot to slap me, or smash a glass on some guy who's chained up. I don't even think he is Rushdie. I been willin' to go along if there was some sure money, but I don't believe he's Rushdie enough to kill him.

**DAN** What about the newspaper? What about all that? Huh?

*Pause. GERALD thinks it through and nods to himself.*

**GERALD** Maybe you set it up.

**DAN** Me? You calling me a liar?

**GERALD** Yeah. Probably. You coulda sent the reply yourself.

**DAN** You want'a get your head kicked in?

**GERALD** I ain't afraid of you.

*GERALD picks up the baseball bat and holds it tight.*

You're only any good if you got someone on the ground or can sucker-punch them. So come on.

*DAN just looks at GERALD.*

Come on!

*GERALD smashes a table with the bat.*

I've hung by you! I've been good to you and what've I ever got? Now I'm telling you I'm not going to do this, so if you want a piece of me, *come on!*

*He hits the table. DAN just stands and watches him.*

**DAN** You're fuckin' worthless. I only let you hang around me 'cause I thought you might have a *shred* of sense rattling around in that pea brain'a yours. But you are the most useless, dim, uncoordinated motherfucker I have ever seen. I was doing you a favour—

**GERALD** —When have you done anyone a *favour*?—

**DAN** —but you are way, way too big a loser. You want to let him go? Let 'im go. But I'm tellin you, he squeals, this is your place, and I'll say it was your plan, and you're the one who'll do time, buddy. I'm coverin' my ass, I ain't goin' to take the fall for this shit.

**GERALD** How's that different from any other time, Dan?

**DAN** I'm outta here. We could'a been rich. But it's probably better this way. If you can't be trusted, better I should cut my losses now. I'm done with you, finished. So, let 'im go.

*DAN withdraws the keys from his pocket and pegs them at GERALD. GERALD fumbles the keys and drops them and when he looks down at them, DAN attacks, kicking GERALD in the groin.*

You're not afraid of me? That it? Not afraid of me. Well, be afraid!

*DAN knees GERALD in the head, then smashes him to the ground. He picks up the baseball bat.*

You were goin' to use this on me? Hey? This make you a big man suddenly?

*DAN hurls the bat out the door. He looks down at GERALD, grabs him by the collar and drags him to the doorway. DAN then takes the door and slams it several times against GERALD's head.*

**GERALD** Oh, fuck man, cut it out. Cut it out.

**DAN** You want me to cut it out? You want me to cut it out! I'll show you fuckin' cuttin' it out! You lame, stupid, glassy-eyed punk. Takin' his side over me!

*DAN grabs GERALD by the feet and drags him out the door.*

**GERALD** No man! No! No!

*GERALD tries to hang onto the door but DAN kicks his fingers and forces him to let go. Then DAN drags GERALD out to the stairwell. We hear DAN beating GERALD and hear GERALD's moans get steadily quieter. As soon as they go out the door, CLARENCE moves his chair over to where the keys are. He tries to grab them, but they slip from his hands and slide down the ventilation shaft.*

**CLARENCE** Oh, fuck.

**DAN** *(offstage)* Big guy! Not afraid of me, right!

**GERALD** *(offstage)* Don't.

*GERALD is thrown down the stairs. We hear GERALD thumping down one stair after another, then hear DAN go after him again. We hear the beating continue and then hear DAN drag GERALD outside. CLARENCE tries to stick his fingers into the ventilation shaft and drag the keys, but can't quite do it. He goes to the bedside table and grabs a fork, returns to the shaft and tries once again to grab the keys. No luck. We hear the door open and shut downstairs and then hear footsteps pounding up the stairs. CLARENCE redoubles his efforts. The door is flung open. ELLIE stands there.*

**ELLIE** Where is he? I'm gonna have his nuts for bookends. He took the money, left me at the mall, I had to thumb a ride and walk – What happened to you? What's been going on here?

**CLARENCE** You told.

**ELLIE** What are you talking about?

**CLARENCE** You told him! Didn't you?

*Slight pause.*

**ELLIE** Yeah. What's been—

**CLARENCE** We've got to get out of here, right now.

**ELLIE** What are you—

**CLARENCE** —Right now! He kicked the crap outta Gerald, he may have killed him. He's coming back. Now help me get the keys to the handcuffs up from the air vent.

*She hesitates.*

Come on! You see that blood? It's Gerald's. He said he's going to kill me. He could be back any minute.

*ELLIE kneels.*

**ELLIE** How'd they get there?

**CLARENCE** Dan threw them down. When Gerald went to pick them up, Dan jumped him.

**ELLIE** What happened to your face?

**CLARENCE** He broke a glass on it.

**ELLIE** I can't reach 'em.

**CLARENCE** Is there a wire or anything?

*ELLIE goes to the closet and grabs a coat hanger. She twists it so that she can fit it down the register.*

You didn't see anyone out there?

**ELLIE** No.

**CLARENCE** You had to tell him.

**ELLIE** I thought he'd want to make a deal.

**CLARENCE** Well, I guess not, eh? Hurry.

**ELLIE** Hold on.

*Enter DAN.*

**DAN** What's going on?

*ELLIE stands up.*

**ELLIE** Where's Gerald?

**DAN** What're you looking for?

**ELLIE** I'm getting the keys and we're leaving and I want to know where Gerald is.

**DAN** You're leaving with him?

**ELLIE** Will you stop asking stupid questions, I said we're leaving and there's only three of us in the room so yeah I'm leaving, with him, now, and where's Gerald? He says you punched him out, what for?

**DAN** So, what's the plan, Ellie?

**ELLIE** What're you talking about?

**DAN** Where're you going to go with him?

**ELLIE** Outta here, somewhere else, doesn't matter.

**DAN** With your precious Mr. Solomon, eh? Mr. *Millionaire.*

*DAN grabs the chair by a leg and flips the chair and CLARENCE over on their backs. ELLIE grabs him by his arm to pull him off.*

**ELLIE** Hey!

*DAN turns and throws a chokehold on ELLIE. She runs him against the wall and elbows him, but he continues choking her.*

**DAN** You and him, eh? The two lovebirds. I don't think so.

*ELLIE has passed out and is limp in DAN's arms. He pushes her into the closet and wedges a chair against the door to lock it. He turns back to CLARENCE, who has by this time managed to get himself back up on the chair and withdraw the keys from the air register.*

You got anything else to say to me? Hey? Any deep insights?

*DAN picks up a piece of broken chair.*

'Cause I'm going to make sure this is the last time you say anything.

*CLARENCE pushes his chair back and scuttles away from DAN. DAN continues relentlessly forward, cutting off the angles. Suddenly, DAN leaps after CLARENCE at the same moment that CLARENCE picks up the can of wasp spray and shoots it directly into DAN's eyes. DAN screams, holds his face and falls backward. CLARENCE tries to unlock his shackles. He realizes he has the wrong set of keys. He looks carefully at them.*

**CLARENCE** You bastard. These are *my* keys. You've been to my place, haven't you? You *know.* You know I'm not Rushdie.

**DAN** You've blinded me. I can't see a thing.

*CLARENCE tries to roll his chair out toward the open door. DAN scrambles along the floor and places himself between CLARENCE and the door.*

**CLARENCE** How long did you know? Couple of days? Three days? What? If you knew already… *why*?

*Realizing.*

This has all been for show, hasn't it? You, trying to impress Ellie, make her think you could do something, run something. Once you got started, you just didn't know how to finish, did you?

*DAN slides back to the door and shuts it. He places his back against it. He slowly begins to stand up, trying to get a sense of where CLARENCE is.*

**DAN** I woulda let you go eventually, but no, you gotta be a smart guy. Gotta be working everything every which way, huh? Saying this, saying that, making your little side deals. Always playing someone off'a someone else, eh?

*Slight pause.*

She comes on the car ride with me tonight and she starts *talking*—oh, all kinds'a shit—'bout some big *deal* she's cutting with *you*. You. You're going to pay us all out, you're going to make it all *okay*, you're going to do this, you're going to do that, and oh, everything's going to be so sweet. And after everything's said and done, suddenly she's the queen telling me how things are going to fly. She's the boss, and suddenly I'm nothing. And who are you but a faking, lying, scamming sonofabitch.

*CLARENCE tosses a pop can over to the other side of the room. DAN shifts to block any escape from that direction. A faint knocking comes from inside the closet.*

**ELLIE** Dan? Dan? Lemme out.

**DAN** You hear that Ellie? *Ellie*? You hear about your great Mr. Rushdie. Your precious Mr. Rushdie? He's *nothing – you hear! Nothing!* I've been to his place. He lives in an apartment smaller than yours! He's nothing but a poser! A scam artist. All those deals you made, you made with Mr. Nothing! Doesn't that just make you sick? You sold me out, and you sold me out for *nothing!*

*CLARENCE uses that moment to propel his chair forward and into DAN's side, knocking DAN over. CLARENCE flings open the door and is wheeling out, but DAN grabs hold of the chair and yanks CLARENCE back into the room.*

I'm gonna kill you!

*They fight.*

**ELLIE** Dan! Dan! Stop it! Let me out! Dan!

*DAN gets the better of CLARENCE and begins to choke him.*

**DAN** You gonna talk your way outta this? Huh? Talk? Tell me what a big shot you are? C'mon!

*Suddenly, DAN is struck down from behind. We see the bloodied GERALD, only barely standing, framed in the doorway. He brings the baseball bat down on DAN once more. DAN stops moving. GERALD waits for DAN to move again, but DAN remains still. GERALD drops the bat. He reaches down and hauls DAN off of CLARENCE. ELLIE continues battering at the door of the closet. GERALD walks over to the door and removes the chair. ELLIE steps out – looks at GERALD.*

**GERALD** Come on out.

**ELLIE** Where's Dan?

*GERALD nods at the body on the ground, then sinks into the chair that had locked the closet shut. ELLIE checks DAN.*

**GERALD** He ain't dead.

**ELLIE** So what's your name? Your real name?

**CLARENCE** Clarence.

*She takes a long, long look at him as it all settles in.*

**ELLIE** Clarence. Clarence what?

**CLARENCE** Mukherjee.

**ELLIE** Mukherjee.

*She slides down the wall until she is sitting.*

You hear that, Gerald, we kidnapped "Clarence Mukherjee."

**GERALD** I heard.

**ELLIE** Well, Clarence, I wish you'd'a been clear about that point earlier on.

**CLARENCE** I tried to tell you.

**ELLIE** Yeah, you did.

**CLARENCE** I need the keys. The real keys.

*ELLIE reaches over and pulls another set of keys out of DAN's pocket.*

**ELLIE** There.

*CLARENCE unlocks himself. He is for the first time that we've seen, free.*

Clarence, can you drive?

**CLARENCE** Yeah.

**ELLIE** These are Dan's car keys. You think you could drop Gerald by the hospital before you call the cops?

**CLARENCE** Yeah.

*CLARENCE stands and GERALD gets up unsteadily.*

You comin'?

**ELLIE** Yeah.

**CLARENCE** What about him?

*She kicks the bottom of DAN's feet.*

**ELLIE** Dan? Hey Dan.

*DAN stirs.*

Here's one idea you didn't come up with.

*She clicks one end of the handcuffs to his wrist, the other to a pipe running along the floor. He starts to come to.*

**DAN** What…? What's going on?

**ELLIE** Mr. Rushdie is leaving the building.

*GERALD, ELLIE and CLARENCE exit. Blackout.*

*The End.*

# Excavations

By Eugene Stickland

# About
# Eugene Stickland

Like many Albertans, Eugene Stickland is a native of Saskatchewan, having taken a detour through Toronto where he completed an MFA in playwriting at York University (1984) before settling in Calgary. For ten years, Eugene was Playwright in Residence at Alberta Theatre Projects. During that time, he wrote six plays for ATP, as well as three one-act plays for Calgary's Lunchbox Theatre. *Excavations* began as a commission from Toronto's Theatre Passe Muraille. An early version of the play won the Alberta Playwriting Award in 1995 and was produced by Edmonton's Theatre Network in 2002. Since leaving Alberta Theatre Projects in 2004, Eugene has written many freelance articles as well as a weekly column for the *Calgary Herald.* In 2007, he adapted his one-act play, *Closer and Closer Apart,* into a full-length work that premiered at Edmonton's Theatre Network. He is working on finalizing a publication of the one-act and full-length plays, along with a writer's journal he kept documenting the process, which will be published by Brindle & Glass in 2009. A new full-length play, *Writer's Block,* "a delusional autobiographical fantasy," opened in Calgary in March 2008, produced by Ground Zero Theatre. Eugene lives in Calgary with his daughter, Johanna Stickland.

*Excavations* was first produced by Theatre Network at the Roxy Theatre in Edmonton, Alberta, opening October 2, 2002, with the following company:

| | |
|---|---|
| NED | Jeff Page |
| FINN | John Wright |
| FUDGE | Steve Pirot |
| CHRISTINA | Caroline Livingstone |
| PIANIST | Roger Admiral |

Directed by Bradley Moss
Designed by Raymond Spittal
Dramaturgy by James DeFelice
Stage Manager: Gina Moe

The playwright acknowledges the support of the Canada Council for the Arts and the Alberta Foundation for the Arts.

Civilization is only chaos taking a rest.

Alan Fletcher

## Characters

NED Fletcher is a palaeontologist.
FINN is a local resident, on whose land NED is working.
The Reverend Clifford FUDGE is a defrocked (if he was ever frocked in the first place), disgraced, alcohol-besotted fundamentalist zealot who is a neighbour to FINN.
CHRISTINA Fudge is FUDGE's sister, an amateur palaeontologist, dying to get away, but with nowhere really to go. So she remains…
The PIANIST, who plays…

## Setting

The setting is meant to depict, somewhat realistically, the area in south-western Saskatchewan or south-eastern Alberta in and around the Cypress Hills. This is rolling ranch land, that is at times traversed by deep ravines and cliff formations typically associated with what we think of as badlands.

Along the upstage wall, there is a fairly steep cliff face about six feet in height (depending on the dimensions of the stage, it could be higher). Within this cliff is the fossil that NED has come to excavate. As such, he can work either at the foot of the cliff, or on top of it. (We're talking about a huge, huge fossil, perhaps forty feet long, stirred within the earth like an omelette, so there's no real right or wrong place for him to be digging.)

Stage right, there is the very rustic front porch of FINN's house, quite rough hewn, unpainted, perhaps with a window looking in on discoloured curtains and a few chipped and cracked knick-knacks on the window sill. On the porch, an old wooden chair that FINN sits in, where he cleans his guns or waxes poetical about the need to cull the human race. From this chair, he must seem to be close enough to NED to converse with him.

Stage left, with the sense that it is geographically removed from FINN's house and NED's work area, the kitchen of the FUDGE household. At first glance, it may seem to be a fairly normal kitchen, yet we should sense some death and decay there somehow. Dried or simply dead flowers in a vase on a wooden table. A functioning toaster. A meteorite in a Plexiglas case, that at first glance may appear to be nothing more than a nondescript rock. Also, on the table, on the floor, along the counter, falling out of the cupboards – many, many, many empty red wine bottles. There are also two straight-backed chairs and not much else.

## Situation

One day, while walking along her own property, and across a field onto her neighbour FINN's property, CHRISTINA Fudge came across a fossilized bone sticking out of the face of a cliff. While she was quite accustomed to finding archaeological artifacts in these fields, this was a first for her. She dutifully contacted the provincial museum in the capital and they in turn sent out a palaeontologist to investigate. He determined that the protruding bone was in fact a rib, a part of a much larger skeleton of a T-Rex and that it would serve the interest of science to excavate it. Following some negotiation between the museum and FINN, the landowner, NED Fletcher has been dispatched to begin the excavation. Meanwhile, back at the FUDGE residence, the Reverend Clifford FUDGE drinks himself into oblivion on a daily basis while CHRISTINA walks the fields, hoping for even greater discoveries.

## Time

Around the beginning of the twenty-first century.

# Excavations

## Overture

*The PIANIST enters and takes his place at the keyboard. He can do this quite formally, as if we were at a recital, or very casually. As for how he may be dressed, and where his instrument is located, I defer to the director and designers. He plays an overture, something representative of the musical themes of the play. And then he finishes.*

*Blackout.*

*End of overture.*

## Act One

### Scene One – We Like to Nail Certain Truths...

*A special reveals the Revered Clifford FUDGE standing in somewhat soiled ecclesiastical robes before some sort of pulpit downstage, in an area not really defined as any of the playing areas. He has with him a huge tumbler of red wine and a big old Bible. Despite the fact that his robes are rather dirty, and he seems awfully fond of his wine, he is quite upbeat and cheery. In his mind, it's a beautiful Sunday morning somewhere far away.*

*The PIANIST plays the last bars of the overture (perhaps for as long as thirty seconds or so) or some sort of solemn hymn, such as "What a Friend We Have in Jesus" (Joseph M. Scriven and Charles Crozat Converse).*

*Throughout this, the beginning of the sermon, FUDGE treats the PIANIST as an elderly organ-playing woman from the community and the audience as his congregation.*

**FUDGE** Thank you, Mrs. Shanahan. That was truly beautiful. Such a gift you have. I swear I can feel the will of the Lord Jayzus just a-squirting out the ends of your fingers when you play like that. It's a beautiful world, so let us rejoice in God's love. Amen. Praise Jayzus. Praise, praise Jayzus!

*He drinks.*

A few announcements before we start. The Lady's Auxiliary has been hard at work preparing a nice tea for all of us today, so, please be sure to join us in the basement after the service. Maybe Mrs. Strong will surprise us all with her lovely Bundt cake... have to be careful how you say that one.... Well, we can only hope.

*He drinks.*

And on a more sombre note… *(He has another quick hit of wine.)* I'm afraid Ken Hucklebuck is in the hospital here in Climax once again… looks like they're going to have to take off his other leg… his remaining leg… the leg we've all been referring to as his good leg since he had to have his bad leg amputated a few months back, you all remember. I guess Jayzus must have some special need for old Ken's legs up there in heaven… I don't know…. On any account, once again, our prayers will go out to Ken and the rest of the Hucklebuck family… Enid, Buck, Varley, Lizzy, Kindersley, Travis, Vamis, Rick, whatever the little one's name is, and of course, Trina…

*At the mention of Trina's name, he twitches.*

Ahh yes. Dear sweet Trina… dear sweet, young, lithe Trina…. Who knew she was only fifteen?

*Drinks more.*

Right. Okay. Okay…

*He recovers himself a bit, enough to begin his actual sermon. As he begins, he gives the nod to Mrs. Shanahan who dutifully begins to play background music for him.*

Jayzus said: "The hour is coming in which all that are in the graves shall hear his voice and shall come forth; they that have done good, unto a resurrection of life, and they that have done evil, unto the resurrection of damnation." John 5:28…

*CHRISTINA enters, upstage from FUDGE. She stands for a moment and watches him.*

Now, it is upon this particular quotation of our Lord Jayzus, that we like to nail certain truths which function as the foundation of our prophesy – and of course, one of those things that we hold as the truth is the knowledge—

*CHRISTINA has approached FUDGE. She takes him by the arm and starts leading him towards their kitchen. The music stumbles to some kind of conclusion.*

What the hay—?

**CHRISTINA** It's okay…

*House lights fade entirely, as does the light FUDGE has been sermonizing in, as the lights come up on their kitchen area. She leads him to the table. The following dialogue virtually overlaps.*

It's okay, Clifford…

**FUDGE** What are you…?

**CHRISTINA** It's okay…

**FUDGE** What are you doing?

**CHRISTINA** Sit down and rest a bit and everything...

**FUDGE** But my sermon...

**CHRISTINA** I know...

**FUDGE** I have to deliver my sermon...

**CHRISTINA** There's no one there...

**FUDGE** The congregation...

**CHRISTINA** There is no congregation...

**FUDGE** My flock...

**CHRISTINA** There is no flock...

**FUDGE** They have to hear...

**CHRISTINA** There's no one to hear...

**FUDGE** But they have to—

**CHRISTINA** Shhh!

**FUDGE** *(whispering)* They have to hear...

*She gets him sitting at his seat at the table (at least by now). She places his Bible and glass of wine on the table before him. He passes out with his face on the open Bible. The PIANIST begins accompanying her, a movement from conventional dialogue into a more poetic and perhaps even abstract duet between piano and voice.*

**CHRISTINA** Too bad
So sad
So sad for me
You see
Stuck in this rut
The person I'm with
Is as crazy
As a shit house rat.
God help me
I've got to get out.
God help me
I got to get unstuck...
I got to get unstuck...

*Lights fade on the FUDGES who both remain in place in their kitchen. The PIANIST creates a bridge to the next scene, as lights fade to blackout.*

## Scene Two – A Beautiful New Beginning

*Lights up on FINN's front porch. He is sitting with a .33 magnum rifle, complete with scope, across his legs. The PIANIST plays FINN's theme, which as I hear it is some transcription of the theme from the Sibelius violin concerto. FINN listens to the PIANIST, almost as though he were listening to an LP on his old stereo. After a few moments, he snaps the gun shut and stands.*

**FINN** You know, every time I hear about a crowded jetliner crashing into some remote and frigid sea, I feel a real wave of joy washing over me…

*Music changes as lights fade on FINN and sneak up on the FUDGE kitchen, so the entire set is now visible in a faint light. The other characters are discernable in a tableau – FUDGE asleep on his Bible, CHRISTINA across the room from him holding an orange, FINN on his front porch holding his gun. NED enters down right. The PIANIST plays NED's theme music as NED comes to centre stage. He is carrying a suitcase and is wearing a backpack. He has a hat on his head. From their places on the stage, the others slowly turn to look at him. The PIANIST plays some kind of hopeful, optimistic theme. NED's lines are spoken in duet with the music.*

**NED** Ahhhhh, yeah. Here we go. Here we go. Here we are. Here we are. The country. The country. So this is good. Sure it is. This is very good. *(He takes in a deep breath through his nostrils.)* Oooooh. That air. And that sky. Man. That's some sky up there. Beautiful. Beautiful sky. Beautiful air. Beautiful country. Beautiful people. Beautiful simple wonderful basic gentle country people living out here in this beauty. Away from the shit and concerns of the city. Beautiful. I am among them now. I am among them now. Beautiful. I am in the country. Among the simple folk. A beautiful new beginning…

*Over the course of his last speech, NED has prepared himself to start working. Suddenly the lights shift to suggest a bright morning on the prairie. FINN is revealed on his porch with his gun, as before. NED is up centre, removing his jacket, rolling up his sleeves, getting ready to dig for the fossil. No piano at this point.*

On any account, Mr. Finn—

**FINN** Finn's fine.

**NED** Finn.

**FINN** That's fine.

**NED** Finn. Right. On any account, Finn – it's very generous of you to allow this excavation to take place on your land.

**FINN** Anything for science.

**NED** Right. You're sure you're okay with it?

**FINN** Oh, yeah. I'm fine, I'm fine.

**NED** Well then, in the name of science, I thank you.

**FINN** Quite all right. Don't mention it. It's quite a boon for the town, you know.

**NED** Yeah. That's what they're hoping.

**FINN** Dig this thing up. Display it. Get those tourist dollars in our local cash registers. You could be a bit of a saviour for this community, you know.

**NED** Really…

**FINN** Yep. No pressure, but chop chop, eh? Better get to work.

**NED** Right.

**FINN** Kidding.

**NED** Right…

*NED prepares to start working. FINN attentively watches his every move. NED stops and gives a little wave. FINN waves back.*

**FINN** Actually, you know…

**NED** What's that?

**FINN** It may come of a bit of a surprise to you, but there are certain aspects of science that I am quite conversant with.

**NED** Is that a fact?

**FINN** Oh, yes.

**NED** That's great.

**FINN** You see, I read a lot, eh?

**NED** Yeah. Reading's good.

**FINN** Yes. Helps pass the time. Which you need to do in a place like this. Pass the time…

**NED** Yeah.

**FINN** Yeah. I myself am particularly interested in the process of extinction.

**NED** That's one of my favourite areas, too.

**FINN** Is that a fact?

**NED** Yeah.

**FINN** Excellent. We're going to have some great conversations, you and I. It's true, for example, that ninety-nine per cent of all species that have ever lived are now extinct? Right? I read that.

**NED** It's true. Got one of them right here.

**FINN** Exactly.

**NED** In fact, Finn, we lose three or four species an hour. Right now. Did you know that?

**FINN** No. Three or four an hour? Serious?

**NED** Yeah. That's eighty a day. Thirty thousand a year. Highest level in sixty-five million years.

**FINN** That's mind boggling.

**NED** Yeah, it is.

**FINN** Whose fault is that?

**NED** Well, ours, I guess.

**FINN** Mankind.

**NED** Yeah.

**FINN** Yeah. Mankind. A cancer on the face of the earth.

**NED** It seems like it at times.

**FINN** Yeah. Well. Plenty of time for us to discuss such weighty matters. You're looking forward to getting at it, I guess?

**NED** Oh, yeah.

**FINN** You're going to be okay out here?

**NED** Sure.

**FINN** You're not going to miss the city too much?

**NED** No. I was getting tired of the city.

**FINN** Yeah. Too many people for my liking.

**NED** I've been looking forward to this, actually. Change of pace. Change of scenery.

**FINN** Well, change is as good as a rest, they say.

**NED** Right…

*NED picks up a pickaxe and finds a spot along the face of the cliff where he wants to work. As he is preparing, the PIANIST prepares to play some kind of accompaniment to his work routine. He's about to take a swing when FINN interrupts him. The PIANIST relaxes and doesn't play.*

**FINN** What's that you're doing?

**NED** Digging?

**FINN** Right. Right. What for?

**NED** I have to dig down to the fossil.

**FINN** Right…

**NED** To see where it is.

**FINN** Of course.

**NED** And to see how it's laid out. It's hard to know, exactly, which way it goes back into the cliff.

**FINN** Is it all in one piece?

**NED** No. It's probably been stirred up, like an omelette. And that's a big omelette.

**FINN** How big?

**NED** We think about forty feet or so, head to tail.

**FINN** *(whistles)* That is a big one…

**NED** Yeah. And it's one of only thirteen in the entire world, Finn. Tyrannosaurus Rex. And it's right here on your land.

**FINN** Unbelievable.

**NED** So I have to dig and poke around here and try to figure out the best way to proceed.

**FINN** I see. Hard work?

**NED** Oh, yeah.

**FINN** Good. I like hard work.

**NED** Is that right?

**FINN** Oh, yeah. I could sit and watch it all day. In fact, I do. I don't even bother working on my land anymore. Rent it out, watch some poor bastard bust his nuts day after day. Yep. I could sit and watch someone else work alllll the live-long day.

*NED prepares to start again. The PIANIST gets ready to play. NED stops and looks at FINN, who, of course, is looking down at him.*

It wasn't actually me that located this thing in the first place.

**NED** No?

**FINN** No. I wouldn't have known what it was.

**NED** Right.

**FINN** Looks like a hunk of rock to me. And the funny thing is, I must have walked past it a million times. And yet I missed it. I never saw it. Funny, eh?

**NED** Well, it may not have been actually sticking out for all that long. Maybe only since the spring run off.

**FINN** Really?

**NED** For sure. Every year, something gets exposed that you couldn't see the year before. It's hard to say.

**FINN** Well, that makes me feel a bit better. You'd hate to think you could miss it, eh? A big old bone like that. How old did you say it was again…?

**NED** About seventy million years. Give or take a few weeks.

**FINN** Unbelievable.

**NED** Yeah.

**FINN** Unbelievable! That's unbelievable to me.

**NED** So, who actually found it, then?

**FINN** The neighbour girl, the next farm over. Christina Fudge. One of the Fudge kids.

**NED** Fudge?

**FINN** That's their last name. Fudge.

**NED** I see.

**FINN** She's a bit of a character around these parts. The whole family is a little eccentric, I guess you might say.

**NED** Oh, yeah?

**FINN** A few bubbles off the plumb line.

**NED** Right.

**FINN** Their old man was a mean prick, fire and brimstone and all that, cheap and miserly. Trying to farm land that was only good for grazing. Stretching his pennies into copper wire. He and I never really got along. Putting it mildly. The mother, on the other hand, when she was younger, was a bright, beautiful, amazing woman. Grace, her name was. Her preserves were famous all over the southern part of the province, she even won ribbons for them at Buffalo Days, year after year. A cultured handsome woman, but he just drove her into the ground and crushed her spirit with his backward old country ways. She ended up wandering around the fields out here in a long, white gown—no shit—in a long, white gown like some kind of ghost, used to see her at night sometimes…. But she's been gone quite some time now. They're both gone now. And all that's left are those two orphaned kids over there…

*Lights cross fade down on NED and FINN, who settle in their places, and up on the FUDGE kitchen.*

*End of scene. Continuous action to next scene.*

## Scene Three – Burnt Offerings

*Lights fully up on the kitchen. CHRISTINA is moving around preparing a breakfast while FUDGE sits at the table reading his Bible, sipping at a cup of coffee with some revulsion. He is bravely waiting for his sister to leave for the day so he can start drinking his wine and, by extension, writing his sermon. She is anxious to leave, as she has seen a truck pass by on the road and knows the man from the museum has returned to FINN's place to begin excavating the dinosaur she has discovered. CHRISTINA begins to peel an orange. The PIANIST, who has given up on the idea that NED is going to do anything, shifts his focus to the kitchen and begins to play something domestic and homespun and cheerful enough, say along the lines of Stephen Foster, although this may soon devolve into something that is not quite right.*

**CHRISTINA** Slice a toast?

**FUDGE** No, thank you…

*She takes a slice of bread from the bag, places it in the toaster.*

**CHRISTINA** Sure about that?

**FUDGE** No, thanks…

**CHRISTINA** Suit yourself then…

*She pushes the handle down. Slight pause.*

You know, it wouldn't hurt you to eat a bit from time to time. Like actual solid food. Something 'sides wine. Something that might actually make its way into your large intestine. Be good for your bowels.

**FUDGE** My bowels are fine.

**CHRISTINA** A piece of toast might be just the thing for your bowels.

**FUDGE** Let's not make my bowels the subject of discussion at the table.

**CHRISTINA** It's just that I can hear you moanin' and groanin' in there every morning.

**FUDGE** I don't want to discuss it.

**CHRISTINA** And the smell you leave behind you! It can't be healthy…

**FUDGE** That's enough!

**CHRISTINA** Okay.

*Slight pause.*

**FUDGE** *(reading)* It must be ready now…

**CHRISTINA** What?

**FUDGE** Your toast.

**CHRISTINA** Not yet.

**FUDGE** *(reading)* I can smell it.

**CHRISTINA** I can't.

**FUDGE** *(reading)* When you can smell it, it's ready.

**CHRISTINA** I like my toast dark.

**FUDGE** *(reading)* You're going to burn it.

**CHRISTINA** I know this toaster. I'm not going to burn it. Christ on a bicycle, you think I don't know this toaster?

**FUDGE** *(slamming his book down)* Language!

**CHRISTINA** Deal with it…

*The toast begins to burn in the toaster.*

**FUDGE** Look! It's burning!

*He goes to pop it up but she grabs his hand.*

**CHRISTINA** Leave it!

**FUDGE** It's burning!

**CHRISTINA** I said leave it!

*He leaves it. She pops the toast up. It is black.*

**FUDGE** There. Are you happy now?

**CHRISTINA** Well. Maybe it is a little burnt.

**FUDGE** You never listen to me.

**CHRISTINA** I can fix it.

*She takes out a knife and starts scraping the toast. It begins as a duet of sorts, between the toast scraping and the piano, but then the other actors on stage take it on as well. FINN creaking in his rocking chair, NED sharpening a shovel with a rasp – all designed to drive FUDGE out of his skull. FUDGE tries to go back to his reading but is too distracted and bothered by the scraping of the toast and the wasps inside his skull.*

**FUDGE** Now what are you doing?

**CHRISTINA** Scraping my toast.

**FUDGE** Why?

**CHRISTINA** It's burnt.

**FUDGE** I know it's burnt.

**CHRISTINA** So what's your point?

**FUDGE** Make a new slice.

**CHRISTINA** No need for that. I'll have this one. After I've scraped it.

*She scrapes. They all scrape. FUDGE tries to read, finally gives up.*

**FUDGE** I find that scraping of your toast to be a little hard on my nerves.

**CHRISTINA** Sorry. *(She scrapes softer.)* How's that?

**FUDGE** It's quite possibly the most annoying sound on the face of the earth.

**CHRISTINA** I find it kind of… homey…

*Pause. More scraping.*

**FUDGE** Don't you have anything to do today?

**CHRISTINA** Oh, yeah.

**FUDGE** You do?

**CHRISTINA** Oh, yeah.

**FUDGE** What?

**CHRISTINA** None of your beeswax.

**FUDGE** You see, I need to get my sermon written…

**CHRISTINA** Yes?

**FUDGE** And you're a little distracting.

**CHRISTINA** Sorry.

**FUDGE** And what would happen? If I didn't get my sermon written?

**CHRISTINA** The same thing that will happen if you do get it written: nothing.

**FUDGE** Because you have no faith… spending your days out searching the fields for your pagan artifacts. Even those forbidden fields upon which Daddy forbade us ever to tread. You're an embarrassment to the family.

**CHRISTINA** I'm an embarrassment to the family.

**FUDGE** That's right.

**CHRISTINA** What are you talking about?

**FUDGE** You know what I'm talking about. Your sordid little episode with the man from the museum.

**CHRISTINA** Aw, for God's sake, not that again.

**FUDGE** Language.

**CHRISTINA** Anyway, Marty will be back any day now, and then you'll see it wasn't just a sordid little episode.

**FUDGE** Dream on, sister.

**CHRISTINA** As for the rest of it, you weren't embarrassed the day I found the meteorite, were you?

**FUDGE** Oh, brother, not this again…

**CHRISTINA** And the photographer came out from *The Courier*? And my picture was on the front page. The front page!

**FUDGE** That was twenty years ago for crying out loud—

**CHRISTINA** Yeah, well, you weren't embarrassed then, were you?

**FUDGE** For heaven's sake—

**CHRISTINA** You said it was Momma's soul—

**FUDGE** I know what I said—

**CHRISTINA** And *The Courier* said it was the most important scientific discovery of this region—

**FUDGE** Do you have to go on about your fifteen minutes of fame yet again?

**CHRISTINA** Well, you're the one going on about Marty. You're just jealous.

**FUDGE** Don't be ridiculous.

**CHRISTINA** I'm not being anything—

**FUDGE** The point remains, sister, I have a very select parish in which to deliver my sermon. And a very select congregation to whom it shall be delivered.

**CHRISTINA** Okay. Okay. What parish?

**FUDGE** None of your business.

**CHRISTINA** I can't imagine anyone wants to listen to you after your sordid little episode with Trina Hucklebuck. And poor old Ken lying in the hospital having his legs sawed off all the while.

**FUDGE** How was I supposed to know she was only fifteen?

**CHRISTINA** So where?

**FUDGE** It hasn't been revealed.

**CHRISTINA** Oh, brother…

**FUDGE** But when it is, Christina, I shall be prepared.

**CHRISTINA** I'm sure you shall.

**FUDGE** But how can I get my sermon written, with you peeling oranges and scraping your toast? How?

**CHRISTINA** Fine. You go ahead and write your sermon. I'm going out.

**FUDGE** Thank God.

**CHRISTINA** Just – just try to hold off on the wine a little bit today, will you? Just a bit, 'til the sun's over the yardarm.

**FUDGE** No problem.

**CHRISTINA** Promise?

**FUDGE** Oh, yes. Absolutely.

**CHRISTINA** Great. See you later.

*She leaves.*

**FUDGE** Hold off on my wine. As if. I can't hold off my wine. I can't write without my wine. No way. That would be next to impossible, trying to write without my wine. What does she know about the writing process anyway…?

*Fade on FUDGE as he pours himself a glass of wine. The PIANIST stops playing. After the glass is full, FUDGE keeps on pouring the wine, until it spills over the tabletop and begins to drip down onto the floor. This sound seems to continue for a very long time.*

*End of scene.*

## Scene Four – Love, or Something Like It…

*Lights up on NED and FINN, as before.*

**FINN** …Yeah…. Just those two orphaned kids over there slowly driving each other mental…

**NED** Right. Well. Back at it, I guess.

**FINN** Oh. Don't let me stop you.

**NED** I won't.

**FINN** Yeah, like I say, I do like hard work. I could sit and watch it all day. Well, maybe I'll mosey on in and rustle us up some lemonade…. It's going to be a hot day. Yep. A hot, hot day…

*FINN leaves, going into his shack. NED takes up his pickaxe. The PIANIST thinks, finally. He and NED may even nod at each other before they begin, as at the start of a duet. NED takes a few cuts at the face of the cliff. The piano starts, perhaps with some sort of paleo-artifact theme. They play in this manner for a few moments before NED stops to take a drink from his canteen. (It may be that after a rather soft winter, NED is not in the best of shape…) CHRISTINA enters and watches him for a moment. When she appears, the PIANIST conjures up some kind of theme of high romance. Finally, NED stops and turns to her. During their scene together, we may see FINN's face in his dirty window, watching. And see FUDGE take a few steps out of his kitchen, watching them.*

**CHRISTINA** Hi.

**NED** Hi.

**CHRISTINA** Hi. Sorry if I startled you.

**NED** That's okay.

**CHRISTINA** Who are you?

**NED** My name's Ned. Ned Fletcher.

**CHRISTINA** Hi. I'm Christina.

**NED** Christina Fudge?

**CHRISTINA** Yeah.

**NED** The one who actually found this?

**CHRISTINA** Yeah.

**NED** Cool.

**CHRISTINA** Yeah, so what happened to Marty?

**NED** Marty?

**CHRISTINA** Right. Marty. What happened to him?

**NED** Nothing happened to him.

**CHRISTINA** He said maybe he was going to come back for a visit but something must of happened, he never made it.

**NED** I don't know.

**CHRISTINA** Is he still married?

**NED** As far as I know. I don't really know him all that well.

**CHRISTINA** So, did he actually decide there was something here? Something worth pursuing?

**NED** Well, the fossil, I guess. Beyond that, it doesn't look like it.

**CHRISTINA** No, it sure doesn't…

**NED** Nope…

**CHRISTINA** So they sent you instead of Marty…

**NED** Yeah.

**CHRISTINA** I don't understand why they didn't send Marty.

**NED** Oh. Well, he has a life, I guess. He couldn't just pick up and live out here for the summer. So they sent me.

**CHRISTINA** So you don't have a life?

**NED** Something like that.

**CHRISTINA** Well, you'll fit right in, here.

**NED** Great…

**CHRISTINA** So, are you going to be doing this all by yourself?

**NED** Yeah, for now. It'd be nice to have a crew but that's probably not going to happen, at least not yet. Budget cuts at the museum, you know how it is. So, I'll hack away for the summer. I'm just picking away, trying to figure out the best way to get at it.

**CHRISTINA** It seems like a big job.

**NED** Yeah. Yeah, it is. It's huge.

*Slight pause.*

**CHRISTINA** So…

**NED** Yeah…

**CHRISTINA** Where are you staying?

**NED** Here.

**CHRISTINA** Out here?

**NED** Yeah. Got my tent. Got my camp stove. Got my excellent battery-operated Coleman reading light. And my Big Sky Bistro coffee press. By MEC.

**CHRISTINA** So, you're by yourself then…

**NED** Oh, yeah.

**CHRISTINA** Didn't bring your family out…

**NED** I don't have one.

**CHRISTINA** Your wife?

**NED** No. I don't have one of those either. No wife. No family. No life. Other than this hill for the rest of the summer.

**CHRISTINA** Hmmm.... Not even a girlfriend?

**NED** Just me.

**CHRISTINA** I see. Interesting. Hey. Can I ask you something?

**NED** I think so.

**CHRISTINA** Do you think Marty's a very trustworthy person?

**NED** I really have no idea.

**CHRISTINA** Me neither. Bastard.... Can I ask you something else?

**NED** Why not?

**CHRISTINA** Like, you're a scientist, right? A palaeontologist, right?

**NED** Right.

**CHRISTINA** How old do you think the world is?

**NED** How old do I think the world is?

**CHRISTINA** Yeah.

**NED** That's what you want to ask me? How old do I think the world is?

**CHRISTINA** Yeah.

**NED** Serious.

**CHRISTINA** Yeah.

**NED** Well, it's hard to say exactly. Of course it is. But the commonly held theory is that it's about four billion years old, or so. Between four and five.

**CHRISTINA** Really?

**NED** Yeah.

**CHRISTINA** And you believe that?

**NED** Absolutely.

**CHRISTINA** That fossil?

**NED** Yeah?

**CHRISTINA** How old?

**NED** Seventy million years or so? Sixty-five to seventy million...

**CHRISTINA** Amazing!

**NED** Somewhere in that neighbourhood.

**CHRISTINA** Interesting. So. If someone were to say to you the world is six thousand years old…

**NED** Yeah?

**CHRISTINA** What would you think?

**NED** I'd think I was talking to a begat counter.

**CHRISTINA** What's that?

**NED** Like in the Bible?

**CHRISTINA** Yeah?

**NED** They count all the "begats" from Adam on down and calculate how old the world is from that.

**CHRISTINA** Right. Gotcha. I know all about it. So what do you think of that?

**NED** Not much. Why?

**CHRISTINA** Just curious. Most people around here actually believe it's true.

**NED** Amazing.

**CHRISTINA** Yeah.

**NED** So, you find other things out here, I guess?

**CHRISTINA** Oh, yeah.

**NED** Like what?

**CHRISTINA** Well, I found a meteorite, just across the way.

**NED** Really?

**CHRISTINA** Oh, yeah. We saw it flash across the sky one night. And I found it a while later. A few days.

**NED** Cool.

**CHRISTINA** Had it displayed, eh? A guy in town, Sandy, he's good at such things, though not to be trusted. Beware of people with red hair. They tend to be bad news.

**NED** Right.

**CHRISTINA** Yeah, it looks really sharp. They came out and did an article for the paper on me. Took my picture. I was a celebrity around here for a little while. I find arrowheads and axes and whatnot. There's lots to be found out here. But I totally like the meteorite the best.

**NED** And you found this, too. That's amazing.

**CHRISTINA** Yeah. And here you are.

**NED** Yep. Here I am.

*FINN comes out of his place. He is carrying a little serving tray with two glasses of pink lemonade.*

**FINN** Hello!

**NED** Hey, Finn.

**FINN** This is a surprise. Hi, Christina.

**CHRISTINA** Hi, Finn.

**FINN** How are you?

**CHRISTINA** Good. I actually just dropped by to see how things are going out here. I should probably be getting back.

**FINN** Stay for a lemonade. I've got plenty.

**CHRISTINA** No, thanks. I should probably be getting back.

**FINN** How's that brother of yours doing?

**CHRISTINA** He's doing really well, thanks, Finn. Really well. Stronger every day. Thanks for asking.

**FINN** That's good to hear. Is he going to be able to work again soon?

**CHRISTINA** Any day now. Any day. He's looking for something now. Checks the paper out every day.

**FINN** That's great.

**CHRISTINA** Yeah.

**FINN** I'm glad to hear that. And how are you?

**CHRISTINA** Good.

**FINN** Yeah?

**CHRISTINA** Yeah.

**FINN** That's good.

**CHRISTINA** Yeah.

**FINN** Anything you need?

**CHRISTINA** No. Not really. I'm okay.

**FINN** Good.

**CHRISTINA** Yeah.

**FINN** Sure you won't stay?

**CHRISTINA** No, thank you. I have some things to do. *(to NED)* It was nice meeting you.

**NED** Yeah. You too. Drop by anytime. Next time I'll put you to work.

**CHRISTINA** Okay. I will drop by. Thanks. Bye, Finn…

**FINN** Take care…

*She leaves. They watch her go. FINN crosses over to NED and gives him a glass of lemonade. They drink, still watching her go.*

What'd you think?

**NED** About what?

**FINN** What do you think about her?

**NED** She's not bad.

**FINN** Nope. In fact, she could be quite a looker if only she'd take care of herself a bit better. You know? They've got some awfully nice things over at Sears that she could look quite smart in. Maybe a nice sundress, something a bit more feminine…

**NED** Are there any others around here? Any other women?

**FINN** No, really.

**NED** Serious?

**FINN** No, and that's the tragedy of it, eh? To find another woman even approaching her quality, you'd have to travel all the way to Sifton.

**NED** How far away is that?

**FINN** Forty-three klicks.

**NED** Great…

**FINN** And even in a major centre like Sifton, it's pretty thin pickings. All the kids from around here move away. And all the good looking women. They're the first to go. And I don't blame them. There's nothing for them here…

**NED** I suppose not…

**FINN** Next year country, eh? That's what they call it. Next year country… always waiting to see what next year will bring. And usually, all it brings is just more of the same… more and more of the same old thing…

*They finish their lemonades. FINN takes the glasses and goes back inside the house. NED picks up his pickaxe and takes a couple of whacks at the ground as the lights fade. PIANIST joins in with him, playing a transition from this scene to the next. Blackout.*

*End of scene.*

## Scene Five – Travels with Fudge

*The FUDGE kitchen. During the last scene, FUDGE has been drinking, writing in his notebook, pacing, glancing over at the scene between CHRISTINA and NED. He finds a coat – something from a tractor company, or an old Saskatchewan Roughriders windbreaker. He puts on a hat of similar origin and a pair of sunglasses. He takes out an aerosol breath freshener and has about ten squirts. He leaves the kitchen and hops on his bicycle, a vintage gearless thing from the fifties. As he rides his bicycle, he does all kinds of dips and turns and near crashes into the ditch. The PIANIST accompanies him throughout this scene with some kind of travel music; initially perhaps as he prepares to leave, something reminiscent of the "Mission: Impossible" theme. A film of prairie back roads may be projected in behind him to give a sense of his journey from his own house, over to FINN's land and the excavation site. Of course, as he rides, he speaks. In the first part of the scene, as he is getting ready for the journey, he mutters "fingers and legs" over and over again in some kind of duet with the PIANIST.*

**FUDGE** *(as he's getting ready)* Fingers and legs… fingers and legs… fingers and legs… fingers and legs… *(Etc., ad lib with PIANIST. As he mounts his bicycle, just before takeoff, he has the following revelation.)* There must be a special room in heaven, or a field or something, full of the fingers and legs we lose along the way… *(And so the journey begins, FUDGE bobbing and weaving on the bike 'til he arrives at the site.)*

Fingers and legs, fingers and legs.
Fudge land, Fudge land.
Fingers and legs, fingers and legs.
Fudge land, Fudge land.

Still all Fudge land, Daddy!
Praise the Lord.
Rest in peace.
I sincerely mean that,
Rest in Peace.
Still all Fudge land…

Daddy and those cut off fingers of his
In the Kingdom of Heaven.
The fourth and fifth fingers of the left hand
Because the twine was wrapped around the axel
And the tractor slipped into gear
And Daddy's fingers were sliced clean through.

*He holds up his hand and collapses his fourth and fifth fingers. Then he peddles on, managing to have a drink of wine from one of two or three bottles he has with him in an old fashioned bicycle basket. The hit of wine is followed by much spraying of the aerosol breath freshener.*

This field is
The field where
Daddy lost his wedding band the night he lost his fingers
And maybe Jayzus had a special need of his fingers.
Maybe we'll never know.
Maybe Jayzus needed old Ken's legs.
Maybe we'll never know.
Maybe there's a special room in heaven
Full of the fingers and legs we lose along the way.
Maybe we'll never know.

Because the twine was wrapped around the axel
And the tractor slipped into gear
And Daddy's fingers were sliced clean through.

It was speculated and postulated that
Daddy's wedding band
Had flown from the finger at the moment of slicing
And it lay still under the tractor
In the hay field.

*He stops the bicycle and dismounts. The film freezes into a still of a hay field. He drinks from his wine and then squirts with the breath freshener.*

The field in this hay land that dries too slow for cereal.
The very field the tractor was left that night the fingers were lost.
This field, right here.

All he had left of her was that ring
And he would have it, nothing else would do. So
We walked out here
Looking for Daddy's ring
Moon out
Silhouette of tractor
Sound of footsteps
Smell of rum
Trouble of breathing
Nothing said.

He bade me kneel
Beneath the tractor
I shone the beam.
Tufts of grass
All shadow changing with the angle of the light

And there it—
My God.
There it was.
A little ring of gold
There on the soil.
And I knew there was a God.
Tiny golden ring
Middle of five thousand acres of land.

Yes, there is a God.

I handed the ring to Daddy
Whose fingers art in heaven.

Fingers and legs
Fingers and legs…

Permission to enter Finn-land, Daddy!
Here I go!
Finn Land!

*FUDGE spits and pedals on, nearly falling, righting himself again. He arrives, and as he does, the background film fades and the lights come up on NED who is digging with his back to FUDGE, who gets off his bike, walks around a bit and has a few more hits of breath freshener. Sensing that someone is there, NED looks down.*

**NED** Hey!

**FUDGE** Hello, friend.

**NED** Hi.

**FUDGE** How goes it?

**NED** Good, thanks.

**FUDGE** That's good. Where's Marty?

**NED** He's not here.

**FUDGE** Then there is a God!

**NED** What's that?

**FUDGE** Have you seen my dog?

**NED** Hang on a sec. I'll come down.

**FUDGE** Don't let me disturb you!

**NED** No, no. Hang on. I'm coming down.

*NED comes down as FUDGE furiously freshens his breath.*

Hey.

**FUDGE** Hey. So how's she goin' up there?

**NED** Slow but steady, I guess.

**FUDGE** Oh, yeah.

**NED** Yeah.

**FUDGE** Found somethin', did ya?

**NED** Yeah.

**FUDGE** What is it?

**NED** T-Rex.

**FUDGE** Oooooh. Just like in that movie!

**NED** Yeah.

**FUDGE** Wow.

**NED** Yeah. It's a big one.

**FUDGE** So, how's she comin'?

**NED** Well, it's big, it's just me out here, no crew, so it's going to be a while.

**FUDGE** Yep. Gosh sakes. Big old dinosaur, eh?

**NED** That's right.

**FUDGE** Who'd a thought? Right here. You know? Right here. Lived here all my life and never knew what was in the ground beneath my feet. Big old dinosaur. Who'd a thought? Fingers and legs, fingers and legs…

**NED** What's that?

**FUDGE** I'm amazed, I'm amazed.

**NED** Right…

**FUDGE** Who'd a thought? Big old dinosaur right here…

**NED** We tend to find earlier fossils around here.

**FUDGE** Is that a fact?

**NED** Yeah. Sea creatures, mostly. Plesiosaurs, what not.

**FUDGE** Sea creatures?

**NED** From the time of the inland sea.

**FUDGE** What inland sea?

**NED** The sea that covered the prairies.

**FUDGE** Here?

**NED** Yeah.

**FUDGE** Here where we stand?

**NED** Yeah.

**FUDGE** An inland sea?

**NED** Yeah.

**FUDGE** When?

**NED** About eighty million years ago.

**FUDGE** Are you pulling my leg?

**NED** No.

**FUDGE** You have a very vivid imagination.

**NED** It's science.

**FUDGE** The devil you say…

**NED** Right.

**FUDGE** Science.

**NED** Yes. Anyway…. My name's Ned. I'm with the museum. Sorry I'm not Marty, but I'm not.

**FUDGE** Well, a scientist is a scientist is a scientist. Cliff.

**NED** Hi, Cliff.

**FUDGE** Hi, Ned.

*They shake hands. Slight pause.*

I tell you something, Ned.

**NED** What's that, Cliff?

**FUDGE** It's going to be a long, hot summer.

**NED** Is it?

**FUDGE** Oh, yeah. We fear the drought in these parts. I myself have seen these very fields on fire.

**NED** Really?

**FUDGE** Really. You can predict such things from the activity of the hoppers.

**NED** Can you really?

**FUDGE** Oh, yeah. I tell you something else, Ned.

**NED** What's that?

**FUDGE** Hoppers goin' a be bad this summer, you can feel it. Hoppers goin' a be bad.

**NED** Is that right?

**FUDGE** Oh, yeah. Real bad this year, I'd say. You can feel it, eh? I myself have seen years so bad the hoppers ate the green paint from the shingles.

**NED** Really?

**FUDGE** Oh, yeah. And I feel it now. I feel a devastation is at hand. Impending and relentless.

**NED** Jesus...

**FUDGE** Language.

**NED** Sorry.

*Slight pause.*

So, did you want to come up and look at the work I'm doing? I'm getting some of it exposed up there, the legs, one of the claws...

**FUDGE** Oh! Well, that's mighty kind but I don't want to hold you up.

**NED** You sure?

**FUDGE** That's a pretty big climb for someone with an artificial leg like I got. Yep, that's a big climb for me.

**NED** Okay. Suit yourself.

**FUDGE** No. I just wanted to drop by and say welcome to the neighbourhood. You may find that some people keep a bit of an eye on you but it's a small town and small towns is like that.

**NED** Right. Thanks.

**FUDGE** I won't hold you up anymore. From the important work you're doing.

**NED** Right.

**FUDGE** Science.

**NED** Right.

**FUDGE** You are a man of science.

**NED** Right.

**FUDGE** Right. You take good care of yourself out here, man of science. Ned.

**NED** Thanks, Cliff.

**FUDGE** You make sure.

**NED** I will. You take care, too.

**FUDGE** Oh, I will. Yep. I sure will. Adios, amigo.

**NED** Yeah. See ya…

*NED walks back up the cliff. FUDGE goes back to his bicycle, muttering "fingers and legs" under his breath. He turns the bicycle around, starts riding home again and the background film rolls. When he is sure he's out of NED's sight, he takes a bottle of wine from the basket and has a huge drink and calms himself from the ordeal of his undercover investigation. After a moment, he stops peddling and stares out across a field.*

**FUDGE** And then there's this field.
This one here.
This field
In which my mother
Took her own life.

Another sin
To add to the rich heap
Of Momma's sins.

Known as Momma's field.
The field into which she bled.
Alone and cold
After Daddy found out about
Her dalliance with the unnameable neighbour.

To whom of whom we must not speak.
Upon whose land we must not set our feet
Of all our fields gives me the creeps…
Of all our fields gives me the creeps…

*FUDGE arrives back at his house. He goes to pour himself a glass of wine but the bottle is empty. All the bottles are empty. He makes his way over to the cupboard, opens it, only to discover that the cupboard is bare. The PIANIST follows his journey as he starts to tear apart the cupboards, breaking plates and cups and spilling boxes of cereal and whatnot. There is not a bottle to be found. Finally, somewhere in the back of his brain he remembers a bottle he has hidden for just such an emergency. He climbs up onto the counter and reaches into some unlikely place and triumphantly produces a bottle of red. He slinks down to the floor, cradling the bottle in his arms. Slow fade on FUDGE. End of scene.*

## Scene Six – The Flu, The Common Flu

*The site. NED digging and hacking away at the earth with his pickaxe. (Perhaps in the name of variety we could expect something from the PIANIST at this point along the lines of "Chain Gang" or perhaps some Negro work song.)*

**FINN** So what do you think really happened?

**NED** What's that?

**FINN** The dinosaurs. What do you think really happened to them?

**NED** Well, there's lots of theories.

**FINN** But what do you think?

**NED** I favour the asteroid theory myself.

**FINN** Ah, yes. A heavenly visitation. Havoc on earth. The endless winter and the blotting out of the sun.

**NED** You know about it?

**FINN** Oh, yeah. I study such things. Even comment on them from time to time. In print. There's not much of a dialogue to be had out here. Well, until you showed up. Let me ask you this.

**NED** Yes?

**FINN** Do you think that there's any possibility it was viral?

**NED** Viral?

**FINN** Yeah.

**NED** Well, most of the species that were alive went extinct at roughly the same time. So that would have had to have been one hell of a virus.

**FINN** Well, viruses are pretty amazing creatures, wouldn't you say?

**NED** I guess…

**FINN** I have a lot of hope for them.

**NED** Hope?

**FINN** Yeah.

**NED** What are you talking about, hope?

**FINN** Well, I subscribe to some theories that some find to be a tad contentious.

**NED** Oh, yeah?

**FINN** Yep.

**NED** Are you going to share them?

**FINN** Yeah, I guess, if you think you're up to it.

**NED** I think I may be.

**FINN** Okay. And just so you know who you're talking to, I'll have you know I've actually managed to publish a few papers expounding on my meditations.

*He pulls a bunch of ancient, worn-out folded pieces of paper from his pocket.*

**NED** Really?

**FINN** Oh, yeah. Lot's of clippings. Quite an eclectic array of thoughts and publishers. Publish or perish, they say.

**NED** Tell me about it…

**FINN** What?

**NED** Same in my field. Trouble is, there's nothing particularly noteworthy about this excavation. I don't see any opportunity to further my career out here. I only see an opportunity to break my back—

**FINN** Ned?

**NED** Yeah, Finn?

**FINN** This isn't about you right now.

**NED** Sorry.

**FINN** I was telling you about my publications.

**NED** Right.

**FINN** And I'm only showing you these, not to brag, but so you don't think I'm some kind of rube with no credentials.

**NED** I see. Okay… *(He checks over the papers FINN has given him.)* Wow. *Globe and Mail.*

**FINN** I rest my case.

**NED** Very impressive.

**FINN** Thank you.

**NED** So what are these theories of yours?

**FINN** Well, basically, and I shouldn't have to tell you this given your occupation, but I believe that the world can't possibly hope to sustain its current human population. And if you look at the projections, they're absolutely terrifying. You said yourself, mankind is a cancer on the face of the planet.

**NED** I didn't say that.

**FINN** Sure you did.

**NED** No, I didn't. You did.

**FINN** Yeah, well, whatever. Clearly something has to be done. I believe that action has to be taken.

**NED** What for?

**FINN** To reduce the world's population.

**NED** What kind of action?

**FINN** Something. Anything.

**NED** Like what?

**FINN** Some agent of change.

**NED** What kind of change?

**FINN** Death, I suppose.

**NED** You're talking about reducing the world's population?

**FINN** That's right.

**NED** By how much?

**FINN** Twenty-five percent. For starters.

**NED** Over a billion people.

**FINN** For starters.

**NED** So how do you see this happening?

**FINN** Well, there's lots of scenarios that cross through my mind when I'm sitting out here thinking. But obviously, one of the most efficient is the viruses. That's why I hold them in such high regard. Oh, yeah. The haemorrhagic fevers: Erlichia, Marburg, Ebola, Junin, Machupo—

**NED** What do you know about the Ebola virus?

**FINN** I know that it's fast and efficient.

**NED** That's your word for it? Efficient?

**FINN** Yeah...

**NED** Your internal organs liquefying, bleeding through every orifice in your body, including your eyes... tears of blood, Finn... tears of blood...

**FINN** The ultimate killing machine.

**NED** You think so, do you?

**FINN** I know so. I've done the research.

**NED** It's deeply flawed.

**FINN** What are you talking about?

**NED** It's not an efficient virus.

**FINN** Sure it is.

**NED** No, it's not.

**FINN** Why do you say that?

**NED** It kills its host too quickly.

**FINN** That makes it inefficient?

**NED** Yes.

**FINN** I don't see how.

**NED** I thought you were a published expert on this.

**FINN** I didn't say I was an expert. I just said I published a few of my thoughts and feelings on a very serious subject...

**NED** Well, that would imply that you're some kind of expert.

**FINN** Whatever...

*At this point, something distracts FINN's attention. He picks up his rifle and looks through the scope, starts tracking something as NED continues to speak.*

**NED** The problem is, Finn, you don't even know your basic biology. I don't know if you've ever heard of Stephen Jay Gould, but I've got some of his stuff with me and I think you might find it worth your while to read some of it. You see, Finn, the goal of a virus, as with any organism, is to procreate and ensure the survival of its species—

*FINN fires the gun. A huge explosion, scaring NED half to death.*

Jeezus!

**FINN** Damn things.

**NED** What?!

**FINN** Damned mangy things.

**NED** What?!?!

**FINN** Coyotes.

**NED** Christ!

**FINN** Skulking around. Can't stand 'em.

**NED** You have to shoot them?

Jeff Page and John Wright
*photo by Ian Jackson*

**FINN** That's what you do with them, Ned. You shoot them. What did you think?

**NED** Well, uh, I don't—

**FINN** Anyway, you were saying…

**NED** I was?

**FINN** About the inefficiency of the Ebola virus…

**NED** Oh, yeah. Right. Jeezus – you done? Anything else you wanted to shoot?

**FINN** No. Go ahead.

**NED** Okay. I was talking about the goal of organisms. In this case, viruses.

**FINN** Right. Go on…

**NED** Well, you see, that they happen to kill their host organism is incidental. And in the case of the Ebola virus, unfortunate. Because once the host is dead, the virus is toast.

**FINN** Fascinating…

**NED** Something that works slower is more efficient, ultimately. Something that insidiously attaches itself to a host, without giving itself away too soon, so the virus is passed on. If that's what you really want. If you really want the viruses to win out, at the expense of mankind – in fact, forget the Ebola virus. The deadliest virus in recorded history – you know what it is?

**FINN** The plague?

**NED** Influenza. The common flu.

**FINN** Really…

**NED** Oh, yeah. You want something that's good at killing people, that's it. The flu. You don't need designer viruses for what you're talking about. The flu does the job just fine.

**FINN** I hadn't thought of that.

**NED** You don't think much of life, do you?

**FINN** That's not true. I think about it entirely too much. And that's why I've come to the conclusion that I've come to.

**NED** Well, if the Ebola virus ever mutates, and becomes airborne, then that'll probably happen. In a matter of weeks. Or if there's ever a return of the Spanish flu. Or if this West Nile takes off the way everyone thinks it's going to…

**FINN** Hallelujah…

**NED** I think you're seriously misguided. I can't believe you've managed to publish.

**FINN** Yeah? Well, as long as you're standing on my land day in, day out, all I ask is that you at least consider my opinion, even if you don't embrace it wholeheartedly.

**NED** Fine!

**FINN** Fine.

*They stare at each other a moment. FINN walks off. After a moment, NED has a drink from his canteen, sits on the cliff and lights a cigar. Slow fade.*

*End of scene.*

## Scene Seven – Tractor Factor

*CHRISTINA returns to the FUDGE residence. FUDGE is sitting in a straight-backed chair at the table. The big Bible lies open. He is voraciously drinking his last bottle of wine, while making random notes in his notebook. The PIANIST plays some drunken, wobbly piece – for some reason "Onward Christian Soldiers" (Sabine Baring-Gould and Arthur Sullivan), comes to mind. FUDGE has had a few more drinks.*

**FUDGE** Where have you been?

**CHRISTINA** Out.

**FUDGE** Where out?

**CHRISTINA** Out out.

**FUDGE** Where?

**CHRISTINA** Just out.

**FUDGE** I don't like it when you're out scavenging around. You know how the neighbours talk. I'm serious about this. I have some very disturbing news.

**CHRISTINA** Oh?

**FUDGE** Once again, there is a heathen come into our midst.

**CHRISTINA** Really?

**FUDGE** A blasphemer. In the name of science: another one. After your sordid episode with the last one, Marty, you are to stay away from this one, you hear me?

**CHRISTINA** You must be talking about Ned.

**FUDGE** How do you know his name?

**CHRISTINA** He told me.

**FUDGE** You've actually met him?

**CHRISTINA** Yes.

**FUDGE** How?

**CHRISTINA** I went over…

**FUDGE** And?

**CHRISTINA** He's cute.

**FUDGE** Cute?!

**CHRISTINA** Yes. He's cute. Well, at least he's someone new to look at around here.

**FUDGE** Who the hell cares what he looks like?!

**CHRISTINA** More to the point. He's smart.

**FUDGE** Smart?! Ha! Smoke and mirrors, that's all scientists deal in. And you're gullible enough to be taken in by it all.

**CHRISTINA** He seems to think that your quaint little idea that the world is six thousand years old is bullshit. Just like Marty thought.

**FUDGE** Lies. And watch your language.

**CHRISTINA** He seems to think that this dinosaur he's digging up is seventy million years old.

**FUDGE** Impossible.

**CHRISTINA** Seventy million years.

**FUDGE** No way.

**CHRISTINA** And the world is four billion years old!

**FUDGE** Fantasy.

**CHRISTINA** It's science, Clifford.

**FUDGE** Well, it's wrong.

**CHRISTINA** What makes you think that you're right? What makes you think you could possibly be right?

**FUDGE** The Bible tells me so!

**CHRISTINA** Right. Of course. And everything in the Bible is true.

**FUDGE** God's word, sister. The word of God. It's bad enough that you don't believe in it, but now you've been out consorting with an agent of the devil. Again.

**CHRISTINA** Yeah, yeah. Whatever…

**FUDGE** Digging through the earth for his old bones like a lice-ridden, mangy mongrel hell hound…

**CHRISTINA** He's a nice guy!

**FUDGE** He's evil. His work is blasphemy. You're not to see him again, you understand?

**CHRISTINA** I'll see him if I bloody well want to see him.

**FUDGE** And he's not to be referred to in this house from this moment hence.

**CHRISTINA** You brought him up.

**FUDGE** Well, now I'm un-bringing him up.

**CHRISTINA** Right. Okay. Great. Was there anything else you wanted to share?

**FUDGE** No. Yes.

**CHRISTINA** Well?

**FUDGE** *(smiling a sickly smile)* How have you been, dear?

**CHRISTINA** Why?

**FUDGE** Just curious. And mindful of your well-being. You're a very special person, you know. In my eyes. In God's eyes, even.

**CHRISTINA** What is it, Clifford?

**FUDGE** What is what?

**CHRISTINA** What's on your mind? Why are you talking to me like this?

**FUDGE** I'm your brother.

**CHRISTINA** Talk to me then.

**FUDGE** Okay. Well, you see, Chris. There is a bit of a problem in this house.

**CHRISTINA** What now?

**FUDGE** It's the wine.

**CHRISTINA** The wine?

**FUDGE** Indeed.

**CHRISTINA** What about the wine?

**FUDGE** We have a wine problem.

**CHRISTINA** We do, do we?

**FUDGE** Yes, we do. In fact, it's beyond being a problem, even. It's become a situation, one might say. Full-blown and grave.

**CHRISTINA** What is the situation?

**FUDGE** We're down to our last bottle.

**CHRISTINA** We're down?

**FUDGE** To our last bottle. You hear me?! Our last bottle!

**CHRISTINA** Good.

**FUDGE** What will we do?

**CHRISTINA** Stop drinking.

**FUDGE** Oh.

**CHRISTINA** Simple enough.

**FUDGE** I don't think I can do that.

**CHRISTINA** Sure you can.

**FUDGE** No. I can't do that. I can't stop drinking my wine. No. I can't do that. I wouldn't be able to find the way to get my work done without my wine.

**CHRISTINA** Well, I'm not giving you any more money.

**FUDGE** Why not?

**CHRISTINA** Not for wine.

**FUDGE** But I need my wine.

**CHRISTINA** Things are tight enough as it is. We have no cash flow. We have no crops. No cattle. No food in the fridge. No water in the well—

**FUDGE** You make it all sound so grim—

**CHRISTINA** All we have is the revenue from the oil companies and we're not spending any more of that on wine.

**FUDGE** I was worried you might say that. But I've had a thought that might mitigate against your unreasonableness…

**CHRISTINA** What's your thought?

**FUDGE** Well… because we don't in fact use it anymore—

**CHRISTINA** What?

**FUDGE** Well, I was wondering if it wouldn't perhaps be prudent to unburden ourselves of the tractor, and in doing so, increase our cash flow in a very significant manner.

**CHRISTINA** Sell the tractor?

**FUDGE** Yes.

**CHRISTINA** Sell the tractor?!

**FUDGE** That old John Deere. Yes.

**CHRISTINA** That'd be a good trick.

**FUDGE** Why do you say that?

**CHRISTINA** You don't know?

**FUDGE** Know what?

**CHRISTINA** I say that would be a good trick, to sell the tractor, and you don't know why?

**FUDGE** No. Enlighten me.

**CHRISTINA** I say it would be a good trick, because you already sold it.

**FUDGE** Nonsense.

**CHRISTINA** No. It's not nonsense. You sold it.

**FUDGE** No, I didn't.

**CHRISTINA** Yes, you did. You sold it to that low-life Sandy. For a case of wine and a cooked ham. Sandy's still bragging about it—

**FUDGE** Do you honestly think that I could have undertaken such a complex negotiation as selling our tractor and have no memory of it?

**CHRISTINA** I would have hoped that wouldn't have been possible. But is seems that it is.

**FUDGE** But I saw the tractor only the other day.

**CHRISTINA** Where?

**FUDGE** In the Quonset.

**CHRISTINA** I don't think so.

**FUDGE** I did! I saw it with my own two eyes.

**CHRISTINA** Maybe it didn't like Sandy and came home to you. Like Lassie.

**FUDGE** If you'll excuse me for a moment.

**CHRISTINA** Where are you going?

**FUDGE** I'll be right back.

**CHRISTINA** *(blocking his way)* You're not going to check?!

**FUDGE** *(moving her out of his way)* Let me go!

*He leaves for the Quonset.*

**CHRISTINA** *(calling after him)* You're going to check, aren't you?!

*CHRISTINA goes to the table and sits in the straight-backed chair.*

How can you not remember selling a tractor? Christ's sake…

*The PIANIST and CHRISTINA reprise their beautiful aria from the beginning of the play, which thanks to the beauty of "cut and paste," the author reprints here and now…*

Too bad
So sad
So sad for me
You see
Stuck in this rut
The person I'm with
Is as crazy
As a shit house rat.
God help me
I've got to get out.
God help me
I got to get unstuck…
I got to get unstuck…

*FUDGE trudges into the kitchen. It is obvious he has discovered he no longer owns a tractor. He sits and drops his head to the table. She makes no movement to help him. He peeks up at her.*

**FUDGE** This is a desperate time, sister. I could use some succour.

*She puts her hand on his neck and starts to stroke him. She is extremely seductive in this scene. The PIANIST plays something along the lines of "New York, New York" (Frank Sinatra).*

**CHRISTINA** Well, you know, darling brother, there is a way.

**FUDGE** Oh?

**CHRISTINA** Could be a way.

**FUDGE** Oh?

**CHRISTINA** Pretty simple solution to your problem, actually.

**FUDGE** What is it?

**CHRISTINA** Sell the farm.

**FUDGE** No!—

**CHRISTINA** *(placing a finger to his lips)* Shhh. Listen to me for a sec, will you? Listen to me for a sec. Okay? *(whispering into his ear seductively)* We sell the farm. You know what it's worth. We sell the farm and we take the money. All that money. We just walk away from it and we take the money. We set you up in a sharp little apartment over in Sifton. One with cable TV. Maybe some kind of sectional couch, you know? A book case, for your book. A working toilet. Think of that! We could get you an account over at the liquor store, that one that you like so much. When you're in town like that, you can even get them to deliver. Right to your door. Plus: they take away the empties for you. Think about it, Clifford. Wouldn't that be nice? Wouldn't that be better than living like this?

*He looks up at her. She believes for a heartbeat that maybe he's actually heard her. The PIANIST comes up under this story of Daddy's death with something suitably gothic.*

**FUDGE** When Daddy died, and you weren't there but I was, and let me tell you it was – well, words can't account.... The room was dark and so close, the walls closing in like the room was reduced to a closet and it smelled so intense like him, only more even like him than he smelled himself. All I could do was wait for his last breath. I sat there for hours and hours through the night and then suddenly he reached up his claw hand, and grabbed onto my arm with the remaining fingers and thumb like hot wires grabbing onto me, and he drew me into him, my face on his chest and his voice hot and dry in my ear, and he said, "This is Fudge land, son, and a fuck of a lot of it, seven sections of it, and don't fuck with that, or I'll come back and fuck with you, from the other side, I'll haunt you 'til your final breath, you little fuck, you sell one square foot." And died. Still holding onto me with that claw. My ear pressed up against his dead mouth. So what am I going to do? What am I supposed to do? Am I supposed to fuck with my father? Do you want me to fuck with the dying of my father? Our father. Our Father. Fuck. Fuck! I don't know. I don't know. Sifton sounds pretty damned good to me too, sister, but what am I supposed to do?

*She moves away from him. Then she moves back to him. She hugs him. Then she hits him.*

**CHRISTINA** I don't know, Clifford. But we've got to start doing something other than this. I'm not going to do this anymore.

**FUDGE** I don't know...

**CHRISTINA** Something has to change. I'm sorry, but I've had enough. I've got to get the fuck outta here...

*She leaves. The PIANIST plays something reminiscent of the search for the hidden bottle. FUDGE looks up from the tear-stained Bible. He tries to pour another glass of wine, but the bottle is empty. His gaze falls on the meteorite in its case. He rises and puts on a large black overcoat. He grabs the meteorite.*

**FUDGE** Mamma!

*He hides the meteorite under his coat and leaves, as the PIANIST plays an end o' act flourish.*

*End of Act One.*

## Act Two

### Scene One – Confounded by Certain Truths

*The PIANIST plays some variation of NED's tune. We are seeing NED at work for a few moments, happily working away at the preliminary phase of his excavation, i.e. determining exactly where he needs to dig. He is on top of the cliff with a shovel. He takes out a few shovelfuls of dirt from the ground, and then gets down on his hands and knees, sifting through it. Every once in a while, something captures his attention. A small fragment of a bone, perhaps. He studies it, touches it to his tongue, either discards it or puts it into a Ziploc bag. After a few moments, FINN steps out on his porch with two glasses of pink lemonade. He looks around for NED, but can't see him as he is kneeling down. Finally NED peeks over the top and sees FINN.*

**FINN** Brought you a drink. Little peace offering…

**NED** Great. Thanks.

*NED comes down (whatever his route might be) and FINN gives him his lemonade and returns to his special chair.*

**FINN** Don't mention it. It's a hot day.

**NED** Yeah, it sure is.

**FINN** You need to replenish your liquids, otherwise you'll dry up out here.

**NED** Right.

**FINN** Yep…

**NED** So what have you been doing this morning?

**FINN** Oh, you know. Making lemonade. Listening to the news.

**NED** The news, eh? I've kinda forgotten about the news. The rest of the world seems so far away or something.

**FINN** Tell me about it.

**NED** Anything exciting happening out there?

**FINN** Well, same old, same old. They're still killing each other in the Middle East. But that probably goes without saying.

**NED** No doubt.

**FINN** Beyond that, well… North Korea seems to be heating up again.

**NED** Oh, yeah…

**FINN** The U.S.-Iraq thing is looking good. You gotta like that.

**NED** I don't, actually.

**FINN** Well, I find it pretty exciting.

**NED** Well, I don't.

**FINN** Well, I do.

**NED** Well, I don't.

**FINN** Well, I do.

**NED** Oh, brother. I don't know. I don't know. What do I know anyway? I stand all day on the side of a hill, digging and poking. Wondering if I'm ever going to get laid again. Ever. No money. No fame. No love. No support. Just your voice, endlessly droning on and on about wiping half the population off the face of the earth. Funny the things your life throws at you.

**FINN** Who pooped in your porridge? Sorry if I upset you. We don't have to talk about it, if it makes you uncomfortable. We can talk about something else.

**NED** Yeah?

**FINN** Oh, yeah.

**NED** Suits me.

**FINN** Sure. We can find lots of different things to talk about…

**NED** Great.

**FINN** How's your lemonade?

**NED** It's fine.

**FINN** That's good. Man needs a cool drink on a hot day. Yep. That's for sure. Sit down. Take a load off.

*Pause. They think for a few moments of something else to talk about.*

You mind me asking you something?

**NED** Now what?

**FINN** This is something kind of personal. Nothing to do with my work.

**NED** Oh. Okay. Go ahead.

**FINN** Well, it's just to do with the paucity of attractive women out here…

**NED** Right…

**FINN** I was kinda wondering if you, uh… if you get much into the masturbation thing.

*Pause.*

**NED** I can't believe you're asking me this.

**FINN** If it's too touchy for you, I'll back off.

**NED** No…

**FINN** Well then?

**NED** Well, I mean from time to time, it comes up. As it were. You know. And I can see that the nights get long and there's no one around. So out here, I have to say, sure, I do.

*Slight pause.*

Do you?

**FINN** Oh, yeah. Oh, yeah. I quite like it.

**NED** What's not to like?

**FINN** Exactly. Tell me…

**NED** Yes?

**FINN** Do you, uh… do you tend to conjure up a mental image, or do you prefer to have something in front of you? A magazine, say.

**NED** Either way…. I guess I like the pictures.

**FINN** Me, too… depictions of lingerie, girdles, that kind of thing…

**NED** Yeah…

*Long pause.*

**FINN** You didn't happen to bring anything with you, did you? Any magazines, that kind of thing?

**NED** Sorry.

**FINN** Right. Well. That's unfortunate. You see, it's such a small town. Only the one store, eh? I don't dare buy a magazine. Everyone knows your business around here, eh?

**NED** Right. Well, that's no biggie. Next time I go to the store, I'll pick something up for you…

**FINN** Yeah?

**NED** Sure, why not?

**FINN** They keep them behind the counter. In a special rack. You have to ask specifically for them. The ones wrapped in plastic cost more, but they're worth every penny.

**NED** Okay.

**FINN** You'd be comfortable doing that? Even the plastic ones?

**NED** I think I can handle it.

**FINN** Well, that would be much appreciated. I mean, it doesn't have to be anything kinky, if you know what I mean. Hell, even a new Sears catalogue would be nice.

**NED** I'll see what I can do.

*Pause.*

**FINN** I used to have room in my head for… I don't know. Bigger things. Better things. Like love, maybe. Something lofty like that. Some state of grace that was worth aspiring to, striving towards. I don't know. Maybe somehow I just missed it. Because I can honestly say I don't care anymore…. Just the physical sensation, that small bit of personal pleasure. That's all that matters. As for the rest of it, I really don't know if I give a shit.

**NED** I don't know if I'm there yet, Finn. But I'm starting to think that I might be on my way.

**FINN** You had someone, eh?

**NED** Yeah.

**FINN** Recent?

**NED** How do you know?

**FINN** Just guessing. There's a trace of a ring on your finger there, couldn't help but notice.

**NED** Oh, yeah…

**FINN** Pretty much gone now, though, eh? A little hard work with your hands, a few days in the sun…

**NED** I guess.

**FINN** Thing you have to remember is, you're always better off not being in a relationship. People in relationships lie awake at night dreaming up ways to get out of them. And whether she toasted you or you kissed her off, you have to admit, at some point you were secretly thrilled to find yourself alone again, eh? Free again.

**NED** Maybe…

**FINN** Eh?!

**NED** Yeah… probably.

**FINN** And so you come out here, thinking it might be a good place to start over…

**NED** Something like that.

**FINN** Yeah, well. Good luck on that one…. At least maybe you won't make the same mistake I did.

**NED** What's that?

**FINN** Kids.

**NED** God. Don't tell me you have kids.

**FINN** Something wrong with that?

**NED** I wouldn't have thought you'd be comfortable increasing the world population.

**FINN** Yeah, well, in this case it was personal. I had two of 'em. Two of 'em I talk about, anyway. But they left. A long time ago.

*FINN takes a small, wrinkled photograph from his wallet. The PIANIST conjures up some kind of wistful melody, time gone by.*

That's Kirsten. And that's Michael.

**NED** Who's that?

**FINN** That was me.

**NED** What happened?

**FINN** Well, that's the problem with being a writer. When you're confounded by certain truths you feel a compulsion to share. Their mother didn't understand some of the things I was writing about. The courts felt the same way. So she packed up the kids and hauled her ass out of here.

**NED** I'm sorry…

**FINN** Yeah. I let it shut me up for a long time. But no more. I won't be silenced anymore. Your coming out here has rekindled my desire to share my thoughts again.

**NED** Oh, yeah…

**FINN** Yeah. I have to thank you for that, Ned.

**NED** Great!

*FINN puts the photo back in his wallet.*

Well… back at it, I guess.

**FINN** Don't let me hold you up.

*NED gets up, takes up the pickaxe and starts working again, and the PIANIST joins him.*

Oh.

**NED** *(stopping)* Yeah?

**FINN** If you want anything… if you want to pop in for some more lemonade… or a nice cup of tea… or to have a shower or anything, whatever… that'd be okay.

**NED** Thanks.

*FINN leaves. NED watches him go for a minute, then resumes work. The PIANIST joins in with him and then plays a transition into the next scene. Slow fade.*

*End of scene.*

## Scene Two – Lunch is Served

*NED on top of the cliff. As the piano plays, he works away with his pickaxe, digging down towards the fossil from up above. It is hard work on a hot day. CHRISTINA appears upstage. She is carrying a white plastic bag. The PIANIST plays her theme. She looks beautiful in the prairie breeze. She approaches NED.*

**CHRISTINA** Hi!

**NED** Hey. How's it going?

**CHRISTINA** Good, thanks. How are you making out?

**NED** Slow but steady, I guess.

**CHRISTINA** You've got a lot of digging to do.

**NED** Yeah. I realize that…

**CHRISTINA** I brought you some lunch.

**NED** Really? That's great. Thank you.

**CHRISTINA** *(handing him the bag)* It's not much, but I thought it might hit the spot.

**NED** *(opening the bag)* Thanks…

*He opens the lunch bag. It contains two slices of Wonder Bread, an orange and two of those puffy, chocolate-coated marshmallow cookies, also known as Dream Puffs. The PIANIST plays throughout the eating of this stuff, something reminiscent of a Parisian café.*

Great…

**CHRISTINA** That's an orange. They're very nice. And I took the liberty of buttering your bread, I hope that's okay.

**NED** It's fine.

**CHRISTINA** And the Dream Puffs. A little sugar for energy.

**NED** Right…

**CHRISTINA** Is it okay?

**NED** Oh, yeah. It's fine.

*NED begins to eat his slices of bread as she describes the famous Esso chef's salad.*

**CHRISTINA** I haven't actually got any groceries for a while. I don't know how to cook and my brother hasn't eaten any solid food in years so it's not much fun. I get hungry enough, I go out to the Esso on the highway. I like it out there, full of people on their way somewhere, somewhere else. They have a nice chef's salad there. You should see it. They've got the nice bed of lettuce underneath everything. A nice, crisp iceberg lettuce. And the nice thick slices of roast beef. And the boiled egg. And some strips of ham. And some nice cheddar cheese. And the ranch dressing. Oh, yeah. That's a nice salad, all right. All for $5.95 and that includes your coffee. We could go there sometime, if you wanted. If you were hungry. I could show you.

**NED** That'd be great.

**CHRISTINA** Yeah. It's just a small town, it's not what you're used to, but people tend to congregate there to a certain extent. The food is reliable and it's always open…

**NED** What else do people around here do for excitement?

**CHRISTINA** Well, there's drinking…

**NED** That's good.

**CHRISTINA** And then there's more drinking.

**NED** Okay…

**CHRISTINA** Then there's drinking and driving around and getting into fights and on a really special night there could be a few cows tipped.

**NED** Fascinating.

**CHRISTINA** Oh, yeah. Lives lived…

**NED** Yeah…

*Slight pause.*

**CHRISTINA** Am I keeping you from your work?

**NED** No. Not really.

**CHRISTINA** I should probably get going pretty soon anyway.

**NED** Why?

**CHRISTINA** My brother.

**NED** What about him?

**CHRISTINA** He had a bit of a, you know. One of those things. An incident. I don't like to leave him on his own for too long…

**NED** Another few minutes won't make any difference.

**CHRISTINA** I guess…

**NED** It's just that I feel a connection. With you. Not through the bone, because you found it and here I am. But you know…

**CHRISTINA** What?

**NED** Other stuff?

**CHRISTINA** Like what?

**NED** I don't know. We both like to play in the dirt.

**CHRISTINA** Yeah.

**NED** I've always thought that's a pretty cool thing about what I do. I get paid to play in the dirt.

**CHRISTINA** I'd like to, someday. Get paid for this. You should see. I have a whole suitcase full of stuff. Marty suggested we take them to Vegas some weekend and maybe try to sell them. But, of course, that never happened.

**NED** Probably for the best.

**CHRISTINA** Yeah. And then. There's my meteorite, which I really want to show you sometime.

**NED** Yeah, I'd like to see it.

**CHRISTINA** I'll bring it out with me next time. I guess it's special because we saw it flash across the sky just after my mom died.… My brother thought maybe it was her soul, maybe. Maybe it was, but if it was her soul, all that's left of it now is that rock. I paid a little money and got it displayed properly. And the paper came out and took my picture, put it on the front page. I may have mentioned that already…

*She takes out a crumpled page from a newspaper and shows it to him. FINN comes out of his place with the tray and two glasses of pink lemonade and a small plate of the same cookies that CHRISTINA has packed in the lunch. As he approaches, and NED is watching him, CHRISTINA silently disappears. FINN crosses over and sets down the lemonade and cookies.*

**FINN** Chow time!

**NED** Hey, Finn. *(to CHRISTINA who is not there)* Do you want a glass – Oh.

**FINN** What?

**NED** She came back for a visit, but she disappeared.

*FINN tracks her with his scope.*

**FINN** There she goes… man, she moves fast. *(giving NED the gun)* See…. She's just coming out of that coulee.

**NED** Oh, yeah.

**FINN** You see, she's growing up to be just like her mother, out prowling around the fields night and day. Won't be long 'til she starts skulking around the fields in some kind of diaphanous white nightgown. And it's too bad, because in her case there's something there, something special. And, really, you know, she could be quite a handsome young woman if she'd just do some of the womanly things on herself. Like wearing some makeup or something. Some rouge or something. A little blue eye shadow. All men respond to a little blue eye shadow, don't you think?

**NED** You like the blue eye shadow, do you?

**FINN** Well, yeah, you?

**NED** It's okay. Do you know why you like it?

**FINN** I don't know – I just know I like it.

**NED** But there's a reason you like it.

**FINN** There is?

**NED** Yeah.

**FINN** What?

**NED** Well, they say that when a woman has an orgasm, her eyelids kind of flush, and turn a very delicate shade of blue. Kind of a periwinkle. And blue eye shadow—they say—brings this to mind in the eye of the male beholder. Making the wearer of the eye shadow extremely attractive and even beguiling.

**FINN** Serious.

**NED** Yeah.

**FINN** You're not having me off here?

**NED** It's not an exact science. But that's what they say. I read it somewhere…

**FINN** Hmmmm… I'm going to have to think about that one for a bit.

*FINN wanders back to his porch, sits and rocks and thinks about women's makeup, while NED takes up his pickaxe and gets back to work. The PIANIST resumes the work theme. Lights fade on the work area as a small light comes up on FUDGE at his table.*

*End of scene.*

## Scene Three – And Lot Came Out of Zoar

*The PIANIST plays a happy, domestic piece as we discover FUDGE entering with a case of wine. He dances with it. Hides a bottle in his special hiding place. He sets it down, sits down himself with a fresh bottle, and looks over at the case with love and admiration. He reads the Bible, deeply. CHRISTINA enters.*

**CHRISTINA** Hello.

**FUDGE** Hello.

**CHRISTINA** How was your day?

**FUDGE** Grrreat! How was yours?

**CHRISTINA** It was fine. Just fine.

**FUDGE** You've been out fornicating with that digger of bones?

**CHRISTINA** Oh, boy, would you look at that?

**FUDGE** What?

**CHRISTINA** You've managed to get yourself another case of wine.

**FUDGE** Yeah…

**CHRISTINA** How did you manage that?

**FUDGE** I prayed. The miracle came. That's how it works. It's called faith.

**CHRISTINA** That's great. Just great. Well, I see you won't be needing anything from me, so I guess I'll turn in. Good night, Clifford.

**FUDGE** Good night.

*She leaves for her room, which would seem to be on the other side of the kitchen wall (far left wall). FUDGE takes a great gulp of wine and picks up his Bible, moves down to the spot where we first saw him, with his special (maybe even the pulpit, to begin with). The PIANIST plays some appropriate Old Testament music in behind his reading.*

"And Lot went up out of Zoar, and dwelt in the mountain, and his daughters with him; for he feared to dwell in Zoar: and he dwelt in a cave, he and his two daughters.

And the firstborn said unto the younger, Our father is old, and there is not a man in the earth to come in unto us after the manner of all the earth:

Come, let us make out father drink wine, and we will lie with him, that we may preserve the seed of our father.

And they made their father drink wine that night: and the firstborn went in, and lay with her father..."

*FUDGE stops. Music stops. Then they resume again.*

"And they made their father drink wine that night: and the firstborn went in, and lay with her father..."

*They stop again. The PIANIST resumes as FUDGE mouths these same words. A light bulb turns on over his head. He walks over to the wall and pounds on it.*

**CHRISTINA** *(off)* What?

**FUDGE** I've just had a thought.

**CHRISTINA** *(off)* What?!

**FUDGE** I've just had a thought!

**CHRISTINA** *(off)* What thought?

**FUDGE** A thought about the future of this family!

**CHRISTINA** *(off)* Go to bed.

**FUDGE** No! I've had a deep thought. Maybe even a revelation! Come out, little rabbit. Come out of your hole! I have something to share with you!

*CHRISTINA enters, wearing a diaphanous white nightgown.*

**CHRISTINA** This had better be good.

**FUDGE** Oh, it's good, it's good, it's good all right. Comes from my reading of Genesis.

**CHRISTINA** Great...

**FUDGE** Ohhh... where was I? Oh, right. Yeah. Listen to this...

**CHRISTINA** I'm listening.

**FUDGE** "And they made their father drink wine that night." And the firstborn went in. You see?

**CHRISTINA** No, I don't see.

**FUDGE** They made their father drink wine that night. Father in this case meaning the patriarch. Like, the guy who was around. The only guy. The guy with the seed. Get it? The seed? In this case, Lot. They wanted him to drink wine, so that he might relax, and they in turn might lay with him, that his seed might come unto them. Get it?

**CHRISTINA** Go to bed.

**FUDGE** Don't you see?

**CHRISTINA** Get some sleep.

**FUDGE** "...and the firstborn went in." You see?

**CHRISTINA** No.

**FUDGE** They were coming to the end of their race. They had to do something to keep the race alive. Or face extinction.

*She comes further into the room, in a rather threatening manner. FUDGE returns to the table and drinks some more wine.*

**CHRISTINA** So what's your point?

**FUDGE** Well... it makes the point that given the right set of circumstances... sometimes it's justified...

**CHRISTINA** It?

**FUDGE** Yeah.

**CHRISTINA** This is severely sick and twisted even for you, Clifford.

**FUDGE** It's the word of God.

**CHRISTINA** It's twisted. You've twisted it.

**FUDGE** It's in the Bible.

**CHRISTINA** Everything's in the Bible.

**FUDGE** They were coming to the end of their race – don't you see? So in some cases it's justified— *(He stands and grabs her by the shoulders.)* It's justified, if you're at the end of your race.

**CHRISTINA** Let go of me.

**FUDGE** I have a bold new plan for us, sister.

**CHRISTINA** Clifford. I'm warning you now: let go of me.

**FUDGE** Because we're at the end of our race, you see. We're at the end of the Fudge race—

*She knees him in the groin. He goes down, whimpering on the floor.*

**CHRISTINA** Don't you ever—ever—touch me again. You hear me? Ever!

*No response.*

I'm going out. I won't be back tonight. For God's sake, get some sleep.

*She looks around the room for her meteorite but, of course, she doesn't find it.*

Where's my meteorite? Clifford? Huh? Where is it? What have you done – Oh, my God. Oh my God. You took it, didn't you? You took my meteorite. I get it. You took it over to Sandy and sold it, didn't you. That weasel, he's wanted it ever since I found it, so you took my meteorite and pawned it for a case of wine, didn't you? Didn't you? The most important scientific discovery of this region and you sold it? Even worse, you saw Momma in it, Clifford. You said so. You said it contained her soul. And yet you turned around and sold it? And for what? For wine? For wine? You bastard. You lousy, drunken, pathetic bastard, you stole my meteorite. I hate you. I hate you. I wish you were dead. I wish you'd just die. Why don't you just die! Why don't you do the world a favour and die?! You stupid fucking bastard! *Fuck!*

*She takes a bottle of wine and pours it over him. She leaves. The PIANIST plays the theme we associate with FUDGE and his madness. After a moment, FUDGE reaches up and grabs his bottle of wine. He drinks as the lights fade.*

*End of scene.*

## Scene Four – Consummation

*The site. NED is sitting, reading by the light of a Coleman lantern. The cry of a coyote can be heard very close to him. A series of other coyote calls echo away and fade. The coyote sound is made by FUDGE who is lying with his bottle on his kitchen floor. NED hears it as coyotes. The PIANIST plays some lovely nacht musik.*

**NED** Jesus…

*He goes back to reading. CHRISTINA looms up in the light, still in her nightgown, so the audience and FINN, of course, can see her but NED cannot. The coyote again.*

Man…. This is getting to be like some kind of bad Disney movie…

*CHRISTINA moves forward. NED sees her and screams.*

**CHRISTINA** Hi!

**NED** Aigh!

**CHRISTINA** Oh. Did I startle you?

**NED** My God. Don't ever do that to a person. I could have had a heart attack!

**CHRISTINA** Sorry.

**NED** What the hell are you doing out here?

**CHRISTINA** Well, I was just passing by and it seemed kind of strange not to say hi.

**NED** Passing by? Out here? Like that?

**CHRISTINA** Yeah. Kinda.

**NED** Right.... Right.

**CHRISTINA** Sorry. I can just go if you want me to.

**NED** No, no. It's okay. I'm sorry. You just scared the shit out of me. You know? I was already freaked out by the coyotes. And then you showed up. So you scared me. But it's okay. It's nice to see you. I'm glad you're here. It's all good. Really.

**CHRISTINA** You sure?

**NED** Absolutely. Here.

*He pulls out a camp stool for her.*

Here. Sit. Make yourself at home.

**CHRISTINA** Thanks.

**NED** Want a drink of something?

**CHRISTINA** Sure. What do you have?

**NED** Rum. And rum.

**CHRISTINA** Okay.

**NED** Cool. *(rummaging through his stuff)* Find you something that's not too grossly contaminated here... *(He pulls out a tin cup.)* Voila.

*He pours some rum into the cups, hands her one.*

Cheers.

**CHRISTINA** Cheers.

*They drink. Coyotes again.*

*(to herself)* Stupid bastard...

**NED** You okay?

**CHRISTINA** Yeah.

**NED** Yeah?

**CHRISTINA** Yeah. Are you?

**NED** Yeah. I'm better now. It's nice to have company.

*Slight pause.*

**CHRISTINA** So how are you making out up here?

**NED** Good.

**CHRISTINA** Yeah?

**NED** Yeah.

**CHRISTINA** Amazing view.

**NED** Yeah. You can start feeling pretty insignificant out here…

**CHRISTINA** We are insignificant, Ned.

**NED** Maybe we are.

**CHRISTINA** No one's going to come looking for our bones in a million years.

**NED** No. Probably not.

*FUDGE/coyote is heard.*

**CHRISTINA** Coyotes…

**NED** Yeah. They're not so bad. A bit noisy, but they tend to keep to themselves. Finn shoots them, did you know that?

**CHRISTINA** So?

**NED** Seems like a shame.

**CHRISTINA** Everybody shoots coyotes, Ned.

**NED** Why?

**CHRISTINA** Why? Why, they're nothing but mangy, rabid, chicken-stealin' scavengers, that's why. You shoot them. That's what you do with them.

**NED** Really?

**CHRISTINA** Well, yeah.

**NED** Right.

*Slight pause. NED stifles a yawn.*

**CHRISTINA** Am I keeping you awake?

**NED** Sorry. It's all this fresh air or something. That and digging out here all day, you know. I've got to tell you, I'm not in the best of shape.

**CHRISTINA** Right…

**NED** I was actually thinking of turning in, just before you showed up.

**CHRISTINA** Yeah…

**NED** Hitting the old hay. I've been pretty much getting up when the sun comes up which isn't that long from now.

**CHRISTINA** You're a smooth-talkin' devil, you know that?

**NED** I am?

**CHRISTINA** Where do you sleep?

**NED** In the tent.

**CHRISTINA** I like tents.

**NED** Oh, yeah?

**CHRISTINA** I like sleeping in tents.

**NED** Is that right?

**CHRISTINA** Totally.

**NED** The problem is, though… I only have the one sleeping bag, eh?

**CHRISTINA** Works for me.

**NED** Works for you?

**CHRISTINA** Yeah.

**NED** Right. Okay. Well then. Do you want to stay the night, is that what I'm hearing?

**CHRISTINA** Yes, please.

**NED** Well then. Okay…

**CHRISTINA** Yeah.

*She crawls into the tent. NED has another quick hit of rum. He extinguishes the Coleman lamp and crawls in behind her. A flashlight comes on inside the tent and we are treated to a silhouette show of passion and adventure, the likes of which are seldom seen in the prairie west, while the PIANIST plays a theme celebrating the grandeur of love and romance. At the same time, FINN and FUDGE watch the play of light and shadow on the tent. Suddenly the light switches off.*

*Blackout.*

*End of scene.*

## Scene Five – The Death of Fudge

*FINN on the porch looking at things through the scope of his gun. NED standing on top of the cliff with a cup of coffee. FUDGE approaches the base of the cliff. He is wearing a long black coat and has a bottle of wine in one of the pockets. He has now, over the course of the last few days, consumed several bottles of wine without really eating or sleeping, and yet it's possible he has drunk and fretted himself into a state resembling lucidity. The PIANIST plays something that perhaps puts us in mind of Sergio Leone, complete with the rattlesnake sound effect.*

**FUDGE** "Circumcise yourselves to the Lord, and take away the foreskins of your heart, ye men of Saskatchewan!"

*He looks around him and spits.*

Finn-land.

**FINN** Well, well, well. The Revered Fudge. What brings you here?

**FUDGE** I cannot speak to you.

**FINN** No. And you shouldn't be on my land, either. According to your daddy. But he's dead. And you're here. So talk to me. What brings you out here?

**FUDGE** The prophets.

**FINN** No shit.

**FUDGE** I talk to them. They talk to me. We talk.

**FINN** Is that a fact?

**FUDGE** Absolutely.

**FINN** Just don't touch anything.

**FUDGE** Okay.

**FINN** We got science going on here.

**FUDGE** Okay. I won't touch nothing.

**FINN** See that you don't.

**FUDGE** Okay. I won't. For I, too, am a man of science…

*He wanders over to the base of the cliff and shouts up at NED.*

For I, too, am a man of science!

**NED** What's that?

**FUDGE** I say, for I, too, am a man of science.

**NED** Right. How you doing, Cliff?

**FUDGE** Good, thanks, Ned. Good, good, good.

**FINN** You two know each other?

**NED** Yeah.

**FINN** How?

**NED** Cliff came out and visited me. Why?

**FINN** *(whispering to NED, so that FUDGE doesn't hear, if that's possible)* That's Clifford Fudge, Christina's brother. *(makes the sign of his index finger twirling around his temple)*

**NED** Right…

**FUDGE** You know, Ned, I, too, am a man of science, given to sober introspection and circumspection and and and and and mindful contemplation of the mystery of creation. Yes, indeed. A man of science… like yourself.

**NED** Right…

**FUDGE** For what is science? But a name given to our consuming and passionate desire to achieve a quantitative cognition of our circumambient universe…

**NED** Good point.

**FUDGE** Thank you. Tell me something, Ned…

**NED** What's that?

**FUDGE** Where is my sister?

**NED** Your sister. Well, uh, gee, Cliff…

**FUDGE** I fear she has cleaved to you.

**NED** Cleaved?

**FINN** Cleaved?

**FUDGE** And you have cleaved to her. What have you done with her?

*CHRISTINA pokes her head out of NED's tent.*

**CHRISTINA** Clifford!

**FUDGE** Ahhh, there you are, my blood and my bones. There you are.

**CHRISTINA** What are you doing here?

**FUDGE** An inspection, sister. Nothing for you to worry your little head about.

**CHRISTINA** Give me a sec and I'll take you back home, okay?

**FUDGE** But I'm not finished my little exploration here.

*CHRISTINA disappears back inside the tent and comes right back out wearing one of NED's shirts over the famous and even hereditary diaphanous white nightgown.*

*(to NED)* We men of science. Isn't that right?

**NED** What's that?

**FUDGE** We men of science! Sniffing around the edges of our incomprehensive misundergivings and shnivings and quivings and etc. etc. etc. etc. etc. etc. etc. etc. etc. etc. etc…

*He appears to be stuck on "etc.," which he pronounces as "eckt." CHRISTINA crosses over to him.*

**CHRISTINA** Okay. Time to go home, Cliffy, okay?

**FUDGE** *(pushing her away)* No. I'm not done here. Damned though I may be to even stand here. I am not done.

*She walks over and sits on the porch steps by FINN, who is standing on the porch, holding his rifle, suddenly in an extremely protective manner.*

*(to NED)* You know what you are?

**NED** No.

**FUDGE** You know what you are?

**NED** No.

**FUDGE** You are a fossil cowboy! Shooting the lights out of our misguided comprehension. Six guns blazing for the truth. Ride on. Right on!

**CHRISTINA** Clifford, let's just go home.

**FUDGE** *(to CHRISTINA)* Hang on, hang on. *(to NED)* I need to ask you something.

**NED** Yes?

**FUDGE** I wanna ask you something.

**NED** Yes?

**FUDGE** Hang on. I'm coming up.

*Like some kind of bat he starts to crawl up the side of the cliff. He gets about halfway up and stops and has a huge belt of wine.*

Do you believe in God, cowboy?

**NED** Are you asking me that?

**FUDGE** Yes.

**NED** I don't know.

**FUDGE** You don't know?

**NED** I don't know if I believe or not. You asked. I'm telling you.

**FUDGE** You're wrong, you know.

**NED** About what?

**FUDGE** Evolution.

**NED** I don't think I am.

**FUDGE** All the fossil record proves, again and again, is that a turtle is still a turtle, a snake is still a snake and the hoofed animals of the field are still the hoofed animals of the field. And a man is still a man. As time goes by, there is no progression from one species to another. The conclusion is clear: no amount of accidental genetic modification can cause one kind of life to turn into another.

These bones you dig up prove that, again and again. There is no missing link. Every particle of life complete, inviolate, in and of itself, lovingly crafted by a compassionate and omnipotent God. What you're doing proves it.

**NED** That's your opinion.

**FUDGE** Someday, it will be made known to you. Someday, you'll be made to know how terribly wrong you have been. Someday, you will be turned away, even as you have turned away. Access denied, cowboy.

*He comes the rest of the way up the cliff.*

**NED** Listen, Cliff. I think the tour's over for today. Okay?

**FUDGE** It need not be too late, friend.

**NED** What are you talking about—?

**FUDGE** On your knees, sinner!

**NED** Up yours!

*FUDGE grabs NED by the shoulders, trying to force him down.*

**FUDGE** Fall on your knees and open up your heart to Jayzus! That ye may be saved. Repent, man of science.

**NED** No!

**FUDGE** I say repent!

**NED** No! Leave me alone!

*He pushes FUDGE away. FUDGE falls. NED turns to say something to FINN and CHRISTINA. With surprising quickness, FUDGE picks up the pickaxe and follows him. He's about to nail him from behind. FINN jumps up and shoots right at the two of them. FUDGE falls.*

**FUDGE** Motherfucker!

*His soul, pure and white, can be seen shooting up to heaven, even as he drops to the ground. Quick blackout. Continuous action to the next scene.*

## Scene Six – And the Rocks Were Rent

*As the gunshot reverberates, the lights change, going into some kind of strobe effect. Somehow, perhaps through the use of film, the rocks on the cliff face begin to bleed. A wind effect, sweeping everything from the stage, threatens to blow the actors off their feet. Thunder and lightning. The PIANIST plays something suitably surreal and even abstract throughout this scene, windblown though he may be. There may also be the opportunity here for recorded music as well. We hear also the sound of a shovel in gravel. The sound of empty bottles rattling against each other. The sound of breathing throughout. In the semi darkness, we wish to create some kind of exotic movement/voice/sound piece depicting the death of FUDGE.*

*CHRISTINA kneels, holding the dying FUDGE, who quotes from Matthew 24/33–35…*

**FUDGE** *(His voice, at least, on tape, looping, so these words can repeat, they can be manipulated to slow down and speed up again, depending on the eight million other things going on. If there were a significant budget attached to this moment, there may be a mighty chorus to back him, seventy-five Trina look-alikes, but maybe our PIANIST can, as they say, fake it…. Are there still tapes?!)* Wherefore, ye be witnesses unto yourselves, that ye are the children of them which killed the prophets./Fill ye up then the measure of your fathers./Ye serpents. Ye generation of vipers, how can you escape the damnation of hell? How can you escape the damnation of hell? How can you escape the damnation of hell? How can you escape the damnation of hell… *(Etc…)*

*Light on FINN standing by his cabin.*

**FINN** I can't believe I took him down like that, first shot.

*Lights down on FINN and up on NED who is struggling with his tent.*

**NED** That is not what I mean by a summer in the country!

*Eventually, the storm passes and order is restored to the world. The voices and other sound effects, like of the storm, fade. The lights start to come back up, on the characters, with the exception of FUDGE, standing around the makeshift grave. The music distills into something simple and melodic, either of his own composition or from the repertoire, e.g. the Chopin prelude (in, I believe, C minor).*

*Continuous action to next scene.*

## Scene Seven – The Earthly Paradise

*Lights continue to come up to full value as the PIANIST continues the funeral song, revealing FINN, NED and CHRISTINA at the base of the cliff. Stocking out of the ground, one of FUDGE's feet, showing the ankle, sock and shoe. They look at the foot and look at one another.*

**FINN** *(more to himself than anyone else)* Oh boy, oh boy. Boy, oh boy, oh boy. I can't believe I took him down like that, first shot.

*Silence.*

Because it was in my mind to just scare him or whatever, but there's something I guess, some force at work when your finger's on the trigger, that says go for it, go for the kill. What could I do? What could I do but shoot? Oh boy. I don't know…

*Silence. We may hear the prairie wind if there are sound effects, or the piano may recreate them somehow.*

**CHRISTINA** *(to NED)* So, that's the best you could do?

**NED** What?

**CHRISTINA** That's the best you could do, burying him?

**NED** Yeah…

**CHRISTINA** Couldn't fit all of him in the hole?

**NED** I tried.

**CHRISTINA** Couldn't dig a bigger hole?

**NED** I panicked.

**CHRISTINA** I thought you were like a professional.

**NED** What are you talking about?

**CHRISTINA** Digging. That's what you do.

**NED** I'm a palaeontologist. Not a gravedigger.

**CHRISTINA** Same skills.

**NED** Yeah, well, usually I'm digging things out of the ground, not trying to put them back in.

*Slight pause.*

**FINN** I can't believe I got him like that. That he just went down like that. That it all just finishes like that, completes itself.… And what's left but a shoe we scuffled across the dirt?

*Slight pause.*

**CHRISTINA** Coyote's likely to come and chew on his ankle we just leave him like this.

**NED** Yeah, okay. I'll pile some dirt on him later, okay?

**CHRISTINA** Okay.

**NED** Give me a break. I should never have gotten involved in the first place.

**CHRISTINA** Yeah, well, you're involved now. Don't think you're not. You're involved as much as me and Finn are. Isn't that right, Finn?

**FINN** *(not hearing her)* And to make such a clean, precise shot like that, it's really unbelievable…

**CHRISTINA** Tell him he's involved, Finn. Tell him he's as much involved in this as we are.

**FINN** Oh, he's involved, all right.

**CHRISTINA** Tell 'im.

**FINN** You're involved all right, Ned. Oh, yes, you are. We're all in this together.

**NED** Okay…

**CHRISTINA** What could we do anyways?

**FINN** Nothing.

**CHRISTINA** What could have made it any different than it was?

**FINN** Nothing.

**CHRISTINA** It was only a matter of time…

**FINN** Yep…

**CHRISTINA** Only a matter of time…

**FINN** Yep.

*The three drift away. FINN to his place, NED and CHRISTINA over to the FUDGE home. The PIANIST begins playing "What a Friend We Have in Jesus" or "Onward Christian Soldiers" or some other piece that we identify with FUDGE. The special comes up and FUDGE appears, only now his robe is clean and his hair is combed and his face is as fresh as a cherub's. He looks at the three "mourners" and shakes his head.*

**FUDGE** Sad, really. Can't even muster up a decent prayer to help speed a man to the Sweet Hereafter. Sad. This is what happens, when you have no faith. When you can't believe in anything other than the empirical, and can't see what's beyond the tip of your nose… sad…

For I have seen the heavenly paradise and I have been invited in, all for the simple reason that I invited Jayzus into my heart.

As I recall, it went something like this. I felt the fiery pain as the bullet from Finn's gun singed my flesh. I felt my vigour draining from my body. I felt my heart begin to cool, and my light to fade, like I was lost in the depths of some vast ocean. But then I did open my eyes and saw a great and mighty orb. And it did surge with heat and light and it was beautiful, beyond words or even understanding. And I could hear the singing of a celestial chorus of souls like myself, who had gathered to welcome me to paradise.

Paradise, where I was greeted by the family members made whole again, fingers and legs attached and functioning again. All were there to greet me. And I was made to sip lemonade and eat of Nanaimo bars, and I definitely caught a glimpse of God on His throne, and I am here to tell you that no matter what it might seem at times, all is well with the universe.

Now, before I head on back, in case you haven't figured it out yet, let me put it in as simple terms as I know how, because for some of you here, I've gotta believe there's still hope. It goes like this:

Those of us who have chosen the Lord Jayzus as our personal Saviour will enjoy eternal life in paradise. And the rest of you can go to hell.

*FUDGE holds up his hands the way the Pope holds up his hands, bestowing a blessing on the audience. The music swells, echoing the heavenly chorus. FUDGE disappears in such a way that he seems to transforms into a ghost.*

*Fade to blackout on entire set.*

*End of scene.*

## Scene Eight – One Too Many

*Lights upon the FUDGE kitchen. NED is now sitting in FUDGE's chair, reading, drinking a cup of coffee. CHRISTINA sits at another chair, transfixed. The PIANIST may wish to create some sort of surreal version of what we heard in the Burnt Offerings Scene – hominess gone seriously awry (if it wasn't before).*

**CHRISTINA** Whatcha reading there, honey?

**NED** The Bible.

**CHRISTINA** What?!

**NED** Well, that's what I call it. It's called *The Structure of Evolutionary Theory.* By Stephen Jay Gould.

**CHRISTINA** Who's that?

**NED** You've never heard of Stephen Jay Gould?

**CHRISTINA** No.

**NED** He was the most influential scientific mind in history. Well, after Darwin. My hero. I can't believe you've never heard of him.

**CHRISTINA** Well, now I have…

**NED** Yep. Now you have…

*Pause. The PIANIST begins making a tick-tock sound that gradually gets slower and slower.*

**CHRISTINA** Shouldn't you be out there?

**NED** Where?

**CHRISTINA** Out at Finn's. At your excavation?

**NED** I don't know. Looks like it might rain.

**CHRISTINA** What are you talking about? It doesn't rain here.

**NED** Well, it looks like it to me.

**CHRISTINA** It's just that, the sooner you get done your digging, the sooner we can get out of here and start seeing the world…

**NED** It's a long process.

**CHRISTINA** What do you mean?

**NED** That excavation?

**CHRISTINA** Yes?

**NED** It's a long process.

**CHRISTINA** How long?

**NED** It'll take years.

**CHRISTINA** Years?

**NED** Years and years.

**CHRISTINA** I thought you'd be done this summer.

**NED** Oh, no. I'm going to be here a good long time. Yep. A good… long… time.

**CHRISTINA** Years…

**NED** Yep…

**CHRISTINA** Years…

**NED** Years and years…

*She swoons and falls from her chair. NED doesn't notice. The tick-tock stops and the PIANIST plays some music that helps her get up from the floor and finally take some action. She leaves. He reads. After a moment, CHRISTINA returns with an old suitcase. She throws it on the table and opens it. Inside, hundreds of archaeological artifacts she has collected over the years. She is now wearing a nice sun dress, the kind FINN dreams about. She puts on a hat, a coat and a pair of sunglasses. She takes a few papers from one of the drawers and puts them in her bag.*

What are you doing?

**CHRISTINA** I'm leaving.

**NED** Where are you going?

**CHRISTINA** I don't know.

**NED** But…

**CHRISTINA** What?

**NED** You can't leave.

**CHRISTINA** Yes, I can, actually.

**NED** But you live here.

**CHRISTINA** Not really.

**NED** You belong here.

**CHRISTINA** No, I don't.

**NED** It's your house. Your stuff.

**CHRISTINA** So?

**NED** You can't just walk away.

**CHRISTINA** Yes, I can. Yes, I can.

**NED** No, you can't.

**CHRISTINA** Just you watch me. I've had enough. I'm going to sell this Fudge land and I'm going to spend the rest of my life acting like I was never here, never once.

**NED** But what about your brother?

**CHRISTINA** What about him?

**NED** People will ask about him.

**CHRISTINA** No one cares.

**NED** Okay. About him.

**CHRISTINA** Yeah.

**NED** But what about… you know?

**CHRISTINA** What?

**NED** You and me?

**CHRISTINA** I'm sorry, honey. There's just too much sadness…

**NED** But we can change that. We can move on.

**CHRISTINA** No.

**NED** Why not?

**CHRISTINA** It's too late. And it's sad, really. I know I'll never meet another man like you, as fine as you. But I can't stay here. There's too much sadness on this land…

*She kisses him and leaves, passing by FINN's place.*

*NED starts to cross the set to FINN's place.*

*End of scene. Continuous action to next scene.*

## Scene Nine – The Mission

*NED crosses the stage, over to FINN's house. FUDGE's foot still protrudes from the earth, near the actual excavation site, but everything else, his tent, shovels, etc., is now gone. The PIANIST plays a forlorn version of whatever his theme has been throughout the play.*

*Lights alter in the area of FINN's cabin. A bit of smoke, making everything seem unreal. FINN appears up behind his porch. He is wearing a long coat and a hat and is carrying an old suitcase. NED sees him and takes no notice, at first, that there is something unusual about him.*

**NED** Hey, Finn.

**FINN** So, she left?

**NED** Yeah.

**FINN** You let her get away.

**NED** Yeah…

**FINN** Too bad.

**NED** What's up with you?

**FINN** I'm leaving.

**NED** What do you mean, you're leaving?

**FINN** What I said, I'm leaving.

**NED** But you can't.

**FINN** Why not?

**NED** This is your place.

**FINN** My work here is done. Time to move on.

**NED** Where are you going to go?

**FINN** Where I'm needed.

**NED** Needed? For what?

**FINN** For my work.

**NED** Your work?

**FINN** My life's work.

**NED** What are you talking about?

**FINN** You know damn well what I'm talking about.

**NED** What? That? No. No way. You can't be serious.

**FINN** I'm very serious, Ned.

**NED** Yeah, but that's not work, it's just an opinion.

**FINN** Listen to me.

**NED** Yeah, I have been—

**FINN** I believe in what I've been saying all these years. With my heart and my soul. But naturally, I've never thought of doing anything about it before. Oh, sure, I published a few articles. Spoke to an extension class over at the community college a couple of times. But I never really thought of putting my words into action. But I have to tell you, potting old Fudge there seemed to open the gates or something. Seemed to bring me closer to my destiny.

**NED** So what are you going to do?

**FINN** What am I going to do? I'm going to kill people, that's what I'm going to do. This is what I was meant to do. It's time for me to fulfill my destiny. I am an agent of change.

**NED** That's crazy.

**FINN** Uh huh.

**NED** You can't just—

**FINN** What?

**NED** There's no way.

**FINN** There's lots of ways. Lots and lots of ways.

**NED** But you can't go out and start killing people.

**FINN** Why can't I?

**NED** The law, for one thing.

**FINN** Pfft! The law! It don't matter.... I'll be around in the dark. I'll be everywhere – wherever you look. Wherever there's a fight so hungry people can eat, I'll be there, cheering for a drought. Oh, yeah. I'll be there all right. I've wasted enough time out here. I've got work to do. Keep your eye on the news. I've got a feeling they'll be covering my career. Pay special attention to the medical reports. That unexpected outbreak of Ebola along some forgotten river bank. Far away from here. Or a contaminated water supply, somewhere, somewhere closer to home. An unexpected case of Creutzfeldt-Jakob. Whatever. Remember, I like to work with microbes. I have a lot of faith in 'em. Take care of yourself, son. Good luck with your excavation.

*FINN leaves in a little more smoke. Fade on NED.*

*End of scene.*

## Scene Ten – The End

*The stage appears exactly as it did at the beginning of the play. Characters in their same positions. The only difference, FUDGE is wearing a silk Armani suit, a 44" tall. (Don't worry; the author will graciously buy it at the end of the production.) NED enters exactly as he did at the beginning, with the same bags and equipment. This scene is, of course, the same as NED's first appearance, which is reflected not only in the blocking but also in what the PIANIST does here. The implication is that he is now just arriving, and that what we just saw was a bit of a dream NED had/has on first arriving, as he imagined what it might be like out here.*

**NED** Ahhhhh, yeah. Here we go. Here we go. Here we are. Here we are. The country. The country.... Beautiful country.... Beautiful people. Beautiful simple wonderful basic country people living out here in this beauty.... I am among them now.... I am in the country.... Among the simple folk. A beautiful new beginning...

*Lights fade to blackout over entire set, except for the PIANIST who plays some kind of finale. When he has finished, his light fades to blackout.*

*The End.*

# The Exquisite Hour

By Stewart Lemoine

# About
# Stewart Lemoine

Stewart Lemoine has been writing and directing for Teatro La Quindicina in Edmonton, Alberta since 1982 and is the author of more than fifty plays including *Cocktails at Pam's*, *Evelyn Strange*, *Neck-Breaking Car-Hop*, *Shockers Delight!*, *The Margin of the Sky*, *A Grand Time in the Rapids* and *The Vile Governess and Other Psychodramas*. His annual productions at the Edmonton Fringe Theatre Festival between 1982 and 2002 were consistent sell-outs. Since 1994, he and Teatro have been resident at Edmonton's Varscona Theatre, and their productions have also been successfully mounted in many other Canadian centres, including Toronto, Ottawa, Calgary, and Winnipeg, as well as in New York City.

Stewart is a five-time winner of Edmonton's Elizabeth Sterling Haynes Award for his work with Teatro, most recently for Outstanding New Play for *At the Zenith of the Empire*. He has also won Toronto's Dora Mavor Moore Award for *The Vile Governess and Other Psychodramas*. His play *Pith!* won the New York International Fringe Festival's Award for Excellence in Playwriting following its appearance at the Festival in 2004, and was remounted there in August 2006 as part of the FringeNYC tenth anniversary celebrations. In May 2003, he was honored with the Queen's Golden Jubilee Medal by the Lieutenant Governor of Alberta, Lois Hole.

*The Exquisite Hour* was first produced by Teatro La Quindicina at the Edmonton Fringe Festival, August 16–25, 2002 with the following company:

| | |
|---|---|
| ZACHARY Teale | Jeff Haslam |
| HELEN Darimont | Kate Ryan |

Directed and Stage Managed by Stewart Lemoine

---

The play was revived by Teatro La Quindicina at the Varscona Theatre in Edmonton from July 12–28, 2007 with the same cast and director. On this occasion the set and lighting were designed by Mike Takats and the stage manager was Rachel Rudd.

## Characters

ZACHARY
HELEN

## Setting

ZACHARY Teale's backyard at around 6 p.m. on a late summer day in 1962.

# The Exquisite Hour

*In ZACHARY Teale's backyard at around 6 p.m. on a late summer day in 1962. There is a pair of patio chairs and a small table on which rests a pitcher of lemonade and some glasses. There are some potted flowers on the ground. ZACK is discovered standing with a glass of lemonade. He has a sip and looks up at the sky, then at the potted flowers. He pokes the dirt in one of the pots, then picks up a watering can and gives the flower a little water. He sits down, picks up his lemonade, has another sip, and looks off, happily and also a little blankly. After a moment, HELEN Darimont enters. She's wearing a bright floaty summer dress with hat and gloves and carries a shoulder bag and some envelopes.*

**HELEN** Excuse me. Good afternoon.

**ZACK** Oh, hello there.

**HELEN** You're Mr. Teale? Mr. Zachary Teale?

**ZACK** *(standing)* Zack. Yes.

**HELEN** Mr. Teale, my name is Mrs. Darimont. I'm sorry to just barge into your yard like this, but I've been ringing the front doorbell without result and thought it best to explore other options.

**ZACK** I see. Do I know you, Mrs. Darimont?

**HELEN** You don't, and I should probably tell you that this isn't a social call.

**ZACK** Oh. Are things going to be unpleasant?

**HELEN** I hope not. I didn't mean I'd be unsociable. Quite the opposite in fact. I'm here in a professional capacity.

**ZACK** Are you serving me papers? Is this a legal thing? I paid that parking ticket.

**HELEN** Oh, please, Mr. Teale, you're terrifying yourself without reason. This is just your mail.

**ZACK** Oh. Well… why do you have it?

**HELEN** It was sticking out of your mailbox in an ungainly way. I was afraid something might have been inappropriately creased. Here you go.

**ZACK** Thank you.

*He takes it and puts it aside.*

**HELEN** Aren't you going to look at it? What if there's an invitation or a cheque?

**ZACK** I pick up my cheque at the personnel office where I work. I expect what I've got there are bills and advertising.

**HELEN** No letters?

**ZACK** People don't write to me. Everyone I know lives nearby.

**HELEN** That's a shame, Mr. Teale.

**ZACK** Is it?

**HELEN** It's good to hear how things are progressing elsewhere every now and then. At least that's what I find. And there's nothing like finding a letter from a friend when you thought you were just coming back to an empty house.

**ZACK** That does sound nice.

**HELEN** You're a bachelor, Mr. Teale?

**ZACK** You're correct, ma'am.

**HELEN** And that's how you like it?

**ZACK** Sure it is. Mrs. Darimont, I'm still not sure why you're here. You said it's a professional matter, but I don't suppose anyone's paying you to just have a visit with me in my yard.

**HELEN** Well, no.

**ZACK** Oh. You're not… a religious person, are you?

**HELEN** Oh, no, not at all. Actually, I suppose I do have an abiding faith but you won't find me talking about it. That's absolutely not why I'm here.

**ZACK** Well, good. I respect a person's beliefs in that area but my goodness, those folks that come to the door sometimes, they're always about three steps ahead of you by the time you've said good evening. You're just washing some cups or something and the doorbell rings and you think maybe it's the paper boy collecting but instead… "Are you aware, sir, that you may be headed for an eternity of perdition in the arms of Satan the Devil?" You're just all of a sudden damned, right through the porch screen.

**HELEN** I call that presumptuous.

**ZACK** Ya got that right. About all you can do is say thanks for the bulletin and shut the inside door. Then you watch them go to the neighbour's because apparently they're damned as well. So, Mrs. Darimont, I apologize. You were going to tell me why you're here.

**HELEN** Yes, it really is time for that, isn't it. Mr. Teale, I think it might not surprise you if I say that I'd like to sell you something.

**ZACK** Hm, no, you're right. That did cross my mind. I can't imagine what it is, though.

**HELEN** I'd like to explain that to you, but it does take a little time. You don't have a commitment in the next while?

**ZACK** Well, I was going to head down to The Dixie Chop House for dinner, but I don't like to get there 'til after the rush. *(looking at his watch)* I guess I have an hour or so.

**HELEN** Mr. Teale, will you give it to me? Will you let me have this hour?

**ZACK** I… I suppose it wouldn't kill me.

**HELEN** Oh, I can promise you that.

**ZACK** Actually, Mrs. Darimont, I believe I can be more positive. You've been extremely considerate and I think it'll be my privilege to hear what you've come to tell me.

**HELEN** You're very kind. Thank you.

**ZACK** Would you like some lemonade, Mrs. Darimont?

**HELEN** Oh, that'd be lovely. Thank you.

*He picks up the pitcher and a glass and is about to pour.*

**ZACK** *(stopping)* Oh.

**HELEN** Something's wrong?

**ZACK** It has bourbon in it.

**HELEN** Really?

**ZACK** Yes. Not an enormous amount. It's a little thing in my family. We like a little less sugar and a tiny bit of a kick.

**HELEN** Well, I don't mind a little kick.

**ZACK** I'm glad to hear it.

*He pours and hands her a glass.*

**HELEN** Thank you. Cheers.

*They drink.*

Oh, that's just lovely.

**ZACK** Isn't it. I keep extra glasses out here because the neighbours often seem to drop by at this hour.

**HELEN** *(looking happily at her drink)* Well, that's no surprise. This is so refreshing… and sort of soothing.

**ZACK** Don't you think lemonade should always be like this?

**HELEN** Birthday parties for children would certainly be more manageable. You probably wouldn't even need cake.

**ZACK** *(after a pause)* Do you have children, Mrs. Darimont?

**HELEN** No. No, I don't.

*She takes another sip, then puts her drink down.*

Well now, mustn't guzzle. It's time to begin. Mr. Teale.... Are you satisfied with what you know?

**ZACK** About?

**HELEN** Things in general. Would you say you have a broad base of knowledge?

**ZACK** I suppose I.... No. I'll just say no. I get by just fine, but I'm not one of those extremely informed types who knows the capital of every place and how a bill becomes a law. Back in high school I was good with the sports trivia, but I can't say it's stayed with me. Too trivial I guess.

**HELEN** Do you think so? I have an opinion about that. The things that people call trivia always seem to relate to winners of titles and awards and so forth. But these people's accomplishments put them at the top of their field. There's nothing trivial about winning a pennant or a cup, or even an Academy Award or the Nobel prize.

**ZACK** No, I guess there isn't.

**HELEN** Knowledge shouldn't be all absolutes. It's not about collecting facts so that you can complete a list.

**ZACK** All right. So what is it instead?

**HELEN** What is knowledge? Let's not think that we have to say. Let's just know that it exists and we're going to try to find out a bit more about how it works and what it can do for us.

**ZACK** We're going to learn about knowledge?

**HELEN** Certainly. But first Mr. Teale, I want to know a little more about you. What is... your work?

**ZACK** My job?

**HELEN** Yes!

**ZACK** I'm the supervisor of merchandise receiving at Abernathy's department store.

**HELEN** Oh, that's impressive. I adore shopping at Abernathy's.

**ZACK** Yes, well, we do have a good selection of just about all there is.

**HELEN** And you're responsible for that at some level?

**ZACK** Well, I wouldn't exactly say so. I just collect the merchandise orders from the department managers after they get submitted and then I account for everything as it comes in or if it gets back-ordered and so forth.

**HELEN** So really, every item in the store is your responsibility at some point.

**ZACK** I guess you could say that it all passes under my nose sooner or later.

**HELEN** And you're required to have a great deal of knowledge about all the things that Abernathy's sells.

**ZACK** You'd think that. But I mostly know serial numbers and various sizes of boxes and crates. You have to know what should go on a pallet and what should be in a bunk cart. We have a first-rate group of sales clerks who get to know the products and who can tell you what's the best chair for holding your guests up or what kind of sweater looks good on your shape.

**HELEN** But you don't need to know those things to do your job?

**ZACK** No, I'd say that I don't.

**HELEN** Hmm.

*She reflects for a moment and takes a sip of lemonade.*

**ZACK** Am I coming up short here? Mrs. Darimont?

**HELEN** No, no, I'm just thinking. I'm processing what I've learned about you and what I haven't.

**ZACK** Pardon me?

**HELEN** I just need information. I'm not making any judgments.

**ZACK** All right. But if you have to, you should just go ahead and do that.

**HELEN** *(smiling)* Thank you, Mr. Teale. I may. Tell me, you're a single man. You have your own little house. Marriage doesn't figure in your plans. Starting a family…?

**ZACK** Oh… well now…

*He chuckles and looks away, a little flustered.*

**HELEN** I'm not embarrassing you am I?

**ZACK** Mrs. Darimont, I think you are, but I can't say there's a good reason why that should be. I know you just want simple answers.

**HELEN** That's right. So what's the simple answer?

*He looks at her. She smiles encouragingly.*

**ZACK** Well, I guess…. No, I know… that I haven't gotten to know a girl who I wanted to marry. Or maybe… I haven't talked to a girl and ever thought… "This one might like to marry me."

**HELEN** *(rather incredulous)* What? Never?

**ZACK** Well, basically, yeah. You wanted a simple answer.

**HELEN** Is there a more complicated answer?

**ZACK** Probably, sure. Okay, sometimes my sister Pat and her husband will invite me over for dinner and there'll be a single woman there who they think I might like to meet and they're usually pretty nice girls, but then Pat'll just talk so much all night that nobody gets to know anything about anybody. She tries though. She keeps telling us about each other. "Zack wired his own basement. Can you imagine that?" or "Zack, Nancy here, took her holidays in Oregon last year. Doesn't that sound interesting?" But the thing is always that the girl doesn't care about the wiring and, frankly, I didn't even enjoy doing it and she mostly just read a book while she was in Oregon anyway since the ocean's a bit cold for swimming, and that's how it always goes. So I guess it's still pretty simple. We get dinner but we don't get married.

**HELEN** But tell me one thing. If you could talk more with these girls, would you like that?

**ZACK** I can't… I can't… I can't… say. Yes.

**HELEN** You could arrange to see them again. After the dinner. Away from your sister.

**ZACK** Yes, I know that.

**HELEN** But you never do.

**ZACK** Mrs. Darimont, I think I'd need to be pretty certain of what I had to say to a girl before I'd start making demands of her time.

**HELEN** Oh my. Don't you think she might have something to say to you?

**ZACK** *(after a careful pause)* That's not a prediction that I can make with confidence.

**HELEN** *(standing abruptly)* Oh!

**ZACK** What's wrong? We're not done are we?

**HELEN** No, I'm just digesting what I've learned. I need a little moment.

**ZACK** Can I top up your lemonade?

**HELEN** Yes, please.

*He fills her glass. She paces a little and stands facing upstage.*

**ZACK** *(holding the glass out)* Did you want this over there?

**HELEN** *(turning)* Oh, I'll take it. Thank you.

*She takes the glass and has a sip. He sits and watches her, a little puzzled, yet still smiling expectantly.*

*(turning)* Mr. Teale—

**ZACK** Please, you can call me Zack.

**HELEN** Mmm... *(shaking her head)* ...Mr. Teale, I really believe it would be wonderful if you became aware of a great many more things.

**ZACK** Things. Facts?

**HELEN** Not just facts. None of that trivia. I think you need a broad base of general knowledge and you need to have a point of view about every single thing you know.

**ZACK** You're saying I need to be smarter?

**HELEN** I'd say that of anyone, Mr. Teale. In your case I believe that you have an innate intelligence that's languishing for lack of stimulus.

**ZACK** *(after a pause)* Mrs. Darimont, everything you say seems to stop a little bit short of hurting my feelings. I don't think that's what you're wanting to do, so, maybe you need to be a bit more clear. I still can't quite imagine what it is you're here to sell.

**HELEN** Well, let me just tell you then. I am a representative for a collected body of knowledge. It's called the *Universal Compendium of Information* and it's a beautifully bound and illustrated set of twenty-two volumes containing informed articles on every imaginable subject.

**ZACK** You're.... You're selling encyclopedias?

**HELEN** Simply put, I am.

**ZACK** You want me to buy a set of encyclopedias.

**HELEN** I surely do.

**ZACK** Could you not have said this a while back?

**HELEN** I could always say it at the outset if I thought it was the place to start. You respect the clerks at Abernathy's who know how to determine what a customer needs. I think I've done a good job of this in the short time I've been here. It's true that I'd like you to buy the books, Mr. Teale, but more than that I want you to own them and use them.

**ZACK** Use them for what? In school, encyclopedias were for looking things up that you'd been told you needed to know.

**HELEN** You think that's the limit of their use? Oh, no, no. Acquiring knowledge is a privilege, Mr. Teale, not an obligation. I think you could open any volume of the *Universal Compendium* on any page and read the information contained there, and before long you'd be grateful. You'd be grateful because you would be able to ask yourself the one thing that keeps us all moving forward. You'd say, "All right now, what do I think about that?"

**ZACK** I would?

**HELEN** You're going to.

**ZACK** When?

**HELEN** Right now. Within the hour you've given me. We're going to put the *Compendium* to use.

**ZACK** You have it here? You brought a set of encyclopedias?

**HELEN** Well, no. I'm afraid even I would find knowledge cumbersome if I tried to tote the whole set around with me. *(opening her bag)* I've randomly selected a single volume. It is the eighth of the series and is entitled "*H.*"

*She holds out a book.*

**ZACK** Can I just look at that?

**HELEN** Certainly.

**ZACK** *(examining it)* It's a fine looking book. I like the gold trim.

**HELEN** Each volume has that. When you have them set all in a row, they catch the light in a remarkable way. They create a shimmering band of knowledge on your shelf.

**ZACK** *(opening to an early page)* 1959. This is three years out of date.

**HELEN** Current events aren't the *Compendium*'s province. In fact, the 1959 edition has been acknowledged as the best ever.

**ZACK** Like the '57 Chev.

**HELEN** Exactly. So shall we poke our noses inside and see what's what.

**ZACK** Sure. Should we start on page one here? "Haag, Den, Netherlands: see Hague, The." Already we're gettin' the run-around here.

**HELEN** I find it's more fun to dive in at random points. Why not just open to a page and see what you find.

**ZACK** All righty. I'll even close my eyes.

*He opens to a page, then flips some more pages randomly and finally drops his finger in the middle of a page.*

Let's see now… "Hubert." Flemish saint, born 656, died 727. So, Saint Hubert?

**HELEN** Hubert, I think. *(pronounced Hu-bare)*

**ZACK** Ah. "As a young man Hubert was given to a life of debauchery and pleasure, but while out hunting on Good Friday he beheld the vision of a stag with a burning crucifix between its antlers. The stag spoke to him saying, 'Unless you turn to the Lord and lead a holy life, you shall quickly go down to hell.' It was a conversion experience for Hubert." Well, that's no great surprise. If those door-to-door types who come by had antlers and fire on their heads I might be more inclined to give them a listen. Let's see, what else…. "His association with the hunt led to his patronage of furriers and trappers, and against rabies and bad behaviour in dogs." Now there's more details here… ancestors he had and other saints that he knew, and all these good works. Should I read them?

**HELEN** You don't have to right now. I think what you read there is already rather stimulating.

**ZACK** How so? Am I supposed to go out and hope it'll all happen to me, too? 'Cause I think—

**HELEN** No. Now we're at the part where you ask the question I mentioned earlier. The important one. You know that Hubert had a remarkable experience in the forest and that his life changed because of it. So you say to yourself…

**ZACK** Hey! How about that! No, no, it was a question. It was…. Ah…. What do I think about that?

**HELEN** That's right. So? And?

**ZACK** Uhh… *(nodding seriously)* Interesting.

**HELEN** No, no, that isn't quite it.

**ZACK** It's not interesting?

**HELEN** Of course it's interesting. But why?

**ZACK** Now that's a whole different question.

**HELEN** Actually, it isn't.

**ZACK** Oh-oh. *(taking a sip of lemonade)* Mrs. Darimont, I'm a little lost.

**HELEN** Well, we'll fix that. What I'm asking you to do is to take those simple facts and conjecture about them. It's implied that what happened to Saint Hubert was a miracle, but why that particular miracle. Or better yet, what if there was another explanation for what he saw?

**ZACK** You're saying I need to do some guesswork here?

**HELEN** Well, sure. Use what you know to help you learn more.

**ZACK** I'm afraid I can't do that.

**HELEN** Of course you can.

**ZACK** No, I know that I can't. I don't want to try. I have good reasons.

**HELEN** Can I hear them?

**ZACK** Sure you can. They're kind of embarrassing, but I want to get the point across, so…

*He takes a little sip of lemonade, then has a little breath and begins.*

Way back in school, probably fourth grade, we were asked by our teacher to explain something. She told us that when Thomas Edison was asked to account

Jeff Haslam and Kate Ryan
*photographer unknown*

for the secret of his success as an inventor and discoverer of so many things, he said it was all because there wasn't a clock where he worked. We were supposed to explain why this was significant, so I thought about it and it seemed pretty simple to me, and I put up my hand and said I figured what might have happened was that he really wanted a clock and for whatever reason his folks wouldn't get him one so maybe he just went ahead and invented one. He just built himself a clock and it worked great and he enjoyed doing it and he started thinking, "Inventing. That's what I like. I'm going to keep at this." And next thing you knew he was whippin' up telegraph transmitters and light bulbs and all on account of his needing to know the time. I was proud of that answer but wouldn't you know I was just wrong. "Not a bad guess," said my teacher. "Only it's pretty well-known that Edison didn't invent the clock."

Well, I didn't say that he did, only that he might have made one and I started to explain that but then this loud kid named Kirby just barrelled over me and said that the significant thing was that because Edison didn't have a clock he never knew when it was time to quit working. "Right you are Kirby!" says the teacher and moves on to something else, while I just sat there stunned. I could see the logic of it but at the same time it just went against the grain of everything I'd learned so far in my life. I was brought up to always know the time. I got a watch in first grade. You couldn't be late for school. You weren't supposed to miss dinner. You didn't get to stay up late 'cause you were busy. So why would I ever have thought of the right answer? That teacher should have just told us.

**HELEN** But then you wouldn't have thought of your own answer which was interesting and completely plausible.

**ZACK** And also useless.

**HELEN** Didn't it make you wonder who did invent the clock, or if Edison had built one, what it maybe would have been like?

**ZACK** No, I pretty much dropped the whole notion. I kept my hand on my desk after that.

**HELEN** Oh, Mr. Teale, that's awful. I'm sorry that happened to you, but you have to believe me when I tell you that your reasoning was entirely sound.

**ZACK** And you think that's good enough?

**HELEN** Absolutely. It's great to have a questioning nature, but I think the truly brave people are those willing to suggest answers.

**ZACK** I see what you're saying, but I'm thinking now I need to take that back to old Saint Hubert, and I'm not sure how to work it.

**HELEN** All right, let's walk through it. We'll imagine a little situation where you run into me and we find ourselves discussing the great saint. We're outside so why don't we pretend we're at a company picnic. Does Abernathy's have those?

**ZACK** They do. I usually go for the baseball part.

**HELEN** Well, we'll say this is after. We meet, we exchange some pleasantries and then… informed discussion.

**ZACK** Got it.

**HELEN** All right, here we go.

*She steps away, turns around, then turns back.*

Hi there! Lovely afternoon, isn't it?

**ZACK** It sure is.

**HELEN** Are you enjoying the picnic?

**ZACK** I sure am.

**HELEN** I saw you on the field out there. Good catch in that last inning.

**ZACK** Aw, heck, that was only a fluke.

**HELEN** Well, it looked skillful to me. Oh, there's the punch bowl. I could go for a glass of that.

**ZACK** Me, too, as well. Let me pour one for you and then one for myself.

**HELEN** Oh, how kind.

*He pours them a little more lemonade.*

**ZACK** Here you go.

**HELEN** Thank you. *(raising here glass)* Here's to a pleasant day.

**ZACK** Yes. Pleasant.

*There is a pause. She clears her throat softly and smiles at him. She nods very discreetly. There's another little pause.*

I'd like to talk to you about Saint Hubert.

**HELEN** Oh! I'd rather not discuss religion here at the picnic.

**ZACK** What? You… you're shutting me down.

**HELEN** No, I'm not.

**ZACK** You did it again. Mrs. Darimont, I—

**HELEN** I'm not Mrs. Darimont.

**ZACK** Aaaa! I'm lost. I have to go!

**HELEN** No, no. All right, Zack, listen. I am Mrs. Darimont, but I'm pretending to be somebody else, a girl at the picnic.

**ZACK** But I'm me? Zack?

**HELEN** Yes. But what I was trying to indicate to you is that you have to introduce the topic a bit more carefully. People are wary of strangers who get too serious, too quickly.

**ZACK** You're right. That's obvious. I think I can do better. Can I just…

*He scoots over to the book and reviews it quickly. He puts it down and returns.*

Okay, I think I'm ready. I've just given you your punch.

**HELEN** Thank you.

**ZACK** By the way, my name is Zack.

**HELEN** Pleased to meet you Zack. My name is Lorelei.

**ZACK** Really. Isn't that… Flemish?

**HELEN** It's German.

**ZACK** Oh, I thought maybe… uhhh…

**HELEN** Oh! Well, maybe it could be—

**ZACK** No, no. I've got it. *(taking a breath)* I'm pleased to meet you, Lorelei. Say, those kids sure are having fun with that golden retriever out there.

**HELEN** They are, aren't they.

**ZACK** Still, chasing a dog around and around can be a bit dangerous. Get him a little too excited and suddenly someone's getting bit.

**HELEN** Oh, yes, I've seen it happen.

**ZACK** I guess a little prayer to St. Hubert wouldn't be amiss here.

**HELEN** Really? Why him particularly?

**ZACK** Well, he's the saint who looks out for bad canine behaviour, apparently.

**HELEN** I didn't know that.

**ZACK** Oh, yes. You see I was reading a little about him not long ago and he was a very interesting fellow. Flemish.

**HELEN** Oh?

**ZACK** Yes, a nobleman in fact, and a bit of scamp initially. But then one day, out in the woods he's winding up to pierce a stag with his bow and arrow when he sees a burning cross between its antlers and hears it telling him he's got to shape up or face a pretty nasty reward in the hereafter. Fairly remarkable, huh?

**HELEN** I'll say. *(shaking her head and chuckling a bit)* A talking animal, a burning cross…

**ZACK** You don't buy it? It was a miracle. Those are supposed to be pretty deluxe.

**HELEN** I suppose they are. But the deer alone would probably have done it. You know, when they look at you that special way…

*She demonstrates.*

"Why Hubert? Why this path? Alas?"

**ZACK** *(putting down his glass)* Okey-doke, no more ale today!

*They laugh.*

**HELEN** Actually, I doubt it was that quick.

**ZACK** No, you're probably right. Do it again. Be the deer.

**HELEN** All right.

*She backs up and assumes an even more convincing deer-like stance. ZACK also steps back and turns away, then turns back to look at her.*

**ZACK** Aha! Yon stag looks ripe for the slaying. I'll approach.

*He approaches HELEN slowly. She stares around absently, eyes wide, mouth chewing gently.*

*(crouching)* I'll crouch and aim.

*He pulls back the string of his imaginary bow. She turns her head toward him.*

**HELEN** Bonjour, Hubert.

**ZACK** What the heck? Who said that? Is there someone in the woods? Helloo! Hellooo! Be quiet here, won't you! I've cornered a big animal.

**HELEN** You'll not shoot me, Hubert.

**ZACK** *(gasping)* Oh! It's you. The stag! You're talking to me?

**HELEN** Yes, it seems unlikely, but it's true.

**ZACK** This is obviously witchcraft. I'm going to shoot you right away. Ha!

**HELEN** No, don't!

*She hops away. He chases her to one side and aims.*

**ZACK** Once more I aim! And now I'll shoot!

**HELEN** No, you won't!

**ZACK** Aaa! You spoke again! I'm never going to get used to that.

*She hops back to the other side.*

Oooo. I've got to kill the witchie stag thing.

**HELEN** What are you waiting for, Hubert? I'm right here.

**ZACK** Hey! How do you know my name?

**HELEN** You're a famous local hunter. All the forest creatures know who you are.

**ZACK** That's prep… pre… prepr…

**HELEN** Preposterous?

**ZACK** There ya go. I can normally say that, but I just had a lager.

**HELEN** Right, so what else is new?

**ZACK** You're a saucy critter. I don't like that.

**HELEN** All right then, shoot me. *(indicating)* Here between my big brown eyes.

**ZACK** If that's what you want. *(aiming)* Oh, those eyes are sure pretty and gentle. It's hard not to stare into them.

**HELEN** Go ahead. I don't mind.

**ZACK** *(covering his eyes)* No, no, I can't. I've got to kill her.

**HELEN** Him.

**ZACK** What?

**HELEN** I'm a boy.

**ZACK** Of course you are. You're a stag. Hence the antlers.

**HELEN** Yes, yes. Regard my antlers, Hubert.

**ZACK** Pretty impressive. They'll look good mounted in my rumpus hall.

**HELEN** You think so?

*She makes a cross with her fingers over her head.*

**ZACK** *(stepping back)* But what do I see? A cross of fire! Stag, your head is burning.

*He flaps his hands around her head and blows on the fire to put it out. She pulls back.*

**HELEN** You cannot extinguish these flames, Hubert. They are ignited by the cleansing fires of heaven!

**ZACK** Oh, no! Not that!

**HELEN** Yes! Yes! Are you afraid, Hubert?

**ZACK** I'm very afraid, but confused as well. I associate fire not so much with heaven as with the other place.

**HELEN** Oh, no, we've got it up above as well. We're just much more discriminating in its use.

**ZACK** So you're from there? You're one of heaven's deer?

**HELEN** I surely am. I was selected to bring you a message from on high.

**ZACK** All right, let's have it.

**HELEN** Well, Hubert, it's time to stop with the drinking and carousing. The Lord has better plans for you.

**ZACK** But I've been so happy!

**HELEN** Have you? Really? Haven't your days all been pretty much alike? Hasn't it been getting harder and harder to remember what you did on any particular one of them?

**ZACK** Sure, but how important is that really?

**HELEN** Think of your poor neglected wife.

**ZACK** I'm married? I have a wife?

**HELEN** Do you see what I mean?

**ZACK** No, seriously.... Did I know that? I have to think, yes, pace and think...

*He paces a little and, crossing by the table where the encyclopedia lies open, he surreptitiously glances down. He scans quickly then exclaims.*

Alas! Poor Floribanne! How have I mistreated you!

*He kneels and beats his breast.*

Stag! I'll do as you say. I'll stop with the drink.

**HELEN** It won't be easy. Flemish ale is awfully tasty.

**ZACK** I despise it now. It made me forget my wife.

**HELEN** Actually, you may have to renounce her as well.

**ZACK** Cripes, really?

**HELEN** At least we know you can. Anyway, the rewards will be worth it.

**ZACK** Really? What would some of those be?

**HELEN** Oh, I can't tell you that. It isn't the reason we do good works. You just concentrate on not being bad for the time being. Then gradually, your path will become clear. Speaking of which, I think I should be going. I'm not really from this neck of the woods and it's getting dark. Best of luck to you, Hubert.

**ZACK** Thank you, stag. Say, do you have a name?

**HELEN** A name? *(brief pause)* No. No, I don't.

*She hops away.*

**ZACK** Well, I guess I better go be good.

**HELEN** *(returning)* All right, I'll admit, it's probably more exciting with the burning cross.

**ZACK** What?

**HELEN** I had thought it was excessive, but I think that's probably part of the whole package when you start seeing things that aren't really there.

**ZACK** Oh! It's you, Lorelei! So, you think it didn't really happen?

**HELEN** Well, don't you think maybe that some of the things earlier peoples saw as miracles might have had more rational explanations?

**ZACK** Well… *(pause)* You mean… *(pause, then very slowly and deliberately)* A man who's quite a drinker… sees an animal with fire on its head… and it's talking at him… *(brightly)* Coulda just been the DT's.

**HELEN** You see, that I can believe for certain, and I don't think it detracts from the value of what happened to Saint Hubert, or from the good works that he later accomplished.

**ZACK** So… you think something came from inside him that made him realize there was a way for him to be a better man?

**HELEN** I do.

**ZACK** His conscience maybe!

**HELEN** You're probably right. The talking deer was a manifestation of his conscience.

**ZACK** So it wasn't actually there?

**HELEN** That's right. It was an hallucination.

**ZACK** And yet it seemed so real. Hey!

*He crosses over to the encyclopedia, picks it up and starts flipping through pages.*

**HELEN** What are you doing?

**ZACK** Oh, sorry. Look over there!

**HELEN** It's all right, Mr. Teale. We don't have to be at the picnic anymore.

**ZACK** But I wouldn't really just run off like that. I wouldn't do that to Lorelei. She was a nice girl. I'm just looking up…. "Hallucination… false sensory impression lacking external stimulus… many behavioural scientists consider hallucinations to be symbolic of repressed wishes…." So that seems familiar.

**HELEN** It does indeed.

**ZACK** Now it goes on for quite a bit… "chemically induced hallucination… sleep deprivation… dissociative mechanisms… internal metabolic disturbances…" See also "hysteria." Hey now, that's in this volume as well. But you know… *(shaking his head)* I hate to say it…

**HELEN** Yes?

**ZACK** I don't think I'm interested.

**HELEN** What? You mean you don't want to—

**ZACK** Oh, no, no, no. The book's great. The *Compendium*, I mean. It's just this topic. The waters are seeming a little deep. Hysteria and all.

**HELEN** Mr. Teale, I'm right with you. I'm hoping that my point has been made and that our exploration of one simple topic has demonstrated some of the potential that the *Compendium* holds for you.

**ZACK** I'd say so. I'm pleased about the conclusion we came to and as I say, I did enjoy meeting your friend Lorelei.

**HELEN** Well, I'm sure the pleasure was mutual. She's very big on discussing ideas.

**ZACK** I'd say she doesn't back away from horsin' around either.

**HELEN** Some girls choose to have it all.

**ZACK** That's.... That's just very exciting. So, what's next?

**HELEN** Well, I think maybe you could make another random selection and we'll see where it takes us.

**ZACK** I've no objection. Here goes.

*He flips open the book and selects an entry without looking.*

Well now... "Hohen... Hohenst...

**HELEN** Staufen." *(pronounced shtaufen)*

**ZACK** Hohenstaufen? Hohenstaufen. Isn't that a sausage? Well, let's see. "The name of a village and castle in Swabia, now in the kingdom of..."

*He points. She looks.*

**HELEN** Wurttemburg.

**ZACK** "...which gave its name to the celebrated Swabian family of Hohenstaufen, members of which were emperors or German kings from 1138 to 1208, and again from 1214 to 1254. The earliest known ancestor was Frederick, whose son Frederick built a castle at Staufen and...." I don't see much more than a lot of pretty chewy names coming up here.

**HELEN** You might want to pass on this one.

**ZACK** Can I? I don't know that I should. Mrs. Darimont, you've encouraged me to rise to challenges rather than backing away from them and so far it's done me nothing but good.

**HELEN** Well, let's give 'er a whirl.

**ZACK** Righty-o. But I'm keeping the book open. I think I'll need a cheat sheet.

**HELEN** I'll allow it.

**ZACK** So... we're going to have a conversation. Where will we be?

**HELEN** I don't know. You decide this time. Where would you find yourself in a position to chat with a young lady?

**ZACK** Well… maybe in the dentist's office. In the waiting room, I mean. Not in the chair.

**HELEN** Perfect. So you'll be there already?

**ZACK** And you come in.

**HELEN** Got it.

*She crosses away. He puts the chairs close together and lays the book on a table beside him. He sits and looks ahead and twiddles his thumbs in both directions. After a moment HELEN approaches. He looks up and smiles.*

**ZACK** Good day to you.

**HELEN** Mmm. Mm-hm.

*She sits next to him.*

**ZACK** Guess there's a bit of a wait today.

*HELEN looks away. She covers one side of her mouth and moans repeatedly.*

Oh, my. Everything all right?

**HELEN** *(from one side of her mouth)* Sorry. I'm in very acute pain.

**ZACK** Well, of course you are. That's why you're at the dentist.

**HELEN** Never neglect your oral hygiene!

**ZACK** Oh, I sure don't. I'm here for a checkup. I can't imagine what it's like to— I'll bet you don't want to talk about it particularly. Your pain.

**HELEN** Oh, but what else? It start's here and…. Ohaohaohaoha… goes up here… and the…. Aaaaooooowww…. It's back here again.

**ZACK** I'm sorry. You need to take your mind off that right now. Isn't there something else you can think about? Happy memories. Nice places you've been. The mountains maybe. Or the seashore? Or Swabia?

**HELEN** Swabia?

**ZACK** Yes, that's quite the place. Has been for a while. Lot of history… there.

**HELEN** Uhhhhhhheeeewwwww…

**ZACK** Yeah, I don't remember all of it just now though. I…

*He exhales and turns away. She begins making little high-pitched sounds.*

Shouldn't be long now. I'll recommend that the doctor sees you first.

*She nods gratefully and whimpers a little more.*

My name is Zachary.

**HELEN** De… De… Desiree.

**ZACK** Oh? That's sure pretty.

*HELEN contorts her face in a hideous grimace.*

Just like you are.

*Pause.*

So Desiree, I know it's hard to look on the bright side of things at a time like this but I'd say now is when I'd probably be most grateful that we're not living nine hundred years ago, but in fact… now. I can't imagine there'd have been much dental relief available to anyone back then. No, sir, not even to members of so important a group as the Hohenstaufen clan who held sway there in the aforementioned Swabia. Still, I guess they persevered. Certainly for a couple of hundred years from the time… *(glancing at the book)* …Frederick the First was succeeded by his one-eyed son, also called Frederick, whose mother was called…. Hmmm.

*He reads for a moment, interested and a little perplexed.*

**HELEN** Owwwwwwww!

**ZACK** *(turning)* I'm sorry. I don't know that I'm going to be able to help you. Not with my talking.

*She shudders and sits very still. Her eyes are wide open.*

What's happening now? Are you better?

**HELEN** I… I… I can't feel my legs. Now I can! They're on fire! Now I can't feel them at all! My arms are tingling. Ow! Ow! I have an earache! My foot's asleep! My stomach hurts! Where are my legs?

**ZACK** They're there. Those are them. Those two. What's happening?

**HELEN** I don't know. Pain! Everywhere pain! Now none! Now it's back! Ahhhhh!

**ZACK** You've got to stay calm, Desiree!

**HELEN** What kind of advice is that? Look at what's happening to me!

**ZACK** I can't tell what it is. Nurse! Nurse! Miss Nurse! Where have they all gone?

**HELEN** *(hoarsely)* Smoking!

**ZACK** Well, I'm sure someone'll be right back, and it'll turn out to be nothing serious and really just all related to the tooth and—

**HELEN** *(hyperventilating)* No! No! No! No!

**ZACK** I have to say, getting hysterical isn't what's going to help you here. You can maybe blow off a little steam, but…. Wait a minute! Hysterical? See also… hysteria. Excuse me, Desiree.

*He picks up the book and begins flipping furiously through the pages. He finds the one he wants and reads quickly and with interest.*

Uh-huh. Uh-huh. Uh-huh… "highly emotional and irrational conduct…"

**HELEN** *(sputtering)* Woo-hoo-hoo-hoo!

**ZACK** "…psychological conflict converted into a bodily disturbance…"

*She flings an arm repeatedly into the air.*

I have to tell you, Desiree, your ailment may be imaginary.

**HELEN** *(pointing at her mouth)* Not my toothache.

**ZACK** All right, not that one, but anxiety over that pain is causing you to imagine all sorts of worse symptoms.

**HELEN** *(touching various parts of her body)* Ow! Oo! Eee! Er! Can nothing be done?

**ZACK** Uhhh. *(reading)* Yes! *(flipping pages and quickly finding the one he seeks)* See "Hypnotism"!

**HELEN** Oh! Yes! Hurry!

**ZACK** *(reading)* "…artificially induced state of relaxation… hypnotized patients are subject to extreme suggestibility… symptoms of hysteria may be alleviated…"

*HELEN is vibrating excitedly.*

All right so… *(turning pages)* …where the heck are the directions? Ohhh, this is frustrating! *(reading)* "…monotonous gestures… soothing tone…." Oh dear… *(looking at HELEN)* You have to look at me now, Desiree. Watch my fingers.

*He spreads two fingers and moves them toward her eyes and back again. This causes her to wince and yowl.*

Oh, wait a minute…

*He moves one finger back from side to side. She moves her head along with it, moaning in ever-greater distress. Eventually he just stops and sighs.*

All right, we'll have to try something a little different. Can you close your eyes, Desiree?

*Whimpering, she obliges.*

Now, just breathe and listen to my voice. Can you do that?

*She nods and groans a little. He takes up the book and finds another page.*

All right now… *(very calmly and deliberately)* I'm just going to talk. It seems that the first Duke of Hohenstaufen was Frederick and he was named for his father, also Frederick and, of course, his son was called Frederick, too and the wife of the middle Frederick and mother of the third one was named Agnes and she was known as Agnes von Hohenstaufen, which isn't a big surprise. Now if you skip a hundred or so years you get to another interesting development where a duke known by the name of Henry the Long also marries a girl named Agnes, whose father was Henry the Lion and they had a son called… uh-huh… also Henry. Henry the Younger. Now he didn't have any kids, so the throne passed over to a cousin, Otto the Illustrious, who married the daughter of… somebody, and her name was Agnes as well, so you can see that a lot of the more significant Swabians have been called Frederick or Henry or Agnes. I guess it's not unusual for dukes to get their father's name, but it's a little strange about all the girls being named Agnes and if you asked me to explain the significance there…. Well, I'd have to say it just might have to do with a lack of imagination in the folks who lived in that part of the world and it'd certainly explain why you don't hardly hear boo about Swabia today. It sure seems—

*HELEN has slowly slumped over and is breathing regularly.*

Oh. I cured her.

*He watches her for a moment.*

I should get her a pillow.

*He touches her hand lightly.*

Beg pardon… Desiree…

**HELEN** *(sitting up brightly)* That was excellent work, Mr. Teale.

**ZACK** Yeah, and hard work too. You really put me through the gears. Or I guess… she did.

**HELEN** You have to realize that meeting someone in a dentist's office places you in circumstances of adversity.

**ZACK** I should have picked somewhere else.

**HELEN** No, no. I think you've proven your mettle under trying circumstances. You've applied your general knowledge to a greater good. You are triumphant, Mr. Teale.

**ZACK** Why, thank you, Mrs. Darimont. So I guess it might be time to ask what kind of a price we're looking at for all these volumes. And would I get the whole set at once or one at a time and—

**HELEN** I really would like to leave those things for the very end. I know my hour is drawing to a close, but I think it might be more interesting to continue our explorations as we've been doing.

**ZACK** Well, sure, but I should tell you I'm pretty much convinced.

**HELEN** You don't want to try another topic?

**ZACK** Oh, no, I sure do, but—

**HELEN** Well, let's just move along then. Anything would be easier than that last one. Go ahead, pick something.

*He flips to a page and picks.*

**ZACK** Hannibal of Carthage.

**HELEN** Oh, perfect! A great man. A ruler and an adventurer. Lots of possibilities. Let's be somewhere easy this time. Any suggestions.

**ZACK** Well… how about outdoors somewhere on a pleasant evening.

**HELEN** That's good. Simple. Maybe in a little park. I'll sit here and you can go look over the entry and then you can just join me. Good?

**ZACK** Sure.

*He crosses away and reads intently. She rearranges the chairs and moves away the table with the lemonade. She then stands and smiles and looks around happily. She picks up the watering can and tends to some of the potted flowers. ZACK stops reading and watches her do this. She looks up, sees him looking and smiles. He returns to his reading and she goes and sits. When he's done, he sets down the book and approaches her.*

Why, hello. I hope you wouldn't mind if I were to sit here.

**HELEN** No, not at all.

*He sits.*

**ZACK** It just seems like a good spot to enjoy the evening.

**HELEN** I certainly agree.

**ZACK** It was a very warm day.

**HELEN** That it was.

**ZACK** Not as warm as say… some parts of… Northern Africa…

**HELEN** Thankfully, no.

*Disappointed with his inspiration thus far, ZACK shakes his head and lowers it briefly. After a moment he looks up and smiles a little.*

**ZACK** The sun's going down there and you can see the way it's just lighting across the tops of those trees.

**HELEN** That's very beautiful.

**ZACK** It's one of my favourite things to look at. *(pause)* It's just a few minutes every day, and they may come at four-thirty in the winter or closer to eight in the mid-summer, but I've always thought that if I was pressed to pick, I'd say that it's one of my favourite times of the day. It's just a good moment that you can always count on even though the day's pretty much played out.

*He looks at her. She smiles, then looks out again.*

But I'm worried now that it's not going to be the same. It's now going to always remind me of this particular moment and it'll never be quite good enough.

*She looks at him intently.*

We're not in a park, Mrs. Darimont. We're in my backyard and the sun's going down and I can't talk to you about elephants crossing the Alps.

**HELEN** That's all right, Mr.—

**ZACK** I'd like to look something else up in the book. It's something specific and I think it should be there because it starts with "H." Will you excuse me for a moment to do that?

**HELEN** Of course.

*He gets up and opens the book. He flips to a page and reads briefly. He lowers the book, looking a little disappointed.*

**ZACK** It's less than I'd hoped for.

**HELEN** What did you look up?

**ZACK** Hour. The word… hour.

**HELEN** And what does it say?

**ZACK** "The twenty-fourth part of a day, equivalent to sixty minutes. See also 'Time Measurement.'" See, that's just like a dictionary.

**HELEN** It's so clear, though. What are you missing?

**ZACK** Everything. Everything that makes an hour remarkable. Everything that makes one different from another. And why is an hour the length that it is? Why are there twenty-four of them? If there were less, then they'd have to last longer, wouldn't they? And why do mine have to be the same length as everyone else's? Okay, that's stupid, that wouldn't work and I guess the thing might be to just throw out the clock like Thomas Edison, but I can't because I have to be on time for work. Mrs. Darimont, I'm just sputtering now and I've got to do better than that.

*He takes a second, breathes, then speaks.*

It's hard to know what to do when you've realized that a particular hour in your life is maybe one of the best you're going to have and that every wonderful minute you get to live of it means there's now one minute less. How can you get that to stop happening? Somebody invented the hour, and I guess the minute and the second as well, and I suppose they thought it'd be great to have all this control over when things happen, but couldn't anyone see how we'd just be losing and losing and losing. I've lost so many hours, Mrs. Darimont. So many hours and days and weeks and years and I hardly took notice of it because they were pretty unexceptional. And what's a few more minutes gone at this point?

Well, I want them. I want to keep them. If having them means losing them, then maybe I'd just rather always be about to have them. Why aren't those kind of hours available? Why can't someone cook up that kind of time?

**HELEN** *(after a pause)* Mr. Teale… Zachary. I've always felt that the wonderful thing about an hour's passing was that you got another one delivered to you right away without your even having to ask for it.

**ZACK** But not in this case.

**HELEN** I'm so happy that you've enjoyed this time as much as you have. I don't even think I need to ask you why you did and you should know by now that that's unusual for me.

*He smiles a little weakly. She touches his face gently.*

**ZACK** You should be careful with me, Mrs. Darimont.

**HELEN** You'd think that, and I suppose with good reason. Listen, I guess what I have to do now is tell you a couple of things and then we'll see where we really are. All right?

**ZACK** *(mildly puzzled)* All right.

**HELEN** The first thing you should know is that I don't really have any encyclopedias to sell you. This one comes from a set that my younger sister owns, and I think she'd be more than happy to just let you have them. My parents gave them to her when she started college, but by the end of her freshman year she was necessarily engaged to the Dean of Arts and no longer has any particular need of them.

**ZACK** Oh. I…

**HELEN** You look disappointed. I just told you the *Compendium* is yours for free.

**ZACK** But you aren't an encyclopedia saleslady. And from what I can tell, you really ought be one.

**HELEN** Thank you. That's a wonderful compliment, but I just don't need to do it. I have a job I like, at Abernathy's department store.

**ZACK** I beg your pardon?

**HELEN** You're surprised? I thought you would be. In fact I was counting on it.

**ZACK** How is it that—

**HELEN** You haven't seen me? Well, that's kind of the crux of the matter. Zack, every single morning you go up to the third floor to get the mail for your department. You come out of the service elevator and you go down the hall and you're usually whistling something.

**ZACK** Uh-huh…

**HELEN** And you pass through the management office and as you come through the first doorway, you walk right in front of three women who are sitting at desks and typing. And you say…

**ZACK** "Mornin' ladies!"

**HELEN** And they say, "Good morning!" And off you go and you get your mail and head back down by the stairwell. Zack, I'm one of those three ladies in the management office. I'm Helen Darimont, the first stenographer you pass as you come in the door, and there's even a little plaque on my desk that says my name.

**ZACK** You're one of those women? Since when?

**HELEN** Probably since, let's see… a year and a half ago.

**ZACK** Oh. Okay, but…

**HELEN** There's more. I get off work a little earlier than you do, but sometimes I linger a bit, so I end up standing down by the bus stop when you leave the store at four-thirty. The first time that happened I looked right at you and smiled because I thought we at least had that kind of acquaintance, but you just kept going. It happened like that a couple more times and so I finally just stopped and looked down. But I'd watch you walk away over to the parkade and you just never seemed to have any kind of a spring in your step at all, not like a man who's done for the day and has somewhere to go. It's just become more and more unbearable to me to see you each morning when the light in your eyes is so bright you can't hardly even see what's in front of you, all the while knowing that by the end of the afternoon that that light's just going to be out.

**ZACK** So, you came here to—

**HELEN** I have to keep going now. I think it's fairly obvious why I came here and why I did everything that I did. I don't even have to say, "Now, what do you think about that?" You've made that very clear. What I want to tell you now is just that… I'm not married. I only said I was in order to make sure that things could start out in a simple and businesslike way between us.

**ZACK** So… there's no Mr. Darimont?

**HELEN** Just m'pappy.

**ZACK** Well! Well!

**HELEN** Exactly. So, now it's time for me to ask the question. I, Helen Darimont, a personable and resourceful employee at a reputable department store, am unattached and what's more, I'm in your yard and it's getting on for six-thirty. What do you think about that?

**ZACK** I…. A lot of words are coming to mind but frankly, none of them are quite… adequate. I think it's… super. No, it's T-riffic. No, how about, I think this is a word…. It's opportune.

**HELEN** Oh, say.

**ZACK** I'm going to stop thinking of answers and trade a question back to you.

**HELEN** Oh? What's that?

**ZACK** Do you care for pork chops, Helen?

**HELEN** That's so easy. Yes, I do.

**ZACK** Well then, in recognition of your impressive salesmanship which should definitely not go unrewarded, and by the way, I surely will take every last volume off your sister's hands, I'd like to take you down to Dixie's and I'll buy you dinner and I'll throw another hour of my life along in with it.

**HELEN** Offer accepted. Thank you.

**ZACK** Shall we go?

**HELEN** Yes. Now. Let's go.

*She starts to go. He follows, then stops.*

**ZACK** Oh, hey.

*He goes back and picks up the encyclopedia.*

**HELEN** No, no, you keep that. I don't need it back.

**ZACK** But it just occurred to me. Helen. You'd be in here. Helen of Troy. She'd rate an entry, right?

**HELEN** Yes, but you don't need to read it. There's nothing about that lady that I can't tell you.

**ZACK** *(putting the book down)* Oh, perfect. So let's have it.

**HELEN** Oh, no. We'll wait for a lull in the conversation.

**ZACK** What if there isn't one?

**HELEN** I don't know. That's a good question.

*They look at one another seriously for a moment, then both smile.*

You know, I think we'll be fine.

*She takes his arm and they exit.*

*The End.*

# Coal Valley: The Making of a Miner

By Katherine Koller

# About
# Katherine Koller

Katherine Koller lives in Edmonton, Alberta and writes for radio, stage and screen. Her first plays were produced at the Edmonton Fringe Festival. Her plays for CBC radio include *Cowboy Boots and a Corsage* and *Magpie*. Jagged Edge Lunchbox Theatre in Edmonton produced three of her one-act comedies: *The Early Worm Club*, *Starter Home* and *Magpie*, and Winnipeg's FemFest produced *Cowboy Boots and a Corsage* in 2003 and *Abby's Place* in 2006. *Coal Valley: the Making of a Miner* was commissioned and produced in Drumheller in 2005. The granddaughter of an underground coal miner, Katherine made many discoveries about the grandfather she hardly knew in the research and writing of *Coal Valley*. *Perdu* and *Intimacy, Inc.* were produced at Walterdale Playhouse in Edmonton and Alumnae Theatre in Toronto, respectively, in 2007. Katherine was awarded a self-directed writing residency and a production residency at The Banff Centre on *The Seed Savers*, a drama about the heroism of farming, forgiving and falling in love, which received its first public reading in Saskatoon. Katherine is currently working on a new play called *Lily of the Prairie*, about the power of one in cataclysmic times, in Workshop West Theatre's Playwrights' Unit.

*Coal Valley: The Making of a Miner* was commissioned by the Town of Drumheller for the Year of the Coal Miner and first produced by the Town of Drumheller and the Atlas Coal Mine National Historic Site at the Royal Tyrrell Museum Theatre in Drumheller, Alberta, in February 2005, with the following company:

| | |
|---|---|
| MINER | Leigh Wardhaugh |
| CHIP | John McIver |
| SLAV | Aaron Krogman |
| HATTIE (and other roles) | Glenda Warkentin |
| ANNA (and other roles) | Cari Russell |
| SAM (and other roles) | Travis Friesen |

Directed by roger hamm
Assistant Director: Rachel Peacock
Assistant Director: Rebecca Wohlgemuth
Sound Designer/Composer: Rachel Peacock
Audiovisual Production by Warren Nicholls
Set Construction by Lothar Malmberg
Costumes by Dawn Crosby
Stage Manager: Julie Serger

Dramaturgy and a pre-production workshop were supported by Alberta Playwrights Network and Rosebud School of the Arts.

## Characters

MINER is a voice in the dark and acts as a mentor.
CHIP is a teenager who wants to be a miner and ages into his seventies.
SLAV is an ageless Polish contract miner.
MOM is Chip's mother.
HATTIE is Chip's friend.
SAM is Chip's friend.
STAN is Slav's friend.
ANNA is a Polish girl.
MARY is Chip's aunt.
KITTY is a miner's wife.
JOE is a cutting machine miner.
SIR BARLOW is head of the 1935 Royal Commission on Coal Mining.
TWO BOYS
TWO STUDENTS
CONSTABLE (voice-over)
HOBO (female)
SERGEANT (voice-over)
MAN
MINE OWNER
MINE MANAGER (voice-over)
MINE MANAGER
MRS. PARAMA
REVEREND
GREENHORN
PIT BOSS
2 HELPERS

Suggested doubling:

MOM / BOY / ANNA / MRS. PARAMA / KITTY / HELPER / GREENHORN

HATTIE / BOY / MARY / STUDENT / REVEREND / HELPER / HOBO

SAM / MAN / STUDENT / CONSTABLE (voice-over) / STAN / MINE MANAGER / MINE MANAGER (voice-over) / SERGEANT (voice-over) / JOE / PIT BOSS / SIR BARLOW / MINE OWNER

## Set

On a bare, black stage, there are lights to depict the railway tracks. There is a small coal car, with one side open. There is a pile of coal lumps. A ledge suggests the hills above town. There is a chain pulley and miners' basket. A solitary piece of standing timber can represent a pole, a lamppost, the mine entrance and a shack.

## Place

In the mining camps around Drumheller in the Red Deer River Valley.

## Time

The time passes from 1914 to 1946.

## Music

There are four short folk songs sung a cappella: "Rock of Ages" (Augustus Montague Toplady and Thomas Hastings), "Lulajze Jesuniu" (traditional), "All the Pretty Little Ponies" (traditional) and "Sto Lat!" (traditional). The rest of the music should be popular music of the period and place.

## Sound

The sounds of a train, horn, gunshots, work whistle, mining blast, cave-in, timbers splintering, rock falling, tipple and pony should be as much as possible reflective of the time and help to create the illusion that the valley has a voice of its own.

# Coal Valley: The Making of a Miner

## Act One

### Scene One – Miner in Black

*In blackout, the MINER speaks.*

**MINER** It pays to listen. You gotta train your ears, 'cause there's no echo here. The walls absorb sound, muffle it. Like a thick blanket. Like a womb. It pays to listen to her. Right, that there. Because Mother Nature, well, she's bigger 'n you, son. Right that there.

### Scene Two – Follow the Leader

*In blackout, CHIP, HATTIE and SAM are kids in a cave.*

**CHIP** *(whispers)* The walls are coal.

**HATTIE** *(whispers)* The roof is coal, too.

**SAM** *(whispers)* Anybody got a match?

**CHIP** No! The gas will blow you to kingdom come!

**HATTIE** Send you to hoodoo heaven!

**SAM** I wonder what the Indians did.

**HATTIE** They didn't have matches, they didn't burn coal and they didn't live in caves.

**SAM** How come they didn't burn coal?

**HATTIE** The coal has spirits in it!

**SAM** Good spirits or bad spirits?

**HATTIE** Underground spirits.

**CHIP** Hey, Hattie, I wonder if this is a coyote den.

**HATTIE** Let's get out of here! Whose turn is it?

**SAM** My turn! Follow the leader!

*Lights up; outside the cave.*

Up the coulee!

*CHIP and HATTIE follow him.*

On the ledge!

**CHIP** Hey. That's a good one.

*CHIP picks up a rock.*

**SAM** Not again! Okay, find a rock!

*HATTIE picks up a piece of coal, throws it down.*

**HATTIE** My turn now! Chip, over here! Jump down the slag heap!

*They jump down and come face-to-face with SLAV, who is picking coal from the slag pile into a potato sack.*

**SLAV** Ho! Watch out, your back!

**SAM** Ow! Hot!

**SLAV** It burns, all the time burning. Like me. I work, all the time working.

**HATTIE** You're new here.

**SLAV** I come here to work.

**HATTIE** Are you a miner?

**SLAV** Contract miner, yah.

**CHIP** I want to be a miner.

**SLAV** You grow, get strong. You be a miner.

**SAM** I want to be a railroad man.

**SLAV** Hah! Good work, too. See lots of country.

**SAM** I want to drive through the mountains!

**SLAV** Hah, I just come from mountains. Beautiful, but cold.

**SAM** Where, Crowsnest Pass?

**SLAV** Yah. Warmer here. Dry. I like. I make a little shack there.

**HATTIE** I want to be a teacher.

**SLAV** Ah! Good. You teach me. What this is?

**HATTIE** Prairie cactus.

**SLAV** Hard word. Cactus.

**HATTIE** It's pokey.

**SLAV** Many picks.

**HATTIE** Spikes.

**SLAV** Spicks. Spikes.

**CHIP** My dad was a miner in the Pass.

**SLAV** Oh? Which mine?

**CHIP** Hillcrest.

**SLAV** Oh. Bad trouble there.

**CHIP** He's in the big grave. As wide and long as the railway track.

*SLAV removes his cap.*

**SLAV** I am sorry for him. I worked at the Bellevue. We have a blast there, too, 1910. Hillcrest 1914 was the worst. One hundred eighty-nine mining men. What's your name?

**CHIP** Chip.

**SLAV** I am Slav. I'm happy to shake the hand of a miner's son.

*SLAV shakes CHIP's hand and walks off with his sack. CHIP opens his hand and finds a quarter.*

**CHIP** Look at that!

**SAM** Wow! Two bits!

**HATTIE** My turn! Follow the leader!

*SAM follows. CHIP looks after SLAV, waves, then follows, his special rock in one hand, his quarter in the other.*

**CHIP** Hey! It's my turn!

*CHIP exits.*

## Scene Three – Apron Strings

*MOM cleans stems and leaves from chokecherries in a bowl. CHIP enters, a little older now.*

**CHIP** It's time.

**MOM** No, it's not.

**CHIP** Come on, Mom. I'm old enough. They're taking guys as young as fourteen.

**MOM** And then what? You start in the tipple, you get coal dust in your skin and it pulls you in until you're down there working on the face. That's how it goes.

**CHIP** What's wrong with that?

**MOM** I don't want you underground. It's too much to bear. I'd be sick with worry.

**CHIP** You don't have time to be sick. Look at you, cooking for the miners, washing for the miners, canning Auntie's garden and keeping her house clean.

**MOM** Work is keeping me alive. And there's no end of work here. You'd think it was the Klondike Gold Rush.

**CHIP** Because the mining is better here, Mom. And safer. Uncle John says there's not so much gas. These are flat, deep-seam mines and the coal is good coal.

**MOM** Uncle John, what does he know?

**CHIP** He's a miner.

**MOM** A miner. Not a mother.

**CHIP** Ah, Mom!

**MOM** By the way, I need another load of that good coal. These chokecherries take an awful lot of heating to gel.

**CHIP** You never sing anymore. Dad used to call you his canary. You sang all the time for him.

**MOM** Well, he's not here anymore.

**CHIP** All the more reason for me to get started. I'm going down to the mine office. Do I look all right?

**MOM** You look fourteen and not afraid of work.

**CHIP** I'd really like to go in with the ponies, if they let me. I hear it's nice and cool in summer and warm in winter. Uncle John says that the temperature of the mine never changes, no matter what's going on outside. That's healthy.

**MOM** I don't want you underground.

**CHIP** If I can earn enough, we could get our own place.

**MOM** There aren't any places to be had. The miners are making good money, and if they're not in a coal door shack, they're cramped up in the bunkhouse like chickens in a coop.

**CHIP** There's talk of some company houses going up next spring. Sam is going to try to get on as a builder's helper.

**MOM** Now why can't you do that?

**CHIP** I'll do both.

**MOM** What about school?

**CHIP** I've had enough of school.

**MOM** Chip, your father would not hold with that.

**CHIP** Yeah, well, he's not here anymore.

*MOM exits.*

## Scene Four – Workline

*CHIP is in the line at the mine office window in front of SAM.*

*The MINER appears and looks CHIP over. CHIP notices him and doesn't hear the MINE MANAGER.*

**MINE MANAGER** *(voice-over)* What's your name?

**MINER** Look sharp, now.

**MINE MANAGER** *(voice-over)* You speak English?

**CHIP** Yes, sir. Chip Clarke, sir. I heard you had work in the tipple.

**MINE MANAGER** *(voice-over)* You got any relatives working here?

**CHIP** My uncle John is driver boss.

**MINE MANAGER** *(voice-over)* So you're his wife's sister's boy. You still going to school?

**CHIP** I'd rather be a miner. Like my dad.

**MINE MANAGER** *(voice-over)* Like your dad, huh? All right young fella, I'm going to give you second shift on the sorting table picking bone. You be here four o'clock sharp every day, starting today. Come September, that's right after school.

**CHIP** If I'm going to be a miner, what do I need school for?

**MINE MANAGER** *(voice-over)* I'm going to give you some advice. I don't often hand it out, so listen up.

**CHIP** Yes, sir.

**MINE MANAGER** *(voice-over)* If you don't want a sore back, make sure you eat oatmeal every morning.

**CHIP** Oatmeal porridge?

**MINE MANAGER** *(voice-over)* That's right. No sugar.

**CHIP** No sugar?

**MINER** If you don't want to hurt your back, use your brain.

**MINE MANAGER** *(voice-over)* And if your back still hurts, even with the oatmeal, then you have to use your brain. That's the key to mining, my boy, use your brain more than your back.

**MINER** If you don't use your brain, the mine will crush you like an egg.

**MINE MANAGER** *(voice-over)* So, school first, then you're here from four o'clock to midnight. Next!

*CHIP looks back at the MINER, who smiles. CHIP turns back to SAM and the MINER is gone.*

**CHIP** Did you see a guy over there just now?

**SAM** Nope. Hey, second shift?

**CHIP** Yeah.

**SAM** Same as me. We got the whole day. How about fishing?

**CHIP** I gotta pick coal for my mom. I thought I saw this guy. Hey, did the mine manager say anything to you about school?

**SAM** Me? No. Just said don't be late.

**CHIP** Only problem with second shift is it's going to cut into our social life.

**SAM** Yeah. How are we going to get girlfriends?

**CHIP** I guess we'll see the girls at school.

**SAM** If our eyes are open. If I'm at school, I'll be sleeping. See ya later. Gotta catch some grasshoppers. I'm going fishing.

*SAM exits.*

*CHIP moves to the slag pile and starts to fill a sack with coal. SLAV comes along with a potato sack and starts to fill it, too.*

**CHIP** Hey, Slav!

**SLAV** Hah. Chip, yes?

**CHIP** You're back!

**SLAV** Oh, yeah. Good mining here. I work on farm all summer, but I come back here, work starting tomorrow. Today, I make another shack.

**CHIP** Your own shack!

**SLAV** If I had little cottage, I could get wife. But for now, I make a shack. Willow, mud and boards.

**CHIP** You're your own boss, hey Slav?

**SLAV** I my own boss.

**CHIP** My dad used to say that, too. Be your own boss.

**SLAV** You want to help build my shack? I show you how. Pay you one dollar.

**CHIP** Wow! Would I! Hey! There's an old raft no one uses anymore down by the pond. Plenty of lumber on it.

**SLAV** What we waiting for?

*CHIP and SLAV drag out a piece of board, which forms the slide in the next scene. SLAV exits.*

## Scene Five – Working in the Tipple

*In the tipple, the sound is thundering. CHIP and SAM are sorting coal that's being sent down the roller. Clapper boards are shaking. The boys are freezing and the dust is all over.*

**SAM** When's break time?

**CHIP** Is it dark out yet?

**SAM** It's dark out.

**CHIP** A while yet.

*The MINER appears again and checks the boys' work. SAM does not see or hear him.*

**MINER** Don't let it get clogged up here. Keep it moving.

**CHIP** Yes, sir.

**SAM** Yes, sir, what?

**CHIP** The pit boss. I mean, I talked to him about building a rink.

**SAM** Yeah?

**CHIP** He's lending us a water pump from the mine. They're looking for players for the miners' team.

**SAM** When are you flooding the rink?

**CHIP** Saturday. You want to help?

**SAM** I'll say.

*SAM gets back to work with renewed vigour. The MINER notices and nods at CHIP before he moves on.*

## Scene Six – The Rink

*CHIP and SAM reset the board for the rink, get their sticks and use lumps of coal for pucks. Two other BOYS join them, and under the light of the moon, the magic of the game takes over. SLAV sits overhead on the cliff, looking down, watching the game and singing a Polish Christmas carol, "Lulajze Jezuniu."*

**SLAV** *(sings) Lulajze, Jezuniu, moja perelko,*
*Lulaj, ulubione me piescidelko,*
*Lulajze Jezuniu, lulajze, lulaj.*
*A Ty Go, Matulu, w placzu utulaj.*

*The game breaks up; the BOYS go home. CHIP goes up to where SLAV sits.*

**CHIP** Hey, Slav?

**SLAV** You are so free. You and your friends.

**CHIP** So are you. You're your own boss, right?

**SLAV** Not in war. Me, Slav, ten years I working. No wife. Yet I am enemy, because Austria takes Poland where I am born. I am no Austrian, I'm Polish.

**CHIP** Can't you tell them that?

**SLAV** I try. They mark me down anyway. Look here, enemy alien. Get stamp every month or go to labour camp and work for twenty-five cents a day! They take Ukrainians to labour camp. They take them up to Munson or to the mountains.

**CHIP** Not the miners.

**SLAV** Miners stay working, no travel, no letters to old country. And get the stamp. See here? I don't get stamp three months now.

**CHIP** Do you have to go to the post office?

**SLAV** The lady there, she no like me.

## Scene Seven – The Post Office

*CHIP and SLAV meet MARY.*

**CHIP** This is Slav.

*MARY looks at SLAV's papers and then at SLAV.*

**SLAV** Please, missus, I working overtime, no time to come here.

*A MAN comes in with letters to mail. MARY serves him first.*

**MARY** Thank you, sir.

**MAN** Good day.

*The MAN leaves.*

**MARY** Yes, Slav. I haven't seen you for a while. But I've heard a lot about you.

**SLAV** Who? What they say?

*MARY takes a look at SLAV, then stamps his paper three times and signs it.*

**MARY** Don't you ever worry about coming here again.

**SLAV** Yes, missus.

**MARY** This war can't last forever. And if it makes you feel any better, half the men in the valley have to come in here for this.

**SLAV** Ten years I am in Canada.

**MARY** Have you ever taken any English lessons?

**SLAV** No. No time. I just work.

**MARY** I'm teaching on Wednesday nights at the Miners' Hall. Mostly miners. Some girls, too.

**SLAV** Polish girls going there?

**MARY** Some. It's free for miners.

*SLAV and CHIP tip their hats.*

**SLAV** That's a good lady.

**CHIP** That's my aunt.

*CHIP exits.*

## Scene Eight – English Lessons

*SLAV is first in the class. MARY smiles at him. Then two more STUDENTS arrive and ANNA. SLAV can't take his eyes off ANNA.*

**MARY** We have a new student tonight, Slav Roj, Roja…

**SLAV** Roginski.

**MARY** Thank you, Mr. Roginski. Now, let's say our alphabet all together for review.

**ALL** A, b, c…

*They begin reciting the alphabet, and during this, folk music is heard. In his fantasy, SLAV takes ANNA for a dance.*

**MARY** One last time, our alphabet all together. Until next week.

*SLAV returns ANNA to her seat, and they are as before.*

**ALL** U, v, w, x, y and z.

*The others leave, but SLAV waits to talk to ANNA.*

**SLAV** Hello. I am Boleslav. They call me Slav.

**ANNA** Yes, I know.

**SLAV** Are you working here?

**ANNA** At the store. They hire me because I know Polish, Russian, Czech, German, Hungarian and even some Ukrainian I know.

**SLAV** And English. You speak beautiful English.

**ANNA** *Dziekuje.*

**SLAV** Where do you live?

**ANNA** I just moved here with my sister and her husband, Stan Blonski.

**SLAV** Stan is your brother-in-law!

*SLAV kisses her hand.*

I know Stan. We work in Crowsnest Pass together. He knows me. Anna, can I walk on you?

**ANNA** You may walk me home.

**SLAV** I mean, walk you home!

**ANNA** *Dobra.* Stan would like to see you.

## Scene Nine – Walking the Tracks

*SLAV and ANNA walk along the tracks. They pass CHIP, who smiles because SLAV doesn't even see him, his eyes are so full of ANNA. When CHIP looks up again, HATTIE is there.*

**HATTIE** Chip?

**CHIP** Hattie, is that you?

**HATTIE** I've been away, working on the farm.

**CHIP** You look so different.

**HATTIE** It's been a while.

**CHIP** So, how was the farm?

**HATTIE** I like it better here. There's more people, and I'm not that good with livestock!

**CHIP** I've been working at the mine.

**HATTIE** I heard. Did you finish school?

**CHIP** Not yet. I gotta get my exams this June, and then I'm done.

**HATTIE** I'm going for my teacher's certificate.

**CHIP** Hey, you could practise on me.

**HATTIE** I'm leaving for Calgary tomorrow. Just having a last look around.

**CHIP** Well, I'm glad you saw me.

**HATTIE** Hey, isn't that the guy we met in the hills?

**CHIP** Slav? Yeah. That's him. He's got a girlfriend now.

**HATTIE** He looks really happy.

**CHIP** He does.

**HATTIE** Well, good luck on your exams, Chip. I'll be back in the fall. If I can find a job here.

**CHIP** That won't be a problem for you. I mean, there's so many kids, and only half of them speak English!

**HATTIE** I know! On the farm, I met a girl from Hungary. She came to Canada all by herself to work. She couldn't speak English at all. No one understood her. She even thought of killing herself! So I taught her after church every Sunday.

**CHIP** You're going to make a great teacher.

**HATTIE** As long as it keeps me off the farm!

**CHIP** You won't be lonely, anyway, with all those people in the city.

**HATTIE** I'll be lonely for our hills.

**CHIP** Hey! I know a great place! It makes you feel like you're on top of the world!

**HATTIE** Show me! I want to memorize this valley. And those crocuses! That shade of purple looks different here than up on the prairie!

*CHIP and HATTIE pass SLAV on their way to the hills. This time, CHIP is the one who is oblivious to SLAV, who nods and smiles.*

## Scene Ten – Saturday Night

*CHIP and SAM are on the busy street. They wave to friends. They see SLAV.*

**CHIP** Hey, Slav, you want to go to the movies?

**SLAV** No. I go back. One beer, a haircut and a little shopping. That's all for me.

**SAM** Have you got a big date?

**SLAV** Oh, yes. Big day.

**CHIP** Must be that girl. You always take the midnight train on Saturday paydays. You'll miss the fights.

**SLAV** I got something better waiting for me. Look, see?

*He opens a ring box.*

**CHIP** Wow.

**SLAV** You think she like?

**CHIP** I think she likes you.

**SLAV** I'm gonna ask her tonight. I look okay?

**CHIP** You look good, Slav. What else did you buy?

**SLAV** I got a little roast here for her sister for Sunday dinner. And for me, Blood Bitters if I get nervous.

*SLAV shows the little bottle of syrup.*

I feel nervous already.

*SLAV takes a little sip.*

**CHIP** Careful, Slav. That stuff can make a rabbit kick a bulldog!

**SAM** Come on, Chip, we'll miss the show!

**CHIP** Sam likes the line-up part, where we can look at the girls.

**SLAV** You go look at girls, I go get a wife!

*SLAV exits, purposefully and CHIP and SAM head the other way.*

## Scene Eleven – The Spanish Influenza

*MARY helps MOM into her bed and mops her brow.*

**MARY** Chip! Chip! I need you!

*CHIP comes running, wildflowers in hand.*

**CHIP** Auntie! What is it?

**MARY** Your mom, Chip, she's taken to bed again! Weak as a chicken!

**CHIP** She was feeling better this morning. She was even talking about going to work.

**MARY** I wouldn't let her. You sit with her. I'm worried. I've got to open the post office. There's nothing like an epidemic to cause a flurry of letter-writing. Stay with your mother today, Chip.

*MARY puts on her face mask and heads out.*

**CHIP** Mom? I'm here.

**MOM** Chip. I'm cold.

*CHIP puts the wildflowers in her hands and pulls more blankets over her.*

**CHIP** I'm going to stay right here, Mom.

**MOM** Who's looking after the miners?

**CHIP** Don't worry about them. Worry about yourself.

**MOM** I couldn't save the ones in the blast that killed your father, but I thought I could save the miners sick with flu.

**CHIP** You've done more than anyone.

**MOM** Have you got any money?

**CHIP** A bit.

**MOM** What I've saved is in that teapot, the one without the handle. Some day, when you have a place of your own, plant a little tree for me. And one for your father. We love you, son.

**CHIP** Mom?

**MOM** Sing for me.

**CHIP** Okay. The one you liked, before.
*(sings)* Rock of ages, cleft for me,
Let me hide myself in Thee,
Let the water and the blood,
From thy side, a healing flood,

*The MINER appears and joins in the singing.*

**CHIP & MINER** *(sing)* Rock of ages, cleft for me,
Let me hide myself in Thee.

*MOM drops the wildflowers. She is dead. The MINER picks up the wildflowers and closes them in MOM's hands. He turns her bed around and pushes the coal car down the tracks. After the car is rolled off, CHIP is alone.*

## Scene Twelve – Gravesite

*SLAV finds CHIP at the gravesite.*

**CHIP** Every time I come here, I see these graves, all these graves I dug myself, even my own mother's grave. They look like closed books. All that's left is the names.

**SLAV** Chip? I am sorry for your trouble. Me and Anna, we wait for the flu to pass and the war to end and now it is all over. We marry on Saturday. Come to the party. Good party. Many cabbage rolls. You eat, you drink. Maybe bring your friend?

**CHIP** What friend?

**SLAV** There. Waiting for you.

*HATTIE approaches CHIP as SLAV exits, and CHIP falls into her arms.*

**HATTIE** Oh, Chip, I'm so sorry.

**CHIP** Thank God, you are safe.

**HATTIE** We had it bad in Calgary, too. Every second person was sick. They say the Spanish Influenza took as many Canadians as the war!

**CHIP** They made the Miners' Hall into a morgue. I was digging graves for weeks.

**HATTIE** It's over now.

**CHIP** Yeah. I guess I'm on my own.

**HATTIE** No, you're not. I mean, you've got your aunt and uncle.

**CHIP** And Slav. He invited us to his wedding.

**HATTIE** Us?

**CHIP** I mean, would you like to go?

**HATTIE** A party?

**CHIP** Just what we need.

**HATTIE** I'd love to go with you, Chip.

**CHIP** Are you walking back?

**HATTIE** The long way. Across the hills.

*CHIP takes HATTIE's hand. They exit.*

## Scene Thirteen – Promotion

*The PIT BOSS calls CHIP over.*

**PIT BOSS** So, young fella, I hear you're good with the girls.

**CHIP** One girl, maybe.

**PIT BOSS** I need a sweet-talking young lad to work with the ponies.

**CHIP** I'll do it. Hauling cars, feeding horses, anything to get down to the face.

**PIT BOSS** I would have put you on it sooner, but for your mother, I didn't dare.

**CHIP** And now?

*The MINER is visible again, watching the scene.*

**MINER** Now it's up to you, son.

**PIT BOSS** Well, now it's up to you. You can get started on your mining papers anytime. We're going to need trained young men. Mines are opening up all over the valley. Pony driving is a good way to learn the business.

**CHIP** I've waited a long time. I appreciate it. Second shift?

**PIT BOSS** If you want to study for your certification, I'll put you on first shift. That will give you your nights for the classes. And a bit of social life, eh?

**CHIP** Thank you, sir.

**PIT BOSS** I was a young lad like you, once. Lost my parents early, had to grow up by the hair on my head. Welcome to the unofficial mining apprenticeship program, Chip. You do well with the ponies and I'll get you on the motor haulage after that.

**MINER** Listen to them ponies. They know the mine inside out.

*CHIP watches the MINER and almost misses what the PIT BOSS says.*

**PIT BOSS** Oh, one last thing. Pony boss wants a guy who can sing.

*The MINER exits.*

**CHIP** Sorry, sir?

**PIT BOSS** So can you? Sing?

**CHIP** My mom taught me, sir!

*The PIT BOSS exits.*

**MOM** *(off, sings)* Hush-a-bye, don't you cry,
Go to sleepy little baby.

**CHIP** *(sings)* When you wake, you shall take,
All the pretty little ponies,
Blacks and bays, dapples and greys,
All the pretty little ponies.

*CHIP throws his hat in the air, then exits.*

## Scene Fourteen – Strike Action

*The sound of gunshots. SLAV and STAN meet in the hills.*

**STAN** Slav! You can see better over here!

**SLAV** Stan, I don't like this hiding like dogs in the hot hills.

**STAN** If we go down, they might shoot us.

**SLAV** They call us Bolsheveki.

**STAN** The mining company is so afraid of the one big union, they have to send soldiers after us.

**SLAV** War-sick soldiers. They get ten dollars a day and we get nothing. They get free liquor and we go thirsty.

**STAN** I thought liquor was illegal.

**SLAV** I thought shooting was illegal.

**STAN** Those veterans got it against us no matter what. To them, we are the enemy. Because we have jobs they want.

**SLAV** What kind of job is this? Three months, already, sleeping with one eye open. And running to the hills when the soldiers are wild and drunk!

**STAN** Who's there?

*The CONSTABLE's megaphoned voice yells up to the hills.*

**CONSTABLE** *(voice-over)* Miners! Return to your homes. Return to the mines. Be advised that the mine companies will give preference first to returned soldiers, next to white men with mining experience, and last to you, the alien element. The companies will not recognize the one big union. Hear this! The instigators of this faction have been tarred and feathered and run out of the valley.

**STAN** Tarred and feathered!

**CONSTABLE** *(voice-over)* When you return to the mines, you must sign a note accepting the United Mine Workers of America as your legal agent. That is all.

**SLAV** So. I'm not going back.

**STAN** I thought you wanted to work?

**SLAV** Not with greenhorns.

**STAN** Blacklegs!

**SLAV** Soldiers who know nothing about mining. I wait.

**STAN** We wait already three months. Longer than the Winnipeg General Strike. That is something, anyway.

**SLAV** For nothing, Stan. One big stupid strike for nothing. And some anniversary for Anna and me.

*CHIP makes his way up the hill to the men. He's using a crutch.*

**CHIP** Hey, Slav! Stan!

**SLAV** Chip! What happened to you?

**CHIP** Pony got me.

**SLAV** See? The company feeds the ponies every day, but they let us starve.

*The MINER appears. CHIP uses his crutch to demonstrate the pony.*

**CHIP** They ordered the ponies underground today. I was so glad to get in that cool tunnel! So I'm singing to her, I'm whispering in her ear, I'm calling her my sugar girl, but that pony would not go for anything.

**STAN** Hah! You should pour some slack down her ear! Then she go!

**CHIP** One thing about them ponies, they can bite you, they can kick you, but you can't kick back or the pony boss would fire you on the spot.

**MINER** Pony's listening to the mine.

*The sound of the pony neighing.*

**CHIP** So that pony kicks me good, and I'm down with the air pushed out of me. I can hardly breathe, but I can hear the timbers creaking and the roof sprinkling down on me! So she's starting to cave, and I can't move for my leg, and the guys had to jack up the roof before they can get me out of there! First day inside and they take me out in a coal car!

**SLAV** Ponies feel the roof with their ears.

**MINER** Pony knows when the roof's no good.

**STAN** What are you going to do now?

**CHIP** Pit boss said he'd put me on haulage. He said they're going to start moving coal again, so I think this strike is over. I thought we should celebrate.

*CHIP hands them some beer.*

**STAN** Where did you get your hands on that?

**CHIP** Hattie knows a farmer who makes his own. We're stocking up for the wedding.

**SLAV** Ah! He's *scarbnik*, yah? Like the one who gives the treasure, we say in Poland.

**STAN** *Scarbnik* is the friend of the miner. He gives you help. Like you say, guardian angel.

**CHIP** Hell, I'm no angel. But, hey, I did some spying. I'm in the infirmary, eh, and the doctor is putting this bandage on, and the pit boss was in there talking to the doc. The pit boss said the soldiers are too nervous for the mine jobs. They can't concentrate. They can't take the sound of the blasting.

**STAN** What did the doctor say?

**CHIP** He said the vets have their war memories riding on their shoulders like a nightmare, and when they go underground, they can't stand the dark. And they're supposed to be heroes, eh? It eats them up.

**SLAV** To be a miner, must be calm. All the time calm. Like a gardener.

**STAN** You don't stay alive in a mine if you're half-dead already.

*During the following, the MINER lights his open-flame lamp.*

**SLAV** No light, dark all around you, what you going to do? A miner, he needs a light inside him, for when the headlamp goes out.

**MINER** In pitch black, you feel for your bag of carbide, pour some in, add the water *(spits)*, strike the flint, get the lamp going again.

**STAN** So, we wait. A few more days. The returned men leave, we come back.

**SLAV** And goodbye to the one big union.

**STAN** *Barborka*, pray for us.

**CHIP** Who's that?

**SLAV** St. Barbara. The saint of miners.

**STAN** She protects from cave-ins, fires, sudden death.

**SLAV** But not strikes.

**CHIP** No wonder you guys are such good miners. Guardian angels and saints!

**MINER** Friends.

**SLAV** And beer!

**STAN** *Sto lat!*

**CHIP** *Sto lat!*

**SLAV** *Sto lat!*

*The MINER exits.*

## Scene Fifteen – Wedding

*ANNA comes to HATTIE with a basket containing a bottle of wine, a sack of salt and a loaf of bread.*

**ANNA** This is for your new house.

**HATTIE** Oh, Anna, it's just a two-room shack.

**ANNA** Like everyone has! Never mind. In Poland, it is a custom for every new home. Bread for health, salt for good luck and wine for joy.

*CHIP, now without a crutch, SLAV and SAM join them. SLAV starts the singing.*

**SLAV** *Sto lat, sto lat,*

**ALL** *niech zyje, zyje nam,*
*sto lat, sto lat,*
*niech zyje zyje nam,*
*jeszcze raz, jeszcze raz,*
*niech zyje, zyje nam!*
*Niech zyje nam!*

*ANNA, SLAV and SAM leave the couple to themselves.*

**CHIP** You know what they're singing?

**HATTIE** Something about good health.

**CHIP** May you live for a hundred years. When you take my mom and my dad together, they didn't even get close to a hundred.

**HATTIE** We will just have to make up for it.

**CHIP** We will.

**HATTIE** We'll plant the little trees for your parents tomorrow, Chip. Side by side, right in front of our own home. Then we'll plant the garden.

**CHIP** Hattie, there's a reason they call this Cactus Flats.

**HATTIE** You can build a water wheel, to bring the water up from the river. Slav would help you, he knows how.

**CHIP** Let's start planting now.

**HATTIE** It's a little dark.

**CHIP** Different kind of planting.

*CHIP takes HATTIE offstage.*

## Scene Sixteen – More Lunch

*ANNA is hanging a sheet on the line as HATTIE runs out with her basket of laundry.*

*The sound of a train coming is heard.*

**ANNA** Oh! There they are again!

*HATTIE helps ANNA quickly take down the sheet again.*

**HATTIE** It doesn't matter how early we are. They go by so often, it's a race to get it up wet and down dry and still clean.

**ANNA** It's a hot wind today. It won't take long to dry once we hang it. I want to finish early in time for Women's Institute tonight.

**HATTIE** I wish we could take our husbands to this one.

**ANNA** Slav thinks I am foolish to go.

**HATTIE** He thinks that because he doesn't know himself. That's why we're going. How often do we get a lawyer from Lethbridge up here?

**ANNA** Slav just doesn't trust anybody. He'd put his money in a hole in the garden if I let him!

**HATTIE** Well, it's about time somebody told us about wills. Look at Lottie and Shirley! Their husbands both killed, no wills and the women get nothing!

**ANNA** It's just not fair.

**HATTIE** Especially when you know that if it wasn't for their wives, the men wouldn't have any savings at all!

**ANNA** At least we did that bake sale. That brought some money in for the widows' fund.

**HATTIE** But there's a law for wives, if the husband has a will! And if the men won't get educated about this, then it's up to us!

**ANNA** Sometimes I think they think they are little gods.

**HATTIE** Immortal.

**ANNA** Sometimes, I let myself believe it, just a little. Enough not to worry.

*On the train, CHIP is stoking the engine with coal. SAM is checking the job list for the day.*

**CHIP** I swear, this monster gobbles it up as fast as we shovel it.

**SAM** We got orders for a couple more loads, Chip. Good loads at the mine mean good loads for us, eh?

**CHIP** I can hardly wait to get down there and put my brass tag on a coal car. That's the way to load up the money.

**SAM** It would still be digging, at the end of a shovel.

**CHIP** But you get your own room, eh? You lay some track, you get paid for that. You timber a room and you get paid for that. You fill as many cars as you want and they pay you your contract on every load of coal.

**SAM** Give me steel and smoke and I'll make her move. I'll make her move mountains. Mountains of coal.

**CHIP** I got my papers. I'm ready to go down this fall, soon as they'll take me.

**SAM** We're coming up the hill. Better blow the whistle for your wife.

*ANNA and HATTIE are waiting for the train to go by. HATTIE has to sit down.*

**ANNA** Are you all right?

**HATTIE** It's just the coal smoke. The smell is bothering me more today.

**ANNA** Ah!

**HATTIE** So, your Slav, he likes it, all day in the dark mine?

**ANNA** He loves it.

**HATTIE** Chip is hell bent on going down. Soon as they'll take him. He's loading coal on the train to work up the muscle.

**ANNA** Chip? He's all muscle already.

**HATTIE** He's eating like a horse, and well, we're very happy.

**ANNA** Expecting, too, yah?

**HATTIE** How did you know?

**ANNA** I am a mother twice already! I know. And now we will have babies at the same time.

**HATTIE** You, too!

**ANNA** I hope a boy this time, for me.

**HATTIE** Oh, Anna. I'm so glad I have you here!

**ANNA** Don't worry about Chip. Slav says the miners, they look out for each other. Just like we do. They help each other.

**HATTIE** Have you ever been down to the mine? I mean, inside it?

**ANNA** Oh, no. Slav says there was a man, he took his girlfriend down to show her, and the next day he was killed.

**HATTIE** Hey! My dad told me that same story.

**ANNA** Maybe it's just a story. But I wouldn't want to go down there, would you?

**HATTIE** Maybe it's better not to know.

**ANNA** Slav says it's like magic. He undermines the wall at the bottom, and the next morning, there's coal waiting for him like a gift, tons and tons of coal, fallen from the face.

**HATTIE** Chip can hardly wait to be his own boss.

**ANNA** They can think they're their own boss, anyway.

*ANNA and HATTIE laugh.*

*CHIP blows a whistle – long-short-long-short-long.*

**HATTIE** Oh, that's Chip! The overtime signal! More lunch!

*HATTIE hurries off. ANNA protects both baskets of laundry from the soot of the train with her skirts. HATTIE hurries back with a sack and runs to meet the train.*

**ANNA** Be careful!

*The men thunder in on the train, blowing ash, noise and steam. HATTIE stands firm, holds out the sack, which CHIP grabs as they pass.*

*The men relax in the train car.*

**SAM** That's some fearless kid you're going to have.

**CHIP** How do you know?

**SAM** With a mother like that, who will stand next to steam-spitting, ash-blowing moving steel, and a father like you, who's itching to get down to the coal face, that kid of yours is gonna twist the devil's tail.

**CHIP** Hey, Sam, let's make this baby move, eh?

*Music.*

*CHIP and SAM shovel coal in a race against each other.*

*ANNA and HATTIE hang a sheet on the line.*

## Scene Seventeen – Underground

*In the mine, STAN adjusts the sheet like a brattice cloth.*

*SLAV and CHIP are behind the brattice, in shadow, at the coal face. SLAV is using the breast auger and gestures to CHIP to push him from behind to make the work go faster.*

**STAN** Hey, Slav, we should show Chip the blasting hole over here.

**SLAV** You mean the one you augered out on Friday?

**STAN** Yeah.

*SLAV comes around in front of the brattice. CHIP follows.*

Sure. Check 'er good, there, Chip. Get your eye right in there, see if she's deep enough.

*CHIP gets up to the hole, at eye level, and peers in. He can't see anything and keeps adjusting his lamp to see better. Then STAN lights a match just about at CHIP's head. Suddenly, CHIP is thrown backward with a "whump," exploding built-up methane gas.*

**SLAV** Whoa, you okay Chip?

**CHIP** Yeah, just burned my eyebrows off.

*The MINER appears in shadow.*

**SLAV** It's the methane gas. She builds up over one, two, days.

**MINER** Can't see it. Can't smell it. Sometimes, you feel it.

**SLAV** You hear it, whoosh, over your head, coming out of the cracks.

**CHIP** Like murmuring?

**SLAV** Like whispering. You hear it, keep your head down. The gas, it pushes out, loosens up the coal and goes to the roof.

**STAN** Okay, boys, in the next room, there, we're going to shoot the coal.

*STAN exits.*

*CHIP and SLAV move away, stand close to the timber.*

*(off)* Fire!

*The sound of a muffled "thwump" is heard, rock falling.*

**SLAV** You wait for dust to go down. Dust can explode, too.

**CHIP** What's that smell?

**SLAV** Fumes. From the powder. No breathe it. You get a headache. We wait a little, then we load.

**CHIP** Does Stan do that to all the new guys?

**SLAV** Yeah. Mining school.

*In the shadows, the MINER nods his head to CHIP.*

**MINER** Listen up, son. In coal mining, you can be killed by all four elements: earth if the rock falls on you, water if the mine floods, air if it's full of methane gas or carbon monoxide and fire if a spark from your pick ignites the dust or the gas.

**CHIP** Hey, Slav?

**SLAV** Yeah?

**CHIP** Can we sing or something?

**SLAV** Better you listen right now. Listen to the sounds. Try out the roof there. Hear that? Nice, like a bell? That's a good roof. Hollow, dull, like a drum? Bad roof. You put up a post right away.

**CHIP** How much longer do we wait?

**SLAV** A little longer.

**MINER** Air ventilation in the coal mine is essential. There are many kinds of foul air: fire damp is methane gas; black damp or afterdamp is almost all carbon dioxide and nitrous oxide left after a burn; white damp is carbon monoxide after incomplete combustion; and choke damp is toxic levels of carbon dioxide. Not all of these you can detect.

**SLAV** Listen.

**MINER** Fire damp will explode into a blue flame. In black damp, the air smells strong and heavy. In the case of white damp, the canary will fall from its perch in two and a half minutes. With choke damp, you have only ninety seconds before you succumb, so if your head feels full, hit the floor and breathe from the ground.

**SLAV** Listen to the air.

Leigh Wardhaugh and John McIver
*photo by Linda Digby*

**MINER** Listen to the mine. She's alive. Just like you.

**CHIP** All I hear is my heart thumping.

**SLAV** In the mine, you and your heart are nothing. Piece of dust. You think like she thinks, feel how she feels.

**CHIP** Who?

**SLAV** The mine.

**MINER** Right that there. Listen. Listen to her breathe. Listen to the mine.

*The MINER exits.*

## Scene Eighteen – Strike Again

*HATTIE enters, removes the sheet from the line, bundles it up, a babe in arms. CHIP and SLAV join HATTIE picketing outside the mine. The MINE OWNER places a banner on the coal car. It says, "No. 1 Alberta Hard Coal Bound for Ontario!" There could also be a Union Jack flag hanging from the car.*

**SLAV** Gonna be a dry, hungry summer.

**CHIP** Between a rock and a hard place.

**SLAV** We're little pieces of dust, remember. They don't care.

*The MINE OWNER steps up into the coal car to speak to the crowd.*

**CHIP** A dollar less a ton is not enough to live on!

**HATTIE** Baby killers!

**SLAV** What kind of union says yes to wage cuts?

**MINE OWNER** Good morning. We have received word that strike action is not endorsed by District 18 of the United Mine Workers. We are asking that you consider a small wage cut, fifteen percent, so that the company can compete with the many other mines in the valley to take our superior coal to market in the east! We ask that you support our patriotic intent and avoid the communist sentiment so prevalent in the valley among recently arrived immigrants.

**SLAV** I been here longer than you, mister.

**CHIP** Fifteen percent! That's still a dollar a ton less!

**MINE OWNER** We will have police escorts for miners coming to work, so there will be no need to worry about your security.

**CHIP** Just our reputations.

**HATTIE** They've brought all the ponies up. That's a bad sign. This will be a long strike. I'm worried, Chip. Maybe you better go back to the railway job.

**CHIP** I'm going to have to cross the line. I have to stick to the miners' union, even with a wage cut. If we don't, we're not going to have a union at all. And then where will we be? Every mine an open shop?

**HATTIE** What about you, Slav?

**SLAV** I wait. Again I wait. I grow my garden. Wait for this to pass like puffs of smoke.

**CHIP** You'd be better off to work once in a while. Just so you don't get the label.

**SLAV** Enemy alien?

**CHIP** Red.

**SLAV** Hah, they see my name, they hear my voice, to them I am already a communist.

**CHIP** Stan is one of the ones stirring it up. You should keep clear of him for a while.

**SLAV** Stan is my brother-in-law. What can I do?

**CHIP** Just don't let them blacklist you.

**SLAV** They tell the new men, just come from the old country, they threaten them and say they won't get citizenship papers.

**HATTIE** I don't know, Chip. If you go to work at the mine, there's a lot of people who will be mad at us. Last time, they broke windows.

**CHIP** What kind of strike is this, anyway? It shouldn't be miners against miners, it should be miners against the company.

**HATTIE** Maybe you should start working on your fire boss certification, Chip. You've always talked about it. Instead of looking for the light on the tipple, you'd be in the mine every day.

**CHIP** You could do it with me, Slav.

**SLAV** Hah, they no hire me for fire boss. I got the wrong name.

**CHIP** There are plenty of mines in the valley.

**SLAV** No, no. I move my house upriver already two times. I like my garden now. Good river soil. I stay. But you, you're young. You do fire boss papers. Do it now. Work every day, even Saturday and Sunday. Every day checking for the gas. Me, I like nobody bother me on Saturday and Sunday.

**HATTIE** It's either work or go on welfare. And watch the companies raise the price of coal this winter!

**SLAV** Look, there's old missus Parama. She speaks no English.

*MRS. PARAMA goes up to the MINE OWNER. She looks at him straight in the eye.*

**CHIP** Who is she?

**HATTIE** She's the mother of the Hungarian lady who owns the little grocery. She came from the old country to take care of her grandchildren.

**SLAV** The Hungarian grocery gives all the miners credit. Even I have a big bill there. Now how am I going to pay?

**CHIP** You should ask your communist brother-in-law.

**MINE OWNER** Yes, ma'am? I'm talking to the miners here.

*MRS. PARAMA continues to stare, silently.*

Ma'am? You're interrupting important business!

*MRS. PARAMA holds out her hand. The MINE OWNER doesn't know what to do so he holds out his hand. She grabs it, and with her other hand, takes a lump of coal out of her pocket and lands it in his hand.*

What is this, ma'am?

**HATTIE** Merry Christmas.

**MINE OWNER** I see. Well. Thank you, Ma'am.

*The MINE OWNER drops the coal lump into the empty coal car, wipes off his hands and leaves, shamefaced, under the stare of MRS. PARAMA, who is led off by HATTIE.*

**SLAV** You and me, we stick together. We go on welfare. We go back to work in the fall, you'll see. I grow my garden. You work the railroad. Stay calm.

**CHIP** Stay calm! I work for less and you work for nothing.

**SLAV** I dig. Inside, outside, it doesn't matter.

**CHIP** I don't want to go railroading, being away up the line every night. Not with a new baby. I've got to build another room on, now we've got kids coming.

**SLAV** And so, we grow our gardens.

**CHIP** What do we eat while the gardens are growing?

**SLAV** Do you like dandelions?

*SLAV laughs and moves off, leaving CHIP alone.*

## Scene Nineteen – The River

*CHIP sits on the riverbank. He half-heartedly opens his book. HATTIE finds him.*

**HATTIE** Chip?

**CHIP** I was just studying.

**HATTIE** Studying for your fire boss papers, or studying the river?

**CHIP** Both, I guess.

**HATTIE** I've thought about what you said. About moving.

**CHIP** I've thought about it, too.

**HATTIE** It's true we have no money, but Chip, no one else does either. And if we move to the city, you've got to start all over again with a new trade, and the way things are going, there's no jobs anywhere.

**CHIP** It's tight all right.

**HATTIE** We're managing.

**CHIP** Just barely.

**HATTIE** We got the house built up this year. We're going to have a good garden. You're going to get your fire boss papers, and then it will be steady. Winter and summer. Strikes or no strikes. Orders or no orders.

**CHIP** When I'm a company man, you know I won't make as much money.

**HATTIE** But it will be steady. And you need that. You don't like being away from the mine for so long.

**CHIP** Why, Hattie? There could be a hurricane on the prairie, or a stampede, or a brush fire in the valley, a flood on the river, or a plague of grasshoppers, but when I'm in the mine, I'm in a place of my own, doing my own work, my way, my speed and nothing penetrates the rock but me. Troubles on the surface just don't follow me down.

**HATTIE** You do your troubling up here.

**CHIP** I'm just thinking about you.

**HATTIE** I'm not a worrier, Chip. If I was, what kind of miner's wife would I be?

**CHIP** But the kids, do you think this is the best for them?

**HATTIE** They've got me to teach them, and you to provide for them, and both of us to love them. They've got piles of other kids to play with, the hills and the river to play in. This is our valley.

**CHIP** Even if our house is just three small rooms, we're in debt to the store half the year and we never take a vacation anywhere else?

**HATTIE** Everyone's the same here, Chip. We're all just feeding our families. But we've got the doctor for free because you're a miner, we've got credit at the store because you're a miner and the school and library we just built is done on miners' money. The kids get Miners' Day every summer and a party at Christmas put on by the miners.

*HATTIE picks up four pieces of coal from the pile.*

Chip, if we went somewhere else, we'd be on our own! Like this. You, me, Mike and Jenny.

*HATTIE throws the pieces of coal in the river.*

**CHIP** Okay. We'll stay. Even if there are more hard times ahead.

**HATTIE** Chip. The valley is full of coal.

*CHIP picks up a piece of coal and throws it back in the pile.*

You're just restless, waiting for spring breakup.

**CHIP** I wouldn't be if I knew I was working all summer.

**HATTIE** You have to pass your test first.

**CHIP** I feel like I just did.

**HATTIE** There's a hard time dance on tonight.

**CHIP** Well, that changes everything!

*Music starts as CHIP and HATTIE dance.*

*CHIP lets HATTIE go and watches her pick up his book and exit before he descends to the mine.*

## Scene Twenty – Cave-in

*CHIP finds SLAV sitting in the mine.*

**SLAV** Finally I working steady again, and no car to load. Waiting to work, all the time waiting. In my dreams, I'm shovelling coal, but when I'm awake I'm waiting, always waiting.

**CHIP** Which way did your helper go?

**SLAV** That way.

**CHIP** I'll go see how he's doing.

**SLAV** Okay, Mr. Fire boss.

**CHIP** Hey, Slav, I'm not your boss.

**SLAV** Yes, you are. Because of you I have work. Stan, he had to move to Canmore. Nobody hires him here. So now he works on his knees, in the water, in the gas, on a pitch! Thirty-five degrees! The seams are three feet, like he's digging in a coffin.

**CHIP** Maybe it's better for you that he's gone.

**SLAV** Not Anna. She's not happy without her sister. I don't want to go to Canmore. I stay up all night thinking about it. I want to make good wages today, make Anna happy.

**CHIP** I'll find you a spare car.

*SLAV sits down for a rest while he waits. He nods off, and as he does, the sound of rain falling down, at first gentle, then harder, amplifies.*

*The MINER appears in the corner of the room.*

**MINER** You'd better move on, now.

*SLAV does not hear.*

*CHIP is in another part of the mine. The MINER appears to him.*

The mine is like a woman in labour, her belly tightening up, contracting. She can't help it. It's Nature, and she'll force you out. You better get back there. The hills are bearing down.

*CHIP watches the floor.*

**CHIP** Mice!

*CHIP hurries back to SLAV and hears the sound of timbers splintering.*

Slav!

*SLAV awakes with a start.*

**SLAV** Mother of God!

**CHIP** Let's get out of here!

**SLAV** Wait! Listen!

**CHIP** Which way?

*SLAV throws up some slack in the air.*

**SLAV** See there? She blows that way.

**CHIP** Through the gob to the next room.

**SLAV** You first.

**CHIP** Don't stop.

*They crawl. The roof crashes down behind them.*

I can see the track. She's still shining. Twisted like a pretzel.

**SLAV** Merciful mother.

**CHIP** Keep going.

**SLAV** I'm right behind you.

**CHIP** There's a car.

**SLAV** Listen!

**CHIP** It's stopped.

*SLAV checks the roof, tapping the top of the timber with his pick.*

**SLAV** Look at this.

**CHIP** Pressure squeezed the turpentine right out.

**SLAV** That track is gonna be a mess to clean up.

**CHIP** We'll leave it for the young guys.

**SLAV** I no like losing my lunch box.

**CHIP** Better that than your head.

**SLAV** You saved me this time, boss.

**CHIP** It wasn't me.

**SLAV** You were there.

**CHIP** I saw the mice run. They saved us both.

**SLAV** I feed them extra from now on. I get a bigger lunch box.

**CHIP** No more sleeping on the job, eh?

**SLAV** Okay, boss. I buy the beer tonight.

*SLAV discovers something in the pile of coal.*

But not for this one!

**CHIP** Who is it?

**SLAV** My helper. I see his leg. Oh, Maria.

**CHIP** Is he moving?

**SLAV** No, no. Piece of petrified wood. As big as a table. Crushed his chest.

**CHIP** Dead and buried before the doctor arrives.

**SLAV** I am sleeping and he is bringing my car.

**CHIP** First man I've lost.

**SLAV** He just married.

**CHIP** Oh, God. I've got to go to the widow.

**SLAV** Fire boss duty.

**CHIP** Let's get him out of here.

*CHIP and SLAV work together to pull off the rock.*

Holy hell, that's a big chunk. I don't think he suffered. At least I can tell that to his wife.

*They get the rock off. They leave it propped up against the coal pile. From the coal car, they take a brattice cloth, roll the body of the HELPER on and lift him into the car.*

**SLAV** At least the body is in one piece.

*The MINER enters and pushes the car down the track. SLAV exits.*

## Scene Twenty-one – Wash House

*The sound of a horn calls the emergency signal, a single blast that sounds, fades and repeats relentlessly under the following.*

*In the wash house, the basket containing the dead man's wallet and comb is lowered. CHIP removes the street clothes from the hooks and folds them over his arm. He replaces the wallet and comb into the pockets of the clothes. He puts the bundle of clothes on a piece of butcher paper, folds the paper over and ties it with a string. He smoothes his own hair and clothes. CHIP exits with the package.*

*The horn stops.*

*The End of Act One.*

# Act Two

## Scene One – At the Bar

*KITTY appears alone.*

**KITTY** He was just a man. Young and eager. Looking for a life. I accepted him, because he was so… earnest. He was an honest man.

*CHIP, SLAV and JOE are drinking at the bar.*

**CHIP** It could have been me.

**SLAV** Or me.

**JOE** Come on, boys. A miss is as good as a mile.

**SLAV** It should have been me. Sleeping!

**CHIP** It could have been all of us.

**KITTY** He could have made me into a good wife. But every day he went to the mine, I knew. I knew there was a chance he wouldn't come back.

**SLAV** Poor kid. Just getting a beard.

**JOE** Married, though. He got the three days a week. I'm just getting the one day right now.

**SLAV** So get married!

**JOE** He was married to one of Fanny's girls.

**KITTY** Fanny told me. She said I should keep working, just in case.

**CHIP** Yeah. She was busy at home when I went over there.

**JOE** What kind of busy?

**CHIP** Well, she was working.

**JOE** The afternoon shift! Working on who?

**CHIP** I didn't see. I sure didn't expect that.

**KITTY** I guess now I'll have to move back to Fanny's.

**JOE** Are we doing a collection?

**SLAV** Yeah. We always do.

**JOE** But considering who she is.

**CHIP** Kitty? Didn't she bring over that bag of groceries for the family of the man killed by a runaway boxcar?

**SLAV** Yeah. And didn't he, my helper, may he rest in peace, didn't he give in the collection for hurt miners, like everybody?

**JOE** It's just that she's… a working girl.

**SLAV** And who are we? Who here has never been to Fanny's?

**JOE** For cards, maybe. Or a good meal. Fanny's got the best cook in the valley.

**SLAV** Hah!

**CHIP** Miners' family is miners' family. No one goes through this alone. We'll take up a collection like we always do.

**JOE** Do we have to go to the funeral?

**CHIP** Funeral is Monday.

**SLAV** Funeral day, no work.

**CHIP** Union says we all have to go. Or take a fine.

**SLAV** Hope that's the last one this winter.

**CHIP** I'll drink to that.

**JOE** Me, too.

## Scene Two – The Funeral

*CHIP, SLAV and JOE follow KITTY to the burial site, where the REVEREND is waiting.*

**REVEREND** Lord, look down on our valley, so rich with the bounty of nature's gift of coal. See this man, one of ours, who has given his life, like many others, so that we can keep warm in the winter and bake our daily bread.

**SLAV** Third one in the valley this year.

**REVEREND** Give peace to the souls who work here day in and day out in the mines of this valley, for the good of people across our great nation.

**CHIP** And for miners everywhere.

**JOE** The International Order of the Black Hat.

**REVEREND** And give mercy to those who are left behind, who are left to grieve the dearly departed.

**CHIP, JOE & SLAV** Amen.

*KITTY comes forward to the headstone, the upturned piece of petrified wood.*

*During the following, CHIP passes a salt sack to SLAV, who deposits a coin, and passes it to JOE. Under scrutiny, JOE adds to the sack.*

**KITTY** He just wanted to be a coal miner. I thought I could be a coal miner's wife.

*KITTY releases a handful of slack coal, sprinkling her husband's grave.*

But I didn't do a very good job.

**REVEREND** He is at peace now.

**KITTY** I guess I just got what I deserve.

**REVEREND** No one deserves to suffer, and you still have a life ahead of you. You can turn a corner.

*CHIP presents the salt sack to KITTY.*

**CHIP** This is from the families of all the miners.

*The REVEREND gets his hands on the sack to feel its weight before it gets into KITTY's hands.*

**REVEREND** It's probably enough for a train ticket.

**KITTY** Is that what I should do? Just go somewhere else?

**REVEREND** If you stay here, you know where you'll go.

**KITTY** And if I go someplace else, what will I do?

**REVEREND** I know some people in Calgary. I could help you find a job.

**KITTY** There's no jobs, Reverend, even for able-bodied men. Even Fanny is going to pull out. There's just not enough to go around.

**REVEREND** I know an elderly lady in Calgary who needs a companion. She likes to look her best, and you, well, you'd be able to help her with that. I've written you a letter of introduction.

*The REVEREND passes KITTY a letter. KITTY takes it. JOE tries to follow her, but she pushes him away and walks down the tracks alone. The REVEREND steers JOE away and exits with him.*

*SLAV and CHIP step on the tracks and look after KITTY.*

**CHIP** I'll never forget my father's grave and I only saw it once, when we buried him with the others. Two rows like a double set of tracks that went on and on, salted with snow, just like today, except it was June. My mother could never look back.

*CHIP and SLAV stop at CHIP's mother's headstone, a ritual. CHIP polishes it.*

**SLAV** Yet your mother brings you here. Another mining town.

**CHIP** She thought she could keep me out of the mines. But Slav, what is it, that magnetic pull? Pulling me in.

**SLAV** It's in the blood, maybe. Your father, my father, both miners. All we know is mining.

*The MINER appears.*

**MINER** You start young, get your pit sense. Pick your friends and keep them. Time each move to the rhythms of dark. The mine melts the fat from your bones so your body fits in small pockets of space, sprung-ready to jump back when the rock falls. You work slow and steady, so you can work just as well the next day and the next.

**CHIP** And the next.

*The MINER nods and exits.*

**SLAV** What, next?

**CHIP** What about our sons?

**SLAV** I don't want Yanusz to work in the mine.

**CHIP** I feel the same about Mike.

**SLAV** But then, we just go to a funeral.

**CHIP** We go to a lot of funerals.

*CHIP and SLAV exit.*

## Scene Three – Guest Appearance

*Two HELPERS are on their knees with their picks, keeping their heads clear of the roof in the cramped space they work. CHIP brings SIR Montague BARLOW into the room to meet the men, who stay down on their knees and keep alert to the roof at all times. SIR BARLOW must remove his top hat to clear the roof.*

**SIR BARLOW** My wife calls this place the valley of desolation. She's quite unimpressed by the quality of the air.

**CHIP** I don't think any of the women ever get used to the dust. It gets into everything. Hey, boys?

**HELPER ONE** Sandwiches don't taste right without dust in 'em.

**HELPER TWO** Never had 'em without dust in 'em.

**SIR BARLOW** Is it all right if I ask the men a few questions?

**CHIP** Go right ahead. The mine owner said to give you the cook's tour. Boys, Sir Barlow here is doing a Royal Commission on the state of coal mining in the province of Alberta. He's visiting all the mine sites and he's gathering information for his report. He's got a few questions for you.

**SIR BARLOW** Right, then. I'd like to ask how you feel about the irregular, seasonal nature of the job.

**HELPER ONE** I looks at it this way, sir. Half a loaf is better than no loaf.

**HELPER TWO** Even when it's coated in coal dust.

**SIR BARLOW** The Drumheller Coal Operators have submitted several requests, including better training and the eight-hour day. What are your thoughts on that?

**HELPER ONE** Quicker you can get us to the face, the better. The more I work, the more money I make.

**SIR BARLOW** I see. And you?

**HELPER TWO** Watch your back, there, sir.

**SIR BARLOW** My back.

**HELPER TWO** Roof's getting saggy.

**CHIP** Maybe we should move on, sir. I'll show you the new mechanized cutter we've got just down the corridor here.

*CHIP and SIR BARLOW exit.*

**HELPER ONE** I heard he's got his wife, an assistant and a personal secretary with him, travelling the province for six months. When they go up to Edmonton, they stay at the Macdonald Hotel.

**HELPER TWO** Thinks he can improve us. Ha. Another Aberhart plan.

**HELPER ONE** Asking everyone for ways to reform the job. Just watch, he'll write a big long book about it and no one will read it.

**HELPER TWO** At least he comes down here to see for himself. I've never seen the mine owner underground.

*CHIP and SIR BARLOW enter. SIR BARLOW is bleeding from the head.*

**CHIP** Just hold it tight there, sir!

**SIR BARLOW** Do you not have hard hats here for the men? The mountain mines are fully equipped.

**CHIP** Extra expense. Some of the men don't like them.

**SIR BARLOW** But why? Being knocked on the head with falling chunks of sharp rock must surely be an incentive?

**HELPER ONE** Soft hats help you feel the roof, sir. Need to feel her to know when she'll fall.

**SIR BARLOW** I am fully amazed.

**CHIP** Maybe we should head up to the doc, now.

**SIR BARLOW** Yes, my wife will chide me to no end for this. Bloody hell! These Drumheller miners are a rare breed indeed.

*CHIP and SIR BARLOW exit. The HELPERS walk off into the dark.*

## Scene Four – Railway Station

*The MINE OWNER checks his watch.*

*The sound of a train approaching is heard.*

*A HOBO jumps off the car into the station, lingers, and watches the following.*

*The sound of another train stopping is heard. A GREENHORN gets off, carrying a potato sack full of clothes.*

**GREENHORN** Hey, is this the Drumheller stop?

**MINE OWNER** Yes, siree. Where are you headed?

**GREENHORN** Looking for mining work. Hear there's dozens of mines here.

**MINE OWNER** Some are better than others. Some are just gopher holes.

**GREENHORN** Could you give me some names?

**MINE OWNER** Do better than that. My mine is just down the track. Get back on the train, get off at the next stop and get yourself a place in the bunkhouse. You can start work tomorrow, in the tipple.

**GREENHORN** What's the tipple?

**MINE OWNER** It's where you sort the coal by size: lumps, eggs, nuts and peas.

**GREENHORN** Wow. You're making me hungry.

**MINE OWNER** I only put honest young men like you on that job. It's the last step before the market. The best place for you!

**GREENHORN** Thank you, sir!

**MINE OWNER** Talk to the pit boss. Give him my card. Tell him I hand picked you.

**GREENHORN** Wait 'til I write them at home! Less than two minutes in Drumheller and I've got a job. Do I need a union card, sir?

**MINE OWNER** No. No union men at my mine.

**GREENHORN** My father told me to make sure I joined a union out here.

**MINE OWNER** At the union mines, someone has to die first before there's an opening.

**GREENHORN** Is that right?

**MINE OWNER** That's a fact. Has been for all the Hungry Thirties.

**GREENHORN** But you've got jobs.

**MINE OWNER** I just got some new orders, big ones, and I need eager new starters like you. To use the phrase of Mr. Emerson, to "make Canada as warm as Calcutta."

**GREENHORN** Wow. Mr. Emerson. Calcutta.

**MINE OWNER** Training's all included. There's ten cents for your ticket. Next stop east.

*The sound of the train whistle.*

**GREENHORN** Next stop! Thank you, sir!

*The GREENHORN runs off.*

*The HOBO startles the MINE OWNER. The HOBO is a woman, which goes unnoticed by the MINE OWNER.*

**HOBO** Got anything for a tired traveller?

**MINE OWNER** I got jobs.

**HOBO** Oh, I'm not here for long.

**MINE OWNER** Where are you going?

**HOBO** Thought I'd sample the valley hospitality down at the pool hall.

**MINE OWNER** Why don't you take a job, man?

**HOBO** Don't have any tools. No clothes. No boots.

**MINE OWNER** Can't you go on Relief and get started?

**HOBO** Been gambling too long, mister.

**MINE OWNER** Mining work is good, hard work.

**HOBO** Dirty and dangerous.

**MINE OWNER** It must be better than riding the rails, living on a bed of foxtails in the corner of a railway car.

**HOBO** I'll take my chances.

**MINE OWNER** You just threw one away here.

**HOBO** I don't think so. Look at this valley. Yella with smoke. Dirt and dust valley, I'd call it.

**MINE OWNER** You're mistaken about this valley. There's a boom going on here. Ten thousand people in five years!

**HOBO** Everywhere else, they call it the Depression.

**MINE OWNER** That's just a temporary setback. People still need to stay warm in the winter and preserve their garden harvest in the fall.

**HOBO** If there is a harvest this year. Mighty dry everywhere I've been.

**MINE OWNER** Too many years in a row.

*KITTY enters, sends a look of recognition to the MINE OWNER and hurries off to catch the train.*

**HOBO** Even the ladies of ease are leaving town, huh? It's going to take something big to turn this around, mister.

**MINE OWNER** Oh, it's coming all right. Sooner than you think.

*Music.*

*The MINE OWNER meets CHIP and ANNA on his way out, and they make way for each other with icy cordiality. The HOBO stops CHIP and gets directions to the pool hall before exiting.*

*SLAV enters alone with his potato sack of clothes.*

*The sound of the train whistle as the music stops.*

## Scene Five – World War II

*CHIP searches for SLAV. ANNA sees him first and runs to him.*

**ANNA** Why do you have to do this?

**SLAV** To prove that I am not an enemy and not an alien.

**ANNA** So you must risk your life?

**SLAV** That is what all the others, the natives they call themselves, are doing. All the men are going.

**CHIP** Mostly single men. Not fathers with children.

**SLAV** I go so nobody points a finger at my children.

**ANNA** It is not right that you should have this obligation.

**SLAV** Canada is my country. I must fight for her.

**ANNA** And what about me, Slav?

**SLAV** You'll see. The women will respect you more if I go.

**ANNA** This is about pride.

**SLAV** So what?

**ANNA** You are so proud.

**SLAV** I will not be called an enemy alien ever again.

**CHIP** You are one of the best miners in the valley. No one considers you an outsider.

**ANNA** So many nationalities are living here in peace. I still speak Russian, Hungarian, Czech, Polish, Ukrainian every day! Let this go, Slav. Let us stay together, as a family.

**SLAV** No. I cannot stay. It would be bad for all of us. Besides, the mines are hardly working enough for us to live on.

**CHIP** That's going to change soon.

**SLAV** It always changes. Like the wind. I do not depend on the wind.

**ANNA** We have little, but it is enough. We are happy. I don't complain.

**SLAV** You are a strong woman. You will manage without me.

**ANNA** My hands may manage, but my heart will break.

**SLAV** It is not forever. Be happy you are not in Poland!

**ANNA** I pray you come back to me. But not like I say every day you go to the mine. This is different.

**SLAV** I know. I am not afraid. I promise, I will be back.

**CHIP** As soon as you can.

**ANNA** Oh!

*SLAV and ANNA embrace and then part at the station. SLAV exits. CHIP takes ANNA off.*

## Scene Six – Fire Bossing

*The sound of the end-of-work whistle.*

*The MINER appears.*

**MINER** The fire boss is responsible for all explosives, inside and outside of the mine.

*The PIT BOSS stops CHIP, who is carrying a Cardox shell, in the office.*

**PIT BOSS** Hey, Chip, how did that new Cardox shell work?

**MINER** Never use a short fuse.

**CHIP** Really good. You just gotta stay clear when the shell blows out of the face. One blew a hole clean through a metal boxcar. But we got a lot more lump coal with the Cardox. And no smell, eh? The men really like that. No waiting. Just blast and start loading right away.

**PIT BOSS** Good.

**MINER** Never light two or more shots at the same time.

**CHIP** I think you could sell this idea to all the mines around here.

**PIT BOSS** We're going to build a compressor station to fill the shells with compressed carbon dioxide right on site.

**MINER** Never return to a shot after it has failed to explode until at least ten minutes after it is lit.

**CHIP** The only problem I can see with these shells is if you get a dud. You're waiting and waiting and she doesn't blow. And you don't want to be in her path, in case she blasts late. Like I said, one of these could put a hole straight through you!

**MINER** Never take permissible explosives into the mine on man trips.

**PIT BOSS** Then we'll have to make sure we have good quality control. The last thing we need is flying bullets in the mine. There's enough of that going on in the war.

*CHIP nods to the MINER and exits with the shell.*

## Scene Seven – Army Camp

*The SERGEANT's voice calls out to the ranks.*

**SERGEANT** *(voice-over)* Any men here who are coal miners by trade are asked to step out of line! (*SLAV steps out.*) You men are to report back to your mining towns and get back to work immediately for the good of the war effort. The war needs coal, and lots of it, for the army, the railway, the nation and the factories manufacturing weapons of war.

**SLAV** Excuse me, Sergeant, sir, are all the coal miners going back?

**SERGEANT** *(voice-over)* Yes.

**SLAV** So, there is no dishonour.

**SERGEANT** *(voice-over)* Absolutely not. This is war and everyone has a job to do. Coal mining has been declared an essential wartime service. We need our experienced men in the mines for maximum production and delivery of coal for the war.

**SLAV** So, the mines will work full time?

**SERGEANT** *(voice-over)* We've put in orders for massive amounts of coal. The faster you get home, the faster we'll get it and the faster we can win this war.

*SLAV salutes before he exits.*

## Scene Eight – Home Again

*SLAV runs to ANNA, who hands him his lunch bucket and miners' hat before he runs off to the hills.*

*HATTIE joins ANNA.*

**HATTIE** Thank God for the coal.

**ANNA** For King and country. I have never seen Slav so happy.

**HATTIE** I just hope this means we won't have any more strikes.

**ANNA** Now they have the war to talk about. They can work and talk about the war. They can talk about the war all they want.

**HATTIE** All we have to do now is keep our sons out of it.

**ANNA** Yanusz wants to be a farmer. But he wants to go to university first. Slav asks, why does a farmer need to go to school? Buy land and work hard, he says. I tell him to go up to the prairie, to the country dances, and find a good farm girl for a wife.

**HATTIE** A girl used to hard work.

**ANNA** Like us!

**HATTIE** What is it today, pickles or cabbages?

**ANNA** I think pickles.

**HATTIE** The kids can sweep grain cars today. I want to fatten up those chickens!

**ANNA** Bring your dill. I've got the garlic! Bring some little carrots to put in, if you want. And tomorrow we better start on your tomatoes!

*ANNA exits. CHIP enters and HATTIE hands him his lunch bucket.*

**HATTIE** I put in some extra. In case you go double shift again. There's lots to share around if you have to.

**CHIP** Good. Might happen again today. I wish I could find a few more diggers.

**HATTIE** Hey, Chip, what about Mike?

**CHIP** Our Mike?

**HATTIE** He wants to work after school, just like you did. I think he'd like to work with you.

**CHIP** No. I told him, no. He's just a kid.

**HATTIE** He's the same age as you were when you started. He'd just like to earn some money.

**CHIP** Then I'll pay him to stay away from the mine.

**HATTIE** But why, Chip?

**CHIP** Well, you taught him just like you said you would, and look how smart he is. He could do anything.

**HATTIE** He will do something, we all know that. But earning some extra pocket money, there's nothing wrong with that.

**CHIP** He should be playing hockey in his spare time.

**HATTIE** You don't want him anywhere near the mine.

**CHIP** No, I don't. Do you?

**HATTIE** I know he'd be safe if he was with you.

**CHIP** Every day, I watch my friends go off in different directions of the dark. I always think of my father going off like that, silent and sure-footed.

*The MINER appears, lights his lamp, nods and heads off down to the mine. CHIP watches him depart, slowly, through the dark.*

**HATTIE** Your father. You've always felt closer to him in the mine.

**CHIP** It's one thing thinking about my father in the mine, but watching my own son walk away in the dark like that, alone with his little lamp, that would be real. And I couldn't do that, Hattie. I just couldn't.

**HATTIE** Maybe that's how your mother felt, without your father there to watch over you.

**CHIP** Maybe. Maybe I'm just starting to understand that. If Mike goes in the mine, I'd be taking my worries underground. I couldn't do my job. Something inside me would die.

**HATTIE** How will we tell him that?

**CHIP** I'll start paying Mike an allowance and we'll make it his college fund.

**HATTIE** What about Jenny?

**CHIP** The same goes for her. She gets the same chance.

*HATTIE hugs him goodbye and runs off.*

## Scene Nine – Progress

*CHIP stops the MINE OWNER in the office.*

**CHIP** What about the new battery lamps for the miners?

**MINE OWNER** I guess we're going to have to do something about that.

**CHIP** The mountain mines switched over from the open flame lamps years ago.

**MINE OWNER** Well, they've got more gas.

**CHIP** But that last blast here, three guys killed? That would not have happened with battery lamps.

**MINE OWNER** That's what the inspector said.

**CHIP** So did he recommend the battery lamps or did he order it?

**MINE OWNER** He ordered it. It's just going to be expensive.

**CHIP** I don't want to lose any more men, sir. It's got to be done.

**MINE OWNER** We'll have to set up the battery charger in the new lamp house, and the men will hand in their lamps at the end of each shift, and pick them up the next day with their tags.

**CHIP** Will the miners pay for each battery charge?

**MINE OWNER** The same as they paid for their carbide!

**CHIP** Some of the miners, the ones from the Pass, say that the battery lamps don't give as much glow as open flame, but I'm not listening to that. The safer we make this mine, the more we can produce.

**MINE OWNER** And productivity is progress. We've got good orders coming in, from the United States even, but we need an edge over the other coal companies.

**CHIP** We've got the best ball team.

**MINE OWNER** We better.

**CHIP** We've got experienced mining men willing to take the night shift just for the chance to work here. We'll be able to fill that third shift on the cutting machines in no time.

**MINE OWNER** We're going to go full blast, Chip! We'll mine that twelve-foot seam all the way to Horseshoe Canyon! We've got a long way to go to get out all that coal and leave the other mines in the dust!

*The MINE OWNER exits.*

**CHIP** Dust. It all comes down to dust. Dust that burns.

*The MINER comes up out of the mine.*

**MINER** Breathe it and eat it and wear it, like a badge of honour.

**CHIP** The dirtier the better.

**MINER** Like a pledge between a brotherhood.

**CHIP** Makes the face of every man in the dark of the mine just like the face of the next man.

**MINER** Dust is the great equalizer.

**CHIP** And at the end of the day, we wash it all off.

**MINER** Not all of it.

**CHIP** The rest we wash down with beer while we go on loading coal in the bar.

*The MINER smiles and retreats.*

## Scene Ten – The Bar

*CHIP, JOE and SLAV are at the bar.*

**CHIP** · How did you do today, Slav?

**SLAV** I got my eight tons. One for me, one for Anna and one for each of the children.

**CHIP** What about you, Joe? How many places did you cut today?

**JOE** Ten.

**CHIP** Really?

**JOE** Oh, yeah.

**SLAV** Wait a minute. Me ten, too. I do extra. I forgot.

**JOE** If you got ten tons, I got fourteen places.

**SLAV** Yeah! You big liar.

**JOE** I always get a few more than you. You're practically a senior citizen!

**SLAV** Yeah, and it will be me digging your grave.

**JOE** By hand.

**SLAV** I like working pick and shovel. I like to hear the roof.

**JOE** Machine loaders get the coal out before the roof has a chance to think about coming down.

**CHIP** But she always comes down. Matter of time.

**SLAV** How about you, Chip? How many blasts today?

**CHIP** What?

**SLAV** How many blasts?

**CHIP** Fifty, maybe. My ears are still ringing.

**SLAV** You going to go for pit boss, Chip?

**CHIP** Thinking about it. Yeah, or go deaf.

**SLAV** You're good with the men. That's half the work right there.

**JOE** You got the gas, the roof, the rock pressure, the water, that part is pretty easy.

**CHIP** Something different every day, that's what I like.

**SLAV** But, the men, you can handle them.

**CHIP** I don't like letting the men down. But how much they work depends on orders for the coal.

**SLAV** They have good orders now. Three shifts a day and it's only August.

**CHIP** Yeah. But that Pennsylvania bitumite is stealing the eastern markets. And the Canadian government won't listen to the union and slap a tariff on it.

**SLAV** Where's the help for miners now, uh? The soldiers, they get free education, and what do we get? *(spits)* Nothing.

**CHIP** And what's going to happen with all this oil? Home heating and cooking are going to change over to gas, just like the railways are switching to diesel.

**JOE** That will be the day. Pff.

**CHIP** I don't know. You ask your wives, would they like to stop shovelling coal and ash?

**SLAV** When we can get coal almost free? Hah!

**CHIP** Here, maybe. But in the cities, they'll convert to gas stoves, and where will we be?

**SLAV** Digging up coal nobody wants. Digging in my garden and using coal for compost.

**CHIP** I think the writing is on the wall. It's good we kept our sons out of the mining business. I wouldn't want to be starting off just to see it shut down.

**SLAV** You really think it's going to shut down?

**CHIP** We've never had this kind of competition before.

**JOE** I don't believe you. There's so much coal in these hills, they can't turn their back on this.

**CHIP** Pumping oil out of the ground is pretty easy next to the workings of a coal mine.

**SLAV** Pump it out like water.

**JOE** I'd like to see that.

**CHIP** If you weren't mining, what else would you do?

**SLAV** Never thought about it.

**CHIP** Think about it.

**JOE** I don't know. I guess I'd go work for the oil companies, if that's where the money's going to be.

**SLAV** Stan, my brother-in-law, he quit mining. Now he works in the briquette plant in Canmore.

**CHIP** How does he like that?

**SLAV** He says, miners, working someplace else, it's like sitting in church with no clothes on.

**JOE** But they got the Japanese contract up in Canmore. They're giving five, six, seven days a week if you want it.

**SLAV** How long is that going to last?

**JOE** What about the electric plants? They need piles of coal.

**CHIP** They're starting up some surface mining up by Edmonton. Not as good as our coal, but the electric company doesn't care.

**JOE** No way. The Canadian Utilities plant here takes our coal.

**CHIP** Instead of loading coal by the ton, they'll load coal by the acre.

**JOE** Ha! I could handle that. An acre to your ton any day.

**SLAV** This is not good, Chip, what you say.

**CHIP** I'm going to try to make sure the company keeps the oldest guys. Younger guys have a better chance of doing something new.

*SLAV and JOE look at each other.*

That's the part I won't like about being pit boss.

**JOE** Gentlemen, let us dissolve the dust.

**SLAV** I need another Pilsner.

*ANNA and HATTIE enter.*

**ANNA** No, you don't.

**SLAV** Aw? I turn to cement inside. *(coughs)* So much dust. One more?

**ANNA** Time to go home. No more.

**SLAV** You see? No more my own boss.

**ANNA** We go.

*SLAV and ANNA exit, ANNA five paces ahead of SLAV.*

**HATTIE** How about a little hill-climb?

**CHIP** Sure. You okay on your own, Joe?

**JOE** Yeah. I've got class. Mine rescue training.

**CHIP** You keep that up. Could come in handy wherever you go.

**JOE** Yeah.

**CHIP** And Labour Day competition is coming up. You're going to win that one for us again, hey Joe?

**JOE** You bet.

**CHIP** Good stuff.

*JOE exits.*

## Scene Eleven – Hill Climb

*HATTIE and CHIP are in the hills. CHIP has trouble keeping up as he coughs.*

**HATTIE** Are you okay, Chip?

**CHIP** When I can't climb for coughing, you'll know I'm crusted up and ready for the box.

**HATTIE** What I want to know is when are you going to be ready for retirement?

**CHIP** What's the point of that?

**HATTIE** We could do this every day. Like we used to, when we were courting.

**CHIP** I do love the hug of these hills. I wonder if the kids will miss them.

**HATTIE** They'll be back. This is where they grew up.

**CHIP** Maybe they'll come home to visit, but not to stay. We sent fifty million tons of coal out of this valley, and we sent our children out with it.

**HATTIE** Kids have to find their own path, Chip. Calgary's not that far away. And we know lots of other people there, now.

**CHIP** I knew it. Every time you bring me up here, you've got a plan.

**HATTIE** Oh, Chip, so much has changed. It's just not the same with everyone moving off.

**CHIP** I miss the people, too.

**HATTIE** Ghost towns up and down the valley.

**CHIP** Tipples torn down, equipment hauled off. Just the red shale to mark where the mines were.

**HATTIE** Not much left. Stores, schools, hospital, all gone.

**CHIP** I want to stay.

**HATTIE** I want to move.

**CHIP** I knew this was coming.

**HATTIE** You're worse than a mule.

**CHIP** It's my instinct for self-preservation. Miner's habit. No one can make me go a way I distrust.

**HATTIE** Like your old pit pony.

**CHIP** Now, she was worse than a mule.

**HATTIE** Chip. I could never leave these hills. But we should move to Drumheller, like everyone else. We need a comfortable place for when the kids and their families and our friends come back for visits. And for when you retire.

**CHIP** Okay, we'll move to town. But I'm not retiring. Not yet.

**HATTIE** If that day ever comes, you'll be the last man in the mine.

*HATTIE walks off ahead and CHIP meets SLAV, who gives him an old miner's pick and hat.*

**SLAV** It will be a relic soon. Old enough for the museum. Like me.

**CHIP** We're closing the last mine this year. Good thing you got out of it when you did.

**SLAV** Yeah. I'd rather be buried on the prairie. More sunshine!

**CHIP** All that fresh air. I don't know how good that can be. Makes me cough!

**SLAV** I get used to it, just like my son, the farmer with a university degree!

**CHIP** He will be a success. It's good land. You're good people. Salt of the earth.

**SLAV** Come see us after you close the mine.

*ANNA comes to say goodbye. HATTIE brings the willow basket for her.*

**HATTIE** For your new house. Bread, so you will never be hungry; salt, so you will always be strong; and wine, so you will have joy.

**ANNA** You come to the farm and visit us soon.

**HATTIE** I hope so.

**ANNA** Slav will like to show off his land, a little piece of Canada that he owns. And me, well, soon there will be grandchildren on the farm and I will be content.

**HATTIE** Goodbye, Anna.

**ANNA** If you could do it all again…

**HATTIE** I wouldn't change a thing.

**ANNA** Me, too. Goodbye, Hattie.

*HATTIE and ANNA exit opposite ways. SLAV follows ANNA.*

## Scene Twelve – The Miner in Black

*CHIP descends down to the black. He's an older, slower man now. A light approaches. THE MINER appears.*

**MINER** They're all gone.

**CHIP** There will never be men like that again. Men you could always count on to lend a strong hand.

**MINER** Working shoulder to shoulder, seam to seam.

**CHIP** I'm going to miss it all. Over fifty years, for me.

**MINER** You did good.

**CHIP** Every man trip down to the face. Every well-squared room, every neat blast. Making every move count, working with men who kept their tools sharp and never left a job undone. All of us working to get those black breasts of coal down and loaded up. And before you know it, quitting time, getting hoisted up at the end of the shift, reborn to the noise of life. The smell of the slag pile burning slow on the surface. The fresh air making you cough up the coal dust, and heading to the wash house to hose off.

**MINER** You know what to do. Now it's up to you.

**CHIP** So, now it's up to me.

*CHIP takes a roll of dynamite and starts laying the line.*

**MINER** Listen. Listen to the mine. Listen to her, getting ready for bed under a black blanket of coal that spreads for miles and miles, layers and layers. Feel the hush of the air, the quiet cushion of the walls, the tight roof. She's going to sleep now. Deep under the footfalls of the miners who came and went. Right that there.

**CHIP** Right, that there.

*As CHIP goes to leave, line in one hand, the MINER takes his hat off, flame still burning, and leaves it. The lights fade to black.*

*Music.*

*The End.*

# Kabloona Talk

By Sharon Pollock

# About
# Sharon Pollock

Sharon Pollock is one of Canada's best-known women playwrights. Produced nationally and internationally, author of a large and varied canon, she has had a long and illustrious career in the theatre. From backstage to onstage, from front of house to director's chair, from actor to author, from teacher and mentor to artistic director of venues both large and small, Sharon Pollock remains an active, controversial and prolific participant in the Canadian theatre scene.

Her plays include *Blood Relations* and *Doc*, for both of which she has received Governor General's Awards, *Whiskey Six Cadenza*, *Fair Liberty's Call*, *Moving Pictures*, *End Dream* and *Angel's Trumpet*. Three volumes of her collected works, edited by Cynthia Zimmerman, are published by Playwrights Canada Press.

*Kabloona Talk*, presented in association with Stuck in a Snowbank Theatre, Yellowknife, was given a staged reading on November 6, 2005 as part of Theatre Alberta and Alberta Playwrights' Network PlayWorks Ink Festival 2005. The reading was at the Glenbow Museum, Calgary, with the following company:

| | |
|---|---|
| JUDGE | Larry Reese |
| PROSECUTOR | Joe-Norman Shaw |
| DEFENCE | Peter Strand Rumpel |
| SMITH | Grant Reddick |

Director and Research Assistance: Ben Nind
Stage Manager: Laura Parken

## Acknowledgements

*Kabloona Talk* was commissioned by Stuck in a Snowbank Theatre, Yellowknife, Artistic Director Ben Nind, with the support of the Canada Council for the Arts and Alberta Playwrights' Network.

## Characters

SMITH
The JUDGE
The PROSECUTOR
The DEFENCE

## Time

Edmonton, Alberta. August 17, 1917. Early afternoon.

## Place

The Provincial Courthouse.

## Setting

A room somewhat claustrophobic as a result of its furnishings, but furnishings and anyone within the room are dwarfed by the extremely high ceilings, eight-foot-high doorways, with any windows of a scale proportionate to the doorways and ceiling height. A key is in the door's lock. Furnishings include a liquor cabinet and a couple of comfortable plush armchairs. Draperies and upholstery are of a rich jewel-like colour. There is a strong impression of the vertical sweeping upwards toward heaven, if heaven there be.

A rectangular, utilitarian (say two and a half by seven feet) table of light-coloured wood sits in the middle of the room. The table is constructed with a slight rake. It looks sterile, out of place in this room, as indeed it is a most recent addition and will be removed once this meeting is over. There is nothing on the table; the expanse of bare, barren tabletop and its rake make its area appear greater than it actually is. Five utilitarian chairs accompanying the table are stacked to one side.

It might seem as if aspects of a royal anteroom, and a church basement's table and chairs have intersected.

# Kabloona Talk

## Act One

*It is a short time after the Jury has announced its verdict in The Crown vs. Sinnisiak case. The public is still milling about and dispersing; officers of the Court are leaving the Court Room.*

*Sound of a crowd of murmuring and excited voices. No specific words can be made out. The crowd is fairly close but is slowly moving away.*

*Light reveals SMITH standing by the door. The door is open; he has just entered the room. He looks the perfect upper level bureaucrat, well and expensively dressed, a summer overcoat over one arm, a hat in his hand, a sleek and somewhat severe cut to his suit. He wears a neutral expression although he appears to be listening to, and evaluating, the crowd's murmur. He radiates stillness, blandness and anonymity. In one hand a rusted .44 Winchester rifle. Under his arm a box marked "Crown vs. Sinnisiak."*

*SMITH shuts the door and any sound of the crowd dies away, followed by a few moments of silence.*

*SMITH puts the rifle and box on the table. He lays his coat down draping it carefully, placing his hat precisely on the coat. He returns to the rifle, hefts it assessing its weight and puts it down on the table. He opens the box. He removes a bloodstained priest's cassock, looks at the inside of the collar. He reads the name written in the back of the collar.*

**SMITH** *(His lips move; his voice is close to inaudible.)* Père… Rouvière O.M.I.

*He removes a few disintegrating pages from the box, scans them for a moment, lays them on the table; removes a human lower jawbone with teeth, studies it for a moment, puts it on the table. He gazes out into space, momentary silence and stillness. He pulls out his pocket watch, snaps it open, checks the time and snaps it shut, returning it to his pocket. Another brief moment, then he moves to the liquor cabinet, his back to us, pours a drink, drinks it, his back still turned to us.*

*The JUDGE enters. He is wearing his robes. He takes in SMITH who glances at the JUDGE but doesn't acknowledge him except for that brief glance. The JUDGE shuts the door. He takes in the items on the table.*

**JUDGE** What's this… what're these doing here?… Who authorized this?

*SMITH looks from his drink to the JUDGE again, but says nothing.*

You know you need proper authorization to—

*SMITH sips his drink.*

Yes. Well… I suppose you have it… in a manner of speaking.

*SMITH does not reply. He finishes his drink, goes to the stack of chairs, lifts one off, places it at the table as the JUDGE gets himself a drink.*

A surprising verdict, wouldn't you say?… Actually more than surprising…. But you never know, do you.

I thought we had a jury of six citizens, good and true. Well…. Hmmn. That was an error in judgment.

*The JUDGE's tiny chuckle elicits no response from SMITH.*

You want one? *(referring to his drink)* …No?…

Sad day for Edmonton – and a worse one for justice. Well, God help the North and anyone who goes there.

*SMITH removes a folded telegram from the inside chest pocket of his suit. It has a red diagonal slash across one corner with the words "Official and Confidential." He places it on the table in front of the chair he has placed at the table, a non-verbal command to sit and read.*

*The JUDGE pointedly ignores the implied directive to sit but acknowledges the telegram.*

Official, eh?… And – unofficial is my guess. Neither, and both. No doubt covering any, and all, eventualities.

*SMITH responds with a flicker of a smile and taps the table twice.*

Oh, I'm not disagreeing… something must be done.

*He picks up the telegram. SMITH takes the JUDGE's unfinished drink and returns the glass to the liquor cabinet. The JUDGE notices this but turns his attention to the telegram. He unfolds it and reads.*

*As the JUDGE is reading, a voice blares outside the room; the specific words can't be made out. The PROSECUTOR, still in his robes, opens the door as he continues speaking to an unseen someone in the hallway.*

**PROSECUTOR** That's good advice, sir, I'll consider it! Thank you! Much appreciated! *(shutting the door and speaking to the JUDGE)* Did you hear that?

**JUDGE** Hear what?

**PROSECUTOR** Those "few suggestions" from that condescending Yankee lawyer. The one who's been "observing the proceedings." Aisle seat! On the right? Four rows back, eagle eyes, pigeon chest, donkey bray of a voice?

A few suggestions, my ass. *(sees SMITH and in a low voice asks the JUDGE)*

Was he in court?

**JUDGE** Just arrived. More or less.

**PROSECUTOR** That was quick. What's all this? *(as he takes in the table and items on it)*

*The JUDGE is about to pass the telegram to the PROSECUTOR whose attention is on the table, but catching a look from SMITH he transfers the action, giving the telegram back to SMITH instead who returns it to his own pocket. The end of this transfer is noticed by the PROSECUTOR.*

Is – that something I should know about?

**JUDGE** In time.

**PROSECUTOR** In time? And how much should I know?

**JUDGE** Not now.

**PROSECUTOR** When?

**JUDGE** Later.

**PROSECUTOR** Later?

**JUDGE** Correct. Before, you were asking about? *(a vague gesture at the table and its items)*

**PROSECUTOR** I wasn't asking anything. What I'm thinking? Now that's another matter.

**JUDGE** Which is?

**PROSECUTOR** You know as well as I do.

**JUDGE** Do I?

**PROSECUTOR** We both heard the Defence's address to the Jury. How would you gauge it?

**JUDGE** Undeniably effective.

**PROSECUTOR** Horse manure! It was sentimental and emotional.

**JUDGE** But effective.

**PROSECUTOR** All right, effective! But I lay that at the jury's door. Six men I formerly respected, six men I know personally, for God's sake.

**JUDGE** Yes.

**PROSECUTOR** And these pillars of the community, chosen for their intelligence and clear heads—what do they do?

**JUDGE** I was as surprised as you were.

**PROSECUTOR** They listen to some – some – words fail me—

**JUDGE** Yes.

**PROSECUTOR** The point is they accepted the Defence's argument. His – his—

**JUDGE** You're thinking legal chicanery?

**PROSECUTOR** Trickery!

**JUDGE** Could be called fallacious and irrelevant argument?

**PROSECUTOR** Whatever we care to call it, they were swayed by it. We can't deny that.

**JUDGE** Most unfortunate.

**PROSECUTOR** The jury ignored your charge for God's sake!

**JUDGE** Most regrettable.

**PROSECUTOR** That's all you have to say? "Most regrettable"? "Most unfortunate"? They deliberately disregarded instruction from the Bench!

**JUDGE** My charge was clear.

**PROSECUTOR** Not clear enough, apparently!

**JUDGE** Yes, well you're upset.

**PROSECUTOR** Oh, brilliant deduction, M'Lord. And who would not be?

**JUDGE** We all are, no one's denying that.

**PROSECUTOR** Why so calm then? You do understand don't you? The jury has taken just one hour to ignore a judge's charge and instructions, the evidence and the law!

**JUDGE** It would seem so.

**PROSECUTOR** They've set a savage free. Acquitted him in the clearest case of murder I've ever prosecuted.

**JUDGE** Still, we do have options.

**PROSECUTOR** What options? This Eskimo Sinnisiak tells us he shot an unarmed Catholic priest in the back while the man was running away!

**JUDGE** Ye-es.

**PROSECUTOR** And a jury of six supposedly intelligent men have set this savage free to take God knows what message back to his people.

**JUDGE** Yes.

**PROSECUTOR** And I can tell you what that message is. Open season on whites. That's it. And you tell me there're options? There are no options.

**JUDGE** There're always options.

**PROSECUTOR** Forget your options. Just tell me this. What was the reasoning in the jury room?

*The JUDGE starts to speak, the PROSECUTOR continues.*

And forget the law! I know the law. They tossed that out the window. But what were they thinking? What on earth was in their minds?

*An elated DEFENCE, in robes and in a celebratory mood, stands in the doorway catching part of this.*

**DEFENCE** I'd guess "Not Guilty"! And I'd say congratulations are in order, the line forms to the right!… well to the Right…. A celebratory drink perhaps? *(seeing the table and its items)* Oh oh, something's in the wind. A closing party with hors d'oeuvres yet to arrive? You shouldn't have.

**PROSECUTOR** We didn't.

**DEFENCE** Nevertheless, I'll partake of some liquid refreshment. Who'll join me? *(as he moves to the liquor cabinet)*

*The JUDGE shuts the door; no one steps forward to join the DEFENCE. SMITH will slip a small leather-covered notebook from his pocket and briefly refer to it.*

**PROSECUTOR** We were just discussing the verdict.

**DEFENCE** I heard. At least a bit of your discussion. But the jury's spoken, the trial is over, gentlemen. Brandy all 'round?

**PROSECUTOR** Not for me, thank you.

**DEFENCE** I know you, you crave a brandy, I can see it in your eyes.

*The DEFENCE sets about the pouring of drinks.*

**PROSECUTOR** Well, this time you read me wrong.

**DEFENCE** Come on. Let's have no poor losers here. Think of cricket, country and Kipling.

**JUDGE** I suggest we leave cricket and Kipling out of it.

**DEFENCE** It's not win or lose, it's how you play the game? Isn't that Kipling?

*The DEFENCE passes the PROSECUTOR a glass of brandy, which he accepts.*

**PROSECUTOR** It's not a game – a fact, along with others, that you may not sufficiently appreciate.

**DEFENCE** Facts not sufficiently appreciated? Well now, that's a statement true of one of us. Acquittal, sir! Not guilty! That's a fact. It restores my faith in man.

**PROSECUTOR** Yes, and I've lost mine.

**DEFENCE** Could this be yours, Judge? *(holding up the JUDGE's unfinished drink)* Surely not. There's some still in it.

**JUDGE** Thank you. *(holding out his hand for the glass)*

**DEFENCE** There must be *(holding up the glass)* a quarter of an inch here. I've never known you to leave a drop undrained before. Feeling a bit off, are you?

**JUDGE** An uncouth remark if ever I heard one.

**DEFENCE** What else can you expect? I'm a poor country boy from the West. Wheat paid for Osgoode, and there I passed Law but failed Breeding. Still, I do what I can. Acquittal, eh Judge. Top it up, shall I?

*He does so and the JUDGE accepts the drink; the DEFENCE turns to SMITH.*

Didn't I see you slip in at the back, sir? Just as the jury gave its verdict? And then whhishh! out again, quick as a bunny. I don't believe we've met.

*SMITH acknowledges this with a flicker of a smile.*

It seems introductions are in order.

**JUDGE** I suppose so.

*A brief pause.*

**DEFENCE** I'm waiting.

**JUDGE** Well—

**DEFENCE** If I may— *(as he removes a note from a pocket)* I'm assuming – and it may be a gross assumption – but if that's the case, my learned colleague here *(the PROSECUTOR)* is sure to raise an objection. And then, I suppose, M'Lord could rule on it – no doubt in the prosecution's favour, M'Lord not wishing to break a well-established practice.

**PROSECUTOR** Ridiculous.

**DEFENCE** Is that an objection to my assumption?

**PROSECUTOR** And disrespectful!

**DEFENCE** And now contempt of court?

**JUDGE** Gentlemen.

**DEFENCE** Gentlemen? I've come up in the world.

**PROSECUTOR** Don't be tiresome, just sit down.

**DEFENCE** But I have yet to state my assumption.

**PROSECUTOR** What's your assumption, get on with it, then sit down and shut up.

**DEFENCE** Oh, a definite lack of decorum!

*The JUDGE bangs the table with his fist a couple of times.*

I feel as if I should make an objection.

**PROSECUTOR** Save the histrionics, there's no jury here.

**DEFENCE** No court room either, yet I see evidentiary items displayed. On whose authority I wonder?

**JUDGE** Proper authority.

**DEFENCE** A bit unusual I'd say. All laid out – the gun, the priest's blood-stained robe, a human jawbone and a few pitiful pages of a diary.

**PROSECUTOR** He's got pity for pages but none for the priest who penned them.

**DEFENCE** What're they doing here?

**JUDGE** Come, gentlemen.

**DEFENCE** I sense no answer is forthcoming, so, on to my assumption.

**PROSECUTOR** At last!

**JUDGE** *(bangs his fist)* Order.

**DEFENCE** I'm assuming this gentleman has something to do with this note *(taking it from a pocket)* furtively passed from the court clerk's clammy hand to mine as I left the court room.

**PROSECUTOR** Another oratorical embellishment?

**DEFENCE** My first thought? It came from some sweet buxom admirer. A secret assignation.

**PROSECUTOR** I'll get the gavel, you can hit him.

**JUDGE** We've serious business here.

**DEFENCE** *(reads from the note)* "Please come directly…" and so on, blah, blah, "Conference Room…" such and such… blah, blah, blah "important matter at hand."

*SMITH has approached as the DEFENCE reads and looks over his shoulder at the note.*

Important matter at hand?

*SMITH takes the note from the DEFENCE's hand.*

Well my hopes are dashed. There's no red-haired buxom sweetie here, no secret assignation— *(SMITH tears the note in pieces.)* Correction. No secret assignation that includes a buxom sweetie—

*SMITH drops the pieces in a wastepaper basket.*

And still no introduction?

**JUDGE** Yes – well – allow me to introduce—

**SMITH** Smith.

**DEFENCE** Smith?

**SMITH** A pleasure, sir. *(They shake hands.)* If that offer of a brandy still stands, I'll take you up on it.

**DEFENCE** Smith, eh? *(moving to get him a drink)* Mister? Smith?

**SMITH** Just Smith.

**DEFENCE** The first name wouldn't happen to be John?

**SMITH** Plain Smith will do.

**DEFENCE** Or the last name Doe?

**SMITH** Simply Smith.

**DEFENCE** I doubt that.

**SMITH** As they say, what's in a name?

**DEFENCE** The very question I'm asking myself.

**SMITH** Might I make a suggestion?

**JUDGE** By all means.

**SMITH** I suggest forgetting all differences, raising our glasses in a toast, then down to business.

**DEFENCE** What business?

**SMITH** First the toast.

**DEFENCE** All right then. To common sense and justice.

**PROSECUTOR** I'll drink to that, though I've not seen much of it today.

**DEFENCE** And to my client's acquittal.

**JUDGE** Must you?

**DEFENCE** Must I what?

**PROSECUTOR** Your "client" shot a fleeing, unarmed, Catholic priest in the back, finished him off with a knife and axe and ate his liver. I don't believe I'll drink to his acquittal.

**DEFENCE** And I believe justice prevailed today, whether you agree with the jury's verdict or not.

**PROSECUTOR** Ah, yes, the jury.

**DEFENCE** You can't complain about the jury.

**PROSECUTOR** Oh, yes, I can. And do.

**DEFENCE** You were happy enough when they were seated. Upstanding citizens, all sons of Solomon, weren't they your words?

**PROSECUTOR** They were not.

**DEFENCE** Or words to that effect. Your happiness knew no bounds – until they delivered their verdict.

**PROSECUTOR** A tainted verdict.

**DEFENCE** Not tainted. Merely not to your liking.

**PROSECUTOR** Tainted! Manipulation of discussion during deliberations in the jury room by one particular individual!

**JUDGE** Speculation, my friend.

**PROSECUTOR** We all know who it is. Meet him on the street, he's aggressive and domineering. Standing in the rain he'd bend your ear and arm 'til you agreed that it was sunny.

**DEFENCE** Jury's deliberations didn't deal with weather, but with a man's life.

**PROSECUTOR** I'm saying this verdict, of which you seem to be so proud, is the result of the jury's arm being twisted by a particular jurist!

**DEFENCE** That particular individual has spent most of his life in the far North, has firsthand knowledge of the land—

**PROSECUTOR** Not my point!

**DEFENCE** Has firsthand knowledge of the land and its people! In fact, a valuable, perhaps most valuable, member of the jury, well qualified to speak on the mindset of the accused, who happens to be a Coppermine Eskimo.

**PROSECUTOR** His motive in acquitting was purely personal!

**DEFENCE** You can't say that.

**PROSECUTOR** I just did. He ran for the local legislature and was defeated. He blames the Bishop from Mackenzie diocese for his defeat. If you don't know that, you're the only man in Edmonton who doesn't know it. He tells anyone who'll listen.

**DEFENCE** What has this to do with the jury's verdict?

**PROSECUTOR** The victim was a Catholic priest! Do I have to draw you a picture?

**DEFENCE** It might help, since I fail to see any other proof of bias.

*SMITH will check his watch and begin to unstack the chairs and place them at the table. The DEFENCE and PROSECUTOR will ignore him, speak 'round him.*

**PROSECUTOR** There's more. I spoke to other jurymen. Two of them.

**DEFENCE** Interesting.

**PROSECUTOR** Both talked about jury discussion and decisions. Based on what? Based on rumour and innuendo!

With a total disregard for evidence and facts presented in court!

**DEFENCE** When?

**PROSECUTOR** And, furthermore, they believed that acquittal would be, and is, the right decision despite this dereliction of proper jury duty.

**DEFENCE** Dereliction of duty?

**PROSECUTOR** By relying on rumour and innuendo! I call that evidence of a tainted, even corrupted, jury.

**DEFENCE** When?

**PROSECUTOR** When what?

**DEFENCE** When did you speak to them?

**PROSECUTOR** To whom?

**DEFENCE** The two jury members!

**PROSECUTOR** What does it matter?

**DEFENCE** It matters to me.

**PROSECUTOR** Just now, on my way down from the court, spoke to what's his name, ah—

**DEFENCE** And?

**PROSECUTOR** And what!

**DEFENCE** And the second juryman?

**PROSECUTOR** What about him?

**DEFENCE** You spoke to him when?

**PROSECUTOR** Wednesday

**DEFENCE** Wednesday? – That would be the second day of the Trial?

**PROSECUTOR** Correct.

**DEFENCE** You saw nothing improper in that?

**PROSECUTOR** It was an accidental meeting.

**DEFENCE** Nothing improper?

**PROSECUTOR** I know the man. It would have been discourteous to pass him by without a word.

**DEFENCE** The prosecutor, during the course of a trial, discussing with a juryman matters pertaining to and arising from the trial? You don't think that's improper?

**PROSECUTOR** Oh, for God's sake. We exchanged a few words and each continued on his way. Nothing improper in it.

**DEFENCE** What do you say, M'Lord?

**PROSECUTOR** You've got your acquittal.

**DEFENCE** A ruling, your Honour.

**PROSECUTOR** What more do you want?

**DEFENCE** I want an acknowledgement that my client, Sinnisiak, a Coppermine Eskimo, was acquitted of the murder of Father Jean Baptiste Rouvière fairly and squarely under the tenets of British Law!

**PROSECUTOR** You won't get that from me.

**DEFENCE** Well, you're a dogmatic fool!

**PROSECUTOR** And you're an equivocating simpleton!

**JUDGE** Both sustained.

**PROSECUTOR** Objection!

**DEFENCE** Absolute objection!

**JUDGE** Agreement at last? *(a brief pause)*

**DEFENCE** ...Right.... Right enough. Agree to disagree. On all but the name-calling.

**PROSECUTOR** Agreed.

**DEFENCE** Thank God. Colleagues, and still friends, of a sort, I hope.

**PROSECUTOR** But you do see the case has implications larger than its specifics.

**DEFENCE** Oh, let it go! You'll have another kick at the can next week.

**SMITH** *(who's been unobtrusively taking it all in)* Excuse me. It's all been most informative. But you refer to?

**DEFENCE** We have two dead priests, Rouvière and Le Roux and two accused, Sinnisiak and his friend Uluksuk.

**SMITH** Yes.

**PROSECUTOR** This trial's dealt with only one victim, Father Rouvière, and one defendant, Sinnisiak, although both Eskimos are charged.

**SMITH** And I understand you have the confessions of both men. They admit, do they not, that they acted together in the killing of Fathers Rouvière and Le Roux?

**PROSECUTOR** They do.

**SMITH** And the Eskimos were not tried jointly?

**PROSECUTOR** My decision. A valid one.

**DEFENCE** Valid or not, no jury will find Uluksuk guilty of Rouvière's murder after Sinnisiak, who's confessed to actually killing Rouvière, has been found innocent. As for Le Roux's death, that was clearly self-defence.

**PROSECUTOR** The point is two priests murdered! And we send the Eskimos who did it back to the North free as the breeze. What do you think this says to their people as to the consequence of killing white men? Or, for that matter, of killing each other?

**JUDGE** Good question.

**DEFENCE** Let's not get into it! Save it for Uluksuk's trial. There's no point in rehashing the Sinnisiak case.

**SMITH** Quite the opposite, my friends.

**DEFENCE** Who exactly are you?

**SMITH** Down to business.

**DEFENCE** What business?

**SMITH** In short, the business, or rehashing, of Rex vs. Sinnisiak—

**DEFENCE** That trial is over!

**SMITH** —and the implications of his acquittal—

**DEFENCE** Do either of you know this man?

*Neither JUDGE nor PROSECUTOR indicates "yes" or "no."*

**SMITH** —followed by *(referring to his notebook)* the creation of a legal strategy for the prosecution of *(referring to his notebook)* Sinnisiak and Uluksuk, two Eskimos charged with the murder of two Oblate priests, Father Rouvière and Father Le Roux, on or about the month of November 1913, at or near Bloody Falls on the Coppermine River in the Northwest Territories.

Shall we begin?

**DEFENCE** Has this man been added to the prosecution's legal team?

*The PROSECUTOR avoids the question.*

Is he here at your invitation, Judge?

*The JUDGE gestures with his hands, which indicates "no" but could possibly mean, "what can I do, it's out of my hands." The DEFENCE believes it's a "no."*

Are you a lawyer, sir?

**SMITH** Please, sit.

**DEFENCE** I take it – not a lawyer. That gives me some consolation. I'd hate to think a member of our profession was so ignorant of double jeopardy. Sinnisiak is innocent of the murder of Father Rouvière.

**SMITH** A clear distinction exists between innocent and not guilty.

**DEFENCE** Distinction or not, he can't be charged again.

**SMITH** Therein lies the rub.

**DEFENCE** Meaning?

**SMITH** And the need for strategy.

**DEFENCE** Strategy? Strategy for what?

**SMITH** As to how best proceed with the legal case against the murderers of Fathers Rouvière and Le Roux.

**DEFENCE** Am I the only one at sea here?

**JUDGE** Please just sit and listen.

**SMITH** I'd appreciate your staying.

**JUDGE** It commits you to nothing.

**SMITH** You see I hadn't the opportunity to attend the trial. Had other commitments in the area—fortunately as it turns out—and a guilty verdict seemed a foregone conclusion.

**DEFENCE** Yes, well there's many a slip twixt the cup and the lip.

**SMITH** As others were well aware. And moved quickly. Thus my presence.

**DEFENCE** And you are—?

**SMITH** Here, with you. Shall we call this a small… assessment and planning session? Your contribution is quite indispensable if I'm to get an accurate picture. However *(moves to the door, opens it a crack and shuts it)* if you wish to leave— *(the key is missing when he turns back from the door)* I'm afraid it's quite impossible… *(seems to drop the key in his pocket)* …Your client's interests dictate your presence.

**DEFENCE** *(to the PROSECUTOR)* And you accuse me of histrionics?

**PROSECUTOR** I'm as much in the dark as you are.

**DEFENCE** You do realize perjury's an indictable offense.

**PROSECUTOR** Oh, sit for God's sake. It's been a long week and I'd like to get home at a decent hour.

**DEFENCE** I could bloody my knuckles, take the key and we can all go home early.

**SMITH** We each must do what each thinks best, given the circumstances.

**JUDGE** What's the harm in listening? You two may be on opposite sides of the fence but surely we can agree this case is of supreme importance.

**DEFENCE** As any case is, to the one accused.

**JUDGE** But this is the first of its kind, the first trial under British Law of two of the North's indigenous primitive peoples. It's of national and international interest, with observers from around the world in court. Are you telling me you don't see this as a seminal legal event?

**DEFENCE** I'm well aware of it.

**JUDGE** For the first time, two Eskimos are charged with the ultimate crime of murder, the murder of two whites, this crime taking place in a great expanse of unexplored Arctic land, the true measure of which is unknown, and over which the Canadian Government is just now extending its Dominion. Do you have any disagreement with this statement?

**DEFENCE** No disagreement factually. Since I don't know where you're going I'm uncertain of its relevance.

**JUDGE** I'm saying we owe it to ourselves, to our community, to King and Country, to at least hear this man out.

**DEFENCE** *(looks at SMITH)* To hear "Smith" out.

**SMITH** I'd appreciate you staying.

**DEFENCE** *(to the PROSECUTOR)* Where do you stand on this?

**PROSECUTOR** I see no harm in listening to what the man says.

**SMITH** In service to your client?

*A brief pause.*

**DEFENCE** Well. Against my better judgment.

**SMITH** If I may—to ensure I understand clearly— *(refers to his notebook for a moment, then puts it away)* Our first victim. Father Rouvière, a member of the Oblates of Mary the Immaculate Order, age early thirties, disposition congenial and affable; in the North four years, before accepting the Bishop's proposal to reach out to the Eskimos on the far side of Great Bear Lake.

**PROSECUTOR** A good man.

**SMITH** Father Rouvière is with us today, a silent witness in his few remaining possessions. *(lifts a page)* Water-soaked and tattered pages of his diary, a last entry written shortly before his death; *(displays the cassock)* a blood-stained cassock, inside the neckband "Père Jean Baptiste Rouvière O.M.I." indelibly written, no doubt by his own hand.

Contradiction?

**DEFENCE** None.

**PROSECUTOR** A gentle man with a sense of humour. Adapted well to life in the Arctic.

**DEFENCE** So, let's get on.

**SMITH** The second victim. Father Guillaume Le Roux, an Oblate priest, a few years younger than Rouvière, highly intelligent and educated, a linguist.

**DEFENCE** True but—

**SMITH** Sent North, to join Rouvière approximately one year before the murders.

**DEFENCE** But nothing like Rouvière.

**SMITH** Disposition irritable, testy, less gracious than Rouvière—

**DEFENCE** Just say it. Le Roux was arrogant, impatient and demanding and—

**PROSECUTOR** You exaggerate.

**DEFENCE** —and the North magnified the most unpleasant aspects of his nature.

**PROSECUTOR** An unfair portrait of the man.

**DEFENCE** Here's the simple truth, Smith. Le Roux's personality gave rise to misinterpretation of his actions within the Eskimo culture and that is crucial to what followed.

**PROSECUTOR** It hardly justifies killing him.

**DEFENCE** It's the crux of the matter.

**PROSECUTOR** It's not the crux of the matter.

**SMITH** At the moment we'll stay with what we know. Le Roux is "less gracious" than Rouvière, as stated by those who knew both men well.

**DEFENCE** So, let's state everything we know. We know conversion of the Eskimos to Catholicism is "not progressing" according to the Bishop.

We know the Protestants and Catholics are in "competition for converts"!

We know the Catholics believe increased contact with the Eskimo will increase conversion!!

We know the Protestants are advancing toward the Eskimos at Coronation Gulf on the Arctic Ocean and the Catholics are hell-bent on getting to them first!!

It's all background. Only background.

What's it got to do with four desperate men stranded near Bloody Falls with too few dogs, low supplies, no game and bad weather?

**SMITH** Not background. Context.

**JUDGE** Context.

**SMITH** Continuing. To increase conversion Rouvière and Le Roux will abandon their cabin to travel with an Eskimo named Kormik and his family, on their annual trek into the Arctic Barrens. This group'll continue down the Coppermine River to Coronation Gulf and the seal hunt well ahead, the priests hope, of the Protestants.

**PROSECUTOR** But you've left out Kormik's relationship with Sinnisiak and Uluksuk.

**DEFENCE** Because it doesn't matter.

**PROSECUTOR** It certainly does.

**SMITH** This relationship was – what?

**DEFENCE** Irrelevant.

**PROSECUTOR** The three men, Uluksuk, Sinnisiak and Kormik were friends, good friends.

**DEFENCE** We don't know that! You've left out this. The Eskimo, Kormik, had lived at the priests' cabin before they left for the Barrens with his family. And Kormik was promised a rifle by the priests for services rendered at the cabin.

**PROSECUTOR** That's what we don't know! It could have been Kormik, it might not have been Kormik living at the cabin. It was "some" Eskimo. No one can tell one from another.

**DEFENCE** No one?

**PROSECUTOR** And we don't know that any rifle was promised to anyone at that time. It is the friendship between Sinnisiak, Uluksuk and Kormik that's important. It suggests premeditation when the two Eskimos killed Rouvière and Le Roux.

**SMITH** Premeditation? *(checks his notebook)*

**DEFENCE** There's no premeditation.

**PROSECUTOR** Evidence suggests it.

**SMITH** What is it we know?

**DEFENCE** We know Kormik was promised a rifle at the cabin.

**PROSECUTOR** That's what we don't know!

**DEFENCE** It stands to reason he was.

**PROSECUTOR** We don't even know he was at the cabin!

**DEFENCE** And the promise of a rifle was repeated to Kormik when the priests set out for the Barrens with Kormik and his family.

**PROSECUTOR** You've nothing to support that first promise of a rifle in return for living at the cabin! The only promise, if made at all, was conditional upon Kormik providing safe conduct to, and habitation at, the Coronation Gulf encampment.

**DEFENCE** There was no understanding of "conditional" on Kormik's part.

**PROSECUTOR** How can you know that?

**DEFENCE** The parties, priest and Eskimo, interpreted any interaction between them through a cultural lens. Everything was prone to misinterpretation by the other.

**SMITH** So – a promise made? No promise made? A conditional promise made? A promise made and broken? We can never know. And in the end, does it really matter?

**DEFENCE** Of course it matters! You want context? Sinnisiak's friend, Kormik—

**PROSECUTOR** Now you admit that friendship!

**DEFENCE** I admit the rifle! Kormik was promised a rifle on two occasions. Le Roux reneged on that promise. Kormik had "earned" that rifle. The circumstances that led to the priests' death were the direct result of Le Roux refusing to give Kormik the rifle Kormik believed he'd earned.

**SMITH** But Kormik isn't charged with murder?

**PROSECUTOR** Well, perhaps he should have been.

**JUDGE** I'm inclined to agree. An accessory at least.

**DEFENCE** But that is not the case! Kormik was never charged with anything.

**SMITH** True, apparently. What we do have – are the remains of Father Le Roux. *(the jawbone)* We identify this jawbone as such because it was found at the site of his murder along with other small fragments of bone left by marauding animals. Of Father Rouvière, killed a short distance away, no significant skeletal remains are found.

And what we do know – is that this rifle belonged to Rouvière and Le Roux and was taken from them by Sinnisiak and Uluksuk at the time of their deaths.

**DEFENCE** Or so we suppose.

**PROSECUTOR** No. Of this, we can be certain.

**DEFENCE** More or less.

**PROSECUTOR** Don't be difficult! The rifle belonged to the priests. It was stolen from them. They retrieved it. They were followed and killed. The rifle was stolen from them again after their death. End of story.

**DEFENCE** Kormik had earned that rifle!

**PROSECUTOR** But Sinnisiak and Uluksuk had not earned it!

**DEFENCE** It is not about the rifle! You try to make it sound so simple.

**PROSECUTOR** And you, so complicated.

**SMITH** If you'd pass me that smaller box you'll find inside the larger—

**DEFENCE** What now?

*The PROSECUTOR gets the small box.*

**SMITH** Thank you.

**DEFENCE** What the hell have you there?

**SMITH** Visual aids. *(as he opens the box)*

**DEFENCE** Your eyesight's impaired?

**SMITH** Twenty-twenty.

**DEFENCE** No vision problems, eh? I find that surprising.

*A look from SMITH.*

In a man of your age.

*The DEFENCE lifts from the box a small replica of the parliament buildings, a small train and a section of track.*

My God. You travel with these—I hesitate to ask but—for business or pleasure?

**SMITH** I find them useful.

**DEFENCE** For business or pleasure?

*(to the other two)* I'm not sure I really want to know.

**SMITH** If you don't mind replacing those *(the train, parliament building etc.)* – I'm sure there's something here adequate for our purposes—

*SMITH will get out items that represent the features of the landscape – ribbons of rivers, pools of lakes, fort and cabins, etc. and lay them out on the table.*

Principal features as they apply to our case. Bear with me… I'm sure I can find… *(He looks at several small buildings, each with the name of a city on it.)* Yes – approximately one thousand miles north of Edmonton. *(A small building titled Edmonton is placed on the extreme edge of the table.)*

We begin. Fort Norman *(placing a small fort)* and the Bishop's Saint Theresa Mission *(a church)* situated between the Mackenzie River *(a ribbon of river)* which is not relevant to us at this time.

**DEFENCE** Then why place it?

**SMITH** Context, situated where the Mackenzie River meets the Bear River and the Bear River… *(placing a ribbon of river)* and… here it is: Great Bear Lake *(placing its representation)* equal in area to Lake Huron including Georgian Bay.

**DEFENCE** Large.

**SMITH** Hence the name "Great." Bear. Lake. Dease Bay here, and here we have Dease River. *(placing a ribbon of river)*

**DEFENCE** Good Lord, Smith.

**SMITH** Yes, the area is immense, and who knows what lies beneath it. Mineral wealth, you know.

*Which is not what the DEFENCE meant. The JUDGE gets a refill of brandy and carries the decanter back with him.*

Now, up the Dease and by land over a divide we have Imaerinik Lake *(lays out the lake)* approximately twenty miles southwest of the northwestern arm of the Dismal Lakes *(laying them out)* of which there are three.

**DEFENCE** So far as we know.

**SMITH** So far as we know. Much is unexplored.

We have Rouvière and Le Roux's cabin here *(laying out the cabin)* at Imaerinik Lake. There.

Note the isolation of the priests from their Mission at Fort Norman, the immense distance between their abode and this small outpost of – whether we call it civilization or not is debatable.

**DEFENCE** And Edmonton? What do we call it?

**SMITH** *(smiles at the DEFENCE)* Debatable.

*(then continues)* Now on their journey from Imaerinik cabin to the winter camp at Coronation Gulf they are crossing the Barrens. A vast area.

Kormik and the priests are joined by other Eskimos. They do not take the Kendall River route *(laying out the two ribbons of river)* to the Coppermine River but the Dismal Lakes trail striking the Coppermine River *(an indicator of the trail)* halfway between Bloody Falls *(places a red cross for the Falls)* and the mouth of the Coppermine flowing into Coronation Gulf *(lays out an expanse of water)* on the Arctic Ocean. And. The. Encampment… where is it…. Ahh. This will do. *(places a small tent)*

Better still. *(removes tent, places an igloo)*

*The layout has taken up the entire area of the table. A pause as the men take it in. SMITH will refer to the layout as he continues.*

Fini.

**DEFENCE** Except for people.

**SMITH** Oh, they're there, they're there. Invisible perhaps, but there.

Seven, eight, possibly twelve, or some days after leaving the cabin at Imaerinik Lake the group of Eskimos and priests arrives at the mouth of the Coppermine. The dogs are thin and weak. There's a shortage of food for both man and animal and the sea ice is not yet strong enough to permit a seal hunt. This is a disastrous discovery. What we believe to be the last entry in Rouvière's diary tells it all. *(the water soaked pages)* Translated from French: "Arrived at mouth of Coppermine River; some families already gone, disappointment from Eskimos"—

**DEFENCE** Wait a minute.

**SMITH** "Disappointment from Eskimos; threatened with starvation and do not know what to do."

**DEFENCE** I said wait. "Disillusioned with Eskimos" is what was quoted at trial.

**PROSECUTOR** The difference being?

**DEFENCE** Perfectly clear.

**PROSECUTOR** Really.

**DEFENCE** Smith translates it as "disappointment from." That suggests the Eskimos are disappointed some families have left prior to their arrival, or perhaps some have left after their arrival.

The trial translation "disillusioned with" suggests tension between the priests and the Eskimos.

**PROSECUTOR** Before, after, with, from, it's not relevant.

**DEFENCE** It's like the rifle, speaks to the situation and motivation.

**PROSECUTOR** What's relevant is "threatened with starvation, do not know what to do."

**JUDGE** We do know what they did.

**SMITH** Yes, that we do know. From statements by a most reliable witness and friend of the priests, an Eskimo called Koeha. He tells us food is scarce, starvation threatens the encampment. Rouvière and Le Roux no longer feel as welcome as they once did.

**PROSECUTOR** They sensed danger.

**SMITH** Perhaps.

**PROSECUTOR** And they were right.

**SMITH** At any rate a decision is made. The priests will take their chances on the land, returning to the cabin by the Coppermine-Kendall River route. They have tea, a few provisions on their sled and four dogs in poor shape. Around thirty miles upriver there's a small stand of spruce, wood for warmth and cooking, even caribou perhaps. If they can make that stand of spruce, things won't look so bad.

**PROSECUTOR** And that's when they discover one of their two rifles missing. Their best rifle is missing!

**DEFENCE** Embellishment!

**PROSECUTOR** Perhaps, to some degree.

**JUDGE** Agreed.

**PROSECUTOR** But not outside the realm of possibility.

**SMITH** The essentials are factual. Le Roux accuses Kormik of stealing the rifle. And indeed he has. His wife has hidden it along with some of the priests' provisions.

**DEFENCE** Not stolen! The rifle was promised to Kormik.

**SMITH** That may be how Kormik feels.

**PROSECUTOR** The rifle, possibly promised, but never given, which makes it theft! Conditionally promised, if at all! And that condition has not been met. The priests are not safe at Coronation Gulf. They're returning to Imaerinik cabin. *(indicating so on the table)* Their lives may well depend on each having the means to kill any game they come across. They owe Kormik nothing!

**SMITH** Be that as it may. Kormik refuses to hand over the rifle. Father Le Roux, hasty and hot tempered, grabs the remaining rifle, loads and throws a cartridge into the breach, threatens Kormik and demands the return of the missing gun. Tragedy is averted by the intervention of the priests' friend, Koeha. Stepping forward he urges Kormik to give up the rifle and allow the priests to depart in peace. Others add their voices to Koeha's. Kormik's mother appears with the missing rifle and passes it to Rouvière. Now the priests must go and go quickly. Koeha helps them pack and accompanies them, possibly for protection, 'til the encampment is almost out of sight. He tells us the priests each shook his hand, and he returned to camp. Rouvière and Le Roux continue on. It appears they find it hard-going and don't get far before stopping for the night.

Now we do have Sinnisiak and Uluksuk's confessions which conform to each other in every respect.

**DEFENCE** The confessions are inadmissible and should have been ruled so.

**JUDGE** You object to my ruling, admitting them?

**DEFENCE** Haven't I said it? I objected, and object.

**PROSECUTOR** The RCMP interpreter warned them three times. Three times he told them they need not confess or even speak. It was carefully explained to them. What their rights were. How anything they said could be used against them.

**DEFENCE** But did they understand him?

**JUDGE** He spoke to them in their own tongue.

**DEFENCE** Yes, I heard your interpreter at trial speak to them "in their own tongue." For ten minutes he tried to convey to Koeha on the witness stand the simple question, "Is this a gun you recognize"? The Defence interpreter had to step in and the language difficulty was cleared up in a minute. Koeha simply could not understand the RCMP interpreter. Possibly the same was true with Sinnisiak and Uluksuk.

**JUDGE** The interpreter's translation was adequate, the confessions voluntary.

**DEFENCE** When I ask, "did they understand," I'm talking about more than inadequate translation. I'm asking did they understand the meaning of the warning? Did they understand to what use a confession would be put? How could they? They have no such thing as courts or laws but merely custom!

**SMITH** The confessions of Sinnisiak and Uluksuk—

**PROSECUTOR** Yes, Sinnisiak, a rogue, a thief, troublemaker and liar. That's how his own people regard him.

**DEFENCE** All hearsay and none of it admissible at trial.

**SMITH** Sinnisiak—

**PROSECUTOR** A friend, a good friend of Kormik's.

**DEFENCE** That's not a crime.

**PROSECUTOR** But it is suggestive!

**SMITH** *(illustrates as necessary using the table and its layout)* Sinnisiak tells us he was not present at the Kormik confrontation but saw the two priests leave camp. The following morning before dawn he sets out with Uluksuk and one dog. Their intention, he tells us, is to help some fellow Eskimos he believes are on their way to the Coppermine on the Dismal Lakes trail.

**PROSECUTOR** Just how did they intend to help these people with one dog, no sled and on foot? And no accurate knowledge as to whether these Eskimo are one day or two days or who knows how many days travel away? In fact how do Sinnisiak and Uluksuk know these Eskimos are even on their way?

**DEFENCE** By means unknown to us.

**PROSECUTOR** I can't believe you seriously propose such nonsense. Their explanation is spurious. The truth is they were after the priests with murder in mind.

**SMITH** Sinnisiak and Uluksuk tell us they follow the priests' trail with the latter eventually becoming aware of their presence. The four meet. The Eskimos are unarmed except for their ever-present big knives.

The Eskimos' explanation for their travel may well have been met with suspicion for they're now a mile or so past where the Dismal Lakes trail hits the Coppermine.

**PROSECUTOR** Exactly. They're well past the Dismal Lake trail which is where they should have turned off if they were really out to assist anyone making their way to the Coppermine. Look! Here! You can see it yourself.

*(indicating the trails)* The priests' Kendall River route – and here the Dismal Lake trail. And here the four men meet.

**DEFENCE** We've no way of knowing exactly where that meeting took place.

**JUDGE** That's true.

**PROSECUTOR** We have Sinnisiak and Uluksuk's own words.

**DEFENCE** Perhaps it wasn't a mile past the Dismal Lake trail. Perhaps it was half a mile before it. Perhaps it was here – or here or here. It's all conjecture, from information given by people who may experience space and distance quite differently from us.

**PROSECUTOR** No one suggests they measure in miles but they do recognize landmarks and geographic features! How else would they get about?

**SMITH** In any case! The weather is bad. The stand of spruce promising warmth and perhaps game seems no closer. Le Roux makes an offer.

If Sinnisiak and Uluksuk step into harness with the dogs and help pull the sled 'til they reach the woods, they will be paid in traps. The Eskimos agree, but by nightfall they have not reached the trees. After an uneasy night—

**DEFENCE** Objection to "uneasy."

**SMITH** Then, for reasons unknown – the men break up; Rouvière and Le Roux continue on alone, Sinnisiak and Uluksuk start back. Their dog sniffs out a cache made at some time by the priests to lighten their sled load. The priests catch sight of the men at the cache, they return to prevent theft. Rouvière gives Le Roux a rifle and moves on ahead. Whatever follows results in Le Roux, rifle in hand, forcing Sinnisiak and Uluksuk back into harness, their understanding being that they will be killed if they refuse. This is clearly stated in both confessions. An unarmed Rouvière travels ahead of the sled dogs and men, Le Roux is with the sled, urging the two Eskimos and dogs on, threatening with the rifle as necessary, placing it on the sled when not put to this use. The Eskimos are cold and frightened. Sinnisiak has a plan.

He manages to communicate it to Uluksuk despite Le Roux's attempts to prevent their speaking together. The two fear they will never see their people again, they will die or be killed on the Barrens. They must kill the priests. Uluksuk refuses to act despite his fears and the increasing cold and difficult conditions. Sinnisiak will act.

The rifle is on the sled. Sinnisiak steps out of harness. Le Roux pushes him back. Sinnisiak takes off his belt, he must relieve himself. Le Roux accepts this. Sinnisiak steps behind the sled. Le Roux looks away for a moment and Sinnisiak's big knife is in and out of Le Roux's back. Le Roux goes for the rifle. Sinnisiak yells to Uluksuk who acts. He steps out of harness and struggles with Le Roux for possession of the gun. Uluksuk has his own big knife which is soon put to use. Le Roux dies. At the same time, Rouvière, seeing the struggle, starts back to the sled. Sinnisiak confronts him with the knife and Rouvière turns and runs. Sinnisiak again calls to Uluksuk, "Give me the rifle!" He does so. The first shot misses. The second doesn't. Rouvière sits down when the bullet hits. Sinnisiak approaches with the knife. Rouvière stands up. Uluksuk joins Sinnisiak. A short discussion between the two as Rouvière sinks down. Both men detail their conversation similarly. Uluksuk says, "Go ahead, put the knife in him." Sinnisiak replies, "No, you, I fixed the other one already." Rouvière is up again. Uluksuk strikes and misses, strikes again and doesn't, Rouvière falls but still breathes. Sinnisiak strikes with an axe he carries; first across the neck and then the legs. Rouvière is dead. Uluksuk cuts open the belly of each priest and the two eat a bit of the livers. Sinnisiak states this is what must be done when white men are killed. Each man takes one of the priests' rifles and some ammunition, and they return to the group's encampment. Sinnisiak goes directly to Kormik's tent, tells him he has killed both Rouvière and Le Roux. The people immediately set out for the site and return with the priests' belongings including crucifixes, altar cloths, vessels, breviaries and cassocks which they'll wear in the following years.

All this is clearly stated in their confessions.

Contradiction?

**DEFENCE** The collection of the priests' belongings? Don't think of it as theft.

**PROSECUTOR** You prefer "a posthumous charitable donation"?

**DEFENCE** Of what use are clothing, religious books, tools, guns or other items to the priests? They're dead; they have no further need of anything. In the Eskimos' culture this seizing of the dead's possessions isn't stealing. So, Sinnisiak and Uluksuk may have taken the priests' rifles after their death, but that, in no way, suggests they killed the priests to obtain the rifles.

**PROSECUTOR** Your point being?

**DEFENCE** Their possession of the rifles can't be viewed as theft or offered as evidence or motivation for the murders.

**PROSECUTOR** But Uluksuk, on returning to the camp after the murders, goes immediately to Kormik's tent and hands over the rifle that Kormik says was promised him. And Sinnisiak even tells us that Kormik previously wanted to kill Le Roux for this rifle. You don't think that smells of conspiracy?

**DEFENCE** It's open to interpretation. I don't know what was in Uluksuk's mind, or Sinnisiak's or Kormik's. Nor do you.

**PROSECUTOR** We can read their actions.

**DEFENCE** We misread them; we're culturally illiterate in their world.

**PROSECUTOR** There is one world, and in our portion of it we've sworn to uphold the rule of law. We're not the ones who're culturally illiterate. Why do you—

**SMITH** A question? If I may?

*(to the PROSECUTOR)* Everything indicates a joint charge would be in order, that is Rex vs. Sinnisiak and Uluksuk for the murder of Le Roux and Rouvière.

**JUDGE** That's what I expected.

**DEFENCE** We all did.

**SMITH** Instead you separate it into four charges, one for each man for each death. Why?

**PROSECUTOR** Frankly—to avoid any hitch—to increase the chances for a successful prosecution.

**DEFENCE** Didn't quite work, did it?

**PROSECUTOR** Separate charges allow me to use the evidence of each against the other.

**DEFENCE** Just in case the old boy's network doesn't come through?

**JUDGE** Pardon?

**DEFENCE** Let me rephrase that – just in case the confessions were ruled inadmissible. With a joint charge the statements of both men could have been thrown out.

**JUDGE** Did you just make a serious accusation of bias?

**DEFENCE** No M'Lord, it was a feeble attempt at humour.

**JUDGE** You know perfectly well I questioned the separation of the charges and court transcripts will show that.

**PROSECUTOR** But to forestall any such objections in court I presented the four charges directly to the Attorney General. And he signed them. Complete agreement, no reservations. Not one joint charge but four separate charges. Good legal strategy.

**DEFENCE** Oh, I'm not complaining. It worked for me.

**PROSECUTOR** How you could plead self-defence and still sleep at night is beyond me.

**DEFENCE** Good legal strategy.

**PROSECUTOR** Fact! Sinnisiak shot an unarmed Father Rouvière in the back as he fled. There's not a shred of evidence that Rouvière ever threatened anyone at any time. Every account speaks of his gentleness. Yet you argue Sinnisiak was justified in killing Rouvière in self-defence!

**DEFENCE** I do.

**PROSECUTOR** In your heart of hearts – do you believe that?

**DEFENCE** It's not whether I believe he was justified, it's whether he believed he was justified.

**PROSECUTOR** Will you never stop pounding that drum?

**DEFENCE** Well, the jury danced to its beat.

**PROSECUTOR** After killing Le Roux they could have left Rouvière on the Barrens to die of exposure or starvation or—

**DEFENCE** You prefer that to a clean shot in the back?

**PROSECUTOR** Followed by a not so clean chop to the legs and a savage blow to the neck!

**JUDGE** I don't know about you two, but I'm going to have another.

*He pours himself another drink; the PROSECUTOR gets a refill as well.*

**PROSECUTOR** How the jury could accept self-defence, how they could acquit is… is… not within my comprehension.

*He knocks back his drink.*

**SMITH** I thought you laid it at the door of undue influence?

**PROSECUTOR** What else? No other explanation.

**DEFENCE** You could have had a new one.

**PROSECUTOR** One what?

**DEFENCE** Jury. I requested a new jury.

**SMITH** Why was that?

**DEFENCE** His opening address. It was inflammatory. And prejudicial. Plus it took bloody hours to deliver!

**PROSECUTOR** I had to give the jury some idea of the geography, the character of the Eskimo people, general conditions, even the RCMP's search and arrest of the defendant. That took nearly four years.

**DEFENCE** Almost as long as he spoke. Sinnisiak and Uluksuk sat there sweltering in caribou and fox fur, with bare feet in pans of ice water, while we struggled to keep from nodding off in our robes. Even you, M'Lord, I saw the head bobbing, the eyes closing.

**JUDGE** Not at all.

**DEFENCE** Oh, yes. You drifted off. I'll swear to it.

**JUDGE** Concentrating. I was concentrating. It was a dense address. And the August heat, the crowded courtroom, stagnant air – I did speak to Crown Counsel regarding the length.

**DEFENCE** And I requested you empanel a new jury, that request denied by you.

**PROSECUTOR** The trial was historic, the address necessary.

**DEFENCE** It was prejudicial and grossly unfair.

**PROSECUTOR** I don't regret giving it. I'll give it again at Uluksuk's trial.

**SMITH** Perhaps not.

**DEFENCE** See, the man didn't hear it and even he suggests editing. If he'd had to sit through it I'd lay money he'd urge it be cut altogether.

**PROSECUTOR** I'm not surprised you don't appreciate its content or delivery, given the crassness of your own address to the jury. Did you not refer to the defendant's cannibalism—

**DEFENCE** I find "cannibalism" prejudicial.

**PROSECUTOR** Did you not refer in court to the eating of the priest's liver as being "hardly in good taste"?

**DEFENCE** I admit to a poor choice of words.

**PROSECUTOR** I rest my case, at least so far as it applies to your ability to evaluate my opening address.

**DEFENCE** This is what it really comes down to, Smith. Despite claims of undue influence, the jury understood that Sinnisiak and Uluksuk had a reasonable belief, culturally founded and honestly held, that their lives were in danger and they acted on that belief to preserve their lives.

**PROSECUTOR** Did you know the Fort Resolute Indian agent met with the prisoners on a number of occasions?

**DEFENCE** What now?

**PROSECUTOR** Did you know that?

**DEFENCE** I did.

**PROSECUTOR** He travelled with them and the arresting officers when they came south? Struck up an acquaintance with them?

**DEFENCE** That's right.

**PROSECUTOR** And met with them during the course of the trial?

**DEFENCE** Yes! I was present at those meetings.

**PROSECUTOR** Always present?

**DEFENCE** Not always present, no.

**PROSECUTOR** Might a real relationship, friendship even, have developed between the two accused and this Indian agent?

**DEFENCE** What're you getting at?

**PROSECUTOR** You saw no coaching of the prisoners?

**DEFENCE** None!

**PROSECUTOR** But then you weren't always present, were you?

**DEFENCE** The Eskimo's legal guardian is the Inspector General of Indian Affairs. The agent acts for him.

**PROSECUTOR** And what about his promotion of the Eskimo's innocence within the Edmonton community? What're your thoughts on that?

**DEFENCE** This agent's been delegated to monitor the trial!

**PROSECUTOR** But not to spread false rumours in the general community!

**SMITH** What rumours?

**JUDGE** A story's been circulating.

**PROSECUTOR** And the agent is the source. I have that from reliable informants.

**DEFENCE** Yes, there're rumours—

**PROSECUTOR** And don't tell me you weren't aware of his efforts on your clients' behalf.

**DEFENCE** I heard the rumours, I didn't attribute them to anyone in particular.

**PROSECUTOR** You might have guessed. You knew where his sympathies lie. You weren't suspicious?

**DEFENCE** I don't act on suspicions.

**PROSECUTOR** Well, I telegrammed the Department of Justice. I believe by now this agent's received a telegram from Ottawa defining the difference between lobbying for the defendants and monitoring the trial. A strong reprimand in his file I hope.

**SMITH** What's the story?

**PROSECUTOR** Rumours of intercourse between the priests and the Eskimos' women, that being the real reason behind the killings.

**DEFENCE** Where's the evidence the jury was swayed by these rumours?

**PROSECUTOR** The juryman I met prior to coming here told me, and I quote, "Even a white man would kill for that!" so he says of course the Eskimos must be acquitted!

**DEFENCE** Why were you talking to a juryman?

**PROSECUTOR** He said there was much discussion on this point in the jury room and the same thing's heard on the street. "The priests behaved improperly with the Eskimos' women, so, of course the two accused must be acquitted."

**DEFENCE** Jury deliberations should be confidential!

**SMITH** Any truth to this story?

**PROSECUTOR** None at all.

**JUDGE** It was an accusation made by some half-breed drunken trader—

**PROSECUTOR** Thoroughly investigated by the RCMP and found groundless. And to cap it all off, the Bishop tells us the Eskimo don't mind sharing their women. If anything the priests' lack of interest could have offended the accused.

**DEFENCE** Doesn't this tell us how little we know of their culture? Of their mindset? Of how they perceive and interpret the actions of the white man when they come into contact with him? What is shared, what is not shared? What offends, what does not offend? What do we strangers, we foreigners, know? We're ass over teakettle when it comes to knowing.

**SMITH** Foreigners you say?

**DEFENCE** We're the foreigners in their land.

**SMITH** In whose land?

**DEFENCE** Look, they're living in small groups dispersed over a vast hostile area; they've lived their lives for hundreds of years by custom, by shifting for themselves, by settling things themselves. There is no government as we know it, but only custom.

You do not load and point a gun at a man unless you intend to shoot him. And if a man intends to shoot you, it is wise to shoot him first.

**SMITH** So, we are to live by their customs and standards of conduct and not they by ours?

**DEFENCE** I simply say if you go to certain places you take your chances. If, as a stranger to the ways of that place, you offend, whether unwittingly or purposively, the price you pay will be the same. It may be death.

**PROSECUTOR** In this case it was. But we cannot hold the accused responsible if they did not appreciate that what they did was wrong!

**JUDGE** No, not so. Our Indians are held accountable under the law, and here, in this very province, there're recent immigrants, foreigners from a range of countries. No matter what customs or laws they once lived under, they must conform to the law of this land, British Law, once they're here. And if not, they're charged.

**PROSECUTOR** Surely you're not suggesting that the Eskimo customs of vengeance and valuation of human life should apply to those who risk going North?

**DEFENCE** Try to understand. Rouvière, when they met him, was the first white man these Eskimos had ever seen. Uluksuk, on the stand, tells us—after some thought—that he is eight years old. The RCMP interpreter, an Eskimo who's had some interaction with white men, is given a watch. He's told when the hands point to a certain time the sun will rise. The next day it does. The following day however is overcast and cloudy. He watches the hands of the watch carefully waiting for them to point to that certain time but the sun cannot be seen behind the clouds. He throws the watch away. It must be broken as it no longer makes the sun rise.

These men are children in our world. A child, as these men are, is incapable of committing a crime. That's what I'm saying. And I believe this is what the jury based its verdict on.

**PROSECUTOR** You may believe your profoundly flawed defence arguments moved the jury to acquit. You may even take some pride in it. I hope pride can soothe a conscience.

**DEFENCE** Your remark's offensive.

**PROSECUTOR** Thank God we're not on the Arctic Barrens. I could be shot, stabbed and lose my liver.

**JUDGE** And if Arctic custom prevailed, the Catholic Bishop would be quite right in seeking out, shooting and killing Sinnisiak and Uluksuk, along with some members of their families for good measure.

**DEFENCE** That's an absurd expansion of my argument.

**JUDGE** Both accused clearly believed such acts of vengeance was to be their fate when the Mounties arrived to arrest them. But no, they have the protection of British Law, are treated well, and tried by civilized standards, with every effort made to assure they have the finest legal defence and a fair prosecution. In addition they have an intelligent jury of respected citizens—

**DEFENCE** Yes! Everything in fine working order. With an acquittal!

**JUDGE** But when one has protection under the law, as the two accused have, one is liable for crimes committed under the law.

**SMITH** I don't find your self-defence plea legally sound.

**DEFENCE** How fortunate for me you've no standing in the court.

**SMITH** You say they acted in self-defence. They believed they were in danger of being killed – for which we only have their word.

I'll take them at their word.

However. They had no immediate threat of death; they may have had a reasonable fear of death.

You say they felt dread and panic which justified their defending themselves, in this state of dread and panic, to the point of killing those whom they feared. And this you say is self-defence.

Legally: though you may fear with good reason, you cannot legally plead self-defence when you prevent what you fear, by killing those you fear, when there is no immediate, no immediate, danger to you.

**DEFENCE** Define "immediate" in this case. It's all opinion and interpretation, isn't it?

**SMITH** Le Roux with the rifle and the events around the sled? Yes, one might argue self-defence. Opinion and interpretation may rule the day with Le Roux. An acquittal for both Eskimos based on a reasonable plea of self-defence with Le Roux.

However this is not the case with Rouvière. Sinnisiak shot an unarmed Rouvière in the back as he was running away. Rouvière was no threat, immediate or otherwise. This is not a question of self-defence or guilt. Sinnisiak's guilt is clear in the killing of Rouvière.

**DEFENCE** But Sinnisiak's been tried. He's been acquitted. It's over. Whether you, or you, or you, approve of the verdict, is immaterial.

**SMITH** It's not over.

**PROSECUTOR** However it is true the Crown has lost the strongest case for conviction.

**JUDGE** With the jury completely disregarding my instructions. I was most direct in stating a self-defence plea was not legally sound in the death of Rouvière.

**DEFENCE** How can you disregard the childlike nature of the two accused, the possible misreading of intentions, the difficulties of communication, the environmental conditions, the extenuating circumstances, how can you disregard these!

**JUDGE** I don't! They're mitigating factors that apply and would be given careful consideration in sentencing! They should not be factors in determining guilt by the jury, but in the determination of the sentence! And I stated this in my instructions to the Jury!

**PROSECUTOR** The jury was well aware, Sinnisiak, if found guilty, ran no risk of hanging. None whatsoever.

**JUDGE** And that justice would be tempered with mercy, an appropriate and merciful sentence of incarceration for some period of time, to be served in the North. That was made clear to the jury.

**DEFENCE** Did you hear that?

**SMITH** Justice tempered with mercy, yes.

**DEFENCE** As you apparently feel qualified to give legal opinions, let me ask you something. This awareness, this clarity as just stated by M'Lord, this understanding that the sentence handed out would not be severe or extreme and incarceration not long in duration—this clear promise made to the jury in the prosecutor's closing address—then referred to and confirmed by the Judge in his charge to the jury when he stated capital punishment does not quote "fit this crime"—

**JUDGE** There was nothing improper in the government's telling me its intention to commute the death sentence!

**DEFENCE** And nothing improper in sharing that information with the prosecution and the jury? What do you say, Smith?

**SMITH** I'm listening.

**DEFENCE** I charge that this promise and referral to mitigation of sentence constituted an effort to unduly influence the jury! It was intended to entice them into rendering a verdict of guilty by guaranteeing that the sentence would be light if they came through with the desired verdict!

**PROSECUTOR** It was not improper! In the interests of a substantial and impartial justice, the public and the jury were made aware of the Government's attitude.

**DEFENCE** Government, attitude, right, proper. Fine words. Very general. Mine are more specific.

I'm asking you, Smith.

Does this promise that Sinnisiak would not be hanged if found guilty constitute an effort to influence and entice the jury into rendering a verdict of guilty?

**SMITH** If so, it was unsuccessful.

**DEFENCE** I'm making an accusation here.

**SMITH** Which I find irrelevant. Your client was acquitted.

**DEFENCE** So, it is over.

**SMITH** Not quite.

**DEFENCE** I remind you yet again. All of you. Double jeopardy protects Sinnisiak from further prosecution in this case.

**SMITH** I'm afraid it's you who's forgetful.

**JUDGE** There remains the other charges – the Crown vs. Uluksuk in the death of Father Rouvière—

**DEFENCE** He'll be acquitted. He was Sinnisiak's pawn and with Sinnisiak's acquittal in the murder of Rouvière they'll never convict Uluksuk.

**PROSECUTOR** But then there's the case of Uluksuk and that of Sinnisiak in the death of Father Le Roux—

**DEFENCE** And I say an acquittal for both men. The Eskimo have the strongest case for self-defence with Le Roux who was threatening them with the rifle. It's a foregone conclusion, gentlemen.

Why, I'd put money on not guilty! Acquittals all 'round.

**SMITH** Yes. With a not guilty verdict for Sinnisiak, who admits shooting, stabbing, mutilating a fleeing and unarmed Rouvière, and even bragging of the deed to other Eskimos, it does seem a guilty verdict for Uluksuk or conviction of either Eskimo in the case of Le Roux, extremely unlikely.

I'm not a betting man.

But—*(placing several bills from his pocket on the table)*

It would be a crime to pass up a sure thing...

My money is on the table.

**DEFENCE** You're betting on what?

**SMITH** Was I not clear? I'm betting on "guilty."

**DEFENCE** You're betting on guilty – that the Eskimos will be found guilty?

**SMITH** I am.

**DEFENCE** Despite what you just said – about the unlikelihood of such a verdict?

**SMITH** In spite of what I just said.

**DEFENCE** My money on acquittal. *(money on the table)*

**PROSECUTOR** You do realize acquittal means the accused were justified in killing the missionaries?

**JUDGE** That they would return to the North as free men?

**PROSECUTOR** And the tale they would tell? That white men think less of killing a white man than the Eskimos, themselves, do.

**JUDGE** That if you do kill, you won't be killed in return for reasons of vengeance or retribution. Instead you'll be sought out, even if it takes years. There'll be no shackles on your journey south, you'll travel in relative comfort, meet the White Chief, see many marvellous things, and be set free to return having had a wonderful time.

**DEFENCE** I'm concerned only with the particulars of this case and so should you be.

**PROSECUTOR** But you've no interest in justice for Rouvière and Le Roux. You've even bet against it.

**DEFENCE** I suggest we leave ultimate justice to a higher power. My expertise, and yours supposedly, is in the field of law.

**SMITH** Here are the facts. As we speak, white men are pouring into the North. We know there's copper there, gold discovered in the past, diamonds might be found tomorrow. Who knows what else lies beneath the surface?

**DEFENCE** I'm not a fool.

**SMITH** Already the Canadian Arctic Expedition's actively exploring by order of the government.

**DEFENCE** Northern development and exploitation is preordained, I know that.

**JUDGE** Explorers, traders, prospectors, entrepreneurs that scent an opportunity, are they to be at the mercy of Arctic custom?

**DEFENCE** I have two clients. Their names are Sinnisiak and Uluksuk. I act in their interests.

**PROSECUTOR** Do you really believe that Eskimo standards of vengeance and valuation of human life apply to any white man who takes the risk of going there? Unwittingly offend, you say, and pay the price of death?

**JUDGE** Surely not.

**DEFENCE** I stated my case at trial. I won it. I look forward to the next one.

**SMITH** I'll speak plainly.

**DEFENCE** And I refuse to engage in discussion of these extraneous matters!

**SMITH** It's necessary the government act quickly to assert its sovereignty and jurisdiction in the North.

We're in the process of determining and extending our borders geographically. An integral aspect of this is the extension of our boundaries morally.

**DEFENCE** So, now we have it! This has nothing to do with seeing two men charged and punished for the crime of murder! This is about proving the efficacy of the King's Law over the Northern territory and the Arctic Ocean!

That, in fact, is what the prosecution is fighting for. Correct?

**PROSECUTOR** I wouldn't put it that way.

**DEFENCE** But that is the way of it.

**PROSECUTOR** The two are intrinsically bound, why can't you see that?

**JUDGE** The Crown vs. Sinnisiak and Uluksuk has a singular importance; the case is significant with implications larger than its particulars.

**DEFENCE** If a jury finds an accused guilty of murder, let that accused pay the supreme penalty, death by hanging.

If found not guilty, send him home free.

A verdict, for reasons of government policy, or for any reason other than that in the judgment of the jury the accused is guilty, is not prosecution or justice. It is persecution.

**SMITH** *(checking his watch)* I've a train to catch. We need to move on.

**DEFENCE** To what?

**SMITH** Request for a change of venue.

**DEFENCE** It'll be denied, you have no grounds.

**SMITH** I'm sure there's something. We have an acquittal here in Edmonton, the Gateway of the North, the city you'd think most sensitive to the safety of those travelling north. How can one explain that acquittal? There had to be extraneous influences on the jury.

**DEFENCE** Your reasoning—

**PROSECUTOR** And media bias.

**DEFENCE** Cite it! I saw only fair reportage.

**SMITH** Be unprecedented if we can't find a headline or two.

But probably insufficient to – but.... Ah, the Indian agent—

**PROSECUTOR** Yes.

**SMITH** That is persuasive.

**PROSECUTOR** His lobbying and spreading false rumours? That did create prejudice against the prosecution.

**SMITH** It would.

**DEFENCE** Gossip, nothing more.

**PROSECUTOR** The talk on the street.

**DEFENCE** You can't avoid it in a case like this.

**PROSECUTOR** They were monkeying around with the women. No truth to it, but heard everywhere.

**DEFENCE** People will speculate, it's human nature.

**SMITH** This was excessive, generated and spread with malice toward the Crown.

**PROSECUTOR** And at Peace River Crossing when the boat carrying the prisoners came through? The entire community turned out to greet them. A real celebration with the victims, Rouvière and Le Roux, forgotten.

**SMITH** Nothing useful there. What about the religious end of things? Protestant versus Catholic, anything there?

**PROSECUTOR** Well… noooo… not…

**DEFENCE** *(to the JUDGE)* Are you in on this?

**PROSECUTOR** I did hear a comment—something like—along the lines of a missionary's death being a professional windfall. I'm not sure that gets us anywhere.

**DEFENCE** *(to the JUDGE)* I said, are you party to this?

**SMITH** No Romans on the jury?

**PROSECUTOR** No. None.

**SMITH** Well, we won't touch that. Our strongest argument: the juryman's statement "Even a white man would kill for that."

**PROSECUTOR** Yes, referring to sexual activity between the priests and the Eskimo women which had no foundation, in fact, was not entered in court and yet became a topic of discussion among the jury members and affected their decision.

**DEFENCE** Must I say it again? You should not be privy to jury deliberations.

**SMITH** And what about the Indian agent's access to, and meeting with the prisoners – did that not include interpreters?

**DEFENCE** I object most strongly to these proceedings!

**PROSECUTOR** We know the agent spread prejudice against the Crown and sympathy and sentiment in favour of the prisoners amongst the public.

**SMITH** As for the interpreters – who knows what influence he might have had on them?

**DEFENCE** *(to the JUDGE)* Are you going to speak up?

**JUDGE** I've left the room.

**SMITH** You've enough for an affidavit here?

**PROSECUTOR** I believe so.

**SMITH** And your associate in court?

**PROSECUTOR** He'll swear a second affidavit affirming mine.

**SMITH** I imagine you're opposed?

**DEFENCE** Yes, I'm opposed!

**SMITH** The statements are truthful. How could what's stated fail to affect and sway jury deliberations?

**DEFENCE** A jury disagreeing with the Crown's opinion is not in itself evidence of improper deliberations or jury tampering or media bias or community prejudice!

**SMITH** We'll leave that to the Chief Justice to decide, won't we.

**DEFENCE** Oh, yes – who fortuitously happens to be—

**SMITH** M'Lord.

**DEFENCE** You have nothing to warrant a change of venue!

**SMITH** M'Lord? A change of venue? Granted? Moved to… to where?

**JUDGE** Calgary?

**PROSECUTOR** Calgary it is.

**SMITH** This is Friday. Affidavits prepared on the weekend; sworn and presented on Monday, that would be the twentieth, we'll go to trial on Wednesday the twenty-second in Calgary. The charge. The charge will be Crown vs. Sinnisiak and Uluksuk, two Eskimos charged with the murder of Father Guillaume Le Roux.

**DEFENCE** You're charging them jointly now with Le Roux's murder?

**PROSECUTOR** That is what I've decided, yes.

**DEFENCE** What you've decided?

**PROSECUTOR** Yes.

**DEFENCE** M'Lord, in the interests of justice—a word much bandied about today—and to assure a fair and impartial hearing for these men, I request you excuse yourself from presiding over their trial.

**JUDGE** For what reason?

**DEFENCE** Your prejudices regarding their guilt, and the government's necessity of finding them so for reasons not germane to the particulars of this case.

**JUDGE** Prejudices you say?

**DEFENCE** You've freely stated them. In fact they're clearly evident in your charge and instructions to the Edmonton Jury.

**JUDGE** I'll consider your request.

**SMITH** The Calgary jury will be sequestered. No contact with relations or friends. No access to newspapers. They will be held incommunicado in an appropriate hotel.

**JUDGE** Request denied. I find no evidence of prejudicial statements on my part, only instructions to the jury as to how the law applies to the facts.

**DEFENCE** M'Lord—

**JUDGE** Even were there merit in your request an insurmountable problem would arise. I am the sole judge in Alberta qualified to hear this case who is not on holiday… did I say request denied?… Yes. So. So, we shall meet again in Calgary. I look forward to it.

**DEFENCE** M'Lord!

**JUDGE** What now?

**DEFENCE** I insist on informing the Calgary jury of what the Edmonton jury demonstrated.

**SMITH** What would that be?

**PROSECUTOR** That they were blind to the faults of the accused? More than kind to their virtues? Completely forgetting the victim?

**DEFENCE** I insist on the right to inform the jury that they may defy the Judge's instructions and the law!

**PROSECUTOR** What now.

**DEFENCE** That they can acquit on grounds other than the evidence!

**PROSECUTOR** Where do you get these ideas?

**DEFENCE** William Penn.

**SMITH** Who?

**DEFENCE** The Quaker William Penn arrested and tried for his religious teachings in 1670.

**PROSECUTOR** In 1670.

**DEFENCE** Correct.

**SMITH** And why should this interest us, or any jury?

**DEFENCE** William Penn, acquitted by the jury despite the Crown's charge and instructions to convict.

**PROSECUTOR** I fear a storm of words coming on.

**DEFENCE** Subsequently, jury members were imprisoned, starved and cruelly mistreated in an effort by the Crown to force a reversal of their decision and to find Penn guilty.

**PROSECUTOR** Hardly relevant, M'Lord, although a temptation.

**DEFENCE** The jury refused and stood firm despite their suffering.

**JUDGE** Ye-es.

**DEFENCE** Eventually the Crown and its prosecutors were obliged to retreat, to free Penn and the jury and to accept the jury verdict of "not guilty." I assume you know what this did.

**SMITH** Which was?

**DEFENCE** It established the independence of the jury in British Law.

**SMITH** Interesting footnote.

**DEFENCE** Hardly a footnote. Ultimately, the Crown must take direction from the people.

And the Calgary jury has a right to know this.

**SMITH** You're a dangerous man.

**DEFENCE** There're a number of dangerous men in this room. Whether I am one of them is a matter of opinion.

**SMITH** Ah, yes. But whose opinion will prevail?

**JUDGE** Your citing of William Penn, this little history lesson… is… is—

**SMITH** Is what, M'Lord?

**JUDGE** Is… irrelevant and without merit in this case. You will not… present it before the Calgary court. The jury's duty and responsibility is to weigh the evidence, to evaluate the facts, and facts found, to follow, to follow the Judge's charge and instructions as to the law applicable to the facts.

**DEFENCE** Yet, Sinnisiak is acquitted! And his acquittal stands!

**SMITH** There's still Le Roux. We'll see what Wednesday brings.

**DEFENCE** I'll fight for their acquittal.

**PROSECUTOR** And I for justice for Rouvière and Le Roux, for British Law and Dominion sovereignty.

**DEFENCE** Sounds noble. It seems you're the servant of many masters.

**PROSECUTOR** I believe their interests coincide.

**DEFENCE** God help us when they don't.

**SMITH** Well, I've a car waiting and a train to catch.

**JUDGE** Yes, it's late.

**PROSECUTOR** The missus won't be happy. It'll be cold meat and salad in the kitchen and a cold shoulder in the parlour.

*The two exit having no problem opening the door. DEFENCE looks at SMITH who gives him the flicker of a smile.*

**SMITH** Now here's an irony. Sinnisiak acquitted of killing Rouvière, and I don't care what you say, forget the courtroom rhetoric. In your heart of hearts you know that that was murder. But – Sinnisiak is found not guilty. *(gets his coat and hat)*

And in the killing of Le Roux? In my heart of hearts I can understand that that was self-defence. But – Sinnisiak and Uluksuk found guilty. A man found not guilty of a crime he did commit, will be found guilty of a crime he did not commit.... Ironic. Don't you agree?

**DEFENCE** They've not been tried yet.

**SMITH** I like a man who goes against the odds, who fights even though he knows he cannot win. I like you. Without men like you the system would never work.

**DEFENCE** I could go to the press. Tell everyone what's happened here today.

**SMITH** Oh, they'd never believe you. It would throw so many things into question. If they believed you they'd have to act. No one really wants to do that. Go along, get along. With a few like you to make it all... look right.

*He's ready to leave; looks at the table with its layout of features and the small pile of cash.*

You do realize it's a sure thing. I hate to take your money.

**DEFENCE** You've taken much more than that.

**SMITH** A sense of humour, too. *(puts the key on the table)*

I do like you. Perhaps we'll meet again. *(He exits, shutting the door.)*

*The DEFENCE looks at the table for a moment and then he restacks the wooden chairs that accompany the table. As he does so the light dims in the room proper but grows brighter on the tabletop. The DEFENCE, finished with the chairs, looks at the tabletop with its pile of cash and layout. He exits, closing the door. Light continues to dim to dark as tabletop light increases.*

*Eventually the tabletop and its small replicas radiate a shimmering white, then blackout.*

*The End.*

Historical note:

CROWN VS. SINNISIAK, accused of the murder of Father Rouvière, found not guilty in Edmonton, August 17, 1917.

CROWN VS. SINNISIAK AND ULUKSUK, accused of the murder of Father Le Roux, found guilty in Calgary, August 24, 1917.

# While My Mother Lay Dreaming

By Doug Curtis

# About
# Doug Curtis

Doug Curtis is the founder and Artistic Director of Calgary's Ghost River Theatre, founded in 1999 to create new Canadian theatre that is innovative, original and highly theatrical. He was the director and collaborator on *An Eye for An Eye*, about the controversial attempts of Wiebo Ludwig to sabotage the oil industry, which won the 2001 Betty Mitchell Award for Outstanding Musical. Ghost River followed that show with *Picnic*, about the day the Ludwig family came to see *An Eye for An Eye.*

As a producer, Doug recently directed the collaboratively-created *The Alan Parkinson's Project*, and wrote and produced *Confessions of a Paperboy*, *While My Mother Lay Dreaming* and *X-Ray*, a collective-creation musical on 9/11 and Guantanamo Bay. As a writer and performer, he has created *The Photo Double* (One Yellow Rabbit/Ghost River); and collaborated on *The Carrot Warrior* Seminar (Halifax, Edmonton, Calgary). He wrote and performed *Mesa* at Workshop West, at Sunshine Theatre and at Magnetic North in 2005. In 2004, Ghost River created programs such as "Performance Storytelling" and "Writing on Your Feet" to help high school students and emerging performers discover their voice.

*While My Mother Lay Dreaming* was first produced by Shadow Theatre, at the Varscona Theatre in Edmonton, October 12-29, 2006 with the following company:

| | |
|---|---|
| BILL | Richard Meen |
| PEGGY | Coralie Cairns |
| HAROLD | Dan Perry |
| DARCY | Kevin Corey |
| DUANE | Jesse Gervais |
| JENNIFER | Lynley Hall |
| VICTOR | Duval Lang |

Directed by John Hudson
Set and Light Design by Kerem Cetinel
Costume Design by Heather Moore
Sound Design by Chris Wynters
Stage Manager: Wayne Paquette

---

A subsequent production was presented by Ghost River Theatre, Calgary, February 1-28, 2008 with the following company:

| | |
|---|---|
| BILL | Richard Meen |
| PEGGY | Karen Johnson-Diamond |
| HAROLD | Dan Perry |
| DARCY | Rick Duthie |
| DUANE | Frank Zotter |
| JENNIFER | Lynley Hall |
| VICTOR | Kevin Rothery |

Directed by John Hudson
Set and Light Design by Carla Ritchie
Costume Design by Heather Moore
Sound Design by Chris Wynters
Stage Manager: Ellen Close

## Characters

BILL is sixteen with noticeable acne.
PEGGY is Bill's mother, age forty-three.
VICTOR is Bill's father and a house developer, age fifty.
HAROLD is Bill's friend, age eighteen. His family has moved from Kelowna to take part in the boom.
DARCY has recently moved to Calgary from Ajax, Ontario, age sixteen.
JENNIFER is a coincidentalist, age sixteen.
DUANE is the neighbourhood drug dealer.

## Setting

January. 1980. Calgary, Alberta. The combination of warm chinook winds and El Niño weather patterns has left Calgary without snow since November. The temperature is remarkably warm and it creates an effect in many people that the possibilities in life are endless. It is a time of great prosperity in Calgary and Alberta. People from across Canada are moving to Alberta in record numbers. Oil and gas prices are at record levels, making many fantastically wealthy. There is a real feeling of people caught up in the frenzy to make a killing. The sky and the warmth and the strong winds are an important aspect of the atmosphere.

Each location appears permanent, but they seem to disappear when our focus has turned elsewhere. Locations include a bedroom, a backyard deck, a funeral chapel and the interior of a Volkswagen Beetle converted into an off-road dune buggy with wall-to-wall carpeting.

## Music

Music is heard in radios, passing car stereos and in scene transitions. Rush should be played wherever possible, and any number of classic rock songs from 1967 to 1980 can also be used, except for Nana Mouskouri, which Victor listens to. Music may also be used for sudden breakouts of air guitar.

# While My Mother Lay Dreaming

## Act One

### Scene One – Nobody Knows

*After midnight. BILL is sitting in the windowsill in his bedroom.*

**BILL** Some strange things are happening, okay? It's the middle of January? And we've had this incredibly warm weather since November. The trees are confused. They think it's spring; they're ready to bud. If it gets cold and starts to snow, it will kill the trees. But nobody knows if it's gonna get cold.

My mom's best friend killed herself last week, because her husband and her son were killed in two separate incidents. And nobody knows why.

Six hundred people are moving to Alberta every day, looking for work and somewhere to sleep, but there is no guarantee. God can give you a brown Christmas. God can make Ronald Reagan president. God can come along and kill your whole family.

*"Gimme Shelter" (Rolling Stones) coming from a truck a half mile away.*

And this! There's this guy in a truck, he has his windows down, and he cuts through our neighbourhood all the time, and he's playing "Gimme Shelter," and he's looped it, so all you hear is the opening riff again and again, and again, and again and again and it's like he thinks this is cool, but it's just annoying. This guy likes to speed through my neighbourhood; he thinks that it's okay to pull up to the four-way stop, wait there for as long as he likes, windows open, no traffic, and without any warning, he will squeal off, playing the same song, again and again and again. And again. And again. Every night for the past month. And nobody knows why.

*Headlights sweep across the room. BILL crouches down, and crawls to a second window, closer to the centre of the room.*

Sugar cubes make a great sound on glass and metal. And they disintegrate on contact, so you can't tell where the shot came from.

*BILL pulls back hard on the slingshot and kneels down by the window.*

How about a little sugar in your coffee? One lump or two? That's not very good for your cavities.

*BILL loads the sugar cubes into a slingshot. He fires, but the cubes fail to connect.*

Shit. Missed again. I know what you're thinking, but he's from Ontario.

Now the downside to having six hundred people move into your hometown, is that eventually they find out where the bush parties are. My brother and sister would talk about these legendary bush parties. And I would meet these girls in grade eleven and twelve—total babes—and then the guys from Ontario show up, and they brought their girlfriends, and then one of our girls will call one of their girls a slut and then they just go ape-shit, and the RC's have it shut down, and I say, "Why don't you just charge the ones from Ontario?" and the RC goes, "How can we tell the difference?"

Something else happened. I thought that all my friends would be with me when we went from grade nine into ten, but they moved away. Their dads got better jobs – and they moved to Houston. Jakarta. Don Mills. All my friends' dads are rich and they don't have to work. My dad works every day. Mom is the manager of Wicker World on MacLeod Trail.

It is 1980. Ronald Reagan has been elected. The first time a senior citizen has been elected to the White House. I lie awake at night and count mushroom clouds.

Oil is thirty dollars a barrel, and I've heard kids in kindergarten say that it's going to hit sixty. Next they'll be saying that a barrel of oil will cost a hundred. It's like there's a comet racing across the sky, and everyone is chasing after it. A comet made of fifties and hundreds.

It is 1980. Ralph Klein is the mayor of Calgary.
I have quit my job as a busboy at Phil's Pancake House.
I have every reason to believe I will find a better job.
Ralph says that all the eastern creeps and bums can just go back home.
Everyone loves Ralph. Even the creeps.
And me.
I'm finally getting sleepy.

*BILL climbs into bed and we hear the truck and "Gimme Shelter" again.*

## Scene Two – Saturday Means Many Things

*The sun rises. PEGGY enters vacuuming. She vacuums around the bed, under the bed and everywhere near it.*

**BILL** Mom. Mom. Mom. Mom! Turn it off! Turn it off!

**PEGGY** *(turns off vacuum)* It's time to get up.

**BILL** Mom—

**PEGGY** It's ten o'clock. Are you going to sleep all day?

**BILL** I got in late.

**PEGGY** Where's your homework?

**BILL** Mom – why won't you let me sleep in?

**PEGGY** Why don't you have any homework?

**BILL** Get out of my room!

*PEGGY turns the vacuum on again.*

Mom. Mom. Mom. Mom!

*She turns the vacuum off. She makes the bed with BILL still in it, tightening the sheets until he is pinned.*

Mom. Mom. Stop.

**PEGGY** Get up.

*She opens the blind – BILL is hit with bright light.*

**BILL** I can't move my arms.

**PEGGY** It's the middle of January and it's ten degrees outside. Phew! It stinks in here. Let's open a window. You need fresh air. Positive ions.

*PEGGY turns the vacuum on again.*

**BILL** Mom. Mom. Mom. Mom!

*She turns the vacuum off.*

**PEGGY** The sun is shining—

**BILL** Mom—

*PEGGY stands there. Then she pulls the sheets out. BILL pulls himself out of the bed and throws on pants, a shirt, jacket and shoes. PEGGY takes the top sheet and keeps flicking it out.*

I swear to God.

**PEGGY** If you get it a certain way you can get it the first time – it's all in the wrist – there's a certain – way – and if you don't get it up in the air, it will not land – the way you want it – to land.

*PEGGY lets the sheet fall and she is still holding on to the corners.*

Well, okay. I'm fine now. I'm okay. Grab the corners.

*They make the bed.*

**BILL** When is the funeral?

**PEGGY** Next week.

**BILL** Where is it?

**PEGGY** St. Gerard's. God, I haven't been there in years. Why would God do this?

**BILL** Maybe he wanted you to go back to church.

**PEGGY** Is that a joke?

**BILL** It was supposed to be.

**PEGGY** Why did this happen? She was a beautiful person.

**BILL** God made a mistake. Or there is no God. What kind of God would take Lorraine's life but also make Ronald Reagan president?

**PEGGY** Don't say that to your father.

**BILL** We have a senior citizen in the White House. Do you have any idea how close we are to nuclear annihilation? Have you heard about the nuclear clock? It's this clock that's at five minutes to midnight, the minute that Reagan was elected—

**PEGGY** Bill, I can't listen—

**BILL** The clock moved two minutes closer to midnight.

**PEGGY** Bill – I can't—

**BILL** It's the closest it's ever been.

**PEGGY** I don't care if we all—

**BILL** Well, you should care.

**PEGGY** —go up in smoke – I don't care.

**BILL** Okay, relax.

*BILL lights a cigarette.*

**PEGGY** I'm glad that you feel comfortable enough around me to just light up.

**BILL** Some kids and their parents? They can't be in the same room together.

**PEGGY** Don't let your father smell you.

**BILL** He never smells me.

**PEGGY** You wouldn't dare light up in front of him, would you?

**BILL** No.

**PEGGY** Lorraine blew smoke in his face. I laughed so hard the first time she did that. She was one of the few people who could make me laugh—

**BILL** Mom—

**PEGGY** We could just look at each other and we would start laughing. I can't stop crying. I don't know if I can get through this.

**BILL** You will get through this.

**PEGGY** And what if I don't?

**BILL** Do you want to kill yourself?

**PEGGY** I've thought about it.

**BILL** Great. Now I'm afraid to leave the house.

**PEGGY** No. No. No. I'll be okay. Okay?

**BILL** Okay.

*BILL gets up to leave.*

**PEGGY** Okay. I'll let you know. *(pause)* Are you going out?

**BILL** Yes.

**PEGGY** Bill, can I say something?

**BILL** I gotta go—

**PEGGY** Are you doing anything about your face?

**BILL** Mom—

**PEGGY** Do you want me to pick up some Clearasil?

**BILL** No.

**PEGGY** Are you eating enough fruit?

**BILL** No.

**PEGGY** Who are you going out with?

**BILL** A friend.

**PEGGY** Tonight is Family Night.

**BILL** Mom.

**PEGGY** What?

**BILL** You need a family to have a Family Night.

**PEGGY** I know that.

**BILL** Is Dad coming?

**PEGGY** He is family.

**BILL** He's going to fall asleep.

**PEGGY** That's what he does, Bill. He works. He eats. And he sleeps. *(pause)*

**BILL** Mom.

**PEGGY** What?

**BILL** Are you going to kill yourself?

**PEGGY** No. It's Family Night. *(pause)* Be home by seven-thirty.

*BILL turns to go. PEGGY takes the sheet and slowly unmakes the bed.*

## Scene Three – Waiting to Begin

*Later that afternoon, outside the Silverball Arcade, a video and pinball arcade that sits on the edge of a new subdivision. HAROLD and BILL outside the arcade. In the distance, we hear "Just My Imagination" (Rolling Stones).*

**BILL** Where's Darcy?

**HAROLD** He said he'd be here.

**BILL** He's not.

**HAROLD** He's probably doing his hair. Be another half an hour.

**BILL** How long does it take to do your hair?

**HAROLD** Three minutes, I timed it.

*Pause.*

**BILL** Our neighbour down the street killed herself.

**HAROLD** No way. That's awful. What happened?

**BILL** She goes skiing with her husband. First run of the day, he has a massive heart attack. He dies in her arms.

**HAROLD** No way. He didn't even get to ski!

**BILL** A week later, her only son dies in a head-on collision.

**HAROLD** That's awful.

**BILL** The next day she goes into her garage.

**HAROLD** Yeah—

**BILL** She runs a hose from the exhaust pipe—

**HAROLD** No.

**BILL** And feeds it into her car.

**HAROLD** No.

**BILL** With garage door down…

*PEGGY holds the sheets in her arms, kneeling and sobbing. HAROLD pulls a joint from his pocket.*

**HAROLD** I'm really sorry.

**BILL** Our families were really close. We would always have these wild hot tub parties.

**HAROLD** You guys have a hot tub?

**BILL** Yeah.

**HAROLD** Maybe we could use it sometime?

**BILL** Sure.

*Pause.*

**HAROLD** How long did it take her to die?

**BILL** I don't know.

**HAROLD** They say you start to fall asleep. You don't even know its happening. If I was going to kill myself, that's how I would do it. Silent monoxide. The silent killer.

**BILL** It's carbon monoxide.

**HAROLD** That's what I said.

**BILL** You said silent monoxide.

**HAROLD** I did?

**BILL** Yeah.

**HAROLD** Well, I meant carbon monoxide. *(beat)* What was her name?

**BILL** Lorraine Tisdale.

**HAROLD** Lorraine Tisdale.... That's a nice name.

**BILL** She was a nice lady.

*PEGGY gets up, remakes the bed.*

**HAROLD** That's what happens in a boom. All these people moving to Calgary, they think they can just cash in.... People want too much stuff. They can't afford it. Then they have to give it back. But they don't want to. So they kill themselves.

**BILL** People don't kill themselves over stuff. They kill themselves for love.

**HAROLD** Then why'd she kill herself?

**BILL** Her family was wiped out, Harold.

**HAROLD** Oh. Yeah. You just said that. Boy, do I have a bad memory. *(beat)* Least she didn't have a beer bottle explode in her face. Whoever heard of a beer bottle exploding after falling six inches? I have the worst luck of anyone I know. Hey, come on, quit hogging.

**BILL** It might have been a faulty bottle.

**HAROLD** That's what my lawyer said! Jeez. It's all wet.

**BILL** You have a lawyer?

**HAROLD** Yeah. We're gonna sue Molson's.

**BILL** Good luck.

**HAROLD** Why?

**BILL** Hello. They're Molson's? They founded this country. They own hockey teams and nuclear power plants; they make more money than most African countries combined.

**HAROLD** I have a good lawyer and he says we have a very good chance. And I have a witness. Darcy was in the car. We were sitting in that lot just over there and I was getting a beer from the trunk—

**BILL** Why were they in the trunk?

**HAROLD** I'm not going to leave an open case in the car. I don't give the police any reason to be suspicious of me. I am very careful, okay? So, I open the trunk, I go for the beer, I close the trunk and then the beer bottle just slips out of my hand, I can get it – it's rolling off the bumper – I got it – I got it, and BOOM everything slows down. Glass and beer and… I should have fallen back. But I didn't. Why did I step forward? That was so stupid! I fell into it. Why did I do that? I feel a sharp sting in my eye and it starts stinging more and more – and then I start screaming. *(beat)* I might have to wear this patch for the rest of my life. It's been forever since I went out with a girl. I probably won't get married. Who's going to marry a Cyclops? I won't have any kids. I won't be able to drive a car, or play any sports – I'll be stuck in Calgary the rest of my life – I hate it here. Everything is so brown. I want to go back to Kelowna. "Canada's Four Season Playground." It's warm and it's green and the girls are friendly. They don't wear so much clothing. In Kelowna, the girls know who you are. They'll say, Hey, Harold! Here they walk right by you, you don't even exist. Christ, I can't even look at girls and when I do my good eye waters up. Every night before I go to bed, I pray to God to give me my eyesight back. But I don't think he's listening. And I just wait.

**BILL** You and my mom always think the worst.

**HAROLD** Gee, Bill. She lost her best friend. I might lose my eye. What have you lost? Nothing bad ever happens to you.

**BILL** I have cystic acne. I might have this the rest of my life. You could get a glass eye, you know. Sammy Davis Jr. has one.

**HAROLD** He does?

**BILL** Yeah. And he's a big star.

**HAROLD** I like Sammy Davis Jr.

**BILL** If you had a glass eye, I bet you would get more dates.

**HAROLD** You think so?

**BILL** Yeah – these glass eyes – they look totally real. Once you get past the— Well. I mean, you tell her – "You were probably wondering – yeah – it's a glass eye." I mean, she's going to like you for you.

**HAROLD** Could you get blue eyes?

**BILL** I guess so. Maybe. I don't know. Why?

**HAROLD** It'd be cool if I could have blue eyes.

**BILL** Your good eye is brown.

**HAROLD** If I had blue eyes, I bet more girls would go out with me.

## Scene Four – Banished from the Arcade

*DARCY Fagen appears. The front of his hair crests like a breaking wave. It is oddly beautiful. He is wearing the same style lumber jacket as BILL and HAROLD, but only a different colour. He is swearing as he is being forced out the door of the arcade. The three boys don't see her, but JENNIFER Lachance comes out of the arcade when they are not looking.*

**DARCY** Don't touch my hair. Don't touch my hair. You touched my hair! You fat ugly hag. Hag – Fat hag, hagolah!

**HAROLD** Oh, no.

**DARCY** My hair is untouchable. You just lost my business. Hag! When my albums get here I won't need you! *(beat)* Nice jackets, boys…

**HAROLD** What happened?

**DARCY** I'm having the best, *the best* Dragon Slayer of my life. I was over a million. There was someone ahead of me; they had a million point five. Their initials JLA. I was closing in.

**HAROLD** No way.

**DARCY** Then it got stuck. The ball's just stuck at the top. Dangling. Right over the jaws of the Fucked Up Monster – I give her a push – I'm right inside her and the ball goes left – right into the jaws – right into triple bonus! – And then it goes black. And for a second, it's like I'm right inside it – I'm breathing it. I've never been to a million. It's quiet. Maybe a million is supposed to be quiet. Then I smell pretzels. Who's eating pretzels? I turn and it's Fat Hag – pretzel dust all over her face, like she looks like – a what – you know – what? A bad nightmare – and I laugh in her face and it's still too quiet – and then she holds up this plug and she's waving this plug in front of my face.

**HAROLD** She unplugged you!

**DARCY** My first time over a million!

**HAROLD** You hit the machine.

**DARCY** It was a love tap.

*Beat.*

**HAROLD** You'll have to apologize.

**DARCY** That'll be Kingdom fuckin' Doomsday. When my albums arrive, two things will happen: One, the Silverball Arcade will no longer be our primary source of entertainment. And two: we will no longer turn to stone whenever we look at Fat Hag. In two days, my stereo and my albums will be here. In two more days we listen to music at my house, in my room, with my albums. *(beat)* Now who's going home to change? *(pause)* Great. Now when we go to get some poontang, they're going to say, "Look at the goofs – they're all wearing the same jackets. We were going to give them some sweet poontang but they're all dressed the same. Tough luck, come on girls, let's go somewhere else."

*DARCY pulls out a joint.*

So, I guess we just stay here looking exactly the same. Light?

*HAROLD is there with a lighter just as fast as he can produce it, lighting the joint. DARCY smokes it, slowly, not offering any to HAROLD or BILL.*

**HAROLD** Oh, come on.

**DARCY** You run home and change jackets and we'll wait for you in the Bug.

**HAROLD** We're using the Bug way too much.

**DARCY** Well, I don't like being outside. It's not good for my hair.

**HAROLD** Oh, you poor thing.

*JENNIFER Lachance enters.*

**JENNIFER** Hey guys. What's up?

**DARCY** Hey Jennifer. What are you doing here?

**JENNIFER** You want to play Dragon Slayer?

**DARCY** No.

**JENNIFER** Afraid of losing again?

**DARCY** I just went over a million.

**HAROLD** Darcy got kicked out.

**BILL** Banished.

**JENNIFER** What happened?

**HAROLD** He hit the machine.

**DARCY** It was a love tap.

**HAROLD** Sure—

**DARCY** But I got over a million.

**JENNIFER** Who's got the top score?

**DARCY** JLA.

**JENNIFER** JLA?

**DARCY** JLA. It's prolly that guy who comes in every afternoon.

**JENNIFER** Are you sure it's a guy?

**DARCY** What?

**JENNIFER** JLA. JLA.

**BILL** JLA. Jennifer Lachance.

**HAROLD** *(beat)* You're JLA!

**BILL** You're in my religion class.

**DARCY** You can beat me anytime, Jennifer.

**JENNIFER** ...Yeah... hey... have you got any smoke?

**DARCY** Here. *(gives the joint to JENNIFER)*

**JENNIFER** Is this the hydroponic?

**DARCY** Yeah.

**JENNIFER** Oh, good. Can I take this one?

**DARCY** Do you want to go get some beer?

**JENNIFER** Sorry, I'm already on a date. I gotta go. Thanks for the joint. I like your eye patch.

**HAROLD** Thanks.

*He turns away, bashful.*

**JENNIFER** Hey, if you guys are going to hang out, you should probably wear different jackets.

See you later!

*JENNIFER exits.*

**HAROLD** She's cool.

**BILL** She's hot.

**HAROLD** She's untouchable.

**BILL** No…

**DARCY** You're treading water in the deep end, boys. Believe me. I tried. Besides, I don't have time for girls… I've got this thing with a woman.

**BILL & HAROLD** A woman?

**HAROLD** A woman?

**DARCY** I just said that.

**HAROLD** Where did you meet this woman?

**DARCY** At school.

**BILL** At school?

*Beat.*

**DARCY** She's a teacher.

**BILL** At our school?

**HAROLD** That's bullshit.

**BILL** Who is she?

**DARCY** I can't tell you. It might jeopardize her job.

**HAROLD** It's bullshit.

**DARCY** No, it isn't.

**HAROLD** Total bullshit.

**BILL** There's no woman.

**HAROLD** Moooo…

**BILL & HAROLD** Mooo…

**DARCY** Okay. I'll tell you.

**HAROLD** Okay.

**BILL** Who is it?

**DARCY** Our religion teacher.

*Beat.*

**BILL** She's a nun.

**DARCY** It's like bagging a lion.

**HAROLD** No way!

**DARCY** Oh, yeah!

**BILL** She's a nun.

**DARCY** I didn't see her wearing any Sally Field flying nun wings. Fuckin' – she had on these tight pants – showing everyone her wicked ass. Nuns do not wear tight jeans. And yesterday, she said we're going to study all the world religions. I look at her and I go, "Can we study the kama sutra?" She's staring right at me. She goes, "Sure. Come to my office after class."

**HAROLD** So what happened?

**DARCY** I waited for her after class. She said, "I think you're going to bring a lot of fresh air to our class discussions."

**BILL** You're going to bring a lot of hot air to the class discussions.

**HAROLD** Darcy, she was giving you detention.

**DARCY** No shit, Sherlock. She was giving me detention so she could get me alone.

**HAROLD** What a loser!

**BILL** Life size!

**DARCY** We're still wearing the same jackets, Bill.

**HAROLD** It's so warm out… I don't need to wear a jacket. *(ties his jacket around his waist)*

**DARCY** Making it a fashion accessory does not escape the fact that we are still three men wearing the same jackets. *(beat)* Okay. More tokes for me.

**HAROLD** Oh, come on.

**DARCY** Fetch me a lager and the rest of the joint is yours.

**HAROLD** Do you have any money?

**DARCY** No.

**HAROLD** You just got paid.

**DARCY** I spent it on this. *(indicates the joint)*

**BILL** Where do you work?

**HAROLD** Darcy works at the bottle depot. With the slow kids!

**DARCY** Duhh… don't forget to take your caps off the pop bottles.

**HAROLD** It's the only job he could find.

**DARCY** You got me the job.

**HAROLD** And they fired me!

**DARCY** Apparently, taking caps off of bottles requires two good eyes.

**BILL** I have some money.

**DARCY** You got a job?

**BILL** I had a job.

**DARCY** Where did you work?

**BILL** I can't say.

**DARCY** Can't be any worse than the bottle depot purgatory—

**HAROLD** Yeah, come on.

**DARCY** Come on.

**BILL** Phil's Pancake House.

**HAROLD** All the pancakes you can eat!

**DARCY** Four kinds of syrup!

**HAROLD** Waiters make good tips—

**BILL** I was a busboy.

**HAROLD** Busboys make good tips.

**BILL** It took me a month to make a hundred bucks.

**HAROLD** A hundred bucks can buy you a lot. You can buy new records, you can get—

**DARCY** A ticket to the Rush concert.

**HAROLD** What? Rush is coming?

**DARCY** Yeah.

**HAROLD** When?

**DARCY** Two weeks.

**HAROLD** Where?

**DARCY** At the Corral.

**HAROLD** No way!

**DARCY** Okay. Here's what we do. We buy an ounce.

**HAROLD** What?

**DARCY** Yeah, we start dealing.

**BILL & HAROLD** Dealing?

**DARCY** Yeah, we'll make a shitload more money than we'd ever make at the bottle depot purgatory. We buy an ounce. We cut it into five quarters, plus a little for our personal stash. We make a profit. We have our own reserve, money to buy beer, money to waste on chicks. And most importantly, money for Rush!

**HAROLD** I can't believe Rush is coming.

**DARCY** We have to go.

**HAROLD** Darcy is a total Rush freak. Ask him anything about Rush.

**DARCY** Ask me anything about Rush. Anything!

**BILL** Why don't you hear Rush on the radio?

**DARCY** Mainstream radio will not play three man bands that sound like five. Mainstream radio is brainwashing everybody into thinking that you need four musicians to play rock 'n roll. With Rush, there's only three. And. They sound like five. Ask me something else. I know all there is to know about Rush. Ask me about Neil Peart. Ask me about Neil Peart. Ask me about Neil Peart. Ask me about Neil Peart.

**HAROLD** Please, just ask him.

**BILL** Who's Neil Peart?

**DARCY** Neil Peart a.k.a. The Professor. The most secretive member of Rush. Nobody knows anything about him. Born September 12, 1952. He starts drumming when he is thirteen. Becomes a member of Rush in June 1974, after playing in a band called Hush. He played in a band called Hush. Don't you find that coincidental that he started out in a band called Hush and ended up in another band called Rush? Ask me about Alex Lifeson. Ask me about Alex Lifeson.

**BILL** Jimmy Page is a better guitarist.

**DARCY** Comparing Alex Lifeson to Jimmy Page is like comparing a tornado to a squall.

**HAROLD** Squall! That's a great word.

**DARCY** Yeah. They are both great artists. But Alex Lifeson is a classically trained guitarist. Go into a music store and look at the sheet music of Rush's 2112 and then look at the notes that Beethoven uses in one of his symphonies. They're the same amount of notes. *(pause)* This is an excellent plan. To review: buy the ounce, cut it into five quarters, make an exponential profit, go to the Rush concert. Any questions? No? Good. I need an alcoholic beverage to slake my thirst. Who's buying?

**BILL** I can't. I gotta go.

**HAROLD** You have to go?

**BILL** I forgot all about dinner with my parents. Every second Saturday, we go out and try to be a family. It's my mom's idea. Sorry guys.

**HAROLD** That's nice.

**DARCY** Are you going to leave us five bucks?

**BILL** Here. Have one on me.

**HAROLD** Think about it, Bill. Are you sure you want to partner up with Darcy?

**DARCY** Hey!

**BILL** I sure as hell don't want to be a busboy.

**DARCY** Do we have a deal?

*Beat.*

**BILL** We have a deal.

*BILL exits.*

**DARCY** Let's get some beer and go to the Bug.

**HAROLD** Let's get some Pilsner.

**DARCY** I don't want Pilsner.

**HAROLD** What's wrong with Pilsner?

**DARCY** Pilsner sucks.

**HAROLD** I'm not drinking Canadian.

**DARCY** Why not?

**HAROLD** We're not drinking the same beer that made me blind in one eye.

## Scene Five

*Later that evening. BILL opens the gate to his backyard and deck. He finds PEGGY lying on the deck, not moving.*

**BILL** Mom. Mom? Are you okay? Mom?

**PEGGY** I slipped.

**BILL** How long have you been lying there?

**PEGGY** I don't know.

**BILL** Does your back hurt?

**PEGGY** I think so.

**BILL** Oh, Jesus. Can you move your toes?

**PEGGY** I don't know.

**BILL** Try and move your toes.

**PEGGY** Okay. *(She does.)* I can move my toes.

**BILL** Can you move your feet?

**PEGGY** Well, I just moved my toes.

**BILL** Okay. I'm going to try and move you.

**PEGGY** I'm not ready to move.

**BILL** We have to get you inside.

**PEGGY** Look at that.

**BILL** Where?

**PEGGY** Lie down and I'll show you. There. Between the trees. *(He lies down beside her.)* See? What is that?

**BILL** That's the North Star.

**PEGGY** I know that. Above the North Star. To the right.

**BILL** I don't have a clue.

**PEGGY** I thought you took astronomy when you were a Cub Scout.

**BILL** We had a section on astronomy, but I didn't want to go.

**PEGGY** What were you doing?

**BILL** I don't know. I just remember I didn't want to be a Cub Scout. I think it was the end of something and I wasn't sure why I wanted to do something different.

*Sidelights appear, sweeping over them. VICTOR brings on two chairs. He sits and waits.*

Speak of the devil.

*VICTOR parks the car but it is still running. VICTOR starts to fall asleep.*

**PEGGY** What's he doing?

*Silence.*

**BILL** I don't know.

**PEGGY** What's he doing?

**BILL** I don't know.

**PEGGY** Bill, stand up. What is he doing?

**BILL** He's just sitting there.

**PEGGY** Why is the engine still running? Turn off the engine. Vic! Turn off the engine!

*VICTOR bobs his head.*

*(at the same time as BILL's next line)* Vic. Vic. Vic! Wake up!

**BILL** Dad! Dad! Wake up!

**PEGGY** Vic. Vic. Vic! Wake up!

*VICTOR opens his eyes, gets out of the chair.*

**VICTOR** *(distracted)* What?

**PEGGY** Why did you leave the car running?

**VICTOR** I was thinking about something.

**PEGGY** What were you thinking about?

**VICTOR** Work. *(pause)* What are you doing down there?

**PEGGY** Looking at the North Star.

**VICTOR** You might see it better with a telescope.

**PEGGY** Oh, really?

**BILL** Mom fell.

**VICTOR** How did you fall?

**PEGGY** The usual way: with a complete lack of dignity.

**VICTOR** Why didn't you chip the ice?

**BILL** There is no ice.

**VICTOR** It's cold enough to slip and fall. Why didn't you salt it?

**BILL** I just got home—

**PEGGY** Vic – did you teach astronomy in Bill's Cub Scout group?

**VICTOR** Yeah. I was their leader.

**PEGGY** That's what I thought—

**VICTOR** You missed that section, Bill. We went out to the edge of the city and we identified all the major stars in the Milky Way. You would have gotten a badge if you were there. But you had something more important to do with your friends. *(pause)* What were you doing?

**BILL** I wasn't doing anything.

**VICTOR** You must have been doing something.

**BILL** I just didn't want to be there.

**PEGGY** Okay—

**VICTOR** Help her up then. Help her up.

**BILL** She wants to lie here and look at the stars.

*They help PEGGY to her feet.*

**PEGGY** Did either of you remember that tonight is Family Night? You forgot, didn't you? Vic?

**VICTOR** Peg – it's late. I'm tired.

**PEGGY** It is eight-thirty on a Saturday night and I have been lying here on this deck since seven – ready to go! If it wasn't for the chinook, I would have frozen to death. Now. There is a new restaurant that just opened on MacLeod Trail. An all-night steak house! I want to go there. I want to have steak. I live in Alberta and I want to have a steak. My best friend, Lorraine, is dead and I would like some steak. My body is screaming for steak. Now help me up.

*VIC and BILL help her to her feet.*

## Scene Six – Smuggler's Cove

*Later that evening. PEGGY, VICTOR and BILL at Smuggler's Cove. A young girl in a wench costume greets them at the door. BILL recognizes her immediately. It is JENNIFER, from his religious studies class but she does not notice him. VICTOR is trying to stay awake.*

**JENNIFER** Hi. Welcome to Smuggler's Cove. I'm Jennifer. I'll be your wench tonight. *(She laughs.)* I mean, I'm your hostess. I'm supposed to say that. We offer a unique dining experience. If you look around, you will see that everything on the wall is a reproduction, and nobody seems to mind. Anyone under ten gets a free eye patch. Is there anyone under ten? No. Well, have a free eye patch anyway. How many of you are there?

**PEGGY** Three.

**VICTOR** Is this one of those singing restaurants?

**JENNIFER** We sing for birthdays, anniversaries, graduations, bar mitzvahs, is someone having a birthday? Would you like us to sing at your table?

**VICTOR & BILL** No!

**PEGGY** It's our Family Night.

**JENNIFER** We don't have a song for Family Night. Maybe we should.

**BILL** Come on, Dad. We're a family.

**JENNIFER** You're in my religion class.

**BILL** Yeah.

**JENNIFER** Ron?

**BILL** No. Bill.

**JENNIFER** Sorry.

**BILL** It's okay. *(beat)* It's Family Night. A very special night.

**JENNIFER** Oh.... So, if you'd like to follow me.

*They walk though what seems like a maze of aisles.*

**PEGGY** Isn't this mysterious? I'll bet there are secret passageways everywhere, just like Pirates of the Caribbean.

**JENNIFER** Here we are.

*They come to the table and sit.*

Our specials tonight are the Baron's Platter, for $14.95, the Queen's Plate for $15.95 and the King's Ransom for $16.95. There's the Buccaneer Burger with Jean Lafitte Fries, and there's the Buried Treasure—a plate of nachos, jalapeños and our blend of red, green and yellow peppers—with three kinds of cheeses, and our Swashbuckler Salad Bar for $12.95.

*VICTOR nods off.*

**PEGGY** Vic?

**VICTOR** What?

**PEGGY** You're falling asleep.

**VICTOR** That's because I'm tired.

**PEGGY** That's because you're up every morning at four-thirty. Why don't you sleep in?

**VICTOR** Because I'm wide awake at four-thirty.

*Pause.*

**JENNIFER** Anyone for an alcoholic beverage?

**BILL** I'll have a beer.

**JENNIFER** Can I see your ID?

**BILL** I don't have it with me.

**JENNIFER** Then I'm afraid I can't serve you.

**VICTOR** I'll have his beer.

**BILL** I'll have a Coke.

**JENNIFER** And what can I get you ma'am?

**PEGGY** It's so mysterious in here. I think I'll have something piratey.

**BILL** Mom.

**JENNIFER** I can bring you something with a cherry and a sword.

**PEGGY** How about a chi-chi?

**JENNIFER** Good choice, very piratey.

**PEGGY** Make it a double.

**BILL** Can I have fruit and a sword, too?

**JENNIFER** I'll still need to see your ID.

*JENNIFER exits to get the drinks.*

**PEGGY** She is cute. You should ask her out.

**BILL** Yeah, Mom, I should be doing a lot of things.

**PEGGY** You should be using that Clearasil, your face will clear right up. It has that Oxy 10.

**VICTOR** What's Oxy 10?

**PEGGY** A new ingredient that clears up cystic acne.

**BILL** Mom, the only thing that will clear up my face is a sandblaster.

**PEGGY** That's an exaggeration.

**BILL** Do you believe everything you see on TV? What? Why are you staring at me?

**PEGGY** You have a big zit that's ready to go—

**BILL** Where?

**PEGGY** Right on your temple. Here. Let me just get—

**BILL** Mom – not here—

**VIC** Peg—

**PEGGY** It's going to go.

*BILL cries out in pain. JENNIFER appears with drinks.*

**JENNIFER** Here we go!

**PEGGY** Got it.

*BILL hides his face behind a menu.*

**JENNIFER** Would you like to order now?

**PEGGY** Tell me, would you go out with a boy who had cystic acne?

**JENNIFER** Pardon?

**PEGGY** Would you go out with a boy who had cystic acne?

**JENNIFER** I might, if he was nice.

**PEGGY** Would you go out with my son? He's feeling very self-conscious these days.

**BILL** *(starts drinking the beer)* I am so sorry.

**JENNIFER** Your mother is very direct. Can I take your orders?

**VICTOR** Three steaks, medium rare, two with baked potatoes, one with fries.

**JENNIFER** I'll be right back. *(leaves)*

**PEGGY** I think she likes you. *(pause)* What?

**BILL** Would you please stop controlling me?

**PEGGY** I'm not controlling you. Is that what you think I am doing?

**VICTOR** Just let him be.

**PEGGY** That's just irresponsible. These next few years are going to be very important, and I want to make sure he becomes a good person. A compassionate person who is thoughtful. Considerate. But look at him. Do you know who he is? We have forgotten about you, Bill, and now… I… want to know what you think. I want to know. I don't know anything about your friends. Do you have friends?

*Pause.*

**BILL** Yes.

**PEGGY** Who are your friends?

*Pause.*

**BILL** Harold. *(pause)* And Darcy.

**PEGGY** What happened to all your friends from last year?

**BILL** They moved away.

**PEGGY** Where did they go?

**BILL** They got rich and left Calgary. Their dads got jobs in New York, London. They all left.

**PEGGY** They all left?

**BILL** They all left.

**VICTOR** They all got rich!

**PEGGY** And what are your new friends like?

**BILL** You've already asked me this.

**PEGGY** And you didn't give me an answer. Why are you being so hostile with me?

**BILL** Why are you picking at me? You're picking at my face, you're picking out girlfriends for me.

**PEGGY** I only want what is best. She seems like a very nice girl.

*JENNIFER re-enters.*

**JENNIFER** Thank you. So? Who ordered the steak? There you go, enjoy your meal.

*She hands out the steaks. Then they all exchange with one another until they get it right. BILL reaches for the ketchup.*

**PEGGY** Thank you. *(to BILL)* Are you going to put ketchup on your steak?

**BILL** Yes.

**PEGGY** No. Don't do that. Have some HP Sauce.

**BILL** I want ketchup.

**JENNIFER** Will there be anything else?

**VICTOR** No.

**JENNIFER** All right then, enjoy. *(exits)*

*Beat.*

**PEGGY** Jackie Onassis does exactly the same thing. She puts ketchup on everything. That is a beautiful steak. How can you put ketchup on it? That will just ruin it.

**VICTOR** Just let the kid have some ketchup on his steak.

**PEGGY** Have you tried HP Sauce before?

**BILL** Yes. Many times. And you know what? I still want ketchup. Can I please have the ketchup? Mom. Can I please have the ketchup? Mom? The ketchup! *(pause)*

**PEGGY** Well. How's your steak, Vic? Would you like some HP Sauce?

**VICTOR** I've got a little bit right here, thanks.

**PEGGY** Bill? How's your ketchup? *(pause)* Ketchup over your steak! Just like the Kennedys. You remember the Russian Tea Room, Vic?

**VICTOR** Of course I remember – how could I forget. We were on our honeymoon. All these Kennedys came crashing through the door – and you could just tell they were Kennedys. One of them had a football, gestured to another, and it looked like he was going to toss it the length of the tea room… and that's exactly what he did. So, he fires the ball, but way too fast and off target and it's headed right towards our table. Your mother's staring like a bunny in the headlights – she's not even moving. So, I'm sitting on her right side and I reach up with my left hand and catch the ball. Everyone in the restaurant starts cheering and I throw the ball right back at him. He wasn't expecting it but catches it and then there was this moment when we just looked at each other, me and Bobby Kennedy. And Peggy said, "There you go, Vic, you're good enough to play ball with the Kennedys."

*Beat.*

**PEGGY** I meant about Jackie and the ketchup!

*Time passes. They devour their food. VICTOR starts to fall asleep in his plate. JENNIFER re-enters.*

**JENNIFER** Excuse me. Sir? Sir? Can I get you a cup of coffee? Sir? Is he a deep sleeper?

**PEGGY** Vic. Vic. It's nine a.m. You've slept in.

**VICTOR** I'm late. I'm late.

*He wakes, gets up to leave.*

**PEGGY** No. You're early, Vic. Seven more hours and you get to go to work.

*Beat.*

**JENNIFER** Anyone for dessert?

**VICTOR** No.

**PEGGY** You always order dessert.

**VICTOR** I have a big day tomorrow.

**PEGGY** Tomorrow is Sunday, Vic.

**VICTOR** I need Sunday to get ready for Monday.

**PEGGY** You get up at four-thirty, you're gone by six and you come home at eight o'clock. You have supper and you're asleep by nine-thirty. With all the time you work, why aren't we living in Eagle Ridge?

**BILL** Mom, it doesn't matter where we live—

**PEGGY** It does matter. I think that if you work so hard, you fall asleep in your dinner, you should live in Eagle Ridge. But I know people from Eagle Ridge and they don't fall asleep in their dinner. Why don't we live in a big house, Vic? You have worked so hard, you should have a big house. Answer me. Why don't we live in a big house?

**VICTOR** Because we re-mortgaged it.

**PEGGY** That's right. We re-mortgaged this one so you could keep the business going. Not once, but twice. Every time I walked into Lorraine's house, there was laughter. Every time. Great, infectious, explosive laughter. And that laughter helped me forget that you were working late, and you were never home for dinner, and you talked me into re-mortgaging the house. And I was okay with it as long as I heard Lorraine's laughter. These last couple of years, I wanted to move in with Lorraine.

*JENNIFER appears.*

**JENNIFER** *(singing)* You have to learn to love each other

'Cause tonight's your special night
Your very special Family Night
Tonight's your special Family Night
To – night's your special Family Night!
Tonight!

Have a good night. Drive safely.

## Scene Seven – Darcy and Harold in the Bug

**HAROLD** Well, I guess I'll call it a night.

**DARCY** It's Saturday night.

**HAROLD** I'm tired.

**DARCY** Don't go in.

**HAROLD** Yeah, I'm going in.

**DARCY** I thought we were going to find some chicks. Come on. It's still early.

**HAROLD** No. Everyone's going to look at my eye patch!

**DARCY** Aaaw. Cindi-loo-hoo hears a freaking one-eyed boo-hoo!

*They backhand each other. It escalates, until HAROLD stops it.*

**HAROLD** Get out. I'll call you tomorrow.

**DARCY** See you later.

*DARCY walks off quickly, leaving HAROLD standing there.*

## Scene Eight

*BILL, VICTOR and PEGGY. BILL takes PEGGY's arm as they go across the deck.*

**PEGGY** I'm wide awake from all that red meat.

**VICTOR** I'm off to bed. Anybody got a problem with that?

*They don't answer. VICTOR exits. BILL waits until he is out of sight, then steps out on to the deck and lights a cigarette. PEGGY finds her original spot on the deck and lies down.*

**BILL** What are you doing?

**PEGGY** I'm looking for Lorraine.

**BILL** You're going to freeze.

**PEGGY** It's surprisingly warm. I could look at these stars forever.

*She hears laughter, clearly. It is coming from the Tisdale's. PEGGY gets up, goes out onto the back deck.*

Who's out there? Hello? Who's out there?

*PEGGY walks over to the Tisdale's. BILL is right behind her. PEGGY hears a noise and turns. BILL surprises her.*

Jesus Christ. Don't sneak up on me like that.

**BILL** What are you doing?

**PEGGY** I heard voices.

**BILL** Where?

**PEGGY** From inside Lorraine's house.

**BILL** Wait. You're not going in there.

**PEGGY** Lorraine gave me a spare key.

**BILL** Wait. You can't go inside!

*PEGGY has already unlocked the front door.*

*Transition.*

*DARCY inside the Bug. He tries to be quiet, but then he begins to sing "The Trees" by Rush, and as he sings louder, he turns the music up, until it is at maximum volume.*

*HAROLD comes out.*

**HAROLD** I knew it was you. What are you doing? You can't stay here.

**DARCY** Why not?

**HAROLD** Why not? Because it's the middle of the night. It's the middle of winter. And this car – this car doesn't belong to you. You're going to freeze out here.

**DARCY** Then ask me in.

**HAROLD** Forget it. You have to go home.

**DARCY** I don't like going home.

**HAROLD** Why not?

**DARCY** Because I don't.

**HAROLD** Look. You can't be in here.

**DARCY** Come on. Come on.

**HAROLD** No.

**DARCY** It's soundproof in here.

**HAROLD** *(reaches in and takes the key)* I could hear you from the house, dicknose. Now go home.

**DARCY** I'm not leaving.

**HAROLD** Darcy, you're driving me crazy – come on.

**DARCY** NO! If I go home… it's just… we're just gonna yell at each other – but I can't yell at him 'cause that'll get his blood pressure up. And he yells at me anyway.

**HAROLD** Move over.

*Transition.*

*PEGGY and BILL. Inside the Tisdale's.*

**PEGGY** I can smell her perfume.

**BILL** Wow. *(beat)* Look.

**PEGGY** What?

**BILL** The kitchen. The living room. It's clean. Spotless. It's like she was planning to go.

*The phone rings. They watch as the answering machine picks it up on the third ring.*

**VOICE-OVER** *(Herb Alpert music in the background)* Hi, hi, hi we're the Tisdales! Lorraine and Bob. We're not here, we're somewhere else. But your call is very important to us. So, tell us what you've called to talk to us about and we'll get right back to you. Promise. Just wait for the beep and our new fancy machine will record it all. Just wait for it…

*There is a beep. The background crackles, and then we hear voices in a vacuum, like they are at a cocktail party, and then we hear Lorraine's laughter, and more voices, then silence.*

**BILL** *(pause)* I think we better go. Mom. I think we better go now.

**PEGGY** It's Lorraine.

**BILL** We should go now.

**PEGGY** She's trying to reach me.

**BILL** I think we better go now.

**PEGGY** Lorraine? Oh my God. I can hear you. You're so close.

*PEGGY reaches out into the darkness, her hand trembling.*

*Blackout.*

*End of Act One.*

# Act Two

## Scene One – Dream Weaver

*Music: "La Villa Strangiato" (Rush, Hemispheres).*

*Early morning. The sun's first light appears on the eastern horizon, while to the west, the massive line of a chinook arch moves across the brightening sky. In the back alley behind HAROLD's, the inside of the Bug is glowing green and silver phosphorescence, while clouds gather. The Bug glows with more intensity, while smoke is escaping from every crevice of the dune buggy. We hear coughing, increasing in intensity until the door opens. It is DARCY hacking and he leans over and spits a lungful of phlegm out on the sidewalk. Finished, VICTOR rises, coughing, hacking and spitting. PEGGY is lying on the ground making a starfish. VICTOR is carefully considering the size of a quarter ounce of grass.*

**VICTOR** On a scale of one to ten, this would be…

**DARCY** Ten.

**VICTOR** Ten.

**DARCY** *(pause)* Yeah.

**VICTOR** Ten? Really.

**DARCY** Ten.

**VICTOR** Ten.

**DARCY** Yeah. Ten.

**VICTOR** Wow.

*VICTOR looks at DARCY.*

**BILL** Dad?

**VICTOR** There are six hundred people moving here every day.

**DARCY** Yes, there are. Once these people have their basic requirements met: food, shelter, they're going to want entertainment.

**VICTOR** I never thought of it as entertainment.

**BILL** Are you going to sell pot with Darcy? Dad, you build houses.

**VICTOR** Not anymore.

**BILL** You're a developer.

**VICTOR** I quit.

**BILL** You can't quit. *(beat)* You're my dad.

**DARCY** Vic. Vic. Vic. Do we have a deal?

**VICTOR** We have a deal.

*They shake on it. VICTOR and DARCY walk away.*

Come on, we're going to be late.

**BILL** What's going on?

**DARCY** Your dad got us tickets to the Rush concert. He's the best dad ever. See you later, Ron!

**BILL** Dad. Dad. Dad. Dad!

**VICTOR** What?

**BILL** You listen to Nana Mouskouri.

**VICTOR** Not anymore.

**HAROLD** Hey, Bill! You're so lucky, man. Nothing bad ever happens to you.

**BILL** That's not true. I have cystic acne.

**HAROLD** If I was in Kelowna right now, I wouldn't have any bad luck. Hey, Bill. Have you ever seen the Okanagan? It's beautiful. We'll go waterskiing, meet some girls and we'll borrow my mom's '67 Barracuda with the top down. Just you and me, okay? What do you say, Bill? Is it a deal? Bill? Is it a deal? Bill? Is it a deal?

*JENNIFER appears out of nowhere.*

**JENNIFER** Hi there.

**BILL** Hi, Jennifer.

**JENNIFER** Kevin.

**BILL** Bill. It's okay…

**JENNIFER** I'm sorry, but you remind me so much of my little brother Kevin.

**BILL** Okay. Stop. I'm not going to get anywhere with you if you think of me as your little brother.

**JENNIFER** We could be really good friends.

*PEGGY sits up.*

**PEGGY** If you become friends then you'll become good lovers. Besides, Bill, sex does not last as long as friendship. It's physically impossible. And friendship is a lot more rewarding.

**BILL** My mother: "The Hallmark Card."

**PEGGY** Hey, you're the girl from Smuggler's! What a coincidence!

**JENNIFER** What's your mom doing?

**BILL** She's counting all the stars in the Milky Way.

**JENNIFER** Is she an astronomer?

**BILL** No. She's the general manager of Wicker World.

*JENNIFER crosses the stage and lies down beside PEGGY.*

**JENNIFER** Is it okay if I lie here?

**PEGGY** You're the girl from Smuggler's!

**JENNIFER** Yes.

**PEGGY** Are you going to stay the night?

**BILL** Jennifer. I want you to know that I think you're great. If you want, you can stay the night.

*He passionately kisses her.*

**JENNIFER** I better go.

*She walks away singing "It Ain't Me Babe" (Bob Dylan).*

**BILL** Oh, man. She tastes like sugar cubes!

**HAROLD** Oh my God! What's happening?

**BILL** What's the matter?

**HAROLD** I can't see. I can't see. I thought I was going to get better. But I've gotten worse. Why did they lie to me? I have to get to Kelowna. Then everything will be fine. Bill, you have to drive me to Kelowna.

**BILL** I only have my learner's.

*In the distance, we hear "Gimme Shelter."*

**HAROLD** I thought I could count on you.

**DARCY** Way to go. He thought he could count on you.

**BILL** I know.

**PEGGY** Friends are more important than sex.

**BILL** I know.

**VICTOR** You're in way over your head, Bill.

*The engine revs higher and higher, tires squealing. Everything grows in intensity! Blackout.*

*Lights up. PEGGY on the deck. BILL in a sweat on his bed. He goes out on the deck.*

**BILL** How many stars have you counted?

**PEGGY** I've lost track.

**BILL** Are you warm enough?

**PEGGY** I think so.

*Pause.*

**BILL** Time to come in, Mom.

*Pause.*

Time to come—

**PEGGY** I'm not ready to come in. *(beat)* She's near me. She's one of those stars and I need to find out which one she is.

**BILL** Let me know if she appears. *(pause)* I'm going out, Mom. I'll see you later.

## Scene Two

*HAROLD, DARCY and BILL on their way to DUANE's.*

**DARCY** Come on, we have two minutes to get there.

**BILL** I'm coming.

**DARCY** We have two minutes to get there.

**BILL** I'm coming.

**HAROLD** You get caught dealing – you go to prison.

**DARCY** Thanks for the tip.

**HAROLD** Don't do the time if you can't do the crime.

**DARCY** Other way around, Eeyore. Come on.

*DARCY starts walking.*

We gotta catch him before he goes out.

**HAROLD** Who?

**DARCY** Duane.

**HAROLD** Duane?

**DARCY** Duane.

**HAROLD** Duane Neidermeyer? *(stops)* You didn't tell me it was Duane.

**DARCY** What's wrong with Duane?

**HAROLD** He gives me the creeps. He stares at my eye patch.

**DARCY** Everybody stares at it. What's the problem?

**HAROLD** We're dealing now. That's the problem. You attract a different breed of human when you start dealing.

**DARCY** Like who?

**HAROLD** Like Duane Neidermeyer.

*Air guitar.*

**DARCY** Harold, we're only selling to people we know. And having you there will make sure everything goes smoothly.

**HAROLD** Smoothly? What – what – what – what – am I supposed to be your – bodyguard?

**DARCY** Yes.

**HAROLD** You guys are just – using me.

**DARCY** Bill, how much 'tang did you get bussing tables?

**BILL** Zero.

**DARCY** Harold. How many girls have you gone out with using your substantial earnings from the bottle depot?

**HAROLD** Wait. Wait. I have to be really careful. I'm suing Molson's. If their lawyers find out I'm part of something like this, I could lose my case.

**DARCY** We only sell to people that we know. *(travelling a bit more)* And here we are. Give me the money.

**BILL** What?

**DARCY** I gotta go alone. He doesn't like meeting people he doesn't know.

**BILL** What if he takes it?

**DARCY** He's not going to rip us off. He's in my automotives class. Give me the money.

*BILL has the money separated in four different pockets.*

Duane always has good grass. Where's the money?

**BILL** I'm getting it.

*Pause.*

**DARCY** Come on. Where's the money? Where's the money? Where's the money?

**BILL** I'm getting it. I'm getting it.

**DARCY** Okay. You guys wait here.

## Scene Three

*The same evening. PEGGY lying on the deck. We hear VICTOR's car pull up. He lets the engine run. VICTOR turns off the car, the headlamps go out. He whistles an old tune, looking for the house key. He stops and sees PEGGY lying on the deck*

**PEGGY** Do you remember the day we moved into this house? It was the hottest July in a hundred years. Lorraine and Bob came up to the front door with their hands behind their backs and said they had a housewarming gift for us. And I was thinking, "That is so nice." And they launched a water balloon right at me. Then another. I was soaked from head to toe. And Lorraine was laughing so hard. It was the first time I heard her laugh. I loved the sound of it, as if she was biting into the air. Then a couple of hours later you and I snuck up on their house and threw water balloons right through their front door. Lorraine tried to catch one but it blew right up in her hand and she got soaked. And we stood there we were all laughing hysterically, even you... I used to love to hear your laughter.

*He goes inside, takes his coat off.*

You don't laugh anymore.

**VICTOR** Of course I do—

**PEGGY** When was the last time you laughed? I mean really laughed. You don't remember.

**VICTOR** I laughed this week. It was Tuesday. I was telling someone in my office about the time Grandpa took me to the Stampede Corral to listen to Trudeau speak at the Liberal convention, and Grandpa drove like a madman to get there early and get a good seat because he wanted everyone to know he was a friend of Tommy Douglas, he knew Tommy Douglas and Grandpa thought Trudeau would be just like Tommy Douglas, but as soon as Trudeau spoke—it must have been only ten minutes—Grandpa stood up so everyone could hear, "Come on, Victor. This is bullshit. This bastard's gonna wreck the country!" And we left. *(laughs)*

**PEGGY** Why do you think that's funny?

**VICTOR** Because it's true.

**PEGGY** What is true?

**VICTOR** What is true is that Trudeau is a goddamned communist.

**PEGGY** What are you talking about?

**VICTOR** He went to Cuba. He was hanging out with Fidel and Mousey Tung. He's a communist. He's giving our wheat away to the Russkies and the Chinks.

*PEGGY gets up to leave.*

**PEGGY** They're Chinese, Vic. People from China are Chinese. Why don't you call them Chinese?

**VICTOR** I didn't know it bothered you so much.

**PEGGY** It makes you sound racist.

**VICTOR** I'm not a racist.

**PEGGY** Vic, I hate to break it to you, but calling a Chinese person a chink is racist.

## Scene Four

*The same evening. Outside DUANE's townhouse. DUANE appears. He has shoulder-length blond hair and is very muscular. He literally kicks DARCY in the ass all the way to the curb, and on the ground, DUANE is about to punch him, but he knocks on his forehead.*

**DUANE** You do not come here! You go to the designated area! Do you understand?

**DARCY** Yes, yes, yes, yes.

**DUANE** The cops are watching me.

*DUANE exits.*

**DARCY** What a fuckhead.

*Beat.*

**BILL** So, did you get any pot?

**DARCY** Yeah. I got some pot, it's right here! *(flips BILL the bird)* No, I didn't get any pot.

**HAROLD** Why not?

**DARCY** 'Cause we didn't go to the designated area.

**HAROLD** Well, how can we go to the designated area if we don't know where it is?

**DARCY** Don't you think I know that? I'm not the Amazing Kreskin. Fuck, he thinks that he's some kind of – He's growing in there. All the windows had tinfoil on them.

**BILL** So where's the designated area?

**DARCY** Fuck! I don't know. He was too busy kickin' my ass to tell me where the designated area was.

**BILL** Do you always have to swear?

**DARCY** Fuck you.

**HAROLD** Nice mouth. I'll go ask.

*HAROLD leaves.*

**DARCY** You're gonna get your ass kicked.

*HAROLD goes up to the door. He rings the bell. DUANE appears.*

**DUANE** Fuck are you?

**HAROLD** I'm Harold.

**DUANE** What do you want?

**HAROLD** You didn't tell us when we're going to meet or where the designated area is.

**DUANE** Who are you?

**HAROLD** I'm with Darcy.

**DUANE** Who's Darcy?

**HAROLD** You just saw him a minute ago. You just kicked his ass.

*Pause.*

**DUANE** Holy Fuck, am I ever stoned. I know you from somewhere. You've been in my dreams. I just had a dream about you. Just now. But I didn't know who you were. But now I know. And my hair was wet. Like it is now. Who are you?

**HAROLD** I'm Harold.

**DUANE** But who are you, Harold?

**HAROLD** I'm Darcy's friend. He's in your automotive class.

**DUANE** Oh, yeah. Darcy. Get out of the light. The police. They just went by. They're always watching me. Every move I make. Give me half an hour, I gotta blow-dry my hair.

**HAROLD** Okay. Where's the designated area?

**DUANE** *(whispers to him)* If you don't mind me asking, what happened to your eye?

**HAROLD** I dropped a beer bottle. It exploded in my eye.

**DUANE** Does it hurt?

**HAROLD** Sometimes.

**DUANE** Does it ever get itchy?

**HAROLD** Sometimes.

**DUANE** Do you ever dream that you still have two eyes?

**HAROLD** All the time.

**DUANE** Can I take a look?

**HAROLD** No.

**DUANE** I respect that. Get out of the light. The police. I can feel them. Is it cold out?

**HAROLD** No. It's beautiful. There's a chinook.

**DUANE** I love chinooks. My hair feathers naturally. *(beat)* Police are on the lookout for guys wearing identical lumber jackets. So, split up.

*HAROLD walks back to BILL and DARCY.*

**DARCY** What did he say?

**HAROLD** He said he'd be half an hour.

**BILL** So, where's the designated area?

**HAROLD** At the elementary school.

**DARCY** He's got a whole shitload of plants in there. I know it.

**HAROLD** So?

**DARCY** So, we could take them.

**HAROLD** What?

**DARCY** Yeah.

**BILL** Are you serious?

*Pause.*

**DARCY** No. I'm just kidding, you guys. *(beat)* I'm just kidding.

**HAROLD** I don't want any trouble, Darcy. I've had enough bad luck. I just want to drink a little beer, get a little high and hang out.

**BILL** And meet some girls.

**HAROLD** And meet some girls.

**BILL** We should be looking for girls.

**DARCY** If we get some grass, then we get some girls.

**BILL** Where are we going to meet them?

**HAROLD** The arcade.

**DARCY** You don't find any girls of quality at the arcade. You find the fat hag and the usual sluts. You know where the babes are? First week of school they were scoping out the guys who have the cars, the hot cars. It's like Darwinism and natural selection. They're warm and dry, they're snuggling; music's loud, something she likes, Journey, REO Speedwagon—some fuckin' shit—Air Supply, Hall and Oates. He doesn't care. She's knobgobbling Mr. Grade Twelve in his new car. That's what a car does, Harold. It opens you up to a whole world of 'tang. *(beat)*

**BILL** I know girls who will take the bus.

**DARCY** Yeah, girls that had to repeat grade eight.

**BILL** What about Jennifer?

**DARCY** Jennifer's different. She's a child prodigy. She's a pinball wizard.

*Music.*

*DUANE appears.*

Hey, Duane, what's up?

**DUANE** Who's this?

**DARCY** This is Bill. It's okay. He's cool. *(beat)*

**DUANE** Who's buying?

**DARCY** We are.

**BILL** I am.

**DUANE** Okay. Which one is it?

**BILL** It's me.

**DARCY** It's him.

**DUANE** I need the money.

**BILL** Can I look at it first?

**DUANE** Oh, man.

*DUANE starts to leave.*

**DARCY** Hey, hey, hey, hey – hang on. Wait, wait, wait, wait. It's cool. It's his first time. Here.

**DUANE** Do I have to count it?

**DARCY** No.

*DUANE takes the money and gives BILL the ounce.*

**BILL** This is Columbian, right?

**DUANE** This is Hydroponic Colombian from Newfoundland. Newfoundland gets some of the brightest sun in the northern hemisphere. You didn't know that did you? You can't trust B.C. and California pot anymore. Too many pesticides. The future is hydro, gentlemen. *(beat)* Did you perm your hair?

**BILL** Yeah.

**DUANE** Yeah. It's not quite your look. Yeah. And Darcy. Your hair. It does this – thing at the front and then it turns into a kind of Ronald McDonald on acid or some shit – *(to HAROLD)* Look at you. The long poodle hair. The eye patch. It's you. *(pause)* Who are you?

**BILL** Bill.

**DUANE** Bill, you gotta be careful with perms. They really stress your hair out. Your hair is your calling card to the world. It says a lot about who you are.

**DARCY** You've got great hair.

**DUANE** Thanks, I take care of it. Johnson's baby shampoo. It's super soft and the ladies like soft hair.

*DUANE lights a joint and passes it to HAROLD.*

Here. Compliments of the house.

**HAROLD** Hey, thanks.

*DUANE exits. The boys start to smoke the joint. HAROLD feels it almost immediately.*

**DARCY** Hey, see you later, Duane. *(pause)*

*HAROLD tokes and passes it on to DARCY and then to BILL.*

**HAROLD** Smooth. *(coughs)*

**DARCY** This is very good. *(coughs)*

**BILL** Very smooth. *(coughs)*

## Scene Five

*PEGGY and VICTOR in a split scene with the boys.*

**VICTOR** Peg. Come on. Get up. There's something I have – something I want to say to you.

Our lives are going to change.

**PEGGY** Really?

**VICTOR** We will never have to work again.

**PEGGY** *(laughs)* Oh, Vic. You have to work. You live to work. It's all you care about. You have no friends; you barely speak to me or Bill. I thought you didn't love me. I thought you had a mistress. So one Saturday morning I followed you. And where did you go? Straight to work! And as I watched you through the window, you were smiling. I haven't seen you that happy at home in years.

**VICTOR** You followed me?

**PEGGY** I thought you were having an affair.

**VICTOR** Jesus Christ, Peggy.

**PEGGY** Who could work that much?

**VICTOR** What the hell is…? I came home with good news.

**PEGGY** What?

**VICTOR** You remember that lousy piece of marshland I bought years ago? They practically gave it to me.

**PEGGY** No.

**VICTOR** Just south of the city. Anyway, the city wants to annex it.

**PEGGY** So?

**VICTOR** Fifty acres, Peg!

**PEGGY** Oh, Vic, I am so tired of hearing—

**VICTOR** You're not even listening to me. Chrissakes, I thought this would help. Can't you just be happy? *(pause)*

**PEGGY** My best friend is dead, Vic. Am I supposed to celebrate?

**VICTOR** No, you are supposed to mourn and move on.

**PEGGY** It has only been a week. This may take me years.

**VICTOR** She's gone.

**PEGGY** No, she isn't!

**VICTOR** Peg—

**PEGGY** It feels like she's still here. Like she's trying to tell me something.

**VICTOR** What? Like what?…

**PEGGY** I don't know – like I need to change my life.

**VICTOR** Good, that's great, I agree, because we've got to move on. Take advantage of our opportunities. I want to tell you something—

**PEGGY** I don't care about your opportunities—

**VICTOR** Peg—

**PEGGY** You want to know what I care about?—

**VICTOR** Peg—

**PEGGY** What I really care about is what is happening to this family.

**VICTOR** Oh, here we go, roll the tape.

**PEGGY** I don't care about your opportunities. You want to know what I care about? What I really care about is what is happening to this family. You care about your work more than you care about the kids.

**VICTOR** The kids don't really need me—

**PEGGY** They need you more than ever—

**VICTOR** Where do you get this?

**PEGGY** I think Bill is into drugs—

**VICTOR** What?

**PEGGY** I think Bill is into drugs.

**VICTOR** How do you know?

**PEGGY** I can smell it on him. When was the last time you smelled him?

**VICTOR** Not since he was a baby. *(laughs)*

**PEGGY** Goddammit, Vic! This is not a joke. I'm scared, he's not working. He sleeps until noon and he's gone all day and night.

**VICTOR** It's just a phase.

**PEGGY** No, it's not just a phase—

**VICTOR** It's just a phase that—

**PEGGY** No. You need to get control of your son. You need to be a father.

**VICTOR** I am a father. Don't you ever tell me that I am not a father. I am a father. I was his Cub Scout leader! I taught him to ride a bike, how to change a flat tire. I stood in the rain and watched his soccer team lose twenty-four to nothing. I built igloos for him in the winter – didn't even want to be a Cub Scout leader. I did it for you. And you know what? I liked it. I was good at it. He was the one who wasn't there the night we drove out to the edge of the city. He could've gotten his astronomy badge if he just applied himself. He could have beaten that Wilson kid for the most badges. So, do not tell me that I am not a father.

**PEGGY** That was ten years ago.

**VICTOR** But it feels like yesterday!

**PEGGY** Vic. That was ten years ago.

*Pause. VICTOR exits.*

## Scene Six – In a Back Alley

**DARCY** I need to hold it. I need to feel it. If I feel it, if I can hold it in my hands, I can tell you if it's right or not!

**BILL** Why do you do this, this constant pecking at people?

**DARCY** What do you mean?

**BILL** People have this space, okay?

**DARCY** What are you talking about?

**BILL** I'm saying, people have this personal space around them. They need that space.

**HAROLD** Yeah…

**DARCY** I wasn't invading your space.

**BILL** You were.

**HAROLD** Yeah, you were.

**BILL** It's like people have a circle around them and you can tell from their body language—

**DARCY** What can you tell? What can you tell?

*DARCY moves closer to BILL, eye to eye.*

I can see your face if I get this close. Look at all those zits. Teenage wasteland.

**BILL** Fuck you.

**DARCY** *(pushes BILL)* You get to say that once to me. And you never say that again.

**HAROLD** Come on guys, play nice.

*They walk until…*

## Scene Seven

*Music: "Hitch a Ride" (Boston).*

*…they arrive at the Bug.*

**DARCY** Okay. Give me the ounce. Give me the ounce. Give me the ounce.

**BILL** Just hang on.

**DARCY** We have to hurry. If I'm not home by eleven, my dad is going to freak. What time is it now?

**BILL** Ten-forty-five.

**DARCY** Do you have any baggies?

**BILL** No.

**DARCY** We don't have any baggies? Way to go. Harold, sneak in to your kitchen and get some baggies.

**HAROLD** My mom is still up. And if I go in the house, I can't come back out.

**BILL** I would prefer it if we just smoked a bud.

**HAROLD** Me, too.

**DARCY** Suit yourself. I'm just trying to help.

*BILL produces a large bud from the bag.*

**BILL** How about this one?

**DARCY** Whoa! Come to Daddy.

*DARCY takes it.*

**BILL** Hey, I want to roll that one.

**DARCY** I have to leave in ten minutes.

**BILL** But I want to roll it.

**DARCY** And I'm faster. Harold, time me.

**HAROLD** Go.

*DARCY rolls the joint while HAROLD times him.*

**DARCY** Time? What was that?

**BILL** Seventeen seconds.

**HAROLD** That's a new record.

**DARCY** Flame!

*HAROLD lights the flame. BILL sees something in the distance. He turns down the music.*

**BILL** Car!

**HAROLD** What?

**DARCY** Get down!

*Headlights sweep across the Bug. We hear "Gimme Shelter." They all duck down. Music trails off.*

**BILL** That's the guy.

**HAROLD** What guy? *(beat)* Someone's coming.

**DARCY** Again?

**HAROLD** They're on foot.

**DARCY** How many?

**HAROLD** Two.

**DARCY** Get down!

*They get down, pause. DARCY reaches over to the stereo and turns it up. HAROLD reacts and turns it down.*

**HAROLD** What are you doing?

**DARCY** You turned it down.

**HAROLD** It might be the cops.

**DARCY** It's the acoustic part. I want to hear it.

**BILL** It looks like Jennifer.

**DARCY** Who's Jennifer?

**HAROLD** The babe from religion?

**BILL** Yeah.

**DARCY** There's someone with her.

**HAROLD** It's another girl.

**DARCY** What did I tell you? Get the grass, get the car and the girls materialize like genies from a lamp.

**HAROLD** It's like we sent a telepathetic message and the girls start to appear.

**BILL** It's telepathic.

**HAROLD** What did I say?

**DARCY** Telepathetic.

**HAROLD** Oh. Well, I meant telepathic.

**BILL** She's pretty tall.

**DARCY** It's her sister.

**HAROLD** She has beautiful hair.

**DARCY** They both have beautiful hair.

*The couple stops to kiss.*

**BILL, HAROLD & DARCY** Whoa.

*Pause.*

**HAROLD** That isn't her sister.

**DARCY** It's Duane.

**BILL** It is?

**HAROLD** Duane knows how to get the girls.

**DARCY** She's got a sweet ass.

**BILL** I can't believe Duane scored her.

**DARCY** It's just as well. Never fall in love with a beautiful girl.

**HAROLD** Why not?

**DARCY** They know they're beautiful and every guy wants them. Plain girls are way more grateful.

**HAROLD** What if the beautiful girl loves you?

**DARCY** That's even worse. Then you're on top of the world. Until she stops loving you. Then you fall harder than you would with an average girl.

**BILL** How do you know?

**DARCY** I went out with a model in Toronto for six months. If she's beautiful and she loves you, then everybody thinks you're a winner. You're sending telepathic messages to everyone you see – you're looking them in the eye like you're saying, "She's giving it to me." And that little voice in you is saying it's forever, but your dark angel says it's going to fall apart. And when she breaks up with you, it's devastating. You're crestfallen.

*Beat.*

**BILL** That's a great word.

**HAROLD** Yeah… crestfallen!

**DARCY** But if she's plain or average, then you know she's going to be faithful.

**HAROLD** At least you guys can get girls. Who's going to go out with me?

**DARCY** Girls who like pirate movies.

**HAROLD** Piss off.

**DARCY** Sorry. No, I'm sorry. Yeah. Out of all of us, you definitely have it the worst.

**HAROLD** Duane doesn't have a car.

**DARCY** Yeah, but he's got charisma. If a guy has a lot of charisma, girls will ignore the fact he doesn't have a car. And his hair is nicer than hers. Women like that. In fact, it's probably more important than anything else.

**HAROLD** He uses baby shampoo.

**BILL** Johnson's baby shampoo.

**DARCY** He looks good.

**BILL** Yeah.

*DUANE and JENNIFER start to exit.*

**DARCY** What time is it?

**BILL** Midnight.

**DARCY** Oh, shit. My dad's going to kill me. I'll see you guys later.

**HAROLD** See you later.

**BILL** See you.

*DARCY exits.*

**HAROLD** I better get in. It's late. Are you going to be okay getting home?

**BILL** Yeah, I'll be fine.

**HAROLD** Okay. G'night. See you tomorrow.

**BILL** G'night, Harold.

## Scene Eight

*PEGGY is on the deck. VICTOR enters with a packed duffle bag.*

**PEGGY** What are you doing?

**VICTOR** I'm not staying here tonight. I can't fix what is wrong with you.

**PEGGY** I don't want you to fix me. *(pause)* I don't know what I want. I don't understand why everyone is trying to get away from me. What have I done? *(beat)* When is the funeral?

**VICTOR** Saturday at two.

**PEGGY** Can you pick me up?

**VICTOR** I'll be here at one thirty. *(exits)*

## Scene Nine – The Arcade

**HAROLD** What do we have?

**DARCY** Five quarters to sell and some left over for personal stash.

**BILL** Okay, so you guys will be here if anyone comes up, right?

**HAROLD** Right.

**BILL** Darcy?

**DARCY** Yeah—

**HAROLD** Rule number two: If we're not together, we don't sell.

*DARCY exits toward the arcade. He comes back.*

**DARCY** Fat hag has the night off. Harold! You up for a game of Dragon Slayer?

**HAROLD** Yeah!

**DARCY** Bill, somebody shows up, you come and get us, okay?

**BILL** Okay.

**HAROLD** Don't sell to anybody, okay?

**BILL** Okay.

*HAROLD and DARCY go in to the arcade. BILL makes rude gestures.*

Fuck you, Darcy. Don't tell me what to do.

*JENNIFER appears.*

**JENNIFER** Hey, Bill, how's it going?

**BILL** Jennifer, hi. What are you doing here?

**JENNIFER** Darcy called, said he bought an ounce and that I should come and have a smoke.

**BILL** Darcy said that? I bought the ounce.

**JENNIFER** Oh… Darcy never said that. He asked me to meet him here.

**BILL** Weren't you going out with…?

**JENNIFER** Who…?

**BILL** I thought I saw you with… Duane.

**JENNIFER** Yeah, we went out, but he's more interested in his hair than me. So… who's got the smoke?

**BILL** I do. I got five quarters to sell right here.

**JENNIFER** Where's Darcy?

**BILL** In the arcade.

**JENNIFER** Great, I'm going to say hi. I'll be right back!

*Suddenly we hear "Gimme Shelter" come up.*

**BILL** It's the guy in the truck. He pulls up slowly. Stops. Rolls down his window. He turns the music down but I can still hear it. I'm being reeled in. Mesmerized. It's one of those moments that you can't control, you know it's going to end badly and everything is going to change. But you're helpless to stop it. He says, "Yeah,

I'm right here." And I look right at him but I can't see his face. He just stares at me. My heart is pounding. He says, "You dealing?" I say, "Yeah." He asks to see one baggie, then another, then another. He just sits there looking down at them. I say, "Are you going to buy?" He says, "I don't know." I say, "Can I have them back, please?" Then there's this long pause. He says, "I'll see you later," and he steps on the gas. The truck surges away and I'm yelling, "What are you doing? Give me my money! Give it back! Give it back!" And I realize that I'm holding onto the door. He goes faster – I feel a fist smashing into my face. I grab his hair. It's greasy and slips through my fingers. He's punching harder. I try to protect my head but it's impossible. I grab the steering wheel. We're now doing thirty miles an hour. The ground is moving so fast under my feet and it just gets faster and faster and faster. I can't hold on, I'm losing my grip. And then it's like every action flick I've ever seen, I push away from the door. I tuck my head in and roll, for about ten feet. The truck veers off to the right and disappears down an alley. The street is empty. There's this girl running toward me and she's screaming.

**JENNIFER** Omigod. Omigod. Omigod. Are you okay? Bill, Bill! Are you okay?

**BILL** Yeah, yeah, I'm okay. My elbow hurts. I think I jammed it.

**JENNIFER** Holy shit! Holy shit! You're lucky to be alive.

**BILL** Asshole took the weed. That asshole took the weed.

**JENNIFER** You're lucky to be alive.

**BILL** Yeah, I guess.

*DARCY and HAROLD come out of the arcade laughing.*

**DARCY** Champion! Still the champion.

**HAROLD** Shut up, I got nine hundred thousand.

*They see BILL and JENNIFER. They run to them.*

What happened?

**BILL** I walked up to the truck. This fuckin' asshole asked me where he could score. I said right here.

**DARCY** No—

**BILL** I pulled out one. I thought…

**DARCY** No—

**HAROLD** Are you okay?

**BILL** I hurt my leg.

**HAROLD** Why didn't you let go?

**BILL** It happened so quickly.

**HAROLD** Why didn't you let go?

**BILL** I didn't want to – it was too much of a rush—

**DARCY** What happened?

**BILL** I pulled out a quarter and he looked at it – he asked if I had another—

**DARCY** Oh, no—

**BILL** I showed him the second one, then a third.

**DARCY** They took our grass?!

**BILL** He grabbed the bags and stepped on the gas. It happened so quickly I didn't know what was happening, so I hung on.

**HAROLD** You held on?

**BILL** He started punching me in the head and I was holding onto the truck with my right hand and hitting him with my left.

**DARCY** How many bags did you show him?

**BILL** Three of them.

**DARCY** Oh, no.

**BILL** Hey, fuck off. I almost got killed.

*DARCY shoves BILL to the ground.*

**DARCY** Don't tell me to fuck off, you fuck off.

**HAROLD** He almost got killed, Darcy. Relax.

**DARCY** Why were you trying to sell without us there?

**BILL** I don't know – I thought I could do it—

**DARCY** Why didn't you wait for us?

**BILL** I wanted to do it on my own.

**DARCY** Rule number one: we don't sell to anyone we don't know. Rule number two: if we're not with you, don't sell.

**BILL** I thought I could do it on my own.

**DARCY** You're too small to do it on your own.

**BILL** Fuck off.

*DARCY sucker-punches BILL. BILL goes down hard.*

**DARCY** I told you not to tell me to fuck off. I told you!

*For the first time, we see HAROLD's strength. He slaps DARCY square in the face three or four times. DARCY falls back.*

**BILL** I'm going home.

**JENNIFER** I'll walk with you.

**BILL** Yeah, okay.

*BILL and JENNIFER leave. HAROLD stands over DARCY, then he turns and goes. DARCY is alone.*

## Scene Ten

*Just before midnight. BILL finds PEGGY lying on the deck, looking up at the sky. She is in her housecoat, with a towel around her head.*

**BILL** Hi, Mom—

*BILL stands in the shadows.*

**PEGGY** What's the name of our galaxy?

**BILL** The Milky Way.

**PEGGY** That's right, you told me.

**BILL** It's a candy bar, too.

**PEGGY** Is that a joke?

**BILL** No, I'm dead serious.

**PEGGY** How can we be in the Milky Way and still see it? How can we be in the middle of something and still see outside of it? *(BILL sniffles.)* Why are you standing over there? *(She looks at him for the first time.)* Oh my God. What happened to you?

**BILL** I got in a fight.

**PEGGY** Did he hit you with a two-by-four?

**BILL** I think it was a four-by-four, actually. Is it bad?

**PEGGY** There is blood streaming down your face and your eyes are bloodshot. *(beat)* What happened to you?

**BILL** I got in a fight. I almost won.

**PEGGY** What happened?

**BILL** I got in a fight. I lost.

**PEGGY** You're too small to get in a fight.

**BILL** Would everybody stop saying I'm too small?

**PEGGY** Who's everybody? Your friends? Did your friends do this to you?

**BILL** I don't want to talk about it.

**PEGGY** Friends stick together. Friends stand up for each other. They defend each other.

**BILL** Your friend killed herself.

**PEGGY** Don't you ever speak ill of Lorraine. Ever. She was my best friend. And I loved her.

**BILL** I'm sorry. I didn't mean it. *(beat)* I was holding onto the…

**PEGGY** Holding on? What do you mean?

**BILL** I mean I held him off—

**PEGGY** Why didn't you run away?

**BILL** Because I'm short. That's what short people do.

**PEGGY** That's just like your father.

**BILL** I'm a chip off the old block.

**PEGGY** The apple doesn't fall far from the tree.

**BILL** No, it hits you right between the eyes. *(BILL gets up to leave.)*

**PEGGY** Where are you going?

**BILL** Clean myself up.

**PEGGY** When I gave birth to you, I didn't expect you to be like your father. *(BILL exits.)* I expected you to be like me.

## Scene Eleven

*Saturday. VICTOR brings on chairs, BILL puts on a jacket and PEGGY goes off and changes. When the three are ready, they sit forward in the chairs.*

**PEGGY** I won't drive with you.

**VICTOR** Why not?

**PEGGY** You make me nervous.

**VICTOR** How do I make you nervous?

**PEGGY** Your driving is erratic.

**VICTOR** How is my driving erratic?

**PEGGY** You're all over the road.

**VICTOR** And when does that happen?

**PEGGY** Every time I drive with you.

**VICTOR** Nonsense.

**PEGGY** It is not nonsense. It is real and I'm not going to die on my way to my friend's funeral.

**VICTOR** Oh, bullshit.

**PEGGY** It is not bullshit, it is the truth. Bill, you drive.

**VICTOR** Get in the car.

**BILL** I only have my learner's.

**PEGGY** That's okay.

**VICTOR** I'm driving.

**PEGGY** Are we going to stand here in the driveway and argue? Vic. Let Bill drive. Let Bill drive. Let Bill drive.

*Pause. VICTOR stares at PEGGY for a moment. Then tosses the keys to BILL.*

## Scene Twelve

**PEGGY** I'll ride in the front. Okay. Keep your foot on the brake when you take the car out of gear. That's it. Shoulder check. Any cars coming? And ease in to traffic. Give her a bit of gas. Easy. Not too much! Good. How are you doing, Vic? Isn't it better when you don't have to drive? Okay. *(beat)* Don't get too close to that car. Bill. You're too close to that car. You're too close to that car! You're too close to that car!

**BILL** Okay!

*Beat.*

**VICTOR** I know a shortcut that will get us there faster.

**PEGGY** It's a funeral, Vic. What's your rush?

**VICTOR** They'll bury her before we get there. *(beat)* There's a shortcut up ahead.

**PEGGY** Stay on this road, Bill.

*Beat.*

**VICTOR** Why are we going so slowly?

**PEGGY** Because we're going the speed limit.

**VICTOR** Step on the gas, Bill.

**BILL** Don't listen to him, Bill.

**VICTOR** We'll get there faster.

**PEGGY** I've timed your shortcuts.

**VICTOR** It's faster.

**PEGGY** In some strange world of yours, you convinced yourself that it's faster, but it's not… and there's the church.

## Scene Thirteen – At the Funeral Chapel

*They get out of their chairs and reorganize them as church pews. VIC looks at his watch. Good church music. They are sitting.*

**PEGGY** Oh… look at the flowers. They're beautiful. *(starts to weep)*

*They get on their knees.*

**VICTOR** What time is this going to end? *(PEGGY looks at VICTOR.)* I was just asking.

**PEGGY** *(starts to weep)* I didn't bring any Kleenex.

*Beat – they all stand and then sit. VIC hands her his handkerchief.*

Thank you. Is it clean?

**VICTOR** You tell me!

**PEGGY** Have you told Bill you've moved out?

**VICTOR** No.

**PEGGY** This might be a good time.

**VICTOR** You think the funeral is a good time?

**PEGGY** It's the only time we could all get together!

**CONGREGATION** Sssssshhhhh!

**VICTOR** Bill, your mother and I are… we… I've moved out.

**BILL** You have?

**VICTOR** Yes.

**BILL** I never noticed.

*They stand.*

**VICTOR** What happened to your face?

**BILL** I have acne.

**PEGGY** He got into a fight.

**VICTOR** Over what?

**BILL** Nothing.

**VICTOR** Who beat you up?

**BILL** No one.

**VICTOR** Why? What were you doing?

**BILL** Nothing.

**VICTOR** You let some punk clean your clock while you were doing nothing? Do you think I'm stupid?

**PEGGY** Quiet!

**CONGREGATION** Sssh!

*Beat.*

**VICTOR** There were a couple of times I had to fight my way out of some bad situations. Playing by the rules was out of the question. You know what I did?

I kicked him in the nuts as hard as I could. Then ran like hell.

*Sign of the cross – they sit.*

**BILL** Mom. Dad. I want to thank you for what's happened so far today. I've learned that the two of you are splitting up and the best way to get out of a fight is to kick the other guy in the nuts.

**CONGREGATION** Shhhh!

*Music. They sing "Amazing Grace" (John Newton). VICTOR drifts off. Funeral starts to break up.*

**PEGGY** You know how I want to be buried?

**VICTOR** In the ground, I presume.

**BILL** I have to go.

**PEGGY** Are you going to be home for dinner?

**BILL** Doubt it.

**PEGGY** I need a minute. Vic, isn't there something you want to say to Bill?

**VICTOR** Bill… don't do drugs.

**PEGGY** Oh, God…

**BILL** Okay, Dad, I won't.

*All overlapping.*

**VICTOR** Peggy, can we – I have a – I have to go, I've got a big meeting.

**PEGGY** Just give me a minute.

**BILL** Mom… Mom.

**PEGGY** Just a minute.

**BILL** I have a date.

**PEGGY & VIC** You have a date!

**BILL** Ah, yeah.

**PEGGY** *(stressed out)* Vic, take him to the car and have the sex talk.

**VICTOR** *(at the same time as BILL's next line)* What?

**BILL** Aw, Mom!

**PEGGY** Just do it… need to say goodbye!

*The sound of murmuring dies off as PEGGY tries to say goodbye. She looks around and everyone has gone. Gently she takes the urn and exits.*

*Music.*

## Scene Fourteen

**JENNIFER** Hey, tough guy, how's it going?

**BILL** I'm still a little sore.

**JENNIFER** You rolled off the truck like a stuntman.

**BILL** I guess so.

**JENNIFER** So, here we are again, synchronicity.

**BILL** What is synchronicity?

**JENNIFER** It's the coincidence of events that seem related but are not obviously caused one by the other.

**BILL** I thought that was coincidence.

**JENNIFER** No, coincidence is something that happens by chance in a surprising or remarkable way. Like when you are thinking about a friend and he calls you up and asks you out.

**BILL** Oh.

**JENNIFER** Come on, let's walk.

**BILL** So… where are you from?

**JENNIFER** My family moved this summer from Ontario. At first I didn't want to go. I didn't want my life uprooted. But my dad got laid off and there are lots of jobs out here. And my dad loved to listen to "Four Strong Winds" by Ian Tyson. He wanted to see the mountains up close.

But I wasn't sure. It's very hard to find a place where you fit in.

**BILL** Yeah, I know.

**JENNIFER** And that's when I learned about synchronicity. We went looking for a realtor to sell our house and out of the blue a woman puts her business card in our mailbox. And guess what her name was?

**BILL** I have no idea.

**JENNIFER** Alberta. The people who bought our house had a new baby named Tyson. Now, was this synchronicity or was it coincidence?

**BILL** Couldn't tell you.

**JENNIFER** So we packed everything into our twelve-year-old Volvo. Me, my little brother Kevin, and my mom and dad. Everything we owned was in that car. We had stuff on the roof, we had a small trailer and, on the first of August, we headed west. And sometimes we couldn't get the radio, so we sang songs. Neil Young, Ian Tyson, Bob Dylan. *(sings)* Jesus must have been watching over us, because my dad finally learned a Bob Dylan song.

**BILL** I can't imagine my dad singing Bob Dylan.

**JENNIFER** And in the car I was reading *The Grapes of Wrath*, and I just got to the part where the Joads's truck breaks down when our Volvo broke down! I freaked out. About twenty minutes later, a tow truck comes along and the name on the truck says: Shell Auto Repair, Henry Fonda Proprietor.

**BILL** No way!

**JENNIFER** So, what do you think the odds are of reading *The Grapes of Wrath*, getting to the part where the Joads's break down, breaking down ourselves and then being picked up by Henry Fonda?

Now was that coincidence? Synchronicity? Or something even bigger?

## Scene Fifteen – At the Bug

**BILL** Here we are.

**JENNIFER** What's this?

**BILL** The Bug.

**JENNIFER** The Bug?

**BILL** It has wall-to-wall carpeting.

**JENNIFER** Wall-to-wall carpeting.

**BILL** It's on the ceiling, too.

**JENNIFER** Were you hoping to make out with me in there?

**BILL** No.

**JENNIFER** Yes, you were.

**BILL** No.

**JENNIFER** Yes, you were.

**BILL** No. I wasn't. *(beat)* Yes, I was.

**JENNIFER** You see? If we're going to hang around together, we have to be honest with each other. Okay?

*Beat.*

**BILL** Okay.

**JENNIFER** Can you believe how warm it is? It's the middle of January. Oh my God! What's that? What is that? It's so beautiful. It's so beautiful. It's a miracle.

**BILL** The northern lights. Haven't you ever seen them before?

**JENNIFER** In magazines, postcards! I don't believe it. You can see them? Was this your plan? Get me high, watch the northern lights and then go for me in the back of your friend's Volkswagen?

**BILL** *(smiles)* There could be fireworks later.

**JENNIFER** It's not happening – you know that.

**BILL** I know that…

**JENNIFER** I usually insist that my date have a car that isn't parked for the winter. That's okay. It's a beautiful night out and I like you.

*DARCY enters.*

**DARCY** Hey.

**JENNIFER** Darcy, what are you doing here?

**DARCY** I was just going for a walk. What are you guys doing here?

**BILL** We're just hanging out.

**DARCY** Is it just you guys, or what?

**JENNIFER** We're on a date.

**DARCY** Oh, you're on a date. That's fun. How is it going?

**BILL** Come on, Jennifer.

**DARCY** What? Do I smell?

**JENNIFER** Why don't you go to the arcade.

**DARCY** I can't. Fat Hag is there.

**JENNIFER** Then go home. I don't know what you're going to do, Darcy, but I'm hanging out with Bill tonight. Is that okay?

**DARCY** That's nice. That's so nice. You two make a really cute couple. I seem to recall that you still have some of the personal stash.

**BILL** Yeah, there's still some.

**DARCY** I want it.

**JENNIFER** Bill, give it to him. Bill. Give him the stash. Right now.

**BILL** Darcy. Me and Jennifer are on a date, okay? Hey, I'm sorry that I didn't listen to you and that I almost got killed. In case you had forgotten, it was my money. Not yours. I thought you were my friend but I guess I was wrong.

**DARCY** If I had money, the beer and tokes would be flowing like Niagara Falls.

**BILL** You've said that.

*JENNIFER and BILL move on.*

Please, don't follow us.

**DARCY** Okay.

## Scene Sixteen

*PEGGY is on the deck. VICTOR enters with a duffle bag.*

**VICTOR** What's that?

*She has Lorraine's ashes in an urn.*

**PEGGY** What's what?

**VICTOR** That.

**PEGGY** That's Lorraine.

**VICTOR** Lorraine?

**PEGGY** Yes.

**VICTOR** Why do you have Lorraine?

**PEGGY** Because nobody took her after the service.

**VICTOR** Nobody?

**PEGGY** Everybody left.

**VICTOR** So you just took her?

**PEGGY** I'll give her back.

*Pause.*

I couldn't just leave her there. She didn't want to be alone. She wanted to be with her family. That's what I want. *(pause)* She wants me to change my life. She doesn't want me to grieve. She wants me to be happy. To know she's with me even though she is not here.

**VICTOR** I want that too, Peg.

**PEGGY** What are you doing home?

**VICTOR** I couldn't sleep.

*Silence. PEGGY looks at VICTOR. She smiles and he joins her up on the deck.*

## Scene Seventeen

*HAROLD, BILL and JENNIFER come back on. DARCY is in the Bug listening to the music loud.*

**HAROLD** Darcy. You can't stay in here without telling me. I'm in a lot of shit. Come on.

**DARCY** There's something I want to show you.

**HAROLD** What is it?

**DARCY** Get in and I'll show you.

**HAROLD** No—

**DARCY** Come on man, I can't show you out there. I have to show you in here.

**HAROLD** No!

**DARCY** Come on, please. Just this once. And I won't ask for anything ever again. Look. I'm sorry about the other night. Okay? I'm sorry. I lost my mind. I lost my mind.

**HAROLD** I'm sorry, too.

**BILL** I'm sorry, too.

*Pause.*

**JENNIFER** Aww. This is so nice. I'm going to cry. *(pause)* You boys are capable of greatness.

**DARCY** Come on, come on, come on. Climb in.

*They climb in to the Bug.*

Okay, everybody just be quiet. Now close your eyes.

*DARCY reaches under the seat of the Bug and brings out a dozen albums.*

*And music.*

*DARCY has cued a Rush song for this moment. The music plays at a low volume. He holds an album in front of his face. The albums are Rush, Pink Floyd, Led Zeppelin, Max Webster, Rolling Stones, Emerson, Lake and Palmer, Van Halen, Triumph and Steely Dan, to name a few.*

**HAROLD** They're records.

**BILL** So?

**DARCY** So? So?

**JENNIFER** Are these your albums?

**DARCY** Rush. Hemispheres. Red vinyl. Pink Floyd. The Wall. Led Zeppelin: Houses of the Holy. 2112 signed by Neil Peart, Alex Lifeson and Geddy Lee.

**HAROLD** Your albums. Your albums! They're here.

**DARCY** They came last night.

**BILL** These are great albums.

**DARCY** Of course. You are all officially invited to my house where I will play these albums.

**HAROLD** When?

**DARCY** Pretty soon. We have to drop acid and listen to Pink Floyd's "The Wall". It's a great album to be on acid with.

**JENNIFER** You are such a freak.

**DARCY** Yeah. I'm going to sell off part of my collection and buy a ticket to Rush.

**HAROLD** But these are your albums. How could you sell them?

**DARCY** I only listen to half of them. And. There's new technology coming out. Laser discs. They're gonna make albums look like eight-track cassettes. So… can we listen to some music.

*2112 starts to play. HAROLD feels something behind his eye patch. He pulls it off, he looks around. He has regained sight in his bad eye. He gets out to look up at the sky.*

**HAROLD** Oh my God. Oh my God. I can see. I can see. Oh, wow. Oh my God. I can see well.

**JENNIFER** What happened?

**HAROLD** I can see well. I can see everything clearer. Oh, wow this is great. Oh, I love this. I didn't think I would ever get better, but I am. I'm getting better.

**JENNIFER** Rush changed your life, Harold!

**BILL** Oh, come on.

**JENNIFER** Don't you believe in miracles?

**HAROLD** I gotta go in and tell my mom. Oh, wow, I love this. I just love this. Mom!

*HAROLD exits.*

**JENNIFER** Wow. We just witnessed a miracle!

**BILL** You think that's a miracle?

**JENNIFER** Don't you?

**BILL** I don't know.

**JENNIFER** *(to BILL)* C'mon, let's go. G'night Darcy.

**DARCY** G'night.

**BILL** *(to DARCY)* We'll see you tomorrow. *(slaps his hand)*

*They leave hand in hand.*

## Scene Eighteen

*BILL arrives home. VICTOR is having a drink. PEGGY is sleeping on the deck.*

**BILL** Mom? Mom?

**VICTOR** Let her sleep. You want a drink?

**BILL** What?

**VICTOR** You want a beer? Scotch?

**BILL** I'll have a beer… no – Scotch…

**VICTOR** Excellent. I'll have that, too. How was your day?

**BILL** Harold got his eyesight back and I had a date with Jennifer and Darcy got his record collection, so, I guess… it was a day of miracles. What about you, Dad?

**VICTOR** I sold some land.

**BILL** Good.

**VICTOR** Yep. *(pause)* I'm supposed to smell you.

**BILL** Why?

**VICTOR** Are you smoking pot, Bill?

**BILL** Yes.

**VICTOR** Are you smoking a lot?

**BILL** Fair amount.

**VICTOR** Okay. Thanks for being honest. Look… lay off that stuff, okay? You need to stop.

**BILL** I think I know that. *(pause)* Why does Mom have Lorraine's urn?

**VICTOR** She wants to be close to her.

*PEGGY wakes up.*

**PEGGY** What are you doing here? What's happened – what's happened? What's happened – did you have a bad date?

**BILL** No, Mom.

**PEGGY** Are you two drinking?

**VICTOR** No, Peg, we're celebrating. I have good news.

**PEGGY** What?

**VICTOR** I sold a little piece of marshland today. We're rich. So…

**PEGGY** I don't feel any different.

**BILL** We're rich?

**VICTOR** Yes.

**BILL** Like are we really rich?

**VICTOR** Yes.

**BILL** Cool. So does that mean we're moving?

**VICTOR** I don't know.

**BILL** Are you guys splitting up?

**VICTOR** I came back to tell you both the good news. And to get my pillow. The one I had last night is not very good.

**BILL** Are you guys going to have a nasty divorce?

**PEGGY** I don't want that.

**VICTOR** Neither do I. Can I take you out for dinner? We can celebrate.

**BILL** Yeah.

**PEGGY** What are we celebrating? That we're rich? I don't feel any different.

Richard Meen, Karen Johnson-Diamond and Kevin Rothery
Ghost River Theatre, Calgary 2007 production
*photo by Sean Dennie*

**BILL** I feel different.

**VICTOR** Come on, let's just go out, we'll have a good meal, and uhm, we'll have a good meal.

**PEGGY** Can we order in?

**VICTOR** Sure. How about… Chinese?

*VICTOR exits into the house.*

*PEGGY opens the urn. She pours a handful of ash into her palm.*

**PEGGY** Why does it look like kitty litter? We start out as water and then we're so soft and fresh and round as babies and then – we end up as pellets in a jar.

*PEGGY pours the handful of ash into a small evergreen tree. Pours some more ash into another small evergreen tree.*

Okay. Okay. This gives me hope. I feel as if my heart is lifting.

**BILL** Mom—

**PEGGY** I want to squeeze this so hard and have it become a diamond. I just want a bit of her to myself. *(pause)* There are things out there you can't even see coming. They can take you out so quickly; you can't even catch your breath. I don't want to lose you.

**BILL** You won't.

**PEGGY** I need you in this world with me.

**BILL** I'm not going anywhere.

**PEGGY** Mean it.

**BILL** I mean it.

*They exit.*

*Blackout.*

*The End.*

## About
# Anne Nothof

Anne Nothof is Professor of English at Athabasca University in Alberta, where she has developed and taught undergraduate and post-graduate distance education courses in literature and drama. She has published critical essays on British and Canadian theatre in journals and books, and edited collections of essays and plays for Guernica, NeWest, and Playwrights Canada Press. She is a board member at NeWest Press and Athabasca University Press, and past president of the Canadian Association for Theatre Research. For twelve years she hosted a weekly radio programme on drama, and developed a television series on world theatre. More recently she has assumed the editorial responsibility for the Canadian Theatre Encyclopedia (www.canadiantheatre.com).